ATHENS: ITS RISE AND FALL

Sir Edward Bulwer Lytton was once Britain's most famous romantic novelist, rivalling and outselling Dickens in his day. His best-known book was the historical novel *The Last Days of Pompeii*, yet he was also responsible for this great work of history.

Athens: Its Rise and Fall, originally published in 1837, was the first radical history of Greece in the spirit of Lord Byron. It ranks with Thomas Babington Macaulay's *History of England* and the works of Thomas Carlyle as one of the greatest intellectual achievements of the Romantic Age, and anticipates the thinking of George Grote and John Stuart Mill on Greek history by more than a decade.

To celebrate the bicentenary of Bulwer Lytton's birth, Routledge is re-issuing this influential work. This new edition publishes, for the first time, the text of a previously forgotten third volume, recently discovered by Oxford academic Oswyn Murray.

Sir Edward Bulwer Lytton, first Baron Lytton (1803–73), dandy and MP, was the most popular novelist of his day, a friend of Disraeli and Dickens, and author of *The Last Days of Pompeii* (1834), amongst many other novels and plays. *Athens: Its Rise and Fall* (1837) was his only historical work.

Oswyn Murray is a Fellow of Balliol College, Oxford and Praefectus of Holywell Manor Graduate Centre. His books include *Early Greece* (1993) and *The Oxford History of the Classical World* (1986).

ATHENS:
ITS RISE AND FALL

With views of the literature,
philosophy, and social life of the
Athenian people

Edward Bulwer Lytton

Bicentenary edition
Edited by Oswyn Murray

Routledge
Taylor & Francis Group

LONDON AND NEW YORK

First published 1837. This edition first published 2004
by Routledge
11 New Fetter Lane, London EC4P 4EE

Simultaneously published in the USA and Canada
by Routledge
29 West 35th Street, New York, NY 10001

Routledge is an imprint of the Taylor & Francis Group

This edition and arrangement © 2004 Oswyn Murray

Previously unpublished material © 2004 Knebworth Estates
www.knebworthhouse.com

Typeset in 11/12pt Garamond 3 by Graphicraft Limited, Hong Kong
Printed and bound in Great Britain by The Cromwell Press, Trowbridge

British Library Cataloguing in Publication Data
A catalogue record for this book is available
from the British Library

Library of Congress Cataloging in Publication Data
Lytton, Edward Bulwer Lytton, Baron, 1803–1873.
Athens : its rise and fall : with views of the literature, philosophy,
and social life of the Athenian people / Edward Bulwer Lytton ;
[edited and with new material by Murray, Oswyn].
p. cm
Includes bibliographical references and index.
1. Athens (Greece)–History. I. Murray, Oswyn. II. Title.

DF285.L992 2004   2003061165

938′.5 — dc22

ISBN 0–415–32087–9

CONTENTS

CONTENTS

CONTENTS

Chapter II   201

Chapter III   213

Chapter IV   233

Chapter V   247

CONTENTS

CONTENTS

CONTENTS

CONTENTS

ILLUSTRATIONS

WELCOME

On the occasion of Edward Bulwer Lytton's 200th birthday in May 2003, scholars and enthusiasts from around the world gathered at the author's home, Knebworth House, in Hertfordshire. In the dusty light of Bulwer Lytton's Jacobean-panelled hall; beneath the frieze painting of his declaration that under this "old roof tree" there be "worth in all, wit in some, laughter open, slander dumb"; in accents American, Italian, German, Dutch, and the occasional English; and in hallmark sentences even longer than this one— favourite passages of Bulwer Lytton were performed with such warmth and enthusiasm that the continuing influence of this great Victorian was firmly and reassuringly established in the twenty-first century.

It was a splendid event. We marvelled at plays, poetry, short stories, novels of all genres, philosophical tracts, literary criticism, political speeches, social histories, ancient histories. The diversity of Bulwer Lytton's contribution to Victorian literature was cited as the one and only reason he is not today fêted as a genius in any one of these fields.

My privileged position as host had a single drawback, the task of cutting short any reader who extended his allotted time. Only one orator gave me trouble. Dr Murray's honey-voiced readings of the virgin passages of *Athens: Its Rise and Fall*—that are now published in this volume—were so rich and hypnotic, that I simply could not stop him. The minutes ticked by, our tea got cold, but we were seduced. The thrill of hearing these beautiful passages transcribed for the very first time from Bulwer Lytton's discarded papers was a highlight of the celebration.

Dr Murray's warmth and enthusiasm for this important work see it here republished by its original publisher, Routledge, including, for the first time, those fragments omitted from earlier editions. All you are missing is the pleasure of Dr Murray reading it to you.

Knebworth House,   The Hon. Henry Lytton Cobbold,
Autumn 2003.   great-great-great-grandson of Edward Bulwer Lytton.

PREFACE

Many friends and colleagues have helped my serendipitous work on this marvellous book. I wish first of all to thank the Lytton family, and especially Lord Cobbold and his son the Hon. Henry Cobbold, who encouraged and facilitated my work in every way as soon as I contacted them. I should also like to record the great pleasure of meeting fellow enthusiasts at the magnificent celebration of Bulwer's bicentennial birthday at Knebworth on the weekend of 25 May 2003.

The frontispiece was provided by Henry Cobbold and is reproduced with the permission of the Knebworth Estates. Mrs Susan Flood, County Archivist of Hertfordshire, arranged for me to view the manuscript of the work, and to borrow the unpublished section on deposit in Balliol College Library. Here my colleagues, the librarian, Dr Penny Bulloch, and her deputy, Alan Tadiello, arranged for me to spend many days transcribing the text, and assisted me with their expertise in nineteenth century handwriting.

It was the online bookshop Scrinium.nl with its list Specimina Septimanalia which first brought the work to my attention. Tom Figueira and Abebooks.com led me to the many American editions. In order to produce a digitally scanned manuscript, I needed to obtain a cheap edition of the book, whose binding could be stretched for scanning: this was made possible by the Abebooks listings, which revealed two physically separated volumes of the first American edition (Harper Brothers 1837), Vol. I in Beaverton, Oregon priced $24, Vol. II in Houston, Texas at $8. For a total of $32 plus shipping, I was the proud possessor of a recreated set, the first volume previously having belonged to "Edward A. and Eugene H. Lynch 1837", the second anonymous; I am happy to report that their sturdy American pioneer bindings stood up remarkably well to subsequent maltreatment by my daughter Ros on the photocopier. The same source helped me to acquire a fine English first edition and other relevant works of Bulwer Lytton's early radical-dandy period.

My colleagues on the Bibliotheca Academica Translationum project of the Arts and Humanities Research Board, Dr Chryssanthi Avlami, Dr Susanne Stark and Hazel Bloss, helped my bibliographical researches, especially into

German translations of the work; I thank the AHRB, the Hulme Surplus Fund of Oxford and the European Commission for grants towards this project. My old friend Carmine Ampolo of the Scuola Normale Superiore di Pisa located and provided a photocopy of part of the almost extinct Italian translation. My researches into the firm of Galignani of Paris were assisted by my colleagues, Roger Lonsdale, Giles Barber, and Dr Philip Rossington. My graduate student, Dr Peter Liddel, and I discussed together the relationship between Bulwer Lytton, Connop Thirlwall and George Grote. Another graduate pupil, Georgiu Kantor, confirmed the non-existence of any Russian translation; while yet another pupil, Paul Kosmin, in his first days in Oxford lent me a battered copy of the Knebworth edition that he had just been given. Dr Tom Harrison of the University of St Andrews guided me to the Knebworth web site and located the Bulwer letter of 1837 about the publication of the work for sale on the web site of Roy Davids Ltd. Sybilla Jane Flower identified its correspondent for me. Dr Tim Rood knew at once of the work of J.A. St John, which I had failed to find in my search of the Bodleian catalogue. During the last stages of the preparation of this book, Dr Catherine Phillips very kindly sent me an advance copy of her essay, "The historical context of *Athens: its Rise and Fall*", to be published in Allan Christensen (ed.), *The Subverting Vision of Bulwer Lytton*, New Jersey: Associated University Presses pp. 228–51. I was delighted to find how close were our views on Bulwer Lytton.

The discovery was presented during 2002–3 to audiences in Sparta, St Andrews (centenary meeting of the Scottish Classical Association), Oxford (two graduate seminars), Dublin (Trinity College Archaeological Society), and at the bicentenary celebrations for Bulwer Lytton at Knebworth. My thanks to the audiences for their interest and help.

I would also like to thank those involved in the production of the book. Peter Hamilton, historian of photography, prepared the scanned text at Bardwell Press. Richard Stoneman, commissioning editor of Routledge and much admired friend of classical publishing, enthusiastically welcomed the return into print of a book by an author whose whole career was bound up with the success of George Routledge's publishing house. For it was the signing of a contract for the republication in their Railway Library of nineteen of Bulwer Lytton's novels for ten years which propelled George Routledge into notoriety in 1852: the advance offered was £20,000, the largest sum paid to any author up to that date; and the investment was a huge success, for by the time of the author's death he had received almost double that sum in royalties. "Those were red-letter days for popular English authors" (F.A. Mumby, *The House of Routledge 1834–1934*, Routledge 1934, pp. 57–60). My thanks too to the production staff at Routledge, and especially to my production editor Liz O'Donnell, and my copy editor (and former pupil) Anne Marriott.

Finally I thank my wife, whose reward for living for nine months with a Bulwer bore was a ticket to the Bulwer Lytton bicentennial birthday celebration at Knebworth in May 2003.

Holywell Manor, Oxford   Oswyn Murray
October 2003

INTRODUCTION

A lost school of history:
ancient Greece in the age of reform

Oswyn Murray

> It was a dark and stormy night; the rain fell in torrents—
> except at occasional intervals, when it was checked by a
> violent gust of wind which swept up the streets (for it is in
> London that our scene lies), rattling along the housetops, and
> fiercely agitating the scanty flame of the lamps that struggled
> against the darkness.
>
> (Bulwer Lytton, *Paul Clifford* (1830) ch. I)

Early in the summer of 2002, I was idly perusing a Dutch book catalogue on
the internet, when my eye was caught by a strange entry:

> BULWER LYTTON, E., Athens; its Rise and Fall. With Views of
> the Literature, Philosophy, and Social Life of the Athenian People.
> Galignani, Paris, 1837. XII, 469p. Bound. Bit rust stained. Ex
> libris. € 29.50

Bulwer Lytton was of course known to me as the author of *The Last Days of
Pompeii,* and other novels, the Knebworth edition of which I had once bought
for £2 in a leather-bound set, in my *fin-de-siècle* days, to decorate my study at
school, and in one of which I had carefully hollowed out a secret container to
hide my cigarettes from a prowling housemaster. But I did not recall ever
having come across any reference to a work of history with such a grandiose
title by this prolific novelist of whom I had not then read a word, and the
entry intrigued me. What was he writing in 1837, and why was his work
published by an Italian living in Paris in that very street, the Rue Vivienne,
where the much revered ancient Bibliothèque Nationale was once housed,
and where I had recently been shown the site of the new Getty-style Institut
national de l'histoire de l'art, which is to be combined with the Centre
Gustav Glotz and the Centre Louis Gernet to create the greatest humanistic

1

research institute in Europe, planned by my friend Alain Schnapp? So after some hesitation, having carefully considered the price and my wife's probable reaction to yet another useless tome, I ordered the book.

Thus began the strange and wonderful story that I am about to relate.

The dandy

> I am perhaps less ignorant than I affect to be: it is *now* my object to be a dandy; hereafter I may aspire to be an orator— a wit, a scholar, or a Vincent. You will see then that there have been many odd quarters of an hour in my life less unprofitably wasted than you imagine.
>
> (Bulwer Lytton, *Pelham* (1828) ch. XLIII)

Bulwer Lytton (or Lytton Bulwer, as he is correctly described on the title page, for he had not yet changed his name in order to lay claim to an Elizabethan heritage) was born in 1803. Having antagonized his mother by making an unsuitable marriage, his allowance was cut off; he decided, like Sir Walter Scott and Lord Archer, to save himself from bankruptcy by writing popular novels, and then buy himself a seat in the House of Commons. Within a decade (1828–37), after twelve novels, two long poems, two works of historical analysis, a play, a political pamphlet and a heap of essays, he had recouped his fortunes; he was a reforming MP, first for the rotten borough of St Ives (1831), and then, after supporting the Great Reform Bill, for Lincoln (1832–41). He became a prominent member of the group of philosophical radicals who supported the secret ballot, a friend of the Utilitarian philosophers around James Mill, and a colleague in Parliament of the future historian of Greece, George Grote, then a banker and MP for the City of London from 1832 to 1841. In 1838 Bulwer Lytton made his most famous speech, advocating the abolition of the last vestiges of slavery—a speech so brilliant that it silenced all opposition. Towards the end of their time in Parliament he and Grote seem to have become more distant: even to close friends like Richard Cobden, Grote appeared a singularly unsuccessful politician who insisted on behaving as if he were in Plato's Republic;[1] while Grote dismissed Bulwer Lytton in a speech as "a literary Whig" (Hansard 40.399). Bulwer Lytton's view of Grote is perhaps best exemplified in his portrait of "Snap, the academical *philosopherling*":

---

1 "A mild and philosophical man, possessing the highest order of moral and intellectual endowments; but wanting something which for need of a better phrase I shall call *devil*. He is too abstract in his tone of reasoning and does not aim to influence others by any proof excepting that of ratiocination" (John Morley, *The Life of Richard Cobden* (London 1906) pp. 136–7).

If our philosopherling enters the House of Commons, he sets up for a *man of business*; he begs to be put upon the dullest committees; he would not lose an hour of twaddle for the world; he affects to despise eloquence, but he never speaks without having learnt every sentence by heart. And oh! such sentences, and such delivery! for the Snaps have no enthusiasm! It is the nature of the material philosophy to forbid that beautiful prodigality of heart; he unites in his agreeable style, the pomp of apathy with the solemnity of dulness. Nine times out of ten our philosopherling is the son of a merchant, his very pulse seems to enter its account in the ledger-book. Ah Plato! Ah Milton! did you mean the lute of philosophy for hands like these![2]

Bulwer Lytton also had family connections with the Philhellenes; for in 1824 his older brother Henry ("a silly supercilious young man") had volunteered to oversee the transfer of £130,000 in gold sovereigns to the provisional Greek government in Nauplion from the London Greek Committee, in order to finance the War of Independence: this gold rapidly disappeared into the hands of brigand leaders, and was to poison Anglo-Greek relations for half a century.[3]

Bulwer Lytton himself was a figure of some social style: at sixteen he had fallen passionately in love with the daughter of a confidence trickster; as a young man he had run away with a gipsy, and had been a lover of Byron's former flame, Lady Caroline Lamb; with his youthful looks and "glitteringly golden hair that, worn in ringlets, played about his shoulders,"[4] he had cut a swathe through the salons of Paris. His first successful novel, *Pelham, or the adventures of a gentleman* (1828), was a fashionable social satire, belonging to the "silver-fork order of fiction", which destroyed the image of the Byronic hero and established the male vogue for black evening dress.[5] The hero was modelled on himself as that newly discovered figure, the dandy:

A fop, a philosopher, a voluptuary and a moralist—a trifler in appearance but rather one to whom trifles are instinctive, than one to whom trifles are natural—an Aristippus on a limited scale, accustomed to draw sage conclusions from the follies he adopts, and while professing

---

2 Edward Lytton Bulwer, *England and the English* (Paris 1833) Bk. IV ch. X. Compare Ruskin's verdict on Grote, below n. 50.

3 For this episode see W. St Clair, *That Greece Might still be Free* (Oxford 1972) ch. 22.

4 T.H.S. Escott, *Edward Bulwer, First Baron Lytton of Knebworth* (London 1910) p. 67. This work remains the best account of Bulwer Lytton's literary career; the family biographies are rather stiff and formal.

5 "*Pelham* caused the black swallow-tail coat to become compulsory for evening wear" (Escott, op.cit. p. 141).

himself a votary of pleasure, desirous in reality to become a disciple of wisdom.[6]

As a figure in the fashionable world Bulwer Lytton prospered: he quit Parliament for a time to devote himself to literature, and was reconciled to his mother, who left him her family's Elizabethan ancestral seat of Knebworth, which he decorated with oriental cupolas. But his marriage to a penniless Irish beauty never recovered from a decade of neglect while he was writing his novels; their relations became one of the scandals of the age: they separated, and began a feud which lasted till his death; she continued to appear at his political meetings with such effect that on one occasion he leaped from the podium into a flower bed to make his escape. In 1852 he had returned to Parliament as a very Tory MP for Hertfordshire, and in 1858 was made Secretary of State for the Colonies; she appeared at his election meeting dressed entirely in lemon yellow silk, with a yellow parasol, rouged face and yellow dyed hair (the colours of the opposition party), mounted the platform and shouted out, "Fiend, villain, monster, cowardly wretch, outcast. I am told", she hissed, "you have been sent to the colonies. If they knew as much about you as I do they would have sent you there long ago." Bulwer Lytton (who had not set eyes on her for twenty-two years) fainted clean away. As a result of this episode he tried to have her incarcerated as a lunatic, and succeeded in creating a public outcry in her favour.[7] It was in fact Bulwer Lytton who sent Gladstone into exile as Governor of the Ionian Islands in 1858, thus being responsible indirectly for introducing cricket and the umbrella to Greece. Appropriately to the work of history I am here presenting, in 1862 on the abdication of King Otto of Bavaria, Bulwer Lytton was even offered the throne of Greece, which (along with many other candidates) he declined. In Scotland his fame is attested by the fact that (without any Scottish connection) he was elected Lord Rector of Glasgow University in 1857. Today Knebworth (or Knobworth as Mick Jagger insists on calling it) is still in the family: it is now a banqueting centre famous as "the stately home of Rock", where since 1974 the Rolling Stones, Queen, Led Zeppelin, Pink Floyd, Oasis and all the rock stars from Freddy Mercury to Eric Clapton have performed.

In his day Bulwer Lytton, "Poet, Essayist, Orator, Statesman, Dramatist, Scholar, Novelist" (*The Times* 1873) was described as "not only the foremost novelist, but the most eminent living writer in English literature" (*Quarterly Review* 1873); the novelist Plumer Ward called him "the most accomplished

---

6 *Pelham*, preface to London 1848 edition, p. iv.
7 There are inevitably many stories about this episode and its consequences; see Escott, op.cit. p. 297, and now especially Leslie Mitchell, *Bulwer Lytton: The Rise and Fall of a Victorian Man of Letters* (London 2003) ch. 3.

writer of the most accomplished era in English letters, practising all classes and styles of composition, novelist, dramatist, poet, historian, moral philosopher, essayist, critic, political pamphleteer—in each superior to all others, and only rivalled by himself."[8] In early life he was a friend and literary model for Disraeli; and later he was a close and much admired friend of Charles Dickens. He was buried in Westminster Abbey, with a sermon by Benjamin Jowett on "one of England's greatest writers and one of the most distinguished men of our time". Now he is remembered (if at all) as the author of two of the most famous phrases in the English language, "Poverty makes for strange bedfellows" and "The pen is mightier than the sword". And of course as Snoopy's favourite author: for it is Snoopy's continual rewriting of that first sentence, "It was a dark and stormy night," which is behind the creation of the annual Bulwer Lytton Fiction Contest for the worst first sentence in any unpublished novel of the year, and so of a flourishing cult in America with its own web site (which I thoroughly recommend).

Enlightenment Greece

The serious study of Greek history began in the eighteenth century. The first substantial narrative history of Greece was the diplomat Temple Stanyan's *The Grecian History*, the first edition of which was published in London in 1739; its importance was immediately recognized across Europe through the French translation of Diderot (Paris 1743). It was this tradition, reinforced by the mutual relationship with the French Enlightenment, that continued into the Scottish Enlightenment. The political message of these works was centred on a comparison between Sparta and Athens, each of which was described from the contrasting accounts in Plutarch's lives of the founders of their constitutions, Lycurgus and Solon. In almost every respect the Spartan system was considered to be the best. Thus the most influential political thinker of the Scottish Enlightenment, Adam Ferguson, in his famous work *An Essay on the History of Civil Society* (1767), describes the virtues of Sparta:

> Every institution of this singular people gave a lesson of obedience, of fortitude, and of zeal for the public: but it is remarkable that they chose to obtain, by their virtues alone, what other nations are fain to buy with their treasure; and it is well known, that, in the course of their history, they came to regard their discipline merely on account of its moral effects. They had experienced the happiness of a mind courageous, disinterested, and devoted to its best affections; and they studied to preserve this character in themselves, by resigning

8 Escott, op.cit p. 239.

the interests of ambition, and the hopes of military glory, even by sacrificing the numbers of their people.[9]

In contrast, Ferguson's picture of democratic Athens was dark and uncomprehending:

> The Athenians retained their popular government under all these defects. The mechanic was obliged, under a penalty, to appear in the public market-place, and to hear debates on the subjects of war, and of peace. He was tempted by pecuniary rewards, to attend on the trial of civil and criminal causes. But notwithstanding an exercise tending so much to cultivate their talents, the indigent came always with minds intent upon profit, or with the habits of an illiberal calling. Sunk under the sense of their personal disparity and weakness, they were ready to resign themselves entirely to the influence of some popular leader, who flattered their passions, and wrought on their fears; or, actuated by envy, they were ready to banish from the state whomsoever was respectable and eminent in the superior order of citizens: and whether from the neglect of the public at one time, or their maladministration at another, the sovereignty was every moment ready to drop from their hands.

This view permeated Scottish educated opinion. To take a couple of typical examples, the little-known William Robertson (1740–1803), namesake and contemporary of the great Scottish historian, published *The History of Ancient Greece* in Edinburgh in 1768.[10] In origin this popular work was a digest adapted for educational purposes from a French work of Alletz, but it had a wide influence in Scottish education, and was republished several times. Robertson set out, in a systematic Appendix to Book I, a comparative account *Of the Spartan and Athenian governments*, which presented much the same picture as Ferguson.[11]

The Scottish tradition continued until at least 1820. In that year at Edinburgh was published a new edition of a book by John Potter, the

9 Adam Ferguson, *An Essay on the History of Civil Society* ed. F. Oz-Salzberger (Cambridge 1995) pp. 142 and 178–9.

10 (Second edition, Edinburgh 1778.) Robertson was secretary to a Scottish laird, in which capacity he was famous for having in 1773 offered Dr Johnson boiled haddocks for breakfast, and a walk through the park. Johnson refused both, the first in disgust, the second because he had come to Scotland to see noble mountains, not civilized parkland. Later Robertson became deputy keeper of the records of Scotland with his brother, and a great expert on the Scottish peerage and Scottish charters. His Life is attached to the 1803 edition of his *History of Ancient Greece*.

11 Part I, pp. 66–82 in the second edition.

antiquarian Elizabethan Archbishop of Canterbury, first published in 1697: John Potter, *Archæologia Græca or the Antiquities of Greece, to which is added an Appendix containing a concise history of the Grecian states by G. Dunbar, F.R.S.E. and Professor of Greek in the University of Edinburgh*.[12] This appendix, separately numerated, is in fact an updated account of 112 pages on the historical institutions and literature of Greece; two sections follow one another, *Of the Spartan Constitution and Government* (pp. 13–42), and *A few Observations on the Athenian Constitution and Government* (pp. 42–55). They explicitly follow the views of Adam Ferguson, especially in the section devoted to Lycurgus, whose legislation was based on two principles, "that all free men were equal, and that slaves were necessary to relieve them from every servile employment" (p. 3). But for the first time in the Scottish tradition, under Ferguson's influence, Dunbar confronts directly the question of how one man could impose such an ideal state on his fellow citizens. Before Lycurgus the Spartans were pirates and warriors:

> It is at least probable, that the government of Sparta took its rise in a great measure from the situation and genius of the people; for no legislator in a free country could, all at once, efface the memory of old institutions, root up inveterate habits, and give a totally new temper and tone to the spirits of the people. . . . An eloquent philosopher (Dr A. Ferguson) has with truth asserted, "that the founders of nations only acted a superior part among numbers who were disposed to the same institutions, and that they left to posterity a renown, pointing them out as the inventors of many practices which had been already in use, and which helped to form their own manners and genius as well as those of their countrymen."

The reign of Mitford

> May I remind you that it is uncertain whether Greek history was invented in England or in Scotland. The two claimants are the Englishman William Mitford who published the first

---

12 George Dunbar (1774–1851) was the child of humble parents. He was apprenticed as a gardener but injured himself falling from a tree; he attracted the notice of a neighbouring proprietor who helped him acquire a classical education. He studied at Edinburgh around 1800, and while tutor in the family of the Lord Provost, was selected to act as assistant to the Professor of Greek, Andrew Dalzell; on his death in 1806, Dunbar became Professor of Greek until his death in 1851 (though in later years a substitute fulfilled his duties). He was not a historian; he wrote books on grammar, language, dictionaries, and textbooks. "As a classical scholar Dunbar did not leave behind him a very enduring reputation, and the bulk of his work has little permanent value. His industry however was very great. His best work was the compilation of lexicons" (*Dictionary of National Biography* (Oxford 1885–)).

volume of his *History of Greece* in 1784 but did not finish his
work until 1810, and the Royal Historiographer of Scotland,
John Gillies, who in 1786 published a complete Greek history
in two volumes in quarto and by 1778 had already published
a discourse "on the history, manners, and character of the
Greeks from the conclusion of the Peloponnesian War to the
battle of Chaeronea."

This was the starting point of the famous inaugural lecture of Arnaldo
Momigliano as Professor of Ancient History at University College London in
1952.[13] His account of the development of Greek history privileges modern narrative histories over more or less systematic accounts of antiquities;
and it is true that both Gillies and Mitford were acutely conscious of the
new demands of continuous narrative history. John Gillies was a disciple
of William Robertson, the official Historiographer Royal of Scotland, and
rival of David Hume as one of the two great historians of the age; Gillies
succeeded to Robertson's official position in 1793. He is described as "a man
of good intentions, a passable scholar, an indefatigable reader, and a most
respectable character, but there was no touch of genius in his writings"
which were "written in a readable but somewhat pompous style." His *History
of Greece* is in fact a rather disappointing production in relation to other
works of the Scottish Enlightenment, and does not live up to the grandiose
political claims in its dedication to King George III:

> Sir,
> The History of Greece exposes the dangerous turbulence of
> Democracy, and arraigns the despotism of tyrants. By describing
> the incurable evils inherent in every form of Republican policy, it
> evinces the inestimable benefits, resulting to Liberty itself, from the
> lawful dominion of hereditary Kings, and the steady operation of
> well-regulated Monarchy. That your Majesty may long reign the
> illustrious Guardian of public freedom, and the unrivalled Patron of
> useful learning, is the fervent prayer of Your Majesty's Most dutiful
> Subject and Servant, John Gillies. London Feb. 10, 1786.

William Mitford's *History of Greece* is also a product of the new historiography of the late eighteenth century. But his model was English—Edward
Gibbon, his fellow officer in the Hampshire Militia, with whom he shared

---

13 Reprinted in *Studies in Historiography* (London 1966) pp. 56–74. Momigliano went on of
course to modify this statement a little by discussing the reasons why the predecessors of
Mitford and Gillies could not be regarded as true historians of Greece, and by discussing
their backgrounds in the antiquarian tradition.

the doubtful privilege of having failed to acquire an education at Oxford from 1761 (where he belonged to the same breakfast club as Jeremy Bentham, who thought "his conversation commonplace"). Like Gibbon, his formative experience had been his encounter with the French *érudit* tradition: the death of his wife and a serious illness led to a trip to France in 1776 where he met M de Meusnier and M de Villoison, and the Baron de Saint Croix, and spent time with the latter at Mourmoiron near Avignon. He returned to live the life of a country gentleman at his family estate of Exbury in Hampshire, and joined the Hampshire Militia as captain under Edward Gibbon as major. His brother (see n. 14 below) recorded: "Their conversations, in those hours of leisure which the militia service afforded, frequently turned on ancient history; and Mr Gibbon, finding the eagerness of his friend in the pursuit of Grecian literature, urged him to undertake the History of Greece."

Mitford's *History of Greece* (published in five volumes at intervals between 1784 and 1810) was an important work which deserved its long reign; it was based on considerable knowledge of the ancient texts, and a refreshing ability (like his friend and model Gibbon) to use comparative studies of other societies, derived from wide reading, as well as from serious reflection on the history of his own country. In fact he was an original historian in terms both of historical method and of his approach to the question of the usefulness of parallels between ancient and modern history. His *History of Greece* was rightly regarded as greatly superior to that of Gillies; it "remained popular and had the merit of supplying a laborious English work on a neglected subject" for almost two generations (*DNB* XIII p. 534): it was last republished in 1835.[14] But it was highly idiosyncratic in a number of ways, not least in its style which was ridiculed by contemporaries such as Lord Byron, being based on principles of grammar and orthography invented by himself out of his study of the "saxon language."

Mitford was therefore the standard history of Greece in the age of reform. In this new climate he was of course attacked for his political views. But these attacks were not wholly fair; it was not that Mitford had sought to distort Greek history in order to provide examples for modern history. Quite the opposite: he opposed all such attempts, and believed firmly that the experience of all Greek states was "not suited to the extensive territory and the free condition of the British islands". In Greece, "true freedom, the freedom of all, such as he conceived British freedom long to have been, never existed"; in contemporary Britain, unlike ancient Greece, there was security of person and property, and absence of slavery. Mitford belonged to the

---

14 In Balliol College Library I was able to use Benjamin Jowett's copy of the new edition of 1835, with a biographical introduction by Mitford's brother Lord Redesdale (ancestor of the Mitford sisters: the historian's papers are still in the hands of the family). The quotations in defence of Mitford are taken from his brother's preface, dated 1829.

generation formed by the experiences of the American and French revolutions, and held the traditional opinions of the landed gentry; he was against the subversive utopian principles of the French and other enlightenments. According to the defence of him by his brother, he rejected the views of "some distinguished persons of the freedom enjoyed by all in the Grecian republics, whose institutions were represented as tending more to the happiness of man than those which had prevailed in this country" (p. xxiii); he "attempted to show the evils that had arisen from institutions adopted by the most distinguished Grecian states, he has sought to impress on the minds of his countrymen that such institutions, even if suited to the condition of those states, were not suited to the condition of his own country; to warn them against the influence of that seduction which the splendid display of talent in the Grecian character might produce." (p. xxviii).

To Mitford the question of the freedom of the individual was crucial. "They [the British] were therefore never objects of that oppression which, in other countries, where slavery has existed to a great extent, has been produced by fear; as in Greece, and especially in Sparta, where a systematic tyranny, of the most atrocious kind, was practised, to prevent the danger, more than once seriously felt, and which at all times was dreaded, from the number of those in bondage, giving them physical power superior to the physical power of the freemen, the sole possessors of political power." (pp. xlvi–xlvii). Similarly Athens: the Athenian constitution was not really a democracy because of slavery.[15] Four hundred thousand slaves made democracy "not so absolutely absurd and impracticable among the Greeks as it would be where no slavery is." Mitford could therefore idealize neither Sparta nor Athens, because for him the only free society was that which had been created through the historical development of English institutions; and there was nothing comparable in the ancient world.

This robust, commonsensical, but parochial view was of course anathema to those who wished to idealize antiquity. In the next generation it was especially his view of Athens to which they objected, because it was especially Athens which they wanted to appropriate as a model of radical democracy. Mitford's consistent use of modern parallels made it easy to accuse him of writing with a modern bias, and George Grote's famous attack on Mitford in the *Westminster Review* of 1826 is fundamentally an attack on his political prejudices:

> The qualities desirable in an historian may be divided into two classes; those which qualify him to trace out and report the facts of the period which he selects; and those which qualify him to embody the facts into results, to survey the general characteristics of society

15 Ch. V sec. IV.

among the people of whom he treats, and to ascertain the comparative degree of civilization which their habits and institutions evince them to have reached.

To appreciate the success of Mr Mitford as an historian, we must examine in what degree he possesses the great mental qualities above described.

And first with regard to the higher philosophising powers: a mere inspection of the titles of his chapters, almost without perusing the body of his work, would suffice to show, that so far from having employed them, he is insensible even to the necessity of employing them in order to elicit the genuine and valuable results of history. He has hardly attempted any analysis of the great social and political characteristics of Greece. His account of the political institutions of Lycurgus is the nearest approximation to such an undertaking, and evinces a greater freedom from his usual prejudices than is to be found any where else throughout his work. If even that, however, falls very short of what it ought to be and might be, the sketch which he has professed to give of the Athenian constitution is still more lamentably defective. We can hardly wonder that this sketch should be very incomplete and meagre, even as a description, since the author confesses himself to have borrowed it entirely from Potter's Antiquities, and has attempted no collation of the authorities for himself: and, when we compare this avowal of Mr Mitford with the new lights which Niebuhr's ingenious and original researches have thrown upon the constitution of Rome, we are made painfully sensible of the difference between the real knowledge of the ancient world possessed or inquired for by a German public, and the appearance of knowledge which suffices here. Nor has Mr Mitford accompanied his imperfect sketch with any philosophical exposition of the tendency of Athenian institutions; of the extent to which they failed in providing securities for good government; and of the reasons which occasioned their failure. . . .

There is a strong tendency in the human mind to the worship of power: a principle which has been explained by Adam Smith with as much philosophy as eloquence in his Theory of Moral Sentiments. Everything in an English education tends to nourish, to strengthen, and to perpetuate this tendency; and in the mind of Mr Mitford, a mind priding itself on adherence to every thing English, it has become absolute idolatry. The whole of his favourable affections are turned towards the man of power. He is devoted to kingly government, and to kings, not only with preference, but even with passion and bigotry; the average kingly character is in his eye a compound of perfections, from which indeed there may be, in individual cases, a few rare and unaccountable deviations; but the worst king that ever existed appears to him better, than the best system possible with no king at all. . . .

But the bias of Mr Mitford exhibits itself still more copiously on the side of his hatred than on the side of his love; partly because the language of blame is so much more poignant than that of praise, partly because Grecian history deals so much more with republics than with monarchs. The number of images and epithets, indicating hatred and contempt, which he has heaped upon the democratical communities, in one part or another of his history, is truly surprising. He is not even solicitous to preserve these images in consistency one with the other, provided each will separately conduce towards his object. Sometimes he describes the sovereign assembly at Athens as composed of fullers, shoemakers, braziers, &c. at other times he tells us that "a sovereign people would not work"; sometimes he reproaches them as inspired with a restless thirst of conquest, at other times he arraigns their self-indulgence and luxury, because they will not serve on expeditions for conquest; in one place he talks awfully of the irresistible might of the sovereign assembly, in another he exhibits to us the "inherent impotence" of the most renowned ancient democracies. He exclaims loudly against the extortions of the Athenian commanders in the Aegean, and terms them (generally, we believe, with justice) "the greatest of pirates." But this is only so long as they are acting in the name of the democracy, and while the democracy can be charged with the guilt of their acts; for when any of these commanders return home, and are brought to trial for the very peculations which he has described as habitually practised, Mr Mitford's tone instantly changes, and he depicts them as innocent sufferers under the scourge of democratical jealousy and ingratitude. If they are tried and acquitted, this he urges as a proof of the uncommon licence of false accusation; if they are found guilty, it is a proof of that still, but it is besides a proof of the greediness and malevolence of a democratical tribunal.[16]

Grote's long article marked a turning point in historical scholarship; it was essentially a defence of ancient democracy against its ancient and modern critics, and was part of a widespread new movement in the British re-evaluation of Sparta and Athens. The attack is usually thought to have begun with Grote; but from John Stuart Mill's *Autobiography* it is clear that James Mill was already warning his small son against the dangers of Mitford at least ten years earlier, and Grote was preceded in at least some of his

16 *Westminster Review* April 1826 pp. 280–5.

criticisms by the young Macaulay.[17] However justified, Grote's attack showed the characteristic arrogance of the Utilitarians in thinking that everyone ought to hold the same views as themselves, and in their complete failure to understand the generation influenced by the American and French Revolutions, or the difference between the mercantile culture of the nineteenth and the still largely agrarian culture of the eighteenth century. Nevertheless it was true that Mitford's scholarship was now out of date, and that his work lacked even the intellectual background of the Scottish Enlightenment that had been provided by writers such as Adam Ferguson.

Grote was in fact denying the right of Mitford to declare the autonomy of ancient history, and asserting the right of the radical tradition to appropriate Athens for the modern world; the strength of his position, as was to become apparent twenty years later, lay not in his political views as such, but in the way that he proceeded to combine them with the tools of German scholarship, and perhaps most clearly in his ability to separate myth from history.

Meanwhile from around 1830 the influence of the new German historical scholarship was beginning to be felt. It arrived through two channels; one is associated with the Cambridge translators and disciples of Niebuhr's *History of Rome*, Julius Hare and Connop Thirlwall (first edition 1828–32). From 1835 Thirlwall began publishing his own *History of Greece*, modelled on Niebuhr's principles: this contains a fascinating attempt to analyse Lycurgan Sparta and Solonian Athens—an amalgamation of the new science with older views, which lacks the fervour but has many analogies with his exact contemporary Bulwer Lytton.[18]

More important was the translation of Carl Ottfried Müller's *History of the Doric Race*, by two future radical politicians, Henry Tufnell and George Cornewall Lewis (1830, second edition 1839), who were contemporaries at what was then the leading intellectual institution in England, Christ Church, Oxford. Cornewall Lewis was the first and most important of the translators from the German;[19] while still a student at Oxford he had translated Boeckh's *Public Economy of Athens* (1828, 1842), and published it anonymously with a long critique of its economic doctrines along Utilitarian lines; in 1830 he attended the lectures of John Austin, the famous Utilitarian Professor of Law at University College London. He also translated Müller's *History of Greek Literature* (1840–2), and later wrote a critique of Niebuhr's theories on early Roman history. He was a leading Utilitarian politician, from 1833 commissioner on a wide range of government reports, author of one of the best critiques of the British Empire (*Essay of the Government of Dependencies* (1841, 1891)), Liberal MP from 1855, editor of the *Edinburgh Review*, and finally Chancellor of the Exchequer under Lord Palmerston. He died aged fifty-six; otherwise he might well have succeeded Gladstone as leader of his party. His philosophy of life is summed up in his famous remark, "Life would be tolerable but for its amusements."

The first thing the new German science of Müller required was that we should forget Lycurgus the founder of Sparta: "If now we apply the method above stated to the history of Lycurgus, we shall find that we have absolutely no account of him as an *individual person*" (*History of the Doric Race* Book I ch. 7 sec. 6). The second lesson to be learned was based on F. Schlegel's theories of the superiority of the Doric race over the Ionian: the Spartan constitution was not specific to Sparta, but simply the most perfect example of a common Dorian way of life:

> In the genuine Doric form of government there were certain pre-dominant ideas, which were peculiar to that race, and were also expressed in the worship of Apollo, viz., those of *harmony* and *order* (τὸ εὔκοσμον), of *self-control* and *moderation* (σωφροσύνη), and of *manly virtue* (ἀρετή). Accordingly, the constitution was formed for the education as well of the old as of the young, and in a Doric state education was upon the whole a subject of greater importance than government. And for this reason all attempts to explain the legislation of Lycurgus, from partial views and considerations, have necessarily failed.[20]

This exposition of a new German version of an idealized Sparta, quite different from the pre-existing French and Scottish theoretical approaches, caused much discussion in Britain: even the translators felt obliged to dissociate themselves from some of Müller's views in their preface; and the racial element in his theories was discussed without ever really gaining acceptance. However, the relegation of Lycurgus to the status of myth, and the question of the relation between the Spartan social system and those of other Dorian states became central. Müller was also partly responsible for the British rejection of Sparta in favour of Athens: his Prussian racially defined Dorians lacked any appeal to the British urban elite of the age of reform, who were choosing rather to identify themselves with democracy and Athens.

Until now it has been held that this shift in consciousness towards both German scholarship and idealization of Athenian society was consummated in Grote's *History of Greece* (the first two volumes of which were published in

20 *History of the Doric Race* Book III ch. 1 sec. 10.

1846, but which was not completed until 1856). But the rediscovery of Bulwer Lytton's *Athens* reveals a different picture.

Radical history

> His knowledge of the liberty of Greece was not drawn from the ignorant historian of her Republics;* nor did he find in the contemplative and gentle philosophy of the ancients, nothing but a sanction for modern bigotry and existing abuses.
>
> *It is really a disgrace to our University, that any of its colleges should accept as a reference, or even tolerate as an author, the presumptuous bigot who has bequeathed to us, in his "History of Greece," the master piece of a declaimer without energy, and of a pedant without learning.
>
> (Bulwer Lytton, *Pelham* (1828) ch. XLIII)

Back to Bulwer Lytton and Athens: what is this unknown work of history? And why is it so obscure that it escaped all the greatest scholars of nineteenth-century historical writing, from Arnaldo Momigliano, to Richard Jenkyns and Frank Turner, the respective authors of the two standard works, *The Victorians and Ancient Greece* (Oxford 1980) and *The Greek Heritage in Victorian Britain* (New Haven and London 1981)? It does not even appear in the ferociously learned work of Martin Bernal, *Black Athena* (London 1987), despite its central importance for his theme.[21]

The answer is given in part in the preface to the later reprint, the Knebworth edition of Bulwer Lytton's *Miscellaneous Works* (1874):

> No more than half the author's original design was ever realised. The Rise of Athens alone, it will be seen, is herein described: the Fall is only dimly foreshadowed. When the manuscript of the present unfinished work was already in the hands of its publishers, the appearance of Mr Thirlwall's "History of Greece" induced the author

---

21 Jenkyns mentions the title (p. 74); Turner briefly misrepresents the book (pp. 210–11). Elizabeth Rawson dismisses it in a footnote: "Lytton also wrote a history of Athens, pre-Thirlwall, and wisely left it unfinished" (*The Spartan Tradition in European Thought* (Oxford 1969) p. 360); doubtless she did not like its denunciation of Sparta. Recently K.N. Demetriou in his excellent and learned monograph on George Grote devoted four pages to Bulwer Lytton (*George Grote on Plato and Athenian Democracy* (Frankfurt 1999) pp. 47–50; see also his article cited above (n. 18) at pp. 63–5. But I am puzzled by his claim that Bulwer's work is "divided into two parts, one historical and the other dealing with the arts and literature of the Athenians. The plan of a literary section already forms a glaring innovation." Such a division was in fact commonplace; the originality of Bulwer lies in the fact that there is no such division in his book, but rather an integration of the two aspects.

of "Athens" to suspend his labours; and he finally abandoned them in consequence of Mr Grote's great work upon the same subject. In his Preface to that work, Mr Grote himself had frankly declared, "If my early friend Dr Thirlwall's 'History of Greece,' had appeared a few years sooner, I should probably never have conceived the design of the present work at all; I should certainly not have been prompted to the task by any deficiencies such as those which I felt and regretted in Mitford." But it was from a strong sense of those deficiencies that Lord Lytton had commenced his narrative of Athenian history; and, therefore, he had no motive to continue it when the historical method he had employed was being exhaustively applied by Mr Grote to the same field of historical research.

So the book, being incomplete and apparently superseded, was forgotten, and has completely disappeared from all accounts of the development of historical writing in the nineteenth century. That is a pity as we shall see, for it is the first serious History of Greece in modern Europe, and the most important work from that most important period of what Bernal has described as the transition from the ancient model to the Aryan model of Greek history. It also provides the earliest and most significant work of the English Romantic school of history, hitherto exemplified by Carlyle and Macaulay, and constitutes the most original English contribution to the continental movement that began the great age of history.

However, the book is not as incomplete as it may seem. For following up a clue in one of the biographies of Bulwer Lytton, I was led to the Hertfordshire Archives, where, in the autumn of 2002, I opened a dusty brown paper parcel —to discover not only the original manuscript of the first two volumes, but also a manuscript of several hundred pages containing the first draft of Volume III, on the "Fall of Athens". Much of this manuscript is of course a retelling of the narrative of Thucydides. But I have been able to transcribe, and here publish for the first time, enough to prove that Bulwer Lytton had anticipated by a decade most of the radical views on Athenian history hitherto attributed to George Grote. For example, Cleon is for the first time recognized as a talented and truly democratic politician. There is a full account of the Pylos affair, in which Cleon "the able demagogue" is recast as the hero of the story long before Grote attempted the same:

> Thro' his whole course on this occasion one cannot but suspect that he was in secret correspondence with Demosthenes and acted by his intelligence and advice. We have seen before the little unison that existed between Demosthenes and the Commanders of the Fleet Eurymedon and Sophocles. It is highly probable, that among the reasons which deterred Demosthenes from assault on Sphacteria,

was the non co-operation of the two commanders. From what follows Cleon evidently had been acquainted with the plan formed by Demosthenes—he names him as his Colleague in the Expedition. What more likely than that Demosthenes really stood in need of Cleon's influence with the popular Assembly to force the rival commanders to the measures he meditated?

If Thucydides is not clear in this somewhat obscure business we must remember that he was in opposition to Cleon and that the most penetrating investigator cannot discover all the true springs of conduct in the Party he opposes.

The introduction to the unpublished Volume III reveals in fact most clearly the ultimate purpose of this fundamental rewriting of Greek history:

We have traced the rise of the Athenian Commonwealth—we have now before us its meridian and decline. In the Peloponnesian War we approach events not more memorable in the Annals of the Ancient World, than instructive to the Societies of the Modern. For as it has been justly said, "there is an ancient and a modern period in the History of every People, the ancient differing, and the modern in many essential points agreeing with that in which we live".[22] In Greece then, as through Europe now, a great Popular spirit was at work. To the earlier times, when Aristocracy protects freedom from the single tyrant, to the later æra of civilization when wealth becomes the innovating principle and enfeebles by extending the privileges of Nobility and Birth, now succeeded the graver struggle between Property and Numbers—that struggle which has produced the greatest calamities in the Past, and with which unreasoning Fanaticism and Speculative Philosophy have alike threatened the Futures of existing Nations. Whatever our several opinions and predilections, we can only profit by the lessons which the history of this struggle in the most brilliant period of Grecian civilization should bestow, by preserving the disproportionate judgment which distinguishes the guide who bequeathed to Mankind the narrative of the Peloponnesian War—κτῆμα ἐς αἰεί—"an everlasting possession," not to subserve the aims of malignant partizans, but to enrich the experience of every statesman and warn the factions of every Land.

---

22 "Thus the largest portion of that history which we commonly call ancient is practically modern, as it describes society in a stage analogous to that in which it now is; while on the other hand, much of what is called modern history is practically ancient, as it relates to a state of things which has passed away. Appendix I. Arnold's Thucyd. vol. I. p. 630."

As was already apparent from the two published volumes, Bulwer Lytton's work belongs to his reforming days as a Radical and a Utilitarian. His aim was to make Greek history live and serve the radical cause. While he was fully acquainted with the latest German scholarship, he also sought to create a history that would stir his contemporaries: as one of his biographers says, "His Athens sensibly promoted the English interest in Greek civilization, history, art, and letters first excited by Byron. In politics there was no question of the time about which, on the Whig or Radical side, he had not written or spoken with destructiveness and effect."[23] Bulwer Lytton's *Athens* is in fact the earliest and most forthright of those histories of Greece that set out to destroy the reputation of William Mitford.

The unfinished book was immensely popular at home and abroad throughout the nineteenth century: Escott in 1910 writes that "some thirty years ago . . . Northumbrian miners and Midland artisans I then found to be well-acquainted with, not only Bulwer-Lytton's fictions, but the serious historical sketches contained in his essays and his Athens."[24] The book was translated into German apparently three times in 1837 (Bulwer Lytton is one of the major British influences on the German novel);[25] it was issued in a popular Tauchnitz (Leipzig) edition for railway travellers (1843), and twice pirated in his collected works.[26] In the United States copies can be found in a variety of American editions in many libraries (I have reports of editions of 1837, 1847, 1852, 1860, and 1874). There is an Italian translation of 1838, of which three copies still exist, in the public libraries of Milan and Bergamo, and in the archbishop's library in Turin.[27] The Royal Library in Copenhagen records a Danish translation of 1856 in three volumes, as part of the collected

---

23 Escott, op.cit. p. 225.

24 Escott, op.cit. pp. 7–8.

25 1. *Athen, seine Erhebung und sein Fall, nebst Ueberblicken ueber die Literatur, die Philosophie und das buergerliche und gesellige Leben des athenischen Volks* (im Verlage der J.B. Metzler'schen Buchhandlung, 1837–1838) trans. by Dr Gustav Pfizer. 2. *Athens Grösse und Verfall, nebst Untersuchungen über die Literatur, die Philosophie und das gesellige Leben des Athenienischen Volkes* Aachen 1837, Mayer (Sämmtliche Werke Bd. 23/24 & 25/26), 4 pts in 2 vols, trans. by O. v. Czarnowski. 3. (no translator specified) *Athens Aufschwung und Fall, mit Hinblick auf die Literatur, die Philosophie und das gesellige Leben des Atheniensischen Volkes*, 5 parts; Parts 1–4: Zwickau 1837, Gebrüder Schumann in Leipzig (E.L. Bulwer, Werke Teil 40–43); Part 5: In: Edward Bulwer Lytton, *Athens Aufschwung und Fall, mit Hinblick auf die Literatur, die Philosophie und das gesellige Leben des Atheniensischen Volkes*, Teil 5 — Ernst Maltravers, Zwickau: Gebrüder Schumann in Leipzig (E.L. Bulwer, Werke Teil 44–48) (1837).

26 *Athens, its rise and fall* (English text) Leipzig 1837, Fleischer (The Complete Works of E.L. Bulwer vol. XII/XIII), 2 vols. *Athens, its rise and fall* (English text) (extracts from text) Leipzig 1884 (Siegismund & Volkening).

27 *Atene, il suo innalzamento e sua caduta*, prima versione italiana di Francesco Ambrosoli, Milano: Vedova di Andrea Stella e figlio, 1838 (information from Carmine Ampolo).

works of Bulwer Lytton, which run to sixty-nine volumes in all.[28] The edition
that I had purchased is indeed evidence of this popularity, for it is an edition
printed by the man whom Byron affectionately called "the old pirate
Galignani", a publisher in Paris who from 1800 to 1852, before the copy-
right agreement between Britain and France, made a speciality of reprinting,
within a month and at one fifth of the price, the works of the most famous
English authors of the Romantic age, like Byron, Shelley, Coleridge and
even a very scholarly first collected edition of Keats. Giovanni Antonio
Galignani, an Italian who had married the daughter of an English publisher
during a period of refuge in London from the French Revolution, returned
to Paris to run a publishing house, a coffee shop and reading room, and a
series of journals for British tourists; his dynasty survives today, and the bookshop Galignani in the Rue de Rivoli now proudly boasts of being the oldest
English-language bookshop on the continent.[29]

The relationship between Bulwer Lytton's *Athens* and contemporary
Utilitarian views on Greek history is however more difficult to unravel. It
is universally believed that the shift in consciousness towards both German
scholarship and idealization of Athenian society was consummated in George
Grote's *History of Greece*, whose influence was dominant in British attitudes to
classical Greece for almost a century, and whose work remains the only serious
full-scale history of Greece in English. But as we have seen, Bulwer Lytton's
book shows that the ideas expressed by Grote were already widespread at least
a decade before he began publishing in 1846, and reveals how much had
changed and become common knowledge in the period between the death of
Lord Byron in 1824 and the start of the reign of Grote—precisely in the age
marked within Britain by the Great Reform Bill of 1832, and externally by
the activity of the British Philhellenes in the Greek War of Independence.

Athens is especially important because of the author's recognition that he
stands at the turning point of the writing of Greek history, and because his
aim is to present to a popular audience the current state of modern controversy.
He offers for instance the most reasoned view that I have yet discovered for
what Martin Bernal has called "the ancient model" of the origins of Greek
culture, the view that it results from Egyptian colonization. Bulwer Lytton
argues explicitly and persuasively for the ancient view that Cecrops was
Egyptian, and for the proposition that many high cultures have derived from

28 *Athenen, dets Opkomst og Fald: med Udsigt over det atheniensiske Folks Litteratur, Philosophie og sociale Liv* trans. Joachim Chr. Møller, Bulwers Skrifter pp. 33–6, Copenhagen, Chr. Steen & Søns Forlag. I owe this information to Mogens Herman Hansen.
29 See the magnificent article by Giles Barber, "Galignani's and the publication of English books in France from 1800 to 1852", *The Library* 16 (1961) pp. 267–86; also the bicentenary volume published by the firm—Diana Cooper-Richet and Emily Bourgeaud, *Galignani* (Paris 1999). Bulwer Lytton himself mentions Galignani's "reading room" in his novel *Pelham* (ch. XXII).

colonization by a more civilized power. But his second chapter is devoted to "the unimportant Consequences to be deduced from the Admission that Cecrops might be Egyptian". He stands therefore exactly at that turning point between the "ancient" and the "Aryan" model of Greek history which Bernal had hypothesized without being able to find the evidence. This age of transition certainly existed; one of Bulwer Lytton's reviewers noticed it explicitly:[30]

> With regard to one species of foreign influence—that exerted by Egypt—Mr Bulwer properly characterises it as "faint and evanescent." Yet the early intrusion of Egyptian settlers on the Attic soil must, we think, be admitted as a fact—not upon the direct testimony of Greek writers, but upon the much stronger, though more oblique evidence of some remarkable traces in Athenian religion, policy, and art. On this head we agree with Frederick Thiersch, Dr Arnold, and Mr Bulwer himself, rather than with Mr Keightley, Mr Thirlwall, and the Germans whom they follow.

Similarly in 1842, J.A. St John, in a dedication to his son, rather poignantly claims to have lost his eyesight in pursuing the Egyptian origins of Greek civilization:[31]

> Whithersoever we have travelled, the wrecks of Grecian literature have accompanied us, and the studies to which these pages owe their existence have been pursued under the influence of almost every climate in Europe. Nay if I pushed my researches still further and visited the portion of Africa commonly supposed to have been the cradle of Hellenic civilisation, it was solely in the hope of qualifying myself to speak with some degree of confidence on the subject of those arts which represent to the Modern World so much of the grandeur and genius of Greece. Here, probably, the action of pestilential winds, and of the sands and burning glare of the desert commenced that dimming of the "visual ray," which, in all likelihood, will wrap me gradually in complete darkness, and veil forever from my sight those forms of the beautiful which have been incarnated, if I may so speak, in marble. This is a language which neither you nor your sister can read to me.

In like fashion Bulwer has read and rejected the opinions of Müller on the Dorian race; he considers German views of the origins of Greek religion,

---

30 *Edinburgh Review* July 1837 p. 164.
31 *The History of the Manners and Customs of Ancient Greece* (3 vols, London 1842) p. vi.

only to reject them in favour of a rationalizing interpretation along French lines. He has read the first two volumes of Thirlwall, but dedicates his work to the last (and maddest) representative of the English tradition of pseudo-exact scholarship, Henry Fynes Clinton, author of the once famous *Fasti Hellenici* (1824–7), a treatise on chronology which Bulwer Lytton compared later to Bayle's Dictionary or Gibbon's History, "a book to which thousands of books had contributed, only to make the originality of the single mind more bold and clear."[32]

Athens versus Sparta

As we have seen, it was traditional in French and English (and even more in Scottish) works on Greek history of the eighteenth century to present a contrast between Sparta and Athens, based respectively on the accounts in Plutarch's Lives of Lycurgus and Solon: Sparta usually wins by a large margin. What is most interesting about Bulwer Lytton's book is his use of this contrast. It is expressed with the rhetorical force of a professional politician skilled in persuading; and it seeks to create a public opinion which should lead to action; his work is designed "not for colleges and cloisters, but for the general and miscellaneous public." His views therefore represent and also seek to influence the public opinion of contemporary British society; they are politically of far greater importance than those of professional historians. It seems indeed to have been partly the difficulty of combining scholarship with political views, and his sense of the increasing dominance of professionalism in historical studies, especially the prospect of competition with the scholarship of Thirlwall, that caused Bulwer Lytton to abandon his projected history after the first two volumes, which carry the story down to the death of Pericles, and an appreciation of Sophocles. For he had intended originally to carry the work down to "the period when the annals of the world are merged into the chronicle of the Roman Empire."[33]

Bulwer Lytton's aim is clearly presented in his title: he sees the history of Greece both conceptually, and in its relation to the modern age, as a history of the rise and fall of Athens, on which the histories of all other Greek cities

---

32 Bulwer Lytton, *The Caxtons* (Edinburgh and London 1849) i.160. For the melancholy Clinton, see my sketch in ch. 15 of *The History of the University of Oxford vol. VI, Nineteenth-Century Oxford, Part 1* ed. M.G. Brock and M.C. Curthoys (Oxford 1997) pp. 523–5.

33 See his Advertisement. This finishing point is found for instance in William Robertson; it was also Mitford's original intention, although he never reached beyond Alexander. The death of Philip (Stanyan) or of Alexander (Gillies, Grote) are more usual; Thirlwall ostensibly carried his narrative down to the modern age, though in a very perfunctory fashion. Bulwer Lytton later wrote an unfinished and, in the view of Elizabeth Rawson, "to the modern reader, unfinishable" novel, *Pausanias the Spartan*, in which the hero betrays Sparta but has sympathy with the Helots—published posthumously in 1876.

are dependent. By his very denial of the charge, his preface already admits that his interpretation is likely to be regarded as politically motivated:

> As the history of the Greek Republics has been too often corruptly pressed into the service of heated political partisans, may I be pardoned the precaution of observing, that whatever my own political code, as applied to England, I have nowhere sought knowingly to pervert the lessons of the past to fugitive interests and party purposes. Whether led sometimes to censure, or more often to vindicate, the Athenian People, I am not conscious of any other desire than that of strict, faithful, impartial justice.

Bulwer Lytton's description of Sparta is traditional in its approach, although he is aware of the views of the recently translated C.O. Müller; for instance on the legend of the Return of Heraclidae he rejects his opinion: "The true nature of this revolution has only been rendered more obscure by modern ingenuity; which has abandoned the popular accounts for suppositions still more improbable and romantic" (Book I ch. VI sec. I). But under the influence of Müller he abandons the view that Lycurgus is responsible for the Spartan constitution (sec. IV):

> I enter not into the discussion whether he framed an entirely new constitution, or whether he restored the spirit of one common to his race and not unfamiliar to Sparta. Common sense seems to me sufficient to assure us of the latter. Let those who please believe that one man, without the intervention of arms—not as a conqueror but a friend— could succeed in establishing a constitution, resting not upon laws, but manners—not upon force, but usage—utterly hostile to all the tastes, desires, and affections of human nature: . . . . For my part, I know that all history furnishes no other such example; and I believe that no man was ever so miraculously endowed with the power to conquer nature.

Lycurgus' aim was to restore not create; Crete already had Dorian customs, and the regulations of Lycurgus must be regarded as not "peculiar to Sparta but as the most perfect development of the Dorian constitutions, as we learn from Pindar."[34]

But rather than follow the principles proposed by the racial typology of Müller, in Book I chapter VI section VI Lytton gives "a brief, but I trust a sufficient outline, of the Spartan constitution, social and political", of a traditional type, until he arrives at "the most active and efficient part of the government, viz the Institution of the Ephors":

---

34 Below p. xx. Here note the reference to "Müller's Dorians".

It is clear that the later authority of the ephors was never designed by Lycurgus, or the earlier legislators. It is entirely at variance with the confined aristocracy which was the aim of the Spartan, and of nearly every genuine Doric constitution. It made a democracy as it were by stealth. This powerful body consisted of five persons, chosen annually by the people. In fact, they may be called the representatives of the popular will . . . Its influence was the result of the vicious constitution of the gerusia, or council. Had that assembly been properly constituted, there would have been no occasion for the ephors. . . . Of two assemblies—the ephors and the gerusia—we see the one elected annually, the other for life—the one responsible to the people, the other not—the one composed of men, busy, stirring, ambitious, in the vigour of life—the other of veterans, past the ordinary stimulus of exertion, and regarding the dignity of office rather as the reward of a life, than the opening to ambition. Of two such assemblies, it is easy to foretell which would lose, and which would augment, authority. . . . The ephoralty was the focus of popular power. Like an American Congress, or an English House of Commons, it prevented the action of the people, by acting in behalf of the people. To representatives annually chosen the multitude cheerfully left the management of their interests. Thus it was true that the ephors prevented the encroachments of the popular assembly; —but how? By encroaching themselves, and in the name of the people! . . . . The ephors gradually destroyed the constitution of Sparta; but, without the ephors, it may be reasonably doubted whether the constitution would have survived half as long. . . . Had the other part of the Spartan constitution (absurdly panegyrized) been so formed as to harmonize with, even in checking, the power of the ephors; and, above all, had it not been for the lamentable error of a social system, which, by seeking to exclude the desire of gain, created a terrible re-action, and made the Spartan magistrature the most venal and corrupt in Greece—the ephors might have sufficed to develop all the best principles of government. For they went nearly to recognize the soundest philosophy of the representative system, being the smallest number of representatives chosen, without restriction, from the greatest number of electors, for short periods, and under strong responsibilities.

The distinction between ancient direct democracy and modern representative democracy was later to become a central theme in Utilitarian political thought: it is here clearly enunciated.[35]

35 See the important study of Nadia Urbinati mentioned below n. 43.

Bulwer Lytton's view of the social system is equally negative (sec. VII):

> If we consider the situation of the Spartans at the time of Lycurgus, and during a long subsequent period, we see at once that to enable them to live at all, they must be accustomed to the life of a camp; —they were a little colony of soldiers, supporting themselves, hand and foot, in a hostile country, over a population that detested them. . . . to be brave, temperate, and hardy, were the only means by which to escape the sword of the Messenian, and to master the hatred of the Helot . . . Accordingly the child was reared, from the earliest age, to a life of hardship, discipline, and privation; he was starved into abstinence;—he was beaten into fortitude;—he was punished without offence, that he might be trained to bear without a groan;—the older he grew, till he reached manhood, the severer the discipline he underwent. The intellectual education was little attended to . . . . The youth . . . was stimulated to condense his thoughts, and to be ready in reply; to say little, and to the point. An aphorism bounded his philosophy. . . . The absorbing love for his native Sparta rendered the citizen singularly selfish towards other states, even kindred to that which he belonged to. Fearless as a Spartan,—when Sparta was unmenaced he was lukewarm as a Greek.

Again he does not believe that there was equality of property in Sparta:

> It is said that Lycurgus forbade the use of gold and silver, and ordained an iron coinage; but gold and silver were at that time unknown as coins in Sparta, and iron was a common medium of exchange throughout Greece. The interdiction of the precious metals was therefore of later origin. . . . A more pernicious regulation it is impossible to conceive. While it effectually served to cramp the effects of emulation—to stint the arts—to limit industry and enterprise—it produced the direct object it was intended to prevent;—it infected the whole state with the desire of gold—it forbade wealth to be spent, in order that wealth might be hoarded; every man seems to have desired gold precisely because he could make very little use of it! From the king to the Helot, the spirit of covetousness spread like a disease. No state in Greece was so open to bribery—no magistracy so corrupt as the ephors. Sparta became a nation of misers precisely because it could not become a nation of spendthrifts. Such are the results which man produces when his legislation deposes nature! . . . (sec. IX)
>
> The whole fabric of the Spartan character rested upon slavery. . . . The motives that render power most intolerant combined in the Spartan in his relations to the Helot—viz. first, necessity for his

services, lost perhaps if the curb were ever relaxed—second, consummate contempt for the individual he debased. . . . Revolt and massacre were perpetually before a Spartan's eyes; and what man will be gentle and unsuspecting to those who wait only the moment to murder him? (sec. XI)

Such are the general outlines of the state and constitution of Sparta—the firmest aristocracy that perhaps ever existed, for it was an aristocracy on the widest base. . . . Although the ephors made the government really and latently democratic, yet the concentration of its action made it seemingly oligarchic; and in its secrecy, caution, vigilance and energy, it exhibited the best of the oligarchic features . . . It was a state of political freedom, but of social despotism (sec. XV).

"With this, I close my introductory chapters and proceed from Dissertation into History" (Book I ch. VIII sec. XVI)—unlike the origins of Sparta, Solon and Athens belong to history; and Bulwer Lytton's long and favourable account of the life and activities of Solon ends with a panegyric (Book II ch. I sec. XVI) of that traditionally most suspect of Athenian institutions, the democratic assembly:

We cannot but allow the main theory of the system to have been precisely that most favourable to the prodigal exuberance of energy, of intellect, and of genius. Summoned to consultation upon all matters, from the greatest to the least, the most venerable to the most trite—today deciding on the number of their warships, tomorrow on that of a tragic chorus; now examining with jealous forethoughts the new barriers to oligarchical ambition;—now appointing, with nice distinction, to various service the various combinations of music;—now welcoming in their forum-senate the sober ambassadors of Lacedæmon or the jewelled heralds of Persia, now voting their sanction to new temples or the reverent reform of worship; compelled to a lively and unceasing interest in all that arouses the mind, or elevates the passions, or refines the taste;—supreme arbiters of the art of the sculptor, as the science of the lawgiver,—judges and rewarders of the limner and the poet, as of the successful negotiator or the prosperous soldier;—we see at once the all-accomplished, all-versatile genius of the nation, and we behold in the same glance the effect and the cause:—every thing being referred to the people, the people learned of every thing to judge. Their genius was artificially forced, and in each of its capacities. They had no need of formal education. Their whole life was one school. . . . All that can inspire the thought or delight the leisure were for the people. Theirs were the portico and the school—theirs

25

the theatre, the gardens, and the baths; they were not, as in Sparta, the tools of the state—they *were* the state! Lycurgus made machines and Solon men. In Sparta the machine was to be wound up by the tyranny of the fixed principle; it could not dine as it pleased—it could not walk as it pleased—it was not permitted to seek its she machine save by stealth and in the dark; its children were not its own—even itself had no property in self. Sparta incorporated under the name of freedom, the worst complexities, the most grievous and the most frivolous vexations, of slavery. And therefore it was that Lacedæmon flourished and decayed, bequeathing to fame men only noted for hardy valour, fanatical patriotism, and profound but dishonourable craft—attracting indeed the wonder of the world, but advancing no claim to its gratitude, and contributing no single addition to its intellectual stores. But in Athens the true blessing of freedom was rightly placed—in the opinions and the soul. Thought was the common heritage which every man might cultivate at his will. This unshackled liberty had its convulsions and its excesses, but producing unceasing emulation and unbounded competition, an incentive to every effort, a tribunal to every claim, it broke into philosophy with the one—into poetry with the other—into the energy and splendour of unexampled intelligence with all. Looking round us at this hour, more than four-and-twenty centuries after the establishment of the constitution we have just surveyed,—in the labours of the student—in the dreams of the poet—in the aspirations of the artist—in the philosophy of the legislator—we yet behold the imperishable blessings we derive from the liberties of Athens and the institutions of Solon. The life of Athens became extinct, but her soul transfused itself, immortal and immortalizing, through the world.

Bulwer Lytton, writing in the age of philhellenism, expressed the values now accepted by the British ruling class. The admiration of Sparta which they had learned from their reading of Plutarch, and from traditional history books written under the influence of French and Scottish models, had disappeared; it had been replaced by a devotion to Athenian democracy, once held only by the most desperate of radicals such as Tom Paine, but now diffused through the entire liberal intelligentsia in the age of the Great Reform Bill, which itself was perceived as making Britain for the first time a true democracy. And most surprisingly of all, the focus of this admiration for the Greek past lay in the newly discovered cultural and educational consequences of that democratic assembly, which in antiquity had been almost universally held in contempt by men such as Thucydides and Aristophanes, Plato and Aristotle, and had been presented as a centre of corruption in the Athenian democratic system even by George Grote in 1826. This was in political

terms the decisive moment in the move from the eighteenth-century idealization of Sparta to the nineteenth-century love affair with Athens. It is no
wonder that, despite the central role played by Maniote leaders (so often
compared to ancient Spartans), in October 1834 the tiny frontier village of
Athens, with no public buildings or hospital or school, rather than Sparta
(or Nauplion, Ægina or Syra) was chosen as the capital of the new Greek
state: as Bulwer's reviewer in the *Edinburgh Review* for 1837 puts it:[36]

> Century after century rolls on in merited obscurity. Athens is insulted
> by the name, without the substance of freedom, until her conquest
> by Omar. She is an appendage of the harem, and "a pander and
> eunuch governs her governor", until the Greeks of our own time
> show something of their fathers' spirit. Then—
>
> > "Last scene of all
> > That ends this strange eventful history—"
>
> A Bavarian prince builds his palace in the city of Theseus—his
> subjects address him in a jargon which mingles Turkish, French,
> Italian, and German with remnants of the lowest Hellenic dialect—
> and the traveller, who has been landed by a steam-boat at the mole
> of the Piræus, returns from a day's shooting in Bœotia to an English
> Hotel in Athens, kept by a native of Wapping!

Athens' rival, Sparta, was rewarded with a neoclassical town plan on its
vacant site by the Bavarian architect Stauffert, a plan which it still possesses,
organized on rational principles with the main square containing town hall,
palace of justice and post office, while religion and crime—the orthodox
cathedral and the prison—were relegated to separate quarters in the wings.[37]

Romantic history

> Consider History with the beginnings of it stretching into the
> remote Time; emerging darkly out of the mysterious Eternity:
> the ends of it enveloping *us* at this hour, whereof we at this hour,
> both as actors and relators, form part! . . . In essence and signi-
> ficance it has been called "the True Epic Poem, and universal

---

36 *Edinburgh Review* July 1837 p. 155.
37 As Chryssanthi Avlami has said to me, if Greece had been freed in the eighteenth
   century, Sparta would now be the capital of Greece; in the nineteenth century it could
   only be Athens. Sparta is now (with Nauplion) the handsomest and best-preserved of the
   neo-hellenic towns of Greece, and there is a lively debate around its conservation: see the
   dossier of town plans and photographs on sale in the city, entitled *Sparta: The Foundation
   and the Urban Planning Development of the Town From 1834 To This Day*, and the conference
   proceedings of 1994, *New Cities for Old: The example of Sparta* (in Greek).

Divine Scripture, whose plenary inspiration no man, out of
Bedlam or in it, shall bring in question."
(Thomas Carlyle, "On History Again" (1833), in *Critical
and Miscellaneous Essays* IV (London 1869) p. 220)

Sir Walter Scott . . . has used those fragments of truth which
historians have scornfully thrown behind them in a manner
which may well excite their envy. He has constructed out of
their gleanings works which, even considered as histories,
are scarcely less valuable than theirs. But a truly great historian would reclaim those materials which the novelist has
appropriated.
(Lord Macaulay, "History" (1828), in *Complete Works
vol VII Essays and Biographies vol I* (London 1913) p. 217)

But the importance of Bulwer Lytton's *Athens* is not just political, in help-
ing to shape the destiny of the new Greek nation. It is also historical and
literary. I have shown how he provides the link between the ancient and the
modern views of Greek history. More significantly his work fits into a vision
of the past which is European in its importance. Sir Walter Scott had
admired Bulwer's first novel; the influence of Scott on the writing of history
is immense: it was he who showed how the old antiquarian and moralizing
history of the previous century could be transformed by the novelist's skill
into a narrative of passion and vigour to inspire the new Romantic age:

These Historical Novels have taught all men this truth, which looks
like a truism, and yet was as good as unknown to writers of history
and others, till so taught: that the bygone ages of the world were
actually filled by living men, not by protocols, state-papers, contro-
versies and abstractions of men. Not abstractions were they, not
diagrams and theorems; but men, in buff or other coats and breeches,
with colour in their cheeks, with passions in their stomach, and the
idioms, features and vitalities of very men. It is a little word this;
inclusive of great meaning! History will henceforth have to take
thought of it.[38]

Throughout Europe the new historical writing was not just inspired by new
standards of scholarship derived from the German tradition. It also learned

38 Carlyle, "Sir Walter Scott" (1838), in *Critical and Miscellaneous Essays* VI (London 1869)
pp. 71f. For Scott's influence in France, note especially Thierry's praise of Scott written in
1834, reprinted in *Philosophie des sciences historiques. Le moment romantique*. Textes réunis et
présentés par Marcel Gauchet (Paris 2002) p. 53. For Carlyle and history, see especially
John D. Rosenberg, *Carlyle and the Burden of History* (Oxford 1985).

from Walter Scott the lesson that history was about the struggle for freedom and the role of individuals in that struggle: Thierry, Guizot, Michelet, and Victor Cousin in France, Niebuhr, Carl Ottfried Müller, and the young Theodor Mommsen in Germany, Sismondi in Geneva, Carlyle and Macaulay in Britain, represent a new school of historiography which swept Europe. But who was the first author to follow Walter Scott in Britain, and where was the Byronic history of the freedom of Greece in this great story? Bulwer Lytton, the disciple of Sir Walter Scott, and like Scott a novelist who understood the power of words, is the missing link in the European school of Romantic history.

Bulwer Lytton's *Athens* should indeed be compared with a far more famous work, published in the same year of 1837—Carlyle's bizarre and compulsively unreadable *French Revolution*, whose relentless addresses to the Reader require him to partake of every event and every emotion, and whose reliance on the minutiae of history to create a sense of vividness exactly follow Macaulay's conception of the significance of Scott's techniques of historical bricolage. Bulwer relies in contrast on the more traditional methods of dialogue and vivid narration, and succeeds in being more effective precisely because he is less outlandish.

The power of Bulwer Lytton's style is that of the professional orator and novelist. Its sources can be found in his long final account of the poet Sophocles. To the modern reader perhaps that analysis reads oddly, although it is wholly in place in the German Romantic tradition which Bulwer Lytton knew well. The centre of Sophocles' art lies in two supreme strengths, those of plot and pathos. His own writing could not be better characterized: Thirlwall saw history as the validation of the Niebuhrian method of research, Grote saw it as the unending demonstration of the rightness of Utilitarian principles; Bulwer Lytton's aim was that of the true Romantic novelist, to make the story immensely vivid, to engage the reader in the action, and to make him suffer with the pathos of successive victories and defeats. Plot and pathos, virtues unknown to Thirlwall and Grote, make his work as vivid as that of any of his contemporaries in Britain or on the continent.

Utilitarian history

It is a remarkable fact, that so numerous and pregnant are the proofs afforded by history in all ages, of the universal and irremediable evils of democratic ascendency, that there is hardly an historical writer of any note, in any country or period of the world, who has not concurred in condemning it as the most dangerous form of government, and the most fatal enemy of that freedom which it professes to support.

([Sir Archibald Allison], review of E.L. Bulwer,
Athens, its Rise and Fall, Blackwood's
Edinburgh Magazine 42 (1837) p. 44)

> History continued to be my strongest predilection and most
> of all ancient history. Mitford's Greece I read continually; my
> father had put me on my guard against the Tory prejudices of
> this writer, and his perversions of facts for the whitewashing
> of despots, and blackening of popular institutions. These points
> he discoursed on, exemplifying them from the Greek orators
> and historians, with such effect that in reading Mitford my
> sympathies were always on the contrary side to those of the
> author, and I could, to some extent, have argued the point
> against him: yet this did not diminish the ever new pleasure
> with which I read the book.
>
> (John Stuart Mill, "Childhood and early education",
> *Autobiography* (1873))

John Stuart Mill was extremely interested in history; the second volume of his *Dissertations and Discussions* contains a number of long essays from the *Edinburgh* and *Westminster Reviews*, dating from the 1840s and 1850s, on the development of modern French historical writing, and two reviews of successive volumes of Grote's *History of Greece*. In the 1830s he knew Bulwer Lytton well, for both were engaged in writing for each other's Radical journals, and Mill (wittingly or unwittingly) contributed an appendix on Jeremy Bentham to Bulwer's British version of de Tocqueville, *England and the English* (1833); Mill persuaded Carlyle to read this book despite his opinion of Bulwer as "a poor fribble".[39] But in October 1835 Mill joked with Carlyle when he heard Bulwer was writing a Greek history: "Perhaps, bye the bye, you did not see, before you went away, the announcement that Bulwer is to publish a History of Athens—what will the world come to! but I much wonder what it will be like."[40] A year later he wrote to Bulwer eagerly anticipating publication.[41] In May or June 1837 he wrote again to Bulwer, "I had not time the other evening to tell you how much I am delighted with 'Athens'—the book is so good, that very few people will see how good."[42]

This was high praise. Mill's fascination with Athens went back to his childhood—he started Greek with his father at the age of three and had read all of Thucydides by the time he was twelve; his particular passion was ancient history: he read Mitford's history of Greece while on his guard against his "Tory prejudices". His father drew his attention to the insight that Demosthenes "afforded into Athenian institutions, and the principles of

---

39 The distinction between dandy and fribble is crucial: Pelham "though a dandy is never a fribble, but always a remarkably shrewd and intellectual man of the world" (Escott, op.cit. p. 59).

40 *The Earlier Letters of John Stuart Mill 1812–1848*, ed. F.E. Mineka (Toronto 1963) no. 147 (17 October 1835).

41 No. 182 (29 November 1836); see also no. 186 (January 1837).

42 No. 206 (May or June 1837).

legislation and government which they often illustrated." Mill's views were indeed the same as those of Bulwer, but they seem to have arrived at them independently: there is no sign of discussion or close involvement, although we may assume that the views of James Mill the elder were widely known in Radical circles. The central importance of democratic Athens for the development of Mill's conception of liberty and political obligation is the subject of a new study by Nadia Urbinati;[43] but it is certainly not true (as she believes) that Mill had to wait for the publication of Grote's *History of Greece* to understand the place of Athens in Radical thought: his own education and Bulwer's *Athens* combined to establish the principles of his political philosophy long before Grote, despite his later lavish praise of Grote.

On its first publication, the importance of Bulwer's work was recognized in both Radical and Tory circles. Everyone remarked in almost identical words on the surprising fact that a fashionable novelist and a dandy should turn to philosophical history: the Radical journals, the *Edinburgh Review* and the *British and Foreign Review* published long and appreciative essays;[44] even the Tory press was respectful,[45]—except for the high Tory satirical journal, *Fraser's Magazine* (patron of Bulwer Lytton's estranged wife), which made fun of the book:

> With that restless ambition of authorship, which the love of glory or of gold can alone keep at fever heat, the honourable member for Lincoln has chosen to appear this season in the character of a learned doctor from the Academy of Athens; having matriculated, we presume, at Pompeii, and taken his A.M. degree at the University of Stinkomalee.

The author went on to attack the "philosophical cutthroats" of the French Revolution who had made a cult of Athens, and to praise the partisan "zeal" of Mitford in his demonstration that "a mob in the agora could act the tiger as well as the autocrat on his throne."

In his explanations of his failure to complete the work Bulwer Lytton defers to Thirlwall and Grote; but his account is disingenuous, and hides a more serious situation. Consider the chronology. It is true that Grote's first

---

43 Nadia Urbinati, *Mill on Democracy: from the Athenian polis to representative government* (Chicago 2002).

44 *Edinburgh Review* July 1837 pp. 151–77 (by Sir D.K. Sandford, 1798–1838, Professor of Greek at Glasgow); *British and Foreign Review* vii (1838) pp. 36–85 (by W.B. Donne, Cambridge Apostle and descendant of the poet).

45 *Blackwood's Edinburgh Magazine* 42 (1837) pp. 44–60 (by Sir Archibald Allison, 1792–1867; reprinted in his *Essays, Political, Historical and Miscellaneous* II (Edinburgh 1850)). *Fraser's Magazine* September 1837 pp. 347–56. The editor and main contributor to *Fraser's Magazine* was the Irish wit and drunkard William Maginn, one of whose infuriated victims resorted to horse-whipping and a duel.

attack on Mitford's excessively reactionary Greek history was in the *Westminster Review* for 1826, and his wife claimed that he had been meditating a Greek history since 1822. But Grote did not begin to publish his history until 1846,[46] nine years after Bulwer Lytton's work; his history was not completed until 1856. Thirlwall's first volumes were indeed published in 1835, in time to be used by Bulwer Lytton; but its publication too extends to 1844. For most of its course Bulwer's book is the earliest of a group of works that represent the great reaction to Mitford, in the light of the new enthusiasm for Greece aroused by Byron and the Philhellenes, and the British discovery of the German Romantic *Wissenschaft* of Niebuhr, August Boeckh, and Carl Ottfried Müller (all, as we have seen, first translated into English in the years from 1828 to 1830).

Moreover something more sinister has happened. George Grote nowhere mentions the work of Bulwer Lytton, despite the fact that it anticipates his approach in most essential respects: it too is in the words of Eduard Meyer "not a history but an apologia for Athens;"[47] it too mounts a sustained attack on Mitford; it too uses German sources consistently, both those in translation and those in the original (Bulwer Lytton met Benjamin Jowett in Germany in 1844, when both were pursuing their interest in German culture); like Grote, Bulwer Lytton sees the reason for Athenian pre-eminence in the sphere of culture as due to the spirit of "unceasing emulation and unbounded competition". Bulwer Lytton presents the first ever panegyric of democratic Athens in Britain; this is indeed the first work to accept the view later made famous by John Stuart Mill, that the Athenian people were "the true hero of the epopee of Greek history, the most gifted community of human beings which the world has yet seen;"[48] and, in its previously unpublished section, a decade before George Grote, it offers the first defence of Cleon as a radical politician, and the first sustained attack on the character of his conservative rival, Nicias; in short Bulwer Lytton presents a view of Greek and especially Athenian history in all essential respects remarkably similar to that of Grote.[49] Yet Bulwer Lytton anticipates the publication of the ideas of Mill and Grote by almost a generation.

46 The writing was apparently begun in 1842; vols 1–2 were published in 1846, vols 3–4 in 1847 and vols 5–6 were reviewed in the *Edinburgh Review* for 1849.
47 Quoted in Karl Popper, *The Open Society and its Enemies* 1 (2nd edn, London 1952) p. 297 n. 15.
48 Review of Grote's *History of Greece* (Spectator, 5 June 1847) in J.S. Mill, *Newspaper Writings* (ed. A.P. and J. Roloson), *Collected Works* 24 (Toronto 1986) p. 1087.
49 Demetriou (above n. 21) devotes six pages (pp. 100–6) to explaining the originality of Grote's treatment of Cleon and Nicias. On the other hand he is correct in asserting the originality of Grote's treatment of the sophists and of Plato: Bulwer's history never reached this point, but it is unlikely that he would have been able to match the depth of Grote's philosophical interests.

The fact is that George Grote, and even more his wife Harriet (in her somewhat mendacious biography), were intent on portraying Grote alone as the founder of the modern study of Greek history: it was he (and of course his wife, who had inspired and encouraged the great work) who had single-handed or together rediscovered the truth about the glorious past of Greece. The passionate history of the man who had once been his friend and colleague (and whose magnificently purple prose far surpassed the leaden tread of the bank clerk from Threadneedle Street)[50] was deliberately written out of history by the cold and cautious Grote.

Bulwer Lytton knew the dangers: in June 2003 I acquired a letter advertised for sale on the web by Roy Davids, and written in Bulwer's characteristic style. The letter is addressed, "London June fourth 1837, Col. D'aguilar Dublin Ireland". George Charles D'Aguilar (1784–1855) was a close friend of Bulwer Lytton, who dedicated the essays collected in *The Student* (1836) to him; he was some twenty years older, and a professional soldier from a military family. He had fought in India and in the Mediterranean during the Napoleonic wars, and later commanded the British troops in China. In 1813–15 he had served as a major in the regiment of Greek Light Infantry raised in the Ionian Islands by the future liberator of Greece, Sir Richard Church, and had moved in the circle of the friends of Byron. By 1837 he was Deputy Adjutant General of the Dublin garrison; he was the author of a standard work on courts martial, and translated the military maxims of Napoleon, as well as Schiller's *Fiesko*; he had a great love of the theatre, and it was in his Dublin house that Bulwer met Macready for the first time. He was just the man to appreciate the new history of Greece:[51]

8 Charles St
Berkeley Sq
June 4

My dear d'Aguilar

I am delighted at your kind & spontaneous criticism on Athens.— I suppose it must be a work of time to secure the public attention to a dry work of that kind. Meanwhile your praise feeds hope. You ask about His Majesty From all I can hear—his illness appears mortal. Water in the Chest.—His state is one cause that keeps the Govt.

---

50 "Grote's History of Greece. . . . There is probably no commercial establishment between Charing Cross and the Bank, whose head clerk could not write a better one, if he had the vanity to waste his time on it." J. Ruskin, *Arrows of the Chace* (1886) in *The Works of John Ruskin*, eds E.T. Cook and A. Wedderburn (London 1903–12) vol. xxxiv, p. 586.

51 Tom Harrison first drew my attention to this letter, which is now displayed at Knebworth. I thank especially Sibylla Jane Flower for identifying the recipient, and providing me with information about him. The new novel referred to is *Ernest Maltravers*.

together as he does not wish the tumult of change at such a time—
If Victoria follow the policy of the Duchess the Whigs will keep a
long sway—if not—the Moderate Tories will repossess themselves.
The loyal feeling for the Princess is astonishing and will probably,
with any popular leaning on her side—retard for years the Movement.

Mrs B. favoured me with a copy of severe verses the other day.
This is all I know of her.— . . . What weather one glimpse of sunshine today. I am going to adopt Wordsworth's advice "Up—up
my friends & leave your Books" & dine at Putney!—so my letter
like my time must be short.—I think you will be pleased with a
Novel I am printing which will be out in 6 weeks The Hero is a
literary cove! Time Modern—Style sentimental o—reflective, o
Germanico!

You will find me ensconced in Charles St with a spare bed for you
when you come to town.

Yrs Ever
EL Bulwer

The work of time for a dry work! It was finally on the bicentenary of
Bulwer Lytton's birth that we celebrated at his ancestral seat of Knebworth
the republication of the (at last almost complete) *Athens: Its Rise and Fall*,
and offered readings from his revolutionary book at the venue that has been
graced by so many rock idols. After 166 years we were able to rock around
the clock to the sound of the newly risen star of Greek history, Bulwer
Lytton.

ATHENS:

ITS RISE AND FALL.

WITH VIEWS OF THE

LITERATURE, PHILOSOPHY, AND SOCIAL LIFE

OF THE

ATHENIAN PEOPLE.

BY EDWARD LYTTON BULWER, ESQ., M.P. A.M.

AUTHOR OF "ENGLAND AND THE ENGLISH," "RIENZI," ETC.

PARIS:

PUBLISHED BY A. AND W. GALIGNANI AND Cº.,
No. 18, RUE VIVIENNE.

—

1837

DEDICATION

TO HENRY FYNES CLINTON, ESQ., &c., &c.
AUTHOR OF "THE FASTI HELLENICI."

MY DEAR SIR,

I am not more sensible of the distinction conferred upon me when you allowed me to inscribe this history with your name, than pleased with an occasion to express my gratitude for the assistance I have derived throughout the progress of my labours from that memorable work, in which you have upheld the celebrity of English learning, and afforded so imperishable a contribution to our knowledge of the Ancient World. To all who in history look for the true connexion between causes and effects, chronology is not a dry and mechanical compilation of barren dates, but the explanation of events and the philosophy of facts. And the publication of the Fasti Hellenici has thrown upon those times, in which an accurate chronological system can best repair what is deficient, and best elucidate what is obscure in the scanty authorities bequeathed to us all, the light of a profound and disciplined intellect, applying the acutest comprehension to the richest erudition, and arriving at its conclusions according to the true spirit of inductive reasoning, which proportions the completeness of the final discovery to the caution of the intermediate process. My obligations to that learning and to those gifts which you have exhibited to the world are shared by all who, in England or in Europe, study the history or cultivate the literature of Greece. But, in the patient kindness with which you have permitted me to consult you during the tedious passage of these volumes through the press—in the careful advice—in the generous encouragement—which have so often smoothed the path and animated the progress—there are obligations peculiar to myself; and in those obligations there is so much that honours me, that, were I to enlarge upon them more, the world might mistake an acknowledgment for a boast.

With the highest consideration and esteem,

Believe me, my dear sir,
Most sincerely and gratefully yours,
EDWARD LYTTON BULWER.

London, March 1837.

ADVERTISEMENT

THE work, a portion of which is now presented to the reader, has occupied me many years—though often interrupted in its progress, either by more active employment, or by literary undertakings of a character more seductive. These volumes were not only written, but actually in the hands of the publisher before the appearance, and even, I believe, before the announcement of the first volume of Mr Thirlwall's History of Greece, or I might have declined going over any portion of the ground cultivated by that distinguished scholar.[1] As it is, however, the plan I have pursued differs materially from Mr Thirlwall, and I trust that the soil is sufficiently fertile to yield a harvest to either labourer.

Since it is the letters, more than the arms or the institutions of Athens, which have rendered her illustrious, it is my object to combine an elaborate view of her literature with a complete and impartial account of her political transactions. The two volumes now published bring the reader, in the one branch of my subject, to the supreme administration of Pericles; in the other, to a critical analysis of the tragedies of Sophocles. Two additional volumes will, I trust, be sufficient to accomplish my task, and close the records of Athens at that period when, with the accession of Augustus, the annals of the world are merged into the chronicle of the Roman empire. In these latter volumes it is my intention to complete the history of the Athenian drama—to include a survey of the Athenian philosophy—to describe the manners, habits, and social life of the people, and to conclude the whole with such a review of the facts and events narrated as may constitute, perhaps, an unprejudiced and intelligible explanation of the *causes* of the rise and fall of Athens.

As the history of the Greek republics has been too often corruptly pressed into the service of heated political partisans, may I be pardoned the precaution of observing that, whatever my own political code, as applied to England,

---

1 In their passage through the press I have, however, had many opportunities to consult and refer to Mr Thirlwall's able and careful work.

I have nowhere sought knowingly to pervert the lessons of a past nor ana-logous time to fugitive interests and party purposes. Whether led sometimes to censure, or more often to vindicate the Athenian people, I am not con-scious of any other desire than that of strict, faithful, impartial justice. Restlessly to seek among the ancient institutions for illustrations (rarely apposite) of the modern, is, indeed, to desert the character of a judge for that of an advocate, and to undertake the task of the historian with the ambition of the pamphleteer. Though designing this work not for colleges and cloisters, but for the general and miscellaneous public, it is nevertheless impossible to pass over in silence some matters which, if apparently trifling in themselves, have acquired dignity, and even interest, from brilliant specu-lations or celebrated disputes. In the history of Greece (and Athenian history necessarily includes nearly all that is valuable in the annals of the whole Hellenic race) the reader must submit to pass through much that is minute, much that is wearisome, if he desire to arrive at last at definite knowledge and comprehensive views. In order, however, to interrupt as little as possible the recital of events, I have endeavoured to confine to the earlier portion of the work such details of an antiquarian or speculative nature as, while they may afford to the general reader, not, indeed, a minute analysis, but perhaps a sufficient notion of the scholastic inquiries which have engaged the atten-tion of some of the subtlest minds of Germany and England, may also prepare him the better to comprehend the peculiar character and circum-stances of the people to whose history he is introduced: and it may be well to warn the more impatient that it is not till the Second Book that disquisition is abandoned for narrative. There yet remain various points on which special comment would be incompatible with connected and popular history, but on which I propose to enlarge in a series of supplementary notes, to be appended to the concluding volume. These notes will also comprise criti-cisms and specimens of Greek writers not so intimately connected with the progress of *Athenian* literature as to demand lengthened and elaborate notice in the body of the work. Thus, when it is completed, it is my hope that this book will combine, with a full and complete history of Athens, Political and Moral, a more ample and comprehensive view of the treasures of the Greek literature than has yet been afforded to the English public. I have ventured on these remarks because I thought it due to the reader, no less than to myself, to explain the plan and outline of a design at present only partially developed.

London, March 1837.

Book I

FROM THE EARLIEST PERIOD TO THE LEGISLATION OF SOLON TO BC 594

CHAPTER I

Situation and soil of Attica—the Pelasgians its earliest inhabitants—their race and language akin to the Grecian—their varying civilization and architectural remains—Cecrops—were the earliest civilizers of Greece foreigners or Greeks?—the foundation of Athens—the improvements attributed to Cecrops—the religion of the Greeks cannot be reduced to a simple system—its influence upon their character and morals, arts, and poetry—the origin of slavery and aristocracy

I. To vindicate the memory of the Athenian people, without disguising the errors of Athenian institutions;—and, in narrating alike the triumphs and the reverses—the grandeur and the decay—of the most eminent of ancient states, to record the causes of her imperishable influence on mankind, not alone in political change or the fortunes of fluctuating war, but in the arts, the letters, and the social habits, which are equal elements in the history of a people;—this is the object that I set before me;—not unreconciled to the toil of years, if, serving to divest of some party errors, and to diffuse through a wider circle such knowledge as is yet bequeathed to us of a time and land, fertile in august examples and in solemn warnings—consecrated by undying names and memorable deeds.

II. In that part of earth termed by the Greeks Hellas, and by the Romans Græcia,[1] a small tract of land known by the name of Attica, extends into

SITUATION AND
SOIL OF ATTICA
the Ægæan Sea—the southeast peninsula of Greece. In its greatest length it is about sixty, in its greatest breadth about twenty-four, geographical miles. In shape it is a rude triangle,—on two sides flows the sea—on the third, the mountain range

---

1 The passage in Aristotle (Meteorol., i. 14), in which, speaking of the ancient Hellas (the country about Dodona and the river Achelous), the author says it was inhabited by a people (along with the Helli, or Selli) then called Græci, now Hellenes (τοτε μεν Γραικοι, νυν δε Ἑλληνες), is well known. The Greek chronicle on the Arundel marbles asserts, that the Greeks were called Græci before they were called Hellenes; in fact, Græci was most probably once a name for the Pelasgi, or for a powerful, perhaps predominant, tribe of the Pelasgi widely extended along the western coast—by them the name was borne into Italy, and (used indiscriminately with that of Pelasgi) gave the Latin appellation to the Hellenic or Grecian people.

of Parnes and Cithæron divides the Attic from the Bœotian territory. It is intersected by frequent but not lofty hills, and, compared with the rest of Greece, its soil, though propitious to the growth of the olive, is not fertile or abundant. In spite of painful and elaborate culture, the traces of which are yet visible, it never produced a sufficiency of corn to supply its population; and this, the comparative sterility of the land, may be ranked among the causes which conduced to the greatness of the people. The principal mountains of Attica are the Cape of Sunium, Hymettus, renowned for its honey, and Pentelicus for its marble; the principal streams which water the valleys are the capricious and uncertain rivulets of Cephisus and Elissus,[2]—streams breaking into lesser brooks, deliciously pure and clear. The air is serene— the climate healthful—the seasons temperate. Along the hills yet breathe the wild thyme, and the odorous plants which, everywhere prodigal in Greece, are more especially fragrant in that lucid sky;—and still the atmosphere colours with peculiar and various tints the marble of the existent temples and the face of the mountain landscapes.

III. I reject at once all attempt to penetrate an unfathomable obscurity for an idle object. I do not pause to inquire whether, after the destruction of Babel, Javan was the first settler in Attica, nor is it reserved for my labours to decide the solemn controversy whether Ogyges was the contemporary of Jacob or of Moses. Neither shall I suffer myself to be seduced into any lengthened consideration of those disputes, so curious and so inconclusive, relative to the origin of the Pelasgi (according to Herodotus the earliest inhabitants of Attica), which have vainly agitated the learned. It may amuse the antiquary to weigh gravely the several doubts as to the derivation of their name from Pelasgus or from Peleg—to connect the scattered fragments of tradition—and to interpret either into history or mythology the language of fabulous genealogies. But our subtlest hypotheses can erect only a fabric of doubt, which, while it is tempting to assault, it is useless to defend. All that it seems to me necessary to say of the Pelasgi is as follows:—They are the earliest race which appear to have exercised a dominant power in Greece. Their kings can be traced by tradition to a time long prior to the recorded genealogy of any other tribe, and Inachus, the father of the Pelasgian Phoroneus, is but another name for the remotest era to which Grecian

THE PELASGIANS ITS EARLI-
EST INHABITANTS—THEIR
RACE AND LANGUAGE AKIN
TO THE GRECIAN

---

2 Modern travellers, in their eloquent lamentations over the now niggard waters of these immortal streams, appear to forget that Strabo expressly informs us that the Cephisus flowed in the manner of a torrent, and failed altogether in the summer. "Much the same", he adds, "was the Ilissus". A deficiency of water was always a principal grievance in Attica, as we may learn from the laws of Solon relative to wells.

chronology can ascend.[3] Whether the Pelasgi were anciently a foreign or a Grecian tribe,[4] has been a subject of constant and celebrated discussion. Herodotus, speaking of some settlements held to be Pelasgic, and existing in his time, terms their language "barbarous;" but Müller, nor with argument insufficient, considers that the expression of the historian would apply only to a peculiar dialect; and the hypothesis is sustained by another passage in Herodotus, in which he applies to certain Ionian dialects the same term as that with which he stigmatizes the language of the Pelasgic settlements. In corroboration of Müller's opinion we may also observe, that the "barbarous-tongued" is an epithet applied by Homer to the Carians, and is rightly construed by the ancient critics as denoting a dialect mingled and unpolished, certainly not foreign. Nor when the Agamemnon of Sophocles upbraids Teucer with "his barbarous tongue,"[5] would any scholar suppose that Teucer is upbraided with not speaking Greek; he is upbraided with speaking Greek inelegantly and rudely. It is clear that they who continued with the least adulteration a language in its earliest form, would seem to utter a strange and unfamiliar jargon to ears accustomed to its more modern construction. And, no doubt, could we meet with a tribe retaining the English of the thirteenth century, the language of our ancestors would be to most of us unintelligible, and seem to many of us foreign. But, however the phrase of Herodotus be interpreted, it would still be exceedingly doubtful whether the settlements he refers to were really and originally Pelasgic, and still more doubtful whether, if Pelasgic, they had continued unalloyed and uncorrupted their ancestral language. I do not, therefore, attach any importance to the expression of Herodotus. I incline, on the contrary, to believe, with the more eminent of English scholars, that the language of the Pelasgi contained at least the elements of that which we acknowledge as the Greek;— and from many arguments I select the following:

First, because, in the states which we know to have been peopled by the Pelasgi (as Arcadia and Attica), and whence the population were not expelled by new tribes, the language appears no less Greek than that of those states from which the Pelasgi were the earliest driven. Had they spoken a totally different tongue from later settlers, I conceive that some unequivocal vestiges of the difference would have been visible even to the historical times.

3 Plato, Timæus. Clinton's Fasti Hellenici, vol. i, p. 5.
4 According to some they were from India, to others from Egypt, to others again from Phœnicia. They have been systematized into Bactrians, and Scythians, and Philistines— into Goths, and into Celts; and tracked by investigations as ingenious as they are futile, beyond the banks of the Danube to their settlements in the Peloponnese. No erudition and no speculation can, however, succeed in proving their existence in any part of the world prior to their appearance in Greece.
5 Sophoc., Ajax, 1251.

Second, because the Hellenes are described as few at first—their progress is slow—they subdue, but they do not extirpate; in such conquests—the conquests of the few settled among the many—the language of the many continues to the last; that of the few would influence, enrich, or corrupt, but never destroy it.

Third, because, whatever of the Grecian language pervades the Latin,[6] we can only ascribe to the Pelasgic colonizers of Italy. In this, all ancient writers, Greek and Latin, are agreed. The few words transmitted to us as Pelasgic betray the Grecian features, and the Lamina Borgiana (now in the Borgian collection of Naples, and discovered in 1783) has an inscription relative to the Siculi or Sicani, a people expelled from their Italian settlements before any received date of the Trojan war, of which the character is Pelasgic—the language Greek.

IV. Of the moral state of the Pelasgi our accounts are imperfect and contradictory. They were not a petty horde, but a vast race, doubtless divided, like every migratory people, into numerous tribes, differing in rank, in civilization,[7] and in many peculiarities of character. The Pelasgi in one country might appear as herdsmen or as savages; in another, in the same age, they might appear collected into cities and cultivating the arts. The history of the East informs us with what astonishing rapidity a wandering tribe, once settled, grew into fame and power; the camp of today—the city of tomorrow—and the "dwellers in the wilderness setting up the towers and the palaces thereof."[8] Thus, while in Greece this mysterious people are often represented as the aboriginal race, receiving from Phœnician and Egyptian settlers the primitive blessings of social life,

THEIR VARYING CIVILIZA-
TION AND ARCHITECTURAL
REMAINS

---

6 All those words (in the Latin) which make the foundation of a language, expressive of the wants or simple relations of life, are almost literally Greek—such as *pater, frater, aratrum, bos, ager*, &c. For the derivation of the Latin from the Æolic dialect of Greece, see "Scheid's Prolegomena to Lennep's Etymologicon Linguæ Græcæ."

7 The Leleges, Dryopes, and most of the other hordes prevalent in Greece, with the Pelasgi, I consider, with Mr Clinton, but as tribes belonging to the great Pelasgic family. One tribe would evidently become more civilized than the rest, in proportion to the social state of the lands through which it migrated—its reception of strangers from the more advanced East—or according as the circumstances of the soil in which it fixed its abode stimulated it to industry, or forced it to invention. The tradition relative to Pelasgus, that while it asserts him to have been the first that dwelt in Arcadia, declares also that he first taught men to build huts, wear garments of skins, and exchange the yet less nutritious food of herbs and roots for the sweet and palatable acorns of the *"fagus"*, justly puzzled Pausanias. Such traditions, if they prove any thing, which I more than doubt, tend to prove that the tribe personified by the word "Pelasgus," migrated into that very Arcadia alleged to have been their aboriginal home, and taught their own rude arts to the yet less cultivated population they found there.

8 See Isaiah, xxiii.

in Italy we behold them the improvers in agriculture[9] and first teachers of letters.[10]

Even so early as the traditional appearance of Cecrops among the savages of Attica, the Pelasgians in Arcadia had probably advanced from the pastoral to the civil life; and this, indeed, is the date assigned by Pausanias to the foundation of that ancestral Lycosura, in whose rude remains (by the living fountain and the waving oaks of the modern Diaphorte) the antiquary yet traces the fortifications of "the first city which the sun beheld."[11] It is in their buildings that the Pelasgi have left the most indisputable record of their name. Their handwriting is yet upon their walls! A restless and various people—overrunning the whole of Greece, found northward in Dacia, Illyria, and the country of the Getæ, colonizing the coasts of Ionia, and long the master-race of the fairest lands of Italy,—they have passed away amid the revolutions of the older earth, their ancestry and their descendants alike unknown;—yet not indeed the last, if my conclusions are rightly drawn: if the primitive population of Greece—themselves Greek—founding the language, and kindred with the blood, of the later and more illustrious Hellenes—they still made the great bulk of the people in the various states, and through their most dazzling age: Enslaved in Laconia—but free in Athens—it was their posterity that fought the Mede at Marathon and Platæa,—whom Miltiades led,—for whom Solon legislated,—for whom

9 The received account of the agricultural skill of the Pelasgi is tolerably well supported. Dionysius tells us that the aboriginals having assigned to those Pelasgi, whom the oracle sent from Dodona into Italy, the marshy and unprofitable land called Velia, they soon drained the fen:—their love of husbandry contributed, no doubt, to form the peculiar character of their civilization and religion.

10 Solinus and Pliny state that the Pelasgi first brought letters into Italy. Long the leading race of Italy, their power declined, according to Dionysius, two generations before the Trojan war.

11 Paus., viii. 38. In a previous chapter (2) that accomplished antiquary observes, that it appeared to him that Cecrops and Lycaon (son of Pelasgus and founder of Lycosura) were contemporaries. By the strong and exaggerating expression of Pausanias quoted in the text, we must suppose, not that he considered Lycosura the first town of the earth, but the first walled and fortified city. The sons of Lycaon were great builders of cities, and in their time rapid strides in civilization appear by tradition to have been made in the Peloponnesus. The Pelasgic architecture is often confounded with the Cyclopean. The Pelasgic masonry is polygonal, each stone fitting into the other without cement; that called the Cyclopean, and described by Pausanias, is utterly different, being composed by immense blocks of stone, with small pebbles inserted in the interstices. (See Gell's Topography of Rome and its Vicinity.) By some antiquaries, who have not made the mistake of confounding these distinct orders of architecture, the Cyclopean has been deemed more ancient than the Pelasgic,—but this also is an error. Lycosura was walled by the Pelasgians between four and five centuries prior to the introduction of the Cyclopean masonry—in the building of the city of Tiryns. Sir William Gell maintains the possibility of tracing walls of Lycosura near the place now called Surias To Kastro.

Plato thought,—whom Demosthenes harangued. Not less in Italy than in Greece the parents of an imperishable tongue, and, in part, the progenitors of a glorious race, we may still find the dim track of their existence wherever the classic civilization flourished,—the classic genius breathed. If in the Latin, if in the Grecian tongue, are yet the indelible traces of the language of the Pelasgi, the literature of the ancient, almost of the modern world, is their true descendant!

V. Despite a vague belief (referred to by Plato) of a remote and perished era of civilization, the most popular tradition asserts the Pelasgic inhabitants of Attica to have been sunk into the deepest ignorance of the elements of social life, when, either from Sais, an Egyptian city, as is commonly supposed, or from Sais a province in Upper Egypt, an Egyptian characterized to posterity by the name of Cecrops is said to have passed into Attica with a band of adventurous emigrants.

CECROPS

The tradition of this Egyptian immigration into Attica was long implicitly received. Recently the bold scepticism of German scholars—always erudite—if sometimes rash—has sufficed to convince us of the danger we incur in drawing historical conclusions from times to which no historical researches can ascend. The proofs upon which rest the reputed arrival of Egyptian colonizers, under Cecrops, in Attica, have been shown to be slender—the authorities for the assertion to be comparatively modern—the arguments against the probability of such an immigration in such an age to be at least plausible and important. Not satisfied, however, with reducing to the uncertainty of conjecture what incautiously had been acknowledged as fact, the assailants of the Egyptian origin of Cecrops presume too much upon their victory, when they demand us to accept as a counter *fact*, what can be, after all, but a counter conjecture. To me, impartially weighing the arguments and assertions on either side, the popular tradition of Cecrops and his colony appears one that can neither be tacitly accepted as history, nor contemptuously dismissed as invention. It would be, however, a frivolous dispute, whether Cecrops were Egyptian or Attican, since no erudition can ascertain that Cecrops ever existed, were it not connected with a controversy of some philosophical importance, viz., whether the early civilizers of Greece were foreigners or Greeks, and whether the Egyptians more especially assisted to instruct the ancestors of a race that have become the teachers and models of the world,—in the elements of religion, of polity, and the arts.

Without entering into vain and futile reasonings, derived from the scattered passages of some early writers, from the ambiguous silence of others—and, above all, from the dreams of etymological analogy or mythological fable, I believe the earliest civilizers of Greece to have been foreign settlers; deducing my belief from the observations of common sense rather than from obscure and unsatisfactory research. I believe it,

WERE THE EARLIEST CIVIL-
IZERS OF GREECE FOR-
EIGNERS OR GREEKS?

First, because, what is more probable than that at very early periods the more advanced nations of the East obtained communication with the Grecian continent and isles! What more probable than that the maritime and roving Phœnicians entered the seas of Greece, and were tempted by the plains, which promised abundance, and the mountains, which afforded a fastness. Possessed of a superior civilization to the hordes they found, they would meet rather with veneration than resistance, and thus a settlement would be obtained by an inconsiderable number, more in right of intelligence than of conquest.

But, though this may be conceded with respect to the Phœnicians, it is asserted that the Egyptians at least were not a maritime or colonizing people: and we are gravely assured, that in those distant times no Egyptian vessel had entered the Grecian seas. But of the remotest ages of Egyptian civilization we know but little. On their earliest monuments (now their books!) we find depicted naval as well as military battles, in which the vessels are evidently those employed *at sea*. According to their own traditions, they colonized in a remote age. They themselves laid claim to Danaus: and the mythus of the expedition of Osiris is not improbably construed into a figurative representation of the spread of Egyptian civilization by the means of colonies. Besides, Egypt was subjected to more than one revolution, by which a large portion of her population was expelled the land, and scattered over the neighbouring regions.[12] And even granting that Egyptians fitted out no maritime expedition—they could easily have transplanted themselves in Phœnician vessels, or Grecian rafts from Asia into Greece. Nor can we forget that Egypt[13] for a time was the habitation, and Thebes the dominion, of the Phœnicians, and hence, perhaps, the origin of the dispute whether certain of the first foreign civilizers of Greece were Phœnicians or Egyptians: The settlers might come from Egypt, and be by extraction Phœnicians: or Egyptian emigrators might well have accompanied the Phœnician.[14]

12 The expulsion of the Hyksos, which was not accomplished by one sudden, but by repeated revolutions, caused many migrations; among others, according to the Egyptians, that of Danaus.

13 The Egyptian monarchs, in a later age, employed the Phœnicians in long and adventurous maritime undertakings. At a comparatively recent date, Neco, king of Egypt, despatched certain Phœnicians on no less an enterprise than that of the circumnavigation of Africa (Herod., iv. 42; Rennell, Geog. of Herod). That monarch was indeed fitted for great designs. The Mediterranean and the Red Sea already received his fleets, and he had attempted to unite them by a canal which would have rendered Africa an island (Herod., ii. 158, 159. Heeren, Phœnicians, ch. iii. See also Diodorus).

14 The general habits of a people can in no age preclude exceptions in individuals. Indian rajahs do not usually travel, but we had an Indian rajah for some years in the Regent's Park; the Chinese are not in the habit of visiting England, but a short time ago some Chinese were in London. Grant that Phœnicians had intercourse with Egypt and with

Second, by the evidence of all history, savage tribes appear to owe their first enlightenment to foreigners: to be civilized, they conquer or are conquered—visit or are visited. For a fact which contains so striking a mystery, I do not attempt to account. I find in the history of every other part of the world, that it is by the colonizer or the conqueror that a tribe neither colonizing nor conquering is redeemed from a savage state, and I do not reject so probable an hypothesis for Greece.

Third, I look to the various arguments of a local or special nature, by which these general probabilities may be supported, and I find them unusually strong: I cast my eyes on the map of Greece, and I see that it is almost invariably on the eastern side that these eastern colonies are said to have been founded: I turn to chronology, and I find the revolutions in the East coincide in point of accredited date with the traditional immigrations into Greece: I look to the history of the Greeks, and I find the Greeks themselves (a people above all others vain of aboriginal descent, and contemptuous of foreign races) agreed in according a general belief to the accounts of their obligations to foreign settlers; and therefore (without additional but doubtful arguments from any imaginary traces of Eastern, Egyptian, Phœnician rites and fables in the religion or the legends of Greece in her remoter age) I see sufficient ground for inclining to the less modern, but more popular belief, which ascribes a foreign extraction to the early civilizers of Greece: nor am I convinced by the reasonings of those who exclude the Egyptians from the list of these primitive benefactors.

It being conceded that no hypothesis is more probable than that the earliest civilizers of Greece were foreign, and might be Egyptian, I do not recognize sufficient authority for rejecting the Attic traditions claiming Egyptian civilizers for the Attic soil, in arguments, whether grounded upon the fact that such traditions, unreferred to by the more ancient, were collected by the more modern of Grecian writers—or upon plausible surmises as to the habits of the Egyptians in that early age. Whether Cecrops were the first—whether he were even one of these civilizers, is a dispute unworthy of philosophical inquirers.[15] But as to the time of Cecrops are referred, both by those who contend for his Egyptian, and those who assert his Attic origin,

Greece, and nothing can be less improbable than that a Phœnician vessel may have contained some Egyptian adventurers. They might certainly be men of low rank and desperate fortunes—they might be fugitives from the law—but they might not the less have seemed princes and sages to a horde of Pelasgic savages.

15 The authorities in favour of the Egyptian origin of Cecrops are—Diodorus (book i); Theopompus; *scholia* Aristophanes; Plutarch; and Suidas. Plato speaks of the ancient connexion between Sais and Athens. Solon finds the names of Erechtheus and Cecrops in Egypt, according to the same authority, I grant a doubtful one (Plato, Critias.) The best positive authority of which I am aware in favour of the contrary supposition that Cecrops was indigenous, is Apollodorus.

certain advances from barbarism, and certain innovations in custom, which would have been natural to a foreigner, and almost miraculous in a native, I doubt whether it would not be our wiser and more cautious policy to leave undisturbed a long accredited conjecture, rather than to subscribe to arguments which, however startling and ingenious, not only substitute no unanswerable hypothesis, but conduce to no important result.[16]

VI. If Cecrops were really the leader of an Egyptian colony, it is more than probable that he obtained the possession of Attica by other means than those of force. To savage and barbarous tribes, the first appearance of men whose mechanical inventions, whose superior knowledge of the arts of life—nay, whose exterior advantages of garb and mien[17]—indicate intellectual eminence, till then neither known nor imagined, presents a something preternatural and divine. The imagination of the wild inhabitants is seduced, their superstitions aroused, and they yield to a teacher—not succumb to an invader. It was probably thus, then, that Cecrops with his colonists would have occupied the Attic plain—conciliated rather than subdued the inhabitants, and united in himself the twofold authority exercised by primeval chiefs —the dignity of the legislator, and the sanctity of the priest. It is evident that none of the foreign settlers brought with them a numerous band. The traditions speak of them with gratitude as civilizers, not with hatred as conquerors. And they did not leave any traces in the establishment of their language:—a proof of the paucity of their numbers, and the gentle nature of their influence—the Phœnician Cadmus, the Egyptian Cecrops, the Phrygian Pelops, introduced no separate and alien tongue. Assisting to civilize the Greeks they then became Greeks; their posterity merged and lost amid the native population.

THE FOUNDATION OF ATHENS

VII. Perhaps, in all countries, the first step to social improvement is in the institution of marriage, and the second is the formation of cities. As Menes in Egypt, as Fohi in China, so Cecrops at Athens is said first to have reduced into sacred limits the irregular intercourse of the sexes,[18] and

THE IMPROVEMENTS AT-TRIBUTED TO CECROPS

16 To enter into all the arguments that have been urged on either side relative to Cecrops would occupy about two hundred pages of this work, and still leave the question in dispute. Perhaps two hundred pages might be devoted to subjects more generally instructive!
17 So, in the Peruvian traditions, the apparition of two persons of majestic form and graceful garments, appearing alone and unarmed on the margin of the Lake Titiaca, sufficed to reclaim a naked and wretched horde from their savage life, to inculcate the elements of the social union, and to collect a people in establishing a throne.
18 "Like the Greeks", says Herodotus (ii. 112), "the Egyptians confine themselves to one wife." Latterly, this among the Greeks, though a common, was not an invariable, restraint; but more on this hereafter.

reclaimed his barbarous subjects from a wandering and unprovidential life, subsisting on the spontaneous produce of no abundant soil. High above the plain, and fronting the sea, which, about three miles distant on that side, sweeps into a bay peculiarly adapted for the maritime enterprises of an earlier age, we still behold a cragged and nearly perpendicular rock. In length its superficies is about eight hundred, in breadth about four hundred, feet.[19] Below, on either side, flow the immortal streams of the Ilissus and Cephisus. From its summit you may survey, here, the mountains of Hymettus, Pentelicus, and, far away, "the silver-bearing Laurium;" below, the wide plain of Attica, broken by rocky hills—there, the islands of Salamis and Ægina, with the opposite shores of Argolis, rising above the waters of the Saronic Bay. On this rock the supposed Egyptian is said to have built a fortress, and founded a city;[20] the fortress was in later times styled the Acropolis, and the place itself, when the buildings of Athens spread far and wide beneath its base, was still designated πόλις or the CITY. By degrees we are told that he extended, from this impregnable castle and its adjacent plain, the limit of his realm, until it included the whole of Attica, and perhaps Bœotia.[21] It is also related that he established eleven other towns or hamlets, and divided his people into twelve tribes, to each of which one of the towns was apportioned—a fortress against foreign invasion, and a court of justice in civil disputes.

If we may trust to the glimmering light which, resting for a moment, uncertain and confused, upon the reign of Cecrops, is swallowed up in all the darkness of fable during those of his reputed successors,—it is to this apocryphal personage that we must refer the elements both of agriculture and law. He is said to have instructed the Athenians to till the land, and to watch the produce of the seasons; to have imported from Egypt the olive-tree, for which the Attic soil was afterward so celebrated, and even to have navigated to Sicily and to Africa for supplies of corn. That such advances from a primitive and savage state were not made in a single generation, is sufficiently clear. With more probability, Cecrops is reputed to have imposed upon the ignorance of his subjects and the license of his followers the curb of impartial law, and to have founded a tribunal of justice (doubtless the sole one for all disputes), in which after times imagined to trace the origin of the solemn Areopagus.

VIII. Passing from these doubtful speculations on the detailed improvements effected by Cecrops in the social life of the Attic people, I shall enter

19 Hobhouse's Travels, Letter 23.
20 It is by no means probable that this city, despite its fortress, was walled like Lycosura.
21 At least Strabo assigns Bœotia to the government of Cecrops. But I confess, that so far from his incorporating Bœotia with Attica, I think that traditions relative to his immediate successors appear to indicate that Attica itself continued to retain independent tribes—soon ripening, if not already advanced, to independent states.

now into some examination of two subjects far more
important. The first is the religion of the Athenians
in common with the rest of Greece; and the second
the origin of the institution of slavery.

The origin of religion in all countries is an inquiry of the deepest interest
and of the vaguest result. For the desire of the pious to trace throughout
all creeds the principles of the one they themselves profess—the vanity of
the learned to display a various and recondite erudition—the passion of the
ingenious to harmonize conflicting traditions—and the ambition of every
speculator to say something new upon an ancient but inexhaustible subject,
so far from enlightening, only perplex our conjectures. Scarcely is the theory
of today established, than the theory of tomorrow is invented to oppose it.
With one the religion of the Greeks is but a type of the mysteries of the
Jews, the event of the deluge, and the preservation of the ark; with another
it is as entirely an incorporation of the metaphysical solemnities of the
Egyptian;—now it is the crafty device of priests, now the wise invention of
sages. It is not too much to say, that after the profoundest labours and the
most plausible conjectures of modern times, we remain yet more uncertain
and confused than we were before. It is the dark boast of every pagan
mythology, as of one of the eldest of the pagan deities, that "none among
mortals hath lifted up its veil!"

After, then, some brief and preliminary remarks, tending to such hypotheses as appear to me most probable and simple, I shall hasten from
unprofitable researches into the Unknown, to useful deductions from what
is given to our survey—in a word, from the origin of the Grecian religion
to its influence and its effects; the first is the province of the antiquary and
the speculator; the last of the historian and the practical philosopher.

IX. When Herodotus informs us that Egypt imparted to Greece the
names of almost all her deities, and that his researches convinced him that
they were of barbarous origin, he exempts from the list of the Egyptian
deities, Neptune, the Dioscuri, Juno, Vesta, Themis, the Graces, and the
Nereids.[22] From Africa, according to Herodotus, came Neptune, from the
Pelasgi the rest of the deities disclaimed by Egypt. According to the same
authority, the Pelasgi learned not their deities, but the names of their deities
(and those at a late period), from the Egyptians.[23] But the Pelasgi were the
first known inhabitants of Greece—the first known inhabitants of Greece
had therefore their especial deities, before any communication with Egypt.
For the rest we must accept the account of the simple and credulous Herodotus
with considerable caution and reserve. Nothing is more natural—perhaps

22 Herod., ii. 1.
23 Ibid., ii. 53.

more certain—than that every tribe,[24] even of utter savages, will invent some deities of their own; and as these deities will as naturally be taken from external objects, common to all mankind, such as the sun or the moon, the waters or the earth, and honoured with attributes formed from passions and impressions no less universal; so the deities of every tribe will have something kindred to each other, though the tribes themselves may never have come into contact or communication.

The mythology of the early Greeks may perhaps be derived from the following principal sources:—First, the worship of natural objects;—and of divinities so formed, the most unequivocally national will obviously be those most associated with their mode of life and the influences of their climate. When the savage first entrusts the seed to the bosom of the earth—when, through a strange and unaccountable process, he beholds what he buried in one season spring forth the harvest of the next—the EARTH itself, the mysterious garner, the benign, but sometimes the capricious reproducer of the treasures committed to its charge—becomes the object of the wonder, the hope, and the fear, which are the natural origin of adoration and prayer. Again, when he discovers the influence of the heaven upon the growth of his labour—when, taught by experience, he acknowledges its power to blast or to mellow—then, by the same process of ideas, the HEAVEN also assumes the character of divinity, and becomes a new agent, whose wrath is to be propitiated, whose favour is to be won. What common sense thus suggests to us, our researches confirm, and we find accordingly that the Earth and the Heaven are the earliest deities of the agricultural Pelasgi. As the Nile to the fields of the Egyptian—earth and heaven to the culture of the Greek. The effects of the SUN upon human labour and human enjoyment are so sensible to the simplest understanding, that we cannot wonder to find that glorious luminary among the most popular deities of ancient nations. Why search through the East to account for its worship in Greece? More easy to suppose that the inhabitants of a land, whom the sun so especially favoured—saw and blessed it, for it was good, than, amid innumerable contradictions and extravagant assumptions, to decide upon that remoter shore, whence was transplanted a deity, whose effects were so benignant, whose worship was so natural, to the Greeks. And in the more plain belief we are also borne out by the more sound inductions of learning. For it is noticeable that neither the

24 That all the Pelasgi—scattered throughout Greece, divided among themselves—frequently at war with each other, and certainly in no habits of peaceful communication—each tribe of different modes of life, and different degrees of civilization, should have concurred in giving no names to their gods, and then have equally concurred in receiving names from Egypt, is an assertion so preposterous, that it carries with it its own contradiction. Many of the mistakes relative to the Pelasgi appear to have arisen from supposing the common name implied a common and united tribe, and not a vast and dispersed people, subdivided into innumerable families, and diversified by innumerable influences.

moon nor the stars—favourite divinities with those who enjoyed the serene nights, or inhabited the broad plains of the East—were (though probably admitted among the Pelasgic deities) honoured with that intense and reverent worship which attended them in Asia and in Egypt. To the Pelasgi, not yet arrived at the intellectual stage of philosophical contemplation, the most sensible objects of influence would be the most earnestly adored. What the stars were to the East, their own beautiful Aurora, awaking them to the delight of their genial and temperate climate, was to the early Greeks.

Of deities thus created from external objects, some will rise out (if I may use the expression) of natural accident and local circumstance. An earthquake will connect a deity with the earth—an inundation with the river or the sea. The Grecian soil bears the marks of maritime revolution; many of the tribes were settled along the coast, and perhaps had already adventured their rafts upon the main. A deity of the sea (without any necessary revelation from Africa) is, therefore, among the earliest of the Grecian gods. The attributes of each deity will be formed from the pursuits and occupations of the worshippers—sanguinary with the warlike—gentle with the peaceful. The pastoral Pelasgi of Arcadia honoured the pastoral Pan for ages before he was received by their Pelasgic brotherhood of Attica. And the agricultural Demeter or Ceres will be recognized among many tribes of the agricultural Pelasgi, which no Egyptian is reputed, even by tradition,[25] to have visited.

The origin of prayer is in the sense of dependance, and in the instinct of self-preservation or self-interest. The first objects of prayer to the infant man will be those on which by his localities he believes himself to be most dependent for whatever blessing his mode of life inclines him the most to covet, or from which may come whatever peril his instinct will teach him the most to deprecate and fear. It is this obvious truth which destroys all the erudite systems that would refer the different creeds of the heathen to some single origin. Till the earth be the same in each region—till the same circumstances surround every tribe—different impressions, in nations yet unconverted and uncivilized, must produce different deities. Nature suggests a God, and man invests him with attributes. Nature and man, the same as a whole, vary in details; the one does not everywhere suggest the same notions—the other cannot everywhere imagine the same attributes. As with other tribes, so with the Pelasgi or primitive Greeks, their early gods were the creatures of their own early impressions.

As one source of religion was in external objects, so another is to be found in internal sensations and emotions. The passions are so powerful in their effects upon individuals and nations, that we can be little surprised to find those effects attributed to the instigation and influence of a supernatural being. Love is individualized and personified in nearly all mythologies; and

25 The connexion of Ceres with Isis was a subsequent innovation.

LOVE therefore ranks among the earliest of the Grecian gods. Fear or terror, whose influence is often so strange, sudden, and unaccountable—seizing even the bravest—spreading through numbers with all the speed of an electric sympathy—and deciding in a moment the destiny of an army or the ruin of a tribe—is another of those passions, easily supposed the afflatus of some preternatural power, and easily, therefore, susceptible of personification. And the pride of men, more especially if habitually courageous and warlike, will gladly yield to the credulities which shelter a degrading and unwonted infirmity beneath the agency of a superior being. TERROR, therefore, received a shape and found an altar probably as early at least as the heroic age. According to Plutarch, Theseus sacrificed to Terror previous to his battle with the Amazons;—an idle tale, it is true, but proving, perhaps, the antiquity of a tradition. As society advanced from barbarism arose more intellectual creations—as cities were built, and as in the constant flux and reflux of martial tribes cities were overthrown, the elements of the social state grew into personification, to which influence was attributed and reverence paid. Thus were fixed into divinity and shape, ORDER, PEACE, JUSTICE, and the stern and gloomy ORCOS,[26] witness of the oath, avenger of the perjury.

This, the second source of religion, though more subtle and refined in its creations, had still its origin in the same human causes as the first, viz., anticipation of good and apprehension of evil. Of deities so created, many, however, were the inventions of poets—(poetic metaphor is a fruitful mother of mythological fable)—many also were the graceful refinements of a subsequent age. But some (and nearly all those I have enumerated) may be traced to the earliest period to which such researches can ascend. It is obvious that the eldest would be connected with the passions—the more modern with the intellect.

It seems to me apparent that almost simultaneously with deities of these two classes would arise the greater and more influential class of personal divinities which gradually expanded into the heroic dynasty of Olympus. The associations which one tribe, or one generation, united with the heaven, the earth, or the sun, another might obviously connect, or confuse, with a spirit or genius inhabiting or influencing the element or physical object which excited their anxiety or awe: And, this creation effected—so what one tribe or generation might ascribe to the single personification of a passion, a faculty, or a moral and social principle, another would just as naturally refer to a personal and more complex deity:—that which in one instance would form the very nature of a superior being, in the other would form only an attribute—swell the power and amplify the character of a Jupiter, a Mars, a Venus, or a Pan. It is in the nature of man, that personal divinities once created and adored, should present more vivid and forcible images to his

---

26 Orcos was the personification of an oath, or the sanctity of an oath.

fancy than abstract personifications of physical objects and moral impressions. Thus, deities of this class would gradually rise into pre-eminence
and popularity above those more vague and incorporeal—and (though I
guard myself from absolutely solving in this manner the enigma of ancient
theogonies) the family of Jupiter could scarcely fail to possess themselves of
the shadowy thrones of the ancestral Earth and the Primeval Heaven.

A third source of the Grecian, as of all mythologies, was in the worship of
men who had actually existed, or been supposed to exist. For in this respect
errors might creep into the calendar of heroes, as they did into the calendar
of saints (the hero-worship of the moderns), which has canonized many
names to which it is impossible to find the owners. This was probably the
latest but perhaps in after times the most influential and popular addition
to the aboriginal faith. The worship of dead men once established, it was
natural to a people so habituated to incorporate and familiarize religious
impressions—to imagine that even their primary gods, first formed from
natural impressions (and, still more, those deities they had borrowed from
stranger creeds) should have walked the earth. And thus among the multitude in the philosophical ages, even the loftiest of the Olympian dwellers
were vaguely supposed to have known humanity;—their immortality but
the apotheosis of the benefactor or the hero.

X. The Pelasgi, then, had their native or aboriginal deities (differing in
number and in attributes with each different tribe), and with them rests the
foundation of the Greek mythology. They required no Egyptian wisdom to
lead them to believe in superior powers. Nature was their primeval teacher.
But as intercourse was opened with the East from the opposite Asia—with
the North from the neighbouring Thrace, new deities were transplanted
and old deities received additional attributes and distinctions, according
as the fancy of the stranger found them assimilate to the divinities he had
been accustomed to adore. It seems to me, that in Saturn we may trace the
popular Phœnician deity—in the Thracian Mars, the fierce war-god of the
North. But we can scarcely be too cautious how far we allow ourselves to be
influenced by resemblance, however strong, between a Grecian and an alien
deity. Such a resemblance may not only be formed by comparatively modern
innovations, but may either be resolved to that general likeness which one
polytheism will ever bear towards another, or arise from the adoption of new
attributes and strange traditions;—so that the deity itself may be homesprung
and indigenous, while bewildering the inquirer with considerable similitude
to other gods, from whose believers the native worship merely received an
epithet, a ceremony, a symbol, or a fable. And this necessity of caution is
peculiarly borne out by the contradictions which each scholar enamoured of
a system gives to the labours of the speculator who preceded him. What one
research would discover to be Egyptian, another asserts to be Phœnician; a
third brings from the North; a fourth from the Hebrews; and a fifth, with
yet wilder imagination, from the far and then unpenetrated caves and woods

of India. Accept common sense as our guide, and the contradictions are less irreconcilable—the mystery less obscure. In a deity essentially Greek, a Phœnician colonist may discover something familiar, and claim an ancestral god. He imparts to the native deity some Phœnician features: an Egyptian or an Asiatic succeeds him—discovers a similar likeness—introduces similar innovations. The lively Greek receives—amalgamates—appropriates all: but the aboriginal deity is not the less Greek. Each speculator may be equally right in establishing a partial resemblance, precisely because all speculators are wrong in asserting a perfect identity.

It follows as a corollary from the above reasonings, that the religion of Greece was much less uniform than is popularly imagined; first, because each separate state or canton had its own peculiar deity; second, because, in the foreign communication of new gods, each stranger would especially import the deity that at home he had more especially adored. Hence to every state its tutelary god—the founder of its greatness, the guardian of its renown. Even in the petty and limited territory of Attica, each tribe, independent of the public worship, had its peculiar deities, honoured by peculiar rites.

The deity said to be introduced by Cecrops is Neith, or more properly Naith[27]—the goddess of Sais, in whom we are told to recognize the Athene, or Minerva of the Greeks. I pass over as palpably absurd any analogy of names by which the letters that compose the word Naith are inverted to the word Athene. The identity of the two goddesses must rest upon far stronger proof. But, in order to obtain this proof, we must know with some precision the nature and attributes of the divinity of Sais—a problem which no learning appears to me satisfactorily to have solved. It would be a strong, and, I think, a convincing argument, that Athene is of foreign origin, could we be certain that her attributes, so eminently intellectual, so thoroughly out of harmony with the barbarism of the early Greeks, were accorded to her at the commencement of her worship. But the remotest traditions (such as her contest with Neptune for the possession of the soil), if we take the more simple interpretation, seem to prove her to have been originally an agricultural deity, the creation of which would have been natural enough to the agricultural Pelasgi;—while her supposed invention of some of the simplest and most elementary arts are sufficiently congenial to the notions of an unpolished and infant era of society. Nor at a long subsequent period is there much resemblance between the formal and elderly goddess of Dædalian sculpture and the glorious and august Glaucopis of Homer—the maiden of celestial beauty as of unrivalled wisdom. I grant that the variety of her attributes renders it more than probable that Athene was greatly indebted, perhaps to the "Divine Intelligence," personified in the Egyptian Naith—perhaps also,

27 Naith in the Doric dialect.

as Herodotus asserts, to the warlike deity of Libya—nor less, it may be, to the Onca of the Phœnicians,[28] from whom in learning certain of the arts, the Greeks might simultaneously learn the name and worship of the Phœnician deity presiding over such inventions. Still an aboriginal deity was probably the nucleus, round which gradually gathered various and motley attributes. And certain it is, that as soon as the whole creation rose into distinct life, the stately and virgin goddess towers, aloof and alone, the most national, the most majestic of the Grecian deities—rising above all comparison with those who may have assisted to decorate and robe her,—embodying in a single form the very genius, multiform, yet individual as it was, of the Grecian people—and becoming among all the deities of the heathen heaven what the Athens she protected became upon the earth.

XI. It may be said of the Greeks, that there never was a people who so completely nationalized all that they borrowed from a foreign source. And whatever, whether in a remoter or more recent age, it *might* have appropriated from the creed of Isis and Osiris, one cause alone would have sufficed to efface from the Grecian the peculiar character of the Egyptian mythology.

The religion of Egypt, as a *science*, was symbolical—it denoted elementary principles of philosophy; its gods were enigmas. It has been asserted (on very insufficient data) that in the earliest ages of the world, one god, of whom the sun was either the emblem or the actual object of worship, was adored universally throughout the East, and that polytheism was created by personifying the properties and attributes of the single deity: "there being one God," says Aristotle, finely, "called by many names, from the various effects which his various power produces."[29] But I am far from believing that a symbolical religion is ever the *earliest* author of polytheism; for a symbolical religion belongs to a later period of civilization, when some men are set apart in indolence to cultivate their imagination, in order to beguile or to instruct the reason of the rest. Priests are the first philosophers—a symbolical religion the first philosophy. But faith precedes philosophy. I doubt not, therefore, that polytheism existed in the East before that age when the priests of Chaldea and of Egypt invested it with a sublimer character by summoning to the aid of invention a wild and speculative wisdom—by representing under corporeal tokens the revolutions of the earth, the seasons,

28 If Onca, or Onga, *was* the name of the Phœnician goddess!—In the "Seven against Thebes", the chorus invoke Minerva under the name of Onca—and there can be no doubt that the Grecian Minerva is sometimes called Onca; but it is not clear to me that the Phœnicians had a deity of that name—nor can I agree with those who insist upon reading Onca for Siga in Pausanias (ix, 12), where he says Siga was the name of the Phœnician Minerva. The Phœnicians evidently had a deity correspondent with the Greek Minerva; but that it was named Onca, or Onga, is by no means satisfactorily proved; and the scholiast on Pindar derives the epithet as applied to Minerva from a Bœotian village.
29 De Mundo, 7.

and the stars, and creating new (or more probably adapting old and sensual) superstitions, as the grosser and more external types of a philosophical creed.[30] But a symbolical worship—the creation of a separate and established order of priests—never is, and never can be, the religion professed, loved, and guarded by a people. The multitude demand something positive and real for their belief—they cannot worship a delusion—their reverence would be benumbed on the instant if they could be made to comprehend that the god to whom they sacrificed was no actual power able to effect evil and good, but the type of a particular season of the year, or an unwholesome principle in the air. Hence, in the Egyptian religion, there was one creed for the vulgar and another for the priests. Again, to invent and to perpetuate a symbolical religion (which is, in fact, an hereditary school of metaphysics) requires men set apart for the purpose, whose leisure tempts them to invention,—whose interest prompts them to imposture. A symbolical religion is a proof of a certain refinement in civilization—the refinement of sages in the midst of a subservient people; and it absorbs to itself those meditative and imaginative minds which, did it not exist, would be devoted to philosophy. Now, even allowing full belief to the legends which bring the Egyptian colonists into Greece, it is probable that few among them were acquainted with the secrets of the symbolical mythology they introduced. Nor, if they were so, is it likely that they would have communicated to a strange and a barbarous population the profound and latent mysteries shrouded from the great majority of Egyptians themselves. Thus, whatever the Egyptian colonizers might have imported of a typical religion, the abstruser meaning would become, either at once or gradually, lost. Nor can we—until the recent age of sophists and refiners—clearly ascertain any period in which did not exist the indelible distinction between the Grecian and Egyptian mythology: viz.—that the first was actual, real, corporeal, household; the second vague, shadowy, and symbolical. This might not have been the case had there been established in the Grecian, as in the Egyptian cities, distinct and separate colleges of priests, having in their own hands the sole care of the religion, and forming a privileged and exclusive body of the state. But among the Greeks (and this should be constantly borne in mind) there never was, at any known historical period, a distinct caste of priests.[31] We may perceive, indeed, that the early colonizers commenced with approaches to that principle, but it was not prosecuted farther. There were sacred families in Athens from which

---

30 The Egyptians supposed three principles: first, one benevolent and universal Spirit; second, matter coeval with eternity; third, nature opposing the good of the universal Spirit. We find these principles in a variety of shapes typified through their deities. Besides their types of nature, as the Egyptians adopted hero gods, typical fables were invented to conceal their humanity, to excuse their errors, or to dignify their achievements.

31 See Heeren's Political History of Greece, in which this point is luminously argued.

certain priesthoods were to be filled—but even these personages were not otherwise distinguished; they performed all the usual offices of a citizen, and were not united together by any exclusiveness of privilege or spirit of party. Among the Egyptian adventurers there were probably none fitted by previous education for the sacred office; and the chief who had obtained the dominion might entertain no irresistible affection for a caste which in his own land he had seen dictating to the monarch and interfering with the government.[32]

Thus, among the early Greeks, we find the chiefs themselves were contented to offer the sacrifice and utter the prayer; and though there were indeed appointed and special priests, they held no imperious or commanding authority. The Areopagus at Athens had the care of religion, but the Areopagites were not priests. This absence of a priestly caste had considerable effect upon the flexile and familiar nature of the Grecian creed, because there were none professionally interested in guarding the purity of the religion, in preserving to what it had borrowed, symbolical allusions, and in forbidding the admixture of new gods and heterogeneous creeds. The more popular a religion, the more it seeks corporeal representations, and avoids the dim and frigid shadows of a metaphysical belief.[33]

The romantic fables connected with the Grecian mythology were, some homesprung, some relating to native heroes, and incorporating native legends, but they were also, in great measure, literal interpretations of symbolical types and of metaphorical expressions, or erroneous perversions of words in other tongues. The craving desire to account for natural phenomena, common to mankind—the wish to appropriate to native heroes the wild tales of mariners and strangers natural to a vain and a curious people—the additions which every legend would receive in its progress from tribe to tribe—and the constant embellishments the most homely inventions would obtain from the competition of rival poets, rapidly served to swell and enrich these primary treasures of Grecian lore—to deduce a history from an allegory—to establish a creed in a romance. Thus the *early* mythology of Greece is to be properly considered in its simple and outward interpretations. The Greeks, as yet in their social infancy, regarded the legends of their faith as a child reads a fairy tale, credulous of all that is supernatural in the agency—unconscious of all that may be philosophical in the moral.

32 Besides, it is not the character of emigrants from a people accustomed to castes to propagate those castes superior to their own, of which they have exported no representatives. Suppose none of that privileged and noble order, called the priests, to have accompanied the Egyptian migrators, those migrators would never have dreamed of instituting that order in their new settlement any more than a colony of the warrior caste in India would establish out of their own order a spurious and fictitious caste of Brahmins.
33 When, in a later age, Karmath, the impostor of the East, sought to undermine Mahometanism, his most successful policy was in declaring its commands to be allegories.

It is true, indeed, that dim associations of a religion, sabæan and element-ary, such as that of the Pelasgi (but not therefore foreign and philosophical), with a religion physical and popular, are, here and there, to be faintly traced among the eldest of the Grecian authors. We may see that in Jupiter they represented the ether, and in Apollo, and sometimes even in Hercules, the sun. But these authors, while, perhaps unconsciously, they hinted at the sym-bolical, fixed, by the vitality and nature of their descriptions, the *actual* images of the gods; and, reversing the order of things, Homer created Jupiter![34]

But most of the subtle and typical interpretations of the Grecian mythology known to us at present were derived from the philosophy of a later age. The explanations of religious fables—such, for instance, as the chaining of Saturn by Jupiter, and the rape of Proserpine by Pluto, in which Saturn is made to signify the revolution of the seasons, chained to the courses of the stars, to prevent too immoderate a speed, and the rape of Proserpine is refined into an allegory that denotes the seeds of corn that the sovereign principle of the earth receives and sepulchres;[35] the moral or physical explanation of legends like these was, I say, the work of the few, reduced to system either from foreign communication or acute invention. For a symbolical religion, created by the priests of one age, is reinstated or remodelled after its corruption by the philosophers of another.

XII. We may here pause a moment to inquire whence the Greeks derived the most lovely and fascinating of their mythological creations—those lesser and more terrestrial beings—the spirits of the mountain, the waters, and the grove.

Throughout the East, from the remotest era, we find that mountains were nature's temples. The sanctity of high places is constantly recorded in the scriptural writings The Chaldæan, the Egyptian, and the Persian, equally believed that on the summit of mountains they approached themselves nearer to the oracles of heaven. But the fountain, the cavern, and the grove, were no less holy than the mountain-top in the eyes of the first religionists of the East. Streams and fountains were dedicated to the Sun, and their exhalations were supposed to inspire with prophecy, and to breathe of the god. The gloom of caverns, naturally the brooding-place of awe, was deemed a fitting

34 Herodotus (ii. 53) observes, that it is to Hesiod and Homer the Greeks owe their theogony; that they gave the gods their titles, fixed their ranks, and described their shapes. And although this cannot be believed literally, in some respects it may metaphorically. Doubt-less the poets took their descriptions from popular traditions; but they made those traditions immortal. Jupiter could never become symbolical to a people who had once pictured to themselves the nod and curls of the Jupiter of Homer.

35 Cicero, de Natura Deorum, ii—most of the philosophical interpretations of the Greek mythology were the offspring of the Alexandrine schools. It is to the honour of Aristarchus that he combated a theory that very much resembles the philosophy that would convert the youthful readers of Mother Bunch into the inventors of allegorical morality.

scene for diviner revelations—it inspired unearthly contemplation and mystic revery. Zoroaster is supposed by Porphyry (well versed in all Pagan lore, though frequently misunderstanding its proper character) to have first inculcated the worship of caverns;[36] and there the early priests held a temple, and primeval philosophy its retreat.[37] Groves, especially those in high places, or in the neighbourhood of exhaling streams, were also appropriate to worship, and conducive to the dreams of an excited and credulous imagination; and Pekah, the son of Remaliah, burnt incense, not only on the hills, but "under every green tree."[38]

These places, then—the mountain, the forest, the stream, and the cavern, were equally objects of sanctity and awe among the ancient nations.

But we need not necessarily suppose that a superstition so universal was borrowed, and not conceived, by the early Greeks. The same causes which had made them worship the earth and the sea, extended their faith to the rivers and the mountains, which in a spirit of natural and simple poetry they called "the children" of those elementary deities. The very soil of Greece, broken up and diversified by so many inequalities, stamped with volcanic features, profuse in streams and mephitic fountains, contributed to render the feeling of local divinity prevalent and intense. Each petty canton had its own Nile, whose influence upon fertility and culture was sufficient to become worthy to propitiate, and therefore to personify. Had Greece been united under one monarchy, and characterized by one common monotony of soil, a single river, a single mountain, alone might have been deemed divine. It was the number of its tribes—it was the variety of its natural features, which produced the affluence and prodigality of its mythological creations.

36 But the worship can be traced to a much earlier date than that most plausibly ascribed to the Persian Zoroaster.

37 So Epimenides of Crete is said to have spent forty-five years in a cavern, and Minos descends into the sacred cave of Jupiter to receive from him the elements of law. The awe attached to woods and caverns, it may be observed, is to be found in the Northern as well as Eastern superstitions. And there is scarcely a nation on the earth in which we do not find the ancient superstition has especially attached itself to the cavern and the forest, peopling them with peculiar demons. Darkness, silence, and solitude are priests that eternally speak to the senses; and few of the most sceptical of us have been lost in thick woods, or entered lonely caverns, without acknowledging their influence upon the imagination: "Ipsa silentia", says beautifully the elder Pliny, "ipsa silentia adoramus." The effect of streams and fountains upon the mind seems more unusual and surprising. Yet, to a people unacquainted with physics, waters imbued with mineral properties, or exhaling mephitic vapours, may well appear possessed of a something preternatural. Accordingly, at this day, among many savage tribes we find that such springs are regarded with veneration and awe. The people of Fiji, in the South Seas, have a well which they imagine the passage to the next world: they even believe that you may see in its waters the spectral images of things rolling on to eternity. Fountains no less than groves, were objects of veneration with our Saxon ancestors.—See Meginhard, Wilkins, &c.

38 2 Kings, xvi. 4.

Nor can we omit from the causes of the teeming, vivid, and universal superstition of Greece, the accidents of earthquake and inundation, to which the land appears early and often to have been exposed. To the activity and caprice of nature—to the frequent operation of causes, unrecognized, unforeseen, unguessed, the Greeks owed much of their disposition to recur to mysterious and superior agencies—and that wonderful poetry of faith which delighted to associate the visible with the unseen. The peculiar character not only of a people, but of its earlier poets—not only of its soil, but of its air and heaven, colours the superstition it creates: and most of the terrestrial demons which the gloomier North clothed with terror and endowed with malice, took from the benignant genius and the enchanting climes of Greece the gentlest offices and the fairest forms;—yet even in Greece itself not universal in their character, but rather the faithful reflections of the character of each class of worshippers: thus the graces,[39] whose "eyes" in the minstrelsy of Hesiod "distilled care-beguiling love," in Lacedæmon were the nymphs of discipline and war!

In quitting this subject, be one remark permitted in digression: the local causes which contributed to superstition might conduct in after times to science. If the Nature that was so constantly in strange and fitful action, drove the Greeks in their social infancy to seek agents for the action and vents for their awe, so, as they advanced to maturer intellect, it was in Nature herself that they sought the causes of effects that appeared at first preternatural. And, in either stage, their curiosity and interest aroused by the phenomena around them—the credulous inventions of ignorance gave way to the eager explanations of philosophy. Often, in the superstition of one age, lies the germ that ripens into the inquiry of the next.

XIII. Pass we now to some examination of the general articles of faith among the Greeks;—their sacrifices and rites of worship.

In all the more celebrated nations of the ancient world, we find established those twin elements of belief by which religion harmonizes and directs the social relations of life, viz., a faith in a future state, and in the providence of superior powers, who, surveying as judges the affairs of earth, punish the wicked and reward the good.[40] It has been plausibly conjectured that the fables of Elysium, the slow Cocytus, and the gloomy Hades, were either invented or allegorized from the names of Egyptian places. Diodorus assures us that by the vast catacombs of Egypt, the dismal mansions of the dead

---

39 Of the three graces, Aglaia, Euphrosyne, and Thalia, the Spartans originally worshipped but one—(Aglaia, splendour) under the name of Phaenna, brightness: they rejected the other two, whose names signify joy and pleasure, and adopted a substitute in one whose name was sound (Cletha)—a very common substitute nowadays!

40 The Persian creed, derived from Zoroaster, resembled the most to that of Christianity. It inculcated the resurrection of the dead, the universal triumph of Ormuzd, the Principle of Light—the destruction of the reign of Ahrimanes, the Evil Principle.

—were the temple and stream, both called Cocytus, the foul canal of Acheron, and the Elysian plains;[41] and, according to the same equivocal authority, the body of the dead was wafted across the waters by a pilot, termed Charon in the Egyptian tongue. But, previous to the embarcation, appointed judges on the margin of the Acheron listened to whatever accusations were preferred by the living against the deceased, and if convinced of his misdeeds, deprived him of the rites of sepulture. Hence it was supposed that Orpheus transplanted into Greece the fable of the infernal regions. But there is good reason to look on this tale with distrust, and to believe that the doctrine of a future state was known to the Greeks without any tuition from Egypt;— while it is certain that the main moral of the Egyptian ceremony, viz., the judgment of the dead, was *not* familiar to the early doctrine of the Greeks. They did not believe that the good were rewarded and the bad punished in that dreary future, which they imbodied in their notions of the kingdom of the shades.[42]

XIV. Less in the Grecian deities than in the customs in their honour, may we perceive certain traces of oriental superstition. We recognize the usages of the older creeds in the chosen sites of their temples—the habitual ceremonies of their worship. It was to the east that the supplicator turned his face, and he was sprinkled, as a necessary purification, with the holy water often alluded to by sacred writers as well as profane—a typical rite entailed from Paganism on the greater proportion of existing Christendom. Nor was any oblation duly prepared until it was mingled with salt—that homely and immemorial offering, ordained not only by the priests of the heathen idols, but also prescribed by Moses to the covenant of the Hebrew God.[43]

XV. We now come to those sacred festivals in celebration of religious mysteries, which inspire modern times with so earnest an interest. Perhaps no subject connected with the religion of the ancients has been cultivated with more laborious erudition, attended with more barren result. And with equal truth and wit, the acute and searching Lobeck has compared the schools of Warburton and St Croix to the Sabines, who possessed the faculty

---

41 Wherever Egyptian, or indeed Grecian colonies migrated, nothing was more natural than that, where they found a coincidence of scene, they should establish a coincidence of name. In Epirus were also the Acheron and Cocytus; and Campania contains the whole topography of the Virgilian Hades.

42 See Book I ch. I sec. XXI.

43 Fire was everywhere in the East a sacred symbol—though it cannot be implicitly believed that the Vulcan or Hephaistus of the Greeks has his prototype or original in the Egyptian Phta or Phtas. The Persian philosophy made fire a symbol of the Divine intelligence—the Persian credulity, like the Grecian, converted the symbol into the god (Max. Tyr., Dissert., 38; Herod., iii. 16). The Jews themselves connected the element with their true Deity. It is in fire that Jehovah reveals himself. A sacred flame was burnt unceasingly in the temples of Israel, and grave the punishment attached to the neglect which suffered its extinction (Maimonides, Tract., vi.).

of dreaming what they wished. According to an ancient and still popular account, the dark enigmas of Eleusis were borrowed from Egypt;—the drama of the Anaglyph.[44] But, in answer to this theory, we must observe, that even if really, at their commencement, the strange and solemn rites which they are asserted to have been—mystical ceremonies grow so naturally out of the connexion between the awful and the unknown—were found so generally among the savages of the ancient world—howsoever dispersed—and still so frequently meet the traveller on shores to which it is indeed a wild speculation to assert that the oriental wisdom ever wandered, that it is more likely that they were the offspring of the native ignorance,[45] than the sublime importation of a symbolical philosophy utterly ungenial to the tribes to which it was communicated and the times to which the institution is referred. And though I would assign to the Eleusinian Mysteries a much earlier date than Lobeck is inclined to affix,[46] I search in vain for a more probable supposition of the causes of their origin than that which he suggests, and which I now place before the reader. We have seen that each Grecian state had its peculiar and favourite deities, propitiated by varying ceremonies. The early Greeks imagined that their gods might be won from them by the more earnest prayers and the more splendid offerings of their neighbours; the Homeric heroes found their claim for divine protection on the number of the offerings they have rendered to the deity they implore. And how far the jealous desire to retain to themselves the favour of tutelary gods was entertained by the Greeks, may be illustrated by the instances specially alluding to the low and whispered voice in which prayers were addressed to the superior powers, lest the enemy should hear the address, and vie with interested emulation for the celestial favour. The Eleusinians, in frequent hostilities with their neighbours, the Athenians, might very reasonably therefore exclude the latter from the ceremonies instituted in honour of their guardian divinities, Demeter and Persephone (i.e., Ceres and Proserpine). And we may here add, that secrecy once established, the rites might at a very early period obtain, and perhaps deserve, an enigmatic and mystic character. But when, after a signal defeat of the Eleusinians, the two states were incorporated, the union was confirmed by a joint participation in

44 The Anaglyph expressed the secret writings of the Egyptians, known only to the priests. The hieroglyph was known generally to the educated.

45 In Gaul, Caesar finds some tribes more civilized than the rest, cultivating the science of sacrifice, and possessed of the dark philosophy of superstitious mysteries; but in certain other and more uncivilized tribes only the elements and the heavenly luminaries (*quos cernunt et quorum opibus aperte juvantur*) were worshipped, and the lore of sacrifice was unstudied. With the Pelasgi as with the Gauls, I believe that such distinctions might have been found simultaneously in different tribes.

46 The arrival of Ceres in Attica is referred to the time of Pandion by Apollodorus.

the ceremony[47] to which a political cause would thus give a more formal and solemn dignity. This account of the origin of the Eleusinian Mysteries is not indeed capable of demonstration, but it seems to me at least the most probable in itself, and the most conformable to the habits of the Greeks, as to those of all early nations.

Certain it is that for a long time the celebration of the Eleusinian ceremonies was confined to these two neighbouring states, until, as various causes contributed to unite the whole of Greece in a common religion and a common name, admission was granted to all Greeks of all ranks, male and female,—provided they had committed no inexpiable offence, performed the previous ceremonies required, and were introduced by an Athenian citizen.

With the growing fame and splendour of Athens, this institution rose into celebrity and magnificence, until it appears to have become the most impressive spectacle of the heathen world. It is evident that a people so imitative would reject no innovations or additions that could increase the interest or the solemnity of exhibition; and still less such as might come (through whatsoever channel) from that antique and imposing Egypt, which excited so much of their veneration and wonder. Nor do I think it possible to account for the great similarity attested by Herodotus and others, between the mysteries of Isis and those of Ceres, as well as for the resemblance in less celebrated ceremonies between the rites of Egypt and of Greece, without granting at once, that mediately, or even immediately, the superstitions of the former exercised great influence upon, and imparted many features to, those of the latter. But the age in which this religious communication principally commenced has been a matter of graver dispute than the question merits. A few solitary and scattered travellers and strangers may probably have given rise to it at a very remote period; but, upon the whole, it appears to me that, with certain modifications, we must agree with Lobeck, and the more rational schools of inquiry, that it was principally in the interval between the Homeric age and the Persian war that mysticism passed into religion—that superstition assumed the attributes of a science—and that lustrations, auguries, orgies, obtained method and system from the exuberant genius of poetical fanaticism.

That in these august mysteries, doctrines contrary to the popular religion were propounded, is a theory that has, I think, been thoroughly overturned.

47 When Lobeck desires to fix the date of this religious union at so recent an epoch as the time of Solon, in consequence of a solitary passage in Herodotus, in which Solon, conversing with Crœsus, speaks of hostilities between the Athenians and Eleusinians, he seems to me to fail in sufficient ground for the assumption. The rite might have been instituted in consequence of a far earlier feud and league—even that traditionally recorded in the Mythic age of Erechtheus and Eumolpus, but could not entirely put an end to the struggles of Eleusis for independence, or prevent the outbreak of occasional jealousy and dissension.

The exhibition of ancient statues, relics, and symbols, concealed from daily adoration (as in the Catholic festivals of this day), probably, made a main duty of the Hierophant. But in a ceremony in honour of Ceres, the blessings of agriculture, and its connexion with civilization, were also very naturally dramatized. The visit of the goddess to the Infernal Regions might form an imposing part of the spectacle: spectral images—alternations of light and darkness—all the apparitions and effects that are said to have imparted so much awe to the mysteries, may well have harmonized with, not contravened, the popular belief. And there is no reason to suppose that the explanations given by the priests did more than account for mythological stories, agreeably to the spirit and form of the received mythology, or deduce moral maxims from the representation, as hackneyed, as simple, and as ancient, as the generality of moral aphorisms are. But, as the intellectual progress of the audience advanced, philosophers, sceptical of the popular religion, delighted to draw from such imposing representations a thousand theories and morals utterly unknown to the vulgar; and the fancies and refinements of later schoolmen have thus been mistaken for the notions of an early age and a promiscuous multitude. The single fact (so often insisted upon), that all Greeks were admissible, is sufficient alone to prove that no secrets incompatible with the common faith, or very important in themselves, could either have been propounded by the priests or received by the audience. And it may be further observed, in corroboration of so self-evident a truth, that it was held an impiety to the *popular* faith to reject the initiation of the mysteries —and that some of the very writers, most superstitious with respect to the one, attach the most solemnity to the ceremonies of the other.

XVI. Sanchoniathon wrote a work, now lost, on the worship of the serpent. This most ancient superstition, found invariably in Egypt and the East, is also to be traced through many of the legends and many of the ceremonies of the Greeks. The serpent was a frequent emblem of various gods—it was often kept about the temples—it was introduced in the mysteries—it was everywhere considered sacred. Singular enough, by the way, that while with us the symbol of the evil spirit, the serpent was generally in the East considered a benefactor. In India, the serpent with a thousand heads; in Egypt, the serpent crowned with the lotos-leaf, is a benign and paternal deity. It was not uncommon for fable to assert that the first civilizers of earth were half man, half serpent. Thus was Fohi of China[48] represented, and thus Cecrops of Athens.

---

48 Kneph, the Agatho demon, or Good Spirit of Egypt, had his symbol in the serpent. It was precisely because sacred with the rest of the world that the serpent would be an object of abhorrence with the Jews. But by a curious remnant of oriental superstition, the early Christians often represented the Messiah by the serpent—and the emblem of Satan became that of the Saviour.

XVII. But the most remarkable feature of the superstition of Greece was her sacred oracles. And these again bring our inquiries back to Egypt. Herodotus informs us that the oracle of Dodona was by far the most ancient in Greece,[49] and he then proceeds to inform us of its origin, which he traces to Thebes in Egypt. But here we are beset by contradictions: Herodotus, on the authority of the Egyptian priests, ascribes the origin of the Dodona and Libyan oracles to two priestesses of the Theban Jupiter—stolen by Phœnician pirates—one of whom, sold into Greece, established at Dodona an oracle similar to that which she had served at Thebes. But in previous passages Herodotus informs us, first, that in Egypt, no priestesses served the temples of any deity, male or female; and second, that when the Egyptians imparted to the Pelasgi the names of their divinities, the Pelasgi consulted the oracle of Dodona on the propriety of adopting them; so that that oracle existed before even the first and fundamental revelations of Egyptian religion. It seems to me, therefore, a supposition that demands less hardy assumption, and is equally conformable with the universal superstitions of mankind (since similar attempts at divination are to be found among so many nations similarly barbarous) to believe that the oracle arose from the impressions of the Pelasgi[50] and the natural phenomena of the spot; though at a subsequent period the manner of the divination was very probably imitated from that adopted by the Theban oracle. And in examining the place it indeed seems as if Nature herself had been the Egyptian priestess! Through a mighty grove of oaks there ran a stream, whose waters supplied a fountain that might well appear, to ignorant wonder, endowed with preternatural properties. At a certain hour of noon it was dry, and at midnight full. Such springs have usually been deemed oracular, not only in the East, but in almost every section of the globe.

At first, by the murmuring of waters, and afterward by noises among the trees, the sacred impostors interpreted the voice of the god. It is an old truth, that mystery is always imposing and often convenient. To plain questions were given dark answers, which might admit of interpretation according to the event. The importance attached to the oracle, the respect paid to the priest, and the presents heaped on the altar, indicated to craft and ambition a profitable profession. And that profession became doubly alluring to its members, because it proffered to the priests an authority in serving the oracles which they could not obtain in the general religion of the people. Oracles increased then, at first slowly, and afterward rapidly, until they grew so numerous that the single district of Bœotia contained no less than twenty-five. The oracle of Dodona long, however, maintained its pre-eminence over

---

49 Herod., ii. 52.4.
50 And this opinion is confirmed by Dionysius and Strabo, who consider the Dodona oracle originally Pelasgic.

the rest, and was only at last eclipsed by that of Delphi,[51] where strong and intoxicating exhalations from a neighbouring stream were supposed to confer prophetic frenzy. Experience augmented the sagacity of the oracles, and the priests, no doubt intimately acquainted with all the affairs of the states around, and viewing the living contests of action with the coolness of spectators, were often enabled to give shrewd and sensible admonitions,— so that the forethought of wisdom passed for the prescience of divinity. Hence the greater part of their predictions were eminently successful; and when the reverse occurred, the fault was laid on the blind misconstruction of the human applicant. Thus no great design was executed, no city founded, no colony planted, no war undertaken, without the advice of an oracle. In the famine, the pestilence, and the battle, the divine voice was the assuager of terror and the inspirer of hope. All the instincts of our frailer nature, ever yearning for some support that is not of the world, were enlisted in behalf of a superstition which proffered solutions to doubt, and remedies to distress.

Besides this general cause for the influence of oracles, there was another cause calculated to give to the oracles of Greece a marked and popular pre-eminence over those in Egypt. A country divided into several small, free, and warlike states, would be more frequently in want of the divine advice, than one united under a single monarchy, or submitted to the rigid austerity of castes and priestcraft;—and in which the inhabitants felt for political affairs all the languid indifference habitual to the subjects of a despotic government. Half a century might pass in Egypt without any political event that would send anxious thousands to the oracle; but in the wonderful ferment, activity, and restlessness of the numerous Grecian towns, every month, every week, there was some project or some feud for which the advice of a divinity was desired. Hence it was chiefly to a political cause that the immortal oracle of Delphi owed its pre-eminent importance. The Dorian worshippers of Apollo (long attached to that oracle, then comparatively obscure), passing from its neighbourhood and befriended by its predictions, obtained the mastership of the Peloponnesus;—their success was the triumph of the oracle. The Dorian Sparta (long the most powerful of the Grecian states), inviolably faithful to the Delphian god, upheld his authority, and spread the fame of his decrees. But in the more polished and enlightened times, the reputation of the oracle gradually decayed; it shone the brightest before and during the Persian war;—the appropriate light of an age of chivalry fading slowly as philosophy arose!

XVIII. But the practice of divination did not limit itself to these more solemn sources—its enthusiasm was contagious—its assistance was ever at

51 Also Pelasgic, according to Strabo.

hand.[52] Enthusiasm operated on the humblest individuals. One person imagined himself possessed by a spirit actually passing into his soul—another
merely inspired by the divine breath—a third was cast into supernatural
ecstasies, in which he beheld the shadow of events, or the visions of a god—
a threefold species of divine possession, which we may still find recognized
by the fanatics of a graver faith! Nor did this suffice; a world of omens
surrounded every man. There were not only signs and warnings in the
winds, the earthquake, the eclipse of the sun or moon, the meteor, or the
thunderbolt—but dreams also were reduced to a science;[53] the entrails of
victims were auguries of evil or of good; the flights of birds, the motions of
serpents, the clustering of bees, had their mystic and boding interpretations.
Even hasty words, an accident, a fall on the earth, a sneeze (for which we still
invoke the ancient blessing), every singular or unwonted event, might become
portentous, and were often rendered lucky or unlucky according to the
dexterity or disposition of the person to whom they occurred.

And although in later times much of this more frivolous superstition
passed away—although Theophrastus speaks of such lesser omens with the
same witty disdain as that with which the Spectator ridicules our fears at the
upsetting of a salt-cellar, or the appearance of a winding-sheet in a candle,
—yet, in the more interesting period of Greece, these popular credulities
were not disdained by the nobler or wiser few, and to the last they retained
that influence upon the mass which they lost with individuals. And it is
only by constantly remembering this universal atmosphere of religion, that
we can imbue ourselves with a correct understanding of the character of the
Greeks in their most Grecian age. Their faith was with them ever—in
sorrow or in joy—at the funeral or the feast—in their uprisings and their

52 "The Americans did not long suppose the efficacy of conjuration to be confined to one
   subject—they had recourse to it in every situation of danger or distress. [. . .] From this
   weakness proceeded likewise the faith of the Americans in dreams, their observation of
   omens, their attention to the chirping of birds and the cries of animals, all which they
   supposed to be indications of future events" (Robertson's History of America, book iv).
      Might not any one imagine that he were reading the character of the ancient Greeks?
   This is not the only point of resemblance between the Americans (when discovered by the
   Spaniards) and the Greeks in their early history; but the resemblance is merely that of a
   civilization in some respects equally advanced.
53 The notion of Democritus of Abdera, respecting the origin of dreams and divination, may
   not be uninteresting to the reader, partly from something vast and terrible in the fantasy,
   partly as a proof of the strange, incongruous, bewildered chaos of thought, from which at
   last broke the light of the Grecian philosophy. He introduced the hypothesis of images
   (εἴδωλα), emanating as it were from external objects, which impress our sense, and
   whose influence creates sensation and thought. Dreams and divination he referred to the
   impressions communicated by images of gigantic and vast stature, which inhabited the
   air and encompassed the world. Yet this philosopher is the original of Epicurus, and
   Epicurus is the original of the modern Utilitarians!

downsittings—abroad and at home—at the hearth and in the market-place—in the camp or at the altar. Morning and night all the greater tribes of the older world offered their supplications on high: and Plato has touchingly insisted on this sacred uniformity of custom, when he tells us that at the rising of the moon and at the dawning of the sun, you may behold Greeks and barbarians—all the nations of the earth—bowing in homage to the gods.

XIX. To sum up, the above remarks conduce to these principal conclusions; first, that the Grecian mythology cannot be moulded into any of the capricious and fantastic systems of erudite ingenuity: as a whole, no mythology can be considered more strikingly original, not only because its foundations appear indigenous, and based upon the character and impressions of the people—not only because at no one period, from the earliest even to the latest date, whatever occasional resemblances may exist, can any *identity* be established between its most popular and essential creations, and those of any other faith; but because, even all that it borrowed it rapidly remodelled and naturalized, growing yet more individual from its very complexity, yet more original from the plagiarisms which it embraced; second, that it differed in many details in the different states, but under the development of a general intercourse, assisted by a common language, the plastic and tolerant genius of the people harmonized all discords—until (catholic in its fundamental principles) her religion united the whole of Greece in indissoluble bonds of faith and poetry—of daily customs and venerable traditions; third, that the influence of other creeds, though by no means unimportant in amplifying the character, and adding to the list of the primitive deities, appears far more evident in the ceremonies and usages than the personal creations of the faith. We may be reasonably sceptical as to what Herodotus heard of the origin of rites or gods from Egyptian priests; but there is no reason to disbelieve the testimony of his experience, when he asserts, that the forms and solemnities of one worship closely resemble those of another; the imitation of a foreign ceremony is perfectly compatible with the aboriginal invention of a national god. For the rest, I think it might be (and by many scholars appears to me to have been) abundantly shown, that the Phœnician influences upon the early mythology of the Greeks were far greater than the Egyptian, though by degrees, and long after the heroic age, the latter became more eagerly adopted and more superficially apparent.

In quitting this part of our subject, let it be observed, as an additional illustration of the remarkable nationality of the Grecian mythology, that our best light to the manners of the Homeric men, is in the study of the Homeric gods. In Homer we behold the mythology of an era, for analogy to which we search in vain the records of the East—that mythology is inseparably connected with the constitution of limited monarchies with the manners of an heroic age:—the power of the sovereign of the aristocracy of heaven is the power of a Grecian king over a Grecian state:—the social life of the gods is the life most coveted by the Grecian heroes;—the uncertain attributes of the deities, rather physical or intellectual than moral—strength and beauty, sagacity mixed with cunning—valour with ferocity—inclination to war, yet faculties for the inventions of peace; such were the attributes most honoured among men, in the progressive, but still uncivilized age which makes the interval so pre-eminently Grecian—between the mythical and historic times. Vain and impotent are all attempts to identify that religion of Achaian warriors with the religion of oriental priests. It was indeed symbolical—but of the character of its believers; typical—but of the restless, yet poetical, daring, yet graceful temperament, which afterward conducted to great achievements and imperishable arts: the coming events of glory cast their shadows before, in fable.

XX. There now opens to us a far more important inquiry than that into the origin and form of the religion of the Greeks; namely, the influences of that religion itself upon their character—their morals—their social and intellectual tendencies.

ITS INFLUENCE UPON THEIR CHARACTER AND MORALS, ARTS, AND POETRY

The more we can approach the Deity to ourselves—the more we can invest him with human attributes—the more we can connect him with the affairs and sympathies of earth, the greater will be his influence upon our conduct—the more fondly we shall contemplate his attributes, the more timidly we shall shrink from his vigilance, the more anxiously we shall strive for his approval. When Epicurus allowed the gods to exist, but imagined them wholly indifferent to the concerns of men, contemplating only their own happiness, and regardless alike of our virtues or our crimes;—with that doctrine he robbed man of the divinity, as effectually as if he had denied his existence. The fear of the gods could not be before the eyes of votaries who believed that the gods were utterly careless of their conduct; and not only the awful control of religion was removed from their passions, but the more beautiful part of its influence, resulting not from terror but from hope, was equally blasted and destroyed: for if the fear of the divine power serves to restrain the less noble natures, so, on the other hand, with such as are more elevated and generous, there is no pleasure like the belief that we are regarded with approbation and love by a Being of ineffable majesty and goodness—who compassionates our misfortunes—who rewards our struggles with ourselves. It is this hope which gives us a pride in our own natures, and which not only restrains us from vice, but inspires us with an emulation to arouse within us all that is great and virtuous, in order the more to deserve his love, and feel the image of divinity reflected upon the soul. It is for this reason that we are not contented to leave the character of a God uncertain and unguessed, shrouded in the darkness of his own infinite power; we clothe him with the attributes of human excellence, carried only to an extent beyond humanity; and cannot conceive a deity not possessed of the qualities—such as justice, wisdom, and benevolence—which are most venerated among mankind. But if we believe that he has passed to earth—that he has borne our shape, that he has known our sorrows—the connexion becomes yet more intimate and close; we feel as if he could comprehend us better, and compassionate more benignly our infirmities and our griefs. The Christ that has walked the earth, and suffered on the cross, can be more readily pictured to our imagination, and is more familiarly before us, than the Dread Eternal One, who hath the heaven for his throne, and the earth only for his footstool.[54] And it is this very human-ness of connexion, so to speak, between man and the Saviour, which gives to the Christian religion, rightly embraced, its peculiar sentiment of gentleness and of love.

But somewhat of this connexion, though in a more corrupt degree, marked also the religion of the Greeks; they too believed (at least the multitude) that most of the deities had appeared on earth, and been the actual dispensers of the great benefits of social life. Transferred to heaven, they could more readily understand that those divinities regarded with interest the nations to which they had been made visible, and exercised a permanent influence over the earth, which had been for a while their home.

Retaining the faith that the deities had visited the world, the Greeks did not however implicitly believe the fables which degraded them by our weaknesses and vices. They had, as it were—and this seems not to have been rightly understood by the moderns—two popular mythologies—the first consecrated to poetry, and the second to actual life. If a man were told to imitate the gods, it was by the virtues of justice, temperance, and bene-volence;[55] and had he obeyed the mandate by emulating the intrigues of Jupiter, or the homicides of Mars, he would have been told by the more enlightened that those stories were the inventions of the poets; and by the more credulous that gods might be emancipated from laws, but men were bound by them—"*Superis sua jura*"[56]—their own laws to the gods! It is true, then, that those fables were preserved—were held in popular respect, but the reverence they excited among the Greeks was due to a poetry which flattered their national pride and enchained their taste, and not to the seri-ous doctrines of their religion. Constantly bearing this distinction in mind, we shall gain considerable insight, not only into their religion, but into seeming contradictions in their literary history. They allowed Aristophanes to picture Bacchus as a buffoon, and Hercules as a glutton, in the same age in which they persecuted Socrates for neglect of the sacred mysteries and contempt of the national gods. To that part of their religion which belonged

54 Isaiah, lxvi. 1.
55 This Lucian acknowledges unawares, when, in deriding the popular religion, he says that a youth who reads of the gods in Homer or Hesiod, and finds their various immoralities so highly renowned, would feel no little surprise when he entered the world, to discover that these very actions of the gods were condemned and punished by mankind.
56 Ovid, Metam., ix.

74

to the poets they permitted the fullest license; but to the graver portion of religion—to the existence of the gods—to a belief in their collective excellence, and providence, and power—to the sanctity of asylums—to the obligation of oaths—they showed the most jealous and inviolable respect. The religion of the Greeks, then, was a great support and sanction to their morals; it inculcated truth, mercy, justice, the virtues most necessary to mankind, and stimulated to them by the rigid and popular belief that excellence was approved and guilt was condemned by the superior powers.[57] And in that beautiful process by which the common sense of mankind rectifies the errors of imagination—those fables which subsequent philosophers rightly deemed dishonourable to the gods, and which the superficial survey of modern historians has deemed necessarily prejudicial to morals—had no unworthy effect upon the estimate taken by the Greeks whether of human actions or of heavenly natures.

XXI. For a considerable period the Greeks did not carry the notion of divine punishment beyond the grave, except in relation to those audacious criminals who had blasphemed or denied the gods; it was by punishments in this world that the guilty were afflicted. And this doctrine, if less sublime than that of eternal condemnation, was, I apprehend, on regarding the principles of human nature, equally effective in restraining crime: for our human and short-sighted minds are often affected by punishments, in proportion as they are human and speedy. A penance in the future world is less fearful and distinct, especially to the young and the passionate, than an unavoidable retribution in this. Man, too fondly or too vainly, hopes, by penitence at the close of life, to redeem the faults of the commencement, and punishment deferred loses more than half its terrors, and nearly all its certainty.

As long as the Greeks were left solely to their mythology, their views of a future state were melancholy and confused. Death was an evil, not a release. Even in their Elysium, their favourite heroes seem to enjoy but a frigid and unenviable immortality. Yet this saddening prospect of the grave rather served to exhilarate life, and stimulate to glory:—"Make the most of existence," say their early poets, "for soon comes the dreary Hades!" And placed beneath a delightful climate, and endowed with a vivacious and cheerful temperament, they yielded readily to the precept. Their religion was eminently glad and joyous; even the stern Spartans lost their austerity in their sacred rites, simple and manly though they were—and the gayer Athenians passed existence in an almost perpetual circle of festivals and holydays.

---

57 So Zaleucus, the disciple of Pythagoras, and the lawgiver of the Locrians of Italy, in the celebrated preamble of his laws, declares that men must hold their souls clear from every vice; that the gods did not accept the offerings of the wicked, but found pleasure only in the just and beneficent actions of the good—see Diod. Siculus, xii. 8.

This uncertainty of posthumous happiness contributed also to the desire of earthly fame. For below at least, their heroes taught them, immortality was not impossible. Bounded by impenetrable shadows to this world, they coveted all that in this world was most to be desired.[58] A short life is acceptable to Achilles, not if it lead to Elysium, but if it be accompanied with glory. By degrees, however, prospects of a future state, nobler and more august, were opened by their philosophers to the hopes of the Greeks. Thales was asserted to be the first Greek who maintained the immortality of the soul, and that sublime doctrine was thus rather established by the philosopher than the priest.[59]

XXII. Besides the direct tenets of religion, the mysteries of the Greeks exercised an influence on their morals, which, though greatly exaggerated by modern speculators, was, upon the whole, beneficial, though not from the reasons that have been assigned. As they grew up into their ripened and mature importance—their ceremonial, rather than their doctrine, served to deepen and diffuse a reverence for religious things. Whatever the licentiousness of other mysteries (especially in Italy), the Eleusinian rites long retained their renown for purity and decorum; they were jealously watched by the Athenian magistracy, and one of the early Athenian laws enacted that the senate should assemble the day after their celebration to inquire into any abuse that might have sullied their sacred character. Nor is it, perhaps, without justice in the later times, that Isocrates lauds their effect on morality, and Cicero their influence on civilization and the knowledge of social principles. The lustrations and purifications, at whatever period their sanctity was generally acknowledged, could scarcely fail of salutary effects. They were supposed to absolve the culprit from former crimes, and restore him, a new man, to the bosom of society. This principle is a great agent of morality, and was felt as such in the earlier era of Christianity: no corrupter is so deadly as despair; to reconcile a criminal with self-esteem is to readmit him, as it were, to virtue.

Even the fundamental error of the religion in point of doctrine, viz., its polytheism, had one redeeming consequence in the toleration which it served to maintain—the grave evils which spring up from the fierce antagonism of religious opinions, were, save in a few solitary and dubious instances, unknown to the Greeks. And this general toleration, assisted yet more by the absence of a separate caste of priests, tended to lead to philosophy through the open and unchallenged portals of religion. Speculations on the

58 A Mainote hearing the Druses praised for their valour, said, with some philosophy, "They would fear death more if they believed in an hereafter!"
59 In the time of Socrates, we may suspect, from a passage in Plato's Phædo, that the vulgar were sceptical of the immortality of the soul, and it may be reasonably doubted whether the views of Socrates and his divine disciple were ever very popularly embraced.

gods connected themselves with bold inquiries into nature. Thought let loose in the wide space of creation—no obstacle to its wanderings—no monopoly of its commerce—achieved, after many a wild and fruitless voyage, discoveries unknown to the past—of imperishable importance to the future. The intellectual adventurers of Greece planted the first flag upon the shores of philosophy; for the competition of errors is necessary to the elucidation of truths; and the imagination indicates the soil which the reason is destined to culture and possess.

XXIII. While such was the influence of their religion on the morals and the philosophy of the Greeks, what was its effect upon their national genius?

We must again remember that the Greeks were the only nation among the more intellectual of that day, who stripped their deities of symbolical attributes, and did not aspire to invent for gods shapes differing (save in loftier beauty) from the aspect and form of man. And thus at once was opened to them the realm of sculpture. The people of the East, sometimes indeed depicting their deities in human forms, did not hesitate to change them into monsters, if the addition of another leg or another arm, a dog's head or a serpent's tail, could better express the emblem they represented. They perverted their images into allegorical deformities; and receded from the beautiful in proportion as they indulged their false conceptions of the sublime. Besides, a painter or a sculptor must have a clear idea presented to him, to be long cherished and often revolved, if we desire to call forth all the inspiration of which his genius may be capable; but how could the eastern artist form a clear idea of an image that should represent the sun entering Aries, or the productive principle of nature? Such creations could not fail of becoming stiff or extravagant, deformed or grotesque. But to the Greek, a god was something like the most majestic or the most beautiful of his own species. He studied the human shape for his conceptions of the divine. Intent upon the natural, he ascended to the ideal.[60]

If such the effect of the Grecian religion upon sculpture, similar and equal its influence upon poetry. The earliest verses of the Greeks appear to have been of a religious, though I see no sufficient reason for asserting that they were therefore of a typical and mystic, character. However that be, the narrative succeeding to the sacred poetry materialized all it touched. The shadows of Olympus received the breath of Homer, and the gods grew at once life-like and palpable to men. The traditions which connected the deities with humanity—the genius which divested them of allegory—gave at once to the epic and the tragic poet the supernatural world. The inhabitants of heaven itself became individualized—bore each a separate character—could be rendered distinct, dramatic, as the creatures of daily life. Thus—an

---

60 It is always by connecting the divine shape with the human that we exalt our creations—
so, in later times, the saints, the Virgin, and the Christ, awoke the genius of Italian art.

advantage which no moderns ever have possessed—with all the ineffable grandeur of deities was combined all the familiar interest of mortals; and the poet, by preserving the characteristics allotted to each god, might make us feel the associations and sympathies of earth, even when he bore us aloft to the unknown Olympus, or plunged below amid the shades of Orcus.

The numerous fables mixed with the Grecian creed, sufficiently venerable, as we have seen, not to be disdained, but not so sacred as to be forbidden, were another advantage to the poet. For the traditions of a nation *are* its poetry! And if we moderns, in the German forest, or the Scottish highlands, or the green English fields, yet find inspiration in the notions of fiend, and sprite, and fairy, not acknowledged by our religion, not appended as an apocryphal adjunct to our belief, how much more were those fables adapted to poetry, which borrowed not indeed an absolute faith, but a certain shadow, a certain reverence and mystery, from religion! Hence we find that the greatest works of imagination which the Greeks have left us, whether of Homer, of Æschylus, or of Sophocles, are deeply indebted to their mythological legends. The Grecian poetry, like the Grecian religion, was at once half human, half divine—majestic, vast, august—household, homely, and familiar. If we might borrow an illustration from the philosophy of Democritus, its earthlier dreams and divinations were indeed the impressions of mighty and spectral images inhabiting the air.[61]

XXIV. Of the religion of Greece, of its rites and ceremonies, and of its influence upon the moral and intellectual faculties—this—already, I fear, somewhat too prolixly told—is all that at present I deem it necessary to say.[62]

We have now to consider the origin of slavery in Greece, an inquiry almost equally important to our accurate knowledge of her polity and manners.

XXV. Wherever we look—to whatsoever period of history—conquest, or the settlement of more enlightened colonizers amid a barbarous tribe, seems the origin of slavery—modified according to the spirit of the times, the humanity of the victor, or the policy of the lawgiver. The aboriginals of Greece were probably its earliest slaves,[63]—yet the aboriginals might be also its earliest lords.

THE ORIGIN OF SLAVERY
AND ARISTOCRACY

---

61 See note 55.

62 In the later age of philosophy I shall have occasion to return to the subject. And in the Appendix, with which I propose to complete the work, I may indulge in some conjectures relative to the Corybantes Curetes, Telchines, &c.

63 Herodotus (vi. 137) speaks of a remote time when the Athenians had no slaves. As we have the authority of Thucydides for the superior repose which Attica enjoyed as compared with the rest of Greece—so (her population never having been conquered) slavery in Attica was probably of later date than elsewhere, and we may doubt whether in that favoured land the slaves were taken from any considerable part of the aboriginal race. I say *considerable* part, for crime or debt would have reduced *some* to servitude. The assertion of Herodotus that the Ionians were indigenous (and not conquerors as Müller pretends) is

Suppose a certain tribe to overrun a certain country—conquer and possess it: new settlers are almost sure to be less numerous than the inhabitants they subdue; in proportion as they are the less powerful in number are they likely to be the more severe in authority: they will take away the arms of the vanquished—suppress the right of meetings—make stern and terrible examples against insurgents—and, in a word, quell by the moral constraint of law those whom it would be difficult to control merely by physical force;—the rigidity of the law being in ratio to the deficiency of the force. In times semi-civilized, and even comparatively enlightened, conquerors have little respect for the conquered—an immense and insurmountable distinction is at once made between the natives and their lords. All ancient nations seem to have considered that the right of conquest gave a right to the lands of the conquered country. William dividing England among his Normans is but an imitator of every successful invader of ancient times. The new-comers having gained the land of a subdued people, that people, in order to subsist, must become the serfs of the land.[64] The more formidable warriors are mostly slain, or exiled, or conciliated by some remains of authority and possessions; the multitude remain the labourers of the soil, and slight alterations of law will imperceptibly convert the labourer into the slave. The earliest slaves appear chiefly to have been the agricultural population. If the possession of the government were acquired by colonizers,[65]—not so much by the force of arms as by the influence of superior arts—the colonizers would in some instances still establish servitude for the multitude, though not under so harsh a name. The laws they would frame for an uncultured and wretched population, would distinguish between the colonizers and the aboriginals, (excepting perhaps only the native chiefs, accustomed arbitrarily to command, though not systematically to enslave the rest). The laws for the aboriginal population would still be an improvement on their previous savage and irregulated state—and generations might pass before they would attain a character of severity, or before they made the final and ineffaceable distinction between the freeman and the slave. The perturbed restlessness and constant migration of tribes in Greece, recorded both by tradition and by history, would consequently tend at a very remote period to the institution and diffusion of slavery: and the Pelasgi of one tribe would become the masters of the Pelasgi of another. There is, therefore, no necessity to look out

very strongly corroborated by the absence in Attica of a class of serfs like the Penestæ of Thessaly and the Helots of Laconia. A race of conquerors would certainly have produced a class of serfs.

64 Or else the land (properly speaking) would remain with the slaves, as it did with the Messenians and Helots—but certain proportions of the produce would be the due of the conquerors.

65 Immigration has not hitherto been duly considered as one of the original sources of slavery.

of Greece for the establishment of servitude in that country by conquest and war. But the peaceful colonization of foreign settlers would (as we have seen) lead to it by slower and more gentle degrees. And the piracies of the Phœnicians, which embraced the human species as an article of their market, would be an example, more prevalent and constant than their own, to the piracies of the early Greeks. The custom of servitude, thus commenced, is soon fed by new sources. Prisoners of war are enslaved, or, at the will of the victor, exchanged as an article of commerce. Before the interchange of money, we have numerous instances of the barter of prisoners for food and arms. And as money became the medium of trade, so slaves became a regular article of sale and purchase. Hence the origin of the slave-market. Luxury increasing, slaves were purchased not merely for the purposes of labour, but of pleasure. The accomplished musician or the beautiful virgin was an article of taste or a victim of passion. Thus, what it was the tendency of barbarism to originate, it became the tendency of civilization to increase.

Slavery, then, originated first in conquest and war, piracy, or colonization: second, in purchase. There were two other and subordinate sources of the institution—the first was crime, the second poverty. If a free citizen committed a heinous offence, he could be degraded into a slave—if he were unable to pay his debts, the creditor could claim his person. Incarceration is merely a remnant and substitute of servitude. The two latter sources failed as nations became more free. But in Attica it was not till the time of Solon, several centuries after the institution of slavery at Athens, that the right of the creditor to the personal services of the debtor was formally abolished.

A view of the moral effects of slavery—of the condition of the slaves at Athens—of the advantages of the system and its evils—of the light in which it was regarded by the ancients themselves, other and more fitting opportunities will present to us.

XXVI. The introduction of an hereditary aristocracy into a particular country, as yet uncivilized, is often simultaneous with that of slavery. A tribe of warriors possess and subdue a territory;—they share its soil with the chief in proportion to their connexion with his person, or their military services and repute—each becomes the lord of lands and slaves—each has privileges above the herd of the conquered population. Suppose again, that the dominion is acquired by colonizers rather than conquerors; the colonizers, superior in civilization to the natives,—and regarded by the latter with reverence and awe, would become at once a privileged and noble order. Hence, from either source, an aristocracy permanent and hereditary.[66] If

---

66 In a horde of savages never having held communication or intercourse with other tribes, there would indeed be men who, by a superiority of physical force, would obtain an ascendency over the rest; but these would not bequeath to their descendants distinct privileges. Exactly because physical power raised the father into rank—the want of

founded on conquest, in proportion to the number of the victors, is that aristocracy more or less oligarchical. The extreme paucity of force with which the Dorians conquered their neighbours, was one of the main causes why the governments they established were rigidly oligarchical.

XXVII. Proceeding onward, we find that in this aristocracy are preserved the seeds of liberty and the germ of republicanism. These conquerors, like our feudal barons, being sharers of the profit of the conquest and the glory of the enterprise, by no means allow undivided and absolute authority to their chiefs. Governed by separate laws—distinguished by separate privileges from the subdued community, they are proud of their own freedom, the more it is contrasted with the servitude of the population: they preserve liberty for themselves—they resist the undue assumptions of the king[67]—and keep alive that spirit and knowledge of freedom which in after times (as their numbers increase, and they become *a people*, distinct still from the aboriginal natives, who continue slaves) are transfused from the nobles to the multitude. In proportion as the new men are warlike will their unconscious spirit be that of republicanism; the connexion between martial and republican tendencies was especially recognized by all ancient writers: and the warlike habits of the Hellenes were the cradle of their political institutions. Thus, in conquest (or sometimes in immigration) we may trace the origin of an aristocracy,[68] as of slavery, and thus, by a deeper inquiry, we may find also

physical power would merge his children among the herd. Strength and activity cannot be hereditary. With individuals of a tribe as yet attaching value *only* to a swift foot or a strong arm, hereditary privilege is impossible. But if one such barbarous tribe conquer another less hardy, and inhabit the new settlement,—then indeed commences an aristocracy—for amid communities, though not among individuals, hereditary physical powers can obtain. One man may not leave his muscles to his son; but one tribe of more powerful conformation than another would generally contrive to transmit that advantage collectively to their posterity. The sense of superiority effected by conquest soon produces too its *moral* effects—elevating the spirit of the one tribe, depressing that of the other, from generation to generation. Those who have denied in conquest or colonization the origin of hereditary aristocracy, appear to me to have founded their reasonings upon the imperfectness of their knowledge of the savage states to which they refer for illustration.

67 Accordingly we find in the earliest records of Greek history—in the stories of the heroic and the Homeric age—that the king possessed but little authority except in matters of war: he was in every sense of the word a limited monarch, and the Greeks boasted that they had never known the unqualified despotism of the East. The more, indeed, we descend from the patriarchal times, the more we shall find that colonists established in their settlements those aristocratic institutions which are the earliest barriers against despotism. Colonies are always the first teachers of free institutions. There is no nation probably more attached to monarchy than the English, yet I believe that if, according to the ancient polity, the English were to migrate into different parts, and establish, in colonizing, their own independent forms of government, there would scarcely be a single such colony not republican!

68 In Attica, immigration, not conquest, must have led to the institution of aristocracy. Thucydides observes, that owing to the repose in Attica (the barren soil of which

that the slavery of a population and the freedom of a state have their date, though dim and undeveloped, in the same epoch.

XXVIII. I have thought that the supposed Egyptian colonization of Attica under Cecrops afforded the best occasion to treat of the above matters, not so much in reference to Cecrops himself as to the migration of Eastern and Egyptian adventurers. Of such migrations the dates may be uncertain—of such adventurers the names may be unknown. But it seems to me impossible to deny the fact of foreign settlements in Greece, in her remoter and more barbarous era, though we may dispute as to the precise amount of the influence they exercised, and the exact nature of the rites and customs they established.

A belief in the early connexion between the Egyptians and Athenians, encouraged by the artful vanity of the one, was welcomed by the lively credulity of the other. Many ages after the reputed sway of the mythical Cecrops, it was fondly imagined that traces of their origin from the solemn Egypt[69] were yet visible among the graceful and versatile people, whose character was as various, yet as individualized, as their religion—who, viewed in whatsoever aspect of their intellectual history, may appear constantly differing, yet remain invariably Athenian. Whether clamouring in the Agora—whether loitering in the Academe—whether, sacrificing to Hercules in the temple—whether laughing at Hercules on the stage—whether with Miltiades arming against the Mede—whether with Demosthenes declaiming against the Macedonian—still unmistakeable, unexampled, original, and alone—in their strength or their weakness, their wisdom or their foibles their turbulent action, their cultivated repose.

---

presented no temptation to the conqueror), the more powerful families expelled from the other parts of Greece, betook themselves for security and refuge to Athens. And from some of these foreigners many of the noblest families in the historical time traced their descent. Before the arrival of these Grecian strangers, Phœnician or Egyptian settlers had probably introduced an aristocratic class.

69 Modern inquirers pretend to discover the Egyptian features in the effigy of Minerva on the earliest Athenian coins. Even the golden grasshopper, with which the Athenians decorated their hair, and which was considered by their vanity as a symbol of their descent from the soil, has been construed into an Egyptian ornament—a symbol of the initiated (Horapoll. Hierogl., ii. 55.) "They are the only Grecian people," says Diodorus, "who swear by Isis, and their manners are very conformable to those of the Egyptians;" and so much truth was there at one time (when what was Egyptian became the fashion) in this remark, that they were reproached by the comic writer that their city was "Egypt and not Athens." But it is evident that all such resemblance as could have been derived from a handful of Egyptians, previous to the age of Theseus, was utterly obliterated before the age of Solon. Even if we accord to the tale of Cecrops all implicit faith, the Atticans would still remain a Pelasgic population, of which a few early institutions—a few benefits of elementary civilization—and, it may be, a few of the nobler families, were probably of Egyptian origin.

CHAPTER II

The unimportant consequences to be deduced from the
admission that Cecrops might be Egyptian—Attic kings
before Theseus—the Hellenes—their genealogy—Ionians and
Achæans Pelasgic—contrast between Dorians and Ionians—
Amphictyonic League

I. In allowing that there does not appear sufficient evidence to induce
us to reject the tale of the Egyptian origin of Cecrops, it will be already

THE UNIMPORTANT CONSE-
QUENCES TO BE DEDUCED
FROM THE ADMISSION
THAT CECROPS MIGHT BE
EGYPTIAN

observed, that I attach no great importance to the
dispute: and I am not inclined reverently to regard
the innumerable theories that have been built on
so uncertain a foundation. An Egyptian may have
migrated to Attica, but Egyptian influence in
Attica was faint and evanescent;—arrived at the

first dawn of historical fact, it is with difficulty that we discover the most
dubious and shadowy vestiges of its existence. Neither Cecrops nor any other
Egyptian in those ages is recorded to have founded a dynasty in Attica—it
is clear that none established a different language—and all the boasted
analogies of religion fade, on a close examination, into an occasional resemblance between the symbols and attributes of Egyptian and Grecian deities,
or a similarity in mystic ceremonies and solemn institutions, which, for the
most part, was almost indisputably formed by intercourse between Greece
and Egypt in a far later age. Taking the earliest epoch at which history
opens, and comparing the whole character of the Athenian people—moral,
social, religious, and political—with that of any Egyptian population, it is
not possible to select a more startling contrast, or one in which national
character seems more indelibly formed by the early and habitual adoption of
utterly opposite principles of thought and action.[1]

---

1 It has been asserted by some that there is evidence in ancient Attica of the existence of
castes similar to those in Egypt and the farther East. But this assertion has been so ably
refuted that I do not deem it necessary to enter at much length into the discussion. It will
be sufficient to observe that the assumption is founded upon the existence of four tribes
in Attica, the names of which etymological erudition has sought to reduce to titles denoting the different professions of warriors, husbandmen, labourers, and (the last much more
disputable and much more disputed) priests. In the first place, it has been cogently

I said that Cecrops founded no dynasty: the same traditions that bring him from Egypt give him Cranaus, a native, for his successor. The darkness

ATTIC KINGS BEFORE
THESEUS

of fable closes over the interval between the reign of Cranaus and the time of Theseus: if tradition be any guide whatsoever, the history of that period was the history of the human race—it was the gradual passage of men from a barbarous state to the dawn of civilization—and the national mythi only gather in wild and beautiful fictions round every landmark in their slow and encumbered progress.

It would be very possible, by a little ingenious application of the various fables transmitted to us, to construct a history of imagined conquests and invented revolutions; and thus to win the unmerited praise of throwing a new light upon those remote ages. But when fable is our only basis—no fabric we erect, however imposing in itself, can be rightly entitled to the name of history. And, as in certain ancient chronicles it is recorded merely of undistinguished monarchs that they "lived and died," so such an assertion is precisely that which it would be the most presumptuous to make respecting the shadowy kings who, whether in Eusebius or the Parian marble, give dates and chronicles to the legendary gloom which preceded the heroic age.

remarked by Mr Clinton (Fasti Hellenici, vol. i, p. 54), that this institution of castes has been very inconsistently attributed to the Greek Ion,—not (as, if Egyptian, it would have been) to the Egyptian Cecrops. Second, if rightly referred to Ion, who did not long precede the heroic age, how comes it that in that age a spirit the most opposite to that of castes universally prevailed—as all the best authenticated enactments of Theseus abundantly prove? Could institutions calculated to be the most permanent that legislation ever effected, and which in India have resisted every innovation of time, every revolution of war, have vanished from Attica in the course of a few generations? Third, it is to be observed, that previous to the divisions referred to Ion, we find the same number of four tribes under wholly different names;—under Cecrops, under Cranaus, under Ericthonius or Erectheus, they received successive changes of appellations, none of which denoted professions, but were moulded either from the distinctions of the land they inhabited, or the names of deities they adored. If remodelled by Ion to correspond with distinct professions and occupations (and where is that social state which does not form different *classes*—a formation widely opposite to that of different *castes*?) cultivated by the majority of the members of each tribe, the name given to each tribe might be but a general title by no means applicable to every individual, and certainly not implying hereditary and indelible distinctions. Fourth, in corroboration of this latter argument, there is not a single evidence— a single tradition, that such divisions ever were hereditary. Fifth, in the time of Solon and the Pisistratidæ we find the four Ionic tribes unchanged, but without any features analogous to those of the oriental castes (Clinton, Fasti Hellenici, vol. i, p. 55). Sixth, I shall add what I have before intimated (see Book I ch. I n. 34), that I do not think it the character of a people accustomed to castes to establish castes mock and spurious in any country which a few of them might visit or colonize. Nay, it is clearly and essentially contrary to such a character to imagine that a handful of wandering Egyptians, even supposing (which

The principal event recorded in these early times, for which there seems some foundation, is a war between Erechtheus of Athens and the Eleusinians; —the last assisted or headed by the Thracian Eumolpus. Erechtheus is said to have fallen a victim in this contest. But a treaty afterward concluded with the Eleusinians confirmed the ascendency of Athens, and, possibly, by a religious ceremonial, laid the foundation of the Eleusinian Mysteries. In this contest is introduced a very doubtful personage, under the appellation of Ion (to whom I shall afterward recur), who appears on the side of the Athenians, and who may be allowed to have exercised a certain influence over them, whether in religious rites or political institutions, though he neither attained to the throne, nor seems to have exceeded the peaceful authority of an ally. Upon the dim and confused traditions relative to Ion, the wildest and most luxuriant speculations have been grafted—prolix to notice, unnecessary to contradict.

II. During this period there occurred—not rapidly, but slowly—the most important revolution of early Greece, viz., the spread of that tribe termed the Hellenes, who gradually established their predominance throughout the land, impressed indelible traces on the national character, and finally converted their own into the national name.

THE HELLENES

I have already expressed my belief that the Pelasgi were not a barbarous race, speaking a barbarous tongue, but that they were akin to the Hellenes, who spoke the Grecian language, and are considered the proper Grecian family. Even the dubious record of genealogy (which, if fabulous in itself,

is absurd) that their party contained members of each different caste observed by their countrymen, would have incorporated with such scanty specimens of each caste any of the barbarous natives—they would leave all the natives to a caste by themselves. And an Egyptian hierophant would as little have thought of associating with himself a Pelasgic priest, as a Brahmin would dream of making a Brahmin caste out of a set of Christian clergymen. But if no Egyptian hierophant accompanied the immigrants, doubly ridiculous is it to suppose that the latter would have raised any of their own body, to whom such a change of caste would be impious, and still less any of the despised savages, to a rank the most honoured and the most reverent which Egyptian notions of dignity could confer. Even the very lowest Egyptians would not touch any thing a Grecian knife had polluted— the very rigidity with which caste was preserved in Egypt would forbid the propagation of castes among barbarians so much below the very lowest caste they could introduce. So far, therefore, from Egyptian adventurers introducing such an institution among the general population, their own spirit of caste must rapidly have died away as intermarriage with the natives, absence from their countrymen, and the active life of an uncivilized home mixed them up with the blood, the pursuits, and the habits of their new associates. Last, if these arguments (which might be easily multiplied) do not suffice, I say it is not for me more completely to destroy, but for those of a contrary opinion more completely to substantiate, an hypothesis so utterly at variance with the Athenian character—the acknowledged data of Athenian history; and which would assert the existence of institutions the most difficult to establish;—when established, the most difficult to modify, much more to efface.

often under the names of individuals typifies the affinity of tribes) makes the Hellenes kindred to the Pelasgi. Deucalion, the founder of the Hellenes, was of Pelasgic origin—son of Prometheus, and nephew of Atlas, king of the Pelasgic Arcadia.

However this may he, we find the Hellenes driven from Phocis, their earliest recorded seat, by a flood in the time of Deucalion. Migrating into Thessaly, they expelled the Pelasgi; and afterward spreading themselves through Greece, they attained a general ascendency over the earlier habitants, enslaving, doubtless, the bulk of the population among which they formed a settlement, but ejecting numbers of the more resolute or the more noble families, and causing those celebrated migrations by which the Pelasgi carried their name and arts into Italy, as well as into Crete and various other isles. On the continent of Greece, when the revolution became complete, the Pelasgi appear to have retained only Arcadia, the greater part of Thessaly,[2] the land of Dodona, and Attica.

There is no reason to suppose the Hellenes more enlightened and civilized than the Pelasgi; but they seem, if only by the record of their conquests, to have been a more stern, warlike, and adventurous branch of the Grecian family. I conclude them, in fact, to have been that part of the Pelasgic race who the longest retained the fierce and vigorous character of a mountain tribe, and who found the nations they invaded in that imperfect period of civilization which is so favourable to the designs of a conqueror—when the first warlike nature of a predatory tribe is indeed abandoned—but before the discipline, order, and providence of a social community are acquired. Like the Saxons into Britain, the Hellenes were invited[3] by the different Pelasgic chiefs as auxiliaries, and remained as conquerors. But in other respects they rather resembled the more knightly and energetic race by whom in Britain the Saxon dynasty was overturned:—the Hellenes were the Normans of antiquity. It is impossible to decide the exact date when the Hellenes obtained the general ascendency, or when the Greeks received from that Thessalian tribe their common appellation. The Greeks were not termed Hellenes in the time in which the Iliad was composed—they were so termed in the time of Hesiod. But even in the Iliad, the word *Pan*hellenes, applied to the Greeks, testifies the progress of the revolution,[4] and in the Odyssey, the Hellenic name is no longer limited to the dominion of Achilles.

2 The Thessali were Pelasgic.
3 Thucyd., i.
4 Homer—so nice a discriminator that he dwells upon the barbarous tongue even of the Carians—never seems to intimate any distinction between the language and race of the Pelasgi and Hellenes, yet he wrote in an age when the struggle was still unconcluded, and when traces of any marked difference must have been sufficiently obvious to detect—sufficiently interesting to notice.

III. The Hellenic nation became popularly subdivided into four principal families, viz., the Dorians, the Æolians, the Ionians, and the Achæans, of which I consider the former two alone genuinely Hellenic.

THEIR GENEALOGY

The fable which makes Dorus, Æolus, and Xuthus the sons of Helen, declares that while Dorus was sent forth to conquer other lands, Æolus succeeded to the domain of Phthiotis, and records no conquests of his own; but attributes to his sons the origin of most of the principal families of Greece. If rightly construed, this account would denote that the Æolians remained for a generation at least subsequent to the first migration of the Dorians, in their Thessalian territories; and thence splitting into various hordes, descended as warriors and invaders upon the different states of Greece. They appear to have attached themselves to maritime situations, and the wealth of their early settlements is the theme of many a legend. The opulence of Orchomenus is compared by Homer to that of Egyptian Thebes. And in the time of the Trojan war, Corinth was already termed "the wealthy." By degrees the Æolians became in a great measure blended and intermingled with the Dorians. Yet so intimately connected are the Hellenes and Pelasgi, that even these, the lineal descendants of Helen through the eldest branch, are no less confounded with the Pelasgic than the Dorian race. Strabo and Pausanias alike affirm the Æolians to be Pelasgic, and in the Æolic dialect we approach to the Pelasgic tongue.

The Dorians, first appearing in Phthiotis, are found two generations afterward in the mountainous district of Histiæotis, comprising within their territory, according to Herodotus, the immemorial Vale of Tempe. Neighboured by warlike hordes, more especially the heroic Lapithæ, with whom their earliest legends record fierce and continued war, this mountain tribe took from nature and from circumstance their hardy and martial character. Unable to establish secure settlements in the fertile Thessalian plains, and ranging to the defiles through which the romantic Peneus winds into the sea, several of the tribe migrated early into Crete, where, though forming only a part of the population of the isle, they are supposed by some to have established the Doric constitution and customs, which in their later settlements served them for a model. Other migrations marked their progress to the foot of Mount Pindus; thence to Dryopis, afterward called Doris; and from Dryopis to the Peloponnesus; which celebrated migration, under the name of the "Return of the Heraclidæ," I shall hereafter more especially describe. I have said that genealogy attributes the origin of the Dorians and that of the Æolians to Dorus and Æolus, sons of Helen. This connects them with the Hellenes and with each other. The adventures of Xuthus, the third son of Helen, are not recorded by the legends of Thessaly, and he seems merely a fictitious creation, invented to bring into affinity with the Hellenes the families, properly Pelasgic, of the Achæans and Ionians. It is by writers comparatively recent that we are told that Xuthus was driven from Thessaly by his brothers—that he took refuge in Attica, and on the plains of Marathon built four towns—Œnoe, Marathon, Probalinthus, and Tricorythus,[5] and that he wedded Creusa, daughter of Erechtheus, king of Attica, and that by her he had two sons, Achæus and Ion. By some we are told that Achæus, entering the eastern side of the Peloponnesus, founded a dominion in Laconia and Argolis; by others, on the contrary, that he conducted a band, partly Athenian, into Thessaly, and recovered the domains of which his father had been despoiled.[6] Both these accounts of Achæus, as the representative of the Achæans, are correct in this, that the Achæans had two settlements from remote periods—the one in the south of Thessaly—the other in the Peloponnesus.

The Achæans were long the most eminent of the Grecian tribes. Possessed of nearly the whole of the Peloponnesus, except, by a singular chance, that

IONIANS AND ACH-
ÆANS PELASGIC

part which afterward bore their name, they boasted the warlike fame of the opulent Menelaus and the haughty Agamemnon, the king of men. The dominant tribe of the heroic age, the Achæans form the kindred link between the several epochs of the Pelasgic and Hellenic sway—their character indeed Hellenic, but their descent apparently Pelasgic. Dionysius of Halicarnassus derives them from Pelasgus himself, and they existed as Achæans before the Hellenic Xuthus was even born. The legend which makes Achæus the brother of Ion tends likewise to prove, that if the Ionians were originally Pelasgic, so also were the Achæans. Let us then come to Ion.

Although Ion is said to have given the name of Ionians to the Atticans, yet long before his time the Iaones were among the ancient inhabitants of the country; and Herodotus (the best authority on the subject) declares that the Ionians were Pelasgic and indigenous. There is not sufficient reason to suppose, therefore, that they were Hellenic conquerors or Hellenic settlers. They appear, on the contrary, to have been one of the aboriginal tribes of Attica:—a part of them proceeded into the Peloponnesus (typified under the migration thither of Xuthus), and these again returning (as typified by the arrival of Ion at Athens), in conjunction with such of their fraternity as had remained in their native settlement, became the most powerful and renowned of the several divisions of the Attic population. Their intercourse with the Peloponnesians would lead the Ionians to establish some of the political institutions and religious rites they had become acquainted within their migration; and thus may we most probably account for the introduction of the worship of Apollo into Attica, and for that peaceful political influence which the mythical Ion is said to have exercised over his countrymen.

At all events, we cannot trace any distinct and satisfactory connexion between this, the most intellectual and brilliant tribe of the Grecian family,

5 Strabo, viii.
6 Paus., viii.

and that roving and fortunate Thessalian horde to which the Hellenes gave the general name, and of which the Dorians were the fittest representative and the most powerful section. Nor, despite the bold assumptions of Müller, is there any evidence of a Hellenic conquest in Attica.[7] And that land which, according to tradition and to history, was the early refuge of exiles, derived from the admission and intercourse of strangers and immigrants those social and political improvements which in other states have been wrought by conquest.

IV. After the Dorians obtained possession of the Peloponnesus, the whole face of Greece was gradually changed. The return of the Heraclidæ was the true consummation of the Hellenic revolution. The tribes hitherto migratory became fixed in the settlements they acquired. The Dorians rose to the rank of the most powerful race of Greece and the Ionians, their sole rivals, possessed only on the continent the narrow soil of Attica, though their colonies covered the fertile coast of Asia Minor. Greece thus reduced to two main tribes, the Doric and the Ionian, historians have justly and generally concurred in noticing between them the strongest and most marked distinctions,—the Dorians grave, inflexible, austere,—the Ionians lively, versatile, prone to change. The very dialect of the one was more harsh and masculine than that of the other; and the music, the dances of the Dorians bore the impress of their severe simplicity. The sentiment of veneration which pervaded their national character taught the Dorians not only, on the one hand, the firmest allegiance to the rites of religion and a patriarchal respect for age—but, on the other hand, a blind and superstitious attachment to institutions merely on account of their antiquity—and an almost servile regard for birth, producing rather the feelings of clanship than the sympathy of citizens. We shall see hereafter, that while Athens established republics, Sparta planted oligarchies. The Dorians were proud of independence, but it was the independence of nobles rather than of a people. Their severity preserved them long from innovation—no less by what was vicious in its excess than by what was wise in its principle. With many great and heroic qualities, they

CONTRAST BETWEEN DORIANS AND IONIANS

---

7 With all my respect for the deep learning and acute ingenuity of Müller, it is impossible not to protest against the spirit in which much of the History of the Dorians is
conceived—a spirit than which nothing can be more dangerous to sound historical inquiry.
A vague tradition, a doubtful line, suffice the daring author for proof of a foreign conquest,
or evidence of a religious revolution. There are German writers who seem to imagine that
the new school of history is built on the maxim of denying what is, and explaining what is
not. Ion is never recorded as supplanting, or even succeeding, an Attic king. He might
have introduced the worship of Apollo; but, as Mr Clinton rightly observes, that worship
never superseded the worship of Minerva, who still remained the tutelary divinity of the
city. However vague the traditions respecting Ion, they all tend to prove an *alliance* with
the Athenians, viz., precisely the reverse of a *conquest* of them.

were yet harsh to enemies—cruel to dependents—selfish to allies. Their whole policy was to preserve themselves as they were; if they knew not the rash excesses, neither were they impelled by the generous emotions which belong to men whose constant aspirations are to be better and to be greater;— they did not desire to be better or to be greater; their only wish was not to be different. They sought in the future nothing but the continuance of the past; and to that past they bound themselves with customs and laws of iron. The respect in which they held their women, as well as their disdain of pleasure, preserved them in some measure from the licentiousness common to states in which women are despised; but the respect had little of the delicacy and sentiment of individual attachment—attachment was chiefly for their own sex.[8] The Ionians, on the contrary, were susceptible, flexile, and more characterized by the generosity of modern knighthood than the sternness of ancient heroism. Them, not the past, but the future, charmed. Ever eager to advance, they were impatient even of the good, from desire of the better. Once urged to democracy—democracy fixed their character, as oligarchy fixed the Spartan. For, to change is the ambition of a democracy— to conserve of an oligarchy. The taste, love, and intuition of the beautiful stamped the Greeks above all nations, and the Ionians above all the Greeks. It was not only that the Ionians were more inventive than their neighbours, but that whatever was beautiful in invention they at once seized and appro- priated. Restless, inquisitive, ardent, they attempted all things, and perfected art—searched into all things, and consummated philosophy.

The Ionic character existed everywhere among Ionians, but the Doric was not equally preserved among the Dorians. The reason is evident. The essence of the Ionian character consisted in the spirit of change—that of the Dorian in resistance to innovation. When any Doric state abandoned its hereditary customs and institutions, it soon lost the Doric character—became lax, effeminate, luxurious—a corruption of the character of the Ionians; but no change could assimilate the Ionian to the Doric; for they belonged to dif- ferent eras of civilization—the Doric to the older, the Ionian to the more advanced. The two races of Scotland have become more alike than hereto- fore; but it is by making the highlander resemble the lowlander—and not by converting the lowland citizen into the mountain Gael. The habits of commerce, the substitution of democratic for oligarchic institutions, were sufficient to alter the whole character of the Dorians. The voluptuous Corinth—the trading Ægina (Doric states)—infinitely more resembled Athens than Sparta.

It is, then, to Sparta, that in the historical times we must look chiefly for the representative of the Doric tribe, in its proper and elementary features;

---

8 That connexion which existed throughout Greece, sometimes pure, sometimes perverted, was especially and originally Doric.

and there, pure, vigorous, and concentrated, the Doric character presents a perpetual contrast to the Athenian. This contrast continued so long as either nation retained a character to itself;—and (no matter what the pretences of hostility) was the real and inevitable cause of that enmity between Athens and Sparta, the results of which fixed the destiny of Greece.

Yet were the contests of that enmity less the contests between opposing tribes than between those opposing principles which every nation may be said to nurse within itself; viz., the principle to change, and the principle to preserve; the principle to popularize, and the principle to limit the governing power; here the genius of an oligarchy, there of a people; here adherence to the past, there desire of the future. Each principle produced its excesses, and furnishes a salutary warning. The feuds of Sparta and Athens may be regarded as historical allegories, clothing the moral struggles, which, with all their perils and all their fluctuations, will last to the end of time.

V. This period is also celebrated for the supposed foundation of that assembly of the Grecian states called the Amphictyonic Confederacy. Genea-

AMPHICTYONIC LEAGUE

logy attributes its origin to a son of Deucalion called Amphictyon.[9] This fable would intimate a Hellenic origin, since Deucalion is the fabled founder of the Hellenes; but out of twelve tribes which composed the confederacy, only three were Hellenic, and the rest Pelasgic. But with the increasing influence of the Dorian oracle of Delphi, with which it was connected, it became gradually considered a Hellenic institution. It is not possible to decipher the first intention of this league. The meeting was held at two places, near Anthela, in the pass of

---

9 Prideaux on the Marbles. The Iones are included in this confederacy; they could not, then, have taken their name from the Hellenic Ion for Ion was not born at the time of Amphictyon. The name Amphictyon is, however, but a type of the thing amphictyony, or association. Leagues of this kind were probably very common over Greece, springing almost simultaneously out of the circumstances common to numerous tribes, kindred with each other, yet often at variance and feud. A common language led them to establish, by a mutual adoption of tutelary deities, a common religious ceremony, which remained in force after political considerations died away. I take the Amphictyonic league to be one of the proofs of the affinity of language between the Pelasgi and Hellenes. It was evidently made while the Pelasgi were yet powerful and unsubdued by Hellenic influences, and as evidently it could not have been made if the Pelasgi and Hellenes were not perfectly intelligible to each other. Mr Clinton (Fasti Hellenici, vol. i, p. 66), assigns a more recent date than has generally been received to the great Amphictyonic league, placing it between the sixtieth and the eightieth year from the fall of Troy. His reason for not dating it before the former year is, that until then the Thessali (one of the twelve nations) did not occupy Thessaly. But, it may be observed consistently with the reasonings of that great authority, first, that the Thessali are not included in the lists of the league given by Harpocratio and Libanius; and, second, that even granting that the great Amphictyonic assembly of twelve nations did not commence at an earlier period, yet that that more celebrated amphictyony might have been preceded by other and less effectual attempts at association, agreeably to the legends of the genealogy. And this Mr Clinton himself implies.

Thermopylæ, and Delphi; at the latter place in the spring, at the former in the autumn. If tradition imputed to Amphictyon the origin of the council, it ascribed to Acrisius, king of Argos,[10] the formation of its proper power and laws. He is said to have founded one of the assemblies, either that in Delphi or Thermopylæ (accounts vary) and to have combined the two, increased the number of the members, and extended the privileges of the body. We can only interpret this legend by the probable supposition, that the date of holding the same assembly at two different places, at different seasons of the year, marks the epoch of some important conjunction of various tribes, and, it may be, of deities hitherto distinct. It might be an attempt to associate the Hellenes with the Pelasgi, in the early and unsettled power of the former race: and this supposition is rendered the more plausible by the evident union of the worship of the Dorian Apollo at Delphi with that of the Pelasgian Ceres at Thermopylæ.[11] The constitution of the league was this—each city belonging to an Amphictyonic state sent usually two deputies—the one called Pylagoras, the other Hieromnemon. The functions of the two deputies seem to have differed, and those of the latter to have related more particularly to whatsoever appertained to religion. On extraordinary occasions more than one pylagoras was deputed—Athens at one time sent no less than three. But the number of deputies sent did not alter the number of votes in the council. Each city had two votes and no more, no matter how many delegates it employed.

All the deputies assembled,—solemn sacrifices were offered at Delphi to Apollo, Diana Latona, and Minerva; at Thermopylæ to Ceres. An oath was then administered, the form of which is preserved to us by Æschines.

> I swear [runs the oath] never to subvert any Amphictyonic city— never to stop the courses of its waters in peace or in war. Those who attempt such outrages I will oppose by arms; and the cities that so offend I will destroy. If any ravages be committed in the territory of the god, if any connive at such a crime, if any conceive a design hostile to the temple, against them will I use my hands, my feet, my whole power and strength, so that the offenders may be brought to punishment.

Fearful and solemn imprecations on any violation of this engagement followed the oath.

These ceremonies performed, one of the hieromnemons[12] presided over the council; to him were entrusted the collecting the votes, the reporting the

---

10 Strabo, ix.
11 Müller's Dorians, vol. i.
12 Probably chosen in rotation from the different cities.

resolutions, and the power of summoning the general assembly, which was a convention separate from the council, held only on extraordinary occasions, and composed of residents and strangers, whom the solemnity of the meeting congregated in the neighbourhood.

VI. Throughout the historical times we can trace in this league no attempt to combine against the aggression of foreign states, except for the purposes of preserving the sanctity of the temple. The functions of the league were limited to the Amphictyonic tribes: and whether or not its early, and undefined, and obscure purpose was to check wars among the confederate tribes, it could not attain even that object. Its offices were almost wholly confined to religion. The league never interfered when one Amphictyonic state exercised the worst severities against the other, curbing neither the ambition of the Athenian fleet nor the cruelties of the Spartan sword. But, upon all matters relative to religion, especially to the worship of Apollo, the assembly maintained an authority in theory supreme—in practice, equivocal and capricious.

As a political institution, the league contained one vice which could not fail to destroy its power. Each city in the twelve Amphictyonic tribes, the most unimportant as the most powerful, had the same number of votes. This rendered it against the interest of the greater states (on whom its consideration necessarily depended) to cement or increase its political influence: and thus it was quietly left to its natural tendency to sacred purposes. Like all institutions which bestow upon man the proper prerogative of God, and affect authority over religious and not civil opinions, the Amphictyonic council was not very efficient in good: even in its punishment of sacrilege, it was only dignified and powerful whenever the interests of the Delphic temple were at stake. Its most celebrated interference was with the town of Crissa, against which the Amphictyons decreed war; the territory of Crissa was then dedicated to the god of the temple.

VII. But if not efficient in good, the Amphictyonic council was not active in evil. Many causes conspired to prevent the worst excesses to which religious domination is prone,—and this cause in particular. It was not composed of a separate, interested, and permanent class, but of citizens annually chosen from every state, who had a much greater interest in the welfare of their own state than in the increased authority of the Amphictyonic council.[13] They were priests but for an occasion—they were citizens by profession. The jealousies of the various states, the constant change in the delegates, prevented that energy and oneness necessary to any settled design of ecclesiastical ambition.

13 Even the hieromnemons (or deputies entrusted with religious cares) must have been as a class very inferior in ability to the pylagoræ; for the first were chosen by lot, the last by careful selection. And thus we learn, in effect, that while the hieromnemon had the higher grade of dignity, the pylagoras did the greater share of business.

Hence, the real influence of the Amphictyonic council was by no means commensurate with its grave renown; and when, in the time of Philip, it became an important political agent, it was only as the corrupt and servile tool of that able monarch. Still it long continued, under the panoply of a great religious name, to preserve the aspect of dignity and power, until, at the time of Constantine, it fell amid the ruins of the faith it had aspired to protect. The creed that became the successor of the religion of Delphi found a mightier Amphictyonic assembly in the conclaves of Rome. The papal institution possessed precisely those qualities for directing the energies of states, for dictating to the ambition of kings, for obtaining temporal authority under spiritual pretexts which were wanting to the pagan.

CHAPTER III

The heroic age—Theseus—his legislative influence upon
Athens—qualities of the Greek heroes—effect of a traditional
age upon the character of a people

I. As one who has been journeying through the dark[1] begins at length to
perceive the night breaking away in mist and shadow, so that the forms of

THE HEROIC AGE

things, yet uncertain and undefined, assume an exaggerated
and gigantic outline, half lost amid the clouds,—so now,
through the obscurity of fable, we descry the dim and mighty outline of the
HEROIC AGE. The careful and sceptical Thucydides has left us, in the commencement of his immortal history, a masterly portraiture of the manners of
those times in which individual prowess elevate the possessor to the rank of
a demigod;—times of unsettled law and indistinct control;—of adventure—
of excitement;—of daring qualities and lofty crime. We recognize in the
picture features familiar to the North: the roving warriors and the pirate
kings who scoured the sea, descended upon unguarded coasts, and deemed
the exercise of plunder a profession of honour, remind us of the exploits of
the Scandinavian Her-Kongr, and the boding banners of the Dane. The seas
of Greece tempted to piratical adventures: their numerous isles, their winding bays and wood-clad shores proffered ample enterprise to the bold—
ample booty to the rapacious; the voyages were short for the inexperienced,
the refuges numerous for the defeated. In early ages, valour is the true
virtue—it dignifies the pursuits in which it is engaged, and the profession
of a pirate was long deemed as honourable in the Ægæan as among the bold
rovers of the Scandinavian race.[2] If the coast was thus exposed to constant
incursion and alarm, neither were the interior recesses of the country more
protected from the violence of marauders. The various tribes that passed into
Greece, to colonize or conquer, dislodged from their settlements many of
the inhabitants, who, retreating up the country, maintained themselves by
plunder, or avenged themselves by outrage. The many crags and mountains,
the caverns and the woods, which diversify the beautiful land of Greece,

1 Milton, Hist. of Eng., book i.
2 No man of rank among the old northern pirates was deemed honourable if not a pirate,
  gloriam sibi acquirens, as the Vatzdæla hath it.

95

afforded their natural fortresses to these barbarous hordes. The chief who had committed a murder, or aspired unsuccessfully to an unsteady throne, betook himself, with his friends, to some convenient fastness, made a descent on the surrounding villages, and bore off the women or the herds, as lust or want excited to the enterprise. No home was safe, no journey free from peril, and the Greeks passed their lives in armour. Thus, gradually, the profession and system of robbery spread itself throughout Greece, until the evil became insufferable—until the public opinion of all the states and tribes, in which society had established laws, was enlisted against the freebooter—until it grew an object of ambition to rid the neighbourhood of a scourge—and the success of the attempt made the glory of the adventurer. Then naturally arose the race of heroes—men who volunteered to seek the robber in his hold—and, by the gratitude of a later age, the courage of the knight-errant was rewarded with the sanctity of the demigod. At that time too, internal circumstances in the different states—whether from the predominance of, or the resistance to, the warlike Hellenes, had gradually conspired to raise a military and fierce aristocracy above the rest of the population; and as arms became the instruments of renown and power, so the wildest feats would lead to the most extended fame.

II. The woods and mountains of Greece were not then cleared of the first rude aboriginals of nature—wild beasts lurked within its caverns;—wolves abounded everywhere—herds of wild bulls, the large horns of which Herodotus names with admiration, were common; and even the lion himself, so late as the invasion of Xerxes, was found in wide districts from the Thracian Abdera to the Acarnanian Achelous. Thus, the feats of the early heroes appear to have been mainly directed against the freebooter or the wild beast; and among the triumphs of Hercules are recorded the extermination of the Lydian robbers, the death of Cacus, and the conquest of the lion of Nemea and the boar of Erymanthus.

Hercules himself shines conspicuously forth as the great model of these useful adventurers. There is no doubt that a prince,[3] so named, actually existed in Greece; and under the title of the Theban Hercules, is to be carefully distinguished both from the god of Egypt and the peaceful Hercules of Phœnicia,[4] whose worship was not unknown to the Greeks previous to the labours of his namesake. As the name of Hercules was given to the Theban hero (originally called Alcæus), in consequence of his exploits, it may be that

---

3 Most probably more than one prince. Greece has three well-accredited pretenders to the name and attributes even of the Grecian Hercules.
4 Herodotus marks the difference between the Egyptian and Grecian deity, and speaks of a temple erected by the Phœnicians to Hercules, when they built Thasus, five hundred years before the son of Amphitryon was known to the Greeks. The historian commends such of the Greeks as erected two temples to the divinity of that name, worshipping in the one as to a god, but in the other observing only the rites as to a hero (ii. 13, 14).

his countrymen recognized in his character or his history something analogous to the traditional accounts of the Eastern god. It was the custom of the early Greeks to attribute to one man the actions which he performed in concert with others, and the reputation of Hercules was doubtless acquired no less as the leader of an army than by the achievements of his personal prowess. His fame and his success excited the emulation of his contemporaries, and pre-eminent among these ranks the Athenian Theseus.

III. In the romance which Plutarch has bequeathed to us, under the title of a "History of Theseus", we seem to read the legends of our own fabulous days of chivalry. The adventures of an Amadis or a Palmerin are not more knightly nor more extravagant.

THESEUS

According to Plutarch, Ægeus, king of Athens, having no children, went to Delphi to consult the oracle how that misfortune might be repaired. He was commanded not to approach any woman till he returned to Athens; but the answer was couched in mystic and allegorical terms, and the good king was rather puzzled than enlightened by the reply. He betook himself therefore to Trœzene, a small town in the Peloponnesus, founded by Pittheus, of the race of Pelops, a man eminent in that day for wisdom and sagacity. He communicated to him the oracle, and besought his interpretation. Something there was in the divine answer which induced Pittheus to draw the Athenian king into an illicit intercourse with his own daughter, Æthra. The princess became with child; and, before his departure from Trœzene, Ægeus deposited a sword and a pair of sandals in a cavity concealed by a huge stone,[5] and left injunctions with Æthra that, should the fruit of their intercourse prove a male child, and able, when grown up, to remove the stone, she should send him privately to Athens with the sword and sandals in proof of his birth; for Ægeus had a brother named Pallas, who, having a large family of sons, naturally expected, from the failure of the direct line, to possess himself or his children of the Athenian throne; and the king feared, should the secret of his intercourse with Æthra be discovered before the expected child had arrived to sufficient strength to protect himself, that either by treason or assassination the sons of Pallas would despoil the rightful heir of his claim to the royal honours. Æthra gave birth to Theseus, and Pittheus concealed the dishonour of his family by asserting that Neptune, the god most honoured at Trœzene, had condescended to be the father of the child:—the gods were very convenient personages in those days. As the boy grew up, he evinced equal strength of body and nobleness of mind; and at length the time arrived when Æthra communicated to him the secret of his birth, and led him to the stone which concealed the tokens of his origin. He easily removed it, and repaired by land to Athens.

---

5 Plut., in Vit. Thes.—Apollod., iii. This story is often borrowed by the Spanish romance-writers, to whom Plutarch was a copious fountain of legendary fable.

At that time, as I have before stated, Greece was overrun by robbers: Hercules had suppressed them for a while; but the Theban hero was now at the feet of the Lydian Omphale, and the freebooters had reappeared along the mountainous recesses of the Peloponnesus; the journey by land was therefore not only longer, but far more perilous, than a voyage by sea, and Pittheus earnestly besought his grandson to prefer the latter. But it was the peril of the way that made its charm in the eyes of the young hero, and the fame of Hercules had long inspired his dreams by night,[6] and his thoughts by day. With his father's sword, then, he repaired to Athens. Strange and wild were the adventures that befell him. In Epidauria he was attacked by a celebrated robber, whom he slew, and whose club he retained as his favourite weapon. In the Isthmus, Sinnis, another bandit, who had been accustomed to destroy the unfortunate travellers who fell in his way by binding them to the boughs of two pine trees (so that when the trees, released, swung back to their natural position, the victim was torn asunder, limb by limb), was punished by the same death he had devised for others; and here occurs one of those anecdotes illustrative of the romance of the period, and singularly analogous to the chivalry of Northern fable, which taught deference to women, and rewarded by the smiles of the fair the exploits of the bold. Sinnis, "the pine-bender", had a daughter remarkable for beauty, who concealed herself amid the shrubs and rushes in terror of the victor. Theseus discovered her, praying, says Plutarch, in childish innocence or folly, to the plants and bushes, and promising, if they would shelter her, never to destroy or burn them. A graceful legend, that reminds us of the rich inventions of Spenser. But Theseus, with all gentle words and soothing vows, allured the maiden from her retreat, and succeeded at last in obtaining her love and its rewards.

Continued adventures—the conquest of Phæa, a wild sow (or a female robber, so styled from the brutality of her life)—the robber Sciron cast headlong from a precipice—Procrustes stretched on his own bed—attested the courage and fortune of the wanderer, and at length he arrived at the banks of the Cephisus. Here he was saluted by some of the Phytalidæ, a sacred family descended from Phytalus, the beloved of Ceres, and was duly purified from the blood of the savages he had slain. Athens was the first place at which he was hospitably entertained. He arrived at an opportune moment; the Colchian Medea, of evil and magic fame, had fled from Corinth and taken refuge with Ægeus, whose affections she had ensnared. By her art she promised him children to supply his failing line, and she gave full trial to the experiment by establishing herself the partner of the royal couch. But it was not likely that the numerous sons of Pallas would regard this connexion with indifference, and faction and feud reigned throughout the city. Medea

6 Plut., in Vit. Thes.

discovered the secret of the birth of Theseus; and, resolved by poison to rid herself of one who would naturally interfere with her designs on Ægeus, she took advantage of the fear and jealousies of the old king, and persuaded him to become her accomplice in the premeditated crime. A banquet, according to the wont of those hospitable times, was given to the stranger. The king was at the board, the cup of poison at hand, when Theseus, wishing to prepare his father for the welcome news he had to divulge, drew the sword or cutlass which Ægeus had made the token of his birth, and prepared to carve with it the meat that was set before him. The sword caught the eye of the king—he dashed the poison to the ground, and after a few eager and rapid questions, recognized his son in his intended victim. The people were assembled—Theseus was acknowledged by the king, and received with joy by the multitude, who had already heard of the feats of the hero. The traditionary place where the poison fell was still shown in the time of Plutarch. The sons of Pallas ill brooked the arrival and acknowledgment of this unexpected heir to the throne. They armed themselves and their followers, and prepared for war. But one half their troops, concealed in ambush, were cut off by Theseus (instructed in their movements by the treachery of a herald), and the other half, thus reduced, were obliged to disperse. So Theseus remained the undisputed heir to the Athenian throne.

IV. It would be vain for the historian, but delightful for the poet, to follow at length this romantic hero through all his reputed enterprises. I can only rapidly sketch the more remarkable. I pass, then, over the tale how he captured alive the wild bull of Marathon, and come at once to that expedition to Crete, which is indissolubly intwined with immortal features of love and poetry. It is related that Androgeus, a son of Minos, the celebrated king of Crete, and by his valour worthy of such a sire, had been murdered in Attica; some suppose by the jealousies of Ægeus, who appears to have had a singular distrust of all distinguished strangers. Minos retaliated by a war which wasted Attica, and was assisted in its ravages by the pestilence and the famine. The oracle of Apollo, which often laudably reconciled the quarrels of princes, terminated the contest by enjoining the Athenians to appease the just indignation of Minos. They despatched, therefore, ambassadors to Crete, and consented, in token of submission, to send every ninth year a tribute of seven virgins and seven young men. The little intercourse that then existed between states, conjoined with the indignant grief of the parents at the loss of their children, exaggerated the evil of the tribute. The hostages were said by the Athenians to be exposed in an intricate labyrinth, and devoured by a monster, the creature of unnatural intercourse, half man half bull; but the Cretans, certainly the best authority in the matter, stripped the account of the fable, and declared that the labyrinth was only a prison in which the youths and maidens were confined on their arrival—that Minos instituted games in honour of Androgeus, and that the Athenian captives were the prize of the victors. The first victor was the chief of the Cretan army, named

Taurus, and he, being fierce and unmerciful, treated the slaves he thus acquired with considerable cruelty. Hence the origin of the labyrinth and the Minotaur. And Plutarch, giving this explanation of the Cretans, cites Aristotle to prove that the youths thus sent were not put to death by Minos, but retained in servile employments, and that their descendants afterward passed into Thrace, and were called Bottiæans. We must suppose, therefore, in consonance not only with these accounts, but the manners of the age, that the tribute was merely a token of submission, and the objects of it merely considered as slaves.[7]

Of Minos himself all accounts are uncertain. There seems no sufficient ground to doubt, indeed, his existence, nor the extended power which, during his reign, Crete obtained in Greece. It is most probable that it was under Phœnician influence that Crete obtained its maritime renown; but there is no reason to suppose Minos himself Phœnician.

After the return of Theseus, the time came when the tribute to Crete was again to be rendered. The people murmured their dissatisfaction. "It was the guilt of Ægeus", said they, "which caused the wrath of Minos, yet Ægeus alone escaped its penalty; their lawful children were sacrificed to the Cretan barbarity, but the doubtful and illegitimate stranger, whom Ægeus had adopted, went safe and free." Theseus generously appeased these popular tumults: he insisted on being himself included in the seven.

V. Twice before had this human tribute been sent to Crete; and in token of the miserable and desperate fate which, according to vulgar belief, awaited the victims, a black sail had been fastened to the ship. But this time, Ægeus, inspired by the cheerful confidence of his son, gave the pilot a white sail, which he was to hoist if, on his return, he bore back Theseus in safety: if not, the black was once more to be the herald of an unhappier fate. It is probable that Theseus did not esteem this among the most dangerous of his adventures. At the court of the wise Pittheus, or in the course of his travels, he had doubtless heard enough of the character of Minos, the greatest and most sagacious monarch of his time, to be convinced that the son of the Athenian king would have little to fear from his severity. He arrived at Crete, and obtained the love of Ariadne, the daughter of Minos. Now follows a variety of contradictory accounts, the most probable and least poetical of which are

---

7 Mr Müller's ingenious supposition, that the tribute was in fact a religious ceremony, and that the voyage of Theseus had originally no other meaning than the landings at Naxos and Delos, is certainly credible, but not a whit more so than, and certainly not so simple as, the ancient accounts in Plutarch; as with mythological, so with historical legends, it is better to take the plain and popular interpretation whenever it seems conformable to the manners of the times, than to construe the story by newly invented allegories. It is very singular that that is the plan which every writer on the early chronicles of France and England would adopt, and yet which so few writers agree to pursue when they are to treat of the obscure records of the Greeks.

given by Plutarch; but as he concludes them all by the remark that none are of certainty, it is a needless task to repeat them: it suffices to relate, that either with or without the consent of Minos, Theseus departed from Crete, in company with Ariadne, and that by one means or the other he thenceforth freed the Athenians from the payment of the accustomed tribute. As it is obvious that with the petty force with which, by all accounts, he sailed to Crete, he could not have conquered the powerful Minos in his own city, so it is reasonable to conclude, as one of the traditions hath it, that the king consented to his alliance with his daughter and, in consequence of that marriage, waived all farther claim to the tribute of the Athenians.[8]

Equal obscurity veils the fate of the loving Ariadne; but the supposition which seems least objectionable is, that Theseus was driven by storm either on Cyprus or Naxos, and Ariadne being then with child, and rendered ill by the violence of the waves, was left on shore by her lover while he returned to take charge of his vessel; that she died in childbed, and that Theseus, on his return, was greatly afflicted, and instituted an annual festival in her honour. While we adopt the story most probable in itself, and most honourable to the character of the Athenian hero, we cannot regret the various romance which is interwoven with the tale of the unfortunate Cretan, since it has given us some of the most beautiful inventions of poetry;—the Labyrinth love-lighted by Ariadne—the Cretan maid deserted by the stranger with whom she fled—left forlorn and alone on the Naxian shore—and consoled by Bacchus and his satyr horde.

VI. Before he arrived at Athens, Theseus rested at Delos, where he is said to have instituted games, and to have originated the custom of crowning the victor with the palm. Meanwhile Ægeus waited the return of his son. On the Cecropian rock that yet fronts the sea, he watched the coming of the vessel and the waving of the white sail: the masts appeared—the ship approached—the white sail was not visible: in the joy and the impatience of the homeward crew, the pilot had forgotten to hoist the appointed signal, and the old man in despair threw himself from the rock and was dashed to pieces. Theseus received the news of his father's death with sorrow and lamentation. His triumph and return were recorded by periodical festivals, in which the fate of Ægeus was typically alluded to, and the vessel of thirty oars with which he had sailed to Crete was preserved by the Athenians to the times of Demetrius the Phalerean—so often new-pieced and repaired, that it furnished a favourite thesis to philosophical disputants, whether it was or was not the *same* vessel which Theseus had employed.

---

8 Plutarch cites Clidemus in support of another version of the tale, somewhat less probable, viz., that, by the death of Minos and his son Deucalion, Ariadne became possessed of the throne, and that she remitted the tribute.

VII. Possessed of the supreme power, Theseus now bent his genius to the task of legislation, and in this part of his life we tread upon firmer ground,

His legislative influ-ence upon Athens

because the most judicious of the ancient his-torians[9] expressly attributes to the son of Ægeus those enactments which so mainly contributed to consolidate the strength and union of the Athenian people.

Although Cecrops is said to have brought the tribes of Attica under one government, yet it will be remembered that he had divided the territory into twelve districts, with a fortress or capital to each. By degrees these several districts had become more and more distinct from each other, and in many cases of emergency it was difficult to obtain a general assembly or a general concurrence of the people; nay, differences had often sprung up between the tribes, which had been adjusted, not as among common cit-izens, by law, but as among jealous enemies, by arms and bloodshed. It was the master policy of Theseus to unite these petty commonwealths in one state. He applied in person, and by all the arts of persuasion, to each tribe: the poor he found ready enough to listen to an invitation which promised them the shelter of a city, and the protection of a single government from the outrage of many tyrants; the rich and the powerful were more jealous of their independent, scattered, and, as it were, feudal life. But these he sought to conciliate by promises that could not but flatter that very prejudice of liberty which naturally at first induced them to oppose his designs. He pledged his faith to a constitution which should leave the power in the hands of the many. He himself, as monarch, desired only the command in war, and in peace the guardianship of laws he was equally bound to obey. Some were induced by his persuasions, others by the fear of his power, until at length he obtained his object. By common consent he dissolved the towns' corporations and councils in each separate town, and built in Athens one common prytaneum or council-hall, existent still in the time of Plutarch. He united the scattered streets and houses of the citadel, and the new town that had grown up along the plain, by the common name of "Athens", and instituted the festival of the Panathenæa, in honour of the guardian goddess of the city, and as a memorial of the confederacy. Adhering then to his promises, he set strict and narrow limits to the regal power, created, under the name of eupatrids or well-born, an hereditary nobility, and divided into two orders (the husbandmen and mechanics) the remainder of the people. The care of religion, the explanation of the laws, and the situations of magistrates were the privilege of the nobles. He thus laid the foundation of a free, though aristocratic, constitution—according to Aristotle, the first who surrendered the absolute sway of royalty, and receiving from the rhetorical Isocrates the praise that it was a contest which should give most,

9 Thucyd., ii. 15.

the people of power, or the king of freedom. As an extensive population was necessary to a powerful state, so Theseus invited to Athens all strangers willing to share in the benefits of its protection, granting them equal security of life and law; and he set a demarcation to the territory of the state by the boundary of a pillar erected in the Isthmus, dividing Ionia from the Peloponnesus. The Isthmian games in honour of Neptune were also the invention of Theseus.

VIII. Such are the accounts of the legislative enactments of Theseus. But of these we must reject much. We may believe from the account of Thucydides that jealousies among some Attic towns—which might either possess, or pretend to, an independence never completely annihilated by Cecrops and his successors, and which the settlement of foreigners of various tribes and habits would have served to increase—were so far terminated as to induce submission to the acknowledged supremacy of Athens as the Attic capital; and that the right of justice, and even of legislation, which had before been the prerogative of each separate town (to the evident weakening of the supreme and regal authority), was now concentrated in the common council-house of Athens. To Athens, as to a capital, the eupatrids of Attica would repair as a general residence.[10] The city increased in population and importance, and from this period Thucydides dates the enlargement of the ancient city, by the addition of the Lower Town. That Theseus voluntarily lessened the royal power, it is not necessary to believe. In the heroic age a warlike race had sprung up, whom no Grecian monarch appears to have attempted to govern arbitrarily in peace, though they yielded implicitly to his authority in war. Himself on a newly won and uncertain throne, it was the necessity as well as the policy of Theseus to conciliate the most powerful of his subjects. It may also be conceded, that he more strictly defined the distinctions between the nobles and the remaining classes, whether yeomen or husband-men, mechanics or strangers; and it is recorded that the honours and the business of legislation were the province of the eupatrids. It is possible that the people might be occasionally convened—but it is clear that they had little, if any, share in the government of the state. But the mere establishment and confirmation of a powerful aristocracy, and the mere collection of the population into a capital, were sufficient to prepare the way for far more democratic institutions than Theseus himself contemplated or designed. For centuries afterward an oligarchy ruled in Athens; but, free itself, that oligarchy preserved in its monopoly the principles of liberty, expanding in their influence with the progress of society. The democracy of Athens was

10 But many Athenians preferred to a much later age the custom of living without the walls—scattered over the country (Thucyd., ii. 15.). We must suppose it was with them as with the moderns—the rich and the great generally preferred the capital, but there were many exceptions.

not an ancient, yet not a sudden, constitution. It developed itself slowly, unconsciously, continuously—passing the allotted orbit of royalty, oligarchy, aristocracy, timocracy, tyranny, till at length it arrived at its dazzling zenith, blazed—waned—and disappeared.

After the successful issue of his legislative attempts, we next hear of Theseus less as the monarch of history than as the hero of song. On these later traditions, which belong to fable, it is not necessary to dwell. Our own *Coeur de Lion* suggests no improbable resemblance to a spirit cast in times yet more wild and enterprising, and without seeking interpretations, after the fashion of allegory or system, of each legend, it is the most simple hypothesis, that Theseus really departed in quest of adventure from a dominion that afforded no scope for a desultory and eager ambition; and that something of truth lurks beneath many of the rich embellishments which his wanderings and exploits received from the exuberant poetry and the rude credulity of the age. During his absence, Menestheus, of the royal race of Attica, who, Plutarch simply tells us, was the first of mankind that undertook the profession of a demagogue, ingratiated himself with the people, or rather with the nobles. The absence of a king is always the nurse of seditions, and Menestheus succeeded in raising so powerful a faction against the hero, that on his return Theseus was unable to preserve himself in the government, and, pouring forth a solemn curse on the Athenians, departed to Scyros, where he either fell by accident from a precipice, or was thrown down by the king. His death at first was but little regarded; in after times, to appease his ghost and expiate his curse, divine honours were awarded to his memory; and in the most polished age of his descendants, his supposed remains, indicated by an eagle in the skeleton of a man of giant stature, with a lance of brass and a sword by his side, were brought to Athens in the galley of Cimon, hailed by the shouts of a joyous multitude, "as if the living Theseus were come again".

X. I have not altogether discarded, while I have abridged, the legends relating to a hero who undoubtedly exercised considerable influence over his country and his time, because in those legends we trace, better than we could do by dull interpretations equally unsatisfactory though more prosaic, the effigy of the heroic age—not unillustrative of the poetry and the romance which at once formed and indicated important features in the character of the Athenians. Much of the national spirit of every people, even in its most civilized epochs, is to be traced to the influence of that age which may be called the heroic. The wild adventurers of the early Greece tended to humanize even in their excesses. It is true that there are many instances of their sternness, ferocity, and revenge;—they were insolent from the consciousness of surpassing strength; —often cruel from that contempt of life common to the warlike. But the darker side of their character is far less commonly presented to us than the

QUALITIES OF THE GREEK HEROES—EFFECT OF A TRADITIONAL AGE UPON THE CHARACTER OF A PEOPLE brighter—they seem to have been alive to generous emotions more readily than any other race so warlike in an age so rude—their affections were fervid as their hatreds—their friendships more remarkable than their feuds. Even their ferocity was not, as with the Scandinavian heroes, a virtue and a boast—their public opinion honoured the compassionate and the clement. Thus Hercules is said first to have introduced the custom of surrendering to the enemy the corpses of their slain; and mildness, justice, and courtesy are no less his attributes than invincible strength and undaunted courage. Traversing various lands, these paladins of an older chivalry acquired an experience of different governments and customs, which assisted on their return to polish and refine the admiring tribes which their achievements had adorned. Like the knights of a Northern mythus, their duty was to punish the oppressor and redress the wronged, and they thus fixed in the wild elements of unsettled opinion a recognized standard of generosity and of justice. Their deeds became the theme of the poets, who sought to embellish their virtues and extenuate their offences. Thus, certain models, not indeed wholly pure or excellent, but bright with many of those qualities which ennoble a national character, were set before the emulation of the aspiring and the young:—and the traditional fame of a Hercules or a Theseus assisted to inspire the souls of those who, ages afterward, broke the Mede at Marathon, and arrested the Persian might in the Pass of Thermopylæ. For, as the spirit of a poet has its influence on the destiny and character of nations, so TIME itself hath his own poetry, preceding and calling forth the poetry of the human genius, and breathing inspirations, imaginative and imperishable, from the great deeds and gigantic images of an ancestral and traditionary age.

CHAPTER IV

The successors of Theseus—the fate of Codrus—the emigration of Nileus—the archons—Draco

I. The reputed period of the Trojan war follows close on the age of Hercules and Theseus; and Menestheus, who succeeded the latter hero on the throne of Athens, led his countrymen to the immortal war. Plutarch and succeeding historians have not failed to notice the expression of Homer, in which he applies the word *demus* or "people" to the Athenians, as a proof of the popular government established in that state. But while the line has been considered an interpolation, as late at least as the time of Solon, we may observe that it was never used by Homer in the popular and political sense it afterward received. And he applies it not only to the state of Athens, but to that of Ithaca, certainly no democracy.[1]

The demagogue king appears to have been a man of much warlike renown and skill, and is mentioned as the first who marshalled an army in rank and file. Returning from Troy, he died in the isle of Melos, and was succeeded by Demophoon, one of the sons of Theseus, who had also fought with the Grecian army in the Trojan siege. In his time a dispute between the Athenians and Argives was referred to fifty arbiters of each nation, called Ephetæ, the origin of the court so styled, and afterward re-established with new powers by Draco.

To Demophoon succeeded his son Oxyntes, and to Oxyntes, Aphidas, murdered by his bastard brother Thymœtes. Thymœtes was the last of the race of Theseus who reigned in Athens. A dispute arose between the Bœotians and the Athenians respecting the confines of their several territories; it was proposed to decide the difference by a single combat between Thymœtes and the king of the Bœotians. Thymœtes declined the contest. A Messenian exile, named Melanthus, accepted it, slew his antagonist by a stratagem, and, deposing the cowardly Athenian, obtained the sovereignty of Athens. With Melanthus, who was of the race of Nestor, passed into Athens two nobles of the same house, Pæon and Alcmæon, who were the founders of the

---

1 For other instances in which the same word is employed by Homer, see Clinton's Fasti Hellenici, vol. i, introduction, p. ix.

Pæonids and Alcmæonids, two powerful families, whose names often occur in the subsequent history of Athens, and who, if they did not create a new order of nobility, at least sought to confine to their own families the chief privileges of that which was established.

II. Melanthus was succeeded by his son Codrus, a man whose fame finds more competitors in Roman than Grecian history. During his reign the Dorians invaded Attica. They were assured of success by the Delphian oracle, on condition that they did not slay the Athenian king. Informed of the response, Codrus disguised himself as a peasant, and, repairing to the hostile force, sought a quarrel with some of the soldiers, and was slain by them not far from the banks of the Ilissus.[2] The Athenians sent to demand the body of their king; and the Dorians, no longer hoping of success, since the condition of the oracle was thus violated, broke up their encampment and relinquished their design. Some of the Dorians had already by night secretly entered the city and concealed themselves within its walls; but, as the day dawned, and they found themselves abandoned by their associates and surrounded by the foe, they fled to the Areopagus and the altars of the Furies; the refuge was deemed inviolable, and the Dorians were dismissed unscathed—a proof of the awe already attached to the rites of sanctuary.[3] Still, however, this invasion was attended with the success of what might have been the principal object of the invaders. Megara,[4] which had hitherto been associated with Attica, was now seized by the Dorians, and became afterward a colony of Corinth. This gallant but petty state had considerable influence on some of the earlier events of Athenian history.

THE FATE OF CODRUS

III. Codrus was the last of the Athenian kings. The Athenians affected the motives of reverence to his memory as an excuse for forbidding to the illustrious martyr the chance of an unworthy successor. But the aristocratic constitution had been morally strengthened by the extinction of the race of Theseus and the jealousy of a foreign line; and the abolition of the monarchy was rather caused by the ambition of the nobles than the popular veneration for the patriotism of Codrus. The name of king was changed into that of archon (magistrate or governor); the succession was still made hereditary, but the power of the ruler was placed under new limits, and he was obliged to render to the people, or rather to the eupatrids, an account of his government whenever they deemed it advisable to demand it.

IV. Medon, the son of Codrus, was the first of these perpetual archons. In that age bodily strength was still deemed an essential virtue in a chief;

---

2 Paus., i. 19; ii. 18.

3 Paus., vii. 25. An oracle of Dodona had forewarned the Athenians of the necessity of sparing the suppliants.

4 Herod. v. 76 cites this expedition of the Dorians for the establishment of a colony at Megara as that of their first incursion into Attica.

THE EMIGRATION OF
NILEUS—THE ARCHONS

and Nileus, a younger brother of Medon, attempted to depose the archon on no other pretence than that of his lameness.

A large portion of the people took advantage of the quarrel between the brothers to assert that they would have no king but Jupiter. At length Medon had recourse to the oracle, which decided in his favour; and Nileus, with all the younger sons of Codrus, and accompanied by a numerous force, departed from Athens, and colonized that part of Asia Minor celebrated in history under the name of Ionia. The rise, power, and influence of these Asiatic colonies we shall find a more convenient opportunity to notice. Medon's reign, thus freed from the more stirring spirits of his time, appears to have been prosperous and popular; it was an era in the ancient world, when the lameness of a ruler was discovered to be unconnected with his intellect! Then follows a long train of archons—peaceable and obscure. During a period estimated at three hundred years, the Athenians performed little that has descended to posterity—brief notices of petty skirmishes, and trivial dissensions with their neighbours, alone diversify that great interval. Meanwhile, the Ionian colonies rose rapidly into eminence and power. At length, on the death of Alcmæon—the thirteenth and last perpetual archon—a new and more popular change was introduced into the government. The sway of the archon was limited to ten years. This change slowly prepared the way to changes still more important. Hitherto the office had been confined to the two Neleid houses of Codrus and Alcmæon;—in the archonship of Hippomones it was thrown open to other distinguished families; and at length, on the death of Eryxias, the last of the race of Codrus, the failure of that ancient house in its direct line (indirectly it still continued, and the blood of Codrus flowed through the veins of Solon) probably gave excuse and occasion for abolishing the investment of the supreme power in one magistrate; nine were appointed, each with the title of archon (though the name was more emphatically given to the chief of the number), and each with separate functions. This institution continued to the last days of Athenian freedom. This change took place in the twenty-fourth Olympiad.

V. In the thirty-ninth Olympiad, Draco, being chief archon, was deputed to institute new laws. He was a man concerning whom history is singularly

DRACO

brief; we know only that he was of a virtuous and austere renown —that he wrote a great number of verses, as little durable as his laws.[5]

---

5 Suidas. One cannot but be curious as to the motives and policy of a person, virtuous as a man, but so relentless as a lawgiver. Although Draco was himself a noble, it is difficult to suppose that laws so stern and impartial would not operate rather against the more insolent and encroaching class than against the more subordinate ones. The attempt shows a very unwholesome state of society, and went far to produce the democratic action which Solon represented rather than created.

As for the latter—when we learn that they were stern and bloody beyond precedent—we have little difficulty in believing that they were insufficient.

VI. I have hastened over this ambiguous and uninteresting period with a rapidity I trust all but antiquaries will forgive. Hitherto we have been in the land of shadow—we approach the light. The empty names of apocryphal beings which we have enumerated are for the most part as spectres, so dimly seen as to be probably delusions—invoked to please a fanciful curiosity, but without an object to satisfy the reason or excuse the apparition. If I am blamed for not imitating those who have sought, by weaving together disconnected hints and subtle conjectures, to make a history from legends, to overturn what has been popularly believed, by systems equally contradictory, though more learnedly fabricated;—if I am told that I might have made the chronicle thus briefly given extend to a greater space, and sparkle with more novel speculation, I answer that I am writing the history of men and not of names—to the people and not to scholars—and that no researches however elaborate, no conjectures however ingenious, could draw any real or solid moral from records which leave us ignorant both of the characters of men and the causes of events. What matters who was Ion, or whence the first worship of Apollo? What matter revolutions or dynasties, ten or twelve centuries before Athens emerged from a deserved obscurity?—they had no influence upon her after greatness; enigmas impossible to solve—if solved, but scholastic frivolities.

Fortunately, as we desire the history of a people, so it is when the Athenians become a people, that we pass at once from tradition into history.

I pause to take a brief survey of the condition of the rest of Greece prior to the age of Solon.

CHAPTER V

A general survey of Greece and the East previous to the time of Solon—the Grecian colonies—the isles—brief account of the states on the continent—Elis and the Olympic Games

I. On the north, Greece is separated from Macedonia by the Cambunian mountains; on the west spreads the Ionian, on the south and east the Ægæan,

Sea. Its greatest length is two hundred and twenty geographical miles; its greatest width one hundred and forty. No contrast can be more startling than the speck of earth which Greece occupies in the map of the world, compared to the space claimed by the Grecian influences in the history of the human mind. In that contrast itself is the moral which Greece has left us—nor can volumes more emphatically describe the triumph of the Intellectual over the Material. But as nations, resembling individuals, do not become illustrious from their mere physical proportions; as in both, renown has its moral sources; so, in examining the causes which conduced to the eminence of Greece, we cease to wonder at the insignificance of its territories or the splendour of its fame. Even in geographical circumstance Nature had endowed the country of the Hellenes with gifts which amply atoned the narrow girth of its confines. The most southern part of the continent of Europe, it contained within itself all the advantages of sea and land; its soil, though unequal in its product, is for the most part fertile and abundant; it is intersected by numerous streams, and protected by chains of mountains; its plains and valleys are adapted to every product most necessary to the support of the human species; and the sun that mellows the fruits of nature is sufficiently tempered not to relax the energies of man. Bordered on three sides by the sea, its broad and winding extent of coast early conduced to the spirit of enterprise; and, by innumerable bays and harbours, proffered every allurement to that desire of gain which is the parent of commerce and the basis of civilization. At the period in which Greece rose to eminence it was in the very centre of the most advanced and flourishing states of Europe and of Asia. The attention of its earlier adventurers was directed not only to the shores of Italy, but to the gorgeous cities of the East, and the wise and hoary institutions of Egypt. If from other nations they borrowed less than has been popularly supposed, the very intercourse with those nations alone sufficed to impel and develop the faculties of an imitative and youthful people;—while, as the spirit of liberty broke out in all the Grecian states, producing a restless competition both among the citizens in each city and the cities one with another, no energy was allowed to sleep until the operations of an intellect, perpetually roused and never crippled, carried the universal civilization to its height. Nature herself set the boundaries of the river and the mountain to the confines of the several states—the smallness of each concentrated power into a focus—the number of all heightened emulation to a fever. The Greek cities had therefore, above all other nations, the advantage of a perpetual collision of mind—a perpetual intercourse with numerous neighbours, with whom intellect was ever at work—with whom experiment knew no rest. Greece, taken collectively, was the only free country (with the exception of Phœnician states and colonies perhaps equally civilized) in the midst of enlightened despotisms; and in the ancient world, despotism invented and sheltered the arts which liberty refined and perfected.[1] Thus considered, her greatness ceases to be a marvel—the very narrowness of her dominions was a principal cause of it—and to the most favourable circumstances of nature were added circumstances the most favourable of time.

If, previous to the age of Solon, we survey the histories of Asia, we find that quarter of the globe subjected to great and terrible revolutions, which

---

1 Hume utters a sentiment exactly the reverse: "To expect", says he, in his Essay on the rise of Arts and Sciences, "that the arts and sciences should take their first rise in a monarchy, is to expect a contradiction"; and he holds, in a subsequent part of the same essay, that though republics originate the arts and sciences, they may be transferred to a monarchy. Yet this sentiment is utterly at variance with the fact; in the despotic monarchies of the East were the elements of the arts and sciences; it was to republics they were transferred, and republics perfected them. Hume, indeed, is often the most incautious and uncritical of all writers. What can we think of an author who asserts that a refined taste succeeds best in monarchies, and then refers to the indecencies of Horace and Ovid as an example of the reverse in a republic—as if Ovid and Horace had not lived under a monarchy! And throughout the whole of this theory he is as thoroughly in the wrong. By refined taste he signifies an avoidance of immodesty of style. Beaumont and Fletcher, Rochester, Dean Swift wrote under monarchies—their pruriencies are not excelled by any republican authors of ancient times. What ancient authors equal in indelicacy the French romances from the time of the Regent of Orleans to Louis XVI? By all accounts, the despotism of China is the very sink of indecencies, whether in pictures or books. Still more, what can we think of a writer who says, that "the ancients have not left us one piece of pleasantry that is excellent, unless one may except the Banquet of Xenophon and the Dialogues of Lucian"? What! has he forgotten Aristophanes? Has he forgotten Plautus! No—but their pleasantry is not excellent to his taste; and he tacitly agrees with Horace in censuring the "coarse railleries and cold jests" of the Great Original of Molière!

confined and curbed the power of its various despotisms. Its empires for the most part built up by the successful invasions of Nomad tribes, contained in their very vastness the elements of dissolution. The Assyrian Nineveh had been conquered by the Babylonians and the Medes; and Babylon, under the new Chaldæan dynasty, was attaining the dominant power of western Asia. The Median monarchy was scarce recovering from the pressure of barbarian foes, and Cyrus had not as yet arisen to establish the throne of Persia. In Asia Minor, it is true, the Lydian empire had attained to great wealth and luxury, and was the most formidable enemy of the Asiatic Greeks, yet it served to civilize them even while it awed. The commercial and enterprising Phœnicians, now foreboding the march of the Babylonian king, who had "taken counsel against Tyre, the crowning city, whose merchants are princes, whose traffickers are the honourable of the earth", at all times were precluded from the desire of conquest by their divided states,[2] formidable neighbours, and trading habits.

In Egypt a great change had operated upon the ancient character; the splendid dynasty of the Pharaohs was no more. The empire, rent into an oligarchy of twelve princes, had been again united under the sceptre of one by the swords of Grecian mercenaries; and Neco, the son of the usurper—a man of mighty intellect and vast designs—while he had already adulterated the old Egyptian customs with the spirit of Phœnician and Greek adventure, found his field of action only in the East. As yet, then, no foreign enemy had disturbed the early rise of the several states of Greece; they were suffered to form their individual demarcations tranquilly and indelibly; and to progress to that point between social amenities and chivalric hardihood, when, while war is the most sternly encountered, it the most rapidly enlightens. The peace that follows the first war of a half-civilized nation is usually the great era of its intellectual eminence.

II. At this time the colonies in Asia Minor were far advanced in civilization beyond the Grecian continent. Along the western coast of that delicious district—on a shore more fertile, under a heaven more bright, than those of the parent states—the Æolians, Ionians, and Dorians, in a remoter age, had planted settlements and founded cities. The Æolian colonies (the result of the Dorian immigrations[3]) occupied the coasts of Mysia and Caria—on the mainland twelve cities— the most renowned of which were Cyme and Smyrna; and the islands of the Heccatonnesi, Tenedos, and Lesbos, the last illustrious above the rest, and consecrated by the muses of Sappho and Alcæus. They had also settlements

THE GRECIAN COLONIES

---

2 Which forbade the concentration of power necessary to great conquests. Phœnicia was not one state, it was a confederacy of states; so, for the same reason, Greece, admirably calculated to resist, was ill fitted to invade.

3 For the dates of these migrations, see Fasti Hellenici, vol. i.

about Mount Ida. Their various towns were independent of each other; but Mitylene, in the isle of Lesbos, was regarded as their common capital. The trade of Mitylene was extensive—its navy formidable.

The Ionian colonies, founded subsequently to the Æolian, but also (though less immediately) a consequence of the Æolian revolution, were peopled not only by Ionians, but by various nations, led by the sons of Codrus. In the islands of Samos and Chios, on the southern coast of Lydia, where Caria stretches to the north, they established their voluptuous settlements known by the name "Ionia". Theirs were the cities of Myus, and Priene, Colophon, Ephesus, Lebedus, Teos, Clazomene, Erythræ, Phocæa, and Miletus:—in the islands of Samos and Chios were two cities of the same name as the isles themselves. The chief of the Ionian cities at the time on which we enter, and second perhaps in trade and in civilization to none but the great Phœnician states, was the celebrated Miletus—founded first by the Carians—exalted to her renown by the Ionians. Her streets were the mart of the world; along the Euxine and the Palus Mæotis, her ships rode in the harbours of a hundred of her colonies. Here broke the first light of the Greek philosophy. But if inferior to this, their imperial city, each of the Ionian towns had its title to renown. Here flourished already music, and art, and song. The trade of Phocæa extended to the coasts of Italy and Gaul. Ephesus had not yet risen to its meridian—it was the successor of Miletus and Phocæa. These Ionian states, each independent of the other, were united by a common sanctuary—the Panionium (Temple of Neptune), which might be seen far off on the headland of that Mycale afterward the witness of one of the proudest feats of Grecian valour. Long free, Ionia became tributary to the Lydian kings, and afterward to the great Persian monarchy.

In the islands of Cos and Rhodes, and on the southern shores of Caria, spread the Dorian colonies—planted subsequently to the Ionian by gradual immigrations. If in importance and wealth the Æolian were inferior to the Ionian colonies, so were the Dorian colonies to the Æolian. Six cities (Ialyssus, Camirus, and Lindus, in Rhodes; in Cos, a city called from the island; Cnidus and Halicarnassus, on the mainland) were united, like the Ionians, by a common sanctuary—the Temple of Apollo Triopius.

Besides these colonies—the Black Sea, the Palus Mæotis, the Propontis, the coasts of Lower Italy, the eastern and southern shores of Sicily,[4] Syracuse, the mightiest of Grecian offspring, and the daughter of Corinth, —the African Cyrene,—not enumerating settlements more probably referable to a later date, attested the active spirit and extended navigation of early Greece.

---

4 To a much later period in the progress of this work I reserve a somewhat elaborate view of the history of Sicily.

The effect of so vast and flourishing a colonization was necessarily prodigious upon the moral and intellectual spirit of the mother land. The seeds scattered over the earth bore their harvests to her garner.

III. Among the Grecian isles, the glory of Minos had long passed from Crete. The monarchical form of government had yielded to the republican, but in its worst shape—the oligarchic. But the old Cretan institu-

THE ISLES

tions still lingered in the habits of private life;—while the jealousies and commotions of its several cities, each independent, exhausted within itself those powers which, properly concentrated and wisely directed, might have placed Crete at the head of Greece.

Cyprus, equally favoured by situation with Crete, and civilized by the constant influence of the Phœnicians, once its masters, was attached to its independence, but not addicted to warlike enterprise. It was, like Crete, an instance of a state which seemed unconscious of the facilities for command and power which it had received from nature. The island of Corcyra (a Corinthian colony) had not yet arrived at its day of power. This was reserved for that period when, after the Persian war, it exchanged an oligarchic for a democratic action, which wore away, indeed, the greatness of the country in its struggles for supremacy, obstinately and fatally resisted by the antagonist principle.

Of the Cyclades—those beautiful daughters of Crete—Delos, sacred to Apollo, and possessed principally by the Ionians, was the most eminent. But Paros boasted not only its marble quarries, but the valour of its inhabitants, and the vehement song of Archilochus.

Eubœa, neighbouring Attica, possessed two chief cities, Eretria and Chalcis, governed apparently by timocracies, and frequently at war with each other. Though of importance as connected with the subsequent history of Athens, and though the colonization of Chalcis was considerable, the fame of Eubœa was scarcely proportioned to its extent as one of the largest islands of the Ægæan;—and was far outshone by the small and rocky Ægina—the rival of Athens, and at this time her superior in maritime power and commercial enterprise. Colonized by Epidaurus, Ægina soon became independent; but the violence of party, and the power of the oligarchy, while feeding its energies, prepared its downfall.

IV. As I profess only to delineate in this work the rise and fall of the Athenians, so I shall not deem it at present necessary to do more than glance

BRIEF ACCOUNT OF THE
STATES ON THE CONTINENT

at the condition of the continent of Greece previous to the time of Solon. Sparta alone will demand a more attentive survey.

Taking our station on the citadel of Athens, we behold, far projecting into the sea, the neighbouring country of Megaris, with Megara for its city. It was originally governed by twelve kings; the last, Hyperion, being assassinated, its affairs were administered by magistrates, and it was one of the earliest of the countries of Greece which adopted republican institutions.

114

Nevertheless, during the reigns of the earlier kings of Attica, it was tributary to them.[5] We have seen how the Dorians subsequently wrested it from the Athenians;[6] and it underwent long and frequent warfare for the preservation of its independence from the Dorians of Corinth. About the year 640 BC, a powerful citizen named Theagenes wrested the supreme power from the stern aristocracy which the Dorian conquest had bequeathed, though the yoke of Corinth was shaken off. The tyrant—for such was the appellation given to a successful usurper—was subsequently deposed, and the democratic government restored; and although that democracy was one of the most turbulent in Greece, it did not prevent this little state from ranking among the most brilliant actors in the Persian war.

V. Between Attica and Megaris we survey the isle of Salamis—the right to which we shall find contested both by Athens and the Megarians.

VI. Turning our eyes now to the land, we may behold, bordering Attica —from which a mountainous tract divides it—the mythological Bœotia, the domain of the Phœnician Cadmus, and the birthplace of Polynices and Œdipus. Here rise the immemorial mountains of Helicon and Cithæron— the haunt of the muses; here Pentheus fell beneath the raging bands of the Bacchanals, and Actæon endured the wrath of the Goddess of the Woods; here rose the walls of Thebes to the harmony of Amphion's lyre—and still, in the time of Pausanias, the Thebans showed, to the admiration of the traveller, the place where Cadmus sowed the dragon-seed—the images of the witches sent by Juno to lengthen the pains of Alcmena—the wooden statue wrought by Dædalus—and the chambers of Harmonia and of Semele. No land was more sanctified by all the golden legends of poetry—and of all Greece no people was less alive to the poetical inspiration. Devoted, for the most part, to pastoral pursuits, the Bœotians were ridiculed by their lively neighbours for an inert and sluggish disposition—a reproach which neither the song of Hesiod and Pindar, nor the glories of Thebes and Platæa, were sufficient to repel. As early as the twelfth century (BC) royalty was abolished in Bœotia—its territory was divided into several independent states, of which Thebes was the principal, and Platæa and Cheronæa among the next in importance. Each had its own peculiar government; and, before the Persian war, oligarchies had obtained the ascendency in these several states. They were united in a league, of which Thebes was the head; but the ambition and power of that city kept the rest in perpetual jealousy, and weakened, by a common fear and ill-smothered dissensions, a country otherwise, from the size of its territories[7] and the number of its inhabitants,

5 Pausanias, in corroboration of this fact, observes, that Peribœa, the daughter of Alcathous, was sent with Theseus with tribute into Crete.

6 When, according to Pausanias, it changed its manners and its language.

7 In length fifty-two geographical miles, and about twenty-eight to thirty-two broad.

calculated to be the principal power of Greece. Its affairs were administered by eleven magistrates, or bœotarchs, elected by four assemblies held in the four districts into which Bœotia was divided.

VII. Beyond Bœotia lies Phocis, originally colonized, according to the popular tradition, by Phocus from Corinth. Shortly after the Dorian irruption, monarchy was abolished and republican institutions substituted. In Phocis were more than twenty states independent of the general Phocian government, but united in a congress held at stated times on the road between Daulis and Delphi. Phocis contained also the city of Crissa, with its harbour and the surrounding territory inhabited by a fierce and piratical population, and the sacred city of Delphi, on the southwest of Parnassus.

VIII. Of the oracle of Delphi I have before spoken—it remains only now to point out to the reader the great political cause of its rise into importance. It had been long established, but without any brilliant celebrity, when happened that Dorian revolution which is called the "Return of the Heraclidæ". The Dorian conquerors had early steered their course by the advice of the Delphian oracle, which appeared artfully to favour their pretensions, and which, adjoining the province of Doris, had imposed upon them the awe, and perhaps felt for them the benevolence, of a sacred neighbour. Their ultimate triumph not only gave a striking and supreme repute to the oracle, but secured the protection and respect of a race now become the most powerful of Greece. From that time no Dorian city ever undertook an enterprise without consulting the Pythian voice; the example became general, and the shrine of the deity was enriched by offerings not only from the piety of Greece, but the credulous awe of barbarian kings. Perhaps, though its wealth was afterward greater, its authority was never so unquestioned as for a period dating from about a century preceding the laws of Solon to the end of the Persian war. Delphi was wholly an independent state, administered by a rigid aristocracy;[8] and though protected by the Amphictyonic council, received from its power none of those haughty admonitions with which the defenders of a modern church have often insulted their charge. The temple was so enriched by jewels, statues, and vessels of gold, that at the time of the invasion of Xerxes its wealth was said to equal in value the whole of the Persian armament: and so wonderful was its magnificence, that it appeared more like the Olympus of the gods than a human temple in their honour. On the ancient Delphi stands now the monastery of Kastri. But still you discover the terraces once crowded by fanes—still, amid gloomy chasms, bubbles the Castalian spring—and yet permitted to the pilgrim's gaze is the rocky bath of the Pythia, and the lofty halls of the Corycian Cave.

8 A council of five presided over the business of the oracle, composed of families who traced their descent from Deucalion.

IX. Beyond Phocis lies the country of the Locrians, divided into three tribes independent of each other—the Locri Ozolæ, the Locri Opuntii, the Locri Epicnemidii. The Locrians (undistinguished in history) changed in early times royal for aristocratic institutions.

The nurse of the Dorian race—the small province of Doris—borders the Locrian territory to the south of Mount Œta; while to the west of Locris spreads the mountainous Ætolia, ranging northward from Pindus to the Ambracian Bay. Ætolia gave to the heroic age the names of Meleager and Diomed, but subsequently fell into complete obscurity. The inhabitants were rude and savage, divided into tribes, nor emerged into importance until the latest era of the Grecian history. The political constitution of Ætolia, in the time referred to, is unknown.

X. Acarnania, the most western country of central Greece, appears little less obscure at this period than Ætolia, on which it borders; with Ætolia it arose into eminence in the Macedonian epoch of Greek history.

XI. Northern Greece contains two countries—Thessaly and Epirus.

In Thessaly was situated the long and lofty mountain of the divine Olympus, and to the more southern extreme rose Pindus and Œta. Its inhabitants were wild and hardy, and it produced the most celebrated breed of horses in Greece. It was from Thessaly that the Hellenes commenced their progress over Greece—it was in the kingdoms of Thessaly that the race of Achilles held their sway; but its later history was not calculated to revive the fame of the Homeric hero; it appears to have shared but little of the republican spirit of the more famous states of Greece. Divided into four districts (Thessaliotis, Pelasgiotis, Phthiotis, and Hestiæotis), the various states of Thessaly were governed either by hereditary princes or nobles of vast possessions. An immense population of serfs, or penestæ, contributed to render the chiefs of Thessaly powerful in war and magnificent in peace. Their common country fell into insignificance from the want of a people—but their several courts were splendid from the wealth of a nobility.

XII. Epirus was of somewhat less extent than Thessaly, and far less fertile; it was inhabited by various tribes, some Greek, some barbarian, the chief of which was the Molossi, governed by kings who boasted their descent from Achilles. Epirus has little importance or interest in history until the sun of Athens had set, during the ascendency of the Macedonian kings. It contained the independent state of Ambracia, peopled from Corinth, and governed by republican institutions. Here also were the sacred oaks of the oracular Dodona.

XIII. We now come to the states of the Peloponnesus, which contained eight countries.

Beyond Megaris lay the territory of Corinth: its broad bay adapted it for commerce, of which it availed itself early; even in the time of Homer it was noted for its wealth. It was subdued by the Dorians, and for five generations the royal power rested with the descendants of Aletes,[9] of the family of the Heraclidæ. By a revolution, the causes of which are unknown to us, the kingdom then passed to Bacchis, the founder of an illustrious race (the Bacchiadæ), who reigned first as kings, and subsequently as yearly magistrates, under the name of Prytanes. In the latter period the Bacchiadæ were certainly not a single family, but a privileged class—they intermarried only with each other—the administrative powers were strictly confined to them—and their policy, if exclusive, seems to have been vigorous and brilliant. This government was destroyed, as under its sway the people increased in wealth and importance; a popular movement, headed by Cypselus, a man of birth and fortune, replaced an able oligarchy by an abler demagogue. Cypselus was succeeded by the celebrated Periander, a man whose vices were perhaps exaggerated, whose genius was indisputable. Under his nephew Psammetichus, Corinth afterward regained its freedom. The Corinthians, in spite of every change in the population, retained their luxury to the last, and the epistles of Alciphron, in the second century after Christ, note the ostentation of the few and the poverty of the many. At the time now referred to, Corinth—the Genoa of Greece—was high in civilization, possessed of a considerable naval power, and in art and commerce was the sole rival on the Grecian continent to the graceful genius and extensive trade of the Ionian colonies.

XIV. Stretching from Corinth along the coast opposite Attica, we behold the ancient Argolis. Its three principal cities were Argos, Mycenæ, and Epidaurus. Mycenæ, at the time of the Trojan war, was the most powerful of the states of Greece; and Argos, next to Sicyon, was reputed the most ancient. Argolis suffered from the Dorian revolution, and shortly afterward the regal power, gradually diminishing, lapsed into republicanism.[10] Argolis contained various independent states—one to every principal city.

XV. On the other side of Corinth, almost opposite Argolis, we find the petty state of Sicyon. This was the most ancient of the Grecian states, and was conjoined to the kingdom of Agamemnon at the Trojan war. At first it was possessed by Ionians, expelled subsequently by the Dorians, and not long after seems to have lapsed into a democratic republic. A man of low birth, Orthagoras, obtained the tyranny, and it continued in his family for a century, the longest tyranny in Greece, because the gentlest. Sicyon was of no marked influence at the period we are about to enter, though governed by an able tyrant, Clisthenes, whose policy it was to break the Dorian nobility, while uniting, as in a common interest, popular laws and regal authority.

XVI. Beyond Sicyon we arrive at Achaia. We have already seen that this district was formerly possessed by the Ionians, who were expelled by some of

9 Great-grandson to Antiochus, son of Hercules.—Paus., ii. 4.
10 But at Argos, at least, the name, though not the substance, of the kingly government was extant as late as the Persian war.

118

the Achæans who escaped the Dorian yoke. Governed first by a king, it was afterward divided into twelve republics, leagued together. It was long before Achaia appeared on that heated stage of action, which allured the more restless spirits of Athens and Lacedæmon.

XVII. We now pause at Elis, which had also felt the revolution of the Heraclidæ, and was possessed by their comrades the Ætolians.

ELIS AND THE OLYMPIC GAMES

The state of Elis underwent the general change from monarchy to republicanism; but republicanism in its most aristocratic form;—growing more popular at the period of the Persian wars, but without the convulsions which usually mark the progress of democracy. The magistrates of the commonwealth were the superintendents of the Sacred Games. And here, diversifying this rapid, but perhaps to the general reader somewhat tedious survey of the political and geographical aspect of the states of Greece, we will take this occasion to examine the nature and the influence of those celebrated contests, which gave to Elis its true title to immortality.

XVIII. The origin of the Olympic Games is lost in darkness. The legends which attribute their first foundation to the times of demigods and heroes are so far consonant with truth, that exhibitions of physical strength made the favourite diversion of that wild and barbarous age which is consecrated to the heroic. It is easy to perceive that the origin of athletic games preceded the date of civilization; that, associated with occasions of festival, they, like festivals, assumed a sacred character, and that, whether first instituted in honour of a funeral, or in celebration of a victory, or in reverence to a god, religion combined with policy to transmit an inspiring custom to a more polished posterity. And though we cannot literally give credit to the tradition which assigns the restoration of these games to Lycurgus, in concert with Iphitus, king of Elis, and Cleosthenes of Pisa, we may suppose at least that to Elis, to Pisa, and to Sparta, the institution was indebted for its revival.

The Dorian oracle of Delphi gave its sanction to a ceremony, the restoration of which was intended to impose a check upon the wars and disorders of the Peloponnesus. Thus authorized, the festival was solemnized at the Temple of Jupiter, at Olympia, near Pisa, a town in Elis. It was held every fifth year; it lasted four days. It consisted in the celebration of games in honour of Jupiter and Hercules. The interval between each festival was called an Olympiad. After the fiftieth Olympiad, the whole management of the games, and the choice of the judges, were monopolized by the Eleans. Previous to each festival, officers, deputed by the Eleans, proclaimed a sacred truce. Whatever hostilities were existent in Greece, terminated for the time; sufficient interval was allowed to attend and to return from the games.[11]

---

11 Those who meant to take part in the athletic exercises were required to attend at Olympia thirty days previous to the games, for preparation and practice.

During this period the sacred territory of Elis was regarded as under the protection of the gods—none might traverse it armed. The Eleans arrogated indeed the right of a constant sanctity to perpetual peace; and the right, though sometimes invaded, seems generally to have been conceded. The people of this territory became, as it were, the guardians of a sanctuary; they interfered little in the turbulent commotions of the rest of Greece; they did not fortify their capital; and, the wealthiest people of the Peloponnesus, they enjoyed their opulence in tranquillity;—their holy character contenting their ambition. And a wonderful thing it was in the midst of those warlike, stirring, restless tribes—that solitary land, with its plane grove bordering the Alpheus, adorned with innumerable and hallowed monuments and statues—unvisited by foreign wars and civil commotion—a whole state one temple!

At first only the foot-race was exhibited; afterward were added wrestling, leaping, quoiting, darting, boxing, a more complicated species of foot-race (the Diaulus and Dolichus), and the chariot- and horse-races. The Pentathlon was a contest of five gymnastic exercises combined. The chariot-races[12] preceded those of the riding horses, as in Grecian war the use of chariots preceded the more scientific employment of cavalry, and were the most attractive and splendid part of the exhibition. Sometimes there were no less than forty chariots on the ground. The rarity of horses, and the expense of their training, confined, without any law to that effect, the chariot-race to the highborn and the wealthy. It was consistent with the vain Alcibiades to decline the gymnastic contests in which his physical endowments might have insured him success, because his competitors were not the equals to the long-descended heir of the Alcmæonid. In the equestrian contests his success was unprecedented. He brought seven chariots into the field, and bore off at the same time the first, second, and fourth prize.[13] Although women,[14] with the exception of the priestesses of the neighbouring fane of Ceres, were not permitted to witness the engagements, they were yet allowed to contend by proxy in the chariot-races; and the ladies of Macedon especially availed themselves of the privilege. No sanguinary contest with weapons, no gratuitous ferocities, no struggle between man and beast (the graceless butcheries of Rome), polluted the festival dedicated to the Olympian god. Even boxing with the cestus was less esteemed than the other athletic exercises, and was

12 It would appear by some Etruscan vases found at Veii, that the Etruscans practised *all* the Greek games—leaping, running, cudgel-playing, &c., and were not restricted, as Niebuhr supposes, to boxing and chariot-races.

13 It however diminishes the real honour of the chariot-race, that the owner of horses usually won by proxy.

14 The indecorum of attending contests where the combatants were unclothed was a sufficient reason for the exclusion of females. The priestess of Ceres, the mighty mother, was accustomed to regard all such indecorums as symbolical, and had therefore refined away any remarkable indelicacy.

excluded from the games exhibited by Alexander in his Asiatic invasions.[15] Neither did any of those haughty assumptions of lineage or knightly blood, which characterize the feudal tournament, distinguish between Greek and Greek. The equestrian contests were indeed, from their expense, limited to the opulent, but the others were impartially free to the poor as to the rich, the peasant as the noble,—the Greeks forbade monopoly in glory. But although thus open to all Greeks, the stadium was impenetrably closed to barbarians. Taken from his plough, the boor obtained the garland for which the monarchs of the East were held unworthy to contend, and to which the kings of the neighbouring Macedon were forbidden to aspire till their Hellenic descent had been clearly proved.[16] Thus periodically were the several states reminded of their common race, and thus the national name and character were solemnly preserved: yet, like the Amphictyonic league, while the Olympic festival served to maintain the great distinction between foreigners and Greeks, it had but little influence in preventing the hostile contests of Greeks themselves. The very emulation between the several states stimulated their jealousy of each other: and still, if the Greeks found their countrymen in Greeks they found also in Greeks their rivals.

We can scarcely conceive the vast importance attached to victory in these games;[17] it not only immortalized the winner, it shed glory upon his tribe. It is curious to see the different honours characteristically assigned to the conqueror in different states. If Athenian, he was entitled to a place by the magistrates in the Prytaneum; if a Spartan, to a prominent station in the field. To conquer at Elis was renown for life, "no less illustrious to a Greek than consulship to a Roman!"[18] The haughtiest nobles, the wealthiest princes,

15 Plut., in Vit. Alex. When one of the combatants with the cestus killed his antagonist by running the ends of his fingers through his ribs, he was ignominiously expelled the stadium. The cestus itself, made of thongs of leather, was evidently meant not to increase the severity of the blow, but for the prevention of foul play by the antagonists laying hold of each other, or using the open hand. I believe that the iron bands and leaden plummets were *Roman* inventions, and unknown at least till the later Olympic games. Even in the pancratium, the fiercest of all the contests—for it seems to have united wrestling with boxing (a struggle of physical strength, without the precise and formal laws of the boxing and wrestling matches), it was forbidden to kill an enemy, to injure his eyes, or to use the teeth.

16 Even to the foot-race, in which many of the competitors were of the lowest rank, the son of Amyntas, king of Macedon, was not admitted till he had proved an Argive descent. He was an unsuccessful competitor.

17 Herodotus relates an anecdote, that the Eleans sent deputies to Egypt, vaunting the glories of the Olympic games, and inquiring if the Egyptians could suggest any improvement. The Egyptians asked if the citizens of Elis were allowed to contend, and, on hearing that they were, declared it was impossible they should not favour their own countrymen, and consequently that the games must lead to injustice—a suspicion not verified.

18 Cic., Quæst. Tusc., 11, 17.

the most successful generals contended for the prize.[19] And the prize (after the seventh Olympiad) was a wreath of the wild olive!

Numerous other and similar games were established throughout Greece. Of these, next to the Olympic, the most celebrated, and the only national ones, were the Pythian at Delphi, the Nemean in Argolis, the Isthmian in Corinth; yet elsewhere the prize was of value; at all the national ones it was but a garland—a type of the eternal truth, that praise is the only guerdon of renown. The olive-crown was nothing!—the shouts of assembled Greece— the showers of herbs and flowers—the banquet set apart for the victor— the odes of imperishable poets—the public register which transmitted to posterity his name—the privilege of a statue in the Altis—the return home through a breach in the walls (denoting by a noble metaphor, "that a city which boasts such men has slight need of walls"[20]), the first seat in all public spectacles; the fame, in short, extended to his native city—bequeathed to his children—confirmed by the universal voice wherever the Greek civilization spread;—this was the true olive-crown to the Olympic conqueror!

No other clime can furnish a likeness to these festivals: born of a savage time, they retained the vigorous character of an age of heroes, but they took every adjunct from the arts and the graces of civilization. To the sacred ground flocked all the power, and the rank, and the wealth, and the intellect, of Greece. To that gorgeous spectacle came men inspired by a nobler ambition than that of the arena. Here the poet and the musician could summon an audience to their art. If to them it was not a field for emulation,[21] it was at least a theatre of display.

XIX. The uses of these games were threefold;—first, the uniting all Greeks by one sentiment of national pride, and the memory of a common race; second, the inculcation of hardy discipline—of physical education throughout every state, by teaching that the body had its honours as well as the intellect—a theory conducive to health in peace—and in those ages when men fought hand to hand, and individual strength and skill were the nerves of the army, to success in war; but, third, and principally, its uses were in sustaining and feeding as a passion, as a motive, as an irresistible incentive— the desire of glory! That desire spread through all classes—it animated all

19 Nero (when the glory had left the spot) drove a chariot of ten horses in Olympia, out of which he had the misfortune to tumble. He obtained other prizes in other Grecian games, and even contended with the heralds as a crier. The vanity of Nero was astonishing, but so was that of most of his successors. The Roman emperors were the sublimest coxcombs in history. In men born to stations which are beyond ambition, all aspirations run to seed.
20 Plut., in Sympos.
21 It does not appear that at Elis there were any of the actual contests in music and song which made the character of the Pythian games. But still it was a common *exhibition* for the cultivation of every art. Sophist, and historian, and orator, poet and painter, found their mart in the Olympic fair.

tribes—it taught that true rewards are not in gold and gems, but in men's opinions. The ambition of the Altis established fame as a common principle of action. What chivalry did for the few, the Olympic contests effected for the many—they made a knighthood of a people.

If, warmed for a moment from the gravity of the historic muse, we might conjure up the picture of this festival, we would invoke the imagination of the reader to that sacred ground decorated with the profusest triumphs of Grecian art—all Greece assembled from her continent, her colonies, her isles—war suspended—a Sabbath of solemnity and rejoicing—the Spartan no longer grave, the Athenian forgetful of the forum—the highborn Thessalian, the gay Corinthian—the lively gestures of the Asiatic Ionian;—suffering the various events of various times to confound themselves in one recollection of the past, he may see every eye turned from the combatants to one majestic figure—hear every lip murmuring a single name[22]—glorious in greater fields: Olympia itself is forgotten. Who is the spectacle of the day? Themistocles, the conqueror of Salamis, and the saviour of Greece! Again —the huzzas of countless thousands following the chariot-wheels of the competitors—whose name is shouted forth, the victor without a rival?—it is Alcibiades, the destroyer of Athens! Turn to the temple of the Olympian god, pass the brazen gates, proceed through the columned aisles,[23] what arrests the awe and wonder of the crowd? Seated on a throne of ebon and of ivory, of gold and gems—the olive-crown on his head, in his right hand the statue of Victory, in his left, wrought of all metals, the cloud-compelling sceptre, behold the colossal masterpiece of Phidias, the Homeric dream imbodied[24]—the majesty of the Olympian Jove! Enter the banquet-room of the conquerors—to whose verse, hymned in a solemn and mighty chorus, bends the listening Spartan—it is the verse of the Dorian Pindar! In that motley and glittering space (the fair of Olympia, the mart of every commerce, the focus of all intellect), join the throng, earnest and breathless, gathered round that sunburnt traveller;—now drinking in the wild account of Babylonian gardens, or of temples whose awful deity no lip may name— now, with clinched hands and glowing cheeks, tracking the march of Xerxes along exhausted rivers, and over bridges that spanned the sea—what moves, what hushes that mighty audience? It is Herodotus reading his history![25]

Let us resume our survey.

22 Plut., in Vit. Them.
23 Paus., v.
24 When Phidias was asked on what idea he should form his statue, he answered by quoting the well-known verses of Homer, on the curls and nod of the thunder god.
25 I am of course aware that the popular story that Herodotus read portions of his history at Olympia has been disputed—but I own I think it has been disputed with very indifferent success against the testimony of competent authorities, corroborated by the general practice of the time.

XX. Midland, in the Peloponnesus, lies the pastoral Arcady. Besides the rivers of Alpheus and Erymanthus, it is watered by the gloomy stream of Styx; and its western part, intersected by innumerable brooks, is the land of Pan. Its inhabitants were long devoted to the pursuits of the herdsman and the shepherd, and its ancient government was apparently monarchical. The Dorian irruption spared this land of poetical tradition, which the oracle of Delphi took under no unsuitable protection, and it remained the eldest and most unviolated sanctuary of the old Pelasgic name. But not very long after the return of the Heraclidæ, we find the last king stoned by his subjects, and democratic institutions established. It was then parcelled out into small states, of which Tegea and Mantinea were the chief.

XXI. Messenia, a fertile and level district, which lies to the west of Sparta, underwent many struggles with the latter power; and this part of its history, which is full of interest, the reader will find briefly narrated in that of the Spartans, by whom it was finally subdued. Being then incorporated with that country, we cannot, at the period of history we are about to enter, consider Messenia as a separate and independent state.[26]

And now, completing the survey of the Peloponnesus, we rest at Laconia, the country of the Spartans.

---

26 We find, indeed, that the Messenians continued to struggle against their conquerors, and that about the time of the battle of Marathon they broke out into a resistance sometimes called the third war (Plato, Leg. 111).

CHAPTER VI

Return of the Heraclidæ—the Spartan constitution and
habits—The first and second Messenian war

I. We have already seen, that while the Dorians remained in Thessaly, the
Achæans possessed the greater part of the Peloponnesus. But, under the title
of the "Return of the Heraclidæ" (or the descendants of

RETURN OF THE
HERACLIDÆ

Hercules), an important and lasting revolution established the
Dorians in the kingdoms of Agamemnon and Menelaus.
The true nature of this revolution has only been rendered more obscure by
modern ingenuity, which has abandoned the popular accounts for suppositions still more improbable and romantic. The popular accounts run thus:
—persecuted by Eurystheus, king of Argos, the sons of Hercules, with their
friends and followers, are compelled to take refuge in Attica. Assisted by
the Athenians, they defeat and slay Eurystheus, and regain the Peloponnesus.
A pestilence, regarded as an ominous messenger from offended heaven,
drives them again into Attica. An oracle declares that they shall succeed
after the third fruit by the narrow passage at sea. Wrongly interpreting
the oracle, in the third year they make for the Corinthian Isthmus. At the
entrance of the Peloponnesus they are met by the assembled arms of
the Achæans, Ionians, and Arcadians. Hyllus, the eldest son of Hercules,
proposes the issue of a single combat. Echemus, king of Tegea, is selected
by the Peloponnesians. He meets and slays Hyllus, and the Heraclidæ
engage not to renew the invasion for one hundred years. Nevertheless,
Cleodæus, the son, and Aristomachus, the grandson, of Hyllus, successively
attempt to renew the enterprise, and in vain. The three sons of Aristomachus
(Aristodemus, Temenus, and Cresphontes), receive from Apollo himself
the rightful interpretation of the oracle. It was by the Straits of Rhium,
across a channel which rendered the distance between the opposing shores
only five stadia, that they were ordained to pass; and by the third fruit,
the third generation was denoted. The time had now arrived:—with the
assistance of the Dorians, the Ætolians, and the Locrians, the descendants
of Hercules crossed the strait, and established their settlement in the
Peloponnesus.

II. Whether in the previous expeditions the Dorians had assisted the
Heraclidæ, is a matter of dispute—it is not a matter of importance. Whether

these Heraclidæ were really descendants of the Achæan prince, and the rightful heritors of a Peloponnesian throne, is a point equally contested and equally frivolous. It is probable enough that the bold and warlike tribe of Thessaly might have been easily allured, by the pretext of reinstating the true royal line, into an enterprise which might plant them in safer and more wide domains, and that while the prince got the throne, the confederates obtained the country.[1] All of consequence to establish is, that the Dorians shared in the expedition, which was successful—that by time and valour they obtained nearly the whole of the Peloponnesus—that they transplanted the Doric character and institutions to their new possessions, and that the Return of the Heraclidæ is, in fact, the popular name for the conquest of the Dorians. Whatever distinction existed between the Achæan Heraclidæ and the Doric race had probably been much effaced during the long absence of the former among foreign tribes, and after their establishment in the Peloponnesus it soon became entirely lost. But still the legend that assigned the blood of Hercules to the royalty of Sparta received early and implicit credence, and Cleomenes, king of that state, some centuries afterward, declared himself not Doric, but Achæan.

Of the time employed in consummating the conquest of the invaders we are unable to determine—but, by degrees, Sparta, Argos, Corinth, and Messene, became possessed by the Dorians; the Ætolian confederates obtained Elis. Some of the Achæans expelled the Ionians from the territory they held in the Peloponnesus, and gave to it the name it afterward retained, of Achaia. The expelled Ionians took refuge with the Athenians, their kindred race.

The fated house of Pelops swept away by this irruption, Sparta fell to the lot of Procles and Eurysthenes,[2] sons of Aristodemus, fifth in descent from Hercules; between these princes the royal power was divided, so that the constitution always acknowledged two kings—one from each of the Heracleid families. The older house was called the Agids, or descendants of Agis, son of Eurysthenes; the latter, the Eurypontids, from Eurypon, descendant of Procles. Although Sparta, under the new dynasty, appears to have soon arrogated the pre-eminence over the other states of the Peloponnesus, it was long before she achieved the conquest even of the

---

1 Suppose Vortigern to have been expelled by the Britons, and to have implored the assistance of the Saxons to reinstate him in his throne, the "Return of Vortigern" would have been a highly popular name for the invasion of the Saxons. So, if the Russians, after Waterloo, had parcelled out France, and fixed a Cossack settlement in her "violet vales," the destruction of the French would have been still urbanely entitled the "Return of the Bourbons".

2 According to Herodotus, the Spartan tradition assigned the throne to Aristodemus himself, and the regal power was not divided till after his death.

cities in her immediate neighbourhood. The Achæans retained the possession of Amyclæ, built upon a steep rock, and less than three miles from Sparta, for more than two centuries and a half after the first invasion of the Dorians. And here the Achæans guarded the venerable tombs of Cassandra and Agamemnon.

III. The consequences of the Dorian invasion, if slowly developed, were great and lasting. That revolution not only changed the character of the Peloponnesus—it not only called into existence the iron race of Sparta—but the migrations which it caused made the origin of the Grecian colonies in Asia Minor. It developed also those seeds of latent republicanism which belonged to the Dorian aristocracies, and which finally supplanted the monarchical government through nearly the whole of civilized Greece. The revolution once peacefully consummated, migrations no longer disturbed to any extent the continent of Greece, and the various tribes became settled in their historic homes.

IV. The history of Sparta, till the time of Lycurgus, is that of a state maintaining itself with difficulty amid surrounding and hostile neighbours; the power of the chiefs diminished the authority of the kings; and while all without was danger, all within was turbulence. Still the very evils to which the Spartans were subjected—their paucity of numbers—their dissensions with their neighbours—their pent up and encompassed situation in their mountainous confines—even the preponderating power of the warlike chiefs, among whom the unequal divisions of property produced constant feuds— served to keep alive the elements of the great Doric character; and left it the task of the first legislative genius rather to restore and to harmonize, than to invent and create.

As I am writing the history, not of Greece, but of Athens, I do not consider it necessary that I should detail the legendary life of Lycurgus. Modern writers have doubted his existence, but without sufficient reason:— such assaults on our belief are but the amusements of scepticism. All the popular accounts of Lycurgus agree in this—that he was the uncle of the king (Charilaus, an infant), and held the rank of protector—that, unable successfully to confront a powerful faction raised against him, he left Sparta and travelled into Crete, where all the ancient Doric laws and manners were yet preserved, vigorous and unadulterated. There studying the institutions of Minos, he beheld the model for those of Sparta. Thence he is said to have passed into Asia Minor, and to have been the first who collected and transported to Greece the poems of Homer,[3] hitherto only partially known in that country. According to some writers, he travelled also into Egypt; and

---

3 He *wrote* or *transcribed* them, is the expression of Plutarch, which I do not literally translate, because this touches upon very disputed ground.

could we credit one authority, which does not satisfy even the credulous Plutarch, he penetrated into Spain and Libya, and held converse with the Gymnosophists of India.

Returned to Sparta, after many solicitations, he found the state in disorder: no definite constitution appears to have existed; no laws were written. The division of the regal authority between two kings must have produced jealousy—and jealousy, faction. And the power so divided weakened the monarchic energy without adding to the liberties of the people. A turbulent nobility—rude, haughty mountain chiefs—made the only part of the community that could benefit by the weakness of the crown, and feuds among themselves prevented their power from becoming the regular and organized authority of a government.[4] Such disorders induced prince and people to desire a reform; the interference of Lycurgus was solicited; his rank and his travels gave him importance; and he had the wisdom to increase it by obtaining from Delphi (the object of the implicit reverence of the Dorians) an oracle in his favour.

Thus called upon and thus encouraged, Lycurgus commenced his task. I enter not into the discussion whether he framed an entirely new constitution, or whether he restored the spirit of one common to his race and not unfamiliar to Sparta. Common sense seems to me sufficient to assure us of the latter. Let those who please believe that one man, without the intervention of arms—not as a conqueror, but a friend could succeed in establishing a constitution, resting not upon laws, but manners—not upon force, but usage—utterly hostile to all the tastes, desires, and affections of human nature: moulding every, the minutest, detail of social life into one system— that system offering no temptation to sense, to ambition, to the desire of pleasure, or the love of gain, or the propensity to ease—but painful, hard, sterile, and unjoyous;—let those who please believe that a system so created could at once be received, be popularly embraced, and last uninterrupted, unbroken, and without exciting even the desire of change for four hundred years, without having had any previous foundation in the habits of a people—without being previously rooted by time, custom, superstition, and character into their breasts. For my part, I know that all history furnishes no

4 "Sometimes the states", says Plutarch, "veered to democracy—sometimes to arbitrary power"; that is, at one time the nobles invoked the people against the king; but if the people presumed too far, they supported the king against the people. If we imagine a confederacy of highland chiefs even a century or two ago—give them a nominal king—consider their pride and their jealousy—see them impatient of authority in one above them, yet despotic to those below—quarrelling with each other—united only by clanship, never by citizenship;—and place them in a half-conquered country, surrounded by hostile neighbours and mutinous slaves—we may then form, perhaps, some idea of the state of Sparta previous to the legislation of Lycurgus.

other such example; and I believe that no man was ever so miraculously endowed with the power to conquer nature.[5]

But we have not the smallest reason, the slightest excuse, for so pliant a credulity. We look to Crete, in which, previous to Lycurgus, the Dorians had established their laws and customs, and we see at once the resemblance to the leading features of the institutions of Lycurgus; we come with Aristotle to the natural conclusion, that what was familiar to the Dorian Crete was not unknown to the Dorian Sparta, and that Lycurgus did not innovate, but restore and develop, the laws and the manners which, under domestic dissensions, might have undergone a temporary and superficial change, but which were deeply implanted in the national character and the Doric habits. That the regulations of Lycurgus were not regarded as peculiar to Sparta, but as the most perfect development of the Dorian constitution, we learn from Pindar,[6] when he tells us that "the descendants of Pamphylus and of the Heraclidæ wish always to retain the Doric institutions of Ægimius". Thus regarded, the legislation of Lycurgus loses its miraculous and improbable character, while we still acknowledge Lycurgus himself as a great and profound statesman, adopting the only theory by which reform can be permanently wrought, and suiting the spirit of his laws to the spirit of the people they were to govern. When we know that his laws were not written, that he preferred engraving them only on the hearts of his countrymen, we know at once that he must have legislated in strict conformity to their early prepossessions and favourite notions. That the laws were unwritten would alone be a proof how little he introduced of what was alien and unknown.

I proceed to give a brief, but I trust a sufficient outline, of the Spartan constitution, social and political, without entering into prolix and frivolous discussions as to what was effected or restored by Lycurgus—what by a later policy.

THE SPARTAN CONSTITU-
TION AND HABITS

There was at Sparta a public assembly of the people (called ἀλία), as common to other Doric states, which usually met every full moon—upon great occasions more often. The decision of peace and war—the final ratification of all treaties with foreign powers—the appointment to the office of counsellor, and other important dignities—the imposition of new laws—a disputed succession to the throne,—were among those matters which required the assent of the people. Thus there was the show and semblance of a democracy, but we shall find that the intention and

---

5 When we are told that the object of Lycurgus was to root out the luxury and effeminacy existent in Sparta, a moment's reflection tells us that effeminacy and luxury could not have existed. A tribe of fierce warriors, in a city unfortified—shut in by rocks—harassed by constant war—gaining city after city from foes more civilized, stubborn to bear, and slow to yield—maintaining a perilous yoke over the far more numerous races they had subdued —what leisure, what occasion had such men to become effeminate and luxurious?

6 See Müller's Dorians, vol. ii, p. 12 (translation).

origin of the constitution were far from democratic. "If the people should opine perversely, the elders and the princes shall dissent." Such was an addition to the Rhetra of Lycurgus. The popular assembly ratified laws, but it could propose none—it could not even alter or amend the decrees that were laid before it. It appears that only the princes, the magistrates, and foreign ambassadors had the privilege to address it.

The main business of the state was prepared by the gerusia, or council of elders, a senate consisting of thirty members, inclusive of the two kings, who had each but a simple vote in the assembly. This council was in its outline like the assemblies common to every Dorian state. Each senator was required to have reached the age of sixty; he was chosen by the popular assembly, not by vote, but by acclamation. The mode of election was curious. The candidates presented themselves successively before the assembly, while certain judges were enclosed in an adjacent room where they could hear the clamour of the people without seeing the person of the candidate. On him whom they adjudged to have been most applauded the election fell. A mode of election open to every species of fraud, and justly condemned by Aristotle as frivolous and puerile.[7] Once elected, the senator retained his dignity for life: he was even removed from all responsibility to the people. That Müller should consider this an admirable institution, "a splendid monument of early Grecian customs", seems to me not a little extraordinary. I can conceive no elective council less practically good than one to which election is for life, and in which power is irresponsible. That the institution was felt to be faulty is apparent, not because it was abolished, but because its more important functions became gradually invaded and superseded by a third legislative power, of which I shall speak presently.

The original duties of the gerusia were to prepare the decrees and business to be submitted to the people; they had the power of inflicting death or degradation: without written laws, they interpreted custom, and were intended to preserve and transmit it. The power of the kings may be divided into two heads—power at home—power abroad: power as a prince—power as a general. In the first it was limited and inconsiderable. Although the kings presided over a separate tribunal, the cases brought before their court related only to repairs of roads, to the superintendence of the intercourse with other states, and to questions of inheritance and adoption.

When present at the council they officiated as presidents, but without any power of dictation; and, if absent, their place seems easily to have been supplied. They united the priestly with the regal character; and to the descendants of a demigod a certain sanctity was attached, visible in the

---

7 In the same passage Aristotle, with that wonderful sympathy in opinion between himself and the political philosophers of our own day, condemns the principle of seeking and canvassing for suffrages.

ceremonies both at demise and at the accession to the throne, which appeared to Herodotus to savour rather of oriental than Hellenic origin. But the respect which the Spartan monarch received neither endowed him with luxury nor exempted him from control. He was undistinguished by his garb—his mode of life, from the rest of the citizens. He was subjected to other authorities, could be reprimanded, fined, suspended, exiled, put to death. If he went as ambassador to foreign states, spies were not unfrequently sent with him, and colleagues the most avowedly hostile to his person associated in the mission. Thus curbed and thus confined was his authority at home, and his prerogative as a king. But by law he was the leader of the Spartan armies. He assumed the command—he crossed the boundaries, and the limited magistrate became at once an imperial despot![8] No man could question—no law circumscribed his power. He raised armies, collected money in foreign states, and condemned to death without even the formality of a trial. Nothing, in short, curbed his authority, save his responsibility on return. He might be a tyrant as a general; but he was to account for the tyranny when he relapsed into a king. But this distinction was one of the wisest parts of the Spartan system; for war requires in a leader all the licence of a despot; and triumph, decision, and energy can only be secured by the unfettered exercise of a single will. Nor did early Rome owe the extent of her conquests to any cause more effective than the unlicensed discretion reposed by the senate in the general.[9]

VI. We have now to examine the most active and efficient part of the government, viz., the institution of the ephors. Like the other components of the Spartan constitution, the name and the office of ephor were familiar to other states in the great Dorian family; but in Sparta the institution soon assumed peculiar features, or rather, while the inherent principles of the monarchy and the gerusia remained stationary, those of the ephors became expanded and developed. It is clear that the later authority of the ephors was never designed by Lycurgus or the earlier legislators. It is entirely at variance with the confined aristocracy which was the aim of the Spartan, and of nearly every genuine Doric[10] constitution. It made a democracy as it were by

8 In this was preserved the form of royalty in the heroic times. Aristotle well remarks, that in the council Agamemnon bears reproach and insult, but in the field he becomes armed with authority over life itself—"Death is in his hand".

9 Whereas the modern republics of Italy rank among the causes which prevented their assuming a widely conquering character, their extreme jealousy of their commanders, often wisely ridiculed by the great Italian historians; so that a baggage-cart could scarcely move, or a cannon be planted, without an order from the senate!

10 Müller rightly observes, that though the ephoralty was a common Dorian magistrature, "yet, considered as an office, opposed to the king and council, it is not for that reason less peculiar to the Spartans; and in no Doric, nor even in any Grecian state is there any thing which exactly corresponds with it."

stealth. This powerful body consisted of five persons, chosen annually by the people. In fact, they may be called the representatives of the popular will—the committee, as it were, of the popular council. Their original power seems to have been imperfectly designed; it soon became extensive and encroaching. At first the ephoralty was a tribunal for civil, as the gerusia was for criminal, causes; it exercised a jurisdiction over the Helots and Periœci, over the public market, and the public revenue. But its character consisted in this:—it was strictly a popular body, chosen by the people for the maintenance of their interests. Agreeably to this character, it soon appears arrogating the privilege of instituting an inquiry into the conduct of all officials except the counsellors. Every eighth year, selecting a dark night when the moon withheld her light, the ephors watched the aspect of the heavens, and if any shooting star were visible in the expanse, the kings were adjudged to have offended the deity, and were suspended from their office until acquitted of their guilt by the oracle of Delphi or the priests at Olympia. Nor was this prerogative of adjudging the descendants of Hercules confined to a superstitious practice: they summoned the king before them, no less than the meanest of the magistrates, to account for imputed crimes. In a court composed of the counsellors (or gerusia), and various other magistrates, they appeared at once as accusers and judges; and, dispensing with appeal to a popular assembly, subjected even royalty to a trial of life and death. Before the Persian war they sat in judgment on the king Cleomenes for an accusation of bribery;—just after the Persian war, they resolved upon the execution of the regent Pausanias. In lesser offences they acted without the formality of this council, and fined or reprimanded their kings for the affability of their manners, or the size[11] of their wives. Over education—over social habits—over the regulations relative to ambassadors and strangers—over even the marshalling of armies and the number of troops, they extended their inquisitorial jurisdiction. They became, in fact, the actual government of the state.

It is easy to perceive that it was in the nature of things that the institution of the ephors should thus encroach until it became the prevalent power. Its influence was the result of the vicious constitution of the gerusia, or council. Had that assembly been properly constituted, there would have been no occasion for the ephors. The gerusia was evidently meant, by the policy of Lycurgus, and by its popular mode of election, for the only representative assembly. But the absurdity of election for life, with irresponsible powers, was sufficient to limit its acceptation among the people. Of two assemblies—the ephors and the gerusia—we see the one elected annually, the other for life—the one responsible to the people, the other not—the one composed of men, busy, stirring, ambitious, in the vigour of life—the other

---

11 They rebuked Archidamus for having married too small a wife. See Müller's Dorians, vol. ii, p. 121 (translation), and the authorities he quotes.

of veterans, past the ordinary stimulus of exertion, and regarding the dignity of office rather as the reward of a life than the opening to ambition. Of two such assemblies it is easy to foretell which would lose, and which would augment, authority. It is also easy to see, that as the ephors increased in importance, they, and not the gerusia, would become the check to the kingly authority. To whom was the king accountable? To the people:—the ephors were the people's representatives! This part of the Spartan constitution has not, I think, been sufficiently considered in what seems to me its true light; namely, that of a representative government. The ephoralty was the focus of the popular power. Like an American Congress or an English House of Commons, it prevented the action of the people by acting in behalf of the people. To representatives annually chosen, the multitude cheerfully left the management of their interests.[12] Thus it was true that the ephors prevented the encroachments of the popular assembly;—but how? by encroaching themselves, and in the name of the people! When we are told that Sparta was free from those democratic innovations constant in Ionian states, we are not told truly. The Spartan populace was constantly innovating, not openly, as in the noisy Agora of Athens, but silently and ceaselessly, through their delegated ephors. And these dread and tyrant five—an oligarchy constructed upon principles the most liberal—went on increasing their authority, as civilization, itself increasing, rendered the public business more extensive and multifarious, until they at length became the agents of that fate which makes the principle of change at once the vital and the consuming element of states. The ephors gradually destroyed the constitution of Sparta; but, without the ephors, it may be reasonably doubted whether the constitution would have survived half as long. Aristotle (whose mighty intellect is never more luminously displayed than when adjudging the practical workings of various forms of government) paints the evils of the ephoral magistrature, but acknowledges that it gave strength and durability to the state. "For",[13] he says, "the people were contented on account of their ephors, who were chosen from the whole body." He might have added, that men so chosen, rarely too selected from the chiefs, but often from the lower ranks, were the ablest and most active of the community, and that the fewness of their numbers gave energy and unity to their councils. Had the other part of the Spartan constitution (absurdly panegyrized) been so formed as to harmonize with, even in checking, the power of the ephors; and, above all, had it not been for the lamentable errors of a social system, which, by seeking to exclude the desire of gain, created a terrible reaction, and made the Spartan magistrature the most venal and corrupt in Greece—the ephors might have sufficed to develop all the best principles of government. For they went

12 Aristot., Pol., ii. 9.
13 Idem.

nearly to recognize the soundest philosophy of the representative system, being the smallest number of representatives chosen, without restriction, from the greatest number of electors, for short periods, and under strong responsibilities.[14]

I pass now to the social system of the Spartans.

VII. If we consider the situation of the Spartans at the time of Lycurgus, and during a long subsequent period, we see at once that to enable them to live at all, they must be accustomed to the life of a camp;—they were a little colony of soldiers, supporting themselves, hand and foot, in a hostile country, over a population that detested them. In such a situation certain qualities were not praiseworthy alone—they were necessary. To be always prepared for a foe—to be constitutionally averse to indolence—to be brave, temperate, and hardy, were the only means by which to escape the sword of the Messenian and to master the hatred of the Helot. Sentinels they were, and they required the virtues of sentinels: fortunately, these necessary qualities were inherent in the bold mountain tribes that had long roved among the crags of Thessaly, and wrestled for life with the martial Lapithæ. But it now remained to mould these qualities into a system, and to educate each individual in the habits which could best preserve the community. Accordingly the child was reared, from the earliest age, to a life of hardship, discipline, and privation; he was starved into abstinence;—he was beaten into fortitude; —he was punished without offence, that he might be trained to bear without a groan;—the older he grew, till he reached manhood, the severer the discipline he underwent. The intellectual education was little attended to: for what had sentinels to do with the sciences or the arts? But the youth was taught acuteness, promptness, and discernment—for such are qualities essential to the soldier. He was stimulated to condense his thoughts, and to be ready in reply; to say little, and to the point. An aphorism bounded his philosophy. Such an education produced its results in an athletic frame, in simple and hardy habits—in indomitable patience—in quick sagacity. But there were other qualities necessary to the position of the Spartan, and those scarce so praiseworthy—viz., craft and simulation. He was one of a scanty, if a valiant, race. No single citizen could be spared the state: it was often better to dupe than to fight an enemy. Accordingly, the boy was trained to cunning as to courage. He was driven by hunger, or the orders of the leader over him, to obtain his food, in house or in field, by stealth;—if undiscovered, he was applauded; if detected, punished. Two main-springs of action

14 These remarks on the democratic and representative nature of the ephoralty are only to be applied to it in connexion with the Spartan people. It must be remembered that the ephors represented the will of that dominant class, and not of the Laconians or Periœci, who made the bulk of the non-enslaved population; and the democracy of their constitution was therefore but the democracy of an oligarchy.

were constructed within him—the dread of shame and the love of country. These were motives, it is true, common to all the Grecian states, but they seem to have been especially powerful in Sparta. But the last produced its abuse in one of the worst vices of the national character. The absorbing love for his native Sparta rendered the citizen singularly selfish towards other states, even kindred to that which he belonged to. Fearless as a Spartan,— when Sparta was unmenaced he was lukewarm as a Greek. And this exaggerated yet sectarian patriotism, almost peculiar to Sparta, was centred, not only in the safety and greatness of the state, but in the inalienable preservation of its institutions;—a feeling carefully sustained by a policy exceedingly jealous of strangers.[15] Spartans were not permitted to travel. Foreigners were but rarely permitted a residence within the city: and the Spartan dislike to Athens arose rather from fear of the contamination of her principles than from envy at the lustre of her fame. When we find (as our history proceeds) the Spartans dismissing their Athenian ally from the siege of Ithomë, we recognize their jealousy of the innovating character of their brilliant neighbour;—they feared the infection of the democracy of the Agora. This attachment to one exclusive system of government characterized all the foreign policy of Sparta, and crippled the national sense by the narrowest bigotry and the obtusest prejudice. Wherever she conquered, she enforced her own constitution, no matter how inimical to the habits of the people, never dreaming that what was good for Sparta might be bad for any other state. Thus, when she imposed the Thirty Tyrants on Athens, she sought, in fact, to establish her own gerusia; and, no doubt, she imagined it would become, not a curse, but a blessing to a people accustomed to the wildest freedom of a popular assembly. Though herself, through the tyranny of the ephors, the unconscious puppet of the democratic action, she recoiled from all other and more open forms of democracy as from a pestilence. The simple habits of the Spartan life assisted to confirm the Spartan prejudices. A costly dinner, a fine house, these sturdy Dorians regarded as a pitiable sign of folly. They had no respect for any other cultivation of the mind than that which produced bold men and short sentences. Them, nor the science of Aristotle, nor the dreams

---

15 Machiavel, (Discourses on the first Decade of Livy, i. 6) attributes the duration of the Spartan government to two main causes—first, the fewness of the body to be governed, allowing fewness in the governors; and second, the prevention of all the changes and corruption which the admission of strangers would have occasioned. He proceeds then to show that for the long duration of a constitution the people should be few in number, and all popular impulse and innovation checked; yet that, for the splendour and greatness of a state, not only population should be encouraged, but even political ferment and agitation be leniently regarded. Sparta is his model for duration, republican Rome for progress and empire. "To my judgment", the Florentine concludes, "I prefer the latter, and for the strife and emulation between the nobles and the people, they are to be regarded indeed as inconveniences, but necessary to a state that would rise to the Roman grandeur."

of Plato were fitted to delight. Music and dancing were indeed cultivated among them, and with success and skill; but the music and the dance were always of one kind—it was a crime to vary an air[16] or invent a measure. A martial, haughty, and superstitious tribe can scarcely fail to be attached to poetry,—war is ever the inspiration of song,—and the eve of battle to a Spartan was the season of sacrifice to the Muses. The poetical temperament seems to have been common among this singular people. But the dread of innovation, when carried to excess, has even worse effect upon literary genius than legislative science; and though Sparta produced a few poets gifted, doubtless, with the skill to charm the audience they addressed, not a single one of the number has bequeathed to us any other memorial than his name. Greece, which preserved, as in a common treasury, whatever was approved by her unerring taste, her wonderful appreciation of the beautiful, regarded the Spartan poetry with an indifference which convinces us of its want of value. Thebes, and not Sparta, has transmitted to us the Dorian spirit in its noblest shape: and in Pindar we find how lofty the verse that was inspired by its pride, its daring, and its sublime reverence for glory and the gods. As for commerce, manufactures, agriculture, the manual arts—such peaceful occupations were beneath the dignity of a Spartan—they were strictly prohibited by law as by pride, and were left to the Periœci or the Helots.

VIII. It was evidently necessary to this little colony to be united. Nothing unites men more than living together in common. The syssitia, or public tables, an institution which was common in Crete, in Corinth,[17] and in Megara, effected this object in a mode agreeable to the Dorian manners. The society at each table was composed of men belonging to the same tribe or clan. New members could only be elected by consent of the rest. Each head of a family in Sparta paid for his own admission and that of the other members of his house. Men only belonged to them. The youths and boys had their own separate table. The young children, however, sat with their parents on low stools, and received a half share. Women were excluded. Despite the celebrated black broth, the table seems to have been sufficiently, if not elegantly, furnished. And the second course, consisting of voluntary gifts, which was supplied by the poorer members from the produce of the chase—by the wealthier from their flocks, orchards, poultry, &c., furnished what by Spartans were considered dainties. Conversation was familiar, and even jocose, and relieved by songs. Thus the public tables (which even the kings were ordinarily obliged to attend) were rendered agreeable and inviting by the attractions of intimate friendship and unrestrained intercourse.

16 Plut., de Musicâ.
17 At Corinth they were abolished by Periander as favourable to an aristocracy, according to Aristotle; but a better reason might be that they were dangerous to tyranny.

IX. The obscurest question relative to the Spartan system is that connected with property. It was evidently the intention of Lycurgus or the earlier legislators to render all the divisions of land and wealth as equal as possible. But no law can effect what society forbids. The equality of one generation cannot be transmitted to another. It may be easy to prevent a great accumulation of wealth, but what can prevent poverty? While the acquisition of lands by purchase was forbidden, no check was imposed on its acquisition by gift or testament; and in the time of Aristotle land had become the monopoly of the few. Sparta, like other states, had consequently her inequalities—her comparative rich and her positive poor—from an early period in her known history. As land descended to women, so marriages alone established great disparities of property. "Were the whole territory", says Aristotle, "divided into five portions, two would belong to the women." The regulation by which the man who could not pay his quota to the syssitia was excluded from the public tables proves that it was not an uncommon occurrence to be so excluded; and indeed that exclusion grew at last so common, that the public tables became an aristocratic instead of a democratic institution. Aristotle, in later times, makes it an objection to the ephoral government that poor men were chosen ephors, and that their venality arose from their indigence—a moral proof that poverty in Sparta must have been more common than has generally been supposed;[18]—men of property would not have chosen their judges and dictators in paupers. Land was held and cultivated by the Helots, who paid a certain fixed proportion of the produce to their masters. It is said that Lycurgus forbade the use of gold and silver, and ordained an iron coinage; but gold and silver were at that time unknown as coins in Sparta, and iron was a common medium of exchange throughout Greece. The interdiction of the precious metals was therefore of later origin. It seems to have only related to private Spartans. For those who, not being Spartans of the city—that is to say, for the Laconians or Periœci—engaged in commerce, the interdiction could not have existed. A more pernicious regulation it is impossible to conceive. While it effectually served to cramp the effects of emulation—to stint the arts—to limit industry and enterprise —it produced the direct object it was intended to prevent;—it infected the whole state with the desire of gold—it forbade wealth to be spent, in order that wealth might be hoarded; every man seems to have desired gold precisely because he could make very little use of it! From the king to the Helot,[19] the

18 "Yet, although goods were appropriated, their uses", says Aristotle, "were freely communicated,—a Spartan could use the horses, the slaves, the dogs, and carriages of another." If this were to be taken literally, it is difficult to see how a Spartan could be poor. We must either imagine that different times are confounded, or that limitations with which we are unacquainted were made in this system of borrowing.

19 See, throughout the Grecian history, the Helots collecting the plunder of the battle-field, hiding it from the gripe of their lords, and selling gold at the price of brass!

spirit of covetousness spread like a disease. No state in Greece was so open to bribery—no magistracy so corrupt as the ephors. Sparta became a nation of misers precisely because it could not become a nation of spendthrifts. Such are the results which man produces when his legislation deposes nature!

X. In their domestic life the Spartans, like the rest of the Greeks, had but little pleasure in the society of their wives. At first the young husband only visited his bride by stealth—to be seen in company with her was a disgrace. But the women enjoyed a much greater freedom and received a higher respect in Sparta than elsewhere; the soft Asiatic distinctions in dignity between the respective sexes did not reach the hardy mountaineers of Lacedæmon; the wife was the mother of men! Brought up in robust habits, accustomed to athletic exercises, her person exposed in public processions and dances, which, but for the custom that made decorous even indecency itself, would have been indeed licentious, the Spartan maiden, strong, hardy, and half a partaker in the ceremonies of public life, shared the habits, aided the emulation, imbibed the patriotism, of her future consort. And, by her sympathy with his habits and pursuits, she obtained an influence and ascendency over him which was unknown in the rest of Greece. Dignified on public occasions, the Spartan matron was deemed, however, a virago in private life; and she who had no sorrow for a slaughtered son, had very little deference for a living husband. Her obedience to her spouse appears to have been the most cheerfully rendered upon those delicate emergencies when the service of the state required her submission to the embraces of another![20]

XI. We now come to the most melancholy and gloomy part of the Spartan system—the condition of the Helots.

The whole fabric of the Spartan character rested upon slavery. If it were beneath a Spartan to labour—to maintain himself—to cultivate land —to build a house—to exercise an art;—to do aught else than to fight an enemy—to choose an ephor—to pass from the chase or the palæstra to the public tables—to live a hero in war—an aristocrat in peace,—it was clearly a supreme necessity to his very existence as a citizen, and even as a human being, that there should be a subordinate class of persons employed in the

20 Aristotle, who is exceedingly severe on the Spartan ladies, says very shrewdly, that the men were trained to submission to a civil by a military system, while the women were left untamed. A Spartan hero was thus made to be henpecked. Yet, with all the alleged severity of the Dorian morals, these sturdy matrons rather discarded the graces than avoided the frailties of their softer contemporaries. Plato (Leges, i and vi) and Aristotle (Pol., ii) give very unfavourable testimonials of their chastity. Plutarch, the blind panegyrist of Sparta, observes with amusing composure, that the Spartan husbands were permitted to lend their wives to each other; and Polybius (in a fragment of the 12th book (Fragm. Vatican., tom. ii, p. 384)) informs us that it was an old-fashioned and common custom in Sparta for three or four brothers to share one wife. The poor husbands!—no doubt the lady was a match for them all! So much for those gentle creatures whom that grave German professor, M. Müller, holds up to our admiration and despair.

occupations rejected by himself, and engaged in providing for the wants of this privileged citizen. Without Helots the Spartan was the most helpless of human beings. Slavery taken from the Spartan state, the state would fall at once! It is no wonder, therefore, that this institution should have been guarded with an extraordinary jealousy—nor that extraordinary jealousy should have produced extraordinary harshness. It is exactly in proportion to the fear of losing power that men are generally tyrannical in the exercise of it. Nor is it from cruelty of disposition, but from the anxious curse of living among men whom social circumstances make his enemies because his slaves, that a despot usually grows ferocious, and that the urgings of suspicion create the reign of terror. Besides the political necessity of a strict and unrelaxed slavery, a Spartan would also be callous to the sufferings, from his contempt for the degradation, of the slave; as he despised the employments abandoned to the Helot, even so would he despise the wretch that exercised them. Thus the motives that render power most intolerant combined in the Spartan in his relations to the Helot—viz., first, necessity for his services, lost perhaps if the curb were ever relaxed—second, consummate contempt for the individual he debased. The habit of tyranny makes tyranny necessary. When the slave has been long maddened by your yoke, if you lighten it for a moment he rebels. He has become your deadliest foe, and self-preservation renders it necessary that him whom you provoke to vengeance you should crush to impotence. The longer, therefore, the Spartan government endured, the more cruel became the condition of the Helots. Not in Sparta were those fine distinctions of rank which exist where slavery is unknown, binding class with class by ties of mutual sympathy and dependance—so that Poverty itself may be a benefactor to Destitution. Even among the poor the Helot had no brotherhood! he was as necessary to the meanest as to the highest Spartan—his wrongs gave its very existence to the commonwealth. We cannot, then, wonder at the extreme barbarity with which the Spartans treated this miserable race; and we can even find something of excuse for a cruelty which became at last the instinct of self-preservation. Revolt and massacre were perpetually before a Spartan's eyes; and what man will be gentle and unsuspecting to those who wait only the moment to murder him?

XII. The origin of the Helot race is not clearly ascertained: the popular notion that they were the descendants of the inhabitants of Helos, a maritime town subdued by the Spartans, and that they were degraded to servitude after a revolt, is by no means a conclusive account. Whether, as Müller suggests, they were the original slave population of the Achæans, or whether, as the ancient authorities held, they were such of the Achæans themselves as had most obstinately resisted the Spartan sword, and had at last surrendered without conditions, is a matter it is now impossible to determine. For my own part, I incline to the former supposition, partly because of the wide distinction between the enslaved Helots and the (merely) inferior Periœci, who were certainly Achæans; a distinction which I do not think the different manner in which the two classes were originally subdued would suffice to account for;—partly because I doubt whether the handful of Dorians who first fixed their dangerous settlement in Laconia could have effectually subjugated the Helots, if the latter had not previously been inured to slavery. The objection to this hypothesis—that the Helots could scarcely have so hated the Spartans if they had merely changed masters, does not appear to me very cogent. Under the mild and paternal chiefs of the Homeric age,[21] they might have been subjected to a much gentler servitude. Accustomed to the manners and habits of their Achæan lords, they might have half forgotten their condition; and though governed by Spartans in the same external relations, it was in a very different spirit. The sovereign contempt with which the Spartans regarded the Helots, they would scarcely have felt for a tribe distinguished from the more honoured Periœci only by a sterner valour and a greater regard for freedom; while that contempt is easily accounted for, if its objects were the previously subdued population of a country the Spartans themselves subdued.

The Helots were considered the property of the state—but they were entrusted and leased, as it were, to individuals; they were bound to the soil; even the state did not arrogate the power of selling them out of the country; they paid to their masters a rent in corn—the surplus profits were their own. It was easier for a Helot than for a Spartan to acquire riches—but riches were yet more useless to him. Some of the Helots attended their masters at the public tables, and others were employed in all public works: they served in the field as light-armed troops: they were occasionally emancipated, but there were several intermediate grades between the Helot and the freeman; their nominal duties were gentle indeed when compared with the spirit in which they were regarded and the treatment they received. That much exaggeration respecting the barbarity of their masters existed is probable enough; but the exaggeration itself, among writers accustomed to the institution of slavery elsewhere, and by no means addicted to an overstrained humanity, is a proof of the manner in which the treatment of the Helots was viewed by the more gentle slave-masters of the rest of Greece. They were branded with ineffaceable dishonour: no Helot might sing a Spartan song; if he but touched what belonged to a Spartan it was profaned—he was the Pariah of Greece. The ephors—the popular magistrates—the guardians of freedom—are reported by Aristotle to have entered office in making a formal declaration of war against the Helots—probably but an idle ceremony of disdain and insult. We cannot believe with Plutarch, that the infamous cryptia was instituted for the purpose he assigns—viz., that it was an ambuscade of the Spartan youths, who dispersed themselves through the

---

21 In Homer the condition of the slave seems, everywhere, tempered by the kindness and indulgence of the master.

country, and by night murdered whomsoever of the Helots they could meet. But it is certain that a select portion of the younger Spartans ranged the country yearly, armed with daggers, and that with the object of attaining familiarity with military hardships was associated that of strict, stern, and secret surveillance over the Helot population. No Helot, perhaps, was murdered from mere wantonness; but who does not see how many would necessarily have been butchered at the slightest suspicion of disaffection, or for the faintest utility of example? These miserable men were the objects of compassion to all Greece. "It was the common opinion", says Ælian, "that the earthquake in Sparta was a judgment from the gods upon the Spartan inhumanity to the Helots." And perhaps in all history (not even excepting that awful calmness with which the Italian historians narrate the cruelties of a Paduan tyrant or a Venetian oligarchy) there is no record of crime more thrilling than that dark and terrible passage in Thucydides which relates how two thousand Helots, the best and bravest of their tribe, were selected as for reward and freedom,—how they were led to the temples in thanksgiving to the gods—and how they disappeared,—their fate notorious—the manner of it a mystery!

XIII. Besides the Helots, the Spartans exercised an authority over the intermediate class called the Periœci. These were indubitably the old Achæan race, who had been reduced, not to slavery, but to dependance. They retained possession of their own towns, estimated in number, after the entire conquest of Messenia, at one hundred. They had their own different grades and classes, as the Saxons retained theirs after the conquest of the Normans. Among these were the traders and manufacturers of Laconia; and thus whatever art attained of excellence in the dominions of Sparta was not Spartan but Achæan. They served in the army, sometimes as heavy-armed, sometimes as light-armed soldiery, according to their rank or callings; and one of the Periœci obtained the command at sea. They appear, indeed, to have been universally acknowledged throughout Greece as free citizens, yet dependent subjects. But the Spartans jealously and sternly maintained the distinction between exemption from the servitude of a Helot, and participation in the rights of a Dorian: the Helot lost his personal liberty—the Periœcus his political.

XIV. The free or purely Spartan population (as not improbably with every Doric state) was divided into three generic tribes—the Hyllean, the Dymanatan, and the Pamphylian: of these the Hyllean (the reputed descendants of the son of Hercules) gave to Sparta both her kings. Besides these tribes of blood or race, there were also five local tribes, which formed the constituency of the ephors, and thirty subdivisions called *obes*—according to which the more aristocratic offices appear to have been elected. There were also recognized in the Spartan constitution two distinct classes—the Equals and the Inferiors. Though these were hereditary divisions, merit might promote a member of the last—demerit degrade a member of the first. The

141

Inferiors, though not boasting the nobility of the Equals, often possessed men equally honoured and powerful: as among the commoners of England are sometimes found persons of higher birth and more important station than among the peers—(a term somewhat synonymous with that of Equal). But the higher class enjoyed certain privileges which we can but obscurely trace.[22] Forming an assembly among themselves, it may be that they alone elected to the senate; and perhaps they were also distinguished by some peculiarities of education—an assertion made by Mr Müller, but not to my mind sufficiently established. With respect to the origin of this distinction between the Inferiors and the Equals, my own belief is, that it took place at some period (possibly during the Messenian wars) when the necessities of a failing population induced the Spartans to increase their number by the admixture either of strangers, but (as that hypothesis is scarce agreeable to Spartan manners) more probably of the Periœci; the new citizens would thus be the Inferiors. Among the Greek settlements in Italy, it was by no means uncommon for a colony, once sufficiently established, only to admit new settlers even from the parent state upon inferior terms; and in like manner in Venice arose the distinction between the gentlemen and the citizens; for when to that sea-girt state many flocked for security and refuge, it seemed but just to give to the prior inhabitants the distinction of hosts, and to consider the immigrators as guests;—to the first a share in the administration and a superior dignity—to the last only shelter and repose.

XV. Such are the general outlines of the state and constitution of Sparta —the firmest aristocracy that perhaps ever existed, for it was an aristocracy on the widest base. If some Spartans were noble, every Spartan boasted himself gentle. His birth forbade him to work, and his only profession was the sword. The difference between the meanest Spartan and his king was not so great as that between a Spartan and a Periœcus. Not only the servitude of the Helots, but the subjection of the Periœci, perpetually nourished the pride of the superior race; and to be born a Spartan was to be born to power. The sense of superiority and the habit of command impart a certain elevation to the manner and the bearing. There was probably more of dignity in the poorest Spartan citizen than in the wealthiest noble of Corinth—the most voluptuous courtier of Syracuse. And thus the reserve, the decorum, the stately simplicity of the Spartan mien could not but impose upon the imagination of the other Greeks, and obtain the credit for correspondent qualities which did not always exist beneath that lofty exterior. To lively nations, affected by externals, there was much in that sedate majesty of demeanour; to gallant nations, much in that heroic valour; to superstitious nations, much in that proverbial regard to religious rites, which characterized the Spartan race. Declaimers on luxury admired their simplicity—the

22 Three of the Equals always attended the king's person in war.

sufferers from innovation, their adherence to ancient manners. Many a victim of the turbulence of party in Athens sighed for the repose of the Lacedæmonian city; and as we always exaggerate the particular evils we endure, and admire most blindly the circumstances most opposite to those by which we are affected, so it was often the fashion of more intellectual states to extol the institutions of which they saw only from afar and through a glass the apparent benefits, without examining the concomitant defects. An Athenian might laud the Spartan austerity, as Tacitus might laud the German barbarism; it was the panegyric of rhetoric and satire, of wounded patriotism or disappointed ambition. Although the ephors made the government really and latently democratic, yet the concentration of its action made it seemingly oligarchic; and in its secrecy, caution, vigilance, and energy, it exhibited the best of the oligarchic features. Whatever was democratic by law was counteracted in its results by all that was aristocratic in custom. It was a state of political freedom, but of social despotism. This rigidity of ancient usages was binding long after its utility was past. For what was admirable at one time became pernicious at another; what protected the infant state from dissension, stinted all luxuriance of intellect in the more matured community. It is in vain that modern writers have attempted to deny this fact—the proof is before us. By her valour Sparta was long the most eminent state of the most intellectual of all countries; and when we ask what she has bequeathed to mankind—what she has left us in rivalry to that Athens, whose poetry yet animates, whose philosophy yet guides, whose arts yet inspire the world—we find only the names of two or three minor poets, whose works have perished, and some half a dozen pages of pithy aphorisms and pointed repartees!

XVI. My object in the above sketch has been to give a general outline of the Spartan character and the Spartan system during the earlier and more brilliant era of Athenian history, without entering into unnecessary conjectures as to the precise period of each law and each change. The social and political

THE FIRST AND SECOND
MESSENIAN WAR

state of Sparta became fixed by her conquest of Messenia. It is not within the plan of my undertaking to retail at length the legendary and for the most part fabulous accounts of the first and second Messenian wars. The first was dignified by the fate of the Messenian hero Aristodemus, and the fall of the rocky fortress of Ithomë; its result was the conquest of Messenia; the inhabitants were compelled to an oath of submission, and to surrender to Sparta half their agricultural produce. After the first Messenian war, Tarentum was founded by a Spartan colony, composed, it is said, of youths,[23] the offspring of Spartan women and Laconian men, who were dissatisfied with

---

23 The institution of the ephors has been, with probability, referred to this epoch—chosen at first as the viceroys in the absence of the kings.

their exclusion from citizenship, and by whom the state was menaced with a formidable conspiracy shared by the Helots. Meanwhile, the Messenians, if conquered, were not subdued. Years rolled away, and time had effaced the remembrance of the past sufferings, but not of the ancient[24] liberties.

It was among the youth of Messenia that the hope of the national deliverance was the most intensely cherished. At length, in Andania, the revolt broke forth. A young man, pre-eminent above the rest for birth, for valour, and for genius, was the head and the soul of the enterprise. His name was Aristomenes. Forming secret alliances with the Argives and Arcadians, he at length ventured to raise his standard, and encountered at Dera, on their own domains, the Spartan force. The issue of the battle was indecisive; still, however, it seems to have seriously aroused the fears of Sparta: no further hostilities took place till the following year; the oracle at Delphi was solemnly consulted, and the god ordained the Spartans to seek their adviser in an Athenian. They sent to Athens and obtained Tyrtæus. A popular but fabulous account[25] describes him a lame teacher of grammar, and of no previous repute. His songs and his exhortations are said to have produced almost miraculous effects. I omit the romantic adventures of the hero Aristomenes, though it may be doubted whether all Grecian history can furnish passages that surpass the poetry of his reputed life. I leave the reader to learn elsewhere how he hung at night a shield in the temple of Chalciœcus, in the very city of the foe, with the inscription, that Aristomenes dedicated to the goddess that shield from the spoils of the Spartans—how he penetrated the secret recesses of Trophonius—how he was deterred from entering Sparta by the spectres of Helen and the Dioscuri—how, taken prisoner in an attempt to seize the women of Ægila, he was released by the love of the priestess of Ceres—how, again made captive, and cast into a deep pit with fifty of his men, he escaped by seizing hold of a fox (attracted thither by the dead bodies), and suffering himself to be drawn by her through dark and scarce pervious places to a hole that led to the upper air. These adventures, and others equally romantic, I must leave to the genius of more credulous historians.

All that seems to me worthy of belief is, that after stern but unavailing struggles, the Messenians abandoned Andania, and took their last desperate station at Ira, a mountain at whose feet flows the river Neda, separating Messenia from Triphylia. Here, fortified alike by art and nature, they sustained a siege of eleven years. But with the eleventh the term of their resistance was completed. The slave of a Spartan of rank had succeeded in engaging the affections of a Messenian woman who dwelt without the walls of the mountain fortress. One night the guilty pair were at the house of the

24 Paus., iv.
25 See Müller's Dorians, vol. i, p. 172, and Clinton's Fasti Hellenici, vol. i, p. 183.

adulteress—the husband abruptly returned—the slave was concealed, and overheard that, in consequence of a violent and sudden storm, the Messenian guard had deserted the citadel, not fearing attack from the foe on so tempestuous a night, and not anticipating the inspection of Aristomenes, who at that time was suffering from a wound. The slave overheard—escaped—reached the Spartan camp—apprized his master Emperamus (who, in the absence of the kings, headed the troops) of the desertion of the guard:—an assault was agreed on: despite the darkness of the night, despite the violence of the rain, the Spartans marched on:—scaled the fortifications:—were within the walls. The fulfilment of dark prophecies had already portended the fate of the besieged; and now the very howling of the dogs in a strange and unwonted manner was deemed a prodigy. Alarmed, aroused, the Messenians betook themselves to the nearest weapons within their reach. Aristomenes, his son Gorgus, Theoclus, the guardian prophet of his tribe (whose valour was equal to his science), were among the first to perceive the danger. Night passed in tumult and disorder. Day dawned, but rather to terrify than encourage—the storm increased—the thunder burst—the lightning glared. What dismayed the besieged encouraged the besiegers. Still, with all the fury of despair, the Messenians fought on: the very women took part in the contest; death was preferable, even in their eyes, to slavery and dishonour. But the Spartans were far superior in number, and, by continual reliefs, the fresh succeeded to the weary. In arms for three days and three nights without respite, worn out with watching, with the rage of the elements, with cold, with hunger, and with thirst, no hope remained for the Messenians: the bold prophet declared to Aristomenes that the gods had decreed the fall of Messene, that the warning oracles were fulfilled. "Preserve", he cried, "what remain of your forces—save yourselves. Me the gods impel to fall with my country!" Thus saying, the soothsayer rushed on the enemy and fell at last covered with wounds and satiated with the slaughter himself had made. Aristomenes called the Messenians round him; the women and the children were placed in the centre of the band, guarded by his own son and that of the prophet. Heading the troop himself, he rushed on the foe, and by his gestures and the shaking of his spear announced his intention to force a passage, and effect escape. Unwilling yet more to exasperate men urged to despair, the Spartans made way for the rest of the besieged. So fell Ira![26] The brave Messenians escaped to Mount Lycæum in Arcadia, and afterward the greater part, invited by Anaxilaus, their own countryman, prince of the Dorian colony at Rhegium in Italy, conquered with him the Zanclæans of Sicily, and named the conquered town Messene. It still preserves the name.[27]

26 For the dates here given of the second Messenian war see Fasi Hellenici, vol. i, p. 190, and Appendix 2.
27 Now called Messina.

But Aristomenes, retaining indomitable hatred to Sparta, refused to join the colony. Yet hoping a day of retribution, he went to Delphi. What counsel he there received is unrecorded. But the deity ordained to Damagetes, prince of Ialysus in Rhodes, to marry the daughter of the best man of Greece. Such a man the prince esteemed the hero of the Messenians, and wedded the third daughter of Aristomenes. Still bent on designs against the destroyers of his country, the patriot warrior repaired to Rhodes, where death delivered the Spartans from the terror of his revenge. A monument was raised to his memory, and that memory, distinguished by public honours, long made the boast of the Messenians, whether those in distant exile, or those subjected to the Spartan yoke. Thus ended the second Messenian war. Such of the Messenians as had not abandoned their country were reduced to Helotism. The Spartan territory extended, and the Spartan power secured, that haughty state rose slowly to pre-eminence over the rest of Greece; and preserved, amid the advancing civilization and refinement of her neighbours, the stern and awing likeness of the heroic age:—in the mountains of the Peloponnesus, the polished and luxurious Greeks beheld, retained from change as by a spell, the iron images of their Homeric ancestry!

CHAPTER VII

I. The Return of the Heraclidæ occasioned consequences of which the most important were the least immediate. Whenever the Dorians forced a settlement, they dislodged such of the previous inhabitants as refused to succumb. Driven elsewhere to seek a home, the exiles found it often in yet fairer climes, and along more fertile soils. The example of these involuntary migrators became imitated wherever discontent prevailed or population was redundant: and hence, as I have already recorded, first arose those numerous colonies, which along the Asiatic shores, in the Grecian isles, on the plains of Italy, and even in Libya and in Egypt were destined to give, as it were, a second youth to the parent states.

GOVERNMENTS IN GREECE

II. The ancient Greek constitution was that of an aristocracy, with a prince at the head. Suppose a certain number of men, thus governed, to be expelled their native soil, united by a common danger and common suffering, to land on a foreign shore, to fix themselves with pain and labour in a new settlement—it is quite clear that a popular principle would insensibly have entered the forms of the constitution they transplanted. In the first place, the power of the prince would be more circumscribed—in the next place, the free spirit of the aristocracy would be more diffused: the first, because the authority of the chief would rarely be derived from royal ancestry, or hallowed by prescriptive privilege; in most cases he was but a noble, selected from the ranks, and crippled by the jealousies, of his order: the second, because all who shared in the enterprise would in one respect rise at once to an aristocracy—they would be distinguished from the population of the state they colonized. Misfortune, sympathy, and change would also contribute to sweep away many demarcations; and authority was transmuted from a birthright into a trust, the moment it was withdrawn from the shelter of ancient custom, and made the gift of the living rather than a heritage from the dead. It was probable, too, that many of such colonies were founded by men, among whom was but little disparity of rank: this would be especially the case with those which were the overflow of a redundant population; —the great and the wealthy are never redundant!—the mass would thus ordinarily be composed of the discontented and the poor, and even where the aristocratic leaven was most strong, it was still the aristocracy of some defeated and humbled faction. So that in the average equality of the emigrators were the seeds of a new constitution; and if they transplanted the form of monarchy, it already contained the genius of republicanism. Hence, colonies in the ancient, as in the modern world, advanced by giant strides towards popular principles. Maintaining a constant intercourse with their father-land, their own constitutions became familiar and tempting to the popula-tion of the countries they had abandoned; and much of whatsoever advant-ages were derived from the soil they selected, and the commerce they found within their reach, was readily attributed only to their more popular constitu-tions;—as, at this day, we find American prosperity held out to our example, not as the result of local circumstances, but as the creature of political institutions.

One principal cause of the republican forms of government that began (as, after the Dorian migration, the different tribes became settled in those seats by which they are historically known) to spread throughout Greece, was, therefore, the establishment of colonies retaining constant intercourse with the parent states. A second cause is to be found in the elements of the previous constitutions of the Grecian states themselves, and the political principles which existed universally, even in the heroic ages: so that, in fact, the change from monarchy to republicanism was much less violent than at the first glance it would seem to our modern notions. The ancient kings, as described by Homer, possessed but a limited authority, like that of the Spartan kings—extensive in war, narrow in peace. It was evidently con-sidered that the source of their authority was in the people. No notion seems to have been more universal among the Greeks than that it was for the com-munity that all power was to be exercised. In Homer's time popular assemblies existed, and claimed the right of conferring privileges on rank. The nobles were ever jealous of the prerogative of the prince, and ever encroaching on his accidental weakness. In his sickness, his age, or his absence, the power of the state seems to have been wrested from his hands—the prey of the chiefs, or the dispute of contending factions. Nor was there in Greece that chivalric fealty to a *person* which characterizes the North. From the earliest times it was not the MONARCH, but the STATE, that called forth the virtue of devotion, and inspired the enthusiasm of loyalty. Thus, in the limited pre-rogative of royalty, in the jealousy of the chiefs, in the right of popular assemblies, and, above all, in the silent and unconscious spirit of political theory, we may recognize in the early monarchies of Greece the germs of their inevitable dissolution. Another cause was in that singular separation of tribes, speaking a common language, and belonging to a common race, which characterized the Greeks. Instead of overrunning a territory in one vast irruption, each section seized a small district, built a city, and formed an independent people. Thus, in fact, the Hellenic governments were not those of a country, but of a town; and the words "state" and "city" were synonymous.[1] Municipal constitutions, in their very nature, are ever more or less republican; and, as in the Italian states, the corporation had only to shake off some power unconnected with, or hostile to it to rise into a republic. To this it may be added, that the true republican spirit is more easily established among mountain tribes imperfectly civilized, and yet fresh from the wildness of the natural life, than among old states, where luxury leaves indeed the desire, but has enervated the power of liberty, "as the marble from the quarry may be more readily wrought into the statue, than that on which the hand of the workman has already been employed."[2]

III. If the change from monarchy to republicanism was not very violent in itself, it appears to have been yet more smoothed away by gradual preparations. Monarchy was not abolished, it declined. The direct line was broken, or some other excuse occurred for exchanging an hereditary for an elective monarchy; then the period of power became shortened, and from monarchy for life it was monarchy only for a certain number of years: in most cases the name too (and how much is there in names!) was changed, and the title of ruler or magistrate substituted for that of king.

Thus, by no sudden leap of mind, by no vehement and short-lived revolutions, but gradually, insensibly, and permanently, monarchy ceased— a fashion, as it were, worn out and obsolete—and republicanism succeeded. But this republicanism at first was probably in no instance purely democratic. It was the chiefs who were the visible agents in the encroachments on the monarchic power—it was an aristocracy that succeeded monarchy. Sometimes this aristocracy was exceedingly limited in number, or the governing power was usurped by a particular faction or pre-eminent families; then it was called an OLIGARCHY. And this form of aristocracy appears generally to have been the most immediate successor to royalty. "The first polity", says Aristotle,[3] "that was established in Greece after the lapse of monarchies, was that of the members of the military class, and those wholly horsemen . . . such republics, though called democracies, had a strong tendency to oligarchy, and even to royalty."[4] But the spirit of change still progressed: whether they

1 In Phocis were no less than twenty-two states ($\pi\acute{o}\lambda\epsilon\iota\varsigma$); in Bœotia, fourteen; in Achaia, ten. The ancient political theorists held no community too small for independence, provided the numbers sufficed for its defence. We find from Plato that a society of five thousand freemen capable of bearing arms was deemed powerful enough to constitute an independent state. One great cause of the ascendency of Athens and Sparta was, that each of those cities had from an early period swept away the petty independent states in their several territories of Attica and Laconia.
2 Machiavel, Discor., i. 2).
3 Aristot., Pol., iv. 13.
4 Aristotle cites among the advantages of wealth, that of being enabled to train horses. Wherever the nobility could establish among themselves a cavalry, the constitution was oligarchical. Yet, even in states which did not maintain a cavalry (as Athens previous to the constitution of Solon), an oligarchy was the first form of government that rose above the ruins of monarchy.

were few or many, the aristocratic governors could not fail to open the door to further innovations. For, if many, they were subjected to dissensions among themselves—if few, they created odium in all who were excluded from power. Thus fell the oligarchies of Marseilles, Ister, and Heraclea. In the one case they were weakened by their own jealousies, in the other by the jealousies of their rivals. The progress of civilization and the growing habits of commerce gradually introduced a medium between the populace and the chiefs. The MIDDLE CLASS slowly rose, and with it rose the desire of extended liberties and equal laws.[5]

IV. Now then appeared the class of DEMAGOGUES. The people had been accustomed to change. They had been led against monarchy, and found they had only resigned the one master to obtain the many:—a demagogue arose, sometimes one of their own order, more often a dissatisfied, ambitious, or impoverished noble. For they who have wasted their patrimony, as the Stagirite shrewdly observes, are great promoters of innovation! Party ran high—the state became divided—passions were aroused—and the popular leader became the popular idol. His life was probably often in danger from the resentment of the nobles, and it was always easy to assert that it was so endangered. He obtained a guard to protect him, conciliated the soldiers, seized the citadel, and rose at once from the head of the populace to the ruler of the state. Such was the common history of the tyrants of Greece, who never supplanted the kingly sway (unless in the earlier ages, when, born to a limited monarchy, they extended their privileges beyond the law, as Pheidon of Argos), but nearly always aristocracies or oligarchies.[6] I need scarcely observe that the word "tyrant" was of very different signification in ancient times from that which it bears at present. It more nearly corresponded to our word "usurper," and denoted one who, by illegitimate means, whether of art or force, had usurped the supreme authority. A tyrant might be mild or cruel—the father of the people, or their oppressor; he still preserved the name, and it was transmitted to his children. The merits of this race of

---

5 One principal method of increasing the popular action was by incorporating the neighbouring villages or wards in one municipality with the capital. By this the people gained both in number and in union.

6 Sometimes in ancient Greece there arose a species of lawful tyrants, under the name of Æsymnetes. These were voluntarily chosen by the people, sometimes for life, sometimes for a limited period, and generally for the accomplishment of some particular object. Thus was Pittacus of Mitylene elected to conduct the war against the exiles. With the accomplishment of the object he abdicated his power. But the appointment of Æsymnetes can hardly be called a regular form of government. They soon became obsolete—the mere creatures of occasion. While they lasted, they bore a strong resemblance to the Roman dictators—a resemblance remarked by Dionysius, who quotes Theophrastus as agreeing with Aristotle in his account of the Æsymnetes.

rulers, and the unconscious benefits they produced, have not been justly appreciated, either by ancient or modern historians. Without her tyrants, Greece might never have established her democracies. As may be readily supposed, the man who, against powerful enemies, often from a low origin and with impoverished fortunes, had succeeded in ascending a throne, was usually possessed of no ordinary abilities. It was almost vitally necessary for him to devote those abilities to the cause and interests of the people. Their favour had alone raised him—numerous foes still surrounded him—it was on the people alone that he could depend.

The wiser and more celebrated tyrants were characterized by an extreme modesty of deportment—they assumed no extraordinary pomp, no lofty titles —they left untouched, or rendered yet more popular, the outward forms and institutions of the government—they were not exacting in taxation—they affected to link themselves with the lowest orders, and their ascendency was usually productive of immediate benefit to the working classes, whom they employed in new fortifications or new public buildings; dazzling the citizens by a splendour that seemed less the ostentation of an individual than the prosperity of a state. But the aristocracy still remained their enemies, and it was against them, not against the people, that they directed their acute sagacities and unsparing energies. Every more politic tyrant was a Louis XI, weakening the nobles, creating a middle class. He effected his former object by violent and unscrupulous means. He swept away by death or banishment all who opposed his authority or excited his fears. He thus left nothing between the state and a democracy but himself; himself removed, democracy ensued naturally and of course. There are times in the history of all nations when liberty is best promoted—when civilization is most rapidly expedited —when the arts are most luxuriantly nourished by a strict concentration of power in the hands of an individual—and when the despot is but the representative of the popular will.[7] At such times did the tyrannies in Greece mostly flourish, and they may almost be said to cease with the necessity which called them forth. The energy of these masters of a revolution opened the intercourse with other states; their interests extended commerce; their policy broke up the sullen barriers of oligarchical prejudice and custom; their fears found perpetual vent for the industry of a population whom they dreaded to leave in indolence; their genius appreciated the arts—their vanity fostered them. Thus they interrupted the course of liberty only to improve, to concentre, to advance its results. Their dynasty never lasted long; the

---

7 For, as the great Florentine has well observed, "to found well a government, one man is the best—once established, the care and execution of the laws should be transferred to many" (Machiavel, Discor., i. 9). And thus a tyranny builds the edifice, which the republic hastens to inhabit.

oldest tyranny in Greece endured but a hundred years[8]—so enduring only from its mildness. The son of the tyrant rarely inherited his father's sagacity and talents: he sought to strengthen his power by severity; discontent ensued, and his fall was sudden and complete. Usually, then, such of the aristocracy as had been banished were recalled, but not invested with their former privileges. The constitution became more or less democratic. It is true that Sparta, who lent her powerful aid in destroying tyrannies, aimed at replacing them by oligarchies—but the effort seldom produced a permanent result: the more the aristocracy was narrowed, the more certain was its fall. If the middle class were powerful—if commerce thrived in the state—the former aristocracy of birth was soon succeeded by an aristocracy of property (called a timocracy), and this was in its nature certain of democratic advances. The moment you widen the suffrage, you may date the commencement of universal suffrage. He who enjoys certain advantages from the possession of ten acres, will excite a party against him in those who have nine; and the arguments that had been used for the franchise of the one are equally valid for the franchise of the other. Limitations of power by property are barriers against a tide which perpetually advances. Timocracy, therefore, almost invariably paved the way to democracy. But still the old aristocratic faction, constantly invaded, remained powerful, stubborn, and resisting, and there was scarcely a state in Greece that did not contain the two parties which we find today in England, and in all free states—the party of the movement to the future, and the party of recurrence to the past; I say the past, for in politics there is no present! Wherever party exists, if the one desire fresh innovations, so the other secretly wishes not to preserve what remains, but to restore what has been. This fact it is necessary always to bear in mind in examining the political contests of the Athenians. For in most of their domestic convulsions we find the cause in the efforts of the anti-popular party less to resist new encroachments than to revive departed institutions. But though in most of the Grecian states were two distinct orders, and the eupatrids, or "well-born", were a class distinct from, and superior to, that of the commonalty, we should err in supposing that the separate orders made the great political divisions. As in England the more ancient of the nobles are often found in the popular ranks, so in the Grecian states many of the eupatrids headed the democratic party. And this division among themselves, while it weakened the power of the well-born, contributed to prevent any deadly or ferocious revolutions: for it served greatly to soften the excesses of the predominant faction, and every collision found mediators between the

---

8 That of Orthagoras and his sons in Sicyon. "Of all governments," says Aristotle, "that of an oligarchy, or of a tyrant, is the least permanent." A quotation that cannot be too often pressed on the memory of those reasoners who insist so much on the brief duration of the ancient republics.

contending parties in some who were at once friends of the people and members of the nobility. Nor should it be forgotten that the triumph of the popular party was always more moderate than that of the antagonist faction —as the history of Athens will hereafter prove.

V. The legal constitutions of Greece were four—Monarchy, Oligarchy, Aristocracy, and Democracy; the illegal was Tyranny in a twofold shape, viz., whether it consisted in an usurped monarchy or an usurped oligarchy. Thus the oligarchy of the Thirty in Athens was no less a tyranny than the single government of Pisistratus. Even democracy had its illegal or corrupt form—in OCHLOCRACY or mob rule; for democracy did not signify the rule of the lower orders alone, but of all the people—the highest as the lowest. If the highest became by law excluded—if the populace confined the legislative and executive authorities to their own order—then democracy, or the government of a whole people, virtually ceased, and became the government of a *part* of the people—a form equally unjust and illegitimate—equally an abuse in itself, whether the dominant and exclusive portion were the nobles or the mechanics. Thus in modern yet analogous history, when the middle class of Florence expelled the nobles from any share of the government, they established a monopoly under the name of liberty; and the resistance of the nobles was the lawful struggle of patriots and of freemen for an inalienable privilege and a natural right.

VI. We should remove some very important prejudices from our minds, if we could once subscribe to a fact plain in itself, but which the contests of modern party have utterly obscured—that in the mere forms of their government, the Greek republics cannot fairly be pressed into the service of those who in existing times would attest the evils, or proclaim the benefits, of constitutions purely democratic. In the first place, they were *not* democracies, even in their most democratic shape;—the vast majority of the working classes were the enslaved population. And, therefore, to increase the popular tendencies of the republic was, in fact, only to increase the liberties of the few. We may fairly doubt whether the worst evils of the ancient republics, in the separation of ranks, and the war between rich and poor, were not the necessary results of slavery. We may doubt, with equal probability, whether much of the lofty spirit, and the universal passion for public affairs, whence emanated the enterprise, the competition, the patriotism, and the glory of the ancient cities, could have existed without a subordinate race to carry on the drudgeries of daily life. It is clear, also, that much of the intellectual greatness of the several states arose from the exceeding smallness of their territories—the concentration of internal power, and the perpetual emulation with neighbouring and kindred states nearly equal in civilization; it is clear, too, that much of the vicious parts of their character, and yet much of their more brilliant, arose from the absence of the PRESS. Their intellectual state was that of men *talked* to, not *written* to. Their imagination was perpetually called forth—their deliberative reason rarely;—they were the fitting audience for an orator, whose art is effective in proportion to the impulse and the passion of those he addresses. Nor must it be forgotten that the representative system, which is the proper conductor of the democratic action, if not wholly unknown to the Greeks,[9] and if unconsciously practised in the Spartan ephoralty, was at least never existent in the more democratic states. And assemblies of the whole people are compatible only with those small nations of which the city is the country. Thus, it would be impossible for us to propose the abstract constitution of any ancient state as a warning or an example to modern countries which possess territories large in extent —which subsist without a slave population—which substitute representative councils for popular assemblies—and which direct the intellectual tastes and political habits of a people, not by oratory and conversation, but through the more calm and dispassionate medium of the press. This principle settled, it may perhaps be generally conceded, that on comparing the democracies of Greece with all other contemporary forms of government, we find them the most favourable to mental cultivation—not more exposed than others to internal revolutions—usually, in fact, more durable,—more mild and civilized in their laws—and that the worst tyranny of the Demus, whether at home or abroad, never equalled that of an oligarchy or a single ruler. That in which the ancient republics are properly models to us consists not in the form, but the spirit of their legislation. They teach us that patriotism is most promoted by bringing all classes into public and constant intercourse—that intellect is most luxuriant wherever the competition is widest and most unfettered—and that legislators can create no rewards and invent no penalties equal to those which are silently engendered by society itself—while it maintains, elaborated into a system, the desire of glory and the dread of shame.

9 Besides the representation necessary to confederacies—such as the Amphictyonic league, &c., a representative system was adopted at Mantinea, where the officers were named by deputies chosen by the people. "This form of democracy", says Aristotle, "existed among the shepherds and husbandmen of Arcadia"; and was probably not uncommon with the ancient Pelasgians. But the μυρίοι of Arcadia had not the legislative power.

CHAPTER VIII

I. Before concluding this introductory portion of my work, it will be necessary to take a brief survey of the intellectual state of Greece prior to that

BRIEF SURVEY OF ARTS, LETTERS, AND PHILOSOPHY IN GREECE, PRIOR TO THE LEGISLATION OF SOLON

wonderful era of Athenian greatness which commenced with the laws of Solon. At this period the *continental* states of Greece had produced little in that literature which is now the heirloom of the world. Whether under her monarchy, or the oligarchical constitution that succeeded it, the depressed and languid genius of Athens had given no earnest of the triumphs she was afterward destined to accomplish. Her literature began, though it cannot be said to have ceased, with her democracy. The solitary and doubtful claim of the birth—but not the song—of Tyrtæus is the highest literary honour to which the earlier age of Attica can pretend; and many of the Dorian states—even Sparta itself—appear to have been more prolific in poets than the city of Æschylus and Sophocles. But throughout all Greece, from the earliest time, was a general passion for poetry, however fugitive the poets. The poems of Homer are the most ancient of profane writings—but the poems of Homer themselves attest that they had many, nor ignoble, precursors. Not only do they attest it in their very excellence—not only in their reference to other poets—but in the general manner of life attributed to chiefs and heroes. The lyre and the song afford the favourite entertainment at the banquet.[1] And Achilles, in the interval of his indignant repose, exchanges the deadly sword for the "silver harp",

---

1   Then to the lute's soft voice prolong the night,
     Music, the banquet's most refined delight.
                    Pope's Odyssey, xxi. 473.

 It is stronger in the original—

     Μολπῇ καὶ φόρμιγγι· τὰ γὰρ τ᾽ἀναθήματα δαιτός.

> And sings
> The immortal deeds of heroes and of kings.[2]

II. Ample tradition and the internal evidence of the Homeric poems prove the Iliad at least to have been the composition of an Asiatic Greek; and though the time in which he flourished is yet warmly debated, the most plausible chronology places him about the time of the Ionic migration, or somewhat less than two hundred years after the Trojan war. The following lines in the speech of Juno in the fourth book of the Iliad are supposed by some[3] to allude to the Return of the Heraclidæ and the Dorian conquests in the Peloponnesus:—

> Three towns are Juno's on the Grecian plains,
> More dear than all th' extended earth contains—
> Mycenæ, Argos, and the Spartan Wall,—
> These may'st thou raze, nor I forbid their fall;
> 'Tis not in me the vengeance to remove—
> The crime's sufficient that they share my love."[4]

And it certainly does seem to me that in a reference so distinct to the three great Peloponnesian cities which the Dorians invaded and possessed, Homer makes as broad an allusion to the conquests of the Heraclidæ, not only as would be consistent with the pride of an Ionic Greek in attesting the triumphs of the national Dorian foe, but as the nature of a theme cast in a distant period, and remarkably removed, in its general conduct, from the historical detail of subsequent events, would warrant to the poet.[5] And here I may observe, that if the date thus assigned to Homer be correct, the very subject of the Iliad might have been suggested by the consequences of the Dorian irruption. Homer relates,

> Achilles' wrath, to Greece the direful spring
> Of woes unnumbered.

But Achilles is the native hero of that Thessalian district, which was the earliest settlement of the Dorian family. Agamemnon, whose injuries he

---

2 Iliad, ix, Pope's translation, line 250.
3 Heyne, F. Clinton, &c.
4 Pope's translation, iv. 75, &c.
5 At least this passage is sufficient to refute the arguments of Mr Mitford, and men more learned than that historian, who, in taking for their premises as an indisputable fact the extraordinary assumption, that Homer never once has alluded to the Return of the Heraclidæ, arrive at a conclusion very illogical, even if the premises were true, viz., that therefore Homer preceded the date of that great revolution.

resents, is the monarch of the great Achæan race, whose dynasty and dominion the Dorians are destined to overthrow. It is true that at the time of the Trojan war the Dorians had migrated from Phthiotis to Phocis—it is true that Achilles was not of Dorian extraction; still there would be an interest attached to the singular coincidence of place; as, though the English are no descendants from the Britons, we yet associate the British history with our own: hence it seems to me, though I believe the conjecture is new, that it is not the *whole* Trojan war, but that *episode* in the Trojan war (otherwise unimportant) illustrated by the wrath of Achilles, which awakens the inspiration of the poet. In fact, if under the exordium of the Iliad there lurk no typical signification, the exordium is scarce appropriate to the subject. For the wrath of Achilles did not bring upon the Greeks woes more mighty than the ordinary course of war would have destined them to endure. But if the Grecian audience (exiles, and the posterity of exiles), to whom, on Asiatic shores, Homer recited his poem, associated the hereditary feud of Achilles and Agamemnon with the strife between the ancient warriors of Phthiotis and Achaia; *then*, indeed, the opening lines assume a solemn and prophetic significance, and their effect must have been electrical upon a people ever disposed to trace in the mythi of their ancestry the legacies of a dark and ominous fatality, by which each present suffering was made the inevitable result of an immemorial cause.[6]

III. The ancients unanimously believed the Iliad the production of a single poet; in recent times a contrary opinion has been started; and in Germany, at this moment, the most fashionable belief is, that that wonderful poem was but a collection of rhapsodies by various poets, arranged and organized by Pisistratus and the poets of his day; a theory a scholar may support, but which no poet could ever have invented! For this proposition the principal reasons alleged are these:—it is asserted as an "indisputable fact":

> that the art of writing, and the use of manageable writing materials,
> were entirely, or all but entirely, unknown in Greece and its islands
> at the supposed date of the composition of the Iliad and Odyssey;
> that, if so, these poems could not have been committed to writing
> during the time of such their composition; that, in a question of
> comparative probabilities like this, it is a much grosser improbabil-
> ity that even the single Iliad, amounting, after all curtailments and
> expungings, to upwards of 15,000 hexameter lines, should have

6 I own that this seems to me the most probable way of accounting for the singular and otherwise disproportioned importance attached by the ancient poets to that episode in the Trojan war, which relates to the feud of Achilles and Agamemnon. As the first recorded enmity between the great Achæans and the warriors of Phthiotis, it would have a solemn and historical interest both to the conquering Dorians and the defeated Achæans, flattering to the national vanity of either people.

been actually conceived and perfected in the brain of one man, with no other help but his own or others' memory, than that it should in fact be the result of the labours of several distinct authors; that if the Odyssey be counted, the improbability is doubled; that if we add, upon the authority of Thucydides and Aristotle, the Hymns and Margites, not to say the Batrachomyomachia, that which was improbable becomes morally impossible! that all that has been so often said as to the fact of as many verses or more having been committed to memory, is beside the point in question, which is not whether 15,000 or 30,000 lines may not be learned by heart from print or manuscript, but whether one man can originally compose a poem of that length, which, rightly or not, shall be thought to be a perfect model of symmetry and consistency of parts, without the aid of writing materials;—that, admitting the superior probability of such an achievement in a primitive age, we know nothing actually similar or analogous to it; and that it so transcends the common limits of intellectual power, as at the least to merit, with as much justice as the opposite opinion, the character of improbability.[7]

And upon such arguments the identity of Homer is to be destroyed! Let us pursue them seriatim. First:

> The art and the use of manageable writing materials were entirely, or all but entirely, unknown in Greece and its islands at the supposed date of the composition of the Iliad and Odyssey.

The whole argument against the unity of Homer rests upon this assertion; and yet this assertion it is impossible to prove! It is allowed, on the contrary, that alphabetical characters were introduced in Greece by Cadmus—nay, inscriptions believed by the best antiquaries to bear date before the Trojan war are found even among the Pelasgi of Italy. Dionysius informs us that the Pelasgi first introduced letters into Italy. But in answer to this, it is said that letters were used only for inscriptions on stone or wood, and not for the preservation of writings so voluminous. If this were the case, I scarcely see why the Greeks should have professed so grateful a reminiscence of the gift of Cadmus,—the mere inscription of a few words on stone would not be so very popular or beneficial an invention! But the Phœnicians had constant intercourse with the Egyptians and Hebrews; among both those nations the art and materials of writing were known. The Phœnicians, far more enterprising than either, must have been fully acquainted with their means of

---

7 I adopt the analysis of the anti-Homer arguments so clearly given by Mr Coleridge in his eloquent Introduction to the Study of the Greek Poets. Homer, p. 39.

written communication—and indeed we are assured that they were so. Now, if a Phœnician had imparted so much of the art to Greece as the knowledge of a written alphabet, is it probable that he would have suffered the communication to cease there? The Phœnicians were a commercial people—their colonies in Greece were for commercial purposes,—would they have wilfully and voluntarily neglected the most convenient mode of commercial correspondence?—importing just enough of the art to suffice for inscriptions of no use but to the natives, would they have stopped short precisely at that point when the art became useful to themselves! And in vindicating that most able people from so wilful a folly, have we no authority in history as well as common sense! We have the authority of Herodotus! When he informs us that the Phœnicians communicated letters to the Ionians, he adds, that by a very ancient custom the Ionians called their books *diptheræ*, or skins, because, at a time when the plant of the biblos or papyrus was *scarce*,[8] they used instead of it the skins of goats and sheep—a custom he himself witnessed among barbarous nations. Were such materials used only for inscriptions relative to a religious dedication, or a political compact? No; for then, wood or stone—the temple or the pillar—would have been the material for the inscription,—they must, then, have been used for a more literary purpose; and verse was the first form of literature. I grant that prior, and indeed long subsequent to the time of Homer, the art of writing (as with us in the dark ages) would be very partially known—that in many parts of Greece, especially European Greece, it might scarcely ever be used but for brief inscriptions. But that is nothing to the purpose;—if known at all—to any Ionian trader—even to any neighbouring Asiatic—even to any Phœnician settler—there is every reason to suppose that Homer himself, or a contemporary disciple and reciter of his verses, would have learned both the art and the use of the materials which could best have ensured the fame of the poet, or assisted the memory of the reciter. And, though Plutarch in himself alone is no authority, he is not to be rejected as a corroborative testimony when he informs us that Lycurgus collected and *transcribed* the poems of Homer; and that writing was then known in Greece is evident by the very ordinance of Lycurgus that his laws should not be written. But Lycurgus is made by Apollodorus contemporary with Homer himself and this belief appears to receive the sanction of the most laborious and profound of modern chronologers.[9] I might adduce various other arguments in support

8 ἐν σπάνει βίβλων, are the words of Herodotus. Leaves and the bark of trees were also used from a very remote period previous to the common use of the papyrus, and when we are told that leaves would not suffice for works of any length or duration, it must not be forgotten that in a much later age it was upon leaves (and mutton bones) that the Koran was transcribed. The rudest materials are sufficient for the preservation of what men deem it their interest to preserve!

9 See Clinton's Fasti Hellenici, vol. i, p. 145.

of those I have already advanced; but I have said enough already to show that it is not an *"indisputable fact"* that Homer could not have been acquainted with writing materials; and that the whole battery erected to demolish the fame of the greatest of human geniuses has been built upon a most uncertain and unsteady foundation. It may be impossible to prove that Homer's poems were written, but it is equally impossible to prove that they were not—and if it were necessary for the identity of Homer that his poems should have been written, that necessity would have been one of the strongest proofs, not that Homer did *not* exist, but that writing *did!*

But let us now suppose it proved that writing materials for a literary purpose were unknown, and examine the assertions built upon that hypothesis. Second:

> That if these poems could not have been committed to writing during the time of their composition, it is a much grosser improbability that even the single Iliad, amounting, after all curtailments and expungings, to upwards of 15,000 hexameter lines, should have been actually conceived and perfected in the brain of one man, with no other help but his own or others' memory, than that it should, in fact, be the result of the labours of several distinct authors.

I deny this altogether. "The improbability" might be "grosser" if the Iliad had been composed in a day! But if, as any man of common sense would acknowledge, it was composed in parts or "fyttes" of moderate length at a time, no extraordinary power of memory, or tension of thought, would have been required by the poet. Such parts, once recited and admired, became known and learned by a hundred professional bards, and were thus orally published, as it were, in detached sections, years perhaps before the work was completed.

All that is said, therefore, about the difficulty of composing so long a poem without writing materials is but a jargon of words. Suppose no writing materials existed, yet, as soon as portions of a few hundred lines at a time were committed to the memory of other minstrels, the author would, in those minstrels, have living books whereby to refresh his memory, and could even, by their help, polish and amend what was already composed. It would not then have been necessary for the poet himself perfectly and verbally to remember the whole work. He had his tablets of reference in the hearts and lips of others, and even, if it were necessary that he himself should retain the entire composition, the constant habit of recital, the constant exercise of memory, would render such a task by no means impracticable or unprecedented. As for the unity of the poem, thus composed, it would have been, as it is, the unity, not of technical rules and pedantic criticism, but the unity of interest, character, imagery, and thought—a unity which required no written references to maintain it, but which was the essential quality of one master-mind, and ought to be, to all plain men, an irrefragable proof that one mind alone conceived and executed the work.

IV. So much for the alleged improbability of one author for the Iliad. But with what face can these critics talk of "probability", when, in order to get rid of one Homer, they ask us to believe in twenty! Can our wildest imagination form more monstrous hypotheses than these, viz., that several poets, all possessed of the very highest order of genius (never before or since surpassed), lived in the same age—that that genius was so exactly similar in each, that we cannot detect in the thoughts, the imagery, the conception and treatment of character, human and divine, as manifest in each, the least variety in these wonderful minds—that out of the immense store of their national legends, they all agreed in selecting one subject, the war of Troy—that of that subject they all agreed in selecting only one portion of time, from the insult of Achilles to the redemption of the body of Hector—that their different mosaics so nicely fitted one into the other, that by the mere skill of an able editor they were joined into a whole, so symmetrical that the acutest ingenuity of ancient Greece could never discover the imposture[10]—and that,

---

10 Critics, indeed, discover some pretended gaps and interpolations; but these, if conceded, are no proof against the unity of Homer; the wonder is, that there should be so few of such interpolations, considering the barbarous age which intervened between their composition and the time in which they were first carefully edited and collected. With more force it is urged against the argument in favour of the unity of Homer, derived from the unity of the style and character, that there are passages which modern critics agree to be additions to the original poems, made centuries afterward, and yet unsuspected by the ancients; and that in these additions—such as the last books of the Iliad, with many others less important—the Homeric unity of style and character is still sustained. We may answer, however, that, in the first place, we have a right to be sceptical as to these discoveries—many of them rest on very insufficient critical grounds; in the second place, if we grant them, it is one thing whether a forged addition be introduced into a poem, and another thing whether the poem be *all additions*; in the third place, we may observe, that successful imitations of the style and characters of an author, however great, may be made many centuries afterward with tolerable ease, and by a very inferior genius, although, at the time he wrote or sung, it is not easy to suppose that half a dozen or more poets shared his spirit or style. It is a very common scholastic trick to imitate, nowadays, and with considerable felicity, the style of the greatest writers, ancient and modern. But the unity of Homer does not depend on the question whether imitative forgeries were introduced into a great poem, but whether a multitude of great poets combined in one school on one subject. An ingenious student of Shakespeare, or the older dramatists, might impose upon the public credulity a new scene, or even a new play, as belonging to Shakespeare, but would that be any proof that a company of Shakespeares combined in the production of Macbeth? I own, by the way, that I am a little doubtful as to our acumen in ascertaining what is Homeric and what is not, seeing that Schlegel, after devoting half a life to Shakespeare (whose works are composed in a living language, the authenticity of each of which works a living nation can attest), nevertheless attributes to that poet a catalogue of plays, of which Shakespeare is perfectly innocent!—but, to be sure, Steevens does the same!

of all these poets, so miraculous in their genius, no single name, save that of Homer, was recorded by the general people to whom they sung, or claimed by the peculiar tribe whose literature they ought to have immortalized? If everything else were wanting to prove the unity of Homer, this prodigious extravagance of assumption, into which a denial of that unity has driven men of no common learning and intellect, would be sufficient to establish it.

Third:

> That if the Odyssey be counted, the improbability is doubled; that if we add, upon the authority of Thucydides and Aristotle the Hymns and Margites, not to say the Batrachomyomachia, that which was improbable becomes morally impossible.

Were these last-mentioned poems Homer's, there would yet be nothing improbable in the invention and composition of minor poems without writing materials; and the fact of his having composed one long poem throws no difficulty in the way of his composing short ones. We have already seen that the author need not himself have remembered them all his life. But this argument is not honest, for the critics who have produced it agree in the same breath, when it suits their purpose, that the Hymns, &c., are not Homer's —and in this I concur with their, and the almost universal, opinion.

The remaining part of the analysis of the hostile argument has already been disposed of in connexion with the first proposition.

It now remains to say a few words upon the authorship of the Odyssey.

V. The question, whether or not the two epics of the Iliad and Odyssey were the works of the same poet, is very different one from that which we have just discussed. Distinct and separate, indeed, are the inquiries whether Greece might produce, at certain intervals of time, two great epic poets, selecting opposite subjects and whether Greece produced a score or two of great poets, from whose desultory remains the mighty whole of the Iliad was arranged. Even the ancients of the Alexandrine school did not attribute the Odyssey to the author of the Iliad. The theme selected—the manners described —the mythological spirit—are all widely different in the two works, and one is evidently of more recent composition than the other. But, for my own part, I do not think it has been yet clearly established that all these acknowledged differences are incompatible with the same authorship. If the Iliad were written in youth, the travels of the poet, the change of mind produced by years and experience, the facility with which an ancient Greek changed or remodelled his pliant mythology, the rapidity with which (in the quick development of civilization in Greece) important changes in society and manners were wrought, might all concur in producing, from the mature age of the poet, a poem very different to that which he composed in youth. And the various undetected interpolations and alterations supposed to be foisted into the Odyssey may have originated such detailed points of difference as present the graver obstacles to this conjecture. Regarding the Iliad and Odyssey as wholes, they are so analogous in all the highest and rarest attributes of genius, that it is almost as impossible to imagine two Homers as it is two Shakespeares. Nor is there such a contrast between the Iliad and the Odyssey as there is between any one play of Shakespeare's and another.[11] Still, I should warn the general reader, that the utmost opposition that can reasonably and effectually be made to those who assign to different authors these several epics, limits itself rather to doubt than to denial.

VI. It is needless to criticize these immortal masterpieces; not that criticism upon them is yet exhausted—not that a most useful, and even novel analysis of their merits and character may not yet be performed, nor that the most striking and brilliant proofs of the unity of each poem, separately considered, may not be established by one who shall, with fitting powers, undertake the delightful task of deducing the individuality of the poet from the individualizing character of his creations, and the peculiar attributes of his genius. With human works, as with the divine, the main proof of the unity of the author is in his fidelity to himself:—not then as a superfluous, but as far too lengthened and episodical a labour, if worthily performed, do I forego at present a critical survey of the two poems popularly ascribed to Homer.

The early genius of Greece devoted itself largely to subjects similar to those which employed the Homeric muse. At a later period—probably dating at the Alexandrian age—a vast collection of ancient poems was arranged into what is termed the "Epic Cycle"; these commenced at the Theogony, and concluded with the adventures of Telemachus. Though no longer extant, the Cyclic poems enjoyed considerable longevity. The greater part were composed between the years 775 BC and 566 BC. They were extant in the time of Proclus (AD 450); the eldest, therefore, endured at least twelve, the most recent ten centuries;—save a few scattered lines, their titles alone remain, solitary tokens, yet floating above the dark oblivion which has swept over the epics of thirty bards! But, by the common assent, alike of the critics and the multitude, none of these approached the remote age, still less the transcendent merits, of the Homeric poems.

VII. But, of earlier date than these disciples of Homer, is a poetry of a class fundamentally distinct from the Homeric, viz., the collection attributed to Hesiod. Of one of these only, a rustic and homely poem called "Works and Days", was Hesiod considered the author by his immediate country-men (the Bœotians of Helicon); but the more general belief assigned to the fertility of his genius a variety of other works, some of which, if we may

---

11 That Pisistratus or his son, assisted by the poets of his day, did more than collect, arrange, and amend poems already in high repute, we have not only no authority to suppose, but much evidence to contradict. Of the true services of Pisistratus to Homer, more hereafter.

judge by the titles, aimed at a loftier vein.[12] And were he only the author of the "Works and Days"—a poem of very insignificant merit[13]—it would be scarcely possible to account for the high estimation in which Hesiod was held by the Greeks, often compared, and sometimes preferred, to the mighty and majestic Homer. We must either, then, consider Hesiod as the author of many writings superior perhaps to what we now possess, or, as is more plausibly and popularly supposed by modern critics, the representative and type, as it were, of a great school of national poetry. And it has been acutely suggested that, viewing the pastoral and lowly occupation he declares himself to pursue[14] combined with the subjects of his muse, and the place of his birth, we may believe the name of Hesiod to have been the representative of the poetry, not of the victor lords, but of the conquered people, expressive of their pursuits, and illustrative of their religion. This will account for the marked and marvellous difference between the martial and aristocratic strain of Homer and the peaceful and rustic verse of Hesiod,[15] as well as for the distinction no less visible between the stirring mythology of the one and the thoughtful theogony of the other. If this hypothesis be accepted, the Hesiodic era might very probably have commenced before the Homeric (although what is now ascribed to Hesiod is evidently of later date than the Iliad and the Odyssey). And Hesiod is to Homer what the Pelasgic genius was to the Hellenic.[16]

VIII. It will be obvious to all who study what I may call the natural history of poetry, that short hymns or songs must long have preceded the gigantic compositions of Homer. Linus and Thamyris, and, more disputably, Orpheus, are recorded to have been the precursors of Homer, though the poems ascribed to them (some of which still remain) were of much later date. Almost coeval with the Grecian gods were doubtless religious hymns in their honour. And the germ of the great lyrical poetry that we now possess was, in the rude chants of the warlike Dorians, to that Apollo who was no less the Inspirer than the Protector. The religion of the Greeks preserved and dignified the

---

12 "The descent of Theseus with Pirithous into hell", &c.—Paus., ix. 31.

13 Especially if with the Bœotians we are to consider the most poetical passage (the introductory lines to the muses) a spurious interpolation.

14 A herdsman.

15 I cannot omit a tradition recorded by Pausanias. A leaden table near the fountain was shown by the Bœotians as that on which the "Works and Days" *was written*. The poems of Hesiod certainly do not appear so adapted to recital as perusal. Yet, by the most plausible chronology, they were only composed about one hundred years after those of Homer!

16 The Aones, Hyantes, and other tribes, which I consider part of the great Pelasgic family, were expelled from Bœotia by Thracian hordes. They afterward returned in the time of the Dorian emigration. Some of the population must, however, have remained—the peasantry of the land; and in Hesiod we probably possess the national poetry, and arrive at the national religion, of the old Pelasgi.

poetry it created; and the bard, "beloved by gods as men", became invested, as well with a sacred character as a popular fame. Beneath that cheerful and familiar mythology, even the comic genius sheltered its licence, and found its subjects. Not only do the earliest of the comic dramatists seem to have sought in mythic fables their characters and plots, but, far before the DRAMA itself arose in any of the Grecian states, comic recital prepared the way for comic representation. In the eighth book of the Odyssey, the splendid Alcinous and the pious Ulysses listen with delight to the story, even broadly ludicrous, how Vulcan nets and exposes Venus and her war-god lover—

> All heaven beholds imprisoned as they lie,
> And unextinguished laughter shakes the sky.

And this singular and well-known effusion shows not only how grave and reverent an example Epicharmus had for his own audacious portraiture of the infirmities of the Olympian family, but how immemorially and how deeply fixed in the popular spirit was the disposition to draw from the same source the elements of humour and of awe.

But, however ancient the lyrical poetry of Greece, its masterpieces of art were composed long subsequent to the Homeric poems; and, no doubt, greatly influenced by acquaintance with those fountains of universal inspiration. I think it might be shown that lyrical poetry developed itself, in its more elaborate form, earliest in those places where the poems of Homer are most likely to have been familiarly known.

The peculiar character of the Greek lyrical poetry can only be understood by remembering its inseparable connexion with music; and the general application of both, not only to religious but political purposes. The Dorian states regarded the lyre and the song as powerful instruments upon the education, the manners, and the national character of their citizens. With them these arts were watched and regulated by the law, and the poet acquired something of the social rank, and aimed at much of the moral design, of a statesman and a legislator while, in the Ionian states, the wonderful stir and agitation, the changes and experiments in government, the rapid growth of luxury, commerce, and civilization, afforded to a poetry which was not, as with us, considered a detached, unsocial, and solitary art, but which was associated with every event of actual life—occasions of vast variety—themes of universal animation. The eloquence of poetry will always be more exciting in its appeals—the love for poetry always more diffused throughout a people, in proportion as it is less written than recited. How few, even at this day, will read a poem!—what crowds will listen to a song! Recitation transfers the stage of effect from the closet to the multitude—the public becomes an audience, the poet an orator. And when we remember that the poetry thus created, embodying the most vivid, popular, animated subjects of interest, was united with all the pomp of festival and show—all the grandest, the most elaborate, and artful effects of music—we may understand why the true genius of lyrical composition has passed for ever away from the modern world.

As early as between BC 708 and 605, Archilochus brought to perfection a poetry worthy of loftier passions than those which mostly animated his headstrong and angry genius. In 625 (thirty-one years before the legislation of Solon) flourished Arion, the Lesbian, who, at Corinth, carried to extraordinary perfection the heroic adaptation of song to choral music. In 611 flourished the Sicilian, Stesichorus—no unworthy rival of Arion;—while simultaneously, in strains less national and Grecian, and more resembling the inspiration of modern minstrels, Alcæus vented his burning and bitter spirit;—and Sappho (whose chaste and tender muse it was reserved for the chivalry of a northern student, five-and-twenty centuries after the hand was cold and the tongue was mute, to vindicate from the longest-continued calumny that genius ever endured)[17] gave to the most ardent of human passions the most delicate colouring of female sentiment. Perhaps, of all that Greece has bequeathed to us, nothing is so perfect in its concentration of real feeling as the fragments of Sappho. In one poem of a few lines—nor that, alas! transmitted to us complete—she has given a picture of the effect of love upon one who loves, to which volumes of the most eloquent description could scarcely add a single new touch of natural pathos—so subtle is it, yet so simple. I cannot pass over in silence the fragments of Mimnermus— they seem of an order so little akin to the usual character of Grecian poetry; there is in them a thoughtful though gloomy sadness, that belongs rather to the deep northern imagination than the brilliant fancies of the West; their melancholy is mixed with something half intellectual—half voluptuous— indicative of the mournful but interesting wisdom of satiety. Mimnermus is a principal model of the Latin elegiac writers—and Propertius compares his love verses with those of Homer. Mimnermus did not invent the elegiac form (for it was first applied to warlike inspiration by another Ionian poet, Callinus); but he seems the founder of what we now call the elegiac spirit in its association of the sentiment of melancholy with the passion of love.

IX. While such was the state of POETRY in Greece—torpid in the Ionian Athens, but already prodigal in her kindred states of Asia and the Isles;— gravely honoured, rather than produced, in Sparta;—splendidly welcomed, rather than home-born, in Corinth;—the Asiatic colonies must also claim the honour of the advance of the sister arts. But in architecture the Dorian states of European Greece, Sicyon, Ægina, and the luxurious Corinth were no unworthy competitors with Ionia.

In the heroic times, the Homeric poems, especially the Odyssey, attest the refinement and skill to which many of the imitative arts of Grecian civilization had attained. In embroidery, the high-born occupation of Helen

17 Welcker.

and Penelope, were attempted the most complex and difficult designs; and it is hard to suppose that these subjects could have been wrought upon garments with sufficient fidelity to warrant the praise of a poet who evidently wrote from experience of what he had seen, if the art of DRAWING had not been also carried to some excellence—although to PAINTING itself the poet makes none but dubious and obscure allusions. Still, if, on the one hand,[18] in embroidery, and upon arms (as the shield of Achilles), delineation in its more complex and minute form was attempted,—and if, on the other hand, the use of colours was known (which it was, as applied not only to garments but to ivory), it could not have been long before two such kindred elements of the same art were united. Although it is contended by many that rude stones or beams were the earliest objects of Grecian worship, and though it is certain that in several places such emblems of the Deity preceded the worship of images, yet to the superstitious art of the rude Pelasgi in their earliest age, uncouth and half-formed statues of Hermes are attributed, and the idol is commemorated by traditions almost as antique as those which attest the sanctity of the *fetiche*.[19] In the Homeric age, SCULPTURE in metals, and on a large scale, was certainly known. By the door of Alcinous, the king of an island in the Ionian Sea, stand rows of dogs in gold and silver—in his hall, upon pedestals, are golden statues of boys holding torches; and that such sculpture was even then dedicated to the gods is apparent by a well-known passage in the earlier poem of the Iliad; which represents Theano, the Trojan priestess of Minerva, placing the offering of Hecuba upon the knees of the statue of the goddess. How far, however, such statues could be called works of art, or how far they were wrought by native Greeks, it is impossible to determine.[20] Certain it is that the memorable and gigantic advance in the art of sculpture was not made till about the fiftieth Olympiad (BC 580), when Dipænus and Scyllis first obtained celebrity in works in marble (wood

---

18 The deadly signs which are traced by Prœtus on the tablets of which Bellerophon was the bearer, and which are referred to in the Iliad, are generally supposed by the learned to have been pictorial, and, as it were, hieroglyphical figures; my own belief, and the easiest interpretation of the passage, is, that they were alphabetical characters—in a word, writing, not painting.

19 Pausanias, i. 27, speaks of a wooden statue in the Temple of Polias, in Athens, said to have been the gift of Cecrops; and, with far more claim to belief, in the previous chapter he tells us that the most holy of all the images was a statue of Minerva, which, by the common consent of all the towns before incorporated in one city, was dedicated in the citadel, or Πόλις. Tradition, therefore, carried the date of this statue beyond the time of Theseus. Plutarch also informs us that Theseus himself, when he ordained divine honours to be paid to Ariadne, ordered two little statues to be made of her—one of silver and one of brass.

20 All that Homer calls the work of Vulcan, such as the dogs in the palace of Alcinous, &c., we may suppose to be the work of foreigners. A poet could scarcely attribute to the gods a work that his audience knew an artificer in their own city had made!

and metals were the earliest materials of sculpture). The great improvements in the art seem to have been coeval with the substitution of the naked for the draped figure. Beauty, and ease, and grace, and power, were the result of the anatomical study of the human form. ARCHITECTURE has bequeathed to us, in the Pelasgic and Cyclopean remains, sufficient to indicate the massive strength it early acquired in parts of Greece. In the Homeric times, the intercourse with Asia had already given something of lightness to the older forms. Columns are constantly introduced into the palaces of the chiefs, profuse metallic ornaments decorate the walls; and the Homeric palaces, with their cornices gayly inwrought with blue—their pillars of silver on bases of brass, rising amid vines and fruit-trees,—even allowing for all the exaggerations of the poet,—dazzle the imagination with much of the gaudiness and glitter of an oriental city.[21] At this period Athens receives from Homer the epithet of "broad-streeted": and it is by no means improbable that the city of the Attic king might have presented to a traveller, in the time of Homer, a more pleasing general appearance than in its age of fame, when, after the Persian devastations, its stately temples rose above narrow and irregular streets, and the jealous effects of democracy forbade to the mansions of individual nobles that striking pre-eminence over the houses of the commonalty which would naturally mark the distinction of wealth and rank, in a monarchical, or even an oligarchical government.

X. About the time on which we now enter, the extensive commerce and free institutions of the Ionian colonies had carried all the arts just referred to far beyond the Homeric time. And, in addition to the activity and development of the intellect in all its faculties which progressed with the extensive trade and colonization of Miletus (operating upon the sensitive, inquiring, and poetical temperament of the Ionian population), a singular event, which suddenly opened to Greece familiar intercourse with the arts and lore of Egypt, gave considerable impetus to the whole Grecian MIND.

In our previous brief survey of the state of the oriental world, we have seen that Egypt, having been rent into twelve principalities, had been again united under a single monarch. The ambitious and fortunate Psammetichus was enabled, by the swords of some Ionian and Carian adventurers (who, bound on a voyage of plunder, had been driven upon the Egyptian shores), not only to regain his own dominion, from which he had been expelled by the jealousy of his comrades, but to acquire the sole sovereignty of Egypt. In gratitude for their services, Psammetichus conferred upon his wild allies certain lands at the Pelusian mouth of the Nile, and obliged some Egyptian children to learn the Grecian language;—from these children descended a class of interpreters, that long afterward established the facilities of familiar intercourse between Greece and Egypt. Whatever, before that time, might have

21 See Odyssey, vii.

been the migrations of Egyptians into Greece, these were the first Greeks whom the Egyptians received among themselves. Thence poured into Greece, in one full and continuous stream, the Egyptian influences, hitherto partial and unfrequent.[22]

In the same reign, according to Strabo, the Asiatic Greeks obtained a settlement at Naucratis, the ancient emporium of Egypt; and the communication, once begun, rapidly increased, until in the subsequent time of Amasis we find the Ionians, the Dorians, the Æolians of Asia, and even the people of Ægina and Samos,[23] building temples and offering worship amid the jealous and mystic priestcrafts of the Nile. This familiar and advantageous intercourse with a people whom the Greeks themselves considered the wisest on the earth, exercised speedy and powerful effect upon their religion and their arts:—in the first it operated immediately upon their modes of divination and their mystic rites—in the last, the influence was less direct. It is true, that they probably learned from the Egyptians many technical rules in painting and in sculpture; they learned how to cut the marble and to blend the colours, but their own genius taught them how to animate the block and vivify the image. We have seen already, that before this event, art had attained to a certain eminence among the Greeks—fortunately, therefore, what they now acquired was not the *foundation* of their lore. Grafted on a Grecian stock, every shoot bore Grecian fruit; and what was borrowed from mechanism was reproduced in beauty.[24] As with the arts, so with the SCIENCES; we have

22 The effect of the arts, habits, and manners of a foreign country is immeasurably more important upon us if we visit that country, than if we merely receive visits from its natives. For example, the number of French emigrants who crowded our shores at the time of the French revolution very slightly influenced English customs, &c. But the effect of the French upon us when, after the peace, our own countrymen flocked to France, was immense.

23 Herod., ii. 178.

24 Grecian architecture seems to have been more free from obligation to any technical secrets of Egyptian art than Grecian statuary or painting. For, in the first place, it is more than doubtful whether the Doric order was not invented in European Greece long prior to the reign of Psammetichus (The earliest known temple at Corinth is supposed by Col. Leake to bear date BC 800, about one hundred and thirty years before the reign of Psammetichus in Egypt.); and, in the second place, it is evident that the first hints and rudiments both of the Doric and the Ionic order were borrowed, not from buildings of the massive and perennial materials of Egyptian architecture, but from wooden edifices; growing into perfection as stone and marble were introduced, and the greater difficulty and expense of the workmanship insensibly imposed severer thought and more elaborate rules upon the architect. But I cannot agree with Müller and others, that because the first hints of the Doric order were taken from wooden buildings, therefore the first invention was necessarily with the Dorians, since many of the Asiatic cities were built chiefly of wood. It seems to me most probable that Asia gave the first notions of these beautiful forms, and that the Greeks carried them to perfection before the Asiatics, not only from their keen perception of the graceful, but because they earlier made a general use of stone. We learn from Herodotus that the gorgeous Sardis was built chiefly of wood, at a time when the marble of Paros was a common material of the Grecian temples.

reason to doubt whether the Egyptian sages, whose minds were swathed and bandaged in the cerements of hereditary rules, never to swell out of the slavery of castes, had any very sound and enlightened philosophy to communicate: their wisdom was probably exaggerated by the lively and credulous Greeks, awed by the mysticism of the priests, the grandeur of the cities, the very rigidity, so novel to them, of imposing and antique custom. What, then, was the real benefit of the intercourse? Not so much in satisfying as in arousing and stimulating the curiosity of knowledge. Egypt, to the Greeks, was as America to Europe—the Egyptians taught them little, but Egypt much. And that that which the Egyptians did directly communicate, was rather the material for improvement than the improvement itself, this one gift is an individual example and a general type;—the Egyptians imparted to the Greeks the use of the papyrus—the most easy and popular material for writing; we are thus indebted to Egypt for a contrivance that has done much to preserve to us—much, perhaps, to create for us—a Plato and an Aristotle; but for the thoughts of Aristotle and Plato we are indebted to Greece alone:—the material Egyptian—the manufacture Greek.

XI. The use of the papyrus had undoubtedly much effect upon the formation of prose composition in Greece, but it was by no means an instantaneous one. At the period on which we now enter (about BC 600), the first recorded prose Grecian writer had not composed his works. The wide interval between prose in its commencement and poetry in its perfection is peculiarly Grecian; many causes conspired to produce it, but the principal one was, that works, if written, being not the less composed to be recited, not read—were composed to interest and delight, rather than formally to instruct. Poetry was, therefore, so obviously the best means to secure the end of the author, that we cannot wonder to find that channel of appeal universally chosen; the facility with which the language formed itself into verse, and the licence that appears to have been granted to the gravest to assume a poetical diction without attempting the poetical spirit, allowed even legislators and moralists to promulgate precepts and sentences in the rhythm of a Homer and a Hesiod. And since laws were not written before the time of Draco, it was doubly necessary that they should be cast in that fashion by which words are most durably impressed on the memory of the multitude. Even on Solon's first appearance in public life, when he inspires the Athenians to prosecute the war with Megara, he addresses the passions of the crowd, not by an oration, but a poem; and in a subsequent period, when prose composition had become familiar, it was still in verse that Hipparchus communicated his moral apophthegms. The origin of prose in Greece is, therefore, doubly interesting as an epoch, not only in the intellectual, but also in the social state. It is clear that it would not commence until a *reading public* was created; and until, amid the poetical many, had sprung up the grave and studious few. Accordingly, philosophy, orally delivered, preceded prose composition—and Thales taught before Pherecydes wrote.[25] To the superficial it may seem surprising that literature, as distinct from poetry, should commence with the most subtle and laborious direction of the human intellect: yet so it was, not only in Greece, but almost universally. In nearly all countries, speculative conjecture or inquiry is the first successor to poetry. In India, in China, in the East, some dim philosophy is the characteristic of the earliest works—sometimes inculcating maxims of morality—sometimes allegorically shadowing forth, sometimes even plainly expressing, the opinions of the author on the mysteries of life—of nature—of the creation. Even with the moderns, the dawn of letters broke on the torpor of the dark ages of the North in speculative disquisition; the Arabian and the Aristotelian subtleties engaged the attention of the earliest cultivators of modern prose (as separated from poetic fiction), and the first instinct of the awakened reason was to grope through the misty twilight after TRUTH. Philosophy precedes even history, men were desirous of solving the enigmas of the world before they disentangled from tradition the chronicles of its former habitants.

If we examine the ways of an infant we shall cease to wonder at those of an infant civilization. Long before we can engage the curiosity of the child in the history of England—long before we can induce him to listen with pleasure to our stories even of Poitiers and Cressy—and (a fortiori) long before he can be taught an interest in Magna Charta and the Bill of Rights, he will of his own accord question us of the phenomena of nature—inquire how he himself came into the world—delight to learn something of the God we tell him to adore—and find in the rainbow and the thunder, in the meteor and the star, a thousand subjects of eager curiosity and reverent wonder. The why perpetually torments him;—every child is born a philosopher!—the child is the analogy of a people yet in childhood.[26]

25 Thales was one of the seven wise men, BC 586, when Pherecydes of Syrus, the first prose writer, was about fourteen years old. Mr Clinton fixes the acme of Pherecydes about BC 572. Cadmus of Miletus flourished BC 530.

26 To this solution of the question, why literature should generally commence with attempts at philosophy, may be added another:—when written first breaks upon oral communication, the *reading* public must necessarily be extremely confined. In many early nations, that reading public would be composed of the caste of priests; in this case philosophy would be cramped by superstition. In Greece, there being no caste of priests, philosophy embraced those studious minds addicted to a species of inquiry which rejected the poetical form, as well as the poetical spirit. It may be observed, that the more limited the reading public, the more abstruse are generally prose compositions; as readers increase, literature goes back to the fashion of oral communication; for if the reciter addressed the multitude in the earlier age, so the writer addresses a multitude in the later; literature, therefore, commences with poetical fiction, and usually terminates with prose fiction. It was so in the ancient world—it will be so with England and France. The harvest of novels is, I fear, a sign of the approaching exhaustion of the soil.

XII. It may follow as a corollary from this problem, that the Greeks of themselves arrived at the stage of philosophical inquiry without any very important and direct assistance from the lore of Egypt and the East. That lore, indeed, awakened the desire, but it did not guide the spirit of speculative research. And the main cause why philosophy at once assumed with the Greeks a character distinct from that of the Oriental world, I have already intimated,[27] in the absence of a segregated and privileged religious caste. Philosophy thus fell into the hands of sages, not of priests. And whatever the Ionian states (the cradle of Grecian wisdom) received from Egypt or the East, they received to reproduce in new and luxuriant prodigality. The Ionian sages took from an older wisdom not dogmas never to be questioned, but suggestions carefully to be examined. It thus fortunately happened that the deeper and maturer philosophy of Greece proper had a kind of intermedium between the systems of other nations and its own. The eastern knowledge was borne to Europe through the Greek channels of Asiatic colonies, and became Hellenized as it passed. Thus, what was a certainty in the East, became a proposition in Ionia, and ultimately a doubt at Athens. In Greece, indeed, as everywhere, religion was connected with the first researches of philosophy. From the fear of the gods, to question of the nature of the gods, is an easy transition. The abundance and variety of popular superstitions served but to stimulate curiosity as to their origin; and since in Egypt the sole philosophers were the priests, a Greek could scarcely converse with an Egyptian on the articles of his religion without discussing also the principles of his philosophy. Whatever opinions the Greek might then form and promulge, being sheltered beneath no jealous and prescriptive priestcraft, all had unfettered right to canvass and dispute them, till by little and little discussion ripened into science.

The distinction, in fine, between the Greeks and their contemporaries was this: if they were not the only people that philosophized, they were the only people that said whatever they pleased about philosophy. Their very plagiarism from the philosophy of other creeds was fortunate, inasmuch as it presented nothing hostile to the national superstition. Had they disputed about the nature of Jupiter, or the existence of Apollo, they might have been persecuted, but they could start at once into disquisitions upon the eternity of matter, or the providence of a pervading mind.

XIII. This spirit of innovation and discussion, which made the characteristic of the Greeks, is noted by Diodorus. "Unlike the Chaldæans", he observes, "with whom philosophy is delivered from sire to son, and all other employment rejected by its cultivators, the Greeks come late to the science—take it up for a short time—desert it for a more active means of subsistence—and the few who surrender themselves wholly to it practise for gain, innovate the

27 See Book I ch. I.

most important doctrines, pay no reverence to those that went before, create new sects, establish new theorems, and, by perpetual contradictions, entail perpetual doubts." Those contradictions and those doubts made precisely the reason why the Greeks became the tutors of the world!

There is another characteristic of the Greeks indicated by this remark of Diodorus. Their early philosophers, *not* being exempted from other employments, were not the mere dreamers of the closet and the cell. They were active, practical, stirring men of the world, They were politicians and moralists as well as philosophers. The practical pervaded the ideal, and was, in fact, the salt that preserved it from decay. Thus legislation and science sprung simultaneously into life, and the age of Solon is the age of Thales.

XIV. Of the seven wise men (if we accept that number) who flourished about the same period, six were rulers and statesmen. They were eminent, not as physical, but as moral, philosophers; and their wisdom was in their maxims and apophthegms. They resembled in much the wary and sagacious tyrants of Italy in the middle ages—masters of men's actions by becoming readers of their minds. Of these seven, Periander of Corinth and Cleobulus of Lindus, tyrants in their lives, and cruel in their actions, were, it is said, disowned by the remaining five.[28] But goodness is not the necessary consequence of intellect, and, despite their vices, these princes deserved the epithet of wise. Of Cleobulus we know less than of Periander; but both governed with prosperity, and died in old age. If we except Pisistratus, Periander was the greatest artist of all that able and profound fraternity, who, under the name of tyrants, concentred the energies of their several states, and prepared the democracies by which they were succeeded. Periander's reputed maxims are at variance with his practice; they breathe a spirit of freedom and a love of virtue which may render us suspicious of their authenticity—the more so as they are also attributed to others. Nevertheless, the inconsistency would be natural, for reason makes our opinions, and circumstance shapes our actions. "A democracy is better than a tyranny", is an aphorism imputed to Periander: but when asked why he continued tyrant, he answered, "Because it is dangerous willingly to resist, or unwillingly to be deposed." His principles were republican, his position made him a tyrant. He is said to have fallen into extreme dejection in his old age; perhaps because his tastes and his intellect were at war with his life. Chilo, the Lacedæmonian ephor, is placed also among the seven. His maxims are singularly Dorian—they breathe reverence of the dead and suspicion of the living. "Love", he said (if we may take the authority of Aulus Gellius), "as if you might hereafter hate, and hate as if you might hereafter love." Another favourite sentence of his was,

28 Instead of Periander of Corinth, is (by Plato, and therefore) more popularly, but less justly, ranked Myson of Chene.

"To a surety loss is at hand."[29] A third, "We try gold by the touchstone. Gold is the touchstone of the mind." Bias, of Priene in Ionia, is quoted, in Herodotus, as the author of an advice to the Ionians to quit their country, and found a common city in Sardinia. He seems to have taken an active part in all civil affairs. His reputed maxims are plain and homely—the elementary principles of morals. Mitylene in Lesbos boasted the celebrated Pittacus. He rose to the tyranny of the government by the free voice of the people; enjoyed it ten years, and voluntarily resigned it, as having only borne the dignity while the state required the direction of a single leader. It was a maxim with him, for which he is reproved by Plato, "That to be good is hard." His favourite precept was, "Know occasion": and this he amplified in another (if rightly attributed to him), "To foresee and prevent dangers is the province of the wise—to direct them when they come, of the brave."

XV. Of Solon, the greatest of the seven, I shall hereafter speak at length. I pass now to Thales;—the founder of philosophy, in its scientific sense —the speculative in contradistinction to the moral:—although an ardent republican, Thales alone, of the seven sages, appears to have led a private and studious life. He travelled into Crete, Asia, and at a later period into Egypt. According to Lærtius, Egypt taught him geometry. He is supposed to have derived his astrological notions from Phœnicia. But this he might easily have done without visiting the Phœnician states. Returning to Miletus, he obtained his title of Wise.[30] Much learning has been exhausted upon his doctrines to very little purpose. They were of small value, save as they led to the most valuable of all philosophies—that of experiment. They were not new probably even in Greece,[31] and of their utility the following brief sketch will enable the reader to judge for himself.

29 Attributed also to Thales; Stob., Serm.
30 Aristotle relates (Pol., i.) a singular anecdote of the means whereby this philosopher acquired wealth. His skill in meteorology made him foresee that there would be one season an extraordinary crop of olives. He hired during the previous winter all the oil-presses in Chios and Miletus, employing his scanty fortune in advances to the several proprietors. When the approaching season showed the ripening crops, every man wished to provide olive-presses as quickly as possible; and Thales, having them all, let them at a high price. His monopoly made his fortune, and he showed to his friends, says Aristotle, that it was very easy for philosophers to be rich if they desire it, though such is not their principal desire;—philosophy does not find the same facilities nowadays.
31 Thus Homer is cited in proof of the progenital humidity,

Ὠκεανὸς ὅσπερ γένεσις παντὰς τετύκται;

The Bryant race of speculators would attack us at once with "the spirit moving on the face of the waters". It was not an uncommon opinion in Greece that chaos was first water settling into slime, and then into earth; and there are good but not sufficient reasons to attribute a similar, and of course earlier, notion to the Phœnicians, and still more perhaps to the Indians.

He maintained that water, or rather humidity, was the origin of all things, though he allowed mind or intellect (νοῦς) to be the impelling principle. And one of his arguments in favour of humidity, as rendered to us by Plutarch and Stobæus, is pretty nearly as follows:—"Because fire, even in the sun and the stars, is nourished by vapours proceeding from humidity,—and therefore the whole world consists of the same." Of the world, he supposed the whole to be animated by and full of, the Divinity—its Creator—that in it was no vacuum—that matter was fluid and variable.[32]

He maintained the stars and sun to be earthly, and the moon of the same nature as the sun, but illumined by it. Somewhat more valuable would appear to have been his geometrical science, could we with accuracy attribute to Thales many problems claimed also, and more probably, by Pythagoras and later reasoners. He is asserted to have measured the pyramids by their shadows. He cultivated astronomy and astrology; and Lærtius declares him to have been the first Greek that foretold eclipses. The yet higher distinction has been claimed for Thales of having introduced among his countrymen the doctrine of the immortality of the soul. But this sublime truth, though connected with no theory of future rewards and punishments, was received in Greece long before his time. Perhaps, however, as the expressions of Cicero indicate, Thales might be the first who attempted to give reasons for what was believed. His reasons were, nevertheless, sufficiently crude and puerile; and having declared it the property of the soul to move itself, and other things, he was forced to give a soul to the loadstone, because it moved iron!

These fantastic doctrines examined, and his geometrical or astronomical discoveries dubious, it may be asked, what did Thales effect for philosophy? Chiefly this: he gave *reasons* for *opinions*—he aroused the dormant spirit of inquiry—he did for truths what the legislators of his age did for the people —left them active and stirring to free and vigorous competition. He took Wisdom out of despotism, and placed her in a republic—he was in harmony with the great principle of his age, which was investigation, and not tradition; and thus he became the first example of that great truth—that to think freely is the first step to thinking well. It fortunately happened, too, that his moral theories, however inadequately argued upon, were noble and exalting. He contended for the providence of a God, as well as for the immortality of man. He asserted vice to be the most hateful, virtue the most profitable of all things.[33] He waged war on that vulgar tenacity of life which is the enemy to all that is most spiritual and most enterprising in our natures, and maintained that between life and death there is no difference—the fitting deduction from a belief in the continuous existence of the soul.[34] His especial maxim

32 Plut.; de Plac. Phil.
33 Ap. Stob., Serm.
34 Laert.

was the celebrated precept, "Know thyself." His influence was vigorous and immediate. How far he created philosophy may be doubtful, but he created philosophers. From the prolific intelligence which his fame and researches called into being, sprang a new race of thoughts, which continued in unbroken succession until they begat descendants illustrious and immortal. Without the hardy errors of Thales, Socrates might have spent his life in spoiling marble, Plato might have been only a tenth-rate poet, and Aristotle an intriguing pedagogue.

XVI. With this I close my introductory chapters, and proceed from dissertation into history;—pleased that our general survey of Greece should conclude with an acknowledgement of our obligations to the Ionian colonies. Soon, from the contemplation of those enchanting climes; of the extended commerce and the brilliant genius of the people—the birthplace of the epic and the lyric muse, the first home of history, of philosophy, of art;—soon, from our survey of the rise and splendour of the Asiatic Ionians, we turn to the agony of their struggles—the catastrophe of their fall. Those wonderful children of Greece had something kindred with the precocious intellect that is often the hectic symptom of premature decline. Originating, advancing nearly all which the imagination or the reason can produce, while yet in that social youth which promised a long and a yet more glorious existence— while even their great parent herself had scarcely emerged from the long pupillage of nations, they fell into the feebleness of age! Amid the vital struggles, followed by the palsied and prostrate exhaustion of her Ionian children, the majestic Athens suddenly arose from the obscurity of the past to an empire that can never perish, until heroism shall cease to warm, poetry to delight, and wisdom to instruct the future.

Book II

FROM THE LEGISLATION OF SOLON TO THE BATTLE OF MARATHON, BC 594–BC 490

CHAPTER I

The conspiracy of Cylon—loss of Salamis—first appearance
of Solon—success against the Megarians in the struggle
for Salamis—Cirrhæan war—Epimenides—political state of
Athens—character of Solon—his legislation—general view
of the Athenian constitution

I. The first symptom in Athens of the political crisis which, as in other of
the Grecian states, marked the transition of power from the oligarchic to
the popular party, may be detected in the laws of Draco.
THE CONSPIRACY   Undue severity in the legislature is the ordinary proof of
OF CYLON   a general discontent: its success is rarely lasting enough to
confirm a government—its failure, when confessed, invariably strengthens
a people. Scarcely had these laws been enacted when a formidable conspiracy broke out against the reigning oligarchy.[1] It was during the archonship
of Megacles (a scion of the great Alcmæonid family, which boasted its
descent from Nestor) that the aristocracy was menaced by the ambition of
an aristocrat.

Born of an ancient and powerful house, and possessed of considerable
wealth, Cylon, the Athenian, conceived the design of seizing the citadel, and
rendering himself master of the state. He had wedded the daughter of
Theagenes, tyrant of Megara, and had raised himself into popular reputation
several years before, by a victory in the Olympic Games.

The Delphic oracle was supposed to have inspired him with the design;
but it is at least equally probable that the oracle was consulted after the
design had been conceived. The divine voice declared that Cylon should
occupy the citadel on the greatest festival of Jupiter. By the event it does not
appear, however, that he selected the proper occasion. Taking advantage of
an Olympic year, when many of the citizens were gone to the games, and
assisted with troops by his father-in-law, he seized the citadel. Whatever

---

1 According to Clinton's chronology, BC 620, viz., one year after the legislation of Draco.
   This emendation of dates formerly received throws considerable light upon the causes of
   the conspiracy, which perhaps took its strength from the unpopularity and failure of Draco's
   laws Following the very faulty chronology which pervades his whole work, Mr Mitford
   makes the attempt of Cylon *precede* the legislation of Draco.

might have been his hopes of popular support—and there is reason to believe that he in some measure calculated upon it—the time was evidently unripe for the convulsion, and the attempt was unskilfully planned. The Athenians, under Megacles and the other archons, took the alarm, and in a general body blockaded the citadel. But they grew weary of the length of the siege; many of them fell away, and the contest was abandoned to the archons, with full power to act according to their judgment. So supine in defence of the liberties of the state are a people who have not yet obtained liberty for themselves!

II. The conspirators were reduced by the failure of food and water. Cylon and his brother privately escaped. Of his adherents, some perished by famine, others betook themselves to the altars in the citadel, claiming, as suppliants, the right of sanctuary. The guards of the magistrates, seeing the suppliants about to expire from exhaustion, led them from the altar and put them to death. But some of the number were not so scrupulously slaughtered—massacred around the altars of the Furies. The horror excited by a sacrilege so atrocious may easily be conceived by those remembering the humane and reverent superstition of the Greeks:—the indifference of the people to the contest was changed at once into detestation of the victors. A conspiracy, hitherto impotent, rose at once into power by the circumstances of its defeat. Megacles—his whole house—all who had assisted in the impiety, were stigmatized with the epithet of "execrable". The faction, or friends of Cylon, became popular from the odium of their enemies—the city was distracted by civil commotions—by superstitious apprehensions of the divine anger—and, as the excesses of one party are the aliment of the other, so the abhorrence of sacrilege effaced the remembrance of a treason.

III. The petty state of Megara, which, since the earlier ages, had, from the dependent of Athens, grown up to the dignity of her rival, taking advantage of the internal dissensions in the latter city, succeeded in wresting from the Athenian government the isle of Salamis. It was not, however, without bitter and repeated struggles that Athens at last submitted to the surrender of the isle. But, after signal losses and defeats, as nothing is ever more odious to the multitude than unsuccessful war, so the popular feeling was such as to induce the government to enact a decree, by which it was forbidden, upon pain of death, to propose reasserting the Athenian claims. But a law, evidently the offspring of a momentary passion of disgust or despair, and which could not but have been wrung with reluctance from a government, whose conduct it tacitly arraigned, and whose military pride it must have mortified, was not likely to bind, for any length of time, a gallant aristocracy and a susceptible people. Many of the younger portion of the community, pining at the dishonour of their country, and eager for enterprise, were secretly inclined to countenance any stratagem that might induce the reversal of the decree.

LOSS OF SALAMIS

At this time there went a report through the city, that a man of distinguished birth, indirectly descended from the last of the Athenian kings, had
incurred the consecrating misfortune of insanity. Suddenly
this person appeared in the market-place, wearing the
peculiar badge that distinguished the sick.[2] His friends
were, doubtless, well prepared for his appearance—a crowd, some predisposed
to favour, others attracted by curiosity, were collected round him—and,
ascending to the stone from which the heralds made their proclamations,
he began to recite aloud a poem upon the loss of Salamis, boldly reproving
the cowardice of the people, and inciting them again to war. His supposed
insanity protected him from the law—his rank, reputation, and the circumstance of his being himself a native of Salamis, conspired to give his exhortations a powerful effect, and the friends he had secured to back his attempt
loudly proclaimed their applauding sympathy with the spirit of the address.
The name of the pretended madman was Solon, son of Execestides, the
descendant of Codrus.

First appearance of Solon

Plutarch (followed by Mr Mitford, Mr Thirlwall, and other modern
historians) informs us that the celebrated Pisistratus then proceeded to
exhort the assembly, and to advocate the renewal of the war—an account
that is liable to this slight objection, that Pisistratus at that time was not
born![3]

2 A cap.
3 The expedition against Salamis under Solon preceded the arrival of Epimenides at Athens,
which was in 596. The legislation of Solon was BC 594—the first tyranny of Pisistratus
BC 560: viz., thirty-four years after Solon's legislation, and at least thirty-seven years
after Solon's expedition to Salamis. But Pisistratus lived thirty-three years after his first
usurpation, so that, if he had acted in the first expedition to Salamis, he would have lived
to an age little short of one hundred, and been considerably past eighty at the time of his
third most brilliant and most energetic government! The most probable date for the birth
of Pisistratus is that assigned by Mr Clinton, about BC 595, somewhat subsequent to
Solon's expedition to Salamis, and only about a year prior to Solon's legislation. According
to this date, Pisistratus would have been about sixty-eight at the time of his death. The
error of Plutarch evidently arose from his confounding two wars with Megara for Salamis,
attended with similar results—the first led by Solon, the second by Pisistratus. I am the
more surprised that Mr Thirlwall should have fallen into the error of making Pisistratus
contemporary with Solon in this affair, because he would fix the date of the recovery of
Salamis at BC 604 (see note to Thirlwall's Greece, vol. ii, p. 25), and would suppose Solon
to be about thirty-two at that time (viz., twenty-six years old in BC 612). (See Thirlwall,
vol. ii, p. 23, note.) Now, as Pisistratus could not have been well less than twenty-one,
to have taken so prominent a share as that ascribed to him by Plutarch and his modern
followers in the expedition, he must, according to such hypothesis, have been only eleven
years younger than Solon, have perpetrated his first tyranny just before Solon died of
old age, and married a second wife when he was near eighty! Had this been the case,
the relations of the lady could not reasonably have been angry that the marriage was not
consummated!

IV. The stratagem and the eloquence of Solon produced its natural effect upon his spirited and excitable audience, and the public enthusiasm per-

SUCCESS AGAINST THE ME-
GARIANS IN THE STRUGGLE
FOR SALAMIS

mitted the oligarchical government to propose and effect the repeal of the law.[4] An expedition was decreed and planned, and Solon was invested with its command. It was but a brief struggle to recover the little island of Salamis: with one galley of thirty oars and a number of fishing-craft, Solon made for Salamis, took a vessel sent to reconnoitre by the Megarians, manned it with his own soldiers, who were ordered to return to the city with such caution as might prevent the Megarians discovering the exchange, on board, of foes for friends; and then with the rest of his force he engaged the enemy by land, while those in the ship captured the city. In conformity with this version of the campaign (which I have selected in preference to another recorded by Plutarch), an Athenian ship once a year passed silently to Salamis—the inhabitants rushed clamouring down to meet it—an armed man leaped ashore, and ran shouting to the Promontory of Sciradium, near which was long existent a temple erected and dedicated to Mars by Solon.

But the brave and resolute Megarians were not men to be disheartened by a single reverse; they persisted in the contest—losses were sustained on either side, and at length both states agreed to refer their several claims on the sovereignty of the island to the decision of Spartan arbiters. And this appeal from arms to arbitration is a proof how much throughout Greece had extended that spirit of civilization which is but an extension of the sense of justice. Both parties sought to ground their claims upon ancient and traditional rights. Solon is said to have assisted the demand of his countrymen by a quotation, asserted to have been spuriously interpolated from Homer's catalogue of the ships, which appeared to imply the ancient connexion of Salamis and Athens;[5] and whether or not this was actually done, the very tradition that it was done, nearly half a century before the first usurpation of Pisistratus, is a proof of the great authority of Homer in that age, and how largely the services rendered by Pisistratus, many years afterward, to the

---

4 We cannot suppose, as the careless and confused Plutarch would imply, that the people, or popular assembly, reversed the decree; the government was not then democratic, but popular assemblies existed, which, in extraordinary cases—especially, perhaps, in the case of war—it was necessary to propitiate, and customary to appeal to. I make no doubt that it was with the countenance and consent of the archons that Solon made his address to the people, preparing them to *receive* the repeal of the decree, which, without their approbation, it might be unsafe to propose.

5 As the quotation from Homer is extremely equivocal, merely stating that Ajax joined the ships that he led from Salamis with those of the Athenians, one cannot but suppose, that if Solon had really taken the trouble to forge a verse, he would have had the common sense to forge one much more decidedly in favour of his argument.

Homeric poems, have been exaggerated and misconstrued. The mode of burial in Salamis, agreeable to the custom of the Athenians and contrary to that of the Megarians, and reference to certain Delphic oracles, in which the island was called "Ionian", were also adduced in support of the Athenian claims. The arbitration of the umpires in favour of Athens only suspended hostilities; and the Megarians did not cease to watch (and shortly afterward they found) a fitting occasion to regain a settlement so tempting to their ambition.

V. The credit acquired by Solon in this expedition was shortly afterward greatly increased in the estimation of Greece. In the Bay of Corinth was situated a town called Cirrha, inhabited by a fierce and law-less race, who, after devastating the sacred territories of Delphi, sacrilegiously besieged the city itself, in the desire to possess themselves of the treasures which the piety of Greece had accumulated in the Temple of Apollo. Solon appeared at the Amphictyonic council, represented the sacrilege of the Cirrhæans, and persuaded the Greeks to arm in defence of the altars of their tutelary god. Clisthenes, the tyrant of Sicyon, was sent as commander-in-chief against the Cirrhæans; and (according to Plutarch) the records of Delphi inform us that Alcmæon was the leader of the Athenians. The war was not very successful at the onset; the oracle of Apollo was consulted, and the answer makes one of the most amusing anecdotes of priestcraft. The besiegers were informed by the god that the place would not be reduced until the waves of the Cirrhæan Sea washed the territories of Delphi. The reply perplexed the army; but the superior sagacity of Solon was not slow in discovering that the holy intention of the oracle was to appro-priate the land of the Cirrhæans to the profit of the temple. He therefore advised the besiegers to attack and to conquer Cirrha, and to dedicate its whole territory to the service of the god. The advice was adopted—Cirrha was taken; it became thenceforth the arsenal of Delphi, and the insulted deity had the satisfaction of seeing the sacred lands washed by the waves of the Cirrhæan Sea. An oracle of this nature was perhaps more effectual than the sword of Clisthenes in preventing future assaults on the divine city! The Pythian Games commenced, or were revived, in celebration of this victory of the Pythian god.

VI. Meanwhile at Athens—the tranquillity of the state was still disturbed by the mortal feud between the party of Cylon and the adherents of the Alcmæonidæ—time only served to exasperate the desire of vengeance in the one, and increase the indisposition to justice in the other. Fortunately, how-ever, the affairs of the state were in that crisis which is ever favourable to the authority of an individual. There are periods in all constitutions when, amid the excesses of factions, every one submits willingly to an arbiter. With the genius that might have made him the destroyer of the liberties of his coun-try, Solon had the virtue to constitute himself their saviour. He persuaded the families stigmatized with the crime of sacrilege, and the epithet of

CIRRHÆAN WAR

"execrable", to submit to the forms of trial; they were impeached, judged, and condemned to exile; the bodies of those whom death had already summoned to a sterner tribunal were disinterred, and removed beyond the borders of Attica. Nevertheless, the superstitions of the people were unappeased. Strange appearances were beheld in the air, and the augurs declared that the entrails of the victims denoted that the gods yet demanded a fuller expiation of the national crime.

At this time there lived in Crete one of those remarkable men common to the early ages of the world, who sought to unite with the honours of the sage

EPIMENIDES the mysterious reputation of the magician. Epimenides, numbered by some among the seven wise men, was revered throughout Greece as one whom a heavenlier genius animated and inspired. Devoted to poetry, this crafty impostor carried its prerogatives of fiction into actual life; and when he declared—in one of his verses, quoted by St Paul in his Epistle to Titus—that "the Cretans were great liars", we have no reason to exempt the venerable accuser from his own unpatriotic reproach. Among the various legends which attach to his memory is a tradition that has many a likeness both in northern and eastern fable:—he is said to have slept forty-seven[6] years in a cave, and on his waking from that moderate repose, to have been not unreasonably surprised to discover the features of the country perfectly changed. Returning to Cnossus, of which he was a citizen, strange faces everywhere present themselves. At his father's door he is asked his business, and at length, with considerable difficulty, he succeeds in making himself known to his younger brother, whom he had left a boy, and now recognized in an old decrepit man. "This story" says a philosophical biographer, very gravely, "made a considerable sensation"—an assertion not to be doubted; but those who were of a more sceptical disposition imagined that Epimenides had spent the years of his reputed sleep in travelling over foreign countries, and thus acquiring from men those intellectual acquisitions which he more piously referred to the special inspiration of the gods. Epimenides did not scruple to preserve the mysterious reputation he obtained from this tale by fables equally audacious. He endeavoured to persuade the people that he was Æacus, and that he frequently visited the earth; he was supposed to be fed by the nymphs—was never seen to eat in public—he assumed the attributes of prophecy—and dying in extreme old age, was honoured by the Cretans as a god.

In addition to his other spiritual prerogatives, this reviler of "liars" boasted the power of exorcism; was the first to introduce into Greece the custom of purifying public places and private abodes, and was deemed peculiarly successful in banishing those ominous phantoms which were so injurious to the tranquillity of the inhabitants of Athens. Such a man was exactly the person

6 Fifty-seven, according to Pliny.

born to relieve the fears of the Athenians, and accomplish the things dictated by the panting entrails of the sacred victims. Accordingly (just prior to the Cirrhæan war), a ship was fitted out, in which an Athenian named Nicias was sent to Crete, enjoined to bring back the purifying philosopher, with all that respectful state which his celebrity demanded. Epimenides complied with the prayer of the Athenians; he arrived at Athens, and completed the necessary expiation in a manner somewhat simple for so notable an exorcist. He ordered several sheep, some black and some white, to be turned loose in the Areopagus, directed them to be followed, and wherever they lay down, a sacrifice was ordained in honour of some one of the gods. "Hence", say the historian of the philosophers "you may still see throughout Athens anonymous altars (i.e. altars uninscribed to a particular god), the memorials of that propitiation."

The order was obeyed—the sacrifice performed—and the phantoms were seen no more. Although an impostor, Epimenides was a man of sagacity and genius. He restrained the excess of funeral lamentation, which often led to unseasonable interruptions of business, and conduced to fallacious impressions of morality; and in return he accustomed the Athenians to those regular habits of prayer and divine worship, which ever tend to regulate and systematize the character of a people. He formed the closest intimacy with Solon, and many of the subsequent laws of the Athenian are said by Plutarch to have been suggested by the wisdom of the Cnossian sage. When the time arrived for the departure of Epimenides, the Athenians would have presented him with a talent in reward of his services, but the philosopher refused the offer; he besought the Athenians to a firm alliance with his countrymen; accepted of no other remuneration than a branch of the sacred olive which adorned the citadel, and was supposed the primeval gift of Minerva, and returned to his native city,—proving that a man in those days might be an impostor without seeking any other reward than the gratuitous honour of the profession.

VII. With the departure of Epimenides, his spells appear to have ceased; new disputes and new factions arose; and, having no other crimes to expiate, the Athenians fell with one accord upon those of the government. Three parties—the Mountaineers, the Lowlanders, and the Coastmen—each advocating a different form of constitution, distracted the state by a common discontent with the constitution that existed,—the three parties, which, if we glance to the experience of modern times, we might almost believe that no free state can ever be without—viz., the respective advocates of the oligarchic, the mixed, and the democratic government. The habits of life ever produce among classes the political principles by which they are severally regulated. The inhabitants of the mountainous district, free, rude, and hardy, were attached to a democracy; the possessors of the plains were the powerful families who inclined to an oligarchy, although, as in all aristocracies, many of them united, but with

POLITICAL STATE OF ATHENS

185

more moderate views, in the measures of the democratic party; and they who, living by the coast, were engaged in those commercial pursuits which at once produce an inclination to liberty, yet a fear of its excess, a jealousy of the insolence of the nobles, yet an apprehension of the licentiousness of the mob, arrayed themselves in favour of that mixed form of government—half oligarchic and half popular—which is usually the most acceptable to the middle classes of an enterprising people. But there was a still more fearful division than these, the three legitimate parties, now existing in Athens: a division, not of principle, but of feeling—that menacing division which, like the cracks in the soil, portending earthquake, as it gradually widens, is the symptom of convulsions that level and destroy,—the division, in one word, of the Rich and the Poor—the Havenots and the Haves. Under an oligarchy, that most griping and covetous of all forms of government, the inequality of fortunes had become intolerably grievous; so greatly were the poor in debt to the rich, that[7] they were obliged to pay the latter a sixth of the produce of the land, or else to engage their personal labour to their creditors, who might seize their persons in default of payment. Some were thus reduced to slavery, others sold to foreigners. Parents disposed of their children to clear their debts, and many, to avoid servitude, in stealth deserted the land. But a large body of the distressed, men more sturdy and united, resolved to resist the iron pressure of the law: they formed the design of abolishing debts—dividing the land—remodelling the commonwealth: they looked around for a leader, and fixed their hopes on Solon. In the impatience of the poor, in the terror of the rich, liberty had lost its charms, and it was no uncommon nor partial hope that a monarchy might be founded on the ruins of an oligarchy already menaced with dissolution.

VIII. Solon acted during these disturbances with more than his usual sagacity, and therefore, perhaps, with less than his usual energy. He held himself backward and aloof, allowing either party to interpret, as it best pleased, ambiguous and oracular phrases, obnoxious to none, for he had the advantage of being rich without the odium of extortion, and popular without the degradation of poverty. "Phanias the Lesbian" (so states the biographer of Solon) "asserts, that to save the state he intrigued with both parties, promising to the poor a division of the lands, to the rich a confirmation of their claims"; an assertion highly agreeable to the finesse and subtlety of his character. Appearing loth to take upon himself the administration of affairs, it was pressed upon him the more eagerly; and at length he was elected to the triple office of archon, arbitrator, and lawgiver; the destinies of Athens were unhesitatingly placed within his hands; all men hoped from him all things; opposing parties concurred in urging him to assume the

---

7 Plut., in Vit. Sol.

supreme authority of king; oracles were quoted in his favour, and his friends asserted, that to want the ambition of a monarch was to fail in the proper courage of a man. Thus supported, thus encouraged, Solon proceeded to his august and immortal task of legislation.

IX. Let us here pause to examine, by such light as is bequeathed us, the character of Solon. Agreeably to the theory of his favourite maxim, which made moderation the essence of wisdom, he seems to

CHARACTER OF SOLON

have generally favoured, in politics, the middle party, and, in his own actions, to have been singular for that energy which is the equilibrium of indifference and of rashness. Elevated into supreme and un-questioned power—urged on all sides to pass from the office of the legislator to the dignity of the prince—his ambition never passed the line which his virtue dictated to his genius. "Tyranny", said Solon, "is a fair field, but it has no outlet." A subtle, as well as a noble saying; it implies that he who has once made himself the master of the state has no option as to the means by which he must continue his power. Possessed of that fearful authority, his first object is to rule, and it becomes a secondary object to rule well. "Tyranny has, indeed, no outlet!" The few, whom in modern times we have seen endowed with a similar spirit of self-control, have attracted our admiration by their honesty rather than their intellect; and the sceptic in human virtue has ascribed the purity of Washington as much to the mediocrity of his genius as to the sincerity of his patriotism:—the coarseness of vulgar ambi-tion can sympathize but little with those who refuse a throne. But in Solon there is no disparity between the mental and the moral, nor can we account for the moderation of his views by affecting doubt of the extent of his powers. His natural genius was versatile and luxuriant. As an orator, he was the first, according to Cicero, who originated the logical and brilliant rhet-oric which afterward distinguished the Athenians. As a poet, we have the assurance of Plato that, could he have devoted himself solely to the art, even Homer would not have excelled him. And though these panegyrics of later writers are to be received with considerable qualification—though we may feel assured that Solon could never have been either a Demosthenes or a Homer, yet we have sufficient evidence in his history to prove him to have been eloquent—sufficient in the few remains of his verses to attest poetical talent of no ordinary standard. As a soldier, he seems to have been a dexter-ous master of the tactics of that primitive day in which military science consisted chiefly in the stratagems of a ready wit and a bold invention. As a negotiator, the success with which, out of elements so jarring and distracted, he created an harmonious system of society and law, is an unanswerable evidence not more of the soundness of his theories than of his practical knowledge of mankind. The sayings imputed to him which can be most reasonably considered authentic evince much delicacy of observation. Whatever his ideal of good government, he knew well that great secret of statesman-ship, never to carry speculative doctrines too far beyond the reach of the age to which they are to be applied. Asked if he had given the Athenians the best of laws, his answer was, "The best laws they are capable of receiving." His legislation, therefore, was no vague collection of inapplicable principles. While it has been the origin of all subsequent law, while, adopted by the Romans, it makes at this day the universal spirit which animates the codes and constitutions of Europe—it was moulded to the habits, the manners, and the condition of the people whom it was intended to enlighten, to harmonize, and to guide. He was no gloomy ascetic, such as a false philosophy produces, affecting the barren sublimity of an indolent seclusion; open of access to all, free and frank of demeanour, he found wisdom as much in the market-place as the cell. He aped no coxcombical contempt of pleasure, no fanatical disdain of wealth; hospitable and even sumptuous, in his habits of life, he seemed desirous of proving that truly to be wise is honestly to enjoy. The fragments of his verses which have come down to us are chiefly egotistical: they refer to his own private sentiments, or public views, and inform us with a noble pride, "that, if reproached with his lack of ambition, he finds a kingdom in the consciousness of his unsullied name." With all these qualities, he apparently united much of that craft and spirit of artifice which, according to all history, sacred as well as profane, it was not deemed sinful in patriarch or philosopher to indulge. Where he could not win his object by reason, he could stoop to attain it by the affectation of madness. And this quality of craft was necessary perhaps, in that age, to accomplish the full utilities of his career. However he might feign or dissimulate, the end before him was invariably excellent and patriotic; and the purity of his private morals harmonized with that of his political ambition. What Socrates was to the philosophy of reflection, Solon was to the philosophy of action.

X. The first law that Solon enacted in his new capacity was bold and decisive. No revolution can ever satisfy a people if it does not lessen their burdens. Poverty disposes men to innovation only because innovation promises relief. Solon therefore applied himself resolutely, and at once, to the great source of dissension between the rich and the poor—namely, the enormous accumulation of debt which had been incurred by the latter, with slavery the penalty of default. He induced the creditors to accept the compromise of their debts: whether absolutely cancelling the amount, or merely reducing the interest and debasing the coin, is a matter of some dispute; the greater number of authorities incline to the former supposition, and Plutarch quotes the words of Solon himself in proof of the bolder hypothesis, although they by no means warrant such an interpretation. And to remove forever the renewal of the greatest grievance in connexion with the past distresses, he enacted a law that no man hereafter could sell himself in slavery for the discharge of a debt. Even such as were already enslaved were emancipated, and those sold by their creditors into foreign countries were ransomed, and restored to their native land. But, though (from the necessity of the times) Solon went to this desperate extent

His legislation

of remedy, comparable in our age only to the formal sanction of a national bankruptcy, he rejected with firmness the wild desire of a division of lands. There may be abuses in the contraction of debts which require far sterner alternatives than the inequalities of property. He contented himself in respect to the latter with a law which set a limit to the purchase of land—a theory of legislation not sufficiently to be praised, if it were possible to enforce it.[8] At first, these measures fell short of the popular expectation, excited by the example of Sparta into the hope of an equality of fortunes; but the reaction soon came. A public sacrifice was offered in honour of the discharge of debt, and the authority of the lawgiver was corroborated and enlarged. Solon was not one of those politicians who vibrate alternately between the popular and the aristocratic principles, imagining that the concession of today ought necessarily to father the denial of tomorrow. He knew mankind too deeply not to be aware that there is no statesman whom the populace suspect like the one who commences authority with a bold reform, only to continue it with hesitating expedients. His very next measure was more vigorous and more unexceptionable than the first. The evil of the laws of Draco was not that they were severe, but that they were inefficient. In legislation, characters of blood are always traced upon tablets of sand. With one stroke Solon annihilated the whole of these laws, with the exception of that (an ancient and acknowledged ordinance) which related to homicide; he affixed, in exchange, to various crimes—to theft, to rape, to slander, to adultery— punishments proportioned to the offence. It is remarkable that in the spirit of his laws he appealed greatly to the sense of honour and the fear of shame, and made it one of his severest penalties to be styled ἄτιμος or unhonoured— a theory that, while it suited the existent, went far to ennoble the future, character of the Athenians. In the same spirit the children of those who perished in war were educated at the public charge—arriving at maturity, they were presented with a suit of armour, settled in their respective callings, and honoured with principal seats in all public assemblies. That is a wise principle of a state which makes us grateful to its pensioners, and bids us regard in those supported at the public charge the reverent memorials of the public service.[9] Solon had the magnanimity to preclude, by his own hand, a dangerous temptation to his own ambition, and assigned death to the man who aspired to the sole dominion of the commonwealth. He put a check to the jobbing interests and importunate canvass of individuals, by allowing no one to propose a law in favour of a single person, unless he had obtained the votes of six thousand citizens; and he secured the quiet of a city exposed to

8 Aristot., Pol., ii. 8.
9 This regulation is probably of later date than the time of Solon. To Pisistratus is referred a law for disabled citizens, though its suggestion is ascribed to Solon. It was, however, a law that evidently grew out of the principles of Solon.

the licence of powerful factions, by forbidding men to appear armed in the streets, unless in cases of imminent exigence.

XI. The most memorable of Solon's sayings illustrates the theory of the social fabric he erected. When asked how injustice should be banished from a commonwealth, he answered, "by making *all* men interested in the injustice done to *each*"; an answer embodying the whole soul of liberty. His innovations in the mere forms of the ancient constitution do not appear to have been considerable; he rather added than destroyed. Thus he maintained or revived the senate of the aristocracy; but to check its authority he created a people. The four ancient tribes,[10] long subdivided into minor sections, were retained. Foreigners, who had transported for a permanence their property and families to Athens, and abandoned all connexion with their own countries, were admitted to swell the numbers of the free population. This made the constituent body. At the age of eighteen, each citizen was liable to military duties within the limits of Attica; at the age of twenty he attained his majority, and became entitled to a vote in the popular assembly, and to all the other rights of citizenship. Every free Athenian of the age of twenty was thus admitted to a vote in the legislature. But the possession of a very considerable estate was necessary to the attainment of the higher offices. Thus, while the people exercised universal suffrage in voting, the choice of candidates was still confined to an oligarchy. Four distinct ranks were acknowledged; not according, as hitherto, to hereditary descent, but the possession of property. They whose income yielded five hundred measures in any commodity, dry or liquid, were placed in the first rank, under the title of Pentacosiomedimnians. The second class, termed Hippeis, knights or horsemen, was composed of those whose estates yielded three hundred measures. Each man belonging to it was obliged to keep a horse for the public service, and to enlist himself, if called upon, in the cavalry of the military

---

10 A tribe contained three phratries, or fraternities—a phratry contained three genea or clans—a genos or clan was composed of thirty heads of families. As the population, both in the aggregate and in these divisions, must have been exposed to constant fluctuations, the aforesaid numbers were most probably what we may describe as a fiction in law, as Boeckh (Pol. Econ. of Athens, vol. i, p. 47, English translation) observes, "in the same manner that the Romans called the captain a centurion, even if he commanded sixty men, so a family might have been called a τριακάς (i.e., a *thirtiad*), although it contained fifty or more persons." It has been conjectured indeed by some, that from a class not included in these families, vacancies in the phratries were filled up; but this seems to be a less probable supposition than that which I have stated above. If the numbers in Pollux were taken from a census in the time of Solon, the four tribes at that time contained three hundred and sixty families, each family consisting of thirty persons; this would give a total population of ten thousand eight hundred free citizens. It was not long before that population nearly doubled itself, but the titles of the subdivisions remained the same. I reserve for an Appendix a more detailed and critical view of the vehement but tedious disputes of the learned on the complicated subject of the Athenian tribes and families.

forces (the members of either of these higher classes were exempt, however, from serving on board ship, or in the infantry, unless entrusted with some command). The third class was composed of those possessing two hundred[11] measures, and called Zeugitæ; and the fourth and most numerous class comprehended, under the name of Thetes, the bulk of the non-enslaved working population, whose property fell short of the qualification required for the Zeugitæ. Glancing over these divisions, we are struck by their similarity to the ranks among our own northern and feudal ancestry, corresponding to the nobles, the knights, the burgesses, and the labouring classes, which have long made, and still constitute, the demarcations of society in modern Europe. The members of the first class were alone eligible to the highest offices as archons, those of the three first classes to the political assembly of the four hundred (which I shall presently describe), and to some minor magistracies; the members of the fourth class were excluded from all office, unless, as they voted in the popular assembly, they may be said to have had a share in the legislature, and to exercise, in extraordinary causes, judicial authority. At the same time no hereditary barrier excluded them from the hopes so dear to human aspirations. They had only to acquire the necessary fortune, in order to enjoy the privileges of their superiors. And, accordingly, we find, by an inscription on the Acropolis, recorded in Pollux, that Anthemion, of the lowest class, was suddenly raised to the rank of knight.[12]

XII. We perceive, from these divisions of rank, that the main principle of Solon's constitution was founded, not upon birth, but wealth. He instituted what was called a timocracy, viz., an aristocracy of property; based upon democratic institutions of popular jurisdiction, election, and appeal. Conformably to the principle which pervades all states, that make property the qualification for office, to property the general taxation was apportioned. And this, upon a graduated scale, severe to the first class, and completely exonerating the lowest. The ranks of the citizens thus established, the constitution acknowledged three great councils or branches of legislature. The first was that of the venerable Areopagus. We have already seen that this institution had long existed among the Athenians; but of late it had fallen

---

11 Boeckh (Pub. Econ. of Athens, book iv, chap. v.) contends, from a law preserved by Demosthenes, that the number of measures for the Zeugitæ was only one hundred and fifty. But his argument, derived from the analogy of the sum to be given to an heiress by her nearest relation if he refused to marry her, is by no means convincing enough to induce us to reject the proportion of two hundred measures, "preserved [as Boeckh confesses] by all writers", especially as in the time of Demosthenes. Boeckh himself, in a subsequent passage, rightly observes, that the names of Zeugitæ, &c., could only apply to new classes introduced in the place of those instituted by Solon.

12 With respect to the value of "a measure" in that time, it was estimated at a drachma, and a drachma was the price of a sheep.

into some obscurity or neglect, and was not even referred to in the laws of Draco. Solon continued the name of the assembly, but remodelled its constitution. Anciently it had probably embraced all the eupatrids. Solon defined the claims of the aspirants to that official dignity, and ordained that no one should be admitted to the Areopagus who had not filled the situation of archon—an ordeal which implied not only the necessity of the highest rank, but, as I shall presently note, of sober character and unblemished integrity.

The remotest traditions clothed the very name of this assembly with majesty and awe. Holding their council on the sacred hill consecrated to Mars, fable asserted that the god of battle had himself been arraigned before its tribunal. Solon exerted his imagination to sustain the grandeur of its associations. Every distinction was lavished upon senators, who, in the spirit of his laws, could only pass from the temple of virtue to that of honour. Before their jurisdiction all species of crime might be arraigned—they had equal power to reward and to punish. From the guilt of murder to the negative offence of idleness,[13] their control extended—the consecration of altars to new deities, the penalties affixed to impiety, were at their decision, and in their charge. Theirs was the illimitable authority, to scrutinize the lives of men—they attended public meetings and solemn sacrifices, to preserve order by the majesty of their presence. The custody of the laws and the management of the public funds, the superintendence of the education of youth, were committed to their care. Despite their power, they interfered but little in the management of political affairs, save in cases of imminent danger. Their duties, grave, tranquil, and solemn, held them aloof from the stir of temporary agitation. They were the last great refuge of the state, to which, on common occasions, it was almost profanity to appeal. Their very demeanour was modelled to harmonize with the reputation of their virtues and the dignity of their office. It was forbidden to laugh in their assembly— no archon who had been seen in a public tavern could be admitted to their order,[14] and for an Areopagite to compose a comedy was a matter of special prohibition.[15] They sat in the open air, in common with all courts having cognizance of murder. If the business before them was great and various, they were wont to divide themselves into committees, to each of which the several causes were assigned by lot so that no man knowing the cause he was to adjudge could be assailed with the imputation of dishonest or partial prepossession. After duly hearing both parties, they gave their judgment with proverbial gravity and silence. The institution of the ballot (a subsequent custom) afforded secrecy to their award—a proceeding necessary

13 The law against idleness is attributable rather to Pisistratus than Solon.
14 Athenæus, xiv.
15 Plut., de Gloria Athen. I do not in this sketch entirely confine myself to Solon's regulations respecting the Areopagus.

amid the jealousy and power of factions, to preserve their judgment unbiased by personal fear, and the abolition of which, we shall see hereafter, was among the causes that crushed for a while the liberties of Athens. A brazen urn received the suffrages of condemnation—one of wood those of acquittal. Such was the character and constitution of the AREOPAGUS.[16]

XIII. The second legislative council ordained or revived by Solon, consisted of a senate, composed, first of four hundred, and many years afterward of five hundred members. To this council all, save the lowest and most numerous class, were eligible provided they had passed or attained the age of thirty. It was rather a chance assembly than a representative one. The manner of its election appears not more elaborate than clumsy. To every ward there was a president, called phylarchus. This magistrate, on a certain day in the year, gave in the names of all the persons within his district entitled to the honour of serving in the council, and desirous of enjoying it. These names were inscribed on brazen tablets, and cast into a certain vessel. In another vessel was placed an equal number of beans; supposing the number of candidates to be returned by each tribe to be (as it at first was) a hundred, there were one hundred white beans put into the vessel—the rest were black. Then the names of the candidates and the beans were drawn out one by one; and each candidate who had the good fortune to have his name drawn out together with a white bean, became a member of the senate. Thus the constitution of each succeeding senate might differ from the last— might, so far from representing the people, contradict their wishes—was utterly a matter of hazard and chance; and when Mr Mitford informs us that the assembly of the people was the great foundation of evil in the Athenian constitution, it appears that to the capricious and unsatisfactory election of this council we may safely impute many of the inconsistencies and changes which that historian attributes entirely to the more popular assembly.[17] To this council were entrusted powers less extensive in theory than those of the Areopagus, but far more actively exerted. Its members inspected the fleet (when a fleet was afterward established)—they appointed jailers of prisons— they examined the accounts of magistrates at the termination of their office; these were minor duties;—to them was allotted also an authority in other departments of a much higher and more complicated nature. To them was

16 The number of the Areopagites depending upon the number of the archons, was necessarily fluctuating and uncertain. An archon was not necessarily admitted to the Areopagus. He previously underwent a rigorous and severe examination of the manner in which he had discharged the duties of his office, and was liable to expulsion upon proofs of immorality or unworthiness.
17 Some modern writers have contended that at the time of Solon the members of the council were not chosen by lot; their arguments are not to me very satisfactory. But if merely a delegation of the eupatrids, as such writers suppose, the council would be still more vicious in its constitution.

given the dark and fearful extent of power which enabled them to examine and to punish persons accused of offences unspecified by any peculiar law[18]— an ordinance than which, had less attention been paid to popular control, the wildest ambition of despotism would have required a broader base for its designs. A power to punish crimes unspecified by law is a power above law, and ignorance or corruption may easily distort innocence itself into crime. But the main duty of the Four Hundred was to prepare the laws to be submitted to the assembly of the people—the great popular tribunal which we are about presently to consider. Nor could any law, according to Solon, be introduced into that assembly until it had undergone the deliberation, and received the sanction, of this preliminary council. With them, therefore, was THE ORIGIN OF ALL LEGISLATION. In proportion to these discretionary powers was the examination the members of the council underwent. Previous to the admission of any candidate, his life, his character, and his actions were submitted to a vigorous scrutiny.[19] The senators then took a solemn oath that they would endeavour to promote the public good, and the highest punishment they were allowed to inflict was a penalty of five hundred drachmæ. If that punishment were deemed by them insufficient, the criminal was referred to the regular courts of law. At the expiration of their trust, which expired with each year, the senators gave an account of their conduct, and the senate itself punished any offence of its members; so severe were its inflictions, that a man expelled from the senate was eligible as a judge—a proof that expulsion was a punishment awarded to no heinous offence.[20]

The members of each tribe presided in turn over the rest,[21] under the name of prytanes. It was the duty of the prytanes to assemble the senate, which was usually every day, and to keep order in the great assembly of the people. These were again subdivided into the prœdri, who presided weekly over the rest, while one of this number, appointed by lot, was the chief president (or epistates) of the whole council; to him were entrusted the keys of the citadel and the treasury, and a wholesome jealousy of this twofold trust limited its exercise to a single day. Each member gave notice in writing of any motion he intended to make—the prytanes had the prior right to propound the question, and afterward it became matter of open discussion —they decided by ballot whether to reject or adopt it; if accepted, it was then submitted to the assembly of the people, who ratified or refused the law which they might not originate.

---

18 Pollux.

19 Æschines, in Timarch.

20 Each member was paid (as in England once, as in America at this day) a moderate sum (one drachma) for his maintenance, and at the termination of his trust, peculiar integrity was rewarded with money from the public treasury.

21 When there were ten tribes, each tribe presided thirty-five days, or five weeks; when the number was afterward increased to twelve, the period of the presidency was one month.

Such was the constitution of the Athenian council, one resembling in many points to the common features of all modern legislative assemblies.

XIV. At the great assembly of the people, to which we now arrive, all freemen of the age of discretion, save only those branded by law with the opprobrium of atimos (unhonoured),[22] were admissible. At the time of Solon, this assembly was by no means of the importance to which it afterward arose. Its meetings were comparatively rare, and no doubt it seldom rejected the propositions of the Four Hundred. But whenever different legislative assemblies exist, and popular control is once constitutionally acknowledged, it is in the nature of things that the more democratic assembly should absorb the main business of the more aristocratic. A people are often enslaved by the accident of a despot, but almost ever gain upon the checks which the constitution is intended habitually to oppose. In the later time, the assembly met four times in five weeks (at least, during the period in which the tribes were ten in number), that is, during the presidence of each prytanea. The first time of their meeting they heard matters of general import, approved or rejected magistrates, listened to accusations of grave political offences,[23] as well as the particulars of any confiscation of goods. The second time was appropriated to affairs relative as well to individuals as the community; and it was lawful for every man either to present a petition or share in a debate. The third time of meeting was devoted to the state audience of ambassadors. The fourth, to matters of religious worship or priestly ceremonial. These four periodical meetings, under the name of Curia, made the common assembly, requiring no special summons, and betokening no extraordinary emergency. But besides these regular meetings, upon occasions of unusual danger, or in cases requiring immediate discussion, the assembly of the people might also be convened by formal proclamation; and in this case it was termed "Sugkletos", which we may render by the word *convocation*. The prytanes, previous to the meeting of the assembly, always placarded in some public place a programme of the matters on which the people were to consult. The persons presiding over the meeting were prœdri, chosen by lot from the nine tribes, excluded at the time being from the office of prytanes; out of their number a chief president (or epistates) was elected also by lot. Every effort was made to compel a numerous attendance, and each man attending received a small coin for his trouble,[24] a practice fruitful in jests to the comedians. The prytanes might forbid a man of notoriously bad character

---

22 "Atimos" means rather unhonoured than dishonoured. He to whom, in its milder degree, the word was applied, was rather withdrawn (as it were) from honour than branded with disgrace. By rapid degrees, however, the word ceased to convey its original meaning; it was applied to offences so ordinary and common, that it sunk into a mere legal term.

23 The more heinous of the triple offences, termed εἰσαγγελία.

24 This was a subsequent law; an obolus, or one penny farthing, was the first payment; it was afterward increased to three oboli, or threepence three farthings.

to speak. The chief president gave the signal for their decision, in ordinary cases they held up their hands, voting openly; but at a later period, in cases where intimidation was possible, such as in the offences of men of power and authority, they voted in secret. They met usually in the vast arena of their market-place.[25]

XV. Recapitulating the heads of that complex constitution I have thus detailed, the reader will perceive that the legislative power rested in three

GENERAL VIEW OF THE
ATHENIAN CONSTITUTION

assemblies—the Areopagus, the council, and the assembly of the people—that the first, notwithstanding its solemn dignity and vast authority, seldom interfered in the active, popular, and daily politics of the state—that the second originated laws, which the third was the great court of appeal to sanction or reject. The great improvement of modern times has been to consolidate the two latter courts in one, and to unite in a representative senate the sagacity of a deliberative council with the interests of a popular assembly;—the more closely we blend these objects, the more perfectly, perhaps, we attain, by the means of wisdom, the ends of liberty.

XVI. But although in a senate composed by the determinations of chance, and an assembly which from its numbers must ever have been exposed to the agitation of eloquence and the caprices of passion, there was inevitably a crude and imperfect principle,—although two courts containing in themselves the soul and element of contradiction necessarily wanted that concentrated oneness of purpose propitious to the regular and majestic calmness of legislation, we cannot but allow the main theory of the system to have been precisely that most favourable to the prodigal exuberance of energy, of intellect, and of genius. Summoned to consultation upon all matters, from the greatest to the least, the most venerable to the most trite—today deciding on the number of their war-ships, tomorrow on that of a tragic chorus; now examining with jealous forethought the new barriers to oligarchical ambition; now appointing, with nice distinction, to various service the various combinations of music;[26]—now welcoming in their forum-senate the sober ambassadors of Lacedæmon or the jewelled heralds of Persia, now voting their sanction to new temples or the reverent reforms of worship; compelled to a lively and unceasing interest in all that arouses the mind, or elevates the passions, or refines the taste;—supreme arbiters of the art of the sculptor, as the science of the lawgiver,—judges and rewarders of the limner and the poet, as of the successful negociator or the prosperous soldier; we see at once the all-accomplished, all-versatile genius of the nation, and we

25 Sometimes, also, the assembly was held in the Pnyx, afterward so celebrated; latterly, also (especially in bad weather), in the temple of Bacchus;—on extraordinary occasions, in whatever place was deemed most convenient or capacious.

26 Plato, ed. Leges.

behold in the same glance the effect and the cause:—every thing being referred to the people, the people learned of every thing to judge. Their genius was artificially forced, and in each of its capacities. They had no need of formal education. Their whole life was one school. The very faults of their assembly, in its proneness to be seduced by extraordinary eloquence, aroused the emulation of the orator, and kept constantly awake the imagination of the audience. An Athenian was, by the necessity of birth, what Milton dreamed that man could only become by the labours of completest education: in peace a legislator, in war a soldier,—in all times, on all occasions, acute to judge and resolute to act. All that can inspire the thought or delight the leisure were for the people. Theirs were the portico and the school—theirs the theatre, the gardens, and the baths; they were not, as in Sparta, the tools of the state—they *were* the state! Lycurgus made machines and Solon men. In Sparta the machine was to be wound up by the tyranny of a fixed principle; it could not dine as it pleased—it could not walk as it pleased—it was not permitted to seek its she machine save by stealth and in the dark; its children were not its own—even itself had no property in self. Sparta incorporated, under the name of freedom, the worst complexities, the most grievous and the most frivolous vexations, of slavery. And therefore was it that Lacedæmon flourished and decayed, bequeathing to fame men only noted for hardy valour, fanatical patriotism, and profound but dishonourable craft—attracting, indeed, the wonder of the world, but advancing no claim to its gratitude, and contributing no single addition to its intellectual stores. But in Athens the true blessing of freedom was rightly placed—in the opinions and the soul. Thought was the common heritage which every man might cultivate at his will. This unshackled liberty had its convulsions and its excesses, but producing unceasing emulation and unbounded competition, an incentive to every effort, a tribunal to every claim, it broke into philosophy with the one—into poetry with the other—into the energy and splendour of unexampled intelligence with all. Looking round us at this hour, more than four-and-twenty centuries after the establishment of the constitution we have just surveyed,—in the labours of the student—in the dreams of the poet—in the aspirations of the artist—in the philosophy of the legislator—we yet behold the imperishable blessings we derive from the liberties of Athens and the institutions of Solon. The life of Athens became extinct, but her soul transfused itself, immortal and immortalizing, through the world.

XVII. The penal code of Solon was founded on principles wholly opposite to those of Draco. The scale of punishment was moderate, though sufficiently severe. One distinction will suffice to give us an adequate notion of its gradations. Theft by day was not a capital offence, but if perpetrated by night the felon might lawfully be slain by the owner. The tendency to lean to the side of mercy in all cases may be perceived from this—that if the suffrages of the judges were evenly divided, it was the custom in all the courts of Athens to acquit the accused. The punishment of death was rare; that of atimia supplied its place. Of the different degrees of atimia it is not my purpose to speak at present. By one degree, however, the offender was merely suspended from some privilege of freedom enjoyed by the citizens generally, or condemned to a pecuniary fine; the second degree allowed the confiscation of goods; the third for ever deprived the criminal and his posterity of the rights of a citizen: this last was the award only of aggravated offences. Perpetual exile was a sentence never passed but upon state criminals. The infliction of fines, which became productive of great abuse in later times, was moderately apportioned to offences in the time of Solon, partly from the high price of money, but partly, also, from the wise moderation of the lawgiver. The last grave penalty of death was of various kinds, as the cross, the gibbet, the precipice, the bowl—afflictions seldom in reserve for the freemen.

As the principle of shame was a main instrument of the penal code of the Athenians, so they endeavoured to attain the same object by the sublimer motive of honour. Upon the even balance of rewards that stimulate, and penalties that deter, Solon and his earlier successors conceived the virtue of the commonwealth to rest. A crown presented by the senate or the people —a public banquet in the hall of state—the erection of a statue in the thoroughfares (long a most rare distinction)—the privilege of precedence in the theatre or assembly—were honours constantly before the eyes of the young and the hopes of the ambitious. The sentiment of honour thus became a guiding principle of the legislation, and a large component of the character of the Athenians.

XVIII. Judicial proceedings, whether as instituted by Solon or as cor-rupted by his successors, were exposed to some grave and vital evils hereafter to be noticed. At present I content myself with observing, that Solon carried into the judicial the principles of his legislative courts. It was his theory, that all the citizens should be trained to take an interest in the state. Every year a body of six thousand citizens was chosen by lot; no qualification save that of being thirty years of age was demanded in this election. The body thus chosen, called Heliæa, was subdivided into smaller courts, before which all offences, but especially political ones, might be tried. Ordinary cases were probably left by Solon to the ordinary magistrates; but it was not long before the popular jurors drew to themselves the final trial and judgment of all causes. This judicial power was even greater than the legislative; for if an act had passed through all the legislative forms, and was, within a year of the date, found inconsistent with the constitution or public interests, the popular courts could repeal the act and punish its author. In Athens there were no professional lawyers; the law being supposed the common interest of citizens, every encouragement was given to the prosecutor—every facility to the obtaining of justice.

Solon appears to have recognized the sound principle, that the strength of law is in the public disposition to cherish and revere it,—and that nothing is more calculated to make permanent the general spirit of a constitution than to render its details flexile and open to reform. Accordingly, he subjected his laws to the vigilance of regular and constant revision. Once a year, proposals for altering any existent law might be made by any citizen—were debated—and, if approved, referred to a legislative committee, drawn by lot from the jurors. The committee then sat in judgment on the law; five advocates were appointed to plead for the old law; if unsuccessful, the new law came at once into operation. In addition to this precaution, six of the nine archons (called thesmothetæ), whose office rendered them experienced in the defects of the law, were authorized to review the whole code, and to refer to the legislative committee the consideration of any errors or inconsistencies that might require amendment.[27]

XIX. With respect to the education of youth, the wise Athenian did not proceed upon the principles which in Sparta attempted to transfer to the state the dearest privileges of a parent. From the age of sixteen to eighteen (and earlier in the case of orphans) the law, indeed, seems to have considered that the state had a right to prepare its citizens for its service; and the youth was obliged to attend public gymnastic schools, in which, to much physical, some intellectual, discipline was added, under masters publicly nominated. But from the very circumstance of compulsory education at that age, and the absence of it in childhood, we may suppose that there had already grown up in Athens a moral obligation and a general custom, to prepare the youth of the state for the national schools.

Besides the free citizens, there were two subordinate classes—the aliens and the slaves. By the first are meant those composed of settlers, who had not relinquished connexion with their native countries. These, as universally in Greece, were widely distinguished from the citizens; they paid a small annual sum for the protection of the state, and each became a kind of client to some individual citizen, who appeared for him in the courts of justice. They were also forbidden to purchase land; but for the rest, Solon, himself a merchant, appears to have given to such aliens encouragements in trade and manufacture not usual in that age; and most of their disabilities were probably rather moral or imaginary than real and daily causes of grievance. The great and paramount distinction was between the freeman and the slave. No slave could be admitted as a witness, *except by torture*; as for him there was no voice in the state, so for him there was no tenderness in the law. But though the slave might not avenge himself on the master, the system of slavery

27 Plutarch assures us that Solon issued a decree that his laws were to remain in force a hundred years: an assertion which modern writers have rejected as incompatible with their constant revision. It was not, however, so contradictory a decree as it seems at first glance—for one of the laws not to be altered was this power of amending and revising the laws. And, therefore, the enactment in dispute would only imply that the constitution was not to be altered except through the constitutional channel which Solon had appointed.

avenged itself on the state. The advantages to the intellect of the free citizens resulting from the existence of a class maintained to relieve them
from the drudgeries of life, were dearly purchased by the constant insecurity
of their political repose. The capital of the rich could never be directed to the
most productive of all channels—the labour of free competition. The noble
did not employ citizens—he purchased slaves. Thus the commonwealth
derived the least possible advantage from his wealth; it did not flow through
the heart of the republic, employing the idle and feeding the poor. As a
necessary consequence, the inequalities of fortune were sternly visible and
deeply felt. The rich man had no connexion with the poor man—the poor
man hated him for a wealth of which he did not (as in states where slavery
does not exist) share the blessings—purchasing by labour the advantages of
fortune. Hence the distinction of classes defied the harmonizing effects of
popular legislation. The rich were exposed to unjust and constant exactions;
and society was ever liable to be disorganized by attacks upon property.
There was an eternal struggle between the jealousies of the populace and
the fears of the wealthy; and many of the disorders which modern historians
inconsiderately ascribe to the institutions of freedom were in reality the
growth of the existence of slavery.

CHAPTER II

The departure of Solon from Athens—the rise of Pisistratus
—return of Solon—his conduct and death—the second and
third tyranny of Pisistratus—capture of Sigeum—colony in
the Chersonesus founded by the first Miltiades—death of
Pisistratus

I. Although the great constitutional reforms of Solon were no doubt
carried into effect during his archonship, yet several of his legislative and
judicial enactments were probably the work of years. When we consider the
many interests to conciliate, the many prejudices to overcome, which in all
popular states cripple and delay the progress of change in its several details,
we find little difficulty in supposing, with one of the most luminous of
modern scholars,[1] that Solon had ample occupation for twenty years after
the date of his archonship. During this period little occurred in the foreign
affairs of Athens save the prosperous termination of the Cirrhæan war, as before
recorded. At home the new constitution gradually took root, although often
menaced and sometimes shaken by the storms of party and the general desire
for further innovation.

The eternal consequence of popular change is, that while it irritates the
party that loses power, it cannot content the party that gains. It is obvious
that each concession to the people but renders them
THE DEPARTURE OF better able to demand concessions more important. The
SOLON FROM ATHENS theories of some—the demands of others—harassed
the lawgiver, and threatened the safety of the laws. Solon, at length, was
induced to believe that his ordinances required the sanction and repose of
time, and that absence—that moral death—would not only free himself
from importunity, but his infant institutions from the frivolous disposition
of change. In his earlier years he had repaired, by commercial pursuits,
estates that had been impoverished by the munificence of his father; and,
still cultivating the same resources, he made pretence of his vocation to
solicit permission for an absence of ten years. He is said to have obtained a
solemn promise from the people to alter none of his institutions during that

1 See Fasti Hellenici, vol. ii, p. 276.

period;[2] and thus he departed from the city, of whose future glories he had laid the solid foundation. Attracted by his philosophical habits to that solemn land, beneath whose mysteries the credulous Greeks revered the secrets of existent wisdom, the still adventurous Athenian repaired to the cities of the Nile, and fed the passion of speculative inquiry from the learning of the Egyptian priests. Departing thence to Cyprus, he assisted, as his own verses assure us, in the planning of a new city, founded by one of the kings of that beautiful island, and afterward invited to the court of Crœsus (associated with his father Alyattes, then living), he imparted to the Lydian, amid the splendours of state and the adulation of slaves, that well-known lesson on the uncertainty of human grandeur, which, according to Herodotus, Crœsus so seasonably remembered at the funeral pile.[3]

II. However prudent had appeared to Solon his absence from Athens, it is to be lamented that he did not rather brave the hazards from which his genius might have saved the state, than incur those which the very removal of a master-spirit was certain to occasion. We may bind men not to change laws, but we cannot bind the spirit and the opinion, from which laws alone derive cogency or value. We may guard against the innovations of a multitude, which a wise statesman sees afar off, and may direct to great ends; but we cannot guard against that dangerous accident—not to be foreseen, not to be directed—the ambition of a man of genius! During the absence of Solon there rose into eminence one of those remarkable persons who give to vicious designs all the attraction of individual virtues. Bold, generous, affable, eloquent, endowed with every gift of nature and fortune—kinsman to Solon, but of greater wealth and more dazzling qualities—the young Pisistratus, son of Hippocrates, early connected himself with the democratic or highland party. The Megarians, who had never relinquished their designs on Salamis, had taken an opportunity, apparently, before the travels, and, according to Plutarch, even before the legislation of Solon, to repossess themselves of the island. When the Athenians were enabled to extend their energies beyond their own great domestic revolution, Pisistratus obtained the command of an expedition against these

THE RISE OF
PISISTRATUS

---

2 Including, as I before observed, that law which provided for any constitutional change in a constitutional manner.

3   Et Crœsum quem vox justi facunda Solonis
    Respicere ad longæ jussit spatia ultima vitæ.
                Juv., Sat. x. 273.

The story of the interview and conversation between Crœsus and Solon is supported by so many concurrent authorities, that we cannot but feel grateful to the modern learning, which has removed the only objection to it in an apparent contradiction of dates. If, as contended for by Larcher, still more ably by Wesseling, and since by Mr Clinton, we agree that Crœsus reigned jointly with his father Alyattes, the difficulty vanishes at once.

dangerous neighbours, which was attended with the most signal success. A stratagem referred to Solon by Plutarch, who has with so contagious an inaccuracy blended into one the two several and distinct expeditions of Pisistratus and Solon, ought rather to be placed to the doubtful glory of the son of Hippocrates.[4] A number of young men sailed with Pisistratus to Colias, and taking the dress of women, whom they there seized while sacrificing to Ceres, a spy was despatched to Salamis, to inform the Megarian guard that many of the principal Athenian matrons were at Colias, and might be easily captured. The Megarians were decoyed, despatched a body of men to the opposite shore, and beholding a group in women's attire dancing by the strand, landed confusedly to seize the prize. The pretended females drew forth their concealed weapons, and the Megarians, surprised and dismayed, were cut off to a man. The victors lost no time in setting sail for Salamis, and easily regained the isle. Pisistratus carried the war into Megara itself, and captured the port of Nisæa. These exploits were the foundation of his after greatness; and yet young, at the return of Solon, he was already at the head of the democratic party. But neither his rank, his genius, nor his popular influence sufficed to give to his faction a decided eminence over those of his rivals. The wealthy nobles of the lowlands were led by Lycurgus—the moderate party of the coastmen by Megacles, the head of the Alcmæonidæ. And it was in the midst of the strife and agitation produced by these great sections of the people that Solon returned to Athens.

III. The venerable legislator was received with all the grateful respect he deserved; but age had dimmed the brilliancy of his powers. His voice could no longer penetrate the mighty crowds of the market-place. New idols had sprung up—new passions were loosed—new interests formed, and amid the roar and stir of the eternal movement, it was in vain for the high-hearted old man to recall those rushing on the future to the boundaries of the past. If unsuccessful in public, he was not discouraged from applying in private to the leaders of the several parties. Of all those rival nobles, none deferred to his advice with so marked a respect as the smooth and plausible Pisistratus. Perhaps, indeed, that remarkable man contemplated the same objects as Solon himself,—although the one desired to effect by the authority of the chief, the order and the energy which the other would have trusted to the development of the people. But, masking his more interested designs, Pisistratus outbid all competition in his seeming zeal for the public welfare. The softness of his

RETURN OF SOLON

4 Plutarch gives two accounts of the recovery of Salamis by Solon; one of them, which is also preferred by Ælian (Var., vii. 19), I have adopted and described in my narrative of that expedition; the second I now give, but refer to Pisistratus, not Solon; in support of which opinion I am indebted to Mr Clinton for the suggestion of two authorities: Æneas Tacticus, in his Treatise on Sieges, chap. iv, and Frontinus, de Stratagem., iv. 7. Justin also favours the claim of Pisistratus to this stratagem, xi. 8.

manners—his profuse liberality—his generosity even to his foes—the splendid qualities which induced Cicero to compare him to Julius Cæsar,[5] charmed the imagination of the multitude, and concealed the selfishness of his views. He was not a hypocrite, indeed, as to his virtues—a dissembler only in his ambition. Even Solon, in endeavouring to inspire him with a true patriotism, acknowledged his talents and his excellences. "But for ambition," said he, "Athens possesses no citizen worthier than Pisistratus." The time became ripe for the aspiring projects of the chief of the democracy.

IV. The customary crowd was swarming in the market-place, when suddenly in the midst of the assembly appeared the chariot of Pisistratus. The mules were bleeding—Pisistratus himself was wounded. In this condition the demagogue harangued the people. He declared that he had just escaped from the enemies of himself and the popular party, who (under the auspices of the Alcmæonidæ) had attacked him in a country excursion. He reminded the crowd of his services in war—his valour against the Megarians—his conquest of Nisæa. He implored their protection. Indignant and inflamed, the favouring audience shouted their sympathy with his wrongs. "Son of Hippocrates," said Solon, advancing to the spot, and with bitter wit, "you are but a bad imitator of Ulysses. He wounded himself to delude his enemies —you to deceive your countrymen."[6] The sagacity of the reproach was unheeded by the crowd. A special assembly of the people was convened, and a partisan of the demagogue moved that a body-guard of fifty men, armed but with clubs, should be assigned to his protection. Despite the infirmities of his age, and the decrease of his popular authority, Solon had the energy to oppose the motion, and predict its results. The credulous love of the people swept away all precaution—the guard was granted. Its number did not long continue stationary; Pisistratus artfully increased the amount, till it swelled to the force required by his designs. He then seized the citadel—the antagonist faction of Megacles fled—and Pisistratus was master of Athens. Amid the confusion and tumult of the city, Solon retained his native courage. He appeared in public—harangued the citizens—upbraided their blindness— invoked their courage. In his speeches he bade them remember that if it be the more easy task to prevent tyranny, it is the more glorious achievement to destroy it. In his verses[7] he poured forth the indignant sentiment which a thousand later bards have borrowed and enlarged: "Blame not Heaven for your tyrants, blame yourselves." The fears of some, the indifference of others, rendered his exhortations fruitless! The brave old man sorrowfully retreated

5 The most sanguine hope indeed that Cicero seems to have formed with respect to the conduct of Cæsar, was that he might *deserve* the title of the Pisistratus of Rome.

6 If we may, in this anecdote, accord to Plutarch (Vit. Sol.) and Ælian (Var., viii. 16) a belief which I see no reason for withholding.

7 His own verses, rather than the narrative of Plutarch, are the evidence of Solon's conduct on the usurpation of Pisistratus.

to his house, hung up his weapons without his door, and consoled himself with the melancholy boast that "he had done all to save his country, and its laws". This was his last public effort against the usurper. He disdained flight; and, asked by his friends to what he trusted for safety from the wrath of the victor, replied, "To old age",—a sad reflection, that so great a man should find in infinity that shelter which he claimed from glory.

V. The remaining days and the latter conduct of Solon are involved in obscurity. According to Plutarch, he continued at Athens, Pisistratus show-

HIS CONDUCT
AND DEATH

ing him the utmost respect, and listening to the counsel which Solon condescended to bestow upon him: according to Diogenes Laertius, he departed again from his native city,[8] indignant at its submission, and hopeless of its freedom, refusing all overtures from Pisistratus, and alleging that, having established a free government, he would not appear to sanction the success of a tyrant. Either account is sufficiently probable. The wisdom of Solon might consent to mitigate what he could not cure, or his patriotism might urge him to avoid witnessing the changes he had no power to prevent. The dispute is of little importance. At his advanced age he could not have long survived the usurpation of Pisistratus, nor can we find any authority for the date of his death so entitled to credit as that of Phanias, who assigns it to the year following the usurpation of Pisistratus. The bright race was already run. According to the grave author- ity of Aristotle, the ashes of Solon were scattered over the isle of Salamis, which had been the scene of his earlier triumphs; and Athens, retaining his immortal, boasted not his perishable remains.

VI. Pisistratus directed with admirable moderation the courses of the revolution he had produced. Many causes of success were combined in his

THE SECOND AND THIRD
TYRANNY OF PISISTRATUS

favour. His enemies had been the supposed enemies of the people, and the multitude doubtless beheld the flight of the Alcmæonidæ (still odious in their eyes by the massacre of Cylon) as the defeat of a foe, while the triumph of the popular chief was recognized as the victory of the people. In all revolu- tions the man who has sided with the people is permitted by the people the greatest extent of licence. It is easy to perceive, by the general desire which the Athenians had expressed for the elevation of Solon to the supreme authority, that the notion of regal authority was not yet hateful to them, and that they were scarcely prepared for the liberties with which they were entrusted. But although they submitted thus patiently to the ascendency of Pisistratus, it is evident that a less benevolent or less artful tyrant would not have been equally successful. Raised above the law, that subtle genius

---

8 This historian fixes the date of Solon's visit to Crœsus and to Cyprus (on which island he asserts him to have died), not during his absence of ten years, but during the final exile for which he contends.

governed only by the law; nay, he affected to consider its authority greater than his own. He assumed no title—no attribute of sovereignty. He was accused of murder, and he humbly appeared before the tribunal of the Areopagus—a proof not more of the moderation of the usurper than of the influence of public opinion. He enforced the laws of Solon, and compelled the unruly tempers of his faction to subscribe to their wholesome rigour. The one revolution did not, therefore, supplant, it confirmed, the other. *"By these means"*, says Herodotus, "Pisistratus mastered Athens, and yet his situation was far from secure."[9]

VII. Although the heads of the more moderate party, under Megacles, had been expelled from Athens, yet the faction, equally powerful and equally hostile, headed by Lycurgus, and embraced by the bulk of the nobles, still remained. For a time, extending perhaps to five or six years, Pisistratus retained his power; but at length, Lycurgus, uniting with the exiled Alcmæonidæ, succeeded in expelling him from the city. But the union that had led to his expulsion ceased with that event. The contests between the lowlanders and the coastmen were only more inflamed by the defeat of the third party, which had operated as a balance of power, and the broils of their several leaders were fed by personal ambition as by hereditary animosities. Megacles, therefore, unable to maintain equal ground with Lycurgus, turned his thoughts towards the enemy he had subdued, and sent proposals to Pisistratus, offering to unite their forces, and to support him in his pretensions to the tyranny, upon condition that the exiled chief should marry his daughter Cœsyra. Pisistratus readily acceded to the terms, and it was resolved by a theatrical pageant to reconcile his return to the people. In one of the boroughs of the city there was a woman named Phya, of singular beauty and lofty stature. Clad in complete armour, and drawn in a chariot, this woman was conducted with splendour and triumph towards the city. By her side rode Pisistratus—heralds preceded their march, and proclaimed her approach, crying aloud to the Athenians "to admit Pisistratus, the favourite of Minerva, for that the goddess herself had come to earth on his behalf."

The sagacity of the Athenians was already so acute, and the artifice appeared to Herodotus so gross, that the simple Halicarnassean could scarcely credit the authenticity of this tale. But it is possible that the people viewed the procession as an ingenious allegory, to the adaptation of which they were already disposed; and that, like the populace of a later and yet more civilized people, they hailed the goddess while they recognized the prostitute.[10] Be that as it may, the son of Hippocrates recovered his authority, and fulfilled

9 Herod., i. 49.
10 The procession of the goddess of Reason in the first French revolution solves the difficulty that perplexed Herodotus.

his treaty with Megacles by a marriage with his daughter. Between the commencement of his first tyranny and the date of his second return, there was probably an interval of twelve years. His sons were already adults. Partly from a desire not to increase his family, partly from some superstitious disinclination to the blood of the Alcmæonidæ, which the massacre of Cylon still stigmatized with contamination, Pisistratus conducted himself towards the fair Cœsyra with a chastity either unwelcome to her affection, or afflicting to her pride. The unwedded wife communicated the mortifying secret to her mother, from whose lips it soon travelled to the father. He did not view the purity of Pisistratus with charitable eyes. He thought it an affront to his own person that that of his daughter should be so tranquilly regarded. He entered into a league with his former opponents against the usurper, and so great was the danger, that Pisistratus (despite his habitual courage) betook himself hastily to flight:—a strange instance of the caprice of human events, that a man could with a greater impunity subdue the freedom of his country, than affront the vanity of his wife![11]

VIII. Pisistratus, his sons and partisans, retired to Eretria in Eubœa: there they deliberated as to their future proceedings—should they submit to their exile or attempt to retrieve their power? The councils of his son Hippias prevailed with Pisistratus; it was resolved once more to attempt the sovereignty of Athens. The neighbouring tribes assisted the exiles with forage and shelter. Many cities accorded the celebrated noble large sums of money, and the Thebans outdid the rest in pernicious liberality. A troop of Argive adventurers came from the Peloponnesus to tender to the baffled usurper the assistance of their swords, and Lygdamis, an individual of Naxos, himself ambitious of the government of his native state, increased his resources both by money and military force. At length, though after a long and tedious period of no less than eleven years, Pisistratus resolved to hazard the issue of open war. At the head of a foreign force he advanced to Marathon, and pitched his tents upon its immortal plain. Troops of the factious or discontented thronged from Athens to his camp, while the bulk of the citizens, unaffected by such desertions, viewed his preparations with indifference. At length, when they heard that Pisistratus had broken up his encampment, and was on his march to the city, the Athenians awoke from their apathy, and collected their forces to oppose him. He continued to advance his troops, halted at the Temple of Minerva, whose earthly representative had once so benignly assisted him, and pitched his tents opposite the fane. He took advantage of that time in which the Athenians, during the heats of the day,

---

11 Mr Mitford considers this story as below the credit of history. He gives no sufficient reason against its reception, and would doubtless have been less sceptical had he known more of the social habits of that time, or possessed more intimate acquaintance with human nature generally.

were at their entertainments, or indulging the noontide repose, still so grateful to the inhabitants of a warmer climate, to commence his attack. He soon scattered the foe, and ordered his sons to overtake them in their flight, to bid them return peacefully to their employments, and fear nothing from his vengeance. His clemency assisted the effect of his valour, and once more the son of Hippocrates became the master of the Athenian commonwealth.

IX. Pisistratus lost no time in strengthening himself by formidable alliances. He retained many auxiliary troops, and provided large pecuniary resources.[12] He spared the persons of his opponents, but sent their children as hostages to Naxos, which he first reduced and consigned to the tyranny of his auxiliary, Lygdamis. Many of his inveterate enemies had perished on the field—many fled from the fear of his revenge. He was undisturbed in the renewal of his sway, and having no motive for violence, pursued the natural bent of a mild and generous disposition, ruling as one who wishes men to forget the means by which his power has been attained. Pisistratus had that passion for letters which distinguished most of the more brilliant Athenians. Although the poems of Homer were widely known and deeply venerated long before his time, yet he appears, by a more accurate collection and arrangement of them, and probably by bringing them into a more general and active circulation in Athens, to have largely added to the wonderful impetus to poetical emulation, which those immortal writings were calculated to give.

When we consider how much, even in our own times, and with all the advantages of the press, the diffused fame and intellectual influence of Shakespeare and Milton have owed to the praise and criticism of individuals, we may readily understand the kind of service rendered by Pisistratus to Homer. The very example of so eminent a man would have drawn upon the poet a less vague and more inquiring species of admiration; the increased circulation of copies—the more frequent public recitals—were advantages timed at that happy season when the people who enjoyed them had grown up from wondering childhood to imitative and studious youth. And certain it is, that from this period we must date the marked and pervading influence of Homer

---

12 Upon which points, of men and money, Mr Mitford, who is anxious to redeem the character of Pisistratus from the stain of tyranny, is dishonestly prevaricating. Quoting Herodotus, who especially insists upon these undue sources of aid, in the following words—Ἐρρίζωσε τὴν τυρραννίδα, ἐπικούροισί τε πολλοῖσι καὶ χρημάτων συνόδοισι, τῶν μὲν, αὐτόθεν, τῶν δὲ, ἀπὸ Στρυμόνος ποταμοῦ συνιόντων: this candid historian merely says, "A particular interest with the ruling parties in several neighbouring states, especially Thebes and Argos, and a *wise and liberal use of a very great private property*, were the resources in which besides he mostly relied." Why he thus slurs over the fact of the auxiliary forces will easily be perceived. He wishes us to understand that the third tyranny of Pisistratus, being wholesome, was also acceptable to the Athenians, and not, as it in a great measure was, supported by borrowed treasure and foreign swords.

upon Athenian poetry; for the renown of a poet often precedes by many generations the visible influence of his peculiar genius. It is chiefly within the last seventy years that we may date the wonderful effect that Shakespeare was destined to produce upon the universal intellect of Europe. The literary obligations of Athens to Pisistratus were not limited to his exertions on behalf of Homer: he is said to have been the first in Greece who founded a public library, rendering its treasures accessible to all. And these two benefits united, justly entitle the fortunate usurper to the praise of first calling into active existence that intellectual and literary spirit which became diffused among the Athenian people, and originated the models and masterpieces of the world. It was in harmony with this part of his character that Pisistratus refined the taste and socialized the habits of the citizens, by the erection of buildings dedicated to the public worship, or the public uses, and laid out the stately gardens of the Lyceum—(in after times the favourite haunt of philosophy), by the banks of the river dedicated to song. Pisistratus did thus more than continue the laws of Solon—he inculcated the intellectual habits which the laws were designed to create. And as in the circle of human events the faults of one man often confirm what was begun by the virtues of another, so perhaps the usurpation of Pisistratus was necessary to establish the institutions of Solon. It is clear that the great lawgiver was not appreciated at the close of his life; as his personal authority had ceased to have influence, so possibly might have soon ceased the authority of his code. The citizens required repose to examine, to feel, to estimate the blessings of his laws—that repose they possessed under Pisistratus. Amid the tumult of fierce and equipoised factions, it might be fortunate that a single individual was raised above the rest, who, having the wisdom to appreciate the institutions of Solon, had the authority to enforce them. Silently they grew up under his usurped but benignant sway, pervading, penetrating, exalting the people, and fitting them by degrees to the liberty those institutions were intended to confer. If the disorders of the republic led to the ascendency of Pisistratus, so the ascendency of Pisistratus paved the way for the renewal of the republic. As Cromwell was the representative of the very sentiments he appeared to subvert—as Napoleon in his own person incorporated the principles of the revolution of France, so the tyranny of Pisistratus concentrated and embodied the elements of that democracy he rather wielded than overthrew.

X. At home, time and tranquillity cemented the new laws; poetry set before the emulation of the Athenians its noblest monument in the epics of Homer; and tragedy put forth its first unmellowed fruits in the rude recitations of Thespis.[13] Pisistratus sought also to counterbalance the growing

---

13 Who, according to Plutarch, first appeared at the return of Solon; but the proper date for his exhibitions is ascertained (Fasti Hellenici, vol. ii, p. 11) several years after Solon's death.

passion for commerce by peculiar attention to agriculture, in which it is not unlikely that he was considerably influenced by early prepossessions, for his party had been the mountaineers attached to rural pursuits, and his adversaries the coastmen engaged in traffic. As a politician of great sagacity, he might also have been aware, that a people accustomed to agricultural employments are ever less inclined to democratic institutions than one addicted to commerce and manufactures; and if he were the author of a law, which at all events he more rigidly enforced, requiring every citizen to give an account of his mode of livelihood, and affixing punishments to idleness, he could not have taken wiser precautions against such seditions as are begot by poverty upon indolence, or under a juster plea have established the superintendence of a concealed police. We learn from Aristotle that his policy consisted much in subjecting and humbling the pediæi, or wealthy nobles of the lowlands. But his very affection to agriculture must have tended to strengthen an aristocracy, and his humility to the Areopagus was a proof of his desire to conciliate the least democratic of the Athenian courts. He probably, therefore, acted only against such individual chiefs as had incurred his resentment, or as menaced his power; nor can we perceive in his measures the systematic and deliberate policy, common with other Greek tyrants, to break up an aristocracy and create a middle class.

XI. Abroad, the ambition of Pisistratus, though not extensive, was successful. There was a town on the Hellespont called Sigeum, which had long been a subject of contest between the Athenians and the Mitylenæans. Some years before the legislation of Solon, the Athenian general, Phryno, had been slain in single combat by Pittacus, one of the seven wise men, who had come into the field armed like the Roman retiarius, with a net, a trident, and a dagger. This feud was terminated by the arbitration of Periander, tyrant of Corinth, who awarded Sigeum to the Athenians, which was then in their possession, by a wise and plausible decree, that each party should keep what it had got. This war was chiefly remarkable for an incident that introduces us somewhat unfavourably to the most animated of the lyric poets. Alcæus, an eminent citizen of Mitylene, and, according to ancient scandal, the unsuccessful lover of Sappho, conceived a passion for military fame: in his first engagement he seems to have discovered that his proper vocation was rather to sing of battles than to share them. He fled from the field, leaving his arms behind him, which the Athenians obtained, and suspended at Sigeum in the Temple of Minerva. Although this single action, which Alcæus himself recorded, cannot be fairly held a sufficient proof of the poet's cowardice, yet his character and patriotism are more equivocal than his genius. Of the last we have ample testimony, —though few remains save in the frigid grace of the imitations of Horace. The subsequent weakness and civil dissensions of Athens were not favourable to the maintenance of this distant conquest—the Mitylenæans regained Sigeum. Against this town Pisistratus now directed his arms—wrested it from the Mitylenæans—and, instead of annexing it to the republic of Athens, assigned its government to the tyranny of his natural son, Hegesistratus,—a stormy dominion, which the valour of the bastard defended against repeated assaults.[14]

XII. But one incident, the full importance of which the reader must wait a while to perceive, I shall in this place relate. Among the most powerful of the Athenians was a noble named Miltiades, son of Cypselus. By original descent he was from the neighbouring island of Ægina, and of the heroic race of Æacus; but he dated the establishment of his house in Athens from no less distant a founder than the son of Ajax. Miltiades had added new lustre to his name by a victory at the Olympic Games. It was probably during the first tyranny of Pisistratus[15] that an adventure, attended with vast results to Greece, befell this noble. His family were among the enemies of Pisistratus, and were regarded by that sagacious usurper with a jealous apprehension which almost appears prophetic. Miltiades was, therefore, uneasy under the government of Pisistratus, and discontented with his position in Athens. One day, as he sat before his door (such is the expression of the enchanting Herodotus, unconscious of the patriarchal picture he suggests),[16] Miltiades observed certain strangers pass by, whose garments and spears denoted them to be foreigners. The sight touched the chief, and he offered the strangers the use of his house, and the rites of hospitality.

COLONY IN THE CHERSONESUS FOUNDED BY THE FIRST MILTIADES

14 These two wars, divided by so great an interval of time,—the one terminated by Periander of Corinth, the other undertaken by Pisistratus,—are, with the usual blundering of Mr Mitford, jumbled together into the same event. He places Alcæus in the war following the conquest of Sigeum by Pisistratus. Poor Alcæus! the poet flourished Olym. 42 (BC 611); the third tyranny of Pisistratus may date somewhere about BC 537, so that Alcæus, had he been alive in the time ascribed by Mr Mitford to his warlike exhibitions, would have been (supposing him to be born twenty-six years before the date of his celebrity in 611) just a hundred years old—a fitting age to commence the warrior! The fact is, Mr Mitford adopts the rather confused account of Herodotus, without taking the ordinary pains to ascertain dates, which to every one else the very names of Periander and Alcæus would have suggested.

15 For the reader will presently observe the share taken by Crœsus in the affairs of this Miltiades during his government in the Chersonesus; now Crœsus was conquered by Cyrus about BC 546—it must, therefore, have been before that period. But the third tyranny of Pisistratus appears to have commenced nine years afterward, viz., BC 537. The second tyranny probably commenced only two years before the fall of the Lydian monarchy, and seems to have lasted only a year, and during that period Crœsus no longer exercised over the cities of the coast the influence he exerted with the people of Lampsacus on behalf of Miltiades; the departure of Miltiades, son of Cypselus, must therefore have been in the first tyranny, in the interval BC 560–BC 554, and probably at the very commencement of the reign, viz., about BC 550.

16 In the East, the master of the family still sits before the door to receive visitors or transact business.

They accepted his invitation, were charmed by his courtesy, and revealed to him the secret of their travel. In that narrow territory which, skirting the Hellespont, was called the Chersonesus, or Peninsula, dwelt the Doloncians, a Thracian tribe. Engaged in an obstinate war with the neighbouring Absinthians, the Doloncians had sent to the oracle of Delphi to learn the result of the contest. The Pythian recommended the messengers to persuade the first man who, on their quitting the temple, should offer them the rites of hospitality, to found a colony in their native land. Passing homeward through Phocis and Bœotia, and receiving no such invitation by the way, the messengers turned aside to Athens; Miltiades was the first who offered them the hospitality they sought; they entreated him now to comply with the oracle, and assist their countrymen; the discontented noble was allured by the splendour of the prospect—he repaired in person to Delphi—consulted the Pythian—received a propitious answer—and collecting all such of the Athenians as his authority could enlist, or their own ambition could decoy, he repaired to the Chersonesus. There he fortified a great part of the isthmus, as a barrier to the attacks of the Absinthians: but shortly afterward, in a feud with the people of Lampsacus, he was taken prisoner by the enemy. Miltiades, however, had already secured the esteem and protection of Crœsus; and the Lydian monarch remonstrated with the Lampsacenes in so formidable a tone of menace, that the Athenian obtained his release, and regained his new principality. In the meanwhile, his brother Cimon (who was chiefly remarkable for his success at the Olympic Games), sharing the political sentiment of his house, had been driven into exile by Pisistratus. By a transfer to the brilliant tyrant of a victory in the Olympic chariot-race, he, however, propitiated Pisistratus, and returned to Athens.

XIII. Full of years, and in the serene enjoyment of power, Pisistratus died. His character may already be gathered from his actions: crafty in the pursuit

DEATH OF PISISTRATUS

of power, but magnanimous in its possession, we have only, with some qualification, to repeat the eulogium on him ascribed to his greater kinsman, Solon—"That he was the best of tyrants, and without a vice save that of ambition."

212

CHAPTER III

The administration of Hippias—the conspiracy of Harmodius and Aristogiton—the death of Hipparchus—cruelties of Hippias—the young Miltiades sent to the Chersonesus—the Spartans combine with the Alcmæonidæ against Hippias—the fall of the tyranny—the innovations of Clisthenes—his expulsion and restoration—embassy to the satrap of Sardis—retrospective view of the Lydian, Median, and Persian monarchies—result of the Athenian embassy to Sardis—conduct of Cleomenes—victory of the Athenians against the Bœotians and Chalcidians—Hippias arrives at Sparta—the speech of Sosicles the Corinthian—Hippias retires to Sardis

I. Upon the death of Pisistratus, his three sons, Hipparchus, Hippias, and Thessalus, succeeded to the government. Nor, though Hippias was the eldest,

THE ADMINISTRATION OF HIPPIAS

does he seem to have exercised a more prominent authority than the rest—since, in the time of Thucydides, and long afterward, it was the popular error to consider Hipparchus the first-born. Hippias was already of mature age; and, as we have seen, it was he who had counselled his father not to despair, after his expulsion from Athens. He was a man of courage and ability worthy of his race. He governed with the same careful respect for the laws which had distinguished and strengthened the authority of his predecessor. He even rendered himself yet more popular than Pisistratus by reducing one half the impost of a tithe on the produce of the land, which that usurper had imposed. Notwithstanding this relief, he was enabled, by a prudent economy, to flatter the national vanity by new embellishments to the city. In the labours of his government he was principally aided by his second brother, Hipparchus, a man of a yet more accomplished and intellectual order of mind. But although Hippias did not alter the laws, he chose his own creatures to administer them. Besides, whatever share in the government was entrusted to his brothers, Hipparchus and Thessalus, his son and several of his family were enrolled among the archons of the city. And they who by office were intended for the guardians of liberty were the necessary servants of the tyrant.

II. If we might place unhesitating faith in the authenticity of the dialogue attributed to Plato under the title of "Hipparchus", we should have, indeed, high authority in favour of the virtues and the wisdom of that prince. And by whomsoever the dialogue was written, it refers to facts, in the passage relative to the son of Pisistratus, in a manner sufficiently positive to induce us to regard that portion of it with some deference. According to the author, we learn that Hipparchus, passionately attached to letters, brought Anacreon to Athens, and lived familiarly with Simonides. He seems to have been inspired with the ambition of a moralist, and distributed Hermæ, or stone busts of Mercury, about the city and the public roads, which, while answering a similar purpose to our mile-stones, arrested the eye of the passenger with pithy and laconic apophthegms in verse; such as, "Do not deceive your friend", and "Persevere in affection to justice";—proofs rather of the simplicity than the wisdom of the prince. It is not by writing the decalogue upon mile-stones that the robber would be terrified, or the adulterer converted.

It seems that the apophthegmatical Hipparchus did not associate with Anacreon more from sympathy with his genius than inclination to the sub-

THE CONSPIRACY OF HARMODIUS AND ARISTOGITON—THE DEATH OF HIPPARCHUS

jects to which it was devoted. He was addicted to pleasure; nor did he confine its pursuits to the more legitimate objects of sensual affection. Harmodius, a young citizen of no exalted rank, but much personal beauty, incurred the affront of his addresses.[1]

Harmodius, in resentment, confided the overtures of the moralist to his friend and preceptor, Aristogiton. While the two were brooding over the outrage, Hipparchus, in revenge for the disdain of Harmodius, put a public insult upon the sister of that citizen, a young maiden. She received a summons to attend some public procession, as bearer of one of the sacred vessels: on presenting herself she was abruptly rejected, with the rude assertion that she never could have been honoured with an invitation of which she was unworthy. This affront rankled deeply in the heart of Harmodius, but still more in that of the friendly Aristogiton, and they now finally resolved upon revenge. At the solemn festival of Panathenæa (in honour of Minerva), it was the custom for many of the citizens to carry arms in the procession: for this occasion they reserved the blow. They entrusted their designs to few, believing that if once the attempt was begun the people would catch the contagion, and rush spontaneously to the assertion of their freedom. The festival arrived. Bent against the older tyrant, perhaps from nobler motives

---

1 Thucyd., vi. 54. The dialogue of Hipparchus, ascribed to Plato, gives a different story, but much of the same nature. In matters of history, we cannot doubt which is the best authority, Thucydides or Plato,—especially an apocryphal Plato.

than those which urged them against Hipparchus,[2] each armed with a dagger concealed in the sacred myrtle bough which was borne by those who joined the procession, the conspirators advanced to the spot in the suburbs where Hippias was directing the order of the ceremonial. To their dismay, they perceived him conversing familiarly with one of their own partisans, and immediately suspected that to be the treason of their friend which in reality was the frankness of the affable prince. Struck with fear, they renounced their attempt upon Hippias, suddenly retreated to the city, and, meeting with Hipparchus, rushed upon him, wounded, and slew him. Aristogiton turned to fly—he escaped the guards, but was afterward seized, and "not mildly treated"[3] by the tyrant. Such is the phrase of Thucydides, which, if we may take the interpretation of Justin and the later writers, means that, contrary to the law, he was put to the torture.[4] Harmodius was slain upon the spot. The news of his brother's death was brought to Hippias. With an admirable sagacity and presence of mind, he repaired, not to the place of the assassination, but towards the procession itself, rightly judging that the conspiracy had only broken out in part. As yet the news of the death of Hipparchus had not reached the more distant conspirators in the procession, and Hippias betrayed not in the calmness of his countenance any signs of his sorrow or his fears. He approached the procession, and with a composed voice commanded them to deposit their arms and file off towards a place which he indicated. They obeyed the order, imagining he had something to communicate to them. Then turning to his guards, Hippias bade them seize the weapons thus deposited, and he himself selected from the procession all whom he had reason to suspect, or on whose persons a dagger was found, for it was only with the open weapons of spear and shield that the procession was lawfully to be made. Thus rose and thus terminated that conspiracy

2 Although it is probable that the patriotism of Aristogiton and Harmodius "the beloved" has been elevated in after times beyond its real standard, yet Mr Mitford is not justified in saying that it was private revenge, and *not any* political motive, that induced them to conspire the death of Hippias and Hipparchus. Had it been so, why strike at Hippias at all?—why attempt to make him the *first* and principal victim?—why assail Hipparchus (against whom only they had a private revenge) suddenly, by accident, and from the impulse of the moment, *after the failure of their* design on the tyrant himself, with whom they had no quarrel? It is most probable that, as in other attempts at revolution, that of Masaniello—that of Rienzi—public patriotism was not *created*—it was stimulated and made passion by private resentment.

3 Mr Mitford has most curiously translated this passage thus:—"Aristogiton escaped the attending guards, but, being taken *by the people* (!!!) was not mildly treated. So Thucydides has expressed himself." Now Thucydides says quite the reverse: he says that, *owing to the crowd of the people*, the guard could not at first seize him. How did Mr Mitford make this strange blunder? The most charitable supposition is, that, not reading the Greek, he was misled by an error of punctuation in the Latin version.

4 "Qui cum *per tormento* conscios cædis nominare cogeretur," &c. (Justin., ii. 9). This author differs from the older writers as to the precise cause of the conspiracy.

which gave to the noblest verse and the most enduring veneration the names of Harmodius and Aristogiton.[5]

III. The acutest sharpener of tyranny is an unsuccessful attempt to destroy it—to arouse the suspicion of power is almost to compel it to cruelty. Hitherto we have seen that Hippias had graced his authority with beneficent moderation; the death of his brother filled him with secret alarm; and the favour of the populace at the attempted escape of Aristogiton—the ease with which, from a personal affront to an obscure individual, a formidable conspiracy had sprung up into life, convinced him that the arts of personal popularity are only to be relied on when the constitution of the government itself is popular.

CRUELTIES OF HIPPIAS

It is also said that, when submitted to the torture, Aristogiton, with all the craft of revenge, asserted the firmest friends of Hippias to have been his accomplices. Thus harassed by distrust, Hippias resolved to guard by terror a power which clemency had failed to render secure. He put several of the citizens to death. According to the popular traditions of romance, one of the most obnoxious acts of his severity was exercised upon a woman worthy to be the mistress of Aristogiton. Leæna, a girl of humble birth, beloved by that adventurous citizen, was sentenced to the torture, and, that the pain might not wring from her any confession of the secrets of the conspiracy, she bit out her tongue. The Athenians, on afterward recovering their liberties, dedicated to the heroine a brazen lioness, not inappropriately placed in the vicinity of a celebrated statue of Venus.[6] No longer depending on the love of the citizens, Hippias now looked abroad for the support of his power; he formed an alliance with Hippoclus, the prince of Lampasacus, by marrying his daughter with the son of that tyrant, who possessed considerable influence at the Persian court, to which he already directed his eyes—whether as a support in the authority of the present, or an asylum against the reverses of the future.[7]

It was apparently about a year before the death of Hipparchus, that Stesagoras, the nephew and successor of that Miltiades who departed from Athens to found a colony in the Thracian Chersonesus, perished by an assassin's blow. Hippias, evidently deeming he had the right, as sovereign of the parent country, to appoint the governor of the colony, sent to the Chersonesus in that capacity the brother of the deceased, a namesake of the

THE YOUNG MILTIADES SENT TO THE CHERSONESUS

---

5 Herodotus says they were both Gephyræans by descent; a race, according to him, originally Phœnician (Herod., v. 57).

6 Mr Mitford too hastily and broadly asserts the whole story of Leæna to be a fable: if, as we may gather from Pausanias, the statue of the lioness existed in his time, we may pause before we deny all authenticity to a tradition far from inconsonant with the manners of the time or the heroism of the sex.

7 Thucyd., vi. 59.

first founder, whose father, Cimon, from jealousy of his power or repute, had been murdered by the sons of Pisistratus.[8] The new Miltiades was a man of consummate talents, but one who scrupled little as to the means by which to accomplish his objects. Arriving at his government, he affected a deep sorrow for the loss of his brother; the principal nobles of the various cities of the Chersonesus came in one public procession to condole with him; the crafty chief seized and loaded them with irons, and, having thus ensnared the possible rivals of his power, or enemies of his designs, he secured the undisputed possession of the whole Chersonesus, and maintained his civil authority by a constant military force. A marriage with Hegesipyle, a daughter of one of the Thracian princes, at once enhanced the dignity and confirmed the sway of the young and aspiring chief. Some years afterward, we shall see in this Miltiades the most eminent warrior of his age—at present we leave him to an unquiet and perilous power, and return to Hippias.

IV. A storm gathered rapidly on against the security and ambition of the tyrant. The highborn and haughty family of the Alcmæonidæ had been expelled from Athens at the victorious return of Pisistratus—their estates in Attica confiscated—their houses razed—their very sepulchres destroyed. After fruitless attempts against the oppressors, they had retired to Lipsydrium, a fortress on the heights of Parnes, where they continued to cherish the hope of return and the desire of revenge. Despite the confiscation of their Attic estates, their wealth and resources, elsewhere secured, were enormous. The temple of Delphi having been destroyed by fire, they agreed with the Amphictyons to rebuild it, and performed the holy task with a magnificent splendour far exceeding the conditions of the contract. But in that religious land, wealth, thus lavished, was no unprofitable investment. The priests of Delphi were not insensible of the liberality of the exiles, and Clisthenes, the most eminent and able of the Alcmæonidæ, was more than suspected of suborning the Pythian. Sparta, the supporter of oligarchies, was the foe of tyrants, and every Spartan who sought the oracle was solemnly invoked to aid the glorious enterprise of delivering the eupatrids of Athens from the yoke of the Pisistratidæ.

THE SPARTANS COMBINE WITH THE ALCMÆONIDÆ AGAINST HIPPIAS

The Spartans were at length moved by instances so repeatedly urged. Policy could not but soften that jealous state to such appeals to her superstition.

---

8 Herod., vi. 103. In all probability, the same jealousy that murdered the father dismissed the son. Hippias was far too acute and too fearful not to perceive the rising talents and daring temper of Miltiades. By the way, will it be believed that Mitford, in his anxiety to prove Hippias and Hipparchus the most admirable persons possible, not only veils the unnatural passions of the last, but is utterly silent about the murder of Cimon, which is ascribed to the sons of Pisistratus by Herodotus, in the strongest and gravest terms. Mr Thirlwall (Hist. of Greece, vol. ii, p. 223) erroneously attributes the assassination of Cimon to Pisistratus himself.

Under the genius of the Pisistratidæ, Athens had rapidly advanced in power, and the restoration of the Alcmæonidæ might have seemed to the Spartan sagacity but another term for the establishment of that former oligarchy which had repressed the intellect and exhausted the resources of an active and aspiring people. Sparta aroused herself, then, at length, and "though in violation" says Herodotus, "of some ancient ties of hospitality", despatched a force by sea against the prince of Athens. That alert and able ruler lost no time in seeking assistance from his allies, the Thessalians; and one of their powerful princes led a thousand horsemen against the Spartans, who had debarked at Phalerum. Joined by these allies, Hippias engaged and routed the enemy, and the Spartan leader himself fell upon the field of battle. His tomb was long visible in Cynosarges, near the gates of Athens—a place rendered afterward more illustrious by giving name to the Cynic philosophers.[9]

Undismayed by their defeat, the Spartans now despatched a more considerable force against the tyrant, under command of their king Cleomenes.

THE FALL OF THE TYRANNY — This army proceeded by land—entered Attica—encountered, defeated, the Thessalian horse[10]—and marched towards the gates of Athens, joined, as they proceeded, by all those Athenians who hoped, in the downfall of Hippias, the resurrection of their liberties. The Spartan troops hastened to besiege the Athenian prince in the citadel, to which he retired with his forces. But Hippias had provided his refuge with all the necessaries which might maintain him in a stubborn and prolonged resistance. The Spartans were unprepared for the siege—the blockade of a few days sufficed to dishearten them, and they already meditated a retreat. A sudden incident, opening to us in the midst of violence one of those beautiful glimpses of human affection which so often adorn and sanctify the darker pages of history, unexpectedly secured the Spartan triumph. Hippias and his friends, fearing the safety of their children in the citadel, resolved to dismiss them privately to some place of greater security. Unhappily, their care was frustrated, and the children fell into the hands of the enemy. All the means of success within their reach (the foe wearied—the garrison faithful), the parents yet resigned themselves at once to the voluntary sacrifice of conquest and ambition.

Upon the sole condition of recovering their children, Hippias and his partisans consented to surrender the citadel and quit the territories of Attica

---

9 Suidas. Laertius iv. 13 &c. Others, as Ammonius and Simplicius ad Aristotelem, derive the name of Cynics given to these philosophers from the ridicule attached to their manners.

10 Whose ardour appears to have been soon damped. They lost but forty men, and then retired at once to Thessaly. This reminds us of the wars between the Italian republics, in which the loss of a single horseman was considered no trifling misfortune. The value of the steed and the rank of the horseman (always above the vulgar) made the cavalry of Greece easily discouraged by what appears to us an inconsiderable slaughter.

within five days. Thus, in the fourth year from the death of Hipparchus, and about fifty years after the first establishment of the tyranny under its brilliant founder, the dominion of Athens passed away from the house of Pisistratus.

V. The party of Hippias, defeated, not by the swords of the enemy, but by the soft impulses of nature, took their way across the stream of the immemorial Scamander, and sought refuge at Sigeum, still under the government of Hegesistratus, the natural brother of the exiled prince.

The instant the pressure of one supreme power was removed, the two parties embodying the aristocratic and popular principles rose into active life. The state was to be a republic, but of what denomination? The nobles naturally aspired to the predominance— at their head was the eupatrid Isagoras; the strife of party always tends to produce popular results, even from elements apparently the most hostile. Clisthenes, the head of the Alcmæonidæ, was by birth even yet more illustrious than Isagoras; for, among the nobles, the Alcmæonid family stood pre-eminent. But, unable to attain the sole power of the government, Clisthenes and his party were unwilling to yield to the more numerous faction of an equal. The exile and sufferings of the Alcmæonidæ had, no doubt, secured to them much of the popular compassion; their gallant struggles against, their ultimate victory over, the usurper, obtained the popular enthusiasm; thus it is probable, that an almost insensible sympathy had sprung up between this highborn faction and the people at large; and when, unable to cope with the party of the nobles, Clisthenes attached himself to the movement of the commons, the enemy of the tyrant appeared in his natural position—at the head of the democracy. Clisthenes was, however, rather the statesman of a party than the legislator for a people—it was his object permanently to break up the power of the great proprietors, not as enemies of the commonwealth, but as rivals to his faction. The surest way to diminish the influence of property in elections is so to alter the constituencies as to remove the electors from the immediate control of individual proprietors. Under the old Ionic and hereditary divisions of four tribes, many ancient associations and ties between the poorer and the nobler classes were necessarily formed. By one bold innovation, the whole importance of which was not immediately apparent, Clisthenes abolished these venerable divisions, and, by a new geographical survey, created ten tribes instead of the former four. These were again subdivided into districts, or demes; the number seems to have varied, but at the earliest period they were not less than one hundred—at a later period they exceeded one hundred and seventy. To these demes were transferred all the political rights and privileges of the divisions they supplanted. Each had a local magistrate and local assemblies. Like corporations, these petty courts of legislature ripened the moral spirit of democracy while fitting men for the exercise of the larger rights they demanded. A consequence of the alteration of the number of the tribes was

THE INNOVATIONS OF CLISTHENES

an increase in the number that composed the senate, which now rose from four to five hundred members.

Clisthenes did not limit himself to this change in the constituent bodies —he increased the total number of the constituents; new citizens were made—aliens were admitted—and it is supposed by some, though upon rather vague authorities, that several slaves were enfranchised. It was not enough, however, to augment the number of the people, it was equally necessary to prevent the ascension of a single man. Encouraged by the example in other states of Greece, forewarned by the tyranny of Pisistratus, Clisthenes introduced the institution of the ostracism.[11] Probably about the same period, the mode of election to public office generally was altered from the public vote to the secret lot.[12] It is evident that these changes, whether salutary or pernicious, were not wanton or uncalled for. The previous constitution had not sufficed to protect the republic from a tyranny: something deficient in the machinery of Solon's legislation had for half a century frustrated its practical intentions. A change was, therefore, necessary to the existence of the free state; and the care with which that change was directed towards the diminution of the aristocratic influence, is in itself a proof that such influence had been the shelter of the defeated tyranny. The Athenians themselves always considered the innovations of Clisthenes but as the natural development of the popular institutions of Solon; and that decisive and energetic noble seems indeed to have been one of those rude but serviceable instruments by which a more practical and perfect action is often wrought out from the incompleted theories of greater statesmen.

VI. Meanwhile, Isagoras, thus defeated by his rival, had the mean ambition to appeal to the Spartan sword. Ancient scandal attributes to Cleomenes, king of Sparta, an improper connexion with the wife of Isagoras, and every one knows that the fondest friend of the cuckold is invariably the adulterer;—the national policy of founding aristocracies was doubtless, however, a graver motive with the Spartan king than his desire to assist Isagoras. Cleomenes by a public herald proclaimed the expulsion of Clisthenes, upon a frivolous pretence that the Alcmæonidæ were still polluted by the hereditary sacrilege of Cylon. Clisthenes privately retired from the city, and the Spartan king, at the head of an inconsiderable troop, re-entered Athens—expelled, at the instance of Isagoras, seven hundred Athenian families, as inculpated in the pretended pollution of Clisthenes—dissolved the senate—and committed all

HIS EXPULSION AND RESTORATION

---

11 Ælian, Var., xiii, 24.

12 Wachsm. i. 1. §273. Others contend for a later date to this most important change; but, on the whole, it seems a necessary consequence of the innovations of Clisthenes, which were all modelled upon the one great system of breaking down the influence of the aristocracy. In the speech of Otanes (Herod., iii. 80), it is curious to observe how much the vote by lot was identified with a republican form of government.

the offices of the state to an oligarchy of three hundred (a number and a council founded upon the Dorian habits), each of whom was the creature of Isagoras. But the noble assembly he had thus violently dissolved refused obedience to his commands; they appealed to the people, whom the valour of liberty simultaneously aroused, and the citadel, of which Isagoras and the Spartans instantly possessed themselves, was besieged by the whole power of Athens. The conspirators held out only two days; on the third, they accepted the conditions of the besiegers, and departed peaceably from the city. Some of the Athenians, who had shared the treason without participating in the flight, were justly executed. Clisthenes, with the families expelled by Cleomenes, was recalled, and the republic of Athens was thus happily re-established.

VII. But the iron vengeance of that nation of soldiers, thus far successfully braved, was not to be foreboded without alarm by the Athenians. They felt

EMBASSY TO THE
SATRAP OF SARDIS

that Cleomenes had only abandoned his designs to return to them more prepared for contest; and Athens was not yet in a condition to brave the determined and never-sparing energies of Sparta. The Athenians looked around the states of Greece—many in alliance with Lacedæmon—some governed by tyrants—others distracted with their own civil dissensions; there were none from whom the new commonwealth could hope for a sufficient assistance against the revenge of Cleomenes. In this dilemma, they resorted to the only aid which suggested itself, and sought, across the boundaries of Greece, the alliance of the barbarians. They adventured a formal embassy to Artaphernes, satrap of Sardis, to engage the succour of Darius, king of Persia.

Accompanying the Athenians in this mission, full of interest, for it was the first public transaction between that republic and the throne of Persia, I pause to take a rapid survey of the origin of that mighty empire, whose destinies became thenceforth involved in the history of Grecian misfortunes and Grecian fame. That survey commences with the foundation of the Lydian monarchy.

VIII. Amid the Grecian colonies of Asia whose rise we have commemorated, around and above a hill commanding spacious and fertile plains

RETROSPECTIVE VIEW OF
THE LYDIAN, MEDIAN, AND
PERSIAN MONARCHIES

watered by the streams of the Cayster and Mæander, an ancient Pelasgic tribe called the Mæonians had established their abode. According to Herodotus, these settlers early obtained the name of Lydians, from Lydus, the son of Atys. The Dorian revolution did not spare these delightful seats, and an Heraclid dynasty is said to have reigned five hundred years over the Mæonians; these in their turn were supplanted by a race known to us as the Mermnadæ, the founder of whom, Gyges, murdered and dethroned the last of the Heraclidæ; and with a new dynasty seems to have commenced a new and less Asiatic policy. Gyges, supported by the oracle of Delphi, was the first barbarian, except one of the many Phrygian kings claiming the name of Midas, who made votive offerings to that Grecian shrine. From his time this motley tribe, the link between Hellas and the East, came into frequent collision with the Grecian colonies. Gyges himself made war with Miletus and Smyrna, and even captured Colophon. With Miletus, indeed, the hostility of the Lydians became hereditary, and was renewed with various success by the descendants of Gyges, until, in the time of his great-grandson Alyattes, a war of twelve years with that splendid colony was terminated by a solemn peace and a strict alliance. Meanwhile, the petty but warlike monarchy founded by Gyges had preserved the Asiatic Greeks from dangers yet more formidable than its own ambition. From a remote period, savage and ferocious tribes, among which are pre-eminent the Treres and Cimmerians, had often ravaged the inland plains—now for plunder, now for settlement. Magnesia had been entirely destroyed by the Treres—even Sardis, the capital of the Mermnadæ, had been taken, save the citadel, by the Cimmerians. It was reserved for Alyattes to terminate these formidable irruptions, and Asia was finally delivered by his arms from a people in whom modern erudition has too fondly traced the ancestors of the Cymry, or ancient Britons.[13] To this enterprising and able king succeeded a yet more illustrious monarch, who ought to have found in his genius the fame he has derived from his misfortunes. At the age of thirty-five Crœsus ascended the Lydian throne. Before associated in the government with his father, he had rendered himself distinguished in military service; and, wise, accomplished, but grasping and ambitious, this remarkable monarch now completed the designs of his predecessors. Commencing with Ephesus, he succeeded in rendering tributary every Grecian colony on the western coat of Asia; and, leaving to each state its previous institutions, he kept by moderation what he obtained by force.

Crœsus was about to construct a fleet for the purpose of adding to his dominions the isles of the Ægæan, but is said to have been dissuaded from his purpose by a profound witticism of one of the seven wise men of Greece. "The islanders", said the sage, "are about to storm you in your capital of Sardis, with ten thousand cavalry."—"Nothing could gratify me more", said the king, "than to see the islanders invading the Lydian continent with horsemen."—"Right", replied the wise man, "and it will give the islanders equal satisfaction to find the Lydians attacking them by a fleet. To revenge their disasters on the land, the Greeks desire nothing better than to meet you on the ocean." The answer enlightened the king, and, instead of fitting out his fleet, he entered into amicable alliance with the Ionians of the isles.[14] But his ambition was only thwarted in one direction to strike its roots in another; and he turned his invading arms against his neighbours on the

13 See Sharon Turner, vol. i., book i.
14 Herod., i. 26.

continent, until he had progressively subdued nearly all the nations, save the Lycians and Cilicians, westward to the Halys. And thus rapidly and majestically rose from the scanty tribe and limited territory of the old Mæonians the monarchy of Asia Minor.

IX. The renown of Crœsus established, his capital of Sardis became the resort of the wise and the adventurous, whether of Asia or of Greece. In many respects the Lydians so closely resembled the Greeks as to suggest the affinity which historical evidence scarcely suffices to permit us absolutely to affirm. The manners and the customs of either people did not greatly differ, save that with the Lydians, as still throughout the East, but little consideration was attached to women;—they were alike in their cultivation of the arts, and their respect for the oracles of religion—and Delphi, in especial, was inordinately enriched by the prodigal superstition of the Lydian kings.

The tradition which ascribes to the Lydians the invention of coined money is a proof of their commercial habits. The neighbouring Tmolus teemed with gold, which the waters of the Pactolus bore into the very streets of the city. Their industry was exercised in the manufacture of articles of luxury rather than those of necessity. Their purple garments—their skill in the workmanship of metals—their marts for slaves and eunuchs—their export trade of unwrought gold—are sufficient evidence both of the extent and the character of their civilization. Yet the nature of the oriental government did not fail to operate injuriously on the more homely and useful directions of their energy. They appear never to have worked the gold-mines, whose particles were borne to them by the careless bounty of the Pactolus. Their early traditional colonies were wafted on Grecian vessels. The gorgeous presents with which they enriched the Hellenic temples seem to have been fabricated by Grecian art, and even the advantages of commerce they seem rather to have suffered than to have sought. But what a people so suddenly risen into splendour, governed by a wise prince, and stimulated perhaps to eventual liberty by the example of the European Greeks, ought to have become, it is impossible to conjecture; perhaps the Hellenes of the East.

At this period, however, of such power and such promise, the fall of the Lydian empire was decreed. Far from the fertile fields and gorgeous capital of Lydia, amid sterile mountains, inhabited by a simple and hardy race, rose the portentous star of the Persian Cyrus.

X. A victim to that luxury which confirms a free but destroys a despotic state, the vast foundations of the Assyrian empire were crumbling into decay, when a new monarchy, destined to become its successor, sprung up among one of its subject nations. Divided into various tribes, each dependent upon the Assyrian sceptre, was a warlike, wandering, and primitive race, known to us under the name of Medes. Deioces, a chief of one of the tribes, succeeded in uniting these scattered sections into a single people, built a city, and founded an independent throne. His son, Phraortes, reduced the Persians to his yoke—overran Asia—advanced to Nineveh—and ultimately perished in battle with a considerable portion of his army. Succeeded by his son Cyaxares, that monarch consummated the ambitious designs of his predecessors. He organized the miscellaneous hordes that compose an oriental army into efficient and formidable discipline, vanquished the Assyrians, and besieged Nineveh, when a mighty irruption of the Scythian hordes called his attention homeward. A defeat, which at one blow robbed this great king of the dominion of Asia, was ultimately recovered by a treacherous massacre of the Scythian leaders. The Medes regained their power and prosecuted their conquests—Nineveh fell—and through the whole Assyrian realm, Babylon alone remained unsubjugated by the Mede. To this new-built and widespread empire succeeded Astyages, son of the fortunate Cyaxares. But it is the usual character of a conquering tribe to adopt the habits and be corrupted by the vices of the subdued nations among which the invaders settle; and the peaceful reign of Astyages sufficed to enervate that vigilant and warlike spirit in the victor race, by which alone the vast empires of the East can be preserved from their natural tendency to decay. The Persians, subdued by the grandsire of Astyages, seized the occasion to revolt. Among them rose up a native hero, the Gengis-khan of the ancient world. Through the fables which obscure his history we may be allowed to conjecture, that Cyrus, or Khosroo, was perhaps connected by blood with Astyages, and, more probably, that he was entrusted with command among the Persians by that weak and slothful monarch. Be that as it may, he succeeded in uniting under his banners a martial and uncorrupted population, overthrew the Median monarchy, and transferred to a dynasty, already worn out with premature old age, the vigorous and aspiring youth of a mountain race. Such was the formidable foe that now menaced the rising glories of the Lydian king.

XI. Crœsus was allied by blood with the dethroned Astyages, and individual resentment at the overthrow of his relation co-operated with his anxious fears of the ambition of the victor. A less sagacious prince might easily have foreseen that the Persians would scarcely be secure in their new possessions, ere the wealth and domains of Lydia would tempt the restless cupidity of their chief. After much deliberation as to the course to be pursued, Crœsus resorted for advice to the most celebrated oracles of Greece, and even to that of the Libyan Ammon. The answer he received from Delphi flattered, more fatally than the rest, the inclinations of the king. He was informed "that if he prosecuted a war with Persia a mighty empire would be overthrown, and he was advised to seek the alliance of the most powerful states of Greece." Overjoyed with a response to which his hopes gave but one interpretation, the king prodigalized fresh presents on the Delphians, and received from them in return, for his people and himself, the honour of priority above all other nations in consulting the oracle, a distinguished seat in the temple, and the right of the citizenship of Delphi. Once more the fated monarch sought the oracle, and demanded if his power should ever fail. Thus replied the Pythian:—"When a mule shall sit enthroned over the

Medes, fly, soft Lydian, across the pebbly waters of the Hermus." The ingenuity of Crœsus could discover in this reply no reason for alarm, confident that a mule could never be the sovereign of the Medes. Thus animated, and led on, the son of Alyattes prepared to oppose, while it was yet time, the progress of the Persian arms. He collected all the force he could summon from his provinces—crossed the Halys—entered Cappadocia—devastated the surrounding country—destroyed several towns—and finally met on the plains of Pteria the Persian army. The victory was undecided; but Crœsus, not satisfied with the force he led, which was inferior to that of Cyrus, returned to Sardis, despatched envoys for succour into Egypt and to Babylon, and disbanded, for the present, the disciplined mercenaries whom he had conducted into Cappadocia. But Cyrus was aware of the movements of the enemy, and by forced and rapid marches arrived at Sardis, and encamped before its walls. His army dismissed—his allies scarcely reached by his ambassadors—Crœsus yet showed himself equal to the peril of his fortune. His Lydians were among the most valiant of the Asiatic nations—dexterous in their national weapon, the spear, and renowned for the skill and prowess of their cavalry.

XII. In a wide plain, in the very neighbourhood of the royal Sardis, and watered "by the pebbly stream of the Hermus", the cavalry of Lydia met, and were routed by the force of Cyrus. The city was besieged and taken, and the wisest and wealthiest of the eastern kings sunk thenceforth into a petty vassal, consigned as guest or prisoner to a Median city near Ecbatana.[15] The prophecy was fulfilled, and a mighty empire overthrown.[16]

The Grecian colonies of Asia, during the Lydian war, had resisted the overtures of Cyrus, and continued faithful to Crœsus; they had now cause to dread the vengeance of the conqueror. The Ionians and Æolians sent to

15 Ctesias. Mr Thirlwall, in my judgment, very properly contents himself with recording the ultimate destination of Crœsus as we find it in Ctesias, to the rejection of the beautiful romance of Herodotus. Justin observes that Crœsus was so beloved among the Grecian cities, that, had Cyrus exercised any cruelty against him, the Persian hero would have drawn upon himself a war with Greece.

16 After his fall, Crœsus is said by Herodotus to have reproached the Pythian with those treacherous oracles that conduced to the loss of his throne, and to have demanded if the gods of Greece were usually delusive and ungrateful. True to that dark article of Grecian faith which punished remote generations for ancestral crimes, the Pythian replied, that Crœsus had been fated to expiate in his own person the crimes of Gyges, the murderer of his master;—that, for the rest, the declarations of the oracle had been verified; the mighty empire, denounced by the divine voice, had been destroyed, for it was his own, and the mule, Cyrus, was presiding over the Lydian realm: a mule might the Persian hero justly be entitled, since his parents were of different ranks and nations. His father a lowborn Persian—his mother a Median princess. Herodotus assures us that Crœsus was content with the explanation—if so, the god of song was more fortunate than the earthly poets he inspires, who have indeed often, imitating his example, sacrificed their friends to a play upon words, without being so easily able to satisfy their victims.

demand the assistance of Lacedæmon, pledged equally with themselves to the Lydian cause. But the Spartans, yet more cautious than courageous, saw but little profit in so unequal an alliance. They peremptorily refused the offer of the colonists, but, after their departure, warily sent a vessel of fifty oars to watch the proceedings of Cyrus, and finally deputed Lacrines, a Spartan of distinction, to inform the monarch of the Persian, Median, and Lydian empires, that any injury to the Grecian cities would be resented by the Spartans. Cyrus asked with polite astonishment of the Greeks about him, "Who these Spartans were?" and having ascertained as much as he could comprehend concerning their military force and their social habits, replied, "that men who had a large space in the middle of their city for the purpose of cheating one another, could not be to him an object of terror": so little respect had the hardy warrior for the decent frauds of oratory and of trade. Meanwhile, he obligingly added, "that if he continued in health, their concern for the Ionian troubles might possibly be merged in the greatness of their own." Soon afterward Cyrus swept onwards in the prosecution of his vast designs, overrunning Assyria, and rushing through the channels of Euphrates into the palaces of Babylon, and the halls of the scriptural Belshazzar. His son, Cambyses, added the mystic Egypt to the vast conquests of Cyrus—and a stranger to the blood of the great victor, by means of superstitious accident or political intrigue, ascended the throne of Asia, known to European history under the name of Darius. The generals of Cyrus had reduced to the Persian yoke the Ionian colonies; the isle of Samos (the first of the isles subjected) was afterward conquered by a satrap of Sardis, and Darius, who, impelled by the ambition of his predecessors, had led with no similar success a vast armament against the wandering Scythians, added, on his return, Lesbos, Chios, and other isles in the Ægæan, to the new monarchy of the world. As, in the often analogous history of Italian republics, we find in every incursion of the German emperor that some crafty noble of a free state joined the banner of a Frederick or a Henry in the hope of receiving from the imperial favour the tyranny of his own city—so there had not been wanting in the Grecian colonies men of boldness and ambition, who flocked to the Persian standard, and, in gratitude for their services against the Scythian, were rewarded with the supreme government of their native cities. Thus was raised Coes, a private citizen, to the tyranny of Mitylene—and thus Histiæus, already possessing, was confirmed by Darius in, that of Miletus. Meanwhile Megabazus, a general of the Persian monarch, at the head of an army of eighty thousand men, subdued Thrace, and made Macedonia tributary to the Persian throne. Having now established, as he deemed securely, the affairs of the empire in Asia Minor, Darius placed his brother Artaphernes in the powerful satrapy of Sardis, and returned to his capital of Susa.

XIII. To this satrap, brother of that mighty monarch, came the ambassadors of Athens. Let us cast our eyes along the map of the ancient world

RESULT OF THE ATHENIAN
EMBASSY TO SARDIS

—and survey the vast circumference of the Persian
realm, stretching almost over the civilized globe.
To the east no boundary was visible before the
Indus. To the north the empire extended to the Caspian and the Euxine seas,
with that steep Caucasian range, never passed even by the most daring of the
early Asiatic conquerors. Eastward of the Caspian, the rivers of Oxus and
Iaxartes divided the subjects of the great king from the ravages of the Tartar;
the Arabian peninsula interposed its burning sands, a barrier to the south—
while the western territories of the empire, including Syria, Phœnicia, the
fertile satrapies of Asia Minor, were washed by the Mediterranean seas.
Suddenly turning from this immense empire, let us next endeavour to discover those dominions from which the Athenian ambassadors were deputed:
far down in a remote corner of the earth we perceive at last the scarce visible
nook of Attica, with its capital of Athens—a domain that in its extremest
length measured sixty geographical miles! We may now judge of the con-
descending wonder with which the brother of Darius listened to the ambassadors of a people, by whose glory alone his name is transmitted to posterity.
Yet was there nothing unnatural or unduly arrogant in his reply. "Send
Darius", said the satrap, affably, "earth and water (the accustomed symbols
of homage), and he will accept your alliance." The ambassadors deliberated,
and, impressed by the might of Persia, and the sense of their own unfriended
condition, they accepted the proposals.

If, fresh from our survey of the immeasurable disparity of power between
the two states, we cannot but allow the answer of the satrap was such as
might be expected, it is not without a thrill of sympathy and admiration we
learn, that no sooner had the ambassadors returned to Athens, than they
received from the handful of its citizens a severe reprimand for their submission. Indignant at the proposal of the satrap, that brave people recurred
no more to the thought of the alliance. In haughty patience, unassisted and
alone, they awaited the burst of the tempest which they foresaw.

XIV. Meanwhile, Cleomenes, chafed at the failure of his attempt on the
Athenian liberties, and conceiving, in the true spirit of injustice, that he had

CONDUCT OF CLEOMENES
—VICTORY OF THE ATHE-
NIANS AGAINST THE BŒO-
TIANS AND CHALCIDIANS

been rather the aggrieved than the aggressor,
levied forces in different parts of the Peloponnesus,
but without divulging the object he had in view.[17]
That object was twofold—vengeance upon Athens,
and the restoration of Isagoras. At length he threw
off the mask, and at the head of a considerable force seized upon the holy
city of Eleusis. Simultaneously, and in concert with the Spartan, the Bœotians
forcibly took possession of Œnoe and Hysiæ—two towns on the extremity
of Attica; while from Chalcis (the principal city of the isle of Eubœa which

17 Herod., v. 74.

fronted the Attic coast) a formidable band ravaged the Athenian territories. Threatened by this threefold invasion, the measures of the Athenians were prompt and vigorous. They left for the present unavenged the incursions of the Bœotians and Chalcidians, and marched with all the force they could collect against Cleomenes at Eleusis. The two armies were prepared for battle, when a sudden revolution in the Spartan camp delivered the Athenians from the most powerful of their foes. The Corinthians, ensnared by Cleomenes into measures of the object of which they had first been ignorant, abruptly retired from the field. Immediately afterward a dissension broke out between Cleomenes and Demaratus, the other king of Sparta, who had hitherto supported his colleague in all his designs, and Demaratus hastily quitted Eleusis and returned to Lacedæmon. At this disunion between the kings of Sparta, accompanied, as it was, by the secession of the Corinthians, the other confederates broke up the camp, returned home, and left Cleomenes with so scanty a force that he was compelled to forego his resentment and his vengeance, and retreat from the sacred city. The Athenians now turned their arms against the Chalcidians, who had retired to Eubœa; but, encountering the Bœotians, who were on their march to assist their island ally, they engaged and defeated them with a considerable slaughter. Flushed by their victory, the Athenians rested not upon their arms—on the same day they crossed that narrow strait which divided them from Eubœa, and obtained a second and equally signal victory over the Chalcidians. There they confirmed their conquest by the establishment of four thousand colonists[18] in the fertile meadows of Eubœa, which had been dedicated by the islanders to the pasturage of their horses. The Athenians returned in triumph to their city. At the price of two minæ each, their numerous prisoners were ransomed, and the captive chains suspended from the walls of the citadel. A tenth part of the general ransom was consecrated, and applied to the purchase of a brazen chariot, placed in the entrance of the citadel, with an inscription which dedicated it to the tutelary goddess of Athens.

"Not from the example of the Athenians only", proceeds the father of history, "but from universal experience, do we learn that an equal form of government is the best. While in subjection to tyrants the Athenians excelled in war none of their neighbours—delivered from the oppressor, they excelled them all; an evident proof that, controlled by one man they exerted themselves feebly, because exertion was for a master; regaining liberty, each man was made zealous, because his zeal was for himself, and his individual interest was the common weal."[19] Venerable praise and accurate distinction![20]

18 If colonists they can properly be called—they retained their connexion with Athens, and all their rights of franchise.
19 Herod., v. 75.
20 Mr Mitford, constantly endeavouring to pervert the simple honesty of Herodotus to a sanction of despotic governments, carefully slurs over this remarkable passage.

XV. The Bœotians, resentful of their defeat, sent to the Pythian oracle to demand the best means of obtaining revenge. The Pythian recommended an alliance with their nearest neighbours. The Bœotians, who, although the inspiring Helicon hallowed their domain, were esteemed but a dull and obtuse race, interpreted this response in favour of the people of the rocky island of Ægina—certainly not their nearest neighbours, if the question were to be settled by geographers. The wealthy inhabitants of that illustrious isle, which, rising above that part of the Ægæan called Sinus Saronicus, we may yet behold in a clear sky from the heights of Phyle, had long entertained a hatred against the Athenians. They willingly embraced the proffered alliance of the Bœotians, and the two states ravaged in concert the coast of Attica. While the Athenians were preparing to avenge the aggression, they received a warning from the Delphic oracle, enjoining them to refrain from all hostilities with the people of Ægina for thirty years, at the termination of which period they were to erect a fane to Æacus (the son of Jupiter, from whom, according to tradition, the island had received its name), and then they might commence war with success. The Athenians, on hearing the response, forestalled the time specified by the oracle by erecting at once a temple to Æacus in their forum. After-circumstances did not allow them to delay to the end of thirty years the prosecution of the war. Meanwhile the unsleeping wrath of their old enemy, Cleomenes, demanded their full attention. In the character of that fierce and restless Spartan, we recognize from the commencement of his career the taint of that insanity to which he subsequently fell a victim.[21] In his earlier life, in a war with the Argives, he had burnt five thousand fugitives by setting fire to the grove whither they had fled—an act of flagrant impiety, no less than of ferocious cruelty, according to the tender superstition of the Greeks. During his occupation of Eleusis, he wantonly violated the mysterious sanctuary of Orgas—the place above all others most consecrated to the Eleusinian gods. His actions and enterprises were invariably inconsistent and vague. He enters Athens to restore her liberties—joins with Isagoras to destroy them; engages in an attempt to revolutionize that energetic state without any adequate preparation—seizes the citadel today to quit it disgracefully tomorrow; invades Eleusis with an army he cannot keep together, and, in the ludicrous cunning common to the insane, disguises from his allies the very enemy against whom they are to fight, in order, as common sense might have expected, to be deserted by them in the instant of battle. And now, prosecuting still further the contradictory tenor of his conduct, he who had driven Hippias from Athens persuades the Spartan assembly to restore the very tyrant the Spartan arms had expelled. In order to stimulate the fears of his countrymen,

---

21 Paus., iii. 5, 6.

Cleomenes[22] asserted, that he had discovered in the Athenian citadel certain oracular predictions, till then unknown, foreboding to the Spartans many dark and strange calamities from the hands of the Athenians.[23] The astute people whom the king addressed were more moved by political interests than religious warnings. They observed, that when oppressed by tyranny, the Athenians had been weak and servile, but, if admitted to the advantages of liberty, would soon grow to a power equal to their own:[24] and in the restoration of a tyrant, their sagacity foreboded the depression of a rival.

XVI. Hippias, who had hitherto resided with his half-brother at Sigeum, was invited to Lacedæmon. He arrived—the Spartans assembled the ambassadors of their various tribes—and in full council thus spoke the policy of Sparta.

HIPPIAS ARRIVES
AT SPARTA

> Friends and allies, we acknowledge that we have erred; misled by deceiving oracles, we have banished from Athens men united to us by ancient hospitality. We restored a republican government to an ungrateful people, who, forgetful that to us they owed their liberty, expelled from among them our subjects and our king. Every day they exhibit a fiercer spirit—proofs of which have been already experienced by the Bœotians, the Chalcidians, and may speedily extend to others, unless they take in time wise and salutary precautions. We have erred—we are prepared to atone for our fault, and to aid you in the chastisement of the Athenians. With this intention we have summoned Hippias and yourselves, that by common counsel and united arms we may restore to the son of Pisistratus the dominion and the dignity of which we have deprived him.

The sentiments of the Spartans received but little favour in the assembly. After a dead and chilling silence, up rose Sosicles, the ambassador for Corinth, whose noble reply reveals to us the true cause of the secession of the Corinthians at Eleusis. "We may expect", said he, with indignant eloquence,

THE SPEECH OF SOSICLES
THE CORINTHIAN

> to see the earth take the place of heaven, since you, oh Spartans, meditate the subversion of equal laws and the restoration of tyrannical

---

22 Mr Mitford, always unduly partial to the Spartan policy, styles Cleomenes "a man violent in his temper, but of considerable abilities". There is no evidence of his abilities. His restlessness and ferocity made him assume a prominent part which he was never adequate to fulfil: he was, at best, a cunning madman.

23 Why, if discovered so long since by Cleomenes, were they concealed till now? The Spartan prince, afterward detected in bribing the oracle itself, perhaps forged these oracular predictions.

24 Herod., v. 91.

governments—a design than which nothing can be more unjust, nothing more wicked. If you think it well that states should be governed by tyrants, Spartans, before you establish tyranny for others, establish it among yourselves! You act unworthily with your allies. You, who so carefully guard against the intrusion of tyranny in Sparta—had you known it as we have done, you would be better sensible of the calamities it entails: listen to some of its effects.

(Here the ambassador related at length the cruelties of Periander, the tyrant of Corinth.) "Such", said he, in conclusion,

such is a tyrannical government—such its effects. Great was our marvel when we learned that it was you, oh Spartans, who had sent for Hippias,—at your sentiments we marvel more. Oh! by the gods, the celestial guardians of Greece, we adjure you not to build up tyrannies in our cities. If you persevere in your purpose—if, against all justice, you attempt the restoration of Hippias, know, at least, that the Corinthians will never sanction your designs.

It was in vain that Hippias, despite his own ability, despite the approval of the Spartans, endeavoured to counteract the impression of this stern harangue,—in vain he relied on the declarations of the oracles,—in vain appealed to the jealousy of the Corinthians, and assured them of the ambition of Athens. The confederates with one accord sympathized with the sentiments of Sosicles, and adjured the Spartans to sanction no innovations prejudicial to the liberties of a single city of Greece.

XVII. The failure of propositions so openly made is a fresh proof of the rash and unthinking character of Cleomenes—eager as usual for all designs, and prepared for none. The Spartans abandoned their design, and Hippias, discomfited but not dispirited, quitted the Lacedæmonian capital. Some of the chiefs of Thessaly, as well as the prince of Macedon, offered him an honourable retreat in their dominions. But it was not an asylum, it was an ally, that the unyielding ambition of Hippias desired to secure. He regained Sigeum, and thence, departing to Sardis, sought the assistance of the satrap, Artaphernes. He who in prosperity was the tyrant, became, in adversity, the traitor of his country; and the son of Pisistratus exerted every effort of his hereditary talent of persuasion to induce the satrap not so much to restore the usurper as to reduce the Athenian republic to the Persian yoke.[25] The arrival and the

HIPPIAS RETIRES
TO SARDIS

---

25 What is the language of Mr Mitford at this treason? "We have seen", says that historian, "the democracy of Athens itself setting the example (among the states of old Greece) of soliciting Persian protection. Will, then, the liberal spirit of patriotism and equal

intrigues of this formidable guest at the court of Sardis soon reached the ears of the vigilant Athenians; they sent to Artaphernes, exhorting him not to place confidence in those whose offences had banished them from Athens. "If you wish for peace", returned the satrap, "recall Hippias." Rather than accede to this condition, that brave people, in their petty share of the extremity of Greece, chose to be deemed the enemies of the vast monarchy of Persia.[26]

government *justify the prejudices of Athenian faction* (!!!) and doom Hippias to peculiar execration, because, at length, he also, with many of his fellow-citizens, despairing of other means for ever returning to their native country, applied to Artaphernes at Sardis?" It is difficult to know which to admire most, the stupidity or dishonesty of this passage. The Athenian democracy applied to Persia for relief against the unjust invasion of their city and liberties by a foreign force; Hippias applied to Persia, not only to interfere in the domestic affairs of a free state, but to reduce that state, his native city, to the subjection of the satrap. Is there any parallel between these cases? If not, what dullness in instituting it! But the dishonesty is equal to the dullness. Herodotus, the only author Mr Mitford here follows, expressly declares (v. 96) that Hippias sought to induce Artaphernes to subject Athens to the sway of the satrap and his master, Darius; yet Mr Mitford says not a syllable of this, leaving his reader to suppose that Hippias merely sought to be restored to his country through the intercession of the satrap.

26 Herod., v. 96.

CHAPTER IV

Histiæus, tyrant of Miletus, removed to Persia—the government of that city deputed to Aristagoras, who invades Naxos with the aid of the Persians—ill success of that expedition—Aristagoras resolves upon revolting from the Persians—repairs to Sparta and to Athens—the Athenians and Eretrians induced to assist the Ionians—burning of Sardis—the Ionian war—the fate of Aristagoras—naval battle of Ladé—fall of Miletus—reduction of Ionia—Miltiades—his character—Mardonius replaces Artaphernes in the Lydian satrapy—hostilities between Ægina and Athens—conduct of Cleomenes—Demaratus deposed—death of Cleomenes—new Persian expedition

I. We have seen that Darius rewarded with a tributary command the services of Grecian nobles during his Scythian expedition. The most remarkable of these deputy tyrants was Histiæus, the tyrant of Miletus. Possessed of that dignity prior to his connexion with Darius, he had received from the generosity of the monarch a tract of land near the river Strymon, in Thrace, sufficing for the erection of a city called Myrcinus. To his cousin, Aristagoras, he committed the government of Miletus—repaired to his new possession, and employed himself actively in the foundations of a colony which promised to be one of the most powerful that Miletus had yet established. The site of the infant city was selected with admirable judgment upon a navigable river, in the vicinity of mines, and holding the key of commercial communication between the long chain of Thracian tribes on the one side, and the trading enterprise of Grecian cities on the other. Histiæus was describing the walls with which the ancient cities were surrounded, when Megabazus, commander of the forces intended to consummate the conquest of Thrace, had the sagacity to warn the Persian king, then at Sardis, of the probable effects of the regal donation. "Have you, sire, done wisely", said he, "in permitting this able and active Greek to erect a new city in Thrace? Know you not that that favoured land, abounding in mines of silver, possesses also every advantage for the construction and equipment of ships; wild Greeks and roving barbarians are mingled there, ripe for enterprise—ready to execute the commands of

HISTIÆUS, TYRANT OF MILETUS, REMOVED TO PERSIA—THE GOVERNMENT OF THAT CITY DEPUTED TO ARISTAGORAS, WHO INVADES NAXOS WITH THE AID OF THE PERSIANS

233

any resolute and aspiring leader? Fear the possibility of a civil war—prevent the chances of the ambition of Histiæus,—have recourse to artifice rather than to force,—get him in your power, and prevent his return to Greece."

Darius followed the advice of his general, sent for Histiæus, loaded him with compliments, and, pretending that he could not live without his counsels, carried him off from his Thracian settlement to the Persian capital of Susa. His kinsman, Aristagoras, continued to preside over the government of Miletus, then the most haughty and flourishing of the Ionian states; but Naxos, beneath it in power, surpassed it in wealth; the fertile soil of that fair isle—its numerous population—its convenient site—its abundant resources, attracted the cupidity of Aristagoras; he took advantage of a civil commotion, in which many of the nobles were banished by the people—received the exiles—and, under the pretence of restoring them, meditated the design of annexing the largest of the Cyclades to the tyranny of Miletus.

He persuaded the traitorous nobles to suffer him to treat with Artaphernes—successfully represented to that satrap the advantages of annexing the gem of the Cyclades to the Persian diadem—and Darius, listening to the advice of his delegate, sent two hundred vessels to the invasion of Naxos, under the command of his kinsman, Megabates. A quarrel ensued, however, between the Persian general and the governor of Miletus. Megabates, not powerful enough to crush the tyrant, secretly informed the Naxians of the meditated attack; and, thus prepared for the assault, they so well maintained themselves in their city, that, after a siege of four months, the pecuniary resources, not only of Megabates, but of Aristagoras, were exhausted, and the invaders were compelled to retreat from the island. Aristagoras now saw that he had fallen into the pit he had digged for others: his treasury was drained—he had incurred heavy debts with the Persian government, which condemned him to reimburse the whole expense of the enterprise—he feared the resentment of Megabates and the disappointment of Artaphernes—and he foresaw that his ill success might be a reasonable plea for removing him from the government of Miletus. While he himself was meditating the desperate expedient of a revolt, a secret messenger from Histiæus suddenly arrived at Miletus. That wily Greek, disgusted with his magnificent captivity, had had recourse to a singular expedient: selecting the most faithful of his slaves, he shaved his skull, wrote certain characters on the surface, and, when the hair was again grown, dismissed this living letter to Aristagoras.[1] The characters commanded the deputy to

ILL SUCCESS OF THAT EXPEDITION

---

1 Aulus Gellius, who relates this anecdote with more detail than Herodotus, asserts that the slave himself was ignorant of the characters written on his skull, that Histiæus selected a domestic who had a disease in his eyes—shaved him, punctured the skin, and sending him to Miletus when the hair was grown, assured the credulous patient that Aristagoras would complete the cure by shaving him a second time. According to this story, we must rather admire the simplicity of the slave than the ingenuity of Histiæus.

commence a revolt; for Histiæus imagined that the quiet of Miletus was the sentence of his exile.

II. This seasonable advice, so accordant with his own views, charmed Aristagoras: he summoned the Milesians, and, to engage their zealous assist-

ance, he divested himself of the tyranny, and established a republic. It was a mighty epoch that, for the stir of thought!—everywhere had awakened a desire for free government and equal laws; and Aristagoras, desirous of conciliating the rest of Ionia, assisted her various states in the establishment of republican institutions. Coës, the tyrant of Mitylene, perished by the hands of the people; in the rest of Ionia, the tyrants were punished but by exile. Thus a spark kindled the universal train already prepared in thought, and the selfish ambition of Aristagoras forwarded the march of a revolution in favour of liberty that embraced all the cities of Ionia. But Aristagoras, evidently a man of a profound, though tortuous policy, was desirous of engaging not only the colonies of Greece, but the mother country also, in the great and perilous attempt to resist the Persian. High above all the states of the older Greece soared the military fame of Sparta; and that people the scheming Milesian resolved first to persuade to his daring project.

Trusting to no ambassador, but to his own powers of eloquence, he arrived in person at Sparta. With a brazen chart of the world, as the known,

in his hand, he sought to inspire the ambition of Cleomenes by pointing out the wide domains—the exhaustless treasures of the Persian realm. He depreciated the valour of its people, ridiculed their weapons, and urged him to the vast design of establishing, by Spartan valour, the insignificant conquest of Asia. The Spartans, always cold to the liberty of other states, were no less indifferent to the glory of barren victories; and when Aristagoras too honestly replied, in answer to a question of the king, that from the Ionian Sea to Susa, the Persian capital, was a journey of three months, Cleomenes abruptly exclaimed, "Milesian, depart from Sparta before sunset;—a march of three months from the sea! —the Spartans will never listen to so frantic a proposal!" Aristagoras, not defeated, sought a subsequent interview, in which he attempted to bribe the king, who, more accustomed to bribe others than be bribed, broke up the conference, and never afterward would renew it.

III. The patient and plotting Milesian departed thence to Athens: he arrived there just at the moment when the Athenian ambassadors had returned from Sardis, charged with the haughty reply of Artaphernes to the mission concerning Hippias. The citizens were aroused, excited, inflamed; equally indignant at the insolence, and fearful of the power, of the satrap. It was a favourable occasion for Aristagoras!

To the imagination of the reader this passage in history presents a striking picture. We may behold the great assembly of that lively, high-souled,

THE ATHENIANS AND ERETRIANS INDUCED TO ASSIST THE IONIANS

sensitive, and inflammable people. There is the Agora;—there the half-built temple to Æacus;—above, the citadel, where yet hang the chains of the captive enemy;—still linger in the ears of the populace, already vain of their prowess, and haughty in their freedom, the menace of the Persian—the words that threatened them with the restoration of the exiled tyrant; and at this moment, and in this concourse, we see the subtle Milesian, wise in the experience of mankind, popular with all free states, from having restored freedom to the colonies of Ionia—every advantage of foreign circumstance and intrinsic ability in his favour,—about to address the breathless and excited multitude. He rose: he painted, as he had done to Cleomenes, in lively colours, the wealth of Asia, the effeminate habits of its people—he described its armies fighting without spear or shield—he invoked the valour of a nation already successful in war against hardy and heroic foes—he appealed to old hereditary ties; the people of Miletus had been an Athenian colony—should not the parent protect the child in the greatest of all blessings—the right to liberty? Now he entreats—now he promises,—the sympathy of the free, the enthusiasm of the brave, are alike aroused. He succeeds; the people accede to his views. "It is easier", says the homely Herodotus, "to gain (or delude) a multitude than an individual; and the eloquence which had failed with Cleomenes enlisted thirty thousand Athenians."[2]

IV. The Athenians agreed to send to the succour of their own colonists, the Ionians, twenty vessels of war. Melanthius, a man of amiable character and popular influence, was appointed the chief. This was the true commencement of the great Persian war.

V. Thus successful, Aristagoras departed from Athens. Arriving at Miletus, he endeavoured yet more to assist his design, by attempting to arouse a certain colony in Phrygia, formed of Thracian captives[3] taken by Megabazus, the Persian general. A great proportion of these colonists seized the occasion to return to their native land—baffled the pursuit of the Persian horse—reached the shore—and were transported in Ionian vessels to their ancient home on the banks of the Strymon. Meanwhile, the Athenian vessels arrived at Miletus, joined by five ships, manned by Eretrians of Eubœa, mindful of former assistance from the Milesians in a war with their fellow-islanders, the Chalcidians, nor conscious, perhaps, of the might of the enemy they provoked.

Aristagoras remained at Miletus, and delegated to his brother the command of the Milesian forces. The Greeks then sailed to Ephesus, debarked at

2 Rather a hyperbolical expression—the total number of free Athenians did not exceed twenty thousand.
3 The Pæonians.

Coressus in its vicinity, and, under the conduct of Ephesian guides, marched along the winding valley of the Cayster—whose rapid course, under a barbarous name, the traveller yet traces, though the swans of the Grecian poets haunt its waves no more—passed over the auriferous Mount of Tmolus, verdant with the vine, and fragrant with the saffron—and arrived at the gates of the voluptuous Sardis. They found Artaphernes unprepared for this sudden invasion—they seized the city;—the satrap and his troops retreated to the citadel.

The houses of Sardis were chiefly built of reeds, and the same slight and inflammable material thatched the roofs even of the few mansions built of brick. A house was set on fire by a soldier—the flames spread throughout the city. In the midst of the conflagration despair gave valour to the besieged—the wrath of man was less fearful than that of the element; the Lydians, and the Persians who were in the garrison, rushed into the market-place, through which flowed the river of Pactolus. There they resolved to encounter the enemy. The invaders were seized with a sudden panic, possibly as much occasioned by the rage of the conflagration as the desperation of the foe; and, retiring to Mount Tmolus, took advantage of the night to retrace their march along the valley of the Cayster.

BURNING OF SARDIS

VI. But the Ionians were not fated to return in safety: from the borders of the river Halys a troop of Persians followed their retreat, and overtaking them when the Ephesian territory was already gained, defeated the Ionians with a great slaughter, amid which fell the leader of the Eretrians.

THE IONIAN WAR

The Athenians were naturally disappointed with the result of this expedition. Returning home, they refused all the overtures of Aristagoras to renew their incursions into Asia. The gallant Ionians continued, however, the hostilities they had commenced against Darius. They sailed to the Hellespont, and reduced Byzantium, with the neighbouring cities. Their forces were joined by the Cyprians, aroused against the Persian yoke by Onesilus, a bold usurper, who had dethroned his brother, the prince of Salamis, in Cyprus; and the conflagration of Sardis dazzling the Carians, hitherto lukewarm, united to the Ionian cause the bulk of that hardy population. The revolt now assumed a menacing and formidable aspect. Informed of these events, Darius summoned Histiæus: "The man", said he, "whom you appointed to the government of Miletus has rebelled against me. Assisted by the Ionians, whom I shall unquestionably chastise, he has burnt Sardis. Had he your approbation? Without it would he have dared such treason? Beware how you offend a second time against my authority." Histiæus artfully vindicated himself from the suspicions of the king. He attributed the revolt of the Ionians to his own absence, declared that if sent into Ionia he would soon restore its inhabitants to their wonted submission, and even promised to render the island of Sardinia tributary to Persia.

VII. Deluded by these professions, Darius dismissed the tyrant of Miletus, requiring only his return on the fulfilment of his promises. Meanwhile, the generals of Darius pressed vigorously on the insurgents. Against Onesilus, then engaged in reducing Amathus (the single city in Cyprus opposed to him), Artybius, a Persian officer, conducted a formidable fleet. The Ionians hastened to the succour of their Cyprian ally—a battle ensued both by land and sea:—in the latter the Ionians defeated, after a severe contest, the Phœnician auxiliaries of Persia—in the former, a treacherous desertion of some of the Cyprian troops gave a victory to the Persian. The brave Onesilus, who had set his fate upon the issue of the field, was among the slain. The Persians proceeded to blockade, and ultimately to regain, the Cyprian cities: of these, Soli, which withstood a siege of five months, proffered the most obdurate resistance; with the surrender of that gallant city, Cyprus once more, after a year of liberty, was subjected to the dominion of the great king.

This success was increased by the reduction of several towns on the Hellespont, and two signal defeats over the Carians, in the last of which the Milesians, who had joined their ally, suffered a prodigious loss. The Carians, however, were not subdued, and in a subsequent engagement they effected a great slaughter among the Persians, the glory of which was enhanced by the death of Daurises, general of the barbarians, and son-in-law to Darius. But this action was not sufficiently decisive to arrest the progress of the Persian arms. Artaphernes, satrap of Sardis, and Otanes, the third general in command, led their forces into Ionia and Æolia:—the Ionian Clazomenæ, the Æolian Cuma, were speedily reduced.

VIII. The capture of these places, with the general fortunes of the war, disheartened even the patient and adventurous Aristagoras. He could not

THE FATE OF ARISTAGORAS

but believe that all attempts against the crushing power of Darius were in vain. He assembled the adherents yet faithful to his arms, and painted to them the necessity of providing a new settlement. Miletus was no longer secure, and the vengeance of Darius was gathering rapidly around them. After some consultation they agreed to repair to that town and territory in Thrace which had been given by Darius to Histiæus.[4] Miletus was entrusted to the charge of a popular citizen named

---

4 Hecatæus, the historian of Miletus, opposed the retreat to Myrcinus, advising his country-men rather to fortify themselves in the isle of Leros, and await the occasion to return to Miletus. This early writer seems to have been one of those sagacious men who rarely obtain their proper influence in public affairs, because they address the reason in opposition to the passions of those they desire to lead. Unsuccessful in this proposition, Hecatæus had equally failed on two former occasions:—first, when he attempted to dissuade the Milesians from the revolt of Aristagoras; second, when, finding them bent upon it, he advised them to appropriate the sacred treasures in the temple at Branchidas to the maintenance of a naval force. On each occasion his advice failed precisely because given without prejudice or passion. The successful adviser must appear to sympathize even with the errors of his audience.

Pythagoras, and these hardy and restless adventurers embarked for Thrace. Aristagoras was fortunate enough to reach in safety the settlement which had seemed so formidable a possession to the Persian general; but his usual scheming and bold ambition, not contented with that domain, led him to the attack of a town in its vicinity. The inhabitants agreed to resign it into his hands, and, probably lulled into security by this concession, he was suddenly, with his whole force, cut off by an incursion of the Thracian foe. So perished the author of many subsequent and mighty events, and who, the more we regard his craft, his courage, his perseverance, and activity, the vastness of his ends, and the perseverance with which he pursued them, must be regarded by the historian as one of the most stirring and remarkable spirits of that enterprising age.

IX. The people of Miletus had not, upon light grounds or with feeble minds, embarked in the perilous attempt to recover their liberties. Deep was the sentiment that inspired—solemn and stern the energy which supported them. The Persian generals

NAVAL BATTLE OF LADÉ

now collected in one body their native and auxiliary force. The Cyprians, lately subdued, were compelled to serve. Egypt and Cilicia swelled the armament, and the skill of the Phœnicians rendered yet more formidable a fleet of six hundred vessels. With this power the barbarians advanced upon Miletus. Most, if not all, of the Ionian states prepared themselves for the struggle—delegates met at the Panionium—it was agreed to shun the Persians upon land—to leave to the Milesians the defence of their city—to equip the utmost naval force they could command—and, assembling in one fleet off the small isle of Ladé, opposite to Miletus, to hazard the battle upon the seas. Three hundred and fifty triremes were provided, and met at the appointed place. The discipline of the navy was not equal to the valour of the enterprise; Dionysius, commander of the Phocæans, attempted, perhaps too rigorously, to enforce it;—jealousy and disgust broke out among the troops—and the Samian leaders, whether displeased with their allies, or tempted by the Persians, who, through the medium of the exiled tyrants of Greece, serving with them, maintained correspondence with the Ionians, secretly agreed to desert in the midst of the ensuing battle. This compact made, the Phœnicians commenced the attack, and the Ionians, unsuspicious of treachery, met them with a contracted line. In the beginning of the engagement, the Samians, excepting only eleven ships (whose captains were afterward rewarded by a public column in their native market-place), fulfilled their pledge, and sailed away to Samos. The Lesbians, stationed next them, followed their example, and confusion and flight became contagious. The Chians alone redeemed the character of the allies, aided, indeed, by Dionysius the Phocæan, who, after taking three of the enemy's ships, refused to retreat till the day was gone, and then, sailing to Phœnicia, sunk several trading-vessels, enriched himself with their spoil, and eventually reaching Sicily, became renowned as a pirate, formidable to the Carthaginian and

239

Tyrsenian families of the old Phœnician foe, but holding his Grecian countrymen sacred from his depredations.

The Persian armament now bent all its vengeance on Miletus; they besieged it both by land and by sea—every species of military machine then known was directed against its walls, and, in the sixth year after the revolt of Aristagoras, Miletus fell—Miletus, the capital of Ionia—the mother of a hundred colonies! Pittacus, Thales, Arctinus, were among the great names she gave to science and to song. Worthy of her renown, she fell amid the ruins of that freedom which she showed how nobly she could have continued to adorn by proving how sternly she could defend. The greater part of the citizens were slain—those who remained, with the women and the children, were borne into slavery by the victors. Their valour and renown touched the heart of Darius, and he established the captives in a city by that part of the Erythræan Sea which receives the waters of the Barbarian Tigris. Their ancient territories were portioned out between the Persians and the Carians of Pedasa.

FALL OF MILETUS

X. The Athenians received the news of this fatal siege with the deepest sorrow, and Herodotus records an anecdote illustrative of the character of that impassioned people, and interesting to the history of their early letters. Phrynichus, a disciple of Thespis, represented on the stage the capture of Miletus, and the whole audience burst into tears. The art of the poet was considered criminal in thus forcibly reminding the Athenians of a calamity which was deemed their own: he was fined a thousand drachmæ, and the repetition of the piece forbidden—a punishment that was but a glorious homage to the genius of the poet and the sensibility of the people.

After innumerable adventures, in which he exhibited considerable but perverted abilities, Histiæus fell into the hands of Artaphernes, and died upon the cross. Darius rebuked the zeal of the satrap, and lamented the death of a man, whose situation, perhaps, excused his artifices.

And now the cloud swept onward—one after one the Ionian cities were reduced—the islands of Chios, Lesbos, Tenedos, depopulated; and all Ionia subjugated and enslaved. The Persian fleet proceeded to subdue all the towns and territories to the left of the Hellespont. At this time their success in the Chersonesus drove from that troubled isthmus a chief, whose acute and dauntless faculties made him subsequently the scourge of Persia and the deliverer of Greece.

REDUCTION OF IONIA

XI. We have seen Miltiades, nephew to the first of that name, arrive at the Chersonesus—by a stroke of dexterous perfidy, seize the persons of the neighbouring chieftains—attain the sovereignty of that peninsula, and marry the daughter of a Thracian prince. In his character was united, with much of the intellect, all the duplicity of the Greek. During the war between Darius and the Scythians, while affecting to follow the Persian army, he had held traitorous intercourse with the foe, and proposed to the Grecian chiefs to destroy the bridge of

MILTIADES—HIS CHARACTER

boats across the Danube confided to their charge; so that, what with the force of the Scythians and the pressure of famine, the army of Darius would have perished among the Scythian wastes, and a mighty enemy have been lost to Greece—a scheme that, but for wickedness, would have been wise. With all his wiles, and all his dishonesty, Miltiades had the art, not only of rendering authority firm, but popular. Driven from his state by the Scythian Nomades, he was voluntarily recalled by the very subjects over whom he had established an armed sovereignty—a rare occurrence in that era of republics. Surrounded by fierce and restless foes, and exercised in constant, if petty warfare, Miltiades had acquired as much the experience of camps as the subtleties of Grecian diplomacy; yet, like many of the wise of small states, he seems to have been more crafty than rash—the first for flight wherever flight was the better policy—but the first for battle if battle were the more prudent. He had in him none of the inconsiderate enthusiasm of the hero— none of the blind but noble subservience to honour. Valour seems to have been for his profound intellect but the summation of chances, and when we afterward find him the most daring soldier, it is only because he was the acutest calculator.

On seeing the Phœnician fleet, under Persia, arrive off the isle of Tenedos, which is opposite the Chersonesus, Miltiades resolved not to wait the issue of a battle as before he had fled the Scythian, so now, without a struggle, he succumbed to the Phœnician sword. He loaded five vessels with his property —with four he eluded the hostile fleet—the fifth, commanded by his eldest son, was pursued and taken.[5] In triumphant safety the chief of the Chersonesus arrived at Athens. He arrived at that free state to lose the dignity of a Thracian prince, and suddenly to be reminded that he was an Athenian citizen. He was immediately prosecuted for the crime of tyranny. His influence or his art, admiration of his genius, or compassion of his reverses, however, procured him an acquittal. We may well suppose that, highborn and wealthy, he lost no occasion of cementing his popularity in his native state.

XII. Meanwhile, the Persians suspended for that year all further hostilities against the Ionians. Artaphernes endeavoured to conciliate the subdued colonies by useful laws, impartial taxes, and MARDONIUS REPLACES ART- benign recommendations to order and to peace. APHERNES IN THE LYDIAN The next year, however, that satrap was recalled, SATRAPY and Mardonius, a very young noble, the son-in-law of Darius, was appointed, at the head of a considerable naval and military

---

5 The humane Darius—whose virtues were his own, his faults of his station—treated the son of Miltiades with kindness and respect, married him to a Persian woman, and endowed him with an estate. It was the habitual policy of that great king to attach to his dominions the valour and the intellect of the Greeks.

force, to the administration of the affairs in that part of the Persian empire. Entering Ionia, he executed a novel, a daring, but no unstatesman-like stroke of policy. He removed all the Ionian tyrants, and everywhere restored republican forms of government; deeming, unquestionably, that he is the securest master of distant provinces who establishes among them the institutions which they best love. Then proceeding to the Hellespont, Mardonius collected his mighty fleets and powerful army, and passed through Europe towards the avowed objects of the Persian vengeance—the cities of Eretria and Athens.

From the time that the Athenians had assisted the forces of Miletus and Ionia in the destruction of Sardis, their offence had rankled in the bosom of Darius. Like most monarchs, he viewed as more heinous offenders the foreign abetters of rebellion, than the rebels themselves. Religion, no doubt, conspired to augment his indignation. In the conflagration of Sardis the temple of the great Persian deity had perished, and the inexpiated sacrilege made a duty of revenge. So keenly, indeed, did Darius resent the share that the remote Athenians had taken in the destruction of his Lydian capital, that, on receiving the intelligence, he is said to have called for his bow, and, shooting an arrow in the air, to have prayed for vengeance against the offenders; and three times every day, as he sat at table, his attendants were commanded to repeat to him, "Sir, remember the Athenians."

XIII. But the design of Mardonius was not only directed against the Athenians and the state of Eretria, it extended also to the rest of Greece: preparations so vast were not meant to be wasted upon foes apparently insignificant, but rather to consolidate the Persian conquests on the Asiatic coasts; and to impress on the neighbouring continent of Europe adequate conceptions of the power of the great king. By sea, Mardonius subdued the islanders of Thasus, wealthy in its gold-mines; by land he added to the Persian dependances in Thrace and Macedonia. But losses, both by storm and battle, drove him back to Asia, and delayed for a season the deliberate and organized invasion of Greece.

In the following year, while the tributary cities Mardonius had subdued were employed in constructing vessels of war and transports for cavalry, ambassadors were despatched by Darius to the various states of Greece, demanding the homage of earth and water—a preliminary calculated to ascertain who would resist, who submit to, his power—and certain to afford a pretext, in the one case for empire, in the other for invasion. Many of the cities of the continent, and all the islands visited by the ambassadors, had the timidity to comply with the terms proposed. Sparta and Athens, hitherto at variance, united at once in a haughty and indignant refusal. To so great a height was the popular rage in either state aroused by the very demand, that the Spartans threw the ambassadors into their wells, and the Athenians, into their pit of punishment, bidding them thence get their earth and water; a singular coincidence of excess in the two states—to be justified by no pretence—to be extenuated only by the reflection, that liberty ever becomes a species of noble madness when menaced by foreign danger.[6]

XIV. With the rest of the islanders, the people of Ægina, less resolute than their near neighbours and ancient foes, the Athenians, acceded to the proposal of tribute. This, more than the pusillanimity of the other states, alarmed and inflamed the Athenians; they suspected that the Æginetans had formed some hostile alliance against them with the Persians, and hastened to accuse them to Sparta of betraying the liberties of Greece. Nor was there slight ground for the suspicions of the Athenians against Ægina. The people of that island had hereditary and bitter feuds with the Athenians, dating almost from their independence of their parent state of Epidaurus; mercantile jealousies were added to ancestral enmity, and the wares of Athens were forbidden all application to sacred uses in Ægina. We have seen the recent occasion on which Attica was invaded by these hostile neighbours, then allied with Thebes; and at that period the naval force of Ægina was such as to exceed the unconscious and untried resources of the Athenians. The latter had thus cause at once to hate and to dread a rival placed by nature in so immediate a vicinity to themselves, that the submission of Ægina to the Persian seemed in itself sufficient for the destruction of Athens.

HOSTILITIES BETWEEN ÆGINA AND ATHENS

XV. The Athenian ambassadors met with the most favourable reception at Sparta. The sense of their common danger, and sympathy in their mutual courage, united at once these rival states; even the rash and hitherto unrelenting Cleomenes eagerly sought a reconciliation with his former foe. That prince went in person to Ægina, determined to ascertain the authors of the suspected treachery; —with that characteristic violence which he never provided the means to support, and which so invariably stamps this unable and headstrong Spartan, as one who would have been a fool, if he had not been a madman— Cleomenes endeavoured to seize the persons of the accused. He was stoutly resisted, and disgracefully baffled, in this impotent rashness; and his fellow-king, Demaratus, whom we remember to have suddenly deserted Cleomenes at Eleusis, secretly connived with the Æginetans in their opposition to his colleague, and furnished them with an excuse, by insinuating that Cleomenes had been corrupted by the Athenians. But Demaratus was little aware of the dark and deadly passions which Cleomenes combined with his constitutional insanity. Revenge made a great component of his character, and the Grecian history records few instances of a nature more vehemently vindictive.

CONDUCT OF CLEOMENES

6 Pausanias says, that Talthybius afterward razed the house of Miltiades, because that chief instigated the Athenians to the execution of the Persian envoys.

There had been various rumours at Sparta respecting the legitimacy of Demaratus. Cleomenes entered into a secret intrigue with a kinsman of his

DEMARATUS DEPOSED

colleague, named Leotychides, who cherished an equal hatred against Demaratus;[7] the conditions between them were, that Cleomenes should assist in raising Leotychides to the throne of Demaratus, and Leotychides should assist Cleomenes in his vengeance against Ægina. No sooner was this conspiracy agreed upon than Leotychides propagated everywhere the report that the birth of Demaratus was spurious. The Spartans attached the greatest value to legitimacy,—they sent to consult the Pythian—and Cleomenes, through the aid of Colon, a powerful citizen of Delphi, bribed the oracle to assert the illegitimacy of his foe. Demaratus was deposed. Sinking at once into the rank of a private citizen, he was elected to some inferior office. His enemy, Leotychides, now upon his throne, sent him, by way of insult, a message to demand which he preferred—his past or his present dignity. Demaratus was stung, and answered, that the question might fix the date of much weal or much woe to Sparta; saying this, he veiled his head—sought his home—sacrificed to Jupiter—and solemnly adjured his mother to enlighten him as to his legitimacy. The parental answer was far from unequivocal, and the matron appeared desirous of imputing the distinction of his birth to the shade of an ancient Spartan hero, Astrobachus, rather than to the earthly embrace of her husband. Demaratus heard, and formed his decision: he escaped from Sparta, baffled his pursuers, and fled into Asia, where he was honourably received and largely endowed by the beneficent Darius.

XVI. Leotychides, elected to the regal dignity, accompanied Cleomenes to Ægina: the people of that isle yielded to the authority they could not

DEATH OF CLEOMENES

effectually resist; and ten of their most affluent citizens were surrendered as hostages to Athens. But, in the meanwhile, the collusion of Cleomenes with the oracle was discovered—the priestess was solemnly deposed—and Cleomenes dreaded the just indignation of his countrymen. He fled to Thessaly, and thence passing among the Arcadians, he endeavoured to bind that people by the darkest oaths to take arms against his native city—so far could hatred stimulate a man consistent only in his ruling passion of revenge. But the mighty power of Persia now lowering over Lacedæmon, the Spartan citizens resolved to sacrifice even justice to discretion; it was not a time to distract their forces by new foes, and they invited Cleomenes back to Sparta, with the offer of his former station. He returned, but his violent career, happily for all, was now closed;

---

7 Demaratus had not only prevented the marriage of Leotychides with a maiden named Percalos, but, by a mixture of violence and artifice, married her himself. Thus, even among the sober and unloving Spartans, woman could still be the author of revolutions.

his constitutional madness, no longer confined to doubtful extravagance, burst forth into incontrollable excess. He was put under confinement, and obtaining a sword from a Helot, who feared to disobey his commands, he deliberately destroyed himself—not by one wound, but slowly gashing the flesh from his limbs until he gradually ascended to the nobler and more mortal parts. This ferocious suicide excited universal horror, and it was generally deemed the divine penalty of his numerous and sacrilegious crimes: the only dispute among the Greeks was, to which of his black offences the wrath of Heaven was the most justly due.[8]

XVII. No sooner did the news of his suicide reach the Æginetans than those proud and wealthy islanders sought, by an embassy to Sparta, to regain their hostages yet detained at Athens. With the death of Cleomenes, the anger of Sparta against Ægina suddenly ceased—or, rather, we must suppose that a new party, in fellowship with the Æginetan oligarchy, came into power. The Spartans blamed Leotychides for his co-operation with Cleomenes; they even offered to give him up to the Æginetans—and it was finally agreed that he should accompany the ambassadors of Ægina to Athens, and insist on the surrender of the hostages. But the Athenians had now arrived at that spirit of independence, when nor the deadly blows of Persia, nor the iron sword of Sparta, nor the treacherous hostilities of their nearest neighbour, could quell their courage or subdue their pride. They disregarded the presence and the orations of Leotychides, and peremptorily refused to surrender their hostages. Hostilities between Ægina and Athens were immediately renewed. The Æginetans captured the sacred vessel then stationed at Sunium, in which several of the most eminent Athenians were embarked for the festival of Apollo; nor could the sanctity of the voyage preserve the captives from the ignominy of irons. The Athenians resolved upon revenge, and a civil dissension in Ægina placed it in their power. An Æginetan traitor, named Nicodromus, offered them his assistance, and, aided by the popular party opposed to the oligarchical government, he seized the citadel. With twenty ships from Corinth, and fifty of their own, the Athenians invaded Ægina; but, having been delayed in making the adequate preparations, they arrived a day later than had been stipulated. Nicodromus fled; the oligarchy restored, took signal and barbarous vengeance upon such of their insurgent countrymen as fell into their hands. Meanwhile, the Athenian fleet obtained a victory at sea, and the war still continued.

XVIII. While, seemingly unconscious of greater dangers, Athens thus practised her rising energies against the little island of Ægina, thrice every

---

8 The national pride of the Spartans would not, however, allow that their king was the object of the anger of the gods, and ascribing his excesses to his madness, accounted for the last by a habit of excessive drinking, which he had acquired from the Scythians.

NEW PERSIAN EXPEDITION day the servants of the Persian king continued to exclaim, "Sir, remember the Athenians!"[9] The traitor, Hippias, constantly about the person of the courteous monarch, never failed to stimulate still further his vengeance by appealing to his ambition. At length, Darius resolved no longer to delay the accomplishment of his designs. He recalled Mardonius, whose energy, indeed, had not been proportioned to his powers, and appointed two other generals—Datis, a native of the warlike Media, and Artaphernes, his own nephew, son to the former satrap of that name. These were expressly ordered to march at once against Eretria and Athens. And Hippias, now broken in frame, advanced in age,[10] and after an exile of twenty years, accompanied the Persian army—sanguine of success, and grasping, at the verge of life, the shadow of his former sceptre.

9 Herod., vi. 94.
10 Ibid., vi. 107.

CHAPTER V

The Persian generals enter Europe—invasion of Naxos,
Carystus, Eretria—the Athenians demand the aid of Sparta
—the result of their mission and the adventure of their
messenger—the Persians advance to Marathon—the plain
described—division of opinion in the Athenian camp—the
advice of Miltiades prevails—the dream of Hippias—battle
of Marathon

I. On the Cilician coast the Persian armament encamped—thence, in a
fleet of six hundred triremes, it sailed to Samos—passed through the midst
of the clustering Cyclades, and along that part
THE PERSIAN GENERALS
ENTER EUROPE—INVASION
OF NAXOS, CARYSTUS,
ERETRIA
of the Ægæan Sea called "the Icarian", from the
legendary fate of the son of Dædalus—invaded
Naxos—burnt her town and temples, and sparing
the sacred Delos, in which the Median Datis rever-
enced the traditional birthplace of two deities analogous to those most
honoured in the Persian creed[1]—awed into subjection the various isles, until
it arrived at Eubœa, divided but by a strait from Attica, and containing
the city of the Eretrians. The fleet first assailed Carystus, whose generous
citizens refused both to aid against their neighbours, and to give hostages
for their conduct. Closely besieged, and their lands wasted, they were compelled, however, to surrender to the Persians. Thence the victorious armament passed to Eretria. The Athenians had sent to the relief of that city the
four thousand colonists whom they had established in the island—but fear,
jealousy, division, were within the walls. Ruin seemed certain, and a chief of
the Eretrians urged the colonists to quit a city which they were unable to
save. They complied with the advice, and reached Attica in safety. Eretria,
however, withstood a siege of six days; on the seventh the city was betrayed
to the barbarians by two of that fatal oligarchical party, who in every
Grecian city seem to have considered no enemy so detestable as the majority
of their own citizens; the place was pillaged—the temples burnt—the
inhabitants enslaved. Here the Persians rested for a few days ere they
embarked for Attica.

1 The sun and moon.

II. Unsupported and alone, the Athenians were not dismayed. A swift-footed messenger was despatched to Sparta, to implore its prompt assistance. On the day after his departure from Athens, he reached his destination, went straight to the assembled magistrates, and thus addressed them: —

THE ATHENIANS DEMAND
THE AID OF SPARTA

> Men of Lacedæmon, the Athenians supplicate your aid; suffer not the most ancient of the Grecian cities to be enslaved by the barbarian. Already Eretria is subjected to their yoke, and all Greece is diminished by the loss of that illustrious city.

The resource the Athenians had so much right to expect failed them. The Spartans, indeed, resolved to assist Athens, but not until assistance would have come too late. They declared that their religion forbade them to commence a march till the moon was at her full, and this was only the ninth day of the month.[2] With this unsatisfying reply, the messenger returned to Athens. But, employed in this arduous enterprise— his imagination inflamed by the greatness of the danger—and its workings yet more kindled by the loneliness of his adventure and the mountain stillness of the places through which he passed, the Athenian messenger related, on his return, a vision less probably the creation of his invention than of his excited fancy. Passing over the Mount Parthenius, amid whose wild recesses gloomed the antique grove dedicated to Telephus, the son of Hercules,[3] the Athenian heard a voice call to him aloud, and started to behold that mystic god, to whom, above the rest of earth, were dedicated the hills and woods of Arcady—the Pelasgic Pan. The god bade him "ask at Athens why the Athenians forgot his worship—he who loved them well—and might yet assist them at their need."

THE RESULT OF THEIR MIS-
SION AND THE ADVENTURE
OF THEIR MESSENGER

Such was the tale of the messenger. The lively credulities of the people believed its truth, and in calmer times dedicated a temple to the deity, venerated him with annual sacrifices, and the race of torches.

III. While the Athenians listened to the dreams of this poetical superstition, the mighty thousands of the Mede and Persian landed on the Attic

---

2 In his attack upon Herodotus, Plutarch asserts that the Spartans *did* make numerous military excursions at the beginning of the month; if this be true, so far from excusing the Spartans, it only corroborates the natural suspicion that they acted in accordance, not with superstition, but with their usual calculating and selfish policy—ever as slow to act in the defence of other states as prompt to assert the independence of their own.

3 Paus., viii, 5.

THE PERSIANS ADVANCE TO MARATHON—THE PLAIN DESCRIBED

coast, and, conducted by Hippias among their leaders, marched to the plain of Marathon, which the traveller still beholds stretching wide and level, amid hills and marshes, at the distance of only ten miles from the gates of Athens. Along the shore the plain extends to the length of six miles—inland it exceeds two. He who surveys it now looks over a dreary waste, whose meagre and arid herbage is relieved but by the scanty foliage of unfrequent shrubs or pear-trees, and a few dwarf pines drooping towards the sea. Here and there may be seen the grazing oxen, or the peasant bending at his plough—a distant roof, a ruined chapel, are not sufficient evidences of the living to interpose between the imagination of the spectator and the dead. Such is the present Marathon—we are summoned back to the past.

IV. It will be remembered that the Athenians were divided into ten tribes at the instigation of Clisthenes. Each of these tribes nominated a general; there were therefore ten leaders to the Athenian army.

DIVISION OF OPINION IN THE ATHENIAN CAMP

Among them was Miltiades, who had succeeded in ingratiating himself with the Athenian people, and obtained from their suffrages a command.[4]

Aided by a thousand men from Platæa, then on terms of intimate friendship with the Athenians, the little army marched from the city, and advanced to the entrance of the plain of Marathon. Here they arrayed themselves in martial order, near the Temple of Hercules, to the east of the hills that guard the upper part of the valley. Thus encamped, and in sight of the gigantic power of the enemy, darkening the long expanse that skirts the sea, divisions broke out among the leaders;—some contended that a battle was by no means to be risked with such inferior forces—others, on the contrary, were for giving immediate battle. Of this latter advice was Miltiades—he

4 The exact number of the Athenians is certainly doubtful. Herodotus does not specify it. Justin estimates the number of *citizens* at ten thousand, besides a thousand Platæans; Nepos at ten thousand in all; Pausanias at nine thousand. But this total, furnished by authorities so equivocal, seems incredibly small. The free population could have been little short of twenty thousand. We must add the numbers, already great, of the resident aliens and the slaves, who, as Pausanias tells us, were then for the first time admitted to military service. On the other hand it is evident, from the speech of Miltiades to Callimachus, and the supposed treachery of the Alcmæonid, that some, nor an inconsiderable, force, was left in reserve at Athens for the protection of the city. Let us suppose, however, that two-thirds of the Athenian citizens of military age, viz., between the ages of twenty and sixty, marched to Marathon (and this was but the common proportion on common occasions), the total force, with the slaves, the settlers, and the Platæan auxiliaries could not amount to less than fifteen or sixteen thousand. But whatever the precise number of the heroes of Marathon, we have ample testimony for the general fact that it was so trifling when compared with the Persian armament, as almost to justify the exaggeration of later writers.

was supported by a man already of high repute, though now first presented to our notice, and afterward destined to act a great and splendid part in the drama of his times. Aristides was one of the generals of the army,[5] and strenuously co-operated with Miltiades in the policy of immediate battle.

Despite, however, the military renown of the one, and the civil eminence of the other, the opposite and more tame opinion seemed likely to prevail, when Miltiades suddenly thus addressed the polemarch Callimachus. That magistrate, the third of the nine archons, was held by virtue of his office equal in dignity to the military leaders, and to him was confided the privilege of a casting vote. "On you, Callimachus", said the chief of the Chersonesus,

THE ADVICE OF MILTIADES PREVAILS

> on you it rests, whether Athens shall be enslaved, or whether from age to age your country, freed by your voice, shall retain in yours a name dearer to her even than those of Aristogiton and Harmodius.[6] Never since the foundation of Athens was she placed in so imminent a peril. If she succumb to the Mede, she is rendered again to the tyranny of Hippias—but if she conquer, she may rise to the first eminence among the states of Greece. How this may be accomplished, and how upon your decision rests the event, I will at once explain. The sentiments of our leaders are divided—these are for instant engagement, those for procrastination. Depend upon it, if we delay, some sedition, some tumult will break out among the Athenians, and may draw a part of them to favour the Medes; but if we engage at once, and before a single dissension takes from us a single man, we may, if the gods give us equal fortune, obtain the victory. Consider the alternative—our decision depends on you.

V. The arguments of Miltiades convinced Callimachus, who knew well the many divisions of the city, the strength which Hippias and the Pisistratidæ still probably possessed within its walls, and who could not but allow that a superior force becomes ever more fearful the more deliberately it is regarded. He interposed his authority. It was decided to give battle. Each general commanded in turn his single day. When it came to the turn of Aristides, he gave up his right to Miltiades, showing his colleagues that it was no disgrace to submit to the profound experience of another. The example once set was universally followed, and Miltiades was thus left in absolute and undivided command. But that able and keen-sighted chief, fearing perhaps

---

5 Plut., in Vit. Arist.; Aristid., pro Quatuor Vias, vol. ii., p. 222, edit. Dindorf.
6 In his graceful work on Athens and Attica, Mr Wordsworth has well observed the peculiar propriety of this reference to the examples of Harmodius and Aristogiton, as addressed to Callimachus. They were from the same borough (Aphidnæ) as the polemarch himself.

that if he took from another his day of command, jealousy might damp the ardour of the general thus deprived and, as it were, degraded, waited till his own appointed day before he commenced the attack.

VI. On the night before Hippias conducted the barbarians to the plains of Marathon, he is said to have dreamed a dream. He thought he was with his

THE DREAM OF HIPPIAS

mother! In the fondness of human hopes he interpreted the vision favourably, and flattered himself that he should regain his authority, and die in his own house of old age. The morning now arrived that was to attest the veracity of his interpretation.

VII. To the left of the Athenians was a low chain of hills, clothed with trees (and which furnished them timber to break the charge of the Persian

BATTLE OF MARATHON

horse)—to their right a torrent;—their front was long, for, to render it more imposing in extent, and to prevent being outflanked by the Persian numbers, the centre ranks were left weak and shallow, but on either wing the troops were drawn up more solidly and strong. Callimachus, the polemarch, commanded the right wing—the Platæans formed the left. They had few, if any, horsemen or archers. The details which we possess of their arms and military array, if not in this, in other engagements of the same period, will complete the picture. We may behold them clad in bright armour, well proof and tempered, which covered breast and back—the greaves, so often mentioned by Homer, were still retained—their helmets were wrought and crested, the cones mostly painted in glowing colours, and the plumage of feathers or horse-hair rich and waving, in proportion to the rank of the wearer. Broad, sturdy, and richly ornamented were their bucklers—the pride and darling of their arms, the loss of which was the loss of honour; their spears were ponderous, thick, and long—a chief mark of contradistinction from the slight shaft of Persia— and, with their short broadsword, constituted their main weapons of offence. No Greek army marched to battle without vows, and sacrifice, and prayer— and now, in the stillness of the pause, the soothsayers examined the entrails of the victims—they were propitious, and Callimachus solemnly vowed to Diana a victim for the slaughter of every foe. Loud broke the trumpets[7]— the standards wrought with the sacred bird of Athens were raised on high;[8] —it was the signal of battle—and the Athenians rushed with an impetuous vehemence upon the Persian power. "The first Greeks of whom I have heard", says the simple Halicarnassean, "who ever ran to attack a foe—the first, too, who ever beheld without dismay the garb and armour of the Medes; for hitherto in Greece the very name of Mede had excited terror."

---

7 The goddess of Athens was supposed to have invented a peculiar trumpet used by her favoured votaries.
8 To raise the standard was the sign of battle (Suidas, Thucyd. Schol., c. 1). On the Athenian standard was depicted the owl of Minerva (Plut., in Vit. Lysand.).

VIII. When the Persian army, with its numerous horse, animal as well as man protected by plates of mail[9]—its expert bowmen—its lines and deep files of turbaned soldiers, gorgeous with many a blazing standard,[10]—headed by leaders well hardened, despite their gay garbs and adorned breastplates, in many a more even field;—when, I say, this force beheld the Athenians rushing towards them, they considered them, thus few, and destitute alike of cavalry and archers,[11] as madmen hurrying to destruction. But it was evidently not without deliberate calculation that Miltiades had so commenced the attack. The warlike experience of his guerrilla life had taught him to know the foe against whom he fought. To volunteer the assault was to forestall and cripple the charge of the Persian horse—besides, the long lances, the heavy arms, the hand-to-hand valour of the Greeks, must have been no light encounter to the more weakly mailed and less formidably armed infantry of the East. Accustomed themselves to give the charge, it was a novelty and a disadvantage to receive it. Long, fierce, and stubborn was the battle. The centre wing of the barbarians, composed of the Sacians and the pure Persian race, at length pressed hard upon the shallow centre of the Greeks, drove them back into the country, and, eager with pursuit, left their own wings to the charge of Callimachus on the one side and the Platæan forces on the other. The brave polemarch, after the most signal feats of valour, fell fighting in the field; but his troops, undismayed, smote on with spear and sword. The barbarians retreated backward to the sea, where swamps and marshes encumbered their movements, and here (though the Athenians did not pursue them far) the greater portion were slain, hemmed in by the morasses, and probably ridden down by their own disordered cavalry. Meanwhile, the two tribes that had formed the centre, one of which was commanded by Aristides,[12] retrieved themselves with a mighty effort, and the two wings, having routed their antagonists, now inclining towards each other, intercepted the barbarian centre, which, thus attacked, front and rear (large trees felled and scattered over the plain obstructing the movements of their cavalry), was defeated with prodigious slaughter. Evening came on:[13]—confused and disorderly, the Persians now only thought of flight: the whole army retired to their ships, hard chased by the Grecian victors, who, amid the carnage, fired the fleet. Cynægirus, brother to Æschylus, the tragic poet (himself highly distinguished for his feats that day), seized one of the vessels by the poop: his hand was severed by an axe;—he died gloriously of his wounds. But to none did the fortunes of that field open a

9 Æschyl., Persæ.
10 Ibid.
11 Herod., vi. xii.
12 Plut., in Vit. Arist.
13 Πρὸς ἑσπέρα, Aristoph., Vesp., 1080.

more illustrious career than to a youth of the tribe Leontis, in whom, though probably then but a simple soldier in the ranks, was first made manifest the nature and the genius destined to command. The name of that youth was Themistocles.[14] Seven vessels were captured—six thousand four hundred of the barbarians fell in the field—the Athenians and their brave ally lost only one hundred and ninety-two; but among them perished many of their bravest nobles. It was a superstition not uncharacteristic of that imaginative people, and evincing how greatly their ardour was aroused, that many of them (according to Plutarch) fancied they beheld the gigantic shade of their ancestral Theseus, completely armed, and bearing down before them upon the foe.

So perished the hopes of the unfortunate Hippias;—obscure and inglorious in his last hour, the exiled prince fell confounded amid the general slaughter.[15]

IX. Despite the capture of some vessels, and the conflagration of others, the Persians still retained a considerable fleet, and, succeeding in boarding their Eretrian plunder (which they had left on the Euboean isle), they passed thence the promontory of Sunium, with the intention of circumventing the Athenians, and arriving at Athens before them—a design which it was supposed they were induced to form by the treachery of some one suspected, without sufficient proof, to belong to the house of the Alcmæonidæ, who held up a shield as a signal to the Persians while they were under sail.[16] But the Athenians were under a prompt and vigilant commander, and while the barbarian fleet doubled the Cape of Sunium, they reached their city, and effectually prevented the designs of the foe. Aristides, with the tribe under his command, was left on the field to guard the prisoners and the booty, and his scrupulous honesty was evinced by his jealous care over the scattered and uncounted treasure.[17] The painter of the nobler schools might find perhaps few subjects worthier of his art than Aristides watching at night amid the torches of his men over the plains of Marathon, in sight of the blue Ægæan, no longer crowded with the barbarian masts;—and the white columns of the Temple of Hercules, beside which the Athenians had pitched their camp.

The Persian fleet anchored off Phalerum, the Athenian harbour, and remaining there, menacing but inactive, a short time, sailed back to Asia.

X. The moon had passed her full, when two thousand Spartans arrived at Athens: the battle was over and the victory won; but so great was their

14 Justin, ii. ix.
15 According, however, to Suidas, he escaped and died at Lemnos.
16 This incident confirms the expressed fear of Miltiades, that delay in giving battle might produce division and treachery among some of the Athenians. Doubtless his speech referred to some particular faction or individuals.
17 Plut., in Vit. Arist.

desire to see the bodies of the formidable Medes, that they proceeded to Marathon, and, returning to Athens, swelled the triumph of her citizens by their applause and congratulations.

XI. The marble which the Persians had brought with them, in order to erect as a trophy of the victory they anticipated, was, at a subsequent period, wrought by Phidias into a statue of Nemesis. A picture of the battle, representing Miltiades in the foremost place, and solemnly preserved in public, was deemed no inadequate reward to that great captain; and yet, conspicuous above the level plain of Marathon, rises a long barrow, fifteen feet in height, the supposed sepulchre of the Athenian heroes. Still does a romantic legend, not unfamiliar with our traditions of the North, give a supernatural terror to the spot. Nightly along the plain are yet heard by superstition the neighings of chargers and the rushing shadows of spectral war.[18] And still, throughout the civilized world (civilized how much by the arts and lore of Athens!) men of every clime, of every political persuasion, feel as Greeks at the name of Marathon. Later fields have presented the spectacle of an equal valour, and almost the same disparities of slaughter; but never, in the annals of earth, were united so closely in our applause, admiration for the heroism of the victors, and sympathy for the holiness of their cause. It was the first great victory of OPINION! and its fruits were reaped, not by Athens only, but by all Greece then, as by all time thereafter, in a mighty and imperishable harvest,—the invisible not less than the actual force of despotism was broken. Nor was it only that the dread which had hung upon the Median name was dispelled—nor that free states were taught their pre-eminence over the unwieldy empires which the Persian conquerors had destroyed,—a greater lesson was taught to Greece, when she discovered that the monarch of Asia could not force upon a petty state the fashion of its government, or the selection of its rulers. The defeat of Hippias was of no less value than that of Darius; and the same blow which struck down the foreign invader smote also the hopes of domestic tyrants.

One successful battle for liberty quickens and exalts that proud and emulous spirit from which are called forth the civilization and the arts that liberty should produce, more rapidly than centuries of repose. To Athens the victory of Marathon was a second Solon.

18 These apparitions, recorded by Pausanias (i. 33), are still believed in by the peasantry.

Book III

FROM THE BATTLE OF MARATHON TO THE BATTLES OF PLATÆA AND MYCALE, BC 490–BC 479

CHAPTER I

The character and popularity of Miltiades—naval expedition
—siege of Paros—conduct of Miltiades—he is accused and
sentenced—his death

I. History is rarely more than the biography of great men. Through a
succession of individuals we trace the character and destiny of nations. THE
PEOPLE glide away from us, a sublime but intangible abstraction, and the
voice of the mighty Agora reaches us only through the medium of its
representatives to posterity. The more democratic the state, the more prevalent this delegation of its history to the few; since it is the prerogative of
democracies to give the widest competition and the keenest excitement to
individual genius: and the true spirit of democracy is dormant or defunct,
when we find no one elevated to an intellectual throne above the rest. In
regarding the characters of men thus concentrating upon themselves our
survey of a nation, it is our duty sedulously to discriminate between their
qualities and their deeds: for it seldom happens that their renown in life was
unattended with reverses equally signal—that the popularity of today was
not followed by the persecution of tomorrow: and in these vicissitudes, our
justice is no less appealed to than our pity, and we are called upon to decide,
as judges, a grave and solemn cause between the silence of a departed people,
and the eloquence of imperishable names.

We have already observed in the character of Miltiades that astute and
calculating temperament common to most men whose lot it has been to

THE CHARACTER AND
POPULARITY OF MILTIADES

struggle for precarious power in the midst of
formidable foes. We have seen that his profound
and scheming intellect was not accompanied by
any very rigid or high-wrought principle; and placed, as the chief of the
Chersonesus had been from his youth upward, in situations of great peril
and embarrassment, aiming always at supreme power, and, in his harassed
and stormy domain, removed far from the public opinion of the free states of
Greece, it was natural that his political code should have become tempered
by a sinister ambition, and that the citizen of Athens should be actuated by
motives scarcely more disinterested than those which animated the tyrant of
the Chersonesus. The ruler of one district may be the hero, but can scarcely
be the patriot, of another. The long influence of years and custom—the

unconscious deference to the opinion of those whom our youth has been taught to venerate, can alone suffice to tame down an enterprising and grasping mind to objects of public advantage, in preference to designs for individual aggrandizement: influence of such a nature had never operated upon the views and faculties of the hero of Marathon. Habituated to the enjoyment of absolute command, he seemed incapable of the duties of civil subordination; and the custom of a life urged him on to the desire of power.[1] These features of his character fairly considered, we shall see little to astonish us in the later reverses of Miltiades, and find additional causes for the popular suspicions he incurred.

II. But after the victory of Marathon, the power of Miltiades was at its height. He had always possessed the affection of the Athenians, which his manners as well as his talents contributed to obtain for him. Affable and courteous—none were so mean as to be excluded from his presence; and the triumph he had just achieved so largely swelled his popularity, that the most unhesitating confidence was placed in all his suggestions.

In addition to the victory of Marathon, Miltiades, during his tyranny in the Chersonesus, had gratified the resentment and increased the dominion of NAVAL EXPEDITION the Athenians. A rude tribe, according to all authority, of the vast and varied Pelasgic family, but essentially foreign to, and never amalgamated with, the indigenous Pelasgians of the Athenian soil, had in very remote times obtained a settlement in Attica. They had assisted the Athenians in the wall of their citadel, which confirmed, by its characteristic masonry, the general tradition of their Pelasgic race. Settled afterward near Hymettus, they refused to blend with the general population —quarrels between neighbours so near naturally ensued—the settlers were expelled, and fixed themselves in the islands of Lemnos and Imbros—a piratical and savage horde. They kept alive their ancient grudge against the Athenians, and, in one of their excursions, landed in Attica, and carried off some of the women while celebrating a festival of Diana. These captives they subjected to their embraces, and ultimately massacred, together with the offspring of the intercourse. "The Lemnian Horrors" became a proverbial phrase—the wrath of the gods manifested itself in the curse of general sterility, and the criminal Pelasgi were commanded by the oracle to repair the heinous injury they had inflicted on the Athenians. The latter were satisfied with no atonement less than that of the surrender of the islands occupied by the offenders. Tradition thus reported the answer of the Pelasgi to so stern a demand—"Whenever one of your vessels, in a single day and with a northern wind, makes its passage to us, we will comply."

Time passed on, the injury was unatoned, the remembrance remained— when Miltiades (then in the Chersonesus) passed from Elæos in a single day

1 "Cum consuetudine ad imperii cupiditatem trahi videretur" (Nepos, in Vit. Milt., 8).

and with a north wind to the Pelasgian islands, avenged the cause of his countrymen, and annexed Lemnos and Imbros to the Athenian sway. The remembrance of this exploit had from the first endeared Miltiades to the Athenians, and, since the field of Marathon, he united in himself the two strongest claims to popular confidence—he was the deliverer from recent perils, and the avenger of hereditary wrongs.

The chief of the Chersonesus was not slow to avail himself of the advantage of his position. He promised the Athenians a yet more lucrative, if less glorious enterprise than that against the Persians, and demanded a fleet of seventy ships, with a supply of men and money, for an expedition from which he assured them he was certain to return laden with spoil and treasure. He did not specify the places against which the expedition was to be directed; but so great was the belief in his honesty and fortune, that the Athenians were contented to grant his demand. The requisite preparations made, Miltiades set sail. Assuming the general right to punish those islands which had sided with the Persian, he proceeded to Paros, which had contributed a trireme to the armament of Datis. But beneath the pretext of national revenge, Miltiades is said to have sought the occasion to prosecute a selfish resentment. During his tyranny in the Chersonesus, a Parian, named Lysagoras, had sought to injure him with the Persian government, and the chief now wreaked upon the island the retaliation due to an individual.

Siege of Paros

Such is the account of Herodotus—an account not indeed inconsistent with the vindictive passions still common to the inhabitants of the western clime, but certainly scarce in keeping with the calculating and politic character of Miltiades: for men go backward in the career of ambition when revenging a past offence upon a foe that is no longer formidable.

Miltiades landed on the island, laid vigorous siege to the principal city, and demanded from the inhabitants the penalty of a hundred talents. The besieged refused the terms, and worked day and night at the task of strengthening the city for defence. Nevertheless, Miltiades succeeded in cutting off all supplies, and the city was on the point of yielding; when suddenly the chief set fire to the fortifications he had erected, drew off his fleet, and returned to Athens, not only without the treasure he had promised, but with an ignominious diminution of the glory he had already acquired. The most probable reason for a conduct[2] so extraordinary was, that by some accident a grove on the continent was set on fire—the flame, visible equally to the besiegers and the besieged, was interpreted alike, by both: each party imagined it a signal from the Persian fleet—the one was dissuaded from yielding, and the other intimitidated from continuing the siege. An additional reason for the retreat was a severe

Conduct of Miltiades

---

2 Nepos, in Vit. Milt., 7.

wound in the leg which Miltiades had received, either in the course of the attack, or by an accident he met with when attempting with sacrilegious superstition to consult the infernal deities on ground dedicated to Ceres.

III. We may readily conceive the amazement and indignation with which, after so many promises on the one side, and such unbounded confidence on the other, the Athenians witnessed the return of this

HE IS ACCUSED AND SENTENCED

fruitless expedition. No doubt the wily and equivocal parts of the character of Miltiades, long cast in shade by his brilliant qualities, came now more obviously in view. He was impeached capitally by Xanthippus, an Athenian noble, the head of that great aristocratic faction of the Alcmæonidæ, which, inimical alike to the tyrant and the demagogue, brooked neither a master of the state nor a hero with the people. Miltiades was charged with having accepted a bribe from the Persians,[3] which had induced him to quit the siege of Paros at the moment when success was assured.

The unfortunate chief was prevented by his wound from pleading his own cause—he was borne into the court stretched upon his couch, while his

HIS DEATH

brother, Tisagoras, conducted his defence. Through the medium of his advocate, Miltiades seems neither vigorously to have refuted the accusation of treason to the state, nor satisfactorily to have explained his motives for raising the siege. His glory was his defence; and the chief answer to Xanthippus was "Marathon and Lemnos". The crime alleged against him was of a capital nature; but, despite the rank of the accuser, and the excitement of his audience, the people refused to pronounce sentence of death upon so illustrious a man. They found him guilty, it is true—but they commuted the capital infliction to a fine of fifty talents. Before the fine was paid, Miltiades expired of the mortification of his wound. The fine was afterward paid by his son, Cimon. Thus ended a life full of adventure and vicissitude.

The trial of Miltiades has often been quoted in proof of the ingratitude and fickleness of the Athenian people. No charge was ever more inconsiderately made. He was accused of a capital crime, *not* by the people, but by a powerful noble. The noble demanded his death—appears to have proved the charge—to have had the law which imposed death wholly on his side—and "the favour of *the people* it was", says Herodotus, expressly, "which saved his life."[4] When we consider all the circumstances of the case—the wound to the popular vanity—the disappointment of excited expectation—the unaccountable conduct of Miltiades himself—and then see his punishment, after a conviction which entailed death, only in the ordinary assessment of

3 Nepos, in Vit. Milt., 7.
4 Herod., vi. 136.

a pecuniary fine,[5] we cannot but allow that the Athenian people (even while vindicating the majesty of law, which in all civilized communities must judge offences without respect to persons) were not in this instance forgetful of the services nor harsh to the offences of their great men.

5 Nepos says the fine was estimated at the cost of the navy he had conducted to Paros; but Boeckh rightly observes, that it is an ignorant assertion of that author that the fine was intended for a compensation, being the usual mode of assessing the offence.

   The case is simply this—Miltiades was accused—whether justly or unjustly no matter —it was clearly as impossible not to receive the accusation and to try the cause, as it would be for an English court of justice to refuse to admit a criminal action against Lord Grey or the Duke of Wellington. Was Miltiades guilty or not? This we cannot tell. We know that he was tried according to the law, and that the Athenians thought him guilty, for they condemned him. So far this is not ingratitude—it is the course of law. A man is tried and found guilty—if past services and renown were to save the great from punishment when convicted of a state offence, society would perhaps be disorganized, and certainly a free state would cease to exist. The question therefore shrinks to this—was it or was it not ungrateful in the people to relax the penalty of death, legally incurred and commute it to a heavy fine? I fear we shall find few instances of greater clemency in monarchies, however mild. Miltiades unhappily died. But nature slew him, not the Athenian people. And it cannot be said with greater justice of the Athenians, than of a people no less illustrious, and who are now their judges, that it was their custom *"de tuer un amiral pour encourager les autres"*.

CHAPTER II

The Athenian tragedy—its origin—Thespis—Phrynichus—
Æschylus—analysis of the tragedies of Æschylus

I. From the melancholy fate of Miltiades, we are now invited to a subject no less connected with this important period in the history of Athens. The interval of repose which followed the battle of Marathon allows us to pause, and notice the intellectual state to which the Athenians had progressed since the tyranny of Pisistratus and his sons.

THE ATHENIAN TRAGEDY

We have remarked the more familiar acquaintance with the poems of Homer which resulted from the labours and example of Pisistratus. This event (for event it was), combined with other causes,—the foundation of a public library, the erection of public buildings, and the institution of public gardens—to create with apparent suddenness, among a susceptible and lively population, a general cultivation of taste. The citizens were brought together in their hours of relaxation,[1] by the urbane and social manner of life, under porticoes and in gardens, which it was the policy of a graceful and benignant tyrant to inculcate; and the native genius, hitherto dormant, of the quick Ionian race, once awakened to literary and intellectual objects, created an audience even before it found expression in a poet. The elegant effeminacy of Hipparchus contributed to foster the taste of the people—for the example of the great is nowhere more potent over the multitude than in the cultivation of the arts. Patronage may not produce poets, but it multiplies critics. Anacreon and Simonides, introduced among the Athenians by Hipparchus, and enjoying his friendship, no doubt added largely to the

---

1 The taste of a people, which is to art what public opinion is to legislation, is formed, like public opinion, by habitual social intercourse and collision. The more men are brought together to converse and discuss, the more the principles of a general national taste will become both diffused and refined. Less to their climate, to their scenery, to their own beauty of form, than to their social habits and preference of the public to the domestic life, did the Athenians, and the Grecian republics generally, owe that wonderful susceptibility to the beautiful and harmonious, which distinguishes them above all nations ancient or modern. Solitude may exalt the genius of a man, but communion alone can refine the taste of a people.

262

influence which poetry began to assume. The peculiar sweetness of those poets imbued with harmonious contagion the genius of the first of the Athenian dramatists, whose works, alas! are lost to us, though evidence of their character is preserved. About the same time the Athenians must necessarily have been made more intimately acquainted with the various wealth of the lyric poets of Ionia and the isles. Thus it happened that their models in poetry were of two kinds, the epic and the lyric; and, in the natural connexion of art, it was but the next step to accomplish a species of poetry which should attempt to unite the two. Happily, at this time, Athens possessed a man of true genius, whose attention early circumstances had directed to a rude and primitive order of histrionic recitation:—Phrynichus, the poet, was a disciple of Thespis, the mime: to him belongs this honour, that out of the elements of the broadest farce he conceived the first grand combinations of the tragic drama.

II. From time immemorial—as far back, perhaps, as the grove possessed an altar, and the waters supplied a reed for the pastoral pipe—poetry and music had been dedicated to the worship of the gods of Greece. At the appointed season of festival to each several deity, his praises were sung, his traditional achievements were recited. One of the divinities last introduced into Greece—the mystic and enigmatical Dionysus, or Bacchus, received the popular and enthusiastic adoration naturally due to the God of the Vineyard, and the "Unbinder of galling cares". His festival, celebrated at the most joyous of agricultural seasons,[2] was associated also with the most exhilarating associations. Dithyrambs, or wild and exulting songs, at first extemporaneous, celebrated the triumphs of the god. By degrees, the rude hymn swelled into prepared and artful measures, performed by a chorus that danced circling round the altar; and the dithyramb assumed a lofty and solemn strain, adapted to the sanctity of sacrifice and the emblematic majesty of the god. At the same time, another band (connected with the phallic procession, which, however outwardly obscene, betokened only, at its origin, the symbol of fertility, and betrays the philosophy of some alien and eastern creed)[3] implored in more lively and homely strains the blessing of the prodigal and jovial deity. These ceremonial songs received a wanton and wild addition, as, in order perhaps more closely to represent and personify the motley march of the Liber Pater, the chorus-singers borrowed the hides and horns from the

ITS ORIGIN

---

2 It seems probable that the principal Bacchic festival was originally held at the time of the vintage—*condita post frumenta*. But from the earliest known period in Attica, all the triple Dionysia were celebrated during the winter and the spring.

3 Egyptian, according to Herodotus, who asserts, that Melampus first introduced the phallic symbol among the Greeks, though he never sufficiently explained its mysterious significations, which various sages since his time had, however, satisfactorily interpreted. It is just to the Greeks to add, that this importation, with the other rites of Bacchus, was considered at utter variance with their usual habits and manners.

vine-browsing goat which they sacrificed, which furnished forth the merry mimicry of the satyr and the faun. Under licence of this disguise, the songs became more obscene and grotesque, and the mummers vied with each other in obtaining the applause of the rural audience by wild buffoonery and unrestricted jest. Whether as the prize of the winner or as the object of sacrifice, the goat (*tragos* in the Greek) was a sufficiently important person-age to bestow upon the exhibition the homely name of TRAGEDY, or GOATSONG, destined afterward to be exalted by association with the proudest efforts of human genius. And while the DITHYRAMB, yet amid the Dorian tribes retained the fire and dignity of its hereditary character—while in Sicyon it rose in stately and mournful measures to the memory of Adrastus, the Argive hero—while in Corinth, under the polished rule of Periander, Arion imparted to the antique hymn a new character and a more scientific music,[4]—gradually, in Attica, it gave way before the familiar and fantastic humours of the satyrs, sometimes abridged to afford greater scope to their exhibitions—sometimes contracting the contagion of their burlesque. Still, however, the reader will observe, that the *tragedy*, or *goatsong*, consisted of two parts—first, the exhibition of the mummers, and, secondly, the dithy-rambic chorus, moving in a circle round the altar of Bacchus. It appears on the whole most probable, though it is a question of fierce dispute and great uncertainty, that not only this festive ceremonial, but also its ancient name of tragedy, or goatsong, had long been familiar in Attica,[5] when, about BC 535, during the third tyranny of Pisistratus, a skilful and ingenious native of Icaria, an Attic village in which the Eleutheria, or Bacchic rites, were

4 Herodotus asserts that Arion *first* named, invented, and taught the dithyramb at Corinth; but, as Bentley triumphantly observes, Athenæus has preserved to us the very verses of Archilochus, his predecessor by a century, in which the song of the dithyramb is named.
5 In these remarks upon the origin of the drama, it would belong less to history than to scholastic dissertation, to enter into all the disputed and disputable points. I do not, therefore, pause with every step to discuss the questions contested by antiquarians—such as, whether the word "tragedy", in its primitive and homely sense, together with the prize of the goat, was or was not known in Attica prior to Thespis (it seems to me that the least successful part of Bentley's immortal work is that which attempts to enforce the latter proposition); still less do I think a grave answer due to those who, in direct opposition to authorities headed by the grave and searching Aristotle, contend that the exhibitions of Thespis were of a serious and elevated character. The historian must himself weigh the evidences on which he builds his conclusions; and come to those conclusions, especially in disputes which bring to unimportant and detached inquiries the most costly expenditure of learning, without fatiguing the reader with a repetition of all the arguments which he accepts or rejects. For those who incline to go more deeply into subjects connected with the early Athenian drama, works by English and German authors, too celebrated to enumerate, will be found in abundance. But even the most careless general reader will do well to delight himself with that dissertation of Bentley on Phalaris, so familiar to students, and which, despite some few intemperate and bold assumptions, will always remain one of the most colossal monuments of argument and erudition.

264

celebrated with peculiar care, surpassed all competitors in the exhibition of these rustic entertainments. He relieved the monotonous pleasantries of the satyric chorus by introducing, usually in his own person, a histrionic tale-teller, who, from an elevated platform, and with the lively gesticulations common still to the popular narrators of romance on the Mole of Naples, or in the bazaars of the East, entertained the audience with some mythological legend. It was so clear that during this recital the chorus remained unnecessarily idle and superfluous, that the next improvement was as natural in itself, as it was important in its consequences. This was to make the chorus assist the narrator by occasional question or remark.

The choruses themselves were improved in their professional art by Thespis. He invented dances, which for centuries retained their popularity on the stage, and is said to have given histrionic disguise to his reciter—at first, by the application of pigments to the face; and afterward, by the construction of a rude linen mask.

THESPIS

III. These improvements, chiefly mechanical, form the boundary to the achievements of Thespis. He did much to create a stage—little to create *tragedy*, in the proper acceptation of the word. His performances were still of a ludicrous and homely character, and much more akin to the comic than the tragic. Of that which makes the essence of the solemn drama of Athens—its stately plot, its gigantic images, its prodigal and sumptuous poetry, Thespis was not in any way the inventor. But Phrynichus, the disciple of Thespis, was a *poet*; he saw, though perhaps dimly and imperfectly, the new career opened to the art, and he may be said to have breathed the immortal spirit into the mere mechanical forms, when he introduced *poetry* into the bursts of the chorus and the monologue of the actor. Whatever else Phrynichus effected is uncertain. The developed plot—the introduction of regular dialogue through the medium of a second actor—the pomp and circumstance—the symmetry and climax of the drama—do not appear to have appertained to his earlier efforts; and the great artistical improvements which raised the simple incident to an elaborate structure of depicted narrative and awful catastrophe, are ascribed, not to Phrynichus, but Æschylus. If the later works of Phrynichus betrayed these excellences, it is because Æschylus had then become his rival, and he caught the heavenly light from the new star which was destined to eclipse him. But everything essential was done for the Athenian tragedy when Phrynichus took it from the satyr and placed it under the protection of the muse—when, forsaking the humours of the rustic farce, he selected a solemn subject from the serious legends of the most vivid of all mythologies—when he breathed into the familiar measures of the chorus the grandeur and sweetness of the lyric ode—when, in a word, taking nothing from Thespis but the stage and the performers, he borrowed his tale from Homer and his melody from Anacreon. We must not, then, suppose, misled by the vulgar accounts of the Athenian drama, that the contest for the goat, and the buffooneries of Thespis, were

PHRYNICHUS

its real origin; born of the epic and the lyric song, Homer gave it character, and the lyrists language. Thespis and his predecessors only suggested the form to which the new-born poetry should be applied.

IV. Thus, under Phrynichus, the Thespian drama rose into poetry, worthy to exercise its influence upon poetical emulation, when a young man of noble family and sublime genius, rendered perhaps more thought-
ÆSCHYLUS
ful and profound by the cultivation of a mystical philosophy,[6] which had lately emerged from the primitive schools of Ionian wisdom, brought to the rising art the united dignity of rank, philosophy, and genius. Æschylus, son of Euphorion, born at Eleusis BC 525, early saturated a spirit naturally fiery and exalted with the vivid poetry of Homer. While yet a boy, and probably about the time when Phrynichus first elevated the Thespian drama, he is said to have been inspired by a dream with the ambition to excel in the dramatic art. But in Homer he found no visionary revelation to assure him of those ends, august and undeveloped, which the actor and the chorus might be made the instruments to effect. For when the idea of scenic representation was once familiar, the epics of Homer suggested the true nature of the drama. The great characteristic of that poet is *individuality*. Gods or men alike have their separate, unmistakeable attributes and distinctions —they converse in dialogue—they act towards an appointed end. Bring Homer on the stage, and introduce two actors instead of a narrator, and a drama is at once effected. If Phrynichus from the first borrowed his story from Homer, Æschylus, with more creative genius and more meditative intellect, saw that there was even a richer mine in the vitality of the Homeric spirit—the unity of the Homeric designs. Nor was Homer, perhaps, his sole though his guiding inspiration. The noble birth of Æschylus no doubt gave him those advantages of general acquaintance with the poetry of the rest of Greece, which an education formed under the lettered dynasty of the Pisistratidæ would naturally confer on the well-born. We have seen that the dithyramb, debased in Attica to the Thespian chorus, was in the Dorian states already devoted to sublime themes, and enriched by elaborate art; and Simonides, whose elegies, peculiar for their sweetness, might have inspired the "ambrosial" Phrynichus, perhaps gave to the stern soul of Æschylus, as to his own pupil Pindar, the model of a loftier music, in his dithyrambic odes.

V. At the age of twenty-five, the son of Euphorion produced his first tragedy. This appears to have been exhibited in the year after the appearance of Aristagoras at Athens,—in that very year so eventful and important, when the Athenians lighted the flames of the Persian war amid the blazing capital of Sardis. He had two competitors in Pratinas and Chœrilus. The last, indeed, preceded Phrynichus, but merely in the burlesques of the rude

6 Æschylus was a Pythagorean. "Veniat Æschylus, sed etiam Pythagoreus" (Cic., Tusc. Disp., ii. 9).

Thespian stage; the example of Phrynichus had now directed his attention to the new species of drama, but without any remarkable talent for its cultivation. Pratinas, the contemporary of Æschylus, did not long attempt to vie with his mighty rival in his own line.[7] Recurring to the old satyr-chorus, he reduced its unmeasured buffooneries into a regular and systematic form; he preserved the mythological tale, and converted it into an artistical burlesque. This invention, delighting the multitude, as it adapted an ancient entertainment to the new and more critical taste, became so popular that it was usually associated with the graver tragedy; when the last becoming a solemn and gorgeous spectacle, the poet exhibited a trilogy (or three tragedies) to his mighty audience, while the satyric invention of Pratinas closed the whole, and answered the purpose of our modern farce.[8] Of this class of the Grecian drama but one specimen remains, in the "Cyclops" of Euripides. It is probable that the birth, no less than the genius of Æschylus, enabled him with greater facility to make the imposing and costly additions to the exhibition, which the nature of the poetry demanded—since, while these improvements were rapidly proceeding, the poetical fame of Æschylus was still uncrowned. Nor was it till the fifteenth year after his first exhibition that the sublimest of the Greek poets obtained the ivy chaplet, which had succeeded to the goat and the ox as the prize of the tragic contests. In the course of a few years, a regular stage, appropriate scenery and costume, mechanical inventions and complicated stage machinery gave fitting illusion to the representation of gods and men. To the monologue of Phrynichus, Æschylus added a second actor;[9] he curtailed the choruses, connected them with the main story, and, more important than all else, reduced to simple but systematic rules the progress and development of a poem, which no longer had for its utmost object to please the ear or divert the fancy, but swept on its mighty and irresistible march, to besiege passion after passion, and spread its empire over the whole soul.

An itinerant platform was succeeded by a regular theatre of wood—the theatre of wood by a splendid edifice, which is said to have held no less an

---

7 Out of fifty plays, thirty-two were satyrical (Suidas, in Prat.).

8 The Tetralogy was the name given to the fourfold exhibition of the three tragedies, or trilogy, and the satyric drama.

9 Yet in Æschylus there are sometimes more than two *speaking* actors on the stage,—as at one time in the "Choephori", Clytemnestra, Orestes, Electra (to say nothing of Pylades, who is silent), and again in the same play, Orestes, Pylades, and Clytemnestra; also in the "Eumenides", Apollo, Minerva, Orestes. It is truly observed, however, that these plays were written after Sophocles had introduced the third actor. The Oresteia tetralogy was exhibited BC 458, only two years before the death of Æschylus and ten years after Sophocles had gained his first prize. Any number of mutes might be admitted, not only as guards, &c., but even as more important personages. Thus, in the "Prometheus", the very opening of the play exhibits to us the demons of Strength and Force, the god Vulcan, and Prometheus himself; but the dialogue is confined to Strength and Vulcan.

audience than thirty thousand persons.[10] Theatrical contests became a matter of national and universal interest. These contests occurred thrice a year, at three several festivals of Bacchus.[11] But it was at the great Dionysia, held at the end of March and commencement of April, that the principal tragic contests took place. At that period, as the Athenian drama increased in celebrity, and Athens herself in renown, the city was filled with visitors, not only from all parts of Greece, but almost from every land in which the Greek civilization was known. The state took the theatre under its protection, as a solemn and sacred institution. So anxious were the people to consecrate wholly to the Athenian name the glory of the spectacle, that at the great Dionysia no foreigner, nor even any metœcus (or alien settler), was permitted to dance in the choruses. The chief archon presided over the performances; to him was awarded the selection of the candidates for the prize. Those chosen were allowed three actors[12] by lot and a chorus, the expense of which was undertaken by the state, and imposed upon one of the principal persons of each tribe, called choragus. Thus, on one occasion, Themistocles was the choragus to a tragedy by Phrynichus. The immense theatre, crowded by thousands, tier above tier, bench upon bench, was open to the heavens, and commanded, from the sloping hill on which it was situated, both land and sea. The actor apostrophized no mimic pasteboard, but the wide expanse of Nature herself—the living sun, the mountain air, the wide and visible Ægæan. All was proportioned to the gigantic scale of the theatre, and the mighty range of the audience. The form was artificially enlarged and heightened; masks of exquisite art and beauty brought before the audience the ideal images of their sculptured gods and heroes, while (most probably) mechanical inventions carried the tones of the voice throughout the various tiers of the theatre. The exhibitions took place in the open day, and the limited length of the plays permitted the performance of probably no less than ten or twelve before the setting of the sun. The sanctity of their origin, and the mythological nature of their stories, added something of religious solemnity to these spectacles, which were opened by ceremonial sacrifice. Dramatic exhibitions, at least for a considerable period, were not, as with us, made hackneyed by constant repetition. They were as rare in their recurrence as they were imposing in their effect; nor was a drama, whether tragic or comic, that had gained the prize, permitted a second time to be exhibited.

---

10 The celebrated temple of Bacchus, built after the wooden theatre had given way beneath the multitude assembled to witness a contest between Pratinas and Æschylus.

11 First, the rural Dionysia, held in the country districts throughout Attica about the beginning of January; second, the Lenæan, or Anthesterial, Dionysia, in the end of February and beginning of March, in which principally occurred the comic contests; and, third, the grand Dionysia of the city, referred to in the text. Afterward dramatic performances were exhibited also in August during the Panathenæa.

12 That is, when *three* actors became admitted on the stage.

A special exemption was made in favour of Æschylus, afterward extended to Sophocles and Euripides. The general rule was necessarily stimulant of renewed and unceasing exertion, and was, perhaps, the principal cause of the almost miraculous fertility of the Athenian dramatists.

VI. On the lower benches of the semicircle sat the archons and magistrates, the senators and priests; while apart, but in seats equally honoured, the gaze of the audience was attracted, from time to time, to the illustrious strangers whom the fame of their poets and their city had brought to the Dionysia of the Athenians. The youths and women[13] had their separate divisions; the rest of the audience were ranged according to their tribes, while the upper galleries were filled by the miscellaneous and impatient populace.

In the orchestra (a space left by the semicircular benches, with wings stretching to the right and left before the scene), a small square platform served as the altar, to which moved the choral dances, still retaining the attributes of their ancient sanctity. The coryphæus, or leader of the chorus, took part in the dialogue as the representative of the rest, and, occasionally, even several of the number were excited into exclamations by the passion of the piece. But the principal duty of the chorus was to diversify the dialogue by hymns and dirges, to the music of flutes, while, in dances far more artful than those now existent, they represented by their movements the emotions that they sung,[14]—thus bringing, as it were, into harmony of action the poetry of language. Architectural embellishments of stone, representing a palace, with three entrances, the centre one appropriated to royalty, the others to subordinate rank, usually served for the scene. But at times, when the plot demanded a different locality, scenes painted with the utmost art and cost were easily substituted; nor were wanting the modern contrivances of artificial lightning and thunder—the clouds for the gods—a variety of inventions for the sudden apparition of demon agents, whether from above or below—and all the adventitious and effective aid which mechanism lends to genius.

VII. Thus summoning before us the external character of the Athenian drama, the vast audience, the unroofed and enormous theatre, the actors themselves enlarged by art above the ordinary proportions of men, the solemn and sacred subjects from which its form and spirit were derived, we turn to Æschylus, and behold at once the fitting creator of its grand and ideal personifications. I have said that Homer was his original; but a more

ANALYSIS OF THE TRA-
GEDIES OF ÆSCHYLUS

---

13 For it is sufficiently clear that women were admitted to the tragic performances, though the arguments against their presence in comic plays preponderate. This admitted, the manners of the Greeks may be sufficient to prove that, as in the arena of the Roman games, they were divided from the men; as, indeed, is indirectly intimated in a passage of the Gorgias of Plato.

14 Schlegel says truly and eloquently of the chorus—"that it was the idealized spectator"— "reverberating to the actual spectator a musical and lyrical expression of his own emotions".

intellectual age than that of the Grecian epic had arrived, and with Æschylus, philosophy passed into poetry. The dark doctrine of fatality imparted its stern and awful interest to the narration of events—men were delineated, not as mere self-acting and self-willed mortals, but as the agents of a destiny inevitable and unseen—the gods themselves are no longer the gods of Homer, entering into the sphere of human action for petty motives and for individual purposes—drawing their grandeur, not from the part they perform, but from the descriptions of the poet;—they appear now as the oracles or the agents of fate—they are visitors from another world, terrible and ominous from the warnings which they convey. Homer is the creator of the material poetry, Æschylus of the intellectual. The corporeal and animal sufferings of the Titan in the epic hell become exalted by tragedy into the portrait of moral fortitude defying physical anguish. The Prometheus of Æschylus is the spirit of a god disdainfully subjected to the misfortunes of a man. In reading this wonderful performance, which in pure and sustained sublimity is perhaps unrivalled in the literature of the world, we lose sight entirely of the cheerful Hellenic worship; and yet it is in vain that the learned attempt to trace its vague and mysterious metaphysics to any old symbolical religion of the East. More probably, whatever theological system it shadows forth, was rather the gigantic conception of the poet himself, than the imperfect revival of any forgotten creed, or the poetical disguise of any existent philosophy. However this be, it would certainly seem, that, in this majestic picture of the dauntless enemy of Jupiter, punished only for his benefits to man, and attracting all our sympathies by his courage and his benevolence, is conveyed something of disbelief or defiance of the creed of the populace—a suspicion from which Æschylus was not free in the judgment of his contemporaries, and which is by no means inconsonant with the doctrines of Pythagoras.

VIII. The conduct of the fable is as follows: two vast demons, Strength and Force, accompanied by Vulcan, appear in a remote plain of earth—an unpeopled desert. There, on a sterile and lofty rock, hard by the sea, Prometheus is chained by Vulcan—"a reward for his disposition to be tender to mankind". The date of this doom is cast far back in the earliest dawn of time, and Jupiter has but just begun his reign. While Vulcan binds him, Prometheus utters no sound—it is Vulcan, the agent of his punishment, that alone complains. Nor is it till the dread task is done, and the ministers of Jupiter have retired, that "the god, unawed by the wrath of gods", bursts forth with his grand apostrophe:—

Oh Air divine! Oh ye swift-winged Winds—
Ye sources of the Rivers, and ye Waves,
That dimple o'er old Ocean like his smiles—
Mother of all—O Earth! and thou the orb,
All-seeing, of the Sun, behold and witness
What I, a god, from the stern gods endure.

270

....

When shall my doom be o'er?—Be o'er!—to me
The Future hides no riddle—nor can woe
Come unprepared! It fits me then to brave
That which must be: for what can turn aside
The dark course of the grim Necessity?

While thus soliloquizing, the air becomes fragrant with odours, and faintly stirs with the rustling of approaching wings. The Daughters of Ocean, aroused from their grots below, are come to console the Titan. They utter many complaints against the dynasty of Jove. Prometheus comforts himself by the prediction that the Olympian shall hereafter require his services, and that, until himself released from his bondage, he will never reveal to his tyrant the danger that menaces his realm; for the vanquished is here described as of a mightier race than the victor, and to him are bared the mysteries of the future, which to Jupiter are denied. The triumph of Jupiter is the conquest of brute force over knowledge.

Prometheus then narrates how, by means of his counsels, Jupiter had gained his sceptre, and the ancient Saturn and his partisans been whelmed beneath the abyss of Tartarus—how he alone had interfered with Jupiter to prevent the extermination of the human race (whom *alone the celestial king disregarded and condemned*)—how he had imparted to them fire, the seed of all the arts, and exchanged in their breasts the terrible knowledge of the future for the beguiling flatteries of hope: and hence his punishment.

At this time Ocean himself appears: he endeavours unavailingly to persuade the Titan to submission to Jupiter. The great spirit of Prometheus, and his consideration for others, are beautifully individualized in his answers to his consoler, whom he warns not to incur the wrath of the tyrant by sympathy with the afflicted. Alone again with the Oceanides, the latter burst forth in fresh strains of pity.

The wide earth echoes wailingly,
　Stately and antique were thy fallen race,
The wide earth waileth thee!
　Lo! from the holy Asian dwelling-place,
Fall for a godhead's wrongs, the mortals' murmuring tears,
　They mourn within the Colchian land,
　　The virgin and the warrior daughters,
　And far remote, the Scythian band,
　　Around the broad Mæotian waters,
　And they who hold in Caucasus their tower,
　　Arabia's martial flower
Hoarse-clamouring 'midst sharp rows of barbed spears.

> One have I seen with equal tortures riven—
> An equal god; in adamantine chains
>   Ever and evermore
> The Titan Atlas, crush'd, sustains
>   The mighty mass of mighty Heaven,
> And the whirling cataracts roar,
> With a chime to the Titan's groans,
> And the depth that receives them moans;
> And from vaults that the earth are under,
> Black Hades is heard in thunder;
> While from the founts of white-waved rivers flow
> Melodious sorrows, wailing with his woe.

Prometheus, in his answer, still farther details the benefits he had conferred on men—he arrogates to himself their elevation to intellect and reason.[15] He proceeds darkly to dwell on the power of Necessity, guided by "the triform fates and the unforgetful Furies", whom he asserts to be sovereign over Jupiter himself. He declares that Jupiter cannot escape his doom: "His doom", ask the daughters of Ocean, "is it not evermore to reign?"—"That thou mayst not learn", replies the prophet; "and in the preservation of this secret depends my future freedom."

The rejoinder of the chorus is singularly beautiful, and it is with a pathos not common to Æschylus that they contrast their present mournful strain with that which they poured

> What time the silence erst was broken,
>   Around the baths, and o'er the bed
> To which, won well by many a soft love-token,
> And hymn'd by all the music of delight,
>   Our Ocean-sister, bright
>   Hesione, was led!

At the end of this choral song appears Io, performing her mystic pilgrimage.[16] The utter woe and despair of Io are finely contrasted with the stern spirit of Prometheus. Her introduction gives rise to those ancestral and traditionary

---

15 In this speech he enumerates, among other benefits, that of numbers, "the prince of wise inventions"—one of the passages in which Æschylus is supposed to betray his Pythagorean doctrines.

16 It is greatly disputed whether Io was represented on the stage as transformed into the actual shape of a heifer, or merely accursed with a visionary frenzy, in which she believes in the transformation. It is with great reluctance that I own it seems to me not possible to explain away certain expressions without supposing that Io appeared on the stage at least partially transformed.

allusions to which the Greeks were so attached. In prophesying her fate, Prometheus enters into much beautiful descriptive poetry, and commemorates the lineage of the Argive kings. After Io's departure, Prometheus renews his defiance to Jupiter, and his stern prophecies, that the son of Saturn shall be "hurled from his realm, a forgotten king". In the midst of these weird denunciations, Mercury arrives, charged by Jupiter to learn the nature of that danger which Prometheus predicts to him. The Titan bitterly and haughtily defies the threats and warnings of the herald, and exults, that whatever be his tortures, he is at least *immortal*,—to be afflicted, but not to die. Mercury at length departs—the menace of Jupiter is fulfilled—the punishment is consummated—and, amid storm and earthquake, both rock and prisoner are struck by the lightnings of the god into the deep abyss.

> The earth is made to reel, and rumbling by,
> Bellowing it rolls, the thunder's gathering wrath!—
> And the fierce fires glare livid; and along
> The rocks the eddies of the sands whirl high,
> Borne by the hurricane, and all the blasts
> Of all the winds leap forth—each hurtling each—
> Met in the wildness of a ghastly war,
> The dark floods blended with the swooping heaven.
> It comes—it comes!—on me it speeds—the Storm,
> The rushing onslaught of the Thunder-god;
> Oh, majesty of earth—my solemn mother!
> And thou that through the universal void,
> Circlest sweet light, all blessing;—EARTH AND ETHER,
> YE I invoke, to know the wrongs I suffer.

IX. Such is the conclusion of this unequalled drama, epitomized somewhat at undue length, in order to show the reader how much the philosophy that had awakened in the age of Solon now actuated the creations of poetry. Not that Æschylus, like Euripides, deals in didactic sentences and oracular aphorisms. He rightly held such pedantries of the closet foreign to the tragic genius.[17] His philosophy is in the spirit, and not in the diction of his works —in vast conceptions, not laconic maxims. He does not preach, but he inspires. The "Prometheus" is perhaps the greatest moral poem in the world —sternly and loftily intellectual—and, amid its darker and less palpable allegories, presenting to us the superiority of an immortal being to all mortal sufferings. Regarded merely as poetry, the conception of the Titan of Æschylus has no parallel except in the Fiend of Milton. But perhaps the representation of a benevolent spirit, afflicted, but not accursed—conquered,

17 Vit. Æsch.

but not subdued by a power, than which it is older, and wiser, and loftier, is yet more sublime than that of an evil demon writhing under the penance deservedly incurred from an irresistible God. The one is intensely moral—at once the more moral and the more tragic, because the sufferings are not deserved, and therefore the defiance commands our sympathy as well as our awe; but the other is but the picture of a righteous doom, borne by a despairing though stubborn will; it affords no excitement to our courage, and forbids at once our admiration and our pity.

X. I do not propose to conduct the reader at length through the other tragedies of Æschylus; seven are left to us, to afford the most striking examples which modern or ancient literature can produce of what perhaps is the true theory of the SUBLIME, viz., elevating the imagination by means of the passions, for a moral end.

Nothing can be more grand and impressive than the opening of the "Agamemnon," with the solitary watchman on the tower, who, for ten long years, has watched nightly for the beacon-fires that are to announce the fall of Ilion, and who now beholds them blaze at last. The description which Clytemnestra gives of the progress of these beacon-fires from Troy to Argos is, for its picturesque animation, one of the most celebrated in Æschylus. The following lines will convey to the general reader a very inadequate reflection, though not an unfaithful paraphrase, of this splendid passage.[18] Clytemnestra has announced to the chorus the capture of Troy. The chorus, half incredulous, demand what messenger conveyed the intelligence. Clytemnestra replies:—

> A gleam—a gleam—from Ida's height,
>   By the fire-god sent, it came;—
> From watch to watch it leapt that light,
>   As a rider rode the Flame!
>   It shot through the startled sky,
>   And the torch of that blazing glory
>   Old Lemnos caught on high,
>   On its holy promontory,
>   And sent it on, the jocund sign,
>   To Athos, Mount of Jove divine.
>   Wildly the while, it rose from the isle,
> So that the might of the journeying Light
>   Skimmed over the back of the gleaming brine!
>   Farther and faster speeds it on,
>   Till the watch that keep Macistus steep—

18 It is the orthodox custom of translators to render the dialogue of the Greek plays in blank verse; but in this instance the whole animation and rapidity of the original would be utterly lost in the stiff construction and protracted rhythm of that metre.

See it burst like a blazing Sun!
   Doth Macistus sleep
   On his tower-clad steep?
No! rapid and red doth the wildfire sweep;
  It flashes afar, on the wayward stream
  Of the wild Euripus, the rushing beam!
It rouses the light on Messapion's height,
And they feed its breath with the withered heath.
   But it may not stay!
   And away—away—
It bounds in its freshening might.

   Silent and soon,
   Like a broadened moon,
It passes in sheen, Asopus green,[19]
And bursts on Cithæron grey!
The warder wakes to the Signal-rays,
And it swoops from the hill with a broader blaze,
  On—on the fiery Glory rode—
  Thy lonely lake, Gorgōpis, glowed—
To Megara's Mount it came;
   They feed it again,
   And it streams amain—
A giant beard of Flame!
The headland cliffs that darkly down
O'er the Saronic waters frown,
Are pass'd with the Swift One's lurid stride,
And the huge rock glares on the glaring tide,
With mightier march and fiercer power
It gain'd Arachne's neighbouring tower—
Thence on our Argive roof its rest it won,
Of Ida's fire the long-descended Son!
  Bright Harbinger of glory and of joy!
So first and last with equal honour crown'd,
In solemn feasts the race-torch circles round.—
And these my heralds! this my SIGN OF PEACE;
Lo! while we breathe, the victor lords of Greece,
  Stalk, in stern tumult, through the halls of Troy![20]

19 Viz., the meadows around Asopus.
20 To make the sense of this detached passage more complete, and conclude the intelligence
    which the queen means to convey, the concluding line in the text is borrowed from the
    next speech of Clytemnestra—following immediately after a brief and exclamatory inter-
    ruption of the chorus.

In one of the earlier choruses, in which is introduced an episodical allu-
sion to the abduction of Helen, occurs one of those soft passages so rare in
Æschylus, nor less exquisite than rare. The chorus suppose the minstrels of
Menelaus thus to lament the loss of Helen:—

> And woe the halls, and woe the chiefs,
>   And woe the bridal bed!—
> And woe her steps—for once she loved
>   The lord whose love she fled!
> Lo! where, dishonour yet unknown,
> He sits—nor deems his Helen flown,
> Tearless and voiceless on the spot:
> All desert, but he feels it not!
> Ah! soon alive, to miss and mourn
> The form beyond the ocean borne
>   Shall start the lonely king!
> And thought shall fill the lost one's room,
> And darkly through the palace gloom
>   Shall stalk a ghostly thing.[21]
>   Her statues meet, as round they rise,
>   The leaden stare of lifeless eyes.
> Where is their ancient beauty gone?—
> Why loathe his looks the breathing stone?
> Alas! the foulness of disgrace,
> Hath swept the Venus from her face!
> And visions in the mournful night,
> Shall dupe the heart to false delight,
>   A false and melancholy;
> For naught with sadder joy is fraught,
> Than things at night by dreaming brought,
>   The Wish'd for and the Holy.
> Swift from the solitary side,
> The Vision and the Blessing glide,
> Scarce welcomed ere they sweep,
>   Pale, bloodless, dreams, aloft
>   On wings unseen and soft,
> Lost wanderers gliding through the paths of Sleep.

But the master-terror of this tragedy is in the introduction of Cassandra, who
accompanies Agamemnon, and who, in the very hour of his return, amid the
pomp and joy that welcome the "king of men", is seized with the prophetic

---

21 Namely, Menelaus, made by grief like the ghost of his former self.

inspiration, and shrieks out those ominous warnings, fated ever to be heard in vain. It is she who recalls to the chorus, to the shuddering audience, that it is the house of the long-fated Atridæ to which their descendant has returned—"that human shamble-house—that bloody floor—that dwelling, abhorred by Heaven, privy to so many horrors against the most sacred ties"; the doom yet hangs over the inexpiable threshold; the curse passes from generation to generation; Agamemnon is the victim of his sires.

Recalling the inhuman banquet served by Atreus to Thyestes of his own murdered children, she starts from the mangled spectres on the threshold:

> See ye those infants crouching by the floor,
> Like phantom dreams, pale nurslings, that have perish'd
> By kindred hands.

Gradually her ravings become clear and clearer, until at last she scents the "blood-dripping slaughter within"; a vapour rises to her nostrils as from a charnel house—her own fate, which she foresees at hand, begins to over-power her—her mood softens, and she enters the palace, about to become her tomb, with thoughts in which frantic terror has yielded to solemn and pathetic resignation:

> Alas for mortals!—what their power and pride?
> A little shadow sweeps it from the earth!
> And if they suffer—why, the Fatal Hour
> Comes o'er the record like a moistened sponge,
> And blots it out; *methinks this latter lot*
> *Affects me deepest—Well! 'tis pitiful!*[22]

Scarcely has the prophetess withdrawn than we hear behind the scene the groans of the murdered king, the palace behind is opened, and Clytemnestra is standing, stern and lofty, by the dead body of her lord. The critics have dwelt too much on the character of Clytemnestra—it is that of Cassandra which is the masterpiece of the tragedy.

XI. The story, which is spread throughout three plays (forming a com-plete trilogy), continues in the opening of the "Chœphori", with Orestes

---

22 The words in italics attempt to convey paraphrastically a new construction of a sentence which has puzzled the commentators, and met with many and contradictory interpreta-tions. The original literally is—"I pity the last the most". Now, at first it is difficult to conjecture why those whose adversity is over, "blotted out with the moistened sponge", should be the most deserving of compassion. But it seems to me that Cassandra applies the sentiments to herself—*she* pities those whose career of grief is over, because it is her own lot which she commiserates, and by reference to which she individualizes a general reflection.

mourning over his father's tomb. If Clytemnestra has furnished would-be critics with a comparison with Lady Macbeth, for no other reason than that one murdered her husband, and the other persuaded her husband to murder somebody else, so Orestes may with more justice be called the Hamlet of the Greeks; but though the character itself of Orestes is not so complex and profound as that of Hamlet, nor the play so full of philosophical beauties as the modern tragedy, yet it has passages equally pathetic, and more sternly and terribly sublime. The vague horror which in the commencement of the play prepares us for the catastrophe by the dream of Clytemnestra—how a serpent lay in swaddling-clothes like an infant, and she placed it in her breast, and it drew blood; the brief and solemn answer of Orestes, "Man's visions never come to him in vain"; the manner in which the avenging parricide interrupts the dream, so that (as in "Macbeth") the prediction inspires the deed that it foretells; the dauntless resolution of Clytemnestra, when she hears in the dark sayings of her servant that "the dead are slaying the living" (i.e., that through the sword of Orestes Agamemnon is avenged on Ægisthus), calls for a weapon, royal to the last, wishing only to

> Know which shall be the victor or the vanquished—
> Since that the crisis of the present horror—

the sudden change from fierce to tender as Orestes bursts in, and, thinking only of her guilty lover, she shrieks forth, "Ah! thou art then no more, beloved Ægisthus"; the advance of the threatening son, the soft apostrophe of the mother as she bares her bosom—

> Hold! and revere this breast on which so oft
> Thy young cheek nestled—cradle of thy sleep,
> And fountain of thy being—

the recoil of Orestes—the remonstrance of Pylades—the renewed passion of the avenger—the sudden recollection of her dream, which the murderess scarcely utters than it seems to confirm Orestes to its fulfilment, and he pursues and slays her by the side of the adulterer; all these passages are full of so noble a poetry, that I do not think the parallel situations in "Hamlet" equal their sustained and solemn grandeur. But the sublimest effort of the imagination is in the conclusion. While Orestes is yet justifying the deed that avenged a father, strange and confused thoughts gradually creep over him. *No eyes see them but his own*—there they are, "the Gorgons, in vestments of sable, their eyes dropping loathly blood!" Slowly they multiply, they approach, still invisible but to their prey—"the angry hell-hounds of his mother". He flies, the fresh blood yet dripping from his hands. This catastrophe—the sudden apparition of the Furies ideally imaged forth to the parricide alone—seems to me greater in conception than the supernatural agency in "Hamlet". The visible ghost is less awful than the unseen Furies.

The plot is continued through the third piece of the trilogy (the "Eumenides"), and out of Æschylus himself, no existing tragedy presents so striking an opening—one so terrible and so picturesque. It is the Temple of Apollo at Delphi. The priestess, after a short invocation, enters the sacred edifice, but suddenly returns. "A man", she says, "is at the marble seat, a suppliant to the god—his bloody hands hold a drawn sword and a long branch of olive. But around the man sleep a wondrous and ghastly troop, not of women, but of things woman-like, yet fiendish; harpies they seem, but are not; black-robed and wingless, and their breath is loud and baleful, and their eyes drop venom—and their garb is neither meet for the shrines of God nor the habitations of men. Never have I seen (saith the Pythian) a nation which nurtured such a race." Cheered by Apollo, Orestes flies while the dread sisters yet sleep; and now within the temple we behold the Furies scattered around, and a pale and lofty shape, the ghost of Clytemnestra, gliding on the stage, awakens the agents of her vengeance. They break forth as they rouse themselves, "Seize—seize—seize." They lament—they bemoan the departure of their victim, they expostulate with Apollo, who expels them from his temple. The scene changes; Orestes is at Athens,—he pleads his cause before the Temple of Minerva. The contest is now shared by gods; Apollo and the Furies are the pleaders—Pallas is the umpire, the Areopagites are the judges. Pallas casts in her vote in favour of Orestes—the lots are equal—he is absolved; the Furies, at first enraged, are soothed by Minerva, and, invited to dwell in Athens, pour blessings on the land. A sacred but joyous procession crowns the whole. Thus the consummation of the trilogy is cheerful, though each of the two former pieces is tragic; and the poet artfully conduces the poem to the honour of his native Athens and the venerable Areopagus.

Regarding the three as one harmonious and united performance, altogether not so long as one play of Shakespeare's, they are certainly not surpassed in greatness of thought, in loftiness of conception, and in sustained vigour of execution, by any poem in the compass of literature; nor, observing their simple but compact symmetry as a whole, shall we do right to subscribe to those who deny to Æschylus the skill of the artist, while they grant him the faculty of the poet. The ingenious Schlegel attributes to these tragedies symbolical interpretations, but to my judgment with signal ill success. These four tragedies—the "Prometheus", the "Agamemnon", the "Chœphori", and the "Eumenides"—are in grandeur immeasurably superior to the remaining three.

XII. Of these last, the "Seven against Thebes" is the best. The subject was one peculiarly interesting to Greece; the War of the Seven was the earliest record of a league among the Grecian princes, and of an enterprise carried on with a regular and systematic design. The catastrophe of two brothers falling by each other's hand is terrible and tragic, and among the most national of the Grecian legends. The fierce and martial spirit of the warrior poet runs throughout the play; his descriptions are animated as with the zeal and passion of battle; the chorus of Theban virgins paint in the most glowing colours the rush of the adverse hosts—the prancing of the chargers—the sound of their hoofs, "rumbling as a torrent lashing the side of cliffs"; we hear the creak of the heavy cars—the shrill whizz of the javelins, "maddening the very air"—the showers of stones crashing over the battlements—the battering at the mighty gates—the uproar of the city—the yells of rapine —the shrieks of infants "strangled by the bubbling blood". Homer himself never accumulated more striking images of horror. The description of Tydeus is peculiarly Homeric—

> Three shadowy crests, the honours of his helm,
> Wave wild, and shrilly from his buckler broad
> The brazen bell rings terror. On the shield
> He bears his haughty ensign—typed by stars
> Gleaming athwart the sky, and in the midst
> Glitters the royal Moon—the Eye of Night.
> Fierce in the glory of his arms, his voice
> Roars by the river banks; and drunk with war
> He pants, as some wild charger, when the trump
> Clangs ringing, as he rushes on the foe.

The proud, dauntless, and warlike spirit of Eteocles, which is designed and drawn with inconceivable power, is beautifully characterized in his reply to the above description:

> Man hath no armour, war hath no array,
> At which this heart can tremble; no device
> Nor blazonry of battle can inflict
> The wounds they menace;—crests and clashing bells
> Without the spear, are toothless, and the night,
> Wrought on yon buckler with the stars of heaven,
> Prophet, perchance, his doom; and if dark Death
> Close round his eyes, are but the ominous signs
> Of the black night that waits him.

The description of each warrior stationed at each gate is all in the genius of Homer, closing as it does with that of Polynices, the brother of the besieged hero, whom, when he hears his name, Eteocles himself resolves to confront. At first, indeed, the latter breaks out into exclamations which denote the awe and struggle of the abhorrent nature; forebodings of his own doom flit before him, he feels the curses of his sire are ripening to their fruit, and that the last storm is yet to break upon the house of Œdipus. Suddenly he checks the impulse, sensible of the presence of the chorus. He passes on to reason with himself, through a process of thought which Shakespeare could not have surpassed. He conjures up the image of that brother, hateful and unjust from infancy to boyhood, from boyhood up to youth—he assures himself that justice would be forsworn if this foe should triumph—and rushes on to his dread resolve.

> 'Tis I will face this warrior; who can boast
> A right to equal mine? Chief against chief—
> Foe against foe!—and brother against brother.
> What, ho! my greaves, my spear, my armour proof
> Against this storm of stones! My stand is chosen.

Eteocles and his brother both perish in the unnatural strife, and the tragedy ends with the decree of the senators to bury Eteocles with due honours, and the bold resolution of Antigone (the sister of the dead) to defy the ordinance which forbids a burial to Polynices—

> For mighty is the memory of the womb
> From which alike we sprung—a wretched mother!

The same spirit which glows through the "Seven against Thebes" is also visible in the "Persians", which, rather picturesque than dramatic, is tragedy brought back to the dithyrambic ode. It portrays the defeat of Xerxes, and contains one of the most valuable of historical descriptions in the lines devoted to the battle of Salamis. The speech of Atossa (the mother of Xerxes), in which she enumerates the offerings to the shade of Darius, is exquisitely beautiful.

> The charms that sooth the dead:
> White milk, and lucid honey, pure-distill'd
> By the wild bee—that craftsman of the flowers;
> The limpid droppings of the virgin fount,
> And this bright liquid from its mountain mother
> Borne fresh—the joy of the time-hallowed vine;
> The pale-green olive's odorous fruit, whose leaves
> Live everlastingly—and these wreathed flowers,
> The smiling infants o' the prodigal earth.

Nor is there less poetry in the invocation of the chorus to the shade of Darius, which slowly rises as they conclude. But the purpose for which the monarch returns to earth is scarcely sufficient to justify his appearance, and does not seem to be in accordance with the power over our awe and terror which the poet usually commands. Darius hears the tale of his son's defeat—

warns the Persians against interfering with the Athenians—tells the mother to comfort and console her son—bids the chorus (who disregard his advice) give themselves to mirth, even though in affliction, "for to the dead riches are no advantage"—and so returns to his repose, which seems very unnecessarily disturbed.

The "Suppliants," which Schlegel plausibly conjectures to have been the intermediate piece of a trilogy, is chiefly remarkable as a proof of the versatility of the poet. All horror has vanished from the scene; the language is soft when compared with the usual diction of Æschylus; the action is peaceful, and the plot extremely simple, being merely the protection which the daughters of Danaus obtain at the court of Pelasgus from the pursuit of the sons of Ægyptus. The heroines of the play, the Danaides, make the chorus, and this serves to render the whole, yet more than the "Persians", a lyric rather than a tragedy. The moral of the play is homely and primitive, and seems confined to the inculcation of hospitality to strangers, and the inviolable sanctity of the shrine. I do not know any passages in the "Suppliants" that equal in poetry the more striking verses of the "Persians", or the "Seven against Thebes".

XIII. Attempts have been made to convey to modern readers a more familiar notion of Æschylus by comparisons with modern poets. One critic likens him to Dante, another to Milton—but he resembles neither. No modern language can convey a notion of the wonderful strength of his diction—no modern poet, of the stern sublimity of his conceptions. The French tragedians may give some weak reflection of Euripides or even of Sophocles, but none have ventured upon the sacred territory of the father of the tragic drama. He defies all imitation. His genius is so near the verge of bombast, that to approach his sublime is to rush into the ridiculous.[23]

Æschylus never once, in the plays that have come down to us, delineates love, except by an expression or two as regards the passion of Clytemnestra for Ægisthus.[24] It was emblematic of a new state of society when Euripides created the "Phædra" and the "Medea". His plots are worked out by the

---

23 Perhaps his mere diction would find a less feeble resemblance in passages of Shelley, especially in the Prometheus of that poet, than in any other poetry existent. But his diction alone. His power is in concentration—the quality of Shelley is diffuseness. The interest excited by Æschylus, even to those who can no longer sympathize with the ancient associations, is startling, terrible, and intense—that excited by Shelley is lukewarm and tedious. The intellectuality of Shelley destroyed, that of Æschylus only increased, his command over the passions.

24 In the comedy of the "Frogs", Aristophanes makes it the boast of Æschylus, that he never drew a single woman influenced by love. Spanheim is surprised that Aristophanes should ascribe such a boast to the author of the "Agamemnon". But the love of Clytemnestra for Ægisthus *is* never drawn—never delineated. It is merely suggested and hinted at—a sentiment lying dark and concealed behind the motives to the murder of Agamemnon ostensibly brought forward, viz., revenge for the sacrifice of Iphigenia, and jealousy of Cassandra.

simplest and the fewest positions. But he had evidently his own theory of art, and studied with care such stage effects as appeared to him most striking and impressive. Thus, in the burlesque contest between Æschylus and Euripides, in the comedy of the "Frogs," the former is censured, not for too rude a neglect, but for too elaborate a cultivation, of theatrical craft—such as introducing his principal characters, his Niobe and Achilles,[25] with their faces hid, and preserving long and obstinate silence, in order by that suspense to sharpen the expectation of the audience. Æschylus, in fact, contrary to the general criticism, was as earnest and thoughtful an artist as Sophocles himself. There was this difference, it is true: one invented the art and the other perfected. But the first requires as intense a study as the last; and they who talk of the savage and untutored genius of Æschylus are no wiser than the critics who applied the phrase of "native wood-notes wild" to the consummate philosophy of "Hamlet", the anatomical correctness of "Othello", the delicate symmetry of "The Tempest". With respect to the language of Æschylus, ancient critics unite with the modern in condemning the straining of his metaphors, and the exaggeration of his images; yet they appear to me a necessary part of his genius, and of the effect it produces. But nothing can be more unsatisfactory and inconclusive than the theory of Schlegel, that such metaphors and images, such rugged boldness and irregular fire, are the characteristics of a literature in its infancy. On the contrary, as we have already seen, Phrynichus, the predecessor of Æschylus, was as much characterized by sweetness and harmony, as Æschylus by grandeur and headlong animation. In our own time, we have seen the cold classic school succeeded by one full of the faults which the German, eloquent but superficial, would ascribe to the infancy of literature. The diction of Æschylus was the distinction of himself, and not of his age; if it require an apology, let us not seek it in false pretences; if he had written after Euripides, his diction would have been equally startling, and his metaphors equally lofty. His genius was one of those which, in any age, can form an era, and not that which an era necessarily forms. He might have enriched his music from the strains of the Dorian lyres, but he required only one poet to have lived before him. The rest of the Greek dramatists required Æschylus—Æschylus required only Homer.

The poet is, indeed, the creator, not of images solely, but of men—not of one race of ideas and characters, but of a vast and interminable posterity scattered over the earth. The origin of what wonderful works, in what distant regions, in what various time, may be traced, step by step, from influence to influence, till we arrive at Homer! Such is the vitality of genius. The true spiritual transmigrator—it passes through all shapes—losing identity, but not life—and kindred to the GREAT INTELLIGENCE, which is the soul of matter—departing from one form only to animate another.

---

25 In plays lost to us.

CHAPTER III

Aristides—his character and position—the rise of Themistocles
—Aristides is ostracized—the ostracism examined—the
influence of Themistocles increases—the silver-mines of Laurion
—their product applied by Themistocles to the increase of the
navy—new direction given to the national character

I. While the progress of the drama and the genius of Æschylus contributed
to the rising renown of Athens, there appeared on the surface of her external
affairs two rival and principal actors, of talents and

ARISTIDES—HIS CHARAC-
TER AND POSITION

designs so opposite, that it soon became evident
that the triumph of one could be only in the defeat
of the other.

Before the battle of Marathon, Aristides had attained a very considerable
influence in Athens. His birth was noble—his connexions wealthy—his own
fortune moderate. He had been an early follower and admirer of Clisthenes,
the establisher of popular institutions in Athens after the expulsion of the
Pisistratidæ, but he shared the predilection of many popular chieftains, and
while opposing the encroachments of a tyranny, supported the power of an
aristocracy. The system of Lycurgus was agreeable to his stern and inflexible
temper. His integrity was republican—his loftiness of spirit was patrician.
He had all the purity, the disinterestedness, and the fervour of a patriot—he
had none of the suppleness or the passion of a demagogue; on the contrary,
he seems to have felt much of that high-spirited disdain of *managing* a
people which is common to great minds conscious that they are serving a
people. His manners were austere, and he rather advised than persuaded men
to his purposes. He pursued no tortuous policy, but marched direct to his
object, fronting, and not undermining, the obstacles in his path. His reputation for truth and uprightness was proverbial, and when some lines in
Æschylus were recited on the stage, implying that "to *be*, and not to seem,
his wisdom was," the eyes of the spectators were fixed at once upon Aristides.
His sternness was only for principles—he had no harshness for men. Priding
himself on impartiality between friends and foes, he pleaded for the very
person whom the laws obliged him to prosecute; and when once, in his
capacity of arbiter between two private persons, one of the parties said that
his opponent had committed many injuries against Aristides, he rebuked
him nobly: "Tell me not," he said, "of injuries against myself, but against

thee. It is thy cause I am adjudging, and not my own." It may be presumed, that with these singular and exalted virtues, he did not seek to prevent the wounds they inflicted upon the self-love of others, and that the qualities of a superior mind were displayed with the bearing of a haughty spirit. He became the champion of the aristocratic party, and before the battle of Marathon he held the office of public treasurer. In this capacity Plutarch asserts that he was subjected to an accusation by Themistocles, and even intimates that Themistocles himself had been his predecessor in that honourable office.[1] But the youth of Themistocles contradicts this statement; and though his restless and ambitious temper had led him already into active life, and he might have combined with others more influential against Aristides, it can scarcely be supposed that, possessing no advantages of birth, he rose into much power or distinction, till he won sudden and popular applause by his gallantry at Marathon.

II. Themistocles was of illegitimate birth, according to the Athenian prejudice, since his mother was a foreigner. His father, though connected with the priestly and highborn house of the Lycomedæ, was not himself a eupatrid. The young Themistocles had many of the qualities which the equivocal condition of illegitimacy often educes from active and stirring minds—insolence, ostentation, the desire to shine, and the invincible ambition to rise. He appears, by a popular tale, to have early associated with his superiors, and to have evinced betimes the art and address which afterward distinguished him. At a meeting of all the illegitimate youths assembled at the wrestling-ring at Cynosarges, dedicated to Hercules, he persuaded some of the young nobles to accompany him, so as to confound as it were the distinction between the legitimate and the baseborn. His early disposition was bold, restless, and impetuous. He paid little attention to the subtleties of schoolmen, or the refinements of the arts; but even in boyhood devoted himself to the study of politics and the arts of government. He would avoid the sports and occupations of his schoolfellows, and compose declamations, of which the subject was the impeachment or defence of some of his young friends. His dispositions prophesied of his future career, and his master was wont to say, "that he was born to be a blessing or a curse to the commonwealth". His strange and precocious boyhood was followed by a wild and licentious youth. He lived in extremes,

THE RISE OF THEMISTOCLES

---

1 I reject the traditions which make Aristides and Themistocles rivals as boys, because chronology itself refutes them. Aristides must have been of mature age at the battle of Marathon, if he was the friend and follower of Clisthenes, one of the ten generals in the action, and archon in the following year. But both Plutarch and Justin assure us that Themistocles was very young at the battle of Marathon, and this assurance is corroborated by other facts connected with his biography. He died at the age of sixty-five, but he lived to see the siege of Cyprus by Cimon. This happened BC 449. If, then, we refer his death to that year, he was born BC 514, and therefore was about twenty-four at the battle of Marathon.

and alternated between the loosest pleasures[2] and the most daring ambition. Entering prematurely into public life, either his restless disposition or his political principles embroiled him with men of the highest rank. Fearless and sanguine, he cared not whom he attacked, or what he adventured; and, whatever his conduct before the battle of Marathon, the popular opinions he embraced could not but bring him, after that event, in constant opposition to Aristides, the champion of the Areopagus.

That splendid victory which gave an opening to his career sharpened his ambition. The loud fame of Miltiades, yet unconscious of reverse, inspired him with a lofty envy. He seems from that period to have forsaken his more youthful excesses. He abstained from his wonted pursuits and pleasures—he indulged much in solitary and abstracted thought—he watched whole nights. His friends wondered at the change, and inquired the cause. "The trophies of Miltiades", said he, "will not suffer me to sleep." From these meditations, which are common to most men in the interval between an irregular youth and an aspiring manhood, he soon seems to have awakened with fixed objects and expanded views. Once emerged from the obscurity of his birth, his success was rapid, for he possessed all the qualities which the people demanded in a leader—not only the talents and the courage, but the affability and the address. He was an agreeable and boon companion—he committed to memory the names of the humblest citizens—his versatility enabled him to be all things to all men. Without the lofty spirit and beautiful mind of Pericles, without the prodigal but effeminate graces of Alcibiades—without, indeed, any of their Athenian poetry in his intellectual composition, he yet possessed much of their powers of persuasion, their ready talent for business, and their genius of intrigue. But his mind, if coarser than that of either of his successors, was yet perhaps more masculine and determined; nothing diverted him from his purpose—nothing arrested his ambition. His ends were great, and he associated the rise of his country with his more selfish objects, but he was unscrupulous as to his means. Avid of glory, he was not keenly susceptible to honour. He seems rather not to have comprehended, than, comprehending, to have disdained the limits which principle sets to action. Remarkably far-sighted, he possessed, more than any of his contemporaries, the prophetic science of affairs: patient, vigilant, and profound, he was always energetic, because always prepared.

Such was the rival of Aristides, and such the rising leader of the popular party at Athens.

III. History is silent as to the part taken by Aristides in the impeachment of Miltiades, but there is no reason to believe that he opposed the measure of
ARISTIDES IS OSTRACIZED   the Alcmæonid party with which he acted, and which seems to have obtained the ascendancy after the death

---

2 Plut., in Vit. Them.; Heraclides et Idomeneus ap. Athen., xii.

of Miltiades. In the year following the battle of Marathon, we find Aristides in the eminent dignity of archon. In this office he became generally known by the title of "the just". His influence, his official rank, the power of the party that supported him, soon rendered him the principal authority of Athens. The courts of the judges were deserted, every litigant repaired to his arbitration—his administration of power obtained him almost the monopoly of it. Still, however, he was vigorously opposed by Themistocles and the popular faction led by that aspiring rival.

By degrees, various reasons, the chief of which was his own high position, concurred to diminish the authority of Aristides; even among his own partisans he lost ground, partly by the jealousy of the magistrates, whose authority he had superseded—and partly, doubtless, from a maxim more dangerous to a leader than any he can adopt, viz., impartiality between friends and foes in the appointment to offices. Aristides regarded not the political opinions, but the abstract character or talents, of the candidates. With Themistocles, on the contrary, it was a favourite saying, "The gods forbid that I should be in power, and my friends no partakers of my success." The tendency of the first policy is to discontent friends, while it rarely, if ever, conciliates foes; neither is it so elevated as it may appear to the superficial; for if we contend for the superiority of one set of principles over another, we weaken the public virtue when we give equal rewards to the principles we condemn as to the principles we approve. We make it appear as if the contest had been but a war of names, and we disregard the harmony which ought imperishably to exist between the opinions which the state should approve and the honours which the state can confer. He who is impartial as to persons must submit to seem lukewarm as to principles. Thus the more towering and eminent the seeming power of Aristides, the more really hollow and insecure were its foundations. To his own party it was unproductive—to the multitude it appeared unconstitutional. The extra-ordinary honours he had acquired—his monopoly of the magistrature—his anti-popular opinions, could not but be regarded with fear by a people so jealous of their liberties. He seemed to their apprehensions to be approaching gradually to the sovereignty of the state—not, indeed, by guards and military force, but the more dangerous encroachments of civil authority. The moment for the attack arrived. Themistocles could count at last upon the chances of a critical experiment, and Aristides was subjected to the ordeal of the ostracism.

IV. The method of the ostracism was this:—each citizen wrote upon a shell, or a piece of broken earthenware, the name of the person he desired to banish. The magistrates counted the shells, and if they amounted to six thousand (a very considerable proportion of the free population, and less than which amount rendered the ostracism invalid), they were sorted, and the man whose name was found on the greater number of shells was exiled for ten years, with full permission to

THE OSTRACISM
EXAMINED

enjoy his estates. The sentence was one that honoured while it afflicted, nor did it involve any other accusation than that of being too powerful or too ambitious for the citizen of a free state. It is a well-known story, that, during the process of voting, an ignorant burgher came to Aristides, whose person he did not know, and requested him to write down the name of Aristides.

"Has he ever injured you?" asked the great man.

"No", answered the clown, "nor do I know him even by sight; but it vexes me to hear him everywhere called 'the Just' ".

Aristides replied not—he wrote his own name on the shell, and returned it to the enlightened voter. Such is a tale to which more importance than is its due has been attached. Yet perhaps we can give a new reading to the honest burgher's reply, and believe that it was not so expressive of envy at the virtue, as of fear at the reputation. Aristides received the sentence of exile with his accustomed dignity. His last words on leaving his native city were characteristic of his generous and lofty nature. "May the Athenian people", he said, "never know the day which shall force them to remember Aristides!"—a wish, fortunately alike for the exile and the people, not realized. That day, so patriotically deprecated, soon came, glorious equally to Athens and Aristides, and the reparation of wrong and the triumph of liberty found a common date.

The singular institution of the ostracism is often cited in proof of the ingratitude of a republic, and the fickleness of a people; but it owed its origin not to republican disorders, but to despotic encroachment—not to a people, but to a tyrant. If we look throughout all the Grecian states, we find that a tyranny was usually established by some able and artful citizen, who, attaching himself either to the aristocratic, or more frequently to the popular party, was suddenly elevated into supreme power, with the rise of the faction he had espoused. Establishing his fame by popular virtues, he was enabled often to support his throne by a moral authority—more dangerous than the odious defence of military hirelings: hence necessarily arose among the free states a jealousy of individuals, whose eminence became such as to justify an undue ambition; and hence, for a long period, while liberty was yet tender and insecure, the (almost) necessity of the ostracism.

Aristotle, who laments and condemns the practice, yet allows that in certain states it was absolutely requisite; he thinks the evil it is intended to prevent "might have been provided for in the earlier epochs of a commonwealth, by guarding against the rise of one man to a dangerous degree of power; but where the habits and laws of a nation are so formed as to render it impossible to prevent the rise, you must then guard against its consequences": and in another part of his Politics he observes, "that even in republics, where men are regarded, not according to their wealth, but worth—where the citizens love liberty and have arms and valour to defend it; yet, should the pre-eminent virtues of one man, or of one family, totally eclipse

288

the merit of the community at large, you have but two choices—the ostracism or the throne."

If we lament the precaution, we ought then to acknowledge the cause. The ostracism was the creature of the excesses of the tyrannical, and not of the popular principle. The bland and specious hypocrisy of Pisistratus continued to work injury long after his death—and the ostracism of Aristides was the necessary consequence of the seizure of the citadel. Such evil hath arbitrary power, that it produces injustice in the contrary principles as a counterpart to the injustice of its own; thus the oppression of our Catholic countrymen for centuries resulted from the cruelties and persecutions of a papal ascendency. We remembered the danger, and we resorted to the rigid precaution. To guard against a second tyranny of opinion, we condemned, nor perhaps without adequate cause, not one individual, but a whole sect, to a moral ostracism. Ancient times are not then so opposite to the present— and the safety of the state may excuse, in a republic as in a monarchy, a thousand acts of abstract injustice. But the banishment of Aristides has peculiar excuses in the critical circumstances of the time. The remembrance of Pisistratus was still fresh—his son had but just perished in an attempt on his country—the family still lived, and still menaced: the republic was yet in its infancy—a hostile aristocracy within its walls—a powerful enemy still formidable without. It is a remarkable fact, that as the republic strengthened, and as the popular power increased, the custom of ostracism was superseded. The democratic party was never so strong as at the time in which it was finally abolished. It is the insecurity of power, whether in a people or a king, that generates suspicion. Habituated to liberty, a people become less rigid and more enlightened as to its precautions.

V. It had been a saying of Aristides, "that if the Athenians desired their affairs to prosper, they ought to fling Themistocles and himself into the barathrum." But fortune was satisfied at this time with a single victim, and reserved the other for a later sacrifice. Relieved from the presence of a rival who had constantly crossed and obstructed his career, Themistocles found ample scope for his genius. He was not one of those who are unequal to the situation it costs them so much to obtain. On his entrance into public life he is said by Theophrastus to have possessed only three talents; but the account is inconsistent with the extravagance of his earlier career, and still more with the expenses to which a man who attempts to lead a party is, in all popular states, unavoidably subjected. More probably, therefore, it is said of him by others, that he inherited a competent patrimony, and he did not scruple to seize upon every occasion to increase it, whether through the open emolument or the indirect perquisites of public office. But, desiring wealth as a means, not an end, he grasped with one hand to lavish with the other. His generosity dazzled and his manners seduced the people, yet he exercised the power he acquired with a considerate and patriotic foresight. From the first

THE INFLUENCE OF THE-
MISTOCLES INCREASES

retreat of the Persian armament he saw that the danger was suspended, and not removed. But the Athenians, who shared a common Grecian fault, and ever thought too much of immediate, too little of distant peril, imagined that Marathon had terminated the great contest between Asia and Europe. They forgot the fleets of Persia, but they still dreaded the galleys of Ægina. The oligarchy of that rival state was the political enemy of the Athenian demos; the ally of the Persian was feared by the conqueror, and every interest, military and commercial, contributed to feed the passionate and jealous hate that existed against a neighbour, too near to forget, too warlike to despise. The thoughtful and profound policy of Themistocles resolved to work this popular sentiment to ulterior objects; and urging upon a willing audience the necessity of making suitable preparations against Ægina, then the mistress of the seas, he proposed to construct a navy, fitted equally to resist the Persian and to open a new dominion to the Athenians.

To effect this purpose he called into aid one of the most valuable sources of her power which nature had bestowed upon Athens.

VI. Around the country by the ancient Thoricus, on the road from the modern Kerratia to the Cape of Sunium, heaps of scoriæ indicate to the traveller that he is in the neighbourhood of the once celebrated silver-mines of Laurion; he passes through pines and woodlands—he notices the indented tracks of wheels which two thousand years have not effaced from the soil—he discovers the ancient shafts of the mines, and pauses before the foundations of a large circular tower and the extensive remains of the castles which fortified the neighbouring town.[3] A little farther, and still passing among mine-banks and hillocks of scoriæ, he beholds upon Cape Colonna the fourteen existent columns of the Temple of Minerva Sunias. In this country, to which the old name is still attached,[4] is to be found a principal cause of the renown and the reverses of Athens—of the victory of Salamis—of the expedition to Sicily.

THE SILVER-MINES OF LAURION

It appears that the silver-mines of Laurion had been worked from a very remote period—beyond even any traditional date. But as it is well and unanswerably remarked, "the scarcity of silver in the time of Solon proves that no systematic or artificial process of mining could at that time have been established".[5] It was, probably, during the energetic and politic rule of the dynasty of Pisistratus that efficient means were adopted to derive adequate advantage from so fertile a source of national wealth. And when, subsequently, Athens, profiting from the lessons of her tyrants, allowed the genius of her free people to administer the state, fresh necessity was created for wealth against the hostility of Sparta—fresh impetus given to general

3 See Dodwell's "Tour through Greece"; Gell's "Itinerary".
4 "Called by some Laurion Oros, or Mount Laurion", Gell's Itinerary.
5 Boeckh's Dissert. on the Silver Mines of Laurium.

industry and public enterprise. Accordingly, we find that shortly after the battle of Marathon the yearly profits of the mines were immense. We learn from the researches of one of those eminent Germans[6] who have applied so laborious a learning with so subtle an acuteness to the elucidation of ancient history, that these mines were always considered the property of the state; shares in them were sold to individuals as tenants in fee farms, and these proprietors paid, besides, an annual sum into the public treasury, amounting to the twenty-fourth part of the produce. The state, therefore, received a regular revenue from the mines, derived from the purchase-moneys and the reserved rents.

This revenue had been hitherto divided among all the free citizens, and the sum allotted to each was by no means inconsiderable, when Themistocles,

THEIR PRODUCT APPLIED BY THEMISTOCLES TO THE INCREASE OF THE NAVY

at an early period of his career (before even the ostracism of Aristides), had the courage to propose that a fund thus lucrative to every individual should be appropriated to the national purpose of enlarging the navy. The feud still carried on with the Æginetans was his pretext and excuse. But we cannot refuse our admiration to the fervent and generous order of public spirit existent at that time, when we find that it was a popular leader who proposed to, and carried through, a popular assembly the motion, that went to impoverish the men who supported his party and adjudged his proposition. Privileged and sectarian bodies never willingly consent to a surrender of pecuniary benefits for a mere public end. But among the vices of a popular assembly, it possesses the redeeming virtue to be generous. Upon a grand and unconscious principle of selfishness, a democracy rarely grudges a sacrifice endured for the service of the state.

The money thus obtained was devoted to the augmentation of the maritime force to two hundred triremes—an achievement that probably exhausted the mine revenue for some years; and the custom once broken, the produce of Laurion does not seem again to have been wasted upon individuals. To maintain and increase the new navy, a decree was passed, either at that time,[7] or somewhat later, which ordained twenty triremes to be built yearly.

VII. The construction of these vessels, the very sacrifice of the citizens, the general interest that must have attached to an undertaking that was at once

NEW DIRECTION GIVEN TO THE NATIONAL CHARACTER

novel in itself, and yet congenial not more to the passions of a people, who daily saw from their own heights the hostile rock of Ægina, "the eyesore of the Piræus", than to the habits of men placed in a sterile land that on three

6 Boeckh's Dissert. on the Silver Mines of Laurium.
7 On this point, see Boeckh's Dissert. On the Silver Mines of Laurium, in reference to the account of Diodorus.

sides tempted to the sea—all combined to assist Themistocles in his master policy—a policy which had for its design gradually to convert the Athenians from an agricultural into a maritime people. What was imputed to him as a reproach became his proudest distinction, viz., that "he first took his countrymen from the spear and shield, and sent them to the bench and oar".

CHAPTER IV

The preparations of Darius—revolt of Egypt—dispute for the
succession to the Persian throne—death of Darius—brief
review of the leading events and characteristics of his reign

I. While, under the presiding genius of Themistocles, Athens was silently
laying the foundation of her naval greatness, and gradually increasing in
influence and renown, the Persian monarch was not forget-
THE PREPARATIONS
OF DARIUS
ful of the burning of Sardis and the defeat of Marathon.
The armies of a despotic power are often slow to collect,
and unwieldy to unite, and Darius wasted three years in despatching emissaries
to various cities, and providing transports, horses, and forage for a new invasion.

The vastness of his preparations, though congenial to oriental warfare, was
probably proportioned to objects more great than those which appear in the
Greek historians. There is no reason, indeed, to suppose that he cherished
the gigantic project afterward entertained by his son—a project no less than
that of adding Europe as a province to the empire of the East. But symptoms
of that revolt in Egypt which shortly occurred, may have rendered it advisable to collect an imposing force upon other pretences; and without being
carried away by any frantic revenge against the remote and petty territory of
Athens, Darius could not but be sensible that the security of his Ionian,
Macedonian, and Thracian conquests, with the homage already rendered to
his sceptre by the isles of Greece, made it necessary to redeem the disgrace
of the Persian arms, and that the more insignificant the foe, the more fatal,
if unpunished, the example of resistance. The Ionian coasts—the entrance
into Europe—were worth no inconsiderable effort, and the more distant the
provinces to be awed, the more stupendous, according to all rules of Asiatic
despotism, should appear the resources of the sovereign. He required an
immense armament, not so much for the sake of crushing the Athenian foe,
as of exhibiting in all its might the angry majesty of the Persian empire.

II. But while Asia was yet astir with the martial preparations of the great
king, Egypt revolted from his sway, and, at the same time, the peace of
Darius was embittered, and his mind engaged, by
REVOLT OF EGYPT—DIS-
PUTE FOR THE SUCCESSION
TO THE PERSIAN THRONE
a contest among his sons for the succession to
the crown. Artabazanes, the eldest of his family,
born to him by his first wife, previous to his own

293

elevation to the throne, founded his claim upon the acknowledged rights of primogeniture; but Xerxes, the eldest of a second family by Atossa, daughter of the great Cyrus, advanced, on the other hand, a direct descent from the blood of the founder of the Persian empire. Atossa, who appears to have inherited something of her father's genius, and who, at all events, exercised unbounded influence over Darius, gave to the claim of her son a stronger support than that which he could derive from argument or custom. The intrigue probably extended from the palace throughout the pure Persian race, who could not but have looked with veneration upon a descendant of Cyrus, nor could there have seemed a more popular method of strengthening whatever was defective in the title of Darius to the crown, than the transmission of his sceptre to a son, in whose person were united the rights of the new dynasty and the sanctity of the old. These reasonings prevailed with Darius, whose duty it was to nominate his own successor, and Xerxes was declared his heir. While the contest was yet undecided, there arrived at the Persian court Demaratus, the deposed and self-exiled king of Sparta. He attached himself to the cause and person of Xerxes, and is even said to have furnished the young prince with new arguments, founded on the usages of Sparta—an assertion not to be wholly disregarded, since Demaratus appeared before the court in the character of a monarch, if in the destitution of an exile, and his suggestions fell upon the ear of an arbiter willing to seize every excuse to justify the resolution to which he had already arrived.

This dispute terminated, Darius in person prepared to march against the Egyptian rebels, when his death consigned to the inexperienced hands of his heir the command of his armies and the execution of his designs.

DEATH OF DARIUS

The long reign of Darius, extending over thirty-six years, was memorable for vast improvements in the administrations of the empire, nor will it, in this place, be an irrelevant digression to glance briefly and rapidly back over some of the events and the innovations by which it was distinguished.

III. The conquest of Cyrus had transplanted, as the ruling people, to the Median empire, a race of brave and hardy, but simple and uncivilized warriors. Cambyses, of whose character no unequivocal evidence remains, since the ferocious and frantic crimes ascribed to him[1] are conveyed to us through the channel of the Egyptian priests, whom he persecuted, most probably, rather as a political nobility than a religious caste, could but slightly have improved the condition of the people, or the administration of the empire, since his reign lasted but seven years and five months,

BRIEF REVIEW OF THE LEADING EVENTS AND CHARACTERISTICS OF HIS REIGN

---

1 If we except the death of his brother, in the Cambyses of Ctesias we find none of the crimes of the Cambyses of Herodotus—and even that fratricide loses its harsher aspect in the account of Ctesias, and Cambyses is represented as betrayed into the crime by a sincere belief in his brother's treason.

during which he was occupied with the invasion of Africa and the subjugation of Egypt. At the conclusion of his reign he was menaced by a singular
conspiracy. The Median magi conspired in his absence from the seat of
empire to elevate a Mede to the throne. Cambyses, under the impulse of
jealous and superstitious fears, had lately put to death Smerdis, his brother.
The secret was kept from the multitude, and known only to a few—among
others, to the magian whom Cambyses had entrusted with the charge of his
palace at Susa, an office as important as confidential. This man conceived a
scheme of amazing but not unparalleled boldness. His brother, a namesake
of the murdered prince, resembled the latter also in age and person. This
brother, the chief of the household, with the general connivance of his
sacerdotal caste, who were naturally anxious to restore the Median dynasty,
suddenly declared to be the true Smerdis, and the impostor, admitted to
possession of the palace, asserted his claim to the sovereign power. The
consent of the magi—the indifference of the people—the absence, not only
of the king, but of the flower of the Persian race—and, above all, the
tranquil possession of the imperial palace, conspired to favour the deceit.[2]
Placed on the Persian throne, but concealing his person from the eyes of the
multitude in the impenetrable pomp of an oriental seraglio, the pseudo-
Smerdis had the audacity to despatch, among the heralds that proclaimed
his accession, a messenger to the Egyptian army, demanding their allegiance. The envoy found Cambyses at Ecbatana in Syria. Neither cowardice
nor sloth was the fault of that monarch; he sprang upon his horse, determined to march at once to Susa, when the sheath fell from his sword, and he
received a mortal wound from the naked blade. Cambyses left no offspring,
and the impostor, believed by the people to be the true son of Cyrus, issued,
from the protecting and august obscurity of his palace, popular proclamations and beneficent edicts. Whatever his present fraud, whatever his previous career, this daring Mede was enabled to make his reign beloved and
respected. After his death he was regretted by all but the Persians, who
would not have received the virtues of a god as an excuse for the usurpation
of a Mede. Known to the vast empire only by his munificence of spirit—by
his repeal of tribute and service, the impostor permitted none to his presence
who could have detected the secret. He never quitted his palace—the nobles
were not invited to his banquets—the women in his seraglio were separated
each from each—and it was only in profound darkness that the partners of
his pleasures were admitted to his bed. The imposture is said by Herodotus

2 The account of this conspiracy in Ctesias seems more improbable than that afforded to us
  by Herodotus. But in both the most extraordinary features of the plot are the same, viz.,
  the striking likeness between the impostor and the dead prince, and the complete success
  which, for a time, attended the fraud. In both narrations, too, we can perceive, behind the
  main personages ostensibly brought forward, the outline of a profound device of the magi
  to win back from the Persian conquerors, and to secure to a Mede, the empire of the East.

to have been first discovered in the following manner:—the magian, according to the royal custom, had appropriated to himself the wives of Cambyses; one of these was the daughter of Otanes, a Persian noble whom the secluded habits of the pretended king filled with suspicion. For some offence, the magian had been formerly deprived of his ears by the order of Cyrus. Otanes communicated this fact, with his suspicions, to his daughter, and the next time she was a partaker of the royal couch, she took the occasion of his sleep to convince herself that the sovereign of the East was a branded and criminal impostor. The suspicions of Otanes verified, he entered, with six other nobles, into a conspiracy, which mainly owed its success to the resolution and energy of one among them, named Darius, who appears to have held a station of but moderate importance among the royal guard, though son of Hystaspes, governor of the province of Persis, and of the purest and loftiest blood of Persia. The conspirators penetrated the palace unsuspected—put the eunuchs who encountered them to death—and reached the chamber in which the usurper himself was seated with his brother. The impostors, though but imperfectly armed, defended themselves with valour; two of the conspirators were wounded, but the swords of the rest sufficed to consummate the work, and Darius himself gave the death-blow to one of the brothers.

This revolution was accompanied and stained by an indiscriminate massacre of the magi. Nor did the Persians, who bore to that Median tribe the usual hatred which conquerors feel to the wisest and noblest part of the conquered race, content themselves with a short-lived and single revenge. The memory of the imposture and the massacre was long perpetuated by a solemn festival, called "the slaughter of the Magi", or Magophonia, during which no magian was permitted to be seen abroad.

The result of this conspiracy threw into the hands of the seven nobles the succession to the Persian throne: the election fell upon Darius, the soul of the enterprise, and who was of that ancient and princely house of the Achæmenids, in which the Persians recognized the family of their ancestral kings. But the other conspirators had not struggled solely to exchange one despot for another. With a new monarchy arose a new oligarchy. Otanes was even exempted from allegiance to the monarch, and his posterity were distinguished by such exclusive honours and immunities, that Herodotus calls them the only Persian family which retained its liberty. The other conspirators probably made a kind of privileged council, since they claimed the right of access at all hours, unannounced, to the presence of the king—a privilege of the utmost value in eastern forms of government—and their power was rendered permanent and solid by certain restrictions on marriage,[3]

---

3 Herodotus says it was resolved that the king could only marry into the family of one of the conspirators; but Darius married two daughters and one grand-daughter of Cyrus. It is more consonant with eastern manners to suppose that it was arranged that the king

which went to maintain a constant alliance between the royal family and their own. While the six conspirators rose to an oligarchy, the tribe of the Pasargadæ—the noblest of those sections into which the pure Persian family was divided—became an aristocracy to officer the army and adorn the court. But though the great body of the conquered Medes were kept in subject inferiority, yet the more sternly enforced from the Persian resentment at the late Median usurpation, Darius prudently conciliated the most powerful of that great class of his subjects by offices of dignity and command, and of all the tributary nations, the Medes ranked next to the Persians.

IV. With Darius, the Persian monarchy progressed to that great crisis in the civilization of those states founded by conquering Nomades, when, after rich possessions are seized, cities built, and settlements established, the unwieldy and enormous empire is divided into provinces, and satrap government reflects in every district the mingled despotism and subservience, pomp and insecurity, of the imperial court. Darius undoubtedly took the most efficient means in his power to cement his sway and organize his resources. For the better collection of tribute, twenty provinces were created, governed by twenty satraps. Hitherto no specific and regular tax had been levied, but the Persian kings had been contented with reluctant presents, or arbitrary extortions. Darius now imposed a limited and annual impost, amounting, according to the computation of Herodotus, to fourteen thousand five hundred and sixty talents, collected partially from Africa, principally from Asia.[4] The Persians, as the conquering and privileged race, were excluded from the general imposition, but paid their moderate contribution under the softer title of gratuity. The Colchians fixed their own burdens— the Ethiopians that bordered Egypt, with the inhabitants of the sacred town of Nyssa, rendered also tributary gratuities—while Arabia offered the homage of her frankincense, and India[5] of her gold. The empire of Darius was the more secure, in that it was contrary to its constitutional spirit to innovate on the interior organization of the distant provinces—they enjoyed their own national laws and institutions—they even retained their monarchs—they resigned nothing but their independence and their tribute. The duty of the satraps was as yet but civil and financial: they were responsible for the

---

should give his own daughters in marriage to members of these six houses. It would have been scarcely possible to claim the monopoly of the royal seraglio, whether its tenants were wives or concubines, and in all probability the king's choice was only limited (nor that very rigidly) to the family of Cyrus, and the numerous and privileged race of the Achæmenids.

4 Besides the regular subsidies, we gather from Herodotus (iii. 92) that the general population was obliged to find subsistence for the king and his armies. Babylon raised a supply for four months, the resources of that satrapy being adequate to a third part of Asia.

5 That comparatively small and frontier part of India known to Darius.

imposts, they executed the royal decrees. Their institution was outwardly designed but for the better collection of the revenue; but when from the ranks of the nobles Darius rose to the throne, he felt the advantage of creating subject principalities, calculated at once to remove and to content the more powerful and ambitious of his former equals. Save Darius himself, no monarch in the known world possessed the dominion or enjoyed the splendour accorded to these imperial viceroys. Babylon and Assyria fell to one—Media was not sufficient for another—nation was added to nation, and race to race, to form a province worthy the nomination of a representative of the great king. His pomp and state were such as befitted the viceroy over monarchs. A measure of silver, exceeding the Attic medimnus, was presented every day to the satrap of Babylon.[6] Eight hundred stallions and sixteen thousand mares were apportioned to his stables, and the tax of four Assyrian towns was to provide for the maintenance of his Indian dogs.

But under Darius, at least, these mighty officers were curbed and kept in awe by the periodical visits of the king himself, or his commissioners; while a broad road, from the western coast to the Persian capital—inns, that received the messengers, and couriers, that transmitted the commands of the king, brought the more distant provinces within the reach of ready intelligence and vigilant control. These latter improvements were well calculated to quicken the stagnant languor habitual to the overgrowth of eastern empire. Nor was the reign of Darius undistinguished by the cultivation of the more elegant arts—since to that period may be referred, if not the foundation, at least the embellishment and increase of Persepolis. The remains of the palace of Chil-Menar, ascribed by modern superstition to the architecture of genii, its graceful columns, its mighty masonry, its terrace-flights, its marble basins, its sculptured designs stamped with the unmistakeable emblems of the magian faith, sufficiently evince that the shepherd-soldiery of Cyrus had already learned to appreciate and employ the most elaborate arts of the subjugated Medes.

During this epoch, too, was founded a more regular military system, by the institution of conscriptions—while the subjection of the skilful sailors of Phœnicia, and of the great maritime cities of Asiatic Greece, brought to the Persian warfare the new arm of a numerous and experienced navy.

V. The reign of Darius is also remarkable for the influence which Grecian strangers began to assume in the Persian court—and the fatal and promiscuous admission of Grecian mercenaries into the Persian service. The manners of the Persians were naturally hospitable, and Darius possessed not only an affable temper, but an inquisitive mind. A Greek physician of Crotona, who succeeded in relieving the king from the effects of a painful accident which had baffled the Egyptian practitioners, esteemed the most skilful the court

6 Forming a revenue of more than 100,000 pounds sterling (Heeren's Persians, chap. ii).

possessed, naturally rose into an important personage. His reputation was increased by a more difficult cure upon the person of Atossa, the daughter of Cyrus, who, from the arms of her brother Cambyses, and those of the magian impostor, passed to the royal marriage-bed. And the physician, though desirous only of returning through some pretext to his own country, perhaps first inflamed the Persian king with the ill-starred wish of annexing Greece to his dominions. He despatched a commission with the physician himself, to report on the affairs of Greece. Many Hellenic adventurers were at that time scattered over the empire, some who had served with Cambyses, others who had sided with the Egyptians. Their valour recommended them to a valiant people, and their singular genius for intrigue took root in every soil. Syloson, a Greek of Samos, brother to Polycrates, the tyrant of that state, who, after a career of unexampled felicity and renown, fell a victim to the hostile treachery of Orœtes, the satrap of Sardis, induced Darius to send over Otanes at the head of a Persian force to restore him to the principality of his murdered brother; and when, subsequently, in his Scythian expedition, Darius was an eyewitness of the brilliant civilization of Ionia, not only did Greece become to him more an object of ambition, but the Greeks of his respect. He sought, by a munificent and wise clemency, to attach them to his throne, and to colonize his territories with subjects valuable alike for their constitutional courage and national intelligence. Nor can we wonder at the esteem which a Hippias or a Demaratus found in the Persian councils, when, in addition to the general reputation of Greeks, they were invested with the dignity of princely rank—for, above all nations,[7] the Persians most venerated the name and the attributes of a king; nor could their oriental notions have accurately distinguished between a legitimate monarch and a Greek tyrant.

VI. In this reign, too, as the empire was concentrated, and a splendid court arose from the warrior camp of Cyrus and Cambyses, the noble elements of the pure Persian character grew confounded with the Median and Assyrian. As the Persians retreated from the manners of a nomad, they lost the distinction of a conquering people. Warriors became courtiers—the palace shrunk into the seraglio—eunuchs and favourites, queens,[8] and above all queen-mothers, rose into pernicious and invisible influence. And while the Greeks, in their small states, and under their free governments, progressed to a civilization, in which luxury only sharpened new energies and created new arts, the gorgeous enervation of a despotism destructive to competition, and an empire too vast for patriotism, rapidly debased and ruined the old

---

7 Such are the expressions of Herodotus. His testimony is corroborated by the anecdotes in his own history, and, indeed, by all other ancient authorities.

8 Dinon (ap. Athen., xiii) observes, that the Persian queen tolerated the multitude of concubines common to the royal seraglio, because they worshipped her, like a divinity.

hardy race of Cyrus,[9] perhaps equal originally to the Greeks in mental, and in many important points far superior to them in moral qualities. With a religion less animated and picturesque, but more simple and exalted, rejecting the belief that the gods partook of a mortal nature, worshipping their GREAT ONE not in statues or in temples, but upon the sublime altar of lofty mountain-tops—or through those elementary agents which are the unidolatrous representatives of his beneficence and power;[10] accustomed, in their primitive and uncorrupted state, to mild laws and limited authority; inured from childhood to physical discipline and moral honesty, "to draw the bow and to speak the truth", this gallant and splendid tribe were fated to make one of the most signal proofs in history, that neither the talents of a despot nor the original virtues of a people can long resist the inevitable effect of vicious political constitutions. It was not at Marathon, nor at Salamis, nor at Platæa, that the Persian glory fell. It fell when the Persians imitated the manners of the slaves they conquered. "Most imitative of all men", says Herodotus, "they are ever ready to adopt the manners of the foreigners. They take from the Medes their robe, from the Egyptians their breastplate". Happy, if to the robe and the breastplate they had confined their appropriations from the nations they despised! Happy, if they had not imparted to their august religion the gross adulterations of the Median magi; if they had not exchanged their mild laws and restricted government, for the most callous contempt of the value of life[11] and the dignity of freedom. The whole of the pure Persian race, but especially the nobler tribe of the Pasargadæ, became raised by conquest over so vast a population, to the natural aristocracy of the

---

9 See, in addition to more familiar authorities, the curious remarks and anecdotes relative to the luxury of the Persian kings, in the citations from Dinon, Heraclides, Agathocles, and Chares of Mitylene, scattered throughout Athenæus, xii, xiii, xiv; but especially xii.

10 Strabo, xv. Herod., i. 131, &c.

11 Among innumerable instances of the disdain of human life contracted after their conquest by those very Persians who, in their mountain obscurity, would neither permit their sovereign to put any one to death for a single offence, nor the master of a household to exercise undue severity to a member of his family (Herod., i. 137), is one recorded by Herodotus, and in the main corroborated by Justin. Darius is at the siege of Babylon; Zopyrus, one of the seven conspirators against the magian, maims himself and enters Babylon as a deserter, having previously concerted with Darius that a thousand men, whose loss he could best spare, should be sent one day to the gate of Semiramis, and two thousand, another day, to the gates of Ninus, and four thousand, a third day, to the Chaldæan gates. All these detachments Zopyrus, at the head of the Babylonians, deliberately butchered. The confidence of the Babylonians thus obtained, Zopyrus was enabled to betray the city to the king. This cold-blooded and treacherous immolation of seven thousand subjects was considered by the humane Darius and the Persians generally a proof of the most illustrious virtue in Zopyrus, who received for it the reward of the satrapy of Babylon. The narrative is so circumstantial as to bear internal evidence of its general truth. In fact, a Persian would care no more for the lives of seven thousand Medes than a Spartan would care for the lives of suspected Helots.

land. But the valuable principle of aristocratic pride, which is the safest curb to monarchic encroachment, crumbled away in the atmosphere of a despotism, which received its capricious checks or awful chastisement only in the dark recesses of a harem. Retaining to the last their disdain of all without the Persian pale, deeming themselves still "the most excellent of mankind",[12] this people, the nobility of the East, with the arrogance of the Spartan, contracting the vices of the East, rapidly decayed from all their national and ancient virtues beneath that seraglio-rule of janissaries and harlots, in which, from first to last, have merged the melancholy destinies of oriental despotism.

VII. Although Darius seems rather to have possessed the ardour for conquest than the genius for war, his reign was memorable for many military triumphs, some cementing, others extending, the foundations of the empire. A formidable insurrection of Babylon, which resisted a siege of twenty-one months, was effectually extinguished, and the new satrap government, aided by the yearly visits of the king, appears to have kept from all subsequent reanimation the vast remains of that ancient empire of the Chaldæan kings. Subsequently an expedition along the banks of the Indus, first navigated for discovery by one of the Greeks whom Darius took into his employ, subjected the highlands north of the Indus, and gave that distant river as a new boundary to the Persian realm. More important, had the fortunes of his son been equal to his designs, was the alarming settlement which the monarch of Asia effected on the European continent, by establishing his sovereignty in Thrace and Macedonia—by exacting homage from the isles and many of the cities of Greece—by breaking up, with the crowning fall of Miletus, the independence and rising power of those Ionian colonies, which ought to have established on the Asiatic coasts the permanent barrier to the irruptions of eastern conquest. Against these successes the loss of six thousand four hundred men at the battle of Marathon, a less number than Darius deliberately sacrificed in a stratagem at the siege of Babylon, would have seemed but a petty counterbalance in the despatches of his generals, set off, as it was, by the spoils and the captives of Eubœa. Nor were the settlements in Thrace and Macedon, with the awe that his vast armament excited throughout that portion of his dominions, an insufficient recompense for the disasters of the expedition, conducted by Darius in person, against the wandering, fierce, and barbarous Mongolian race, that, known to us by the name of Scythians, worshipped their war-god under the symbol of a cimeter, with libations of

12 Herod., i. 134. The Pasargadæ, whom the ancient writers evidently and often confound with the whole Persian population, retained the old education and severe discipline for their youth, long after the old virtues had died away (see Strabo, xv; Herod., i; and the rhetorical romance of Xenophon). But laws and customs, from which the animating spirit of national opinion and sentiment has passed, are but the cenotaphs of dead forms embalmed in vain.

human blood—hideous inhabitants of the inhospitable and barren tracts that interpose between the Danube and the Don.

VIII. Thus the heritage that passed from Darius to Xerxes was the fruit of a long and, upon the whole, a wise and glorious reign. The new sovereign of the East did not, like his father, find a disjointed and uncemented empire of countries rather conquered than subdued, destitute alike of regular revenues and local governments; a wandering camp, shifted to and fro in a wilderness of unconnected nations—Xerxes ascended the throne amid a splendid court, with Babylon, Ecbatana, Persepolis, and Susa for his palaces. Submissive satraps united the most distant provinces with the seat of empire. The wealth of Asia was borne in regular currents to his treasury. Save the revolt of the enfeebled Egyptians, and the despised victory of a handful of men upon a petty foreland of the remote Ægæan, no cloud rested upon the dawn of his reign. As yet unfelt and unforeseen were the dangers that might ultimately result from the very wisdom of Darius in the institution of satraps, who, if not sufficiently supported by military force, would be unable to control the motley nations over which they presided, and, if so supported, might themselves become, in any hour, the most formidable rebels. To whatever prestige he inherited from the fame of his father, the young king added also a more venerable and sacred dignity in the eyes of the Persian aristocracy and perhaps throughout the whole empire, derived, on his mother's side, from the blood of Cyrus. Never, to all external appearance, and, to ordinary foresight, under fairer auspices, did a prince of the East pass from the luxury of a seraglio to the majesty of a throne.

CHAPTER V

Xerxes conducts an expedition into Egypt—he finally resolves on the invasion of Greece—vast preparations for the conquest of Europe—Xerxes arrives at Sardis—despatches envoys to the Greek states, demanding tribute—the bridge of the Hellespont—review of the Persian armament at Abydos— Xerxes encamps at Therme

I. On succeeding to the throne of the East, Xerxes found the mighty army collected by his father prepared to execute his designs of conquest or revenge. In the greatness of that army, in the youth of that prince, various parties beheld the instrument of interest or ambition. Mardonius, warlike and enterprising, desired the subjugation of Greece, and the command of the Persian forces. And to the nobles of the Pasargadæ an expedition into Europe could not but present a dazzling prospect of spoil and power—of satrapies as yet unexhausted of treasure—of garrisons and troops remote from the eye of the monarch, and the domination of the capital.

The persons who had most influence over Xerxes were his uncle Artabanus, his cousin Mardonius, and a eunuch named Natacas.[1] The intrigues of the party favourable to the invasion of Europe were backed by the representations of the Grecian exiles. The family and partisans of the Pisistratidæ had fixed themselves in Susa, and the Greek subtlety and spirit of enterprise maintained and confirmed, for that unprincipled and able faction, the credit they had already established at the Persian court. Onomacritus, an Athenian priest, formerly banished by Hipparchus for forging oracular predictions, was now reconciled to the Pisistratidæ, and resident at Susa. Presented to the king as a soothsayer and prophet, he inflamed the ambition of Xerxes by garbled oracles of conquest and fortune, which, this time, it was not the interest of the Pisistratidæ to expose.

About the same period the Aleuadæ, those princes of Thessaly whose policy seems ever to have been that of deadly hostility to the Grecian republics, despatched ambassadors to Xerxes, inviting him to Greece, and promising assistance to his arms, and allegiance to his sceptre.

---

1 Ctesias, 20.

II. From these intrigues Xerxes aroused himself in the second year of his reign, and, as the necessary commencement of more extended designs, con-

XERXES CONDUCTS AN EXPEDITION INTO EGYPT

ducted in person an expedition against the rebellions Egyptians. That people had neither military skill nor constitutional hardihood, but they were inspired with the most devoted affection for their faith and their institutions. This affection was to them what the love of liberty is in others—it might be easy to conquer them, it was almost impossible to subdue. By a kind of fatality their history, for centuries, was interwoven with that of Greece: their perils and their enemies the same. The ancient connexion which apocryphal tradition recorded between races so opposite seemed a typical prophecy of that which actually existed in the historical times. And if formerly Greece had derived something of civilization from Egypt, she now paid back the gift by the swords of her adventurers; and the bravest and most loyal part of the Egyptian army was composed of Grecian mercenaries. At the same time Egypt shared the fate of all nations that entrust too great a power to auxiliaries. Greeks defended her, but Greeks conspired against her. The adventurers from whom she derived a fatal strength were of a vain, wily, and irritable temperament. A Greek removed from the influence of Greece usually lost all that was honest, all that was noble in the national character; and with the most refining intellect, he united a policy like that of the Italian in the middle ages, fierce, faithless, and depraved. Thus, while the Greek auxiliaries under Amasis, or rather Psammenitus, resisted to the last the arms of Cambyses, it was by a Greek (Phanes) that Egypt had been betrayed. Perhaps, could we thoroughly learn all the secret springs of the revolt of Egypt, and the expedition of Xerxes, we might find a coincidence not of dates alone between Grecian and Egyptian affairs. Whether in Memphis or in Susa, it is wonderful to see the amazing influence and ascendency which the Hellenic intellect obtained. It was in reality the desperate refuse of Europe that swayed the councils, moved the armies, and decided the fate of the mighty dynasties of the East.

III. The arms of Xerxes were triumphant in Egypt, and he more rigorously enforced upon that ill-fated land the iron despotism commenced by

HE FINALLY RESOLVES ON THE INVASION OF GREECE

Cambyses. Intrusting the Egyptian government to his brother Achæmenes, the Persian king returned to Susa, and flushed with his victory, and more and more influenced by the ambitious counsels of Mardonius, he now fairly opened, in the full divan of his counsellors, the vast project he had conceived. The vanity of the Greeks led them too credulously to suppose that the invasion of Greece was the principal object of the great king; on the contrary, it was the least. He regarded Greece but as the threshold of a new quarter of the globe. Ignorant of the nature of the lands he designed to subject, and credulous of all the fables which impart proverbial magnificence to the unknown, Xerxes saw in Europe "regions not inferior to Asia in

304

extent, and far surpassing it in fertility". After the conquest of Greece on either continent, the young monarch unfolded to his counsellors his intention of overrunning the whole of Europe, "until heaven itself should be the only limit to the Persian realm, and the sun should shine on no country contiguous to his own".[2]

IV. These schemes, supported by Mardonius, were opposed only by Artabanus; and the arguments of the latter, dictated by prudence and experience, made considerable impression upon the king. From that time, however, new engines of superstitious craft and imposture were brought to bear upon the weak mind, on whose decision now rested the fatal war between Asia and Europe. Visions and warnings, threats and exhortations, haunted his pillow and disturbed his sleep, all tending to one object, the invasion of Greece. As we learn from Ctesias that the eunuch Natacas was one of the parasites most influential with Xerxes, it is probable that so important a personage in the intrigues of a palace was, with the evident connivance of the magi, the instrument of Mardonius. And, indeed, from this period the politics of Persia became more and more concentrated in the dark plots of the seraglio. Thus superstition, flattery, ambition, all operating upon him, the irresolution of Xerxes vanished. Artabanus himself affected to be convinced of the expediency of the war; and the only object now remaining to the king and his counsellors was to adapt the preparations to the magnitude of the enterprise. Four additional years were not deemed an idle delay in collecting an army and fleet destined to complete the conquest of the world.

"And never", says Herodotus, "was there a military expedition comparable to this. Hard would it be to specify one nation of Asia which did not accompany the Persian king, or any waters, save the great rivers, which were not exhausted by his armament." Preparations for an expedition of three years were made, to guard against the calamities formerly sustained by the Persian fleet. Had the success of the expedition been commensurate with the grandeur of its commencement, perhaps it would have ranked among the sublimest conceptions of military genius. All its schemes were of a vast and gigantic nature. Across the isthmus, which joins the promontory of Athos to the Thracian continent, a canal was formed—a work of so enormous a labour, that it seems almost to have justified the scepticism of later writers,[3] but for the concurrent testimony of Thucydides and Lysias, Plato, Herodotus, and Strabo.

Bridges were also thrown over the river Strymon; the care of provisions was entrusted to the Egyptians and Phœnicians, and stores were deposited in every station that seemed the best adapted for supplies.

VAST PREPARATIONS FOR THE CONQUEST OF EUROPE

---

2 Herod., vii. II.

3 Juvenal, Richardson, &c. The preparations at Mount Athos began three years before Xerxes arrived at Sardis (compare Herod., vii. 21, with 33, 37).

V. While these preparations were carried on, the great king, at the head of his land-forces, marched to Sardis. Passing the river Halys, and the frontiers of Lydia, he halted at Celænæ. Here he was magnificently entertained by Pythius, a Lydian, esteemed, next to the king himself, the richest of mankind. This wealthy subject proffered to the young prince, in prosecution of the war, the whole of his treasure, amounting to two thousand talents of silver, and four millions, wanting only seven thousand, of golden staters of Darius.[4] "My farms and my slaves", he added, "will be sufficient to maintain me."

XERXES ARRIVES AT SARDIS —DESPATCHES ENVOYS TO THE GREEK STATES, DEMANDING TRIBUTE

"My friend", said the royal guest, who possessed all the irregular generosity of princes, "you are the first person, since I left Persia, who has treated my army with hospitality and voluntarily offered me assistance in the war. Accept my friendship; I receive you as my host; retain your possessions, and permit me to supply the seven thousand staters which are wanting to complete the four millions you already possess." A man who gives from the property of the public is seldom outdone in munificence.

At length Xerxes arrived at Sardis, and thence he despatched heralds into Greece, demanding the tribute of earth and water. Athens and Sparta were the only cities not visited by his envoys.

VI. While Xerxes rested at the Lydian city, an enterprise, scarcely less magnificent in conception than that of the canal at Athos, was completed at the sacred passage of the Hellespont. Here was constructed from the coast of Asia to that of Europe a bridge of boats, for the convoy of the army. Scarce was this completed when a sudden tempest scattered the vessels, and rendered the labour vain. The unruly passion of the high-spirited despot was popularly said to have evinced itself at this intelligence, by commanding the Hellespont to receive three hundred lashes and a pair of fetters—a story recorded as a certainty by Herodotus, and more properly condemned as a fable by modern scepticism.

THE BRIDGE OF THE HELLESPONT

A new bridge was now constructed under new artificers, whose industry was sharpened by the fate of their unfortunate predecessors, whom Xerxes condemned to death. These architects completed at last two bridges of vessels, of various kinds and sizes, secured by anchors of great length, and thus protected from the influence of the winds that set in from the Euxine on the one hand, and the south and southeast winds on the other. The elaborate description of this work given by Herodotus proves it to have been no clumsy or unartist-like performance. The ships do not appear so much to have formed the bridge, as to have served for piers to support its weight. Rafters of wood, rough timber, and layers of earth were placed across extended cables, and the

---

4 Differently computed; according to Montfaucon, the sum total may be estimated at thirty-two millions of Louis d'ors.

whole was completed by a fence on either side, that the horses and beasts of burden might not be frightened by the sight of the open sea.

VII. And now the work was finished, the winter was past, and at the dawn of returning spring, Xerxes led his armament from Sardis to Abydos. As the multitude commenced their march, it is said that the sun was suddenly overcast, and an abrupt and utter darkness crept over the face of heaven. The magi were solemnly consulted at the omen; and they foretold, that by the retirement of the sun, the tutelary divinity of the Greeks, was denoted the withdrawal of the protection of Heaven from that fated nation. The answer pleased the king.

On they swept—the conveyance of the baggage, and a vast promiscuous crowd of all nations, preceding; behind, at a considerable interval, came the flower of the Persian army—a thousand horse—a thousand spearmen—the ten sacred steeds, called Nisæan—the car of the great Persian god, drawn by eight snow-white horses, and in which no mortal ever dared to seat himself. Around the person of Xerxes were spearmen and cavalry, whose arms glittered with gold—the ten thousand infantry called "The Immortals", of whom nine thousand bore pomegranates of silver at the extremity of their lances, and one thousand pomegranates of gold. Ten thousand horsemen followed these: and far in the rear, the gorgeous procession closed with the mighty multitude of the general army.

The troops marched along the banks of the Caicus—over the plains of Thebes; and passing Mount Ida to the left, above whose hoary crest broke a storm of thunder and lightning, they arrived at the golden Scamander, whose waters failed the invading thousands. Here it is poetically told of Xerxes, that he ascended the citadel of Priam, and anxiously and carefully surveyed the place, while the magi of the barbarian monarch directed libations to the manes of the Homeric heroes.

VIII. Arrived at Abydos, the king reviewed his army. High upon an eminence, and on a seat of white marble, he surveyed the plains covered with

REVIEW OF THE PERSIAN ARMAMENT AT ABYDOS

countless thousands, and the Hellespont crowded with sails and masts. At first, as he gazed, the lord of Persia felt all the pride and exultation which the command over so many destinies was calculated to inspire. But a sad and sudden thought came over him in the midst of his triumphs, and he burst into tears. "I reflect", said he to Artabanus, "on the transitory limit of human life. I compassionate this vast multitude—a hundred years hence, which of them will still be a living man?" Artabanus replied like a philosopher, "that the shortness of life was not its greatest evil; that misfortune and disease embittered the possession, and that death was often the happiest refuge of the living".[5]

---

5 It must be confessed that the tears of Xerxes were a little misplaced. He wept that men could not live a hundred years, at the very moment when he meditated destroying a tolerable portion of them as soon as he possibly could (Senec., de Brev. Vit., 17).

At early daybreak, while the army yet waited the rising of the sun, they burnt perfumes on the bridge, and strewed it with branches of the triumphal myrtle. As the sun lifted himself above the east, Xerxes poured a libation into the sea, and addressing the rising orb, implored prosperity to the Persian arms, until they should have vanquished the whole of Europe, even to the remotest ends. Then casting the cup, with a Persian cimeter, into the sea, the signal was given for the army to commence the march. Seven days and seven nights were consumed in the passage of that prodigious armament.

IX. Thus entering Europe, Xerxes proceeded to Doriscus (a wide plain of Thrace, commanded by a Persian garrison), where he drew up, and regularly numbered his troops; the fleets ranged in order along the neighbouring coast. The whole amount of the land-force, according to Herodotus, was one million seven hundred thousand. Later writers have been sceptical as to this vast number, but without sufficient grounds for their disbelief. There were to be found the soldiery of many nations:—the Persians in tunics and scale breastplates, the tiara helmet of the Medes, the arrows, and the large bow which was their natural boast and weapon; there were the Medes similarly equipped; and the Assyrians, with barbarous helmets, linen cuirasses, and huge clubs tipped with iron; the Bactrians with bows of reeds, and the Scythian Sacæ, with their hatchets and painted crests. There, too, were the light-clothed Indians, the Parthians, Chorasmians, Sogdians, Gandarians, and the Dadicæ. There were the Caspians, clad in tough hides, with bows and cimeters; the gorgeous tunics of the Sarangæ, and the loose flowing vests (or ziræ) of the Arabians. There were seen the negroes of Æthiopian Nubia with palm bows four cubits long, arrows pointed with flint, and vestures won from the leopard and the lion; a barbarous horde, who, after the wont of savages, dyed their bodies with gypsum and vermilion when they went to war; while the straight-haired Asiatic Æthiopians wore the same armour as the Indians whom they bordered, save that their helmets were formed of the skin of the horse's head,[6] on which the mane was left in the place of plumage. The Libyans were among the horde, and the buskined Paphlagonians, with helms of network; and the Cappadocian Syrians; and the Phrygians; and the Armenians; the Lydians, equipped similarly to the Greeks; the Strymonian Thracians, clad in tunics, below which were flowing robes like the Arabian ziræ or tartan, but of various colours, and buskins of the skins of fawns—armed with the javelin and the dagger; the Thracians, too, of Asia, with helmets of brass wrought with the ears and horns of an ox; the people from the islands of the Red Sea, armed and equipped like Medes; the Mares, and the Colchians, and the Moschi, and other tribes, tedious to enumerate, swelled and diversified the force of Xerxes.

6 Common also to the ancient Germans.

Such were the infantry of the Persian army, forgetting not the ten thousand chosen Persians, called the Immortal Band,[7] whose armour shone with profuse gold, and who were distinguished even in war by luxury—carriages for their women, troops of attendants, and camels and beasts of burden.

Besides these were the Persian cavalry; the nomad Sagartii, who carried with them nooses, in which they sought to entangle their foe; the Medes and the Indian horse, which last had also chariots of war drawn by steeds or wild asses; the Bactrians and Caspians, equipped alike; the Africans, who fought from chariots; the Paricanians; and the Arabians with their swift dromedaries, completed the forces of the cavalry, which amounted to eighty thousand, exclusive even of chariots and the camels.

Nor was the naval unworthy of the land armada. The number of the triremes was one thousand two hundred and seven. Of these the Phœnicians and the Syrians of Palestine furnished three hundred, the serving-men with breastplates of linen, javelins, bucklers without bosses, and helmets fashioned nearly similarly to those of the Greeks; two hundred vessels were supplied by the Egyptians, armed with huge battle-axes, and casques of network; one hundred and fifty vessels came from Cyprus, and one hundred from Cilicia; those who manned the first differing in arms from the Greeks only in the adoption of the tunic, and the Median mitres worn by the chiefs—those who manned the last, with two spears, and tunics of wool. The Pamphylians, clad as the Greeks, contributed thirty vessels, and fifty also were manned by Lycians with mantles of goat-skin and unfeathered arrows of reed. In thirty vessels came the Dorians of Asia; in seventy the Carians, and in a hundred, the subjugated Ionians. The Grecian isles between the Cyaneæ and the promontories of Triopium and Sunium[8] furnished seventeen vessels, and the Æolians sixty. The inhabitants of the Hellespont (those of Abydos alone excepted, who remained to defend the bridges) combined with the people of Pontus to supply a hundred more. In each vessel were detachments of Medes, Persians, and Sacæ; the best mariners were the Phœnicians, especially those of Sidon. The commanders-in-chief of the sea-forces were Ariabignes (son of Darius), Prexaspes, Megabazus (son of Megabates), and Achæmenes (brother of Xerxes, and satrap of Egypt).

Of the infantry, the generals were Mardonius, Tritantæchmes (son of Artabanus), and Smerdones (cousin to Xerxes), Masistes (his brother), Gergis, and Megabazus, son of that celebrated Zopyrus, through whom Darius possessed himself of Babylon.[9]

7 For this reason—whoever died, whether by disease or battle, had his place immediately supplied. Thus their number was invariably the same.
8 Diod. Sic.
9 See ch. IV n. 11.

Harmamithres and Tithæus, who were Medes, commanded the cavalry; a third leader, Pharnouches, died in consequence of a fall from his horse. But the name of a heroine, more masculine than her colleagues, must not be omitted: Artemisia, widow to one of the Carian kings, furnished five ships (the best in the fleet next to those of Sidon), which she commanded in person, celebrated alike for a dauntless courage and a singular wisdom.

X. Such were the forces which the great king reviewed, passing through the land-forces in his chariot, and through the fleet in a Sidonian vessel, beneath a golden canopy. After his survey, the king summoned Demaratus to his presence.

Xerxes encamps at Therme

"Think you", said he, "that the Greeks will presume to resist me?"

"Sire", answered the Spartan, "your proposition of servitude will be rejected by the Greeks; and even if the rest of them sided with you, Lacedæmon still would give you battle; question not in what numbers; had Sparta but a thousand men she would oppose you."

Marching onward, and forcibly enlisting, by the way, various tribes through which he passed, exhausting many streams, and impoverishing the population condemned to entertain his army, Xerxes arrived at Acanthus: there he dismissed the commanders of his fleet, ordering them to wait his orders at Therme, a small town which gave its name to the Thermean Gulf (to which they proceeded, pressing ships and seamen by the way), and afterward, gaining Therme himself, encamped his army on the coast, spreading far and wide its multitudinous array from Therme and Mygdonia to the rivers Lydias and Haliacmon.

CHAPTER VI

The conduct of the Greeks—the oracle relating to Salamis—
art of Themistocles—the Isthmian Congress—embassies to
Argos, Crete, Corcyra, and Syracuse—their ill success—the
Thessalians send envoys to the Isthmus—the Greeks advance
to Tempe, but retreat—the fleet despatched to Artemisium, and
the Pass of Thermopylæ occupied—numbers of the Grecian
fleet—battle of Thermopylæ

I. The first preparations of the Persians did not produce the effect which
might have been anticipated in the Grecian states. Far from uniting against
the common foe, they still cherished a frivolous and unreasonable jealousy of each other. Several readily sent the symbols
of their allegiance to the Persian, including the whole of
Bœotia, except only the Thespians and Platæans. The more timorous states
imagined themselves safe from the vengeance of the barbarian; the more
resolute were overwhelmed with dismay. The renown of the Median arms
was universally acknowledged: for in spite of Marathon, Greece had not yet
learned to despise the foreigner; and the enormous force of the impending
armament was accurately known from the spies and deserters of the Grecian
states, who abounded in the barbarian camp. Even united, the whole navy of
Greece seemed insufficient to contend against such a foe; and, divided among
themselves, several of the states were disposed rather to succumb than to
resist.[1] "And here", says the father of history,

THE CONDUCT
OF THE GREEKS

> I feel compelled to assert an opinion, however invidious it may be
> to many. If the Athenians, terrified by the danger, had forsaken
> their country, or submitted to the Persian, Xerxes would have met
> with no resistance by sea. The Lacedæmonians, deserted by their
> allies, would have died with honour or yielded from necessity, and
> all Greece have been reduced to the Persian yoke. The Athenians
> were thus the deliverers of Greece. They animated the ardour of
> those states yet faithful to themselves; and, next to the gods, they

1 Herod., vii. 138.

311

were the true repellers of the invader. Even the Delphic oracles, dark and ominous as they were, did not shake their purpose, nor induce them to abandon Greece.

When even the deities themselves seemed doubtful, Athens was unshaken. The messengers despatched by the Athenians to the Delphic oracle received indeed an answer well calculated to appal them. "Unhappy men", cried the priestess,

> leave your houses and the ramparts of the city, and fly to the utter-most parts of the earth. Fire and keen Mars, compelling the Syrian chariot, shall destroy, towers shall be overthrown, and temples destroyed by fire. Lo! now, even now, they stand dropping sweat, and their housetops black with blood, and shaking with prophetic awe. Depart and prepare for ill!

II. Cast into the deepest affliction by this response, the Athenians yet, with the garb and symbols of suppliants, renewed their application. "Answer

THE ORACLE RELATING TO SALAMIS

us", they said, "oh supreme God, answer us more pro-pitiously, or we will not depart from your sanctuary, but remain here even until death."

The second answer seemed less severe than the first:

> Minerva is unable to appease the Olympian Jupiter. Again, there-fore, I speak, and my words are as adamant. All else within the bounds of Cecropia and the bosom of the divine Cithæron shall fall and fail you. The wooden wall alone Jupiter grants to Pallas, a refuge to your children and yourselves. Wait not for horse and foot—tarry not the march of the mighty army—retreat, even though they close upon you. Oh Salamis the divine, thou shalt lose the sons of women, whether Ceres scatter or hoard her harvest!

III. Writing down this reply, the messengers returned to Athens. Many and contradictory were the attempts made to interpret the response; some

ART OF THEMISTOCLES

believed that by a wooden wall was meant the citadel, formerly surrounded by a palisade of wood. Others affirmed that the enigmatical expression signified the fleet. But then the concluding words perplexed them. For the apostrophe to Salamis appeared to denote destruction and defeat. At this juncture Themistocles approved himself worthy of the position he had attained. It is probable that he had purchased the oracle to which he found a ready and bold solution. He upheld the resort to the ships, but denied that in the apostrophe to Salamis any evil to Athens was denounced:

Had the prediction of loss and slaughter referred to the Athenians, would Salamis have been called "divine"? Would it not have been rather called the "wretched" if the Greeks were doomed to perish near that isle? The oracle threatens not the Athenians, but the enemy. Let us prepare then to engage the barbarian by sea. Our ships are our wooden walls.

This interpretation, as it was the more encouraging, so it was the more approved. The vessels already built from the revenues of the mines of Laurion were now destined to the safety of Greece.

IV. It was, however, before the arrival of the Persian envoys,[2] and when the Greeks first woke to the certainty, that the vast preparations of Xerxes menaced Greece as the earliest victim, that a congress, perhaps at the onset confined to the Peloponnesian

THE ISTHMIAN CONGRESS

states, met at Corinth. At the head of this confederate council necessarily ranked Sparta, which was the master state of the Peloponnesus. But in policy and debate, if not in arms, she appears always to have met with a powerful rival in Corinth, the diplomacy of whose wealthy and liberal commonwealth often counteracted the propositions of the Spartan delegates. To this congress subsequently came the envoys of all the states that refused tribute and homage to the Persian king. The institution of this Hellenic council, which was one cause of the salvation of Greece, is a proof of the political impotence of the old Amphictyonic League. The synedrion of Corinth (or rather of that Corinthian village that had grown up round the Temple of Neptune, and is styled the "Isthmus" by the Greek writers) was the true historical amphictyony of Hellas.

In the Isthmian congress the genius of Themistocles found an ampler sphere than it had hitherto done among the noisy cabals of Athens. Of all the Greek delegates, that sagacious statesman was most successful in accomplishing the primary object of the confederacy, viz., in removing the jealousies and the dissensions that hitherto existed

EMBASSIES TO ARGOS, CRETE, CORCYRA, AND SYRACUSE

among the states which composed it. In this, perhaps the most difficult, as the most essential, task, Themistocles was aided by a Tegean, named Chileus, who, though he rarely appears upon the external stage of action, seems to have been eminently skilled in the intricate and entangled politics of the time. Themistocles, into whose hands the Athenian republic, at this period, confided the trust not more of its interests than its resentments, set the example of concord; and Athens, for a while, consented to reconciliation and amity with the hated Ægina. All the proceedings of this illustrious congress

2 Müller on the Greek Congress.

were characterized by vigilant prudence and decisive energy. As soon as Xerxes arrived in Sardis, emissaries were despatched to watch the movements of the Persian army, and at the same period, or rather some time before,[3] ambassadors were sent to Corcyra, Crete, Argos, and to Syracuse, then under the dominion of Gelo. This man, from the station of a highborn and powerful citizen of Gela, in Sicily, had raised himself, partly by military talents, principally by a profound and dissimulating policy, to the tyranny of Gela and of Syracuse. His abilities were remarkable, his power great; nor on the Grecian continent was there one state that could command the force and the resources that were at the disposal of the Syracusan prince.

The spies despatched to Sardis were discovered, seized, and would have been put to death, but for the interference of Xerxes, who dismissed them, after directing them to be led round his army, in the hope that their return from the terror of such a spectacle would, more than their death, intimidate and appal their countrymen.

The mission to Argos, which, as a Peloponnesian city, was one of the earliest applied to, was unsuccessful. That state still suffered the exhaustion which followed the horrible massacre perpetrated by Cleomenes, the Spartan king, who had burnt six thousand Argives in the precincts of the sanctuary to which they had fled. New changes of government had followed this fatal loss, and the servile population had been enabled to seize the privileges of the free. Thus, hatred to Sparta, a weakened soldiery, an unsettled internal government, all conspired to render Argos lukewarm to the general cause. Yet that state did not openly refuse the aid which it secretly resolved to withhold. It consented to join the common league upon two conditions: an equal share with the Spartans in the command, and a truce of thirty years with those crafty and merciless neighbours. The Spartans proposed to compromise the former condition, by allowing to the Argive king not indeed half the command, but a voice equal to that of each of their own kings. To the latter condition they offered no objection. Glad of an excuse to retaliate on the Spartans their own haughty insolence, the Argives at once rejected the proposition, and ordered the Spartan ambassador to quit their territories before sunset. But Argos, though the chief city of Argolis, had not her customary influence over the other towns of that district, in which the attachment to Greece was stronger than the jealous apprehensions of Sparta.

The embassy to Sicily was not more successful than that to Argos. Gelo agreed indeed to furnish the allies with a considerable force, but only on the condition of obtaining for Sicily the supreme command, either of the land-force claimed by Sparta, or of the naval force to which Athens already ventured to pretend; an offer to which it was impossible that the Greeks

THEIR ILL SUCCESS

---

3 Müller on the Greek Congress.

should accede, unless they were disposed to surrender to the craft of an auxiliary the liberties they asserted against the violence of a foe. The Spartan and the Athenian ambassadors alike, and with equal indignation, rejected the proposals of Gelo, who, in fact, had obtained the tyranny of his native city by first securing the command of the Gelan cavalry. The prince of Syracuse was little affected by the vehement scorn of the ambassadors. "I see you are in more want of troops than commanders", said he, wittily. "Return, then; tell the Greeks this year will be without its spring." For, as the spring to the year did Gelo consider his assistance to Greece. From Sicily the ambassadors repaired to Corcyra. Here they were amused with flattering promises, but the governors of that intriguing and factious state fitted out a fleet of sixty vessels, stationed near Pylos, off the coast of Sparta, to wait the issue of events, assuring Xerxes, on the one hand, of their indisposition to oppose him, and pretending afterward to the Greeks, on the other, that the adverse winds alone prevented their taking share in the engagement at Salamis. The Cretans were not more disposed to the cause than the Corcyræans; they found an excuse in an oracle of Delphi, and indeed that venerable shrine appears to have been equally dissuasive of resistance to all the states that consulted it; although the daring of the Athenians had construed the ambiguous menace into a favourable omen. The threats of superstition become but incitements to courage when interpreted by the brave.

V. And now the hostile army had crossed the Hellespont, and the Thessalians, perceiving that they were the next objects of attack, despatched ambassadors to the congress at the Isthmus.

THE THESSALIANS SEND ENVOYS TO THE ISTHMUS

Those Thessalian chiefs called the Aleuadæ had, it is true, invited Xerxes to the invasion of Greece. But precisely because acceptable to the chiefs, the arrival of the great king was dreaded by the people. By the aid of the Persians, the Aleuadæ trusted to extend their power over their own country—an ambition with which it is not to be supposed that the people they assisted to subject would sympathize. Accordingly, while Xerxes was to the chiefs an ally, to the people he remained a foe.

These Thessalian envoys proclaimed their willingness to assist the confederates in the defence of their father-land, but represented the imminence of the danger to Thessaly, and demanded an immediate supply of forces. "Without this", they said, "we cannot exert ourselves for you, and our inability to assist you will be our excuse, if we provide for our own safety."

Aroused by these exhortations, the confederates commenced their military movements. A body of infantry passed the Euripus, entered Thessaly, and encamped amid the delights of the vale of Tempe.

THE GREEKS ADVANCE TO TEMPE, BUT RETREAT

Here their numbers, in all ten thousand heavy-armed troops, were joined by the Thessalian horse. The Spartans were led by Euænetus. Themistocles commanded the Athenians. The army did not long, however, remain in the encampment. Alexander, the king of Macedon, sent confidentially advising their retreat, and explaining accurately the force of the enemy. This advice concurred with the discovery that there was another passage into Thessaly through the higher regions of Macedonia, which exposed them to be taken in the rear. And, in truth, it was through this passage that the Persian army ultimately marched. The Greeks, therefore, broke up the camp and returned to the Isthmus. The Thessalians, thus abandoned, instantly treated with the invader, and became among the stanchest allies of Xerxes.

It was now finally agreed in the Isthmian congress, that the most advisable plan would be to defend the pass of Thermopylæ, as being both nearer and narrower than that of Thessaly. The fleet they resolved to send to Artemisium, on the coast of Histiæotis, a place sufficiently neighbouring Thermopylæ to allow of easy communication. Never, perhaps, have the Greeks shown more military skill than in the choice of these stations. But one pass in those mountainous districts permitted the descent of the Persian army from Thessaly, bounded to the west by steep and inaccessible cliffs, extending as far as Mount Œta; to the east by shoals and the neighbouring sea. This defile received its name Thermopylæ, or Hot Gates, from the hot springs which rose near the base of the mountain. In remote times the pastoral Phocians had fortified the place against the incursions of the Thessalians, and the decayed remains of the wall and gates of their ancient garrison were still existent in the middle of the pass; while, by marsh and morass, to render the place yet more impassable, they had suffered the hot springs to empty themselves along the plain, on the Thessalian side, and the quagmire was still sodden and unsteady. The country on either side of the Thermopylæ was so contracted, that before, near the river Phœnix, and behind, near the village of Alpeni, was at that time space only for a single chariot. In such a pass the numbers and the cavalry of the Mede were rendered unavailable; while at the distance of about fifteen miles from Thermopylæ the ships of the Grecian navy rode in the narrow sea, off the projecting shores of Eubœa, equally fortunate in a station which weakened the force of numbers and allowed the facility of retreat.

The sea-station was possessed by the allied ships. Corinth sent forty; Megara twenty; Ægina eighteen; Sicyon twelve; Sparta ten; the Epidaurians contributed eight; the Eretrians seven; the Trœzenians five; the Ityræans and the people of Ceos each two, and the Opuntian Locrians seven vessels of fifty oars. The total of these ships (without reckoning those of fifty oars, supplied by the Locrians, and two barks of the same description, which added to the quota sent by the people of Ceos) amount to one hundred and twenty-four. The Athenian force alone numbered more vessels than all the other confederates, and contributed one hundred and twenty-seven triremes, partly manned by Platæans,

The fleet despatched to Artemisium, and the pass of Thermopylæ occupied

Numbers of the Grecian fleet

besides twenty vessels lent to the Chalcidians, who equipped and manned them. The Athenian fleet was commanded by Themistocles. The land-force at Thermopylæ consisted chiefly of Peloponnesians; its numbers were as follows:—three hundred heavy-armed Spartans; five hundred Tegeans; five hundred Mantinæans; one hundred and twenty Orchomenians; one thousand from the other states of Arcady; two hundred from Phlius; eighty from Mycenæ. Bœotia contributed seven hundred Thespians, and four hundred Thebans; the last had been specially selected by Leonidas, the Spartan chief, because of the general suspicion that the Thebans were attached to the Medes, and he desired, therefore, to approve them as friends, or know them as foes. Although the sentiments of the Thebans were hostile, says Herodotus, they sent the assistance required. In addition to these, were one thousand Phocians, and a band of the Opuntian Locrians, unnumbered by Herodotus, but variously estimated, by Diodorus at one thousand, and, more probably, by Pausanias at no less than seven thousand.

The chief command was entrusted, according to the claims of Sparta, to Leonidas, the younger brother of the frantic Cleomenes,[4] by a different mother, and his successor to the Spartan throne.

There are men whose whole life is in a single action. Of these, Leonidas is the most eminent. We know little of him, until the last few days of his career. He seems, as it were, born but to show how much glory belongs to a brave death. Of his character or genius, his general virtues and vices, his sorrows and his joys, biography can scarcely gather even the materials for conjecture. He passed from an obscure existence into an everlasting name. And history dedicates her proudest pages to one of whom she has nothing but the epitaph to relate.

As if to contrast the little band under the command of Leonidas, Herodotus again enumerates the Persian force, swelled as it now was by many contributions, forced and voluntary, since its departure from Doriscus. He estimates the total by sea and land, thus augmented, at two millions six hundred and forty-one thousand six hundred and ten fighting men, and computes the number of the menial attendants, the motley multitude that followed the armament, at an equal number; so that the son of Darius conducted, hitherto without disaster, to Sepias and Thermopylæ, a body of five millions two hundred and eighty-three thousand two hundred and twenty human

---

4 Anaxandrides, king of Sparta, and father of Cleomenes and Leonidas, had married his niece: she was barren. The ephors persuaded him to take another wife; he did so, and by the second wife Cleomenes was born. Almost at the same time, the first wife, hitherto barren, proved with child. And as she continued the conjugal connexion, in process of time three sons were born; of these Leonidas was the second. But Cleomenes, though the offspring of the second wife, came into the world before the children by the first wife, and therefore had the prior right to the throne.

beings.[5] And out of this wondrous concourse, none in majesty and grace of person, says Herodotus, surpassed the royal leader. But such advantages as belong to superior stature, the kings of Persia obtained by artificial means; and we learn from Xenophon that they wore a peculiar kind of shoe so constructed as to increase their height.

VI. The fleet of Xerxes, moving from Therme, obtained some partial success at sea: ten of their vessels despatched to Sciathos, captured a guard-ship of Trœzene, and sacrificed upon the prow a Greek named Leon; the beauty of his person obtained him that disagreeable preference. A vessel of Ægina fell also into their hands, the crew of which they treated as slaves, save only one hero, Pytheas, endeared even to the enemy by his valour; a third vessel, belonging to the Athenians, was taken at the mouth of the Peneus; the seamen, however, had previously debarked, and consequently escaped. Beacons apprised the Greek station at Artemisium of these disasters, and the fleet retreated for a while to Chalcis, with a view of guarding the Euripus. But a violent storm off the coast of Magnesia suddenly destroying no less than four hundred of the barbarian vessels, with a considerable number of men and great treasure, the Grecian navy returned to Artemisium.

Here they soon made a capture of fifteen of the Persian vessels, which, taking them for friends, sailed right into the midst of them. With this exception, the rest of the barbarian fleet arrived safely at Aphetæ.

VII. Meanwhile the mighty land-force of the great king, passing through Thessaly and Achaia, arrived at last at the wide Trachinian plains, which, stretching along the shores of Thessaly, forty miles in circumference, and adjacent to the straits of Thermopylæ, allowed space for the encampment of his army.

The Greeks at Thermopylæ beheld the approach of Xerxes with dismay; they had anticipated considerable re-enforcements from the confederate states, especially Sparta, which last had determined to commit all her strength to the campaign, leaving merely a small detachment for the defence of the capital. But the Carneian festival in honour of the great Dorian Apollo, at Sparta, detained the Lacedæmonians, and the Olympic Games diverted the rest of the allies, not yet expecting an immediate battle.

The vicinity of Xerxes, the absence of the re-enforcements they expected, produced an alarmed and anxious council; Leonidas dissuaded the confederates from retreat, and despatched messengers to the various states, urging the necessity of supplies, and stating the hopelessness of opposing the Mede effectually with the present forces.

Xerxes, in the meanwhile, who had heard that an insignificant band were assembled under a Spartan descendant of Hercules, to resist his progress,

---

5 It is impossible by any calculations to render this amount more credible to modern scepticism. It is extremely likely that Herodotus is mistaken in his calculation; but who shall correct him?

despatched a spy to reconnoitre their number and their movements. The emissary was able only to inspect those without the entrenchment, who, at that time, happened to be the Spartans; he found that singular race engaged in gymnastic exercises, and dressing their long hair for the festival of battle. Although they perceived the spy, they suffered him to gaze at his leisure, and he returned in safety to the king.

Much astonished at the account he received, Xerxes sent for Demaratus, and detailing to him what the messenger had seen, inquired what it might portend, and whether this handful of men amusing themselves in the defile could seriously mean to resist his arms.

"Sire", answered the Spartan, "it is their intention to dispute the pass, and what your messenger has seen proves that they are preparing accordingly. It is the custom of the Spartans to adorn their hair on the eve of any enterprise of danger. You are advancing to attack the flower of the Grecian valour." Xerxes, still incredulous that opposition could be seriously intended, had the courtesy to wait four days to give the enemy leisure to retreat; in the interim he despatched a messenger to Leonidas, demanding his arms. "Come and take them!", replied the Spartan.

VIII. On the fifth day the patience of Xerxes was exhausted, and he sent a detachment of Medes and Cissians[6] into the pass, with orders to bring its rash and obstinate defenders alive into his presence. The Medes and Cissians were repulsed with considerable loss. The Immortal Band were now ordered to advance, under the command of Hydarnes. But even the skill and courage of that warlike troop were equally unsuccessful; their numbers were crippled by the narrowness of the pass, and their short weapons coped to great disadvantage with the long spears of the Greeks. The engagement was renewed a second day with the like fortune; the loss of the Persians was great, although the scanty numbers of the Spartans were also somewhat diminished.

In the midst of the perplexity which pervaded the king's councils after this defeat, there arrived at the Persian camp one Ephialtes, a Malian. Influenced by the hope of a great reward, this traitor demanded and obtained an audience, in which he offered to conduct the Medes through a secret path across the mountains, into the pass. The offer was joyfully accepted, and Hydarnes, with the forces under his command, was despatched under the guidance of the Malian. At the dusk of evening the detachment left the camp, and marching all night, from the river Asopus, between the mountains of Œta on the right hand, and the Trachinian ridges on the left, they found themselves at the early dawn at the summit of the hill, on which a thousand Phocians had been stationed to defend the pass, for it was not unknown to the Spartans. In the silence of dawn they wound through the

6 The Cissii, or Cissians, inhabited the then fertile province of Susiana, in which was situated the capital of Susa. They resembled the Persians in dress and manners.

thick groves of oak that clad the ascent, and concealed the glitter of their arms; but the exceeding stillness of the air occasioned the noise they made in trampling on the leaves[7] to reach the ears of the Phocians. That band sprang up from the earth on which they had slept, to the consternation and surprise of the invaders, and precipitately betook themselves to arms. The Persians, though unprepared for an enemy at this spot, drew up in battle array, and the heavy onslaught of their arrows drove the Phocians to seek a better shelter up the mountains, not imagining that the passage into the defile, but their own destruction, was the object of the enterprise. The Persians prudently forbore pursuit, but availing themselves of the path now open to their progress, rapidly descended the opposite side of the mountain.

IX. Meanwhile, dark and superstitious terrors were at work in the Grecian camp. The preceding eve the soothsayer (Megistias) had inspected the entrails, and foretold that death awaited the defenders of Thermopylæ in the morning; and on that fatal night a Cumæan deserter[8] from the Persian camp had joined Leonidas, and informed him of the treachery of Ephialtes. At early day their fears were confirmed by the sentinels posted on the mountains, who fled into the defile at the approach of the barbarians.

A hasty council was assembled; some were for remaining, some for flight. The council ended with the resolution of a general retreat, probably with the assent, possibly by the instances, of Leonidas, who was contented to possess the monopoly of glory and of death. The laws of the Spartans forbade them to fly from any enemy, however numerous, and Leonidas did not venture to disobey them. Perhaps his resolution was strengthened by an oracle of that Delphi so peculiarly venerated by the Dorian race, and which foretold either the fall of Sparta, or the sacrifice of a Spartan king of the blood of Hercules. To men whose whole happiness was renown, life had no temptation equal to such a death!

X. Leonidas and his countrymen determined to keep the field. The Thespians alone voluntarily remained to partake his fate; but he detained

BATTLE OF THERMOPYLÆ

also the suspected Thebans, rather as a hostage than an auxiliary. The rest of the confederates precipitately departed across the mountains to their native cities. Leonidas would have dismissed the prophetic soothsayer, but Megistias insisted on his right to remain; he contented himself with sending away his only son, who had accompanied the expedition. Even the stern spirit of Leonidas is said to have yielded to the voice of nature; and he ordered two of his relations to return to Sparta to report the state of affairs. "You prescribe to us the duties of messengers, not of soldiers", was the reply, as the warriors buckled on their shields, and took their posts with the rest.

---

7 So Herodotus (vii. 218); but, as it was summer, the noise was probably made rather by the boughs that obstructed the path of the barbarians, than by leaves on the ground.
8 Diod. Sic., ii. 8.

If history could penetrate from events into the hearts of the agents, it would be interesting even to conjecture the feelings of this devoted band, awaiting the approach of a certain death, in that solitary defile. Their enthusiasm, and that rigid and Spartan spirit which had made all ties subservient to obedience to the law—all excitement tame to that of battle—all pleasure dull to the anticipation of glory—probably rendered the hours preceding death the most enviable of their lives. They might have exulted in the same elevating fanaticism which distinguished afterward the followers of Mahomet; and seen that opening paradise in immortality below, which the Moslemin beheld in anticipation above.

XI. Early on that awful morning, Xerxes offered a solemn libation to his gods, and at the middle of the noon, when Hydarnes might be supposed to be close upon the rear of the enemy, the barbarian troops commenced their march. Leonidas and his band advanced beyond their entrenchment, into the broader part of the defile. Before the fury of their despair, the Persians fell in great numbers; many of them were hurled into the sea, others trodden down and crushed by the press of their own numbers.

When the spears of the Greeks were shivered in pieces they had recourse to their swords, and the battle was fought hand to hand: thus fighting, fell Leonidas, surrounded in death by many of his band, of various distinction and renown. Two half-brothers of Xerxes, mingling in the foremost of the fray, contended for the body of the Spartan king, and perished by the Grecian sword.

For a short time the Spartans repelled the Persian crowd, who, where valour failed to urge them on, were scourged to the charge by the lash of their leaders, and drew the body of Leonidas from the press; and now, winding down the pass, Hydarnes and his detachment descended to the battle. The scene then became changed, the Spartans retired, still undaunted, or rather made yet more desperate as death drew near, into the narrowest of the pass, and, ranged upon an eminence of the strait, they died—fighting, even after their weapons were broken, with their hands and teeth—rather crushed beneath the number than slain by the swords of the foe—"*non victi sed vincendo fatigati*".[9]

XII. Two Spartans of the three hundred, Eurytus and Aristodemus, had, in consequence of a severe disorder in the eyes, been permitted to sojourn at Alpeni; but Eurytus, hearing of the contest, was led by his Helot into the field, and died with his countrymen. Aristodemus alone remained, branded with disgrace on his return to Sparta; but subsequently redeeming his name at the battle of Platæa.[10]

9 Justin, ii. 9.
10 Another Spartan, who had been sent into Thessaly, and was therefore absent from the slaughter of Thermopylæ, destroyed himself.

The Thebans, beholding the victory of the Persians, yielded their arms; and, excepting a few, slain as they approached, not as foes, but as suppliants, were pardoned by Xerxes.

The king himself came to view the dead, and especially the corpse of Leonidas. He ordered the head of that hero to be cut off, and his body suspended on a cross,[11] an instance of sudden passion, rather than customary barbarity. For of all nations the Persians most honoured valour, even in their foes.

XIII. The moral sense of mankind, which places the example of self-sacrifice among the noblest lessons by which our nature can he corrected, has justly immortalized the memory of Leonidas. It is impossible to question the virtue of the man, but we may fairly dispute the wisdom of the system he adorned. We may doubt whether, in fact, his death served his country so much as his life would have done. It was the distinction of Thermopylæ, that its heroes died in obedience to the laws; it was the distinction of Marathon, that its heroes lived to defeat the invader and preserve their country. And in proof of this distinction, we find afterward, at Platæa, that of all the allied Greeks, the Spartans the most feared the conquerors of Thermopylæ; the Athenians the least feared the fugitives of Marathon.

XIV. Subsequently, on the hill to which the Spartans and Thespians had finally retired, a lion of stone was erected by the Amphictyons, in honour of Leonidas; and many years afterward the bones of that hero were removed to Sparta, and yearly games, at which Spartans only were allowed to contend, were celebrated round his tomb. Separate monuments to the Greeks generally, and to the three hundred who had refused to retreat, were built also, by the Amphictyons, at Thermopylæ. Long extant, posterity admired the inscriptions which they bore; that of the Spartans became proverbial for its sublime conciseness.

"Go, stranger", it said, "and tell the Spartans that we obeyed the law—and lie here!"

The private friendship of Simonides the poet erected also a monument to Megistias, the soothsayer, in which it was said truly to his honour, "That the fate he foresaw he remained to brave."

Such is the history of the battle of Thermopylæ.[12]

---

11 The cross was the usual punishment in Persia for offences against the king's majesty or rights. Perhaps, therefore, Xerxes, by the outrage, only desired to signify that he considered the Spartan as a rebel.

12 "Thus fought the Greeks at Thermopylæ", are the simple expressions of Herodotus, vii. 234.

CHAPTER VII

The advice of Demaratus to Xerxes—Themistocles—actions off
Artemisium—the Greeks retreat—the Persians invade Delphi,
and are repulsed with great loss—the Athenians, unaided by
their allies, abandon Athens, and embark for Salamis—the
irresolute and selfish policy of the Peloponnesians—dexterity
and firmness of Themistocles—battle of Salamis—Andros and
Carystus besieged by the Greeks—anecdotes of Themistocles—
honours awarded to him in Sparta—Xerxes returns to Asia—
Olynthus and Potidæa besieged by Artabazus—the Athenians
return home—the ostracism of Aristides is repealed

I. After the victory of Thermopylæ, Demaratus advised the Persian monarch to despatch a detachment of three hundred vessels to the Laconian
coast, and seize the island of Cythera, of which a
Spartan once (foreseeing how easily hereafter that post
might be made to command and overawe the Laconian
capital) had said, "It were better for Sparta if it were sunk into the sea." The
profound experience of Demaratus in the selfish and exclusive policy of his
countrymen made him argue that, if this were done, the fears of Sparta for
herself would prevent her joining the forces of the rest of Greece, and leave
the latter a more easy prey to the invader.

The advice, fortunately for the Greeks, was overruled by Achæmenes.

Meanwhile the Grecian navy, assembled off Artemisium, was agitated by
divers councils. Beholding the vast number of barbarian ships now collected
at Aphetæ, and the whole shores around swarming with hostile troops, the
Greeks debated the necessity of retreat.

The fleet was under the command of Eurybiades, the Spartan. For although
Athens furnished a force equal to all the rest of the allies together, and
might justly, therefore, have pretended to the command, yet
the jealousy of the confederates, long accustomed to yield
to the claims of Sparta, and unwilling to acknowledge a new superiority in
another state, had induced the Athenians readily to forego their claim. And
this especially at the instance of Themistocles. "To him", says Plutarch,
"Greece not only owes her preservation, but the Athenians in particular the
glory of surpassing their enemies in valour and their allies in moderation."
But if fortune gave Eurybiades the nominal command, genius forced

THE ADVICE OF DE-
MARATUS TO XERXES

THEMISTOCLES

323

Themistocles into the actual pre-eminence. That extraordinary man was, above all, adapted to his time; and, suited to its necessities, he commanded its fates. His very fault in the callousness of the moral sentiment, and his unscrupulous regard to expediency, peculiarly aided him in his management of men. He could appeal to the noblest passions—he could wind himself into the most base. Where he could not exalt he corrupted, where he could not persuade he intimidated, where he could not intimidate he bribed.[1]

When the intention to retreat became generally circulated, the inhabitants of the northern coast of Euboea (off which the Athenian navy rode) entreated Eurybiades at least to give them time to remove their slaves and children from the vengeance of the barbarian. Unsuccessful with him, they next sought Themistocles. For the consideration of thirty talents, the Athenian promised to remain at Artemisium, and risk the event of battle. Possessed of this sum, he won over the sturdy Spartan by the gift of five talents, and to Adimantus the Corinthian, the most obstinate in retreat, he privately sent three.[2] The remainder he kept for his own uses;—distinguished from his compeers in this—that he obtained a much larger share of the gift than they; that they were bribed to be brave, and that he was rewarded for bribing them. The pure-minded statesman of the closet cannot but feel some disdain and some regret to find, blended together, the noblest actions and the paltriest motives. But whether in ancient times or in modern, the web of human affairs is woven from a mingled yarn, and the individuals who save nations are not always those most acceptable to the moralist. The share of Themistocles in this business is not, however, so much to his discredit as to that of the Spartan Eurybiades. We cannot but observe that no system contrary to human nature is strong against actual temptation. The Spartan law interdicted the desire of riches, and the Spartans themselves yielded far more easily to the lust of avarice than the luxurious Athenians. Thus a native of Zelea, a city in Asia Minor, had sought to corrupt the Peloponnesian cities by Persian gold: it was not the Spartans, it was the Athenians, who declared this man infamous, and placed his life out of the pale of the Grecian law. With a noble pride Demosthenes speaks of this decree. "The gold", he says, "was brought into the Peloponnesus, not to Athens. But our ancestors

1 Thus the command of the Athenian forces was at one time likely to fall upon Epicydes, a man whose superior eloquence had gained an ascendency with the people, which was neither due to his integrity nor to his military skill. Themistocles is said to have bribed him to forego his pretensions. Themistocles could be as severe as crafty when occasion demanded: he put to death an interpreter who accompanied the Persian envoys, probably to the congress at the Isthmus, for debasing the language of free Greeks to express the demands of the barbarian enemy. (Plutarch implies that these envoys came to Athens, but Xerxes sent none to that city.)

2 Plutarch rejects this story, very circumstantially told by Herodotus, without adducing a single satisfactory argument for the rejection. The scepticism of Plutarch is more frivolous even than his credulity.

extended their care beyond their own city to the whole of Greece."[3] An Aristides is formed by the respect paid to integrity, which society tries in vain—a Demaratus, an Eurybiades, and, as we shall see, a Pausanias, by the laws which, affecting to exclude the influence of the passions, render their temptations novel, and their effects irresistible.

II. The Greeks continued at Euboea; and the Persians, eager to engage so inconsiderable an enemy, despatched two hundred chosen vessels, with

ACTIONS OFF ARTEMISIUM

orders to make a circuitous route beyond Sciathos, and thus, unperceived, to attack the Grecian rear, while on a concerted signal the rest would advance upon the front.

A deserter of Scios escaped, however, from Aphetæ, and informed the Greeks of the Persian plan. Upon this it was resolved at midnight to advance against that part of the fleet which had been sent around Euboea. But as twilight approached, they appeared to have changed or delayed this design, and proceeded at once towards the main body of the fleet, less perhaps with the intention of giving regular battle, than of attempting such detached skirmishes as would make experiment of their hardihood and skill. The Persians, amazed at the infatuation of their opponents, drew out their fleet in order, and succeeded in surrounding the Greek ships.

The night, however, separated the hostile forces, but not until the Greeks had captured thirty of the barbarian vessels; the first ship was taken by an Athenian. The victory, however, despite this advantage, was undecided, when the Greeks returned to Artemisium, the Persians to Aphetæ.

III. But during the night one of those sudden and vehement storms not unfrequent to the summers of Greece broke over the seas. The Persians at Aphetæ heard, with a panic dismay, the continued thunder that burst above the summit of Mount Pelion; and the bodies of the dead and the wrecks of ships, floating round the prows, entangled their oars amid a tempestuous and heavy sea. But the destruction which the Persians at Aphetæ anticipated to themselves, actually came upon that part of the barbarian fleet which had made the circuit round Euboea. Remote from land, exposed to all the fury of the tempest, ignorant of their course, and amid the darkness of night, they were dashed to pieces against those fearful rocks termed "the Hollows", and not a single galley escaped the general destruction.

Thus the fleet of the barbarians was rendered more equal to that of the Greeks. Re-enforced by fifty-three ships from Athens the next day, the Greeks proceeded at evening against that part of the hostile navy possessed by the Cilicians. These they utterly defeated, and returned joyfully to Artemisium.

Hitherto these skirmishes, made on the summer evenings, in order probably to take advantage of the darkening night to break off before any irremediable loss was sustained, seem rather to have been for the sake of practice in the war

---

3 Dem., Philip, 3. See also Æschines, contra Ctesiphon.

—chivalric sorties as it were—than actual and deliberate engagements. But the third day, the Persians, impatient of conquest, advanced to Artemisium. These sea encounters were made precisely on the same days as the conflicts at Thermopylæ; the object on each was the same—the gaining in one of the sea defile, in the other of the land entrance into Greece. The Euripus was the Thermopylæ of the ocean.

IV. The Greeks remained in their station, and there met the shock; the battle was severe and equal; the Persians fought with great valour and firmness, and although the loss upon their side was far the greatest, many of the Greek vessels also perished. They separated as by mutual consent, neither force the victor. Of the Persian fleet the Egyptians were the most distinguished—of the Grecian the Athenians; and of the last none equalled in valour Clinias;—his ship was manned at his own expense. He was the father of that Alcibiades, afterward so famous.

While the Greeks rested at Artemisium, counting the number of their slain, and amid the wrecks of their vessels, they learned the fate of Leonidas.[4]

THE GREEKS RETREAT   This determined their previous consultations on the policy of retreat, and they abandoned the Euripus in steady and marshalled order, the Corinthians first, the Athenians closing the rear. Thus the Persians were left masters of the sea and land entrance into Greece.

But even in retreat, the active spirit of Themistocles was intent upon expedients. It was more than suspected that a considerable portion of the Ionians now in the service of Xerxes were secretly friendly to the Greeks. In the swiftest of the Athenian vessels Themistocles therefore repaired to a watering-place on the coast, and engraved upon the rocks these words, which were read by the Ionians the next day.

> Men of Ionia, in fighting against your ancestors, and assisting to enslave Greece, you act unworthily. Come over to us; or if that may not be, at least retire from the contest, and prevail on the Carians to do the same. If yet neither secession nor revolt be practicable, at least when we come to action exert not yourselves against us. Remember that we are descended from one common race, and that it was on your behalf that we first incurred the enmity of the Persian.

A subtler intention than that which was the more obvious, was couched beneath this exhortation. For if it failed to seduce the Ionians, it might yet induce Xerxes to mistrust their alliance.

---

4 I have said that it might be doubted whether the death of Leonidas was as serviceable to Greece as his life might have been; its immediate consequences were certainly discouraging. If his valour was an example, his defeat was a warning.

When the Persians learned that the Greeks had abandoned their station, their whole fleet took possession of the pass, possessed themselves of the neighbouring town of Histiæa, and, overrunning a part of the isle of Eubœa, received the submission of the inhabitants.

Xerxes now had recourse to a somewhat clumsy, though a very commonly practised artifice. Twenty thousand of his men had fallen at Thermopylæ: of these he buried nineteen thousand, and leaving the remainder uninterred, he invited all who desired it, by public proclamation, to examine the scene of contest. As a considerable number of Helots had joined their Spartan lords and perished with them, the bodies of the slain amounted to four thousand,[5] while those of the Persians were only one thousand. This was a practical despotic bulletin.

V. Of all the neighbouring district, the Phocians had alone remained faithful to the Grecian cause: their territory was now overrun by the Persians, at the instance of their hereditary enemies, the Thessalians, destroying city and temple, and committing all the horrors of violence and rapine by the way. Arrived at Panopeæ, the bulk of the barbarian army marched through Bœotia towards Athens, the great object of revenge, while a separate detachment was sent to Delphi, with a view of plundering the prodigious riches accumulated in that celebrated temple, and of which, not perhaps uncharacteristically, Xerxes was said to be better informed than of the treasures he had left behind in his own palace.

THE PERSIANS INVADE DELPHI, AND ARE REPULSED WITH GREAT LOSS

But the wise and crafty priesthood of Delphi had been too long accustomed successfully to deceive mankind to lose hope or self-possession at the approach even of so formidable a foe. When the dismayed citizens of Delphi ran to the oracle, demanding advice and wishing to know what should be done with the sacred treasures, the priestess gravely replied that "the god could take care of his own possessions, and that the only business of the citizens was to provide for themselves"; a priestly answer, importing that the god considered his possessions, and not the flock, were the treasure. The one was sure to be defended by a divinity, the other might shift for themselves.

5 There were three hundred (Three hundred, for the sake of round numbers—but one of the three hundred—perhaps two—survived the general massacre.) Spartans and four hundred Thespians; supposing that (as it has been asserted) the eighty warriors of Mycenæ also remained with Leonidas, and that one hundred, or a fourth, of the Thebans fell ere their submission was received, this makes a total of eight hundred and eighty. If we take now what at Platæa was the actual ratio of the Helots as compared with the Spartans, i.e., seven to one, we shall add two thousand one hundred Helots, which make two thousand nine hundred and ninety; to which must be added such of the Greeks as fell in the attacks prior to the slaughter of Thermopylæ so that, in order to make out the total of the slain given by Herodotus, more than eleven hundred must have perished before the last action, in which Leonidas fell.

The citizens were not slow in adopting the advice; they immediately removed their wives and children into Achaia—while the males and adults fled—some to Amphissa, some amid the craggy recesses of Parnassus, or into that vast and spacious cavern at the base of Mount Corycus, dedicated to the Muses, and imparting to those lovely deities the poetical epithet of Corycides. Sixty men, with the chief priest, were alone left to protect the sacred city.

VI. But superstition can dispense with numbers in its agency. Just as the barbarians were in sight of the temple, the sacred arms, hitherto preserved inviolable in the sanctuary, were seen by the soothsayer to advance to the front of the temple. And this prodigy but heralded others more active. As the enemy now advanced in the stillness of the deserted city, and impressed doubtless by their own awe (for not to a Persian army could there have seemed no veneration due to the Temple of the Sun!) just by the shrine of Minerva Pronæa, built out in front of the great temple, a loud peal of thunder burst suddenly over their heads, and two enormous fragments of rock (separated from the heights of that Parnassus amid whose recesses mortals as well as gods lay hid) rolled down the mountain-side with a mighty crash, and destroyed many of the Persian multitude. At the same time, from the temple of the warlike goddess broke forth a loud and martial shout, as if to arms. Confused—appalled—panic-stricken by these super-natural prodigies—the barbarians turned to fly; while the Delphians, already prepared and armed, rushed from cave and mountain, and, charging in the midst of the invaders, scattered them with great slaughter. Those who escaped fled to the army in Bœotia. Thus the treasures of Delphi were miraculously preserved, not only from the plunder of the Persian, but also from the clutch of the Delphian citizens themselves, who had been especially anxious, in the first instance, to be permitted to deposit the treasures in a place of safety. Nobody knew better than the priests that treasures always diminish when transferred from one hand to another.

VII. The Grecian fleet anchored at Salamis by the request of the Athenians, who were the more anxious immediately to deliberate on the state of affairs, as the Persian army was now approaching their borders, and they learned that the selfish warriors of the Peloponnesus, according to their customary policy, instead of assisting the Athenians and Greece generally by marching towards Bœotia, were engaged only in fortifying the Isthmus or providing for their own safety.

THE ATHENIANS, UNAIDED BY THEIR ALLIES, ABANDON ATHENS, AND EMBARK FOR SALAMIS

Unable to engage the confederates to assist them in protecting Attica, the Athenians entreated, at least, the rest of the maritime allies to remain at Salamis, while they themselves hastened back to Athens.

Returned home, their situation was one which their generous valour had but little merited. Although they had sent to Artemisium the principal defence of the common cause, now, when the storm rolled towards themselves, none appeared on their behalf. They were at once incensed and discouraged by the universal desertion.[6] How was it possible that, alone and unaided, they could withstand the Persian multitude! Could they reasonably expect the fortunes of Marathon to be perpetually renewed? To remain at Athens was destruction—to leave it seemed to them a species of impiety. Nor could they anticipate victory with a sanguine hope, in abandoning the monuments of their ancestors and the temples of their gods.[7]

Themistocles alone was enabled to determine the conduct of his countrymen in this dilemma. Inexhaustible were the resources of a genius which ranged from the most lofty daring to the most intricate craft. Perceiving that the only chance of safety was in the desertion of the city, and that the strongest obstacle to this alternative was in the superstitious attachment to home ever so keenly felt by the ancients, he had recourse, in the failure of reason, to counter-superstition. In the temple of the citadel was a serpent, dedicated to Minerva, and considered the tutelary defender of the place. The food appropriated to the serpent was suddenly found unconsumed— the serpent itself vanished; and, at the suggestion of Themistocles, the priests proclaimed that the goddess had deserted the city and offered herself to conduct them to the seas. Then, amid the general excitement, Themistocles reiterated his version of the Delphic oracle. Then were the ships reinterpreted to be the wooden walls, and Salamis once more proclaimed "the Divine". The fervour of the people was awakened—the persuasions of Themistocles prevailed—even the women loudly declared their willingness to abandon Athens for the sake of the Athenians; and it was formally decreed that the city should be left to the guardianship of Minerva, and the citizens should save themselves, their women, children, and slaves, as their own discretion might suggest. Most of them took refuge in Trœzene, where they were generously supported at the public expense—some at Ægina—others repaired to Salamis.

A moving and pathetic spectacle was that of the embarkation of the Athenians for the isle of Salamis. Separated from their children, their wives (who were sent to remoter places of safety)—abandoning their homes and altars—the citadel of Minerva—the monuments of Marathon—they set out for a scene of contest, perilous and precarious, and no longer on the site of their beloved father-land. Their grief was heightened by the necessity of leaving many behind, whose extreme age rendered them yet more venerable, while it incapacitated their removal. Even the dumb animals excited all the fond domestic associations, running to the strand, and expressing by their cries their regret for the hands that fed them: one of them, a dog that belonged to Xanthippus, father of Pericles, is said to have followed the ships, and swam to Salamis, to die, spent with toil, upon the sands.

6 Plut., in Vit. Them.
7 Ibid.

VIII. The fleet now assembled at Salamis; the Spartans contributed only sixteen vessels, the people of Ægina thirty—swift galleys and well equipped;

THE IRRESOLUTE AND SELFISH POLICY OF THE PELOPONNESIANS

the Athenians one hundred and eighty; the whole navy, according to Herodotus, consisted of three hundred and seventy-eight[8] ships, besides an inconsiderable number of vessels of fifty oars.

Eurybiades still retained the chief command. A council of war was held. The greater number of the more influential allies were composed of Peloponnesians, and, with the countenance of the Spartan chief, it was proposed to retire from Salamis and fix the station in the Isthmus near the land-forces of the Peloponnesus. This was highly consonant to the interested policy of the Peloponnesian states, and especially to that of Sparta; Attica was considered already lost, and the fate of that territory they were therefore indisposed to consider. While the debate was yet pending, a messenger arrived from Athens with the intelligence that the barbarian, having reduced to ashes the allied cities of Thespiæ and Platæa in Bœotia, had entered Attica; and shortly afterward they learned that (despite a desperate resistance from the handful of Athenians who, some from poverty, some from a superstitious prejudice in favour of the wooden wall of the citadel, had long held out, though literally girt by fire from the burning of their barricades) the citadel had been taken, plundered, and burnt, and the remnant of its defenders put to the sword.

IX. Consternation seized the council; many of the leaders broke away hastily, went on board, hoisted their sails, and prepared to fly. Those who remained in the council determined that an engagement at sea could only be risked near the Isthmus. With this resolve the leaders at night returned to their ships.

It is singular how often, in the most memorable events, the fate and the glory of nations is decided by the soul of a single man. When Themistocles had retired to his vessel, he was sought by Mnesiphilus, who is said to have exercised an early and deep influence over the mind of Themistocles, and to have been one of those practical yet thoughtful statesmen called into existence by the sober philosophy of Solon,[9] whose lessons on the science of government made a groundwork for the rhetorical corruptions of the later sophists. On learning the determination of the council, Mnesiphilus forcibly represented its consequences. "If the allies", said he, "once abandon Salamis, you have lost forever the occasion of fighting for your country. The fleet will certainly separate, the various confederates return home, and Greece will perish. Hasten, therefore, ere yet it be too late, and endeavour to persuade Eurybiades to change his resolution and remain."

8 It is differently stated: by Æschylus and Nepos at three hundred, by Thucydides at four hundred.
9 Plut., in Vit. Them.

This advice, entirely agreeable to the views of Themistocles, excited that chief to new exertions. He repaired at once to Eurybiades; and, by dint of that extraordinary mastery over the minds of others which he possessed, he finally won over the Spartan, and, late as the hour was, persuaded him to reassemble the different leaders.

DEXTERITY AND FIRMNESS OF THEMISTOCLES

X. In that nocturnal council debate grew loud and warm. When Eurybiades had explained his change of opinion and his motives for calling the chiefs together, Themistocles addressed the leaders at some length and with great excitement. It was so evidently the interest of the Corinthians to make the scene of defence in the vicinity of Corinth, that we cannot be surprised to find the Corinthian leader, Adimantus, eager to interrupt the Athenian. "Themistocles", said he, "they who at the public games rise before their time are beaten."

"True", replied Themistocles, with admirable gentleness and temper; "but they who are left behind are never crowned."

Pursuing the advantage which a skilful use of interruption always gives to an orator, the Athenian turned to Eurybiades. Artfully suppressing his secret motive in the fear of the dispersion of the allies, which he rightly judged would offend without convincing, he had recourse to more popular arguments:

> Fight at the Isthmus and you fight in the open sea, where, on account of our heavier vessels and inferior number, you contend with every disadvantage. Grant even success, you will yet lose, by your retreat, Salamis, Megara, and Ægina. You would preserve the Peloponnesus, but remember, that by attracting thither the war, you attract not only the naval, but also the land-forces of the enemy. Fight here, and we have the inestimable advantage of a narrow sea —we shall preserve Salamis, the refuge of our wives and children— we shall as effectually protect the Peloponnesus as by repairing to the Isthmus and drawing the barbarian thither. If we obtain the victory, the enemy will neither advance to the Isthmus nor penetrate beyond Attica. Their retreat is sure.

The orator was again interrupted by Adimantus with equal rudeness. And Themistocles, who well knew how to alternate force with moderation, and menace with persuasion, retorted with an equal asperity, but with a singular dignity and happiness of expression. Said Adimantus, scornfully, alluding to the capture of Athens:

> It becomes you to be silent, and not to advise us to desert our country; you, who no longer have a country to defend! Eurybiades can only be influenced by Themistocles when Themistocles has once more a city to represent.

331

Replied Themistocles, sternly:

> Wretch! We have indeed left our walls and houses—preferring free-
> dom to those inanimate possessions—but know that the Athenians
> still possess a country and a city, greater and more formidable than
> yours, well provided with stores and men, which none of the Greeks
> will be able to resist: our ships are our country and our city.

And he added, once more addressing the Spartan chief:

> If you continue here you will demand our eternal gratitude: fly,
> and you are the destroyers of Greece. In this war the last and sole
> resource of the Athenians is their fleet: reject my remonstrances,
> and I warn you that at once we will take our families on board, and
> sail to that Siris, on the Italian shores, which of old is said to have
> belonged to us, and in which, if the oracle be trusted, we ought to
> found a city. Deprived of us, you will remember my words.

XI. The menace of Themistocles—the fear of so powerful a race, unhoused,
exasperated, and in search of a new settlement—and the yet more immediate
dread of the desertion of the flower of the navy—finally prevailed. Eurybiades
announced his concurrence with the views of Themistocles, and the confederates, wearied with altercation, consented to risk the issue of events at
Salamis.

XII. Possessed of Athens, the Persian king held also his council of war.
His fleet, sailing up the Euripus, anchored in the Attic bay of Phalerum; his
army encamped along the plains around, or within the walls of Athens.
The losses his armament had sustained were already repaired by new re-
enforcements of Malians, Dorians, Locrians, Bœotians, Carystians, Andrians,
Tenedians, and the people of the various isles. "The farther", says Herodotus,
"the Persians penetrated into Greece, the greater the numbers by which they
were followed." It may be supposed, however, that the motley contributions
of an idle and predatory multitude, or of Greeks compelled, not by affection,
but fear, ill supplied to Xerxes the devoted thousands, many of them his own
gallant Persians, who fell at Thermopylæ or perished in the Eubœan seas.

XIII. Mardonius and the leaders generally were for immediate battle. The
heroine Artemisia alone gave a more prudent counsel. She represented to
them, that if they delayed a naval engagement or sailed to the Peloponnesus,[10]
the Greeks, failing of provisions and overruled by their fears, would be
certain to disperse, to retire to their several homes, and, thus detached, fall
an easy prey to Persian arms.

---

10 Here we see additional reason for admiring the sagacity of Themistocles.

Although Xerxes, contrary to expectation, received the adverse opinion of the Carian princess with compliments and praise, he yet adopted the counsel of the majority; and, attributing the ill success at Artemisium to his absence, resolved in person to witness the triumph of his arms at Salamis.

The navy proceeded, in order, to that island; the land-forces on the same night advanced to the Peloponnesus; there, under Cleombrotus, brother to Leonidas, all the strength of the Peloponnesian confederates was already assembled. They had fortified the pass of Sciron, another Thermopylæ in its local character, and protected the Isthmus by a wall, at the erection of which the whole army worked night and day; no materials sufficing for the object of defence were disdained — wood, stones, bricks, and sand — all were pressed into service. Here encamped, they hoped nothing from Salamis—they believed the last hope of Greece rested solely with themselves.[11]

XIV. Again new agitation, fear, and dissension broke out in the Grecian navy. All those who were interested in the safety of the Peloponnesus complained anew of the resolution of Eurybiades—urged the absurdity of remaining at Salamis to contend for a territory already conquered—and the leaders of Ægina, Megara, and Athens were left in a minority in the council.

Thus overpowered by the Peloponnesian allies, Themistocles is said to have bethought himself of a stratagem, not inconsonant with his scheming and wily character. Retiring privately from the debate, yet unconcluded, and summoning the most confidential messenger in his service,[12] he despatched him secretly to the enemy's fleet with this message—

> The Athenian leader, really attached to the king, and willing to see the Greeks subjugated to his power, sends me privately to you. Consternation has seized the Grecian navy; they are preparing to fly; lose not the opportunity of a splendid victory. Divided among themselves, the Greeks are unable to resist you; and you will see, as you advance upon them, those who favour and those who would oppose you in hostility with each other.

The Persian admiral was sufficiently experienced in the treachery and defection of many of the Greeks to confide in the message thus delivered to him; but he scarcely required such intelligence to confirm a resolution already formed. At midnight the barbarians passed over a large detachment to the small isle of Psyttaleia, between Salamis and the continent, and occupying the whole narrow sea as far as the Attic port of Munychia, under cover of the

11 Herod., viii. 74.
12 The tutor of his children, Sicinnus, who had experience of the eastern manners, and spoke the Persian language.

darkness disposed their ships so as to surround the Greeks and cut off the possibility of retreat.

XV. Unconscious of the motions of the enemy, disputes still prevailed among the chiefs at Salamis, when Themistocles was summoned at night from the council, to which he had returned after despatching his messenger to the barbarian. The person who thus summoned him was Aristides. It was the third year of his exile—which sentence was evidently yet unrepealed—or not in that manner, at night and as a thief, would the eminent and highborn Aristides have joined his countrymen. He came from Ægina in an open boat, under cover of the night passed through the midst of the Persian ships, and arrived at Salamis to inform the Greeks that they were already surrounded.

"At any time", said Aristides, "it would become us to forget our private dissensions, and at this time especially, contending only who should most serve his country. In vain now would the Peloponnesians advise retreat; we are encompassed, and retreat is impossible."

Themistocles welcomed the new-comer with joy, and persuaded him to enter the council and acquaint the leaders with what he knew. His intelligence, received with doubt, was presently confirmed by a trireme of Tenians, which deserted to them; and they now seriously contemplated the inevitable resort of battle.

XVI. At dawn all was prepared. Assembled on the strand, Themistocles harangued the troops; and when he had concluded, orders were given to embark.

BATTLE OF SALAMIS

It was in the autumn of BC 480, two thousand three hundred and sixteen years ago, that the battle of Salamis was fought.

High on a throne of precious metals, placed on one of the eminences of Mount Ægaleos, sat, to survey the contest, the royal Xerxes. The rising sun beheld the shores of the Eleusinian Gulf lined with his troops to intercept the fugitives, and with a miscellaneous and motley crowd of such as were rather spectators than sharers of the conflict.[13]

---

13 The number of the Persian galleys, at the lowest computation, was a thousand; that of the Greeks, as we have seen, three hundred and eighty. But the Persians were infinitely more numerously manned, having on board of each vessel thirty men-at-arms, in addition to the usual number of two hundred. Plutarch seems to state the whole number in each Athenian vessel to be fourteen heavy-armed and four bowmen. But this would make the whole Athenian force only three thousand two hundred and forty men, including the bowmen, who were probably not Athenian citizens. It must therefore be supposed, with Mr Thirlwall, that the eighteen men thus specified were *an addition* to the ordinary company. Nepos, Herodotus, and Isocrates compute the total [of Persian galleys] at about twelve hundred; the estimate of one thousand is taken from a dubious and disputed passage in Æschylus, which may be so construed as to signify one thousand, including two hundred and seven vessels, or besides two hundred and seven vessels; viz., twelve hundred and seven in all, which is the precise number given by Herodotus. Ctesias says there were *more* than one thousand.

But not as the Persian leaders had expected was the aspect of the foe; nor did the Greeks betray the confusion or the terror ascribed to them by the emissary of Themistocles. As the daylight made them manifest to the Persian, they set up the loud and martial chorus of the pæan—"the rocks of Salamis echoed back the shout"—and, to use the expression of a soldier of that day,[14] "the trumpet inflamed them with its clangour".

As soon as the Greeks began to move, the barbarian vessels advanced swiftly. But Themistocles detained the ardour of the Greeks until the time when a sharp wind usually arose in that sea, occasioning a heavy swell in the channel, which was peculiarly prejudicial to the unwieldy ships of the Persians; but not so to the light, low, and compact vessels of the Greeks. The manner of attack with the ancient navies was to bring the prow of the vessel, which was fortified by long projecting beaks of brass, to bear upon the sides of its antagonist, and this, the swell of the sea causing the Persian galleys to veer about unwieldily, the agile ships of the Greeks were well enabled to effect.

By the time the expected wind arose, the engagement was begun. The Persian admiral[15] directed his manœuvres chiefly against Themistocles, for on him, as the most experienced and renowned of the Grecian leaders, the eyes of the enemy were turned. From his ship, which was unusually lofty, as from a castle,[16] he sent forth darts and arrows, until one of the Athenian triremes, commanded by Aminias, shot from the rest, and bore down upon him with the prow. The ships met, and, fastened together by their brazen beaks, which served as grappling-irons, Ariabignes gallantly boarded the Grecian vessel, and was instantly slain by the hostile pikes and hurled into the sea.[17] The first who took a ship was an Athenian named Lycomedes. The Grecians keeping to the straits, the Persians were unable to bring their whole armament to bear at once, and could only enter the narrow pass by detachments; the heaviness of the sea and the cumbrous size of their tall vessels frequently occasioned more embarrassment to themselves than the foe—driven and hustling the one against the other. The Athenians maintaining the right wing were opposed by the Phœnicians; the Spartans on the left by the Ionians. The first were gallantly supported by the Æginetans, who, long skilled in maritime warfare, eclipsed even their new rivals the Athenians. The Phœnician line was broken. The Greeks pursued their victory, still preserving the steadiest discipline and the most perfect order. The sea became strewn and covered with the wrecks of vessels and the bodies of the dead;

14 Æschyl., Persæ, 397.
15 The Persian admiral at Salamis is asserted by Ctesias to have been Onaphas, father-in-law to Xerxes. According to Herodotus, it was Ariabignes, the king's brother, who seems the same as Artabazanes, with whom he had disputed the throne. Compare Herod., vii. 2, and viii. 89.
16 Plut., in Vit. Them.
17 Plut., in Vit. Them. The Ariamenes of Plutarch is the Ariabignes of Herodotus.

while, to the left, the Ionians gave way before that part of the allied force commanded by the Spartans, some fighting with great valour, some favouring the Greek confederates. Meanwhile, as the Persians gave way, and the sea became more clear, Aristides, who had hitherto remained on shore, landed a body of Athenians on the isle of Psyttaleia, and put the Persian guard there stationed to the sword.

Xerxes from the mountain, his countless thousands from the shore, beheld, afar and impotent, the confusion, the slaughter, the defeat of the forces on the sea. Anxious now only for retreat, the barbarians retreated to Phalerum; and there, intercepted by the Æginetans, were pressed by them in the rear; by the Athenians, led by Themistocles, in front. At this time the heroine Artemisia, pursued by that Aminias whose vessel had first grappled with the Persians, and who of all the Athenian captains was that day the most eminently distinguished, found herself in the extremest danger. Against that remarkable woman the efforts of the Athenians had been especially directed: deeming it a disgrace to them to have an enemy in a woman, they had solemnly set a reward of great amount upon her capture. Thus pursued, Artemisia had recourse to a sudden and extraordinary artifice. Falling in with a vessel of the Persians, commanded by a Calyndian prince, with whom she had once been embroiled, she bore down against the ship and sunk it—a truly feminine stratagem—deceiving at once a public enemy and gratifying a private hatred. The Athenian, seeing the vessel he had pursued thus attack a barbarian, conceived he had mistaken a friendly vessel, probably a deserter from the Persians, for a foe, and immediately sought new objects of assault. Xerxes beheld and admired the prowess of Artemisia, deeming, in the confusion, that it was a hostile vessel she had sunken.[18]

XVII. The battle lasted till the dusk of evening, when at length the remnant of the barbarian fleet gained the port of Phalerum; and the Greeks beheld along the straits of Salamis no other vestige of the enemy than the wrecks and corpses which were the evidence of his defeat.

XVIII. When morning came, the Greeks awaited a renewal of the engagement; for the Persian fleet were still numerous, the Persian army yet covered the neighbouring shores, and, by a feint to conceal his real purpose, Xerxes had ordered the Phœnician transports to be joined together, as if to connect Salamis to the continent. But a mandate was already issued for the instant

---

18 Mr Mitford, neglecting to observe this error of Xerxes, especially noted by Herodotus, merely observes—"According to Herodotus, though in this instance we may have difficulty to give him entire credit, Xerxes, from the shore where he sat, saw, admired, and applauded the exploit." From this passage one would suppose that Xerxes knew it was a friend who had been attacked, and then, indeed, we could not have credited the account; but if he and those about him supposed it, as Herodotus states, a foe, what is there incredible? This is one instance in ten thousand more important ones, of Mr Mitford's habit of arguing upon one sentence by omitting those that follow and precede it.

departure of the navy for the Hellespont, and a few days afterward the army itself retired into Bœotia.

The victory of Salamis was celebrated by solemn rejoicings, in which, principally remarkable for the beauty of his person, and his accomplishments on the lyre and in the dance, was a youth named Sophocles, destined afterward to share the glory of Æschylus, who, no less a warrior than a poet, distinguished himself in the battle, and has bequeathed to us the most detailed and animated account we possess of its events.

The Grecian conquerors beheld the retreat of the enemy with indignation; they were unwilling that any of that armament which had burnt their hearths and altars should escape their revenge; they pursued the Persian ships as far as Andros, where, not reaching them, they cast anchor and held a consultation. Themistocles is said to have proposed, but not sincerely, to sail at once to the Hellespont and destroy the bridge of boats. This counsel was overruled, and it was decided not to reduce so terrible an enemy to despair:—"Rather", said one of the chiefs (whether Aristides or Eurybiades is differently related), "build another bridge, that Xerxes may escape the sooner out of Europe."

Themistocles affected to be converted to a policy which he desired only an excuse to effect; and, in pursuance of the hint already furnished him, is said to have sent secretly to Xerxes, informing him that it was the intention of the allies to sail to the Hellespont and destroy the bridge, so that, if the king consulted his safety, he would return immediately into Asia, while Themistocles would find pretexts to delay the pursuit of the confederates.

This artifice appears natural to the scheming character of Themistocles; and, from concurrent testimony,[19] it seems to me undoubted that Themistocles maintained a secret correspondence with Xerxes, and even persuaded that monarch that he was disposed to favour him. But it is impossible to believe, with Herodotus, that he had at that time any real desire to conciliate the Persian, foreseeing that he might hereafter need a refuge at the eastern court. Then in the zenith of his popularity, so acute a foresight is not in man. He was one of those to whom the spirit of intrigue is delight in itself, and in the present instance it was exerted for the common cause of the Athenians, which, with all his faults, he never neglected for, but rather incorporated with, his own.

XIX. Diverted from the notion of pursuing the Persians, the Grecian allies, flushed with conquest, were yet eager for enterprise. The isles which had leagued with the Mede were strongly obnoxious to the confederates, and it was proposed to exact from them a fine, in defrayal of the expenses of the war. Siege was laid to Andros, and those islanders were the first who

ANDROS AND CARYSTUS BESIEGED BY THE GREEKS

19 Diod. Sic., xi. 5; Herod., viii. 110; Nepos, et Plut., in Vit. Them.

resisted the demand. Then was it that they made that memorable answer, which may serve as a warning in all times to the strong when pressing on the desperate.

"I bring with me", said Themistocles, "two powerful divinities—Persuasion and Force."

"And we", answered the Andrians, "have two gods equally powerful on our side—Poverty and Despair."

The Andrian deities eventually triumphed, and the siege was raised without effect. But from the Parians and Carystians, and some other islanders, Themistocles obtained enormous sums of money unknown to his colleagues, which, however unjustly extorted, it does not satisfactorily appear that he applied largely to his own personal profit, but, as is more probable, to the rebuilding of Athens. Perhaps he thought, nor without reason, that as the Athenians had been the principal sufferers in the war, and contributed the most largely to its resources, so whatever fines were levied on the seceders were due, not to the confederates generally, but the Athenians alone. The previous conduct of the allies, with so much difficulty preserved from deserting Athens, merited no particular generosity, and excused perhaps the retaliation of a selfish policy.

The payment of the fine did not, however, preserve Carystus from attack. After wasting its lands, the Greeks returned to Salamis and divided the ANECDOTES OF THEMISTOCLES Persian spoils. The first fruits were dedicated to the gods, and the choicest of the booty sent to Delphi. And here we may notice one anecdote of Themistocles, which proves, that whatever, at times and in great crises, was the grasping unscrupulousness of his mind, he had at least no petty and vulgar avarice. Seeing a number of bracelets and chains of gold upon the bodies of the dead, he passed them by, and turning to one of his friends," Take these for yourself", said he, "for you are not Themistocles."[20]

Meanness or avarice was indeed no part of the character of Themistocles, although he has been accused of those vices, because guilty, at times, of extortion. He was profuse, ostentatious, and magnificent above his contemporaries and beyond his means. His very vices were on a large and splendid scale; and if he had something of the pirate in his nature, he had nothing of the miser. When he had to choose between two suitors for his daughter, he preferred the worthy to the wealthy candidate—willing that she should rather marry a man without money than money without a man.[21]

XX. The booty divided, the allies repaired to the Isthmus, according to that beautiful ancient custom of apportioning rewards to such as had been most distinguished. It was in the Temple of Neptune that the leaders met.

20 Plut., in Vit. Them.
21 Ibid. These anecdotes have the stamp of authenticity.

The right of voting was confined to the several chiefs, who were to declare whom they thought the first in merit and whom the second. Each leader wrote his own name a candidate for the first rank; but a great majority of suffrages awarded the second to Themistocles. While, therefore, each leader had only a single suffrage in favour of the first rank, the second rank was unequivocally due to the Athenian.

XXI. But even conquest had not sufficed to remove the jealousies of the confederate leaders—they evaded the decision of a question which could not but be propitious to the Athenians, and returned home without having determined the point which had assembled them at the Isthmus. But Themistocles was not of a temper to brook patiently this fraud upon his honours. Far from sharing the petty and miserable envies of their chiefs, the Greeks generally were loud in praise of his wisdom and services; and, taking advantage of their enthusiasm, Themistocles repaired to Sparta, trusting to the generosity of the principal rival to compensate the injustice of many. His expectations were not ill founded—the customs of Sparta allowed no slight to a Spartan, and they adjudged therefore the prize of valour to their own Eurybiades, while they awarded that of wisdom or science to Themistocles. Each was equally honoured with a crown of olive. Forgetful of all their prejudices, their envy, and their inhospitable treatment of strangers, that nation of warriors were dazzled by the hero whose courage assimilated to their own. They presented him with the stateliest chariot to be found in Sparta, and solemnly conducted him homeward as far as Tegea, by an escort of three hundred chosen Spartans called "the Knights"—the sole example of the Spartans conducting any man from their city. It is said that on his return to Athens, Themistocles was reproached by Timodemus of Aphidna, a Belbinite by origin,[22] and an implacable public enemy, with his visit to Sparta: "The honours awarded you", said Timodemus, "are bestowed from respect, not to you, but to Athens."

"My friend", retorted the witty chief, "the matter stands thus. Had I been a Belbinite, I had not been thus distinguished at Sparta, nor would you, although you had been born an Athenian!"

While the Greeks were thus occupied, the Persian army had retreated with Mardonius into Thessaly. Here that general selected and marshalled the forces with which he intended to renew the war, retaining in his service the celebrated Immortals. The total, including the cavalry, Herodotus estimates at three hundred thousand men.

---

22 Herod., viii. 125. See Wesseling's Comment on Timodemus. Plutarch tells the same anecdote, but makes the baffled rebuker of Themistocles a citizen of Seriphus, an island in which, according to Ælian, the frogs never croaked; the men seem to have made up for the silence of the frogs!

The side note adjacent to paragraph XXI reads: HONOURS AWARDED TO HIM IN SPARTA

Thus occupied, and ere Xerxes departed from Thessaly, the Spartans, impelled by an oracle, sent a messenger to Xerxes to demand atonement for the death of Leonidas.

"Ay", replied the king, laughing, "this man (pointing to Mardonius) shall make you fitting retribution."

Leaving Mardonius in Thessaly, where he proposed to winter, Xerxes now hastened home. Sixty thousand Persians under Artabazus accompanied the king only as far as the passage into Asia; and it was with an inconsiderable force, which, pressed by famine, devastated the very herbage on their way, and which a pestilence and the dysentery diminished as it passed, that the great king crossed the Hellespont, on which the bridge of boats had already been broken by wind and storm. A more abundant supply of provisions than they had yet experienced tempted the army to excesses, to which many fell victims. The rest arrived at Sardis with Xerxes, whence he afterward returned to his more distant capital.

XERXES RETURNS TO ASIA

XXII. The people of Potidæa, on the Isthmus of Pallene, and Olynthus, inhabited by the Bottiæans, a dubious and mongrel race that boasted their origin from those Athenians who, in the traditional ages, had been sent as tributary captives to the Cretan Minos, no sooner learned the dispersion of the fleet at Salamis, and the retreat of the king, than they openly revolted from the barbarian. Artabazus, returning from the Hellespont, laid siege to Olynthus, massacred the inhabitants, and colonized the town with Chalcidians. He then sat down before Potidæa; but a terrible inundation of the sea, with the sallies of the besieged, destroyed the greater number of the unfortunate invaders. The remnant were conducted by Artabazus into Thessaly, to join the army of Mardonius. The Persian fleet, retreating from Salamis, after passing over the king and his forces from the Chersonesus to Abydos, wintered at Cuma; and at the commencement of the spring assembled at Samos.

OLYNTHUS AND POTIDÆA BESIEGED BY ARTABAZUS

Meanwhile the Athenians returned to their dismantled city, and directed their attention to its repair and reconstruction. It was then, too, that in all probability the people hastened, by a formal and solemn reversal of the sentence of ostracism, to reward the services of Aristides, and to restore to the commonwealth the most spotless of its citizens.[23]

THE ATHENIANS RETURN HOME — THE OSTRACISM OF ARISTIDES IS REPEALED

23 See Fasti Hellenici, vol. ii, p. 26.

CHAPTER VIII

Embassy of Alexander of Macedon to Athens—the result of his proposals—Athenians retreat to Salamis—Mardonius occupies Athens—the Athenians send envoys to Sparta—Pausanias succeeds Cleombrotus as regent of Sparta—battle of Platæa— Thebes besieged by the Athenians—battle of Mycale—siege of Sestos—conclusion of the Persian war

I. The dawning spring and the formidable appearance of Mardonius, who, with his Persian forces, diminished indeed, but still mighty, lowered on their confines, aroused the Greeks to a sense of their danger. Their army was not as yet assembled, but their fleet, consisting of one hundred and ten vessels, under the command of Leotychides, king of Sparta, and Xanthippus of Athens, lay off Ægina. Thus anchored, there came to the naval commanders certain Chians, who, having been discovered in a plot against the life of Strattis, a tyrant imposed upon Chios by the Persians, fled to Ægina. They declared that all Ionia was ripe for revolt, and their representations induced the Greeks to advance as far as the sacred Delos.

Beyond they dared not venture, ignorant alike of the localities of the country and the forces of the enemy. Samos seemed to them no less remote than the Pillars of Hercules, and mutual fear thus kept the space between the Persian and the Greek fleet free from the advance of either. But Mardonius began slowly to stir from his winter lethargy. Influenced, thought the Greeks, perhaps too fondly, by a Theban oracle, the Persian general despatched to Athens no less distinguished an ambassador than Alexander, the king of Macedon. That prince, connected with the Persians by alliance (for his sister had married the Persian Bubares, son of Megabazus), was considered an envoy calculated to conciliate the Athenians while he served their enemy. And it was now the object of Mardonius to reconcile the foe whom he had failed to conquer. Aware of the Athenian valour, Mardonius trusted that if he could detach that state from the confederacy, and prevail on the Athenians to unite their arms to his own, the rest of Greece would become an easy conquest. By land he already deemed himself secure of fortune, by sea what Grecian navy, if deprived of the flower of its forces, could resist him?

II. The King of Macedon arrived at Athens; but conscious of the jealous and anxious fear which the news of an embassy from Persia would excite among the confederates, the Athenians delayed to grant him the demanded audience until they had time to send for and obtain deputies from Sparta to be present at the assembly.

Alexander of Macedon then addressed the Athenians:

> Men of Athens! Mardonius informs you, through me, of this mandate from the king: "Whatever injuries", saith he, "the Athenians have done me, I forgive. Restore them their country—let them even annex to it any other territories they covet—permit them the free enjoyment of their laws. If they will ally with me, rebuild the temples I have burnt."

Alexander then proceeded to dilate on the consequences of this favourable mission, to represent the power of the Persian, and urge the necessity of an alliance. "Let my offers prevail with you", he concluded, "for to you alone, of all the Greeks, the king extends his forgiveness, desiring your alliance."

When Alexander had concluded, the Spartan envoys thus spoke through their chief, addressing, not the Macedonian, but the Athenians:

> We have been deputed by the Spartans to entreat you to adopt no measures prejudicial to Greece, and to receive no conditions from the barbarians. This, most iniquitous in itself, would be above all unworthy and ungraceful in you; with you rests the origin of the war now appertaining to all Greece. Insufferable, indeed, if the Athenians, once the authors of liberty to many, were now the authors of the servitude of Greece. We commiserate your melancholy condition—your privation for two years of the fruits of your soil, your homes destroyed, and your fortunes ruined. We, the Spartans, and the other allies, will receive your women and all who may be helpless in the war while the war shall last. Let not the Macedonian, smoothing down the messages of Mardonius, move you. This becomes him; tyrant himself, he would assist in a tyrant's work. But you will not heed him if you are wise, knowing that faith and truth are not in the barbarians.

III. The answer of the Athenians to both Spartan and Persian, the substance of which is no doubt faithfully preserved to us by Herodotus, may

rank among the most imperishable records of that high-souled and generous people. The answer, dictated, and, probably, uttered by Aristides,[1] ran thus:

---

1 Plut., in Vit. Arist.

We are not ignorant that the power of the Mede is many times greater than our own. We required not that ostentatious admonition. Yet, for the preservation of liberty, we will resist that power as we can. Cease to persuade us to contract alliance with the barbarian. Bear back to Mardonius this answer from the Athenians—So long as yonder sun (and the orator pointed to the orb[2]) holds the courses which now it holds—so long will we abjure all amity with Xerxes— so long, confiding in the aid of our gods and heroes, whose shrines and altars he hath burnt, will we struggle against him in battle and for revenge. And thou, beware how again thou bearest such proffers to the Athenians; nor, on the plea of benefit to us, urge us to dishonour; for we would not—ungrateful to thee, our guest and our friend— have any evil befall to thee from the anger of the Athenians.

For you, Spartans! it may be consonant with human nature that you should fear our alliance with the barbarians—yet shamefully you fear it, knowing with what spirit we are animated and act. Gold hath no amount—earth hath no territory, how beautiful soever— that can tempt the Athenians to accept conditions from the Mede for the servitude of Greece. Were we so inclined, many and mighty are our prohibitions; first and chiefly, our temples burnt and overthrown, urging us not to alliance, but to revenge. Next, the whole race of Greece has one consanguinity and one tongue, and common are its manners, its altars, and its gods—base indeed, if Athenians were of these the betrayers! Lastly, learn now, if ye knew it not before, that, while one Athenian shall survive, Athens allies herself not with Xerxes.

We thank you for your providence of us—your offers to protect our families—afflicted and impoverished as we are. We will bear, however, our misfortunes as we may—becoming no burden upon you. Be it your care to send your forces to the field. Let there be no delay. The barbarian will be on us when he learns that we have rejected his proposals. Before he proceed to Attica let us meet him in Bœotia.

IV. On receiving this answer from the Athenians the Spartan ambassadors returned home; and, shortly afterward, Mardonius, by rapid marches, conducted his army towards Attica; fresh supplies of troops recruiting his forces wheresoever he passed. The Thessalian princes, far from repenting their alliance with Mardonius, animated his ardour.

ATHENIANS RETREAT TO SALAMIS — MARDONIUS OCCUPIES ATHENS

2 Ibid.

Arrived in Bœotia, the Thebans endeavoured to persuade the Persian general to encamp in that territory, and to hazard no battle, but rather to seek by bribes to the most powerful men in each city to detach the confederates from the existent alliance. Pride, ambition, and the desire of avenging Xerxes once more upon Athens, deterred Mardonius from yielding to this counsel. He marched on to Attica—he found the territory utterly deserted. He was informed that the inhabitants were either at Salamis or with the fleet. He proceeded to Athens, equally deserted, and, ten months after the first capture by Xerxes, that city a second time was occupied by the Mede.

From Athens Mardonius despatched a Greek messenger to Salamis, repeating the propositions of Alexander. On hearing these offers in council, the Athenians were animated by a species of fury. A counsellor named Lycidas having expressed himself in favour of the terms, he was immediately stoned to death. The Athenian women, roused by a similar passion with the men, inflicted the same fate upon his wife and children—one of those excesses of virtue which become crimes, but for which exigency makes no despicable excuse.[3] The ambassador returned uninjured.

V. The flight of the Athenians to Salamis had not been a willing resort. That gallant people had remained in Attica so long as they could entertain any expectation of assistance from the Peloponnesus; nor was it until compelled by despair at the inertness of their allies, and the appearance of the Persians in Bœotia, that they had removed to Salamis.

The singular and isolated policy of Sparta, which had curbed and crippled, to an exclusive regard for Spartans, all the more generous and daring principles of action, was never, perhaps, so odiously displayed as in the present indifference to an ally that had so nobly preferred the Grecian liberties to its own security. The whole of the Peloponnesus viewed with apathy the occupation of Attica, and the Spartans were employed in completing the fortifications of the Isthmus.

The Athenians despatched messengers to Sparta, as did also Megara and Platæa. These ambassadors assumed a high and reproachful tone of remonstrance.

THE ATHENIANS SEND
ENVOYS TO SPARTA

They represented the conduct of the Athenians in rejecting the overtures of the barbarians—they upbraided the Spartans with perfidy for breaking the agreement to meet the enemy in Bœotia—they declared the resentment of the Athenians at the violation of this compact, demanded immediate supplies, and indicated the plains near Thria, a village in Attica, as a fitting field of battle.

3 The custom of lapidation was common to the earlier ages; it had a kind of sanction, too, in particular offences; and no crime could be considered by a brave and inflamed people equal to that of advice against their honour and their liberties.

The ephors heard the remonstrance, but from day to day delayed an answer. The Spartans, according to Herodotus, were engaged in celebrating the solemnities in honour of Hyacinthus and Apollo; and this ceremonial might have sufficed as a plausible cause for procrastination, according to all the usages and formalities of Spartan manners. But perhaps there might be another and a graver reason for the delayed determination of the ephors.

When the isthmian fortifications were completed, the superstition of the regent Cleombrotus, who had superintended their construction, was alarmed by an eclipse, and he led back to Sparta the detach- ment he had commanded in that quarter. He returned but to die; and his son Pausanias succeeded to the regency during the continued minority of Pleistarchus, the infant heir of Leonidas.[4] If the funeral solemnities on the death of a regent were similar to those bestowed upon a deceased king, we can account at once for the delay of the ephors, since the ten days which passed without reply to the ambassadors exactly correspond in number with the ten days dedicated to public mourning.[5] But whatever the cause of the Spartan de- lay—and the rigid closeness of that oligarchic government kept, in yet more important matters, its motives and its policy no less a secret to contempora- neous nations than to modern inquirers—the delay itself highly incensed the Athenian envoys: they even threatened to treat with Mardonius, and abandon Sparta to her fate, and at length fixed the day of their departure. The ephors roused themselves. Among the deputies from the various states, there was then in Sparta that Chileus, of Tegea, who had been scarcely less serviceable than Themistocles in managing the affairs of Greece in the Isthmian Congress. This able and eminent Arcadian forcibly represented to the ephors the danger of forfeiting the Athenian alliance, and the insuffi- cient resistance against the Persian that the fortifications of the Isthmus would afford. The ephors heard, and immediately acted with the secrecy and the vigilance that belongs to oligarchies. That very night they privately despatched a body of five thousand Spartans and thirty-five thousand Helots (seven to each Spartan), under the command of Pausanias.

The next morning the ephors calmly replied to the angry threats of the Athenians, by protesting that their troops were already on the march, and by this time in Oresteum, a town in Arcadia, about eighteen miles distant from Sparta. The astonished deputies[6] hastened to overtake the Spartan force, and the ephors, as if fully to atone for their past procrastination, gave them the

PAUSANIAS SUCCEEDS CLEOMBROTUS AS RE- GENT OF SPARTA

---

4 See Herod., ix. 10. Also Mr Clinton on the Kings of Sparta, Fasti Hellenici, vol. ii, p. 187.
5 See Herod., vi. 58. After the burial of a Spartan king, ten days were devoted to mourning; nor was any public business transacted in that interval.
6 "According to Aristides' decree", says Plutarch, "the Athenian envoys were Aristides, Xanthippus, Myronides, and Cimon."

escort and additional re-enforcement of five thousand heavy-armed Laconians or Periœci.

VI. Mardonius soon learned from the Argives (who, not content with refusing to join the Greek legion, had held secret communications with the Persians) of the departure of the Spartan troops. Hitherto he had refrained from any outrage on the Athenian lands and city, in the hope that Athens might yet make peace with him. He now set fire to Athens, razed the principal part of what yet remained of the walls and temples,[7] and deeming the soil of Attica ill adapted to his cavalry, and, from the narrowness of its outlets, disadvantageous in case of retreat, after a brief incursion into Megara he retired towards Thebes, and pitched his tents on the banks of the Asopus, extending from Erythræ to Platæa. Here his force was swelled by such of the Greeks as were friendly to his cause.

VII. Meanwhile the Spartans were joined at the Isthmus by the rest of the Peloponnesian allies. Solemn sacrifices were ordained, and the auguries drawn from the victims being favourable, the Greek army proceeded onward; and, joined at Eleusis by the Athenians, marched to the foot of Cithæron, and encamped opposite the Persians, with the river of the Asopus between the armies. Aristides commanded the Athenians, at the head of eight thousand foot; and while the armies were thus situated, a dangerous conspiracy was detected and defeated by that able general.

The disasters of the war—the devastation of lands, the burning of houses— had reduced the fortunes of many of the Athenian nobles. With their property diminished their influence. Poverty, and discontent, and jealousy of new families rising into repute[8] induced these men of fallen fortunes to conspire for the abolition of the popular government at Athens, and, failing that attempt, to betray the cause to the enemy.

This project spread secretly through the camp, and corrupted numbers; the danger became imminent. On the one hand, the conspiracy was not to be neglected; and, on the other, in such a crisis it might be dangerous too narrowly to sift a design in which men of mark and station were concerned. Aristides acted with a singular prudence. He arrested eight of the leaders. Of these he prosecuted only two (who escaped during the proceedings), and, dismissing the rest, appealed to the impending battle as the great tribunal which would acquit them of the charge and prove their loyalty to the state.[9]

---

7 Herodotus speaks of the devastation and ruin as complete. But how many ages did the monuments of Pisistratus survive the ravage of the Persian sword!

8 Plut., in Vit. Arist.

9 This, among a thousand anecdotes, proves how salutary and inevitable was the popular distrust of the aristocracy. When we read of the process of bribing the principal men, and of the conspiracy entered into by others, we must treat with contempt those accusations of the jealousy of the Grecian people towards their superiors which form the staple declamations of commonplace historians.

VIII. Scarce was this conspiracy quelled than the cavalry of the Persians commenced their operations. At the head of that skilful and gallant horse, for which the oriental nations are yet renowned, rode their chief, Masistius, clad in complete armour of gold, of brass, and of iron, and noted for the strength of his person and the splendour of his trappings. Placed on the rugged declivities of Cithæron, the Greeks were tolerably safe from the Persian cavalry, save only the Megarians, who, to the number of three thousand, were posted along the plain, and were on all sides charged by that agile and rapid cavalry. Thus pressed, the Megarians sent to Pausanias for assistance. The Spartan beheld the air darkened with shafts and arrows, and knew that his heavy-armed warriors were ill adapted to act against horse. He in vain endeavoured to arouse those about him by appeals to their honour —all declined the succour of the Megarians—when Aristides, causing the Athenian to eclipse the Spartan chivalry, undertook the defence. With three hundred infantry, mixed with archers, Olympiodorus, one of the ablest of the Athenian officers, advanced eagerly on the barbarian.

Masistius himself, at the head of his troops, spurred his Nisæan charger against the new enemy. A sharp and obstinate conflict ensued; when the horse of the Persian general, being wounded, threw its rider, who could not regain his feet from the weight of his armour. There, as he lay on the ground, with a swarm of foes around him, the close scales of his mail protected him from their weapons, until at length a lance pierced the brain through an opening in his visor. After an obstinate conflict for his corpse, the Persians were beaten back to the camp, where the death of one, second only to Mardonius in authority and repute, spread universal lamentation and dismay.

The body of Masistius, which, by its vast size and beautiful proportions, excited the admiration of the victors, remained the prize of the Greeks; and, placed on a bier, it was borne triumphantly through the ranks.

IX. After this victory, Pausanias conducted his forces along the base of Cithæron into the neighbourhood of Platæa, which he deemed a more convenient site for the disposition of his army and the supply of water. There, near the fountain of Gargaphia,[10] one of the sources of the Asopus (which splits into many rivulets, bearing a common name), and renowned in song for the death of the fabulous Actæon, nor far from the shrine of an old Platæan hero (Androcrates), the Greeks were marshalled in regular divisions, the different nations, some on a gentle acclivity, others along the plain.

BATTLE OF PLATÆA

In the allotment of the several stations a dispute arose between the Athenians and the Tegeans. The latter claimed, from ancient and traditionary prescription, the left wing (the right being unanimously awarded to the

10 Gargaphia is one mile and a half from the town of Platæa (Gell's Itin. 112).

Spartans), and assumed, in the course of their argument, an insolent superiority over the Athenians.

"We came here to fight", answered the Athenians (or Aristides in their name[11]), "and not to dispute. But since the Tegeans proclaim their ancient as well as their modern deeds, fit is it for us to maintain our precedence over the Arcadians."

Touching slightly on the ancient times referred to by the Tegeans, and quoting their former deeds, the Athenians insisted chiefly upon Marathon. "Yet", said their orators, or orator, in conclusion, "while we maintain our right to the disputed post, it becomes us not, at this crisis, to altercate on the localities of the battle. Place us, oh Spartans! wherever seems best to you. No matter what our station; we will uphold our honour and your cause. Command, then—we obey."

Hearing this generous answer, the Spartan leaders were unanimous in favour of the Athenians; and they accordingly occupied the left wing.

X. Thus were marshalled that confederate army, presenting the strongest force yet opposed to the Persians, and comprising the whole might and manhood of the free Grecian states; to the right, ten thousand Lacedæmonians, one half, as we have seen, composed of the Periœci, the other moiety of the pure Spartan race—to each warrior of the latter half were allotted seven armed Helots, to each of the heavy-armed Periœci one serving-man. Their whole force was, therefore, no less than fifty thousand men. Next to the Spartans (a kind of compromise of their claim) were the one thousand five hundred Tegeans; beyond these five thousand Corinthians; and to them contiguous three hundred Potidæans of Pallene, whom the inundation of their seas had saved from the Persian arms. Next in order, Orchomenus ranged its six hundred Arcadians; Sicyon sent three thousand, Epidaurus eight hundred, and Trœzene one thousand warriors. Neighbouring the last were two hundred Lepreatæ, and by them four hundred Myceneans and Tirynthians.[12] Stationed by the Tirynthians came, in successive order, a thousand Phliasians, three hundred Hermionians, six hundred Eretrians and Styreans, four hundred Chalcidians, five hundred Ambracians, eight hundred Leucadians and Anactorians, two hundred Paleans of Cephallenia, and five hundred only of the islanders of Ægina. Three thousand Megarians and six hundred Platæans were ranged contiguous to the Athenians, whose force of eight thousand men, under the command of Aristides, closed the left wing.

Thus the total of the heavy-armed soldiery was thirty-eight thousand seven hundred. To these were added the light-armed force of thirty-five thousand Helots and thirty-four thousand five hundred attendants on the

---

11 Plut., in Vit. Arist.

12 A strange fall from the ancient splendour of Mycenæ, to furnish only four hundred men, conjointly with Tiryns, to the cause of Greece!

Laconians and other Greeks; the whole amounting to one hundred and eight thousand two hundred men, besides one thousand eight hundred Thespians, who, perhaps, on account of the destruction of their city by the Persian army, were without the heavy arms of their confederates.

Such was the force—not insufficient in number, but stronger in heart, union, the memory of past victories, and the fear of future chains—that pitched the tent along the banks of the rivulets which confound with the Asopus their waters and their names.

XI. In the interim Mardonius had marched from his former post, and lay encamped on that part of the Asopus nearest to Platæa. His brave Persians fronted the Lacedæmonians and Tegeans; and, in successive order, ranged the Medes and Bactrians, the Indians and the Sacæ, the Bœotians, Locrians, Malians, Thessalians, Macedonians, and the reluctant aid of a thousand Phocians. But many of the latter tribe about the fastnesses of Parnassus, openly siding with the Greeks, harassed the barbarian outskirts.

Herodotus calculates the hostile force at three hundred and fifty thousand, fifty thousand of which were composed of Macedonians and Greeks. And, although the historian has omitted to deduct from this total the loss sustained by Artabazus at Potidæa, it is yet most probable that the barbarian nearly trebled the Grecian army—odds less fearful than the Greeks had already met and vanquished.

XII. The armies thus ranged, sacrifices were offered up on both sides. It happened, by a singular coincidence, that to either army was an Elean augur. The appearance of the entrails forbade both Persian and Greek to cross the Asopus, and ordained each to act on the defensive.

That the Persian chief should have obeyed the dictates of a Grecian soothsayer is sufficiently probable; partly because a superstitious people rarely despise the superstitions of another faith, principally because a considerable part of the invading army, and that perhaps the bravest and the most skilful, was composed of native Greeks, whose prejudices it was politic to flatter—perilous to affront.

Eight days were consumed in inactivity, the armies confronting each other without motion; when Mardonius, in order to cut off the new forces which every day resorted to the Grecian camp, despatched a body of cavalry to seize the pass of Cithæron. Falling in with a convoy of five hundred beasts of burden, carrying provisions from the Peloponnesus, the barbarians, with an inhumanity sufficient, perhaps, to prove that the detachment was not composed of Persians, properly so speaking, a mild though gallant people—slaughtered both man and beast. The provisions were brought to the Persian camp.

XIII. During the two following days Mardonius advanced nearer to the Asopus, and his cavalry (assisted by the Thebans, who were the right arm of the barbarian army), in repeated skirmishes, greatly harassed the Greeks with much daring and little injury.

At length Mardonius, either wearied of this inactivity or unable to repress the spirit of a superior army, not accustomed to receive the attack, resolved to reject all further compliance with the oracles of this Elean soothsayer, and, on the following morning, to give battle to the Greeks. Acting against one superstition, he sagaciously, however, sought to enlist on his behalf another; and, from the decision of a mortal, he appealed to the ambiguous oracles of the Delphic god, which had ever one interpretation for the enterprise and another for the success.

XIV. Herodotus, in his animated and graphic strain, says,

> The watches of the night were set, the night itself was far advanced —a universal and utter stillness prevailed throughout the army, buried in repose—when Alexander, the Macedonian prince, rode secretly from the Persian camp, and, coming to the outposts of the Athenians, whose line was immediately opposed to his own, demanded an audience of their commanders. This obtained, the Macedonian thus addressed them:—"I am come to inform you of a secret you must impart to Pausanias alone. From remote antiquity I am of Grecian lineage. I am solicitous of the safety of Greece. Long since, but for the auguries, would Mardonius have given battle. Regarding these no longer, he will attack you early on the morning. Be prepared. If he change his purpose, remain as you are—he has provisions only for a few days more. Should the event of war prove favourable, you will but deem it fitting to make some effort for the independence of one who exposes himself to so great a peril for the purpose of apprising you of the intentions of the foe. I am Alexander of Macedon." Thus saying, the horseman returned to the Persian camp. The Athenian leaders hastened to Pausanias, and informed him of what they had heard.

The Spartan does not appear, according to the strong expressions[13] of Herodotus, to have received the intelligence with the customary dauntlessness of his race. He feared the Persians, he was unacquainted with their mode of warfare, and he proposed to the Athenians to change posts with the Lacedæmonians: "For you", said he, "have before contended with the Mede, and your experience of their warfare you learned at Marathon. We, on the other hand, have fought against the Bœotians and Thessalians [opposed to the left wing]. Let us then change our stations."

At first the Athenian officers were displeased at the offer, not from terror, but from pride; and it seemed to them as if they were shifted, like Helots,

13 Herod., ix. 45.

from post to post at the Spartan's pleasure.[14] But Aristides, whose power of persuasion consisted chiefly in appeals, not to the baser, but the loftier passions, and who, in swaying, exalted his countrymen—represented to them that the right wing, which the Spartan proposed to surrender, was, in effect, the station of command.

"And are you", he said, "not pleased with the honour you obtain, nor sensible of the advantage of contending, not against the sons of Greece, but the barbarian invader?"

These words animated those whom the Athenian addressed; they instantly agreed to exchange posts with the Spartans, and "to fight for the trophies of Marathon and Salamis".[15]

XV. As, in the dead of night, the Athenians marched to their new station, they exhorted each other to valour and to the recollection of former victories. But Mardonius, learning from deserters the change of position, moved his Persians opposite the Spartans; and Pausanias again returning to the right, Mardonius pursued a similar manoeuvre. Thus the day was consumed without an action. The troops having resumed their former posts, Mardonius sent a herald to the Spartans, chiding them for their cowardice, and proposing that an allotted number of Persians should meet an equal number of Spartans in battle, and whoever conquered should be deemed victors over the whole adverse army.

This challenge drew no reply from the Spartans. And Mardonius, construing the silence into a proof of fear, already anticipated the victory. His cavalry, advancing upon the Greeks, distressed them from afar and in safety with their shafts and arrows. They succeeded in gaining the Gargaphian fountain, which supplied water to the Grecian army, and choked up the stream. Thus cut off from water, and, at the same time, yet more inconvenienced by the want of provisions, the convoy of which was intercepted by the Persian cavalry, the Grecian chiefs determined to shift the ground, and occupy a space which, being surrounded by rivulets, was termed the island of Oëroë,[16] and afforded an ample supply of water. This island was about a mile from their present encampment: thence they proposed to detach half their army to relieve a convoy of provisions encompassed in the mountains.

About four hours after sunset the army commenced its march; but when Pausanias gave the word to his Spartans, one officer, named Amompharetus,

---

14 Plut., in Vit. Arist.

15 This account, by Herodotus, of the contrast between the Spartan and the Athenian leaders, which is amply supported elsewhere, is, as I have before hinted, a proof of the little effect upon Spartan emulation produced by the martyrdom of Leonidas. Undoubtedly the Spartans were more terrified by the slaughter of Thermopylæ than fired by the desire of revenge.

16 "Here seem to be several islands, formed by a sluggish stream in a flat meadow. (Oëroë?) must have been of that description" (Gell's Itin., 109).

obstinately refused to stir. He alleged the customs and oaths of Sparta, and declared he would not fly from the barbarian foe, nor connive at the dishonour of Sparta.

XVI. Pausanias, though incensed at the obstinacy of the officer, was unwilling to leave him and his troop to perish; and while the dispute was still unsettled, the Athenians, suspicious of their ally, "for they knew well it was the custom of Spartans to say one thing and to think another",[17] despatched a horseman to Pausanias to learn the cause of the delay.

The messenger found the soldiers in their ranks; the leaders in violent altercation. Pausanias was arguing with Amompharetus, when the last, just as the Athenian approached, took up a huge stone with both hands, and throwing it at the feet of Pausanias, vehemently exclaimed, "With this calculus I give my suffrage against flying from the stranger." Pausanias, in great perplexity, bade the Athenian report the cause of the delay, and implore his countrymen to halt a little, that they might act in concert.

At length, towards morning, Pausanias resolved, despite Amompharetus, to commence his march. All his forces proceeded along the steep defiles at the base of Cithæron, from fear of the Persian cavalry; the more dauntless Athenians along the plain. Amompharetus, after impotent attempts to detain his men, was reluctantly compelled to follow.

XVII. Mardonius, beholding the vacant ground before him no longer bristling with the Grecian ranks, loudly vented his disdain of the cowardice of the fugitives, and instantly led his impatient army over the Asopus in pursuit. As yet, the Athenians, who had already passed the plain, were concealed by the hills; and the Tegeans and Lacedæmonians were the sole object of attack.

As the troops of Mardonius advanced, the rest of the Persian armament, deeming the task was now not to fight but to pursue, raised their standards and poured forward tumultuously, without discipline or order.

Pausanias, pressed by the Persian line, and if not of a timorous, at least of an irresolute temper, lost no time in sending to the Athenians for succour. But when the latter were on their march with the required aid, they were suddenly intercepted by the auxiliary Greeks in the Persian service, and cut off from the rescue of the Spartans.

The Spartans beheld themselves thus left unsupported with considerable alarm. Yet their force, including the Tegeans and Helots, was fifty-three thousand men. Committing himself to the gods, Pausanias ordained a solemn sacrifice, his whole army awaiting the result, while the shafts of the Persian bowmen poured on them near and fast. But the entrails presented discouraging omens, and the sacrifice was again renewed. Meanwhile the Spartans evinced their characteristic fortitude and discipline—not one man

17 Herod., ix. 54.

stirring from his ranks until the auguries should assume a more favouring aspect; all harassed, and some wounded, by the Persian arrows, they yet, seeking protection only beneath their broad bucklers, waited with a stern patience the time of their leader and of Heaven. Then fell Callicrates, the stateliest and strongest soldier in the whole army, lamenting, not death, but that his sword was as yet undrawn against the invader.

XVIII. And still sacrifice after sacrifice seemed to forbid the battle, when Pausanias, lifting his eyes, that streamed with tears, to the Temple of Juno that stood hard by, supplicated the tutelary goddess of Cithæron, that if the fates forbade the Greeks to conquer, they might at least fall like warriors.[18] And while uttering this prayer, the tokens waited for became suddenly visible in the victims, and the augurs announced the promise of coming victory.

Therewith the order of battle rang instantly through the army, and, to use the poetical comparison of Plutarch, the Spartan phalanx suddenly stood forth in its strength like some fierce animal—erecting its bristles and preparing its vengeance for the foe. The ground, broken in many steep and precipitous ridges, and intersected by the Asopus, whose sluggish stream[19] winds over a broad and rushy bed, was unfavourable to the movements of cavalry, and the Persian foot advanced therefore on the Greeks.

Drawn up in their massive phalanx, the Lacedæmonians presented an almost impenetrable body—sweeping slowly on, compact and serried— while the hot and undisciplined valour of the Persians, more fortunate in the skirmish than the battle, broke itself into a thousand waves upon that moving rock. Pouring on in small numbers at a time, they fell fast round the progress of the Greeks—their armour slight against the strong pikes of Sparta—their courage without skill—their numbers without discipline; still they fought gallantly, even when on the ground seizing the pikes with their naked hands, and with the wonderful agility which still characterizes the oriental swordsman, springing to their feet and regaining their arms when seemingly overcome—wresting away their enemies' shields, and grappling with them desperately hand to hand.

XIX. Foremost of a band of a thousand chosen Persians, conspicuous by his white charger, and still more by his daring valour, rode Mardonius, directing the attack—fiercer wherever his armour blazed. Inspired by his presence, the Persians fought worthily of their warlike fame, and, even in falling, thinned the Spartan ranks. At length the rash but gallant leader of the Asiatic armies received a mortal wound—his skull was crushed in by a stone from the hand of a Spartan.[20]

18 Plut., in Vit. Arist.
19 Sir W. Gell's Itin. of Greece.
20 Herod., ix. 62.

His chosen band, the boast of the army, fell fighting round him, but his death was the general signal of defeat and flight. Encumbered by their long robes, and pressed by the relentless conquerors, the Persians fled in disorder towards their camp, which was secured by wooden intrenchments, by gates, and towers, and walls. Here, fortifying themselves as they best might, they contended successfully, and with advantage, against the Lacedæmonians, who were ill skilled in assault and siege.

Meanwhile the Athenians obtained the victory on the plains over the Greeks of Mardonius—finding their most resolute enemy in the Thebans (three hundred of whose principal warriors fell in the field)—and now joined the Spartans at the Persian camp. The Athenians are said to have been better skilled in the art of siege than the Spartans; yet at that time their experience could scarcely have been greater. The Athenians were at all times, however, of a more impetuous temper; and the men who had "run to the charge" at Marathon were not to be baffled by the desperate remnant of their ancient foe. They scaled the walls—they effected a breach through which the Tegeans were the first to rush—the Greeks poured fast and fierce into the camp. Appalled, dismayed, stupefied by the suddenness and greatness of their loss, the Persians no longer sustained their fame—they dispersed themselves in all directions, falling, as they fled, with a prodigious slaughter, so that out of that mighty armament scarce three thousand effected an escape. We must except, however, the wary and distrustful Artabazus, who, on the first tokens of defeat, had fled with the forty thousand Parthians and Chorasmians he commanded towards Phocis, in the intention to gain the Hellespont. The Mantineans arrived after the capture of the camp, too late for their share of glory; they endeavoured to atone the loss by the pursuit of Artabazus, which was, however, ineffectual. The Eleans arrived after the Mantineans. The leaders of both these people were afterward banished.

XX. An Æginetan proposed to Pausanias to inflict on the corpse of Mardonius the same insult which Xerxes had put upon the body of Leonidas.

The Spartan indignantly refused. "After elevating my country to fame", said he, "would you have me depress it to infamy by vengeance on the body of the dead? Leonidas and Thermopylæ are sufficiently avenged by this mighty overthrow of the living."

The body of that brave and ill-fated general, the main author of the war, was removed the next day—by whose piety and to what sepulchre is unknown. The tomb of his doubtful fame is alone eternally visible along the plains of Platæa, and above the grey front of the imperishable Cithæron!

XXI. The victory won, the conquerors were dazzled by the gorgeous plunder which remained—tents and couches decorated with precious metals —cups, and vessels, and sacks of gold—and the dead themselves a booty, from the costly ornaments of their chains and bracelets, and cimeters vainly splendid—horses, and camels, and Persian women, and all the trappings and appliances by which despotism made a luxury of war.

Pausanias forbade the booty to be touched,[21] and directed the Helots to collect the treasure in one spot. But those dexterous slaves secreted many articles of value, by the purchase of which several of the Æginetans, whose avarice was sharpened by a life of commerce, enriched themselves—obtaining gold at the price of brass.

Piety dedicated to the gods a tenth part of the booty—from which was presented to the shrine of Delphi a golden tripod, resting on a three-headed snake of brass; to the Corinthian Neptune a brazen statue of the deity, seven cubits high; and to the Jupiter of Olympia a statue of ten cubits. Pausanias obtained also a tenth of the produce in each article of plunder—horses and camels, women and gold—a prize which ruined in rewarding him. The rest was divided among the soldiers, according to their merit.

So much, however, was left unappropriated in the carelessness of satiety, that, in after times, the battlefield still afforded to the search of the Platæans chests of silver and gold, and other treasures.

XXII. Taking possession of the tent of Mardonius, which had formerly been that of Xerxes, Pausanias directed the oriental slaves who had escaped the massacre to prepare a banquet after the fashion of the Persians, and as if served to Mardonius. Besides this gorgeous feast, the Spartan ordered his wonted repast to be prepared; and then, turning to the different chiefs, exclaimed—"See the folly of the Persian, who forsook such splendour to plunder such poverty."

The story has in it something of the sublime. But the austere Spartan was soon corrupted by the very luxuries he affected to disdain. It is often that we despise today what we find it difficult to resist tomorrow.

XXIII. The task of reward to the living completed, the Greeks proceeded to that of honour to the dead. In three trenches the Lacedæmonians were interred; one contained those who belonged to a class in Sparta called "the Knights",[22] of whom two hundred had conducted Themistocles to Tegea (among these was the stubborn Amompharetus); the second, the other Spartans; the third, the Helots. The Athenians, Tegeans, Megarians, Phliasians, each had their single and separate places of sepulture, and, over all, barrows of earth were raised. Subsequently, tribes and states that had shared indeed the final battle or the previous skirmishes, but without the glory of a loss of life, erected cenotaphs to imaginary dead in that illustrious burial-field. Among those spurious monuments was one dedicated to the Æginetans.

---

21 The Tegeans had already seized the tent of Mardonius, possessing themselves especially of a curious brazen manger, from which the Persian's horse was fed, and afterward dedicated to the Alean Minerva.

22 I adopt the reading of Valcknaër, "$\tau o \grave{u}s$ $\dot{i}\pi\pi\acute{e}as$". The Spartan "Knights", in number three hundred, had nothing to do with the cavalry, but fought on foot or on horseback, as required (Dionys. Hal., xi. 13). They formed the royal body-guard.

Aristodemus, the Spartan who had returned safe from Thermopylæ, fell at Platæa, the most daring of the Greeks on that day, voluntarily redeeming a dishonoured life by a glorious death. But to his manes alone of the Spartan dead no honours were decreed.

XXIV. Plutarch relates that a dangerous dispute ensued between the Spartans and Athenians as to their relative claim to the Aristeia, or first military honours; the question was decided by awarding them to the Platæans—a state of which none were jealous; from a similar motive, ordinary men are usually found possessed of the honours due to the greatest.

More important than the Aristeia, had the spirit been properly maintained, were certain privileges then conferred on Platæa. Thither, in a subsequent assembly of the allies, it was proposed by Aristides that deputies from the states of Greece should be annually sent to sacrifice to Jupiter the Deliverer, and confer upon the general politics of Greece. There, every fifth year, should be celebrated games in honour of Liberty; while the Platæans themselves, exempted from military service, should be deemed, so long as they fulfilled the task thus imposed upon them, a sacred and inviolable people. Thus Platæa nominally became a second Elis—its battle-field another Altis. Aristides, at the same time, sought to enforce the large and thoughtful policy commenced by Themistocles. He endeavoured to draw the jealous states of Greece into a common and perpetual league, maintained against all invaders by a standing force of one thousand cavalry, one hundred ships, and ten thousand heavy-armed infantry.

XXV. An earnest and deliberate council was now held, in which it was resolved to direct the victorious army against Thebes, and demand the persons of those who had sided with the Mede. Fierce as had been the hostility of that state to the Hellenic liberties, its sin was that of the oligarchy rather than the people. The most eminent of these traitors to Greece were Timagenidas and Attaginus, and the allies resolved to destroy the city unless those chiefs were given up to justice.

THEBES BESIEGED
BY THE ATHENIANS

On the eleventh day from the battle they sat down before Thebes, and on the refusal of the inhabitants to surrender the chiefs so justly obnoxious, laid waste the Theban lands.

Whatever we may think of the conduct of Timagenidas in espousing the cause of the invaders of Greece, we must give him the praise of a disinterested gallantry, which will remind the reader of the siege of Calais by Edward III, and the generosity of Eustace de St Pierre. He voluntarily proposed to surrender himself to the besiegers.

The offer was accepted. Timagenidas and several others were delivered to Pausanias, removed to Corinth, and there executed—a stern but salutary example. Attaginus saved himself by flight. His children, given up to Pausanias, were immediately dismissed. "Infants", said the Spartan, "could not possibly have conspired against us with the Mede."

While Thebes preserved herself from destruction, Artabazus succeeded in effecting his return to Asia, his troop greatly reduced by the attacks of the Thracians, and the excesses of famine and fatigue.

XXVI. On the same day as that on which the battle of Platæa crushed the land-forces of Persia, a no less important victory was gained over their fleet at Mycale in Ionia.

BATTLE OF MYCALE   It will be remembered that Leotychides, the Spartan king, and the Athenian Xanthippus had conducted the Grecian navy to Delos. There anchored, they received a deputation from Samos, among whom was Hegesistratus, the son of Aristagoras. These ambassadors declared that all the Ionians waited only the moment to revolt from the Persian yoke, and that the signal would be found in the first active measures of the Grecian confederates. Leotychides, induced by these representations, received the Samians into the general league, and set sail to Samos. There, drawn up in line of battle, near the Temple of Juno, they prepared to hazard an engagement.

But the Persians, on their approach, retreated to the continent, in order to strengthen themselves with their land-forces, which, to the amount of sixty thousand, under the command of the Persian Tigranes, Xerxes had stationed at Mycale for the protection of Ionia.

Arrived at Mycale, they drew their ships to land, fortifying them with strong intrenchments and barricades, and then sanguinely awaited the result.

The Greeks, after a short consultation, resolved upon pursuit. Approaching the enemy's station, they beheld the sea deserted, the ships secured by intrenchments, and long ranks of infantry ranged along the shore. Leotychides, by a herald, exhorted the Ionians in the Persian service to remember their common liberties, and that on the day of battle their watchword would be "Hebe".

The Persians, distrusting these messages, though uttered in a tongue they understood not, and suspecting the Samians, took their arms from the latter: and, desirous of removing the Milesians to a distance, entrusted them with the guard of the paths to the heights of Mycale. Using these precautions against the desertion of their allies, the Persians prepared for battle.

The Greeks were anxious and fearful not so much for themselves as for their countrymen in Bœotia, opposed to the mighty force of Mardonius. But a report spreading through the camp that a complete victory had been obtained in that territory (an artifice, most probably, of Leotychides), animated their courage and heightened their hopes.

The Athenians, who, with the troops of Corinth, Sicyon, and Trœzene, formed half the army, advanced by the coast and along the plain—the Lacedæmonians by the more steep and wooded courses; and while the latter were yet on their march, the Athenians were already engaged at the entrenchments.

357

Inspired not more by enmity than emulation, the Athenians urged each other to desperate feats—that they, and not the Spartans, might have the honours of the day. They poured fiercely on—after an obstinate and equal conflict, drove back the foe to the barricades that girt their ships, stormed the entrenchments, carried the wall, and, rushing in with their allies, put the barbarians to disorderly and rapid flight. The proper Persians, though but few in number, alone stood their ground—and even when Tigranes himself was slain, resolutely fought on until the Lacedæmonians entered the intrenchment, and all who had survived the Athenian, perished by the Spartan, sword.

The disarmed Samians, as soon as the fortunes of the battle became apparent, gave all the assistance they could render to the Greeks; the other Ionians seized the same opportunity to revolt and turn their arms against their allies. In the mountain defiles the Milesians intercepted their own fugitive allies, consigning them to the Grecian sword, and active beyond the rest in their slaughter. So relentless and so faithless are men, compelled to servitude, when the occasion summons them to be free.

XXVII. This battle, in which the Athenians were pre-eminently distinguished, was followed up by the conflagration of the Persian ships and the collection of the plunder. The Greeks then retired to Samos. Here deliberating, it was proposed by the Peloponnesian leaders that Ionia should henceforth, as too dangerous and remote to guard, be abandoned to the barbarian, and that, in recompense, the Ionians should be put into possession of the maritime coasts of those Grecian states which had sided with the Mede. The Athenians resisted so extreme a proposition, and denied the power of the Peloponnesians to dispose of Athenian colonies.

The point was surrendered by the Peloponnesians; the Ionians of the continent were left to make their own terms with the barbarian, but the inhabitants of the isles which had assisted against the Mede were received into the general confederacy, bound by a solemn pledge never to desert it. The fleet then sailed to the Hellespont, with the design to destroy the bridge, which they believed still existent. Finding it, however, already broken, Leotychides and the Peloponnesians returned to Greece. The Athenians resolved to attempt the recovery of the colony of Miltiades in the Chersonesus. The Persians collected their whole remaining force at Sestos, the strongest hold in that peninsula—the Athenians laid siege to it, and, after enduring a famine so obstinate that the cordage, or rather straps, of their bedding were consumed for food, the Persians evacuated the town, which the inhabitants then cheerfully surrendered.

SIEGE OF SESTOS

Thus concluding their victories, the Athenians returned to Greece, carrying with them a vast treasure, and, not the least precious relics, the fragments and cables of the Hellespontic bridge, to be suspended in their temples.

XXVIII. Lingering at Sardis, Xerxes beheld the scanty and exhausted remnants of his mighty force, the fugitives of the fatal days of Mycale and

CONCLUSION OF THE
PERSIAN WAR

Platæa. The army over which he had wept in the zenith of his power, had fulfilled the prediction of his tears: and the armed might of Media and Egypt, of Lydia and Assyria, was now no more!

So concluded the great Persian invasion—that war the most memorable in the history of mankind, whether from the vastness or from the failure of its designs. We now emerge from the poetry that belongs to early Greece, through the mists of which the forms of men assume proportions as gigantic as indistinct. The enchanting Herodotus abandons us, and we do not yet permanently acquire, in the stead of his romantic and wild fidelity, the elaborate and sombre statesmanship of the calm Thucydides. Henceforth we see more of the beautiful and the wise, less of the wonderful and vast. What the heroic age is to tradition, the Persian invasion is to history.

Book IV

FROM THE END OF THE PERSIAN INVASION TO THE DEATH OF CIMON, BC 479–BC 449

CHAPTER I

Remarks on the effects of war—state of Athens—interference
of Sparta with respect to the fortification of Athens—
dexterous conduct of Themistocles—the new harbour of the
Piræus—proposition of the Spartans in the Amphictyonic
Council defeated by Themistocles—allied fleet at Cyprus and
Byzantium—Pausanias—alteration in his character—his ambitious views and treason—the revolt of the Ionians from the
Spartan command—Pausanias recalled—Dorcis replaces him—
the Athenians rise to the head of the Ionian league—Delos
made the senate and treasury of the allies—able and prudent
management of Aristides—Cimon succeeds to the command
of the fleet—character of Cimon—Eion besieged—Scyros colonized by Atticans—supposed discovery of the bones of Theseus
—declining power of Themistocles—democratic change in the
constitution—Themistocles ostracized—death of Aristides

I. It is to the imperishable honour of the French philosophers of the last
century, that, above all the earlier teachers of mankind, they advocated those

REMARKS ON THE
EFFECTS OF WAR

profound and permanent interests of the human race which
are inseparably connected with a love of PEACE; that they
stripped the image of WAR of the delusive glory which it
took, in the primitive ages of society, from the passions of savages and the
enthusiasm of poets, and turned our contemplation from the fame of the
individual hero to the wrongs of the butchered millions. But their zeal for
that HUMANITY, which those free and bold thinkers were the first to make
the vital principle of a philosophical school, led them into partial and hasty
views, too indiscriminately embraced by their disciples; and, in condemning
the evils, they forgot the advantages of war. The misfortunes of one generation are often necessary to the prosperity of another. The stream of blood
fertilizes the earth over which it flows, and war has been at once the scourge
and the civilizer of the world: sometimes it enlightens the invader, sometimes the invaded; and forces into sudden and brilliant action the arts and
the virtues that are stimulated by the invention of necessity—matured by
the energy of distress. What adversity is to individuals, war often is to
nations: uncertain in its consequences, it is true that, with some, it subdues
and crushes, but with others it braces and exalts. Nor are the greater and

363

more illustrious elements of character in men or in states ever called prominently forth without something of that bitter and sharp experience which hardens the more robust properties of the mind, which refines the more subtle and sagacious. Even when these—the armed revolutions of the world—are most terrible in their results—destroying the greatness and the liberties of one people—they serve, sooner or later, to produce a counteracting rise and progress in the fortunes of another; as the sea here advances, there recedes, swallowing up the fertilities of this shore to increase the territories of that; and fulfilling, in its awful and appalling agency, that mandate of human destinies which ordains all things to be changed and nothing to be destroyed. Without the invasion of Persia, Greece might have left no annals, and the modern world might search in vain for inspirations from the ancient.

II. When the deluge of the Persian arms rolled back to its eastern bed, and the world was once more comparatively at rest, the continent of Greece rose visibly and majestically above the rest of the civilized earth. Afar in the Latian plains, the infant state of Rome was silently and obscurely struggling into strength against the neighbouring and petty states in which the old Etrurian civilization was rapidly passing to decay. The genius of Gaul and Germany, yet unredeemed from barbarism, lay scarce known, save where colonized by Greeks, in the gloom of its woods and wastes. The pride of Carthage had been broken by a signal defeat in Sicily; and Gelo, the able and astute tyrant of Syracuse, maintained in a Grecian colony the splendour of the Grecian name.

The ambition of Persia, still the great monarchy of the world, was permanently checked and crippled; the strength of generations had been wasted, and the immense extent of the empire only served yet more to sustain the general peace from the exhaustion of its forces. The defeat of Xerxes paralysed the East.

Thus Greece was left secure, and at liberty to enjoy the tranquillity it had acquired, and to direct to the arts of peace the novel and amazing energies which had been prompted by the dangers and exalted by the victories of war.

III. The Athenians, now returned to their city, saw before them the arduous task of rebuilding its ruins and restoring its wasted lands. The

STATE OF ATHENS

vicissitudes of the war had produced many silent and internal as well as exterior changes. Many great fortunes had been broken; and the ancient spirit of the aristocracy had received no inconsiderable shock in the power of new families; the fame of the baseborn and democratic Themistocles, and the victories which a whole people had participated, broke up much of the prescriptive and venerable sanctity attached to ancestral names and to particular families. This was salutary to the spirit of enterprise in all classes. The ambition of the great was excited to restore by some active means their broken fortunes and decaying influence—the energies of the humbler ranks, already aroused by their new importance, were stimulated to maintain and to increase it. It was the very crisis in which a new direction might be given to the habits and the character of a whole people; and to seize all the advantages of that crisis, fate, in Themistocles, had allotted to Athens a man whose qualities were not only pre-eminently great in themselves, but peculiarly adapted to the circumstances of the time. And, as I have elsewhere remarked, it is indeed the nature and prerogative of free states to concentrate the popular will into something of the unity of despotism, by producing, one after another, a series of representatives of the wants and exigencies of the hour—each leading his generation, but only while he sympathizes with its will; and either baffling or succeeded by his rivals, not in proportion as he excels or he is outshone in genius, but as he gives or ceases to give to the widest range of the legislative power the most concentrated force of the executive; thus uniting the desires of the greatest number under the administration of the narrowest possible control; the constitution popular—the government absolute, but responsible.

IV. In the great events of the late campaign, we have lost sight of the hero of Salamis.[1] But the Persian war was no sooner ended than we find Themistocles the most prominent citizen of Athens—a sufficient proof that his popularity had not yet diminished, and that his absence from Platæa was owing to no popular caprice or party triumph.

V. In the sweeping revenge of Mardonius, even private houses had been destroyed, excepting those which had served as lodgments for the Persian nobles.[2] Little of the internal city, less of the outward walls was spared. As soon as the barbarians had quitted their territory, the citizens flocked back with their slaves and families from the various places of refuge; and the first care was to rebuild the city. They were already employed upon this necessary task when ambassadors arrived from Sparta, whose vigilant government, ever jealous of a rival, beheld with no unreasonable alarm the increasing navy and the growing fame of a people hitherto undeniably inferior to the power of Lacedæmon. And the fear that was

INTERFERENCE OF SPARTA
WITH RESPECT TO THE
FORTIFICATION OF ATHENS

---

1 Mr Mitford attributes his absence from the scene to some jealousy of the honours he received at Sparta, and the vainglory with which he bore them. But the vague observations in the authors he refers to by no means bear out this conjecture, nor does it seem probable that the jealousy was either general or keen enough to effect so severe a loss to the public cause. Menaced with grave and imminent peril, it was not while the Athenians were still in the camp that they would have conceived all the petty envies of the forum. The jealousies Themistocles excited were of much later date. It is probable that at this period he was entrusted with the very important charge of watching over and keeping together that considerable but scattered part of the Athenian population which was not engaged either at Mycale or Platæa.

2 Thucyd., i. 89.

secretly cherished by that imperious nation was yet more anxiously nursed by the subordinate allies.[3] Actuated by their own and the general apprehensions, the Spartans therefore now requested the Athenians to desist from the erection of their walls. Nor was it without a certain grace, and a plausible excuse, that the government of a city, itself unwalled, inveighed against the policy of walls for Athens. The Spartan ambassadors urged that fortified towns would become strongholds to the barbarian, should he again invade them; and the walls of Athens might be no less useful to him than he had found the ramparts of Thebes. The Peloponnesus, they asserted, was the legitimate retreat and the certain resource of all; and, unwilling to appear exclusively jealous of Athens, they requested the Athenians not only to desist from their own fortifications, but to join with them in razing every fortification without the limit of the Peloponnesus.

It required not a genius so penetrating as that of Themistocles to divine at once the motive of the demand, and the danger of a peremptory refusal. He persuaded the Athenians to reply that they would send ambassadors to debate the affair; and dismissed the Spartans without further explanation. Themistocles next recommended to the senate[4] that he himself might be one of the ambassadors sent to Sparta, and that those associated with him in the mission (for it was not the custom of Greece to vest embassies in individuals) should be detained at Athens until the walls were carried to a height sufficient, at least, for ordinary defence. He urged his countrymen to suspend for this great task the completion of all private edifices—nay, to spare no building, private or public, from which materials might be adequately selected. The whole population, slaves, women, and children, were to assist in the labour.

VI. This counsel adopted, he sketched an outline of the conduct he himself intended to pursue, and departed for Sparta. His colleagues, no less

DEXTEROUS CONDUCT
OF THEMISTOCLES

important than Aristides, and Abronychus, a distinguished officer in the late war, were to follow at the time agreed on.

Arrived in the Laconian capital, Themistocles demanded no public audience, avoided all occasions of opening the questions in dispute, and screened the policy of delay beneath the excuse that his colleagues were not yet arrived —that he was incompetent to treat without their counsel and concurrence— and that doubtless they would speedily appear in Sparta.

When we consider the shortness of the distance between the states, the communications the Spartans would receive from the neighbouring Æginetans, more jealous than themselves, and the astute and proverbial sagacity of the Spartan council—it is impossible to believe that, for so long

3 Ibid., i. 90.
4 Diod. Sic., xi; Thucyd., i. 90.

a period as, with the greatest expedition, must have elapsed from the departure of Themistocles to the necessary progress in the fortifications, the ephors could have been ignorant of the preparations at Athens or the designs of Themistocles. I fear, therefore, that we must believe, with Theopompus,[5] that Themistocles, the most expert briber of his time, heightened that esteem which Thucydides assures us the Spartans bore him, by private and pecuniary negotiations with the ephors. At length, however, such decided and unequivocal intelligence of the progress of the walls arrived at Sparta, that the ephors could no longer feel or affect incredulity.

Themistocles met the remonstrances of the Spartans by an appearance of candour mingled with disdain. "Why", said he, "give credit to these idle rumours? Send to Athens some messengers of your own, in whom you can confide; let them inspect matters with their own eyes, and report to you accordingly."

The ephors (not unreluctantly, if the assertion of Theopompus may be credited) yielded to so plausible a suggestion, and in the meanwhile the crafty Athenian despatched a secret messenger to Athens, urging the government to detain the Spartan ambassadors with as little semblance of design as possible, and by no means to allow their departure until the safe return of their own mission to Sparta. For it was by no means improbable that, without such hostages, even the ephors, however powerful and however influenced, might not be enabled, when the Spartans generally were made acquainted with the deceit practised upon them, to prevent the arrest of the Athenian delegates.[6]

At length the walls, continued night and day with incredible zeal and toil, were sufficiently completed; and disguise, no longer possible, was no longer useful. Themistocles demanded the audience he had hitherto deferred, and boldly avowed that Athens was now so far fortified as to protect its citizens. "In future", he added, haughtily, "when Sparta or our other confederates send ambassadors to Athens, let them address us as a people well versed in our own interests and the interests of our common Greece. When we deserted Athens for our ships, we required and obtained no Lacedæmonian succours to support our native valour; in all subsequent measures, to whom have we shown ourselves inferior, whether in the council or the field? At present we have judged it expedient to fortify our city, rendering it thus more secure for ourselves and our allies. Nor would it be possible, with a

---

5 Ap. Plut., in Vit. Them.

6 Diodorus (xi) tells us that the Spartan ambassadors, indulging in threatening and violent language at perceiving the walls so far advanced, were arrested by the Athenians, who declared they would only release them on receiving back safe and uninjured their own ambassadors.

strength inferior to that of any rival power, adequately to preserve and equally to adjust the balance of the liberties of Greece.[7]

Contending for this equality, he argued that either all the cities in the Lacedæmonian league should be dismantled of their fortresses, or that it should be conceded, that in erecting fortresses for herself Athens had rightly acted.

VII. The profound and passionless policy of Sparta forbade all outward signs of unavailing and unreasonable resentment. The Spartans, therefore, replied with seeming courtesy, that "in their embassy they had not sought to dictate, but to advise—that their object was the common good"; and they accompanied their excuses with professions of friendship for Athens, and panegyrics on the Athenian valour in the recent war. But the anger they forbore to show only rankled the more bitterly within.[8]

The ambassadors of either state returned home; and thus the mingled firmness and craft of Themistocles, so well suited to the people with whom he had to deal, preserved his country from the present jealousies of a yet more deadly and implacable foe than the Persian king, and laid the foundation of that claim of equality with the most eminent state of Greece, which he hastened to strengthen and enlarge.

The ardour of the Athenians in their work of fortification had spared no material which had the recommendation of strength. The walls everywhere presented, and long continued to exhibit, an evidence of the haste in which they were built. Motley and rough hewn, and uncouthly piled, they recalled, age after age, to the traveller the name of the ablest statesman and the most heroic days of Athens. There, at frequent intervals, would he survey stones wrought in the rude fashion of former times—ornaments borrowed from the antique edifices demolished by the Mede—and frieze and column plucked from dismantled sepulchres; so that even the dead contributed from their tombs to the defence of Athens.

VIII. Encouraged by the new popularity and honours which followed the success of his mission. Themistocles now began to consummate the vast schemes he had formed, not only for the aggrandizement of his country, but for the change in the manners of the citizens. All that is left to us of this wonderful man proves that, if excelled by others in austere virtue or in dazzling accomplishment, he stands unrivalled for the profound and far-sighted nature of his policy. He seems, unlike most of his brilliant countrymen, to have been little influenced by the sallies of impulse or the miserable expediencies of faction —his schemes denote a mind acting on gigantic systems; and it is astonishing with what virtuous motives and with what prophetic art he worked

THE NEW HARBOUR
OF THE PIRÆUS

7 Thucyd., i. 91.
8 Ibid., i. 92.

through petty and (individually considered) dishonest means to grand and permanent results. He stands out to the gaze of time, the model of what a great and fortunate statesman should be, so long as mankind have evil passions as well as lofty virtues, and the state that he seeks to serve is surrounded by powerful and restless foes, whom it is necessary to overreach where it is dangerous to offend.

In the year previous to the Persian war, Themistocles had filled the office of archon,[9] and had already in that year planned the construction of a harbour in the ancient deme of Piræus,[10] for the convenience of the fleet which Athens had formed. Late events had frustrated the continuance of the labour, and Themistocles now resolved to renew and complete it, probably on a larger and more elaborate scale.

The port of Phalerum had hitherto been the main harbour of Athens—one wholly inadequate to the new navy she had acquired; another inlet, Munychia, was yet more inconvenient. But equally at hand was the capacious, though neglected port of Piræus, so formed by nature as to permit of a perfect fortification against a hostile fleet. Of Piræus, therefore, Themistocles now designed to construct the most ample and the most advantageous harbour throughout all Greece. He looked upon this task as the foundation of his favourite and most ambitious project, viz., the securing to Athens the sovereignty of the sea.[11]

9 Schol. ad Thucyd., i. 93. See Clinton, Fasti Hellenici, vol. ii, Introduction, pp. 13 and 14. Mr Thirlwall, vol. ii, p. 401, disputes the date for the archonship of Themistocles given by Mr Clinton and confirmed by the scholiast on Thucydides. He adopts (p. 366) the date which M. Boeckh founds upon Philochorus, viz., BC 493. But the Themistocles who was archon in that year is evidently another person from the Themistocles of Salamis; for in 493 that hero was about twenty-one, an age at which the bastard of Neocles might be driving courtesans in a chariot (as is recorded in Athenæus), but was certainly not archon of Athens. As for M. Boeckh's proposed emendation, quoted so respectfully by Mr Thirlwall, by which we are to read Ὑβριλίδου for Κέβριδος, it is an assumption so purely fanciful as to require no argument for refusing it belief. Mr Clinton's date for the archonship of the great Themistocles is the one most supported by internal evidence—first, by the blanks of the years 481–482 in the list of archons; second, by the age, the position, and repute of Themistocles in BC 481, two years after the ostracism of his rival Aristides. If it were reduced to a mere contest of probabilities between Mr Clinton on one side and M. Boeckh and Mr Thirlwall on the other, which is the more likely, that Themistocles should have been chief archon of Athens at twenty-one or at thirty-three—before the battle of Marathon or after his triumph over Aristides? In fact, a schoolboy knows that at twenty-one (and Themistocles was certainly not older in 493) no Athenian could have been archon. In all probability Κέβριδος is the right reading in Philochorus, and furnishes us with the name of the archon in BC 487 or 486, which years have hitherto been chronological blanks, so far as the Athenian archons are concerned.
10 Paus., i. 1.
11 Diod., Sic., xi.

The completion of the port—the increased navy which the construction of the new harbour would induce—the fame already acquired by Athens in maritime warfare, encouraging attention to naval discipline and tactics—proffered a splendid opening to the ambition of a people at once enterprising and commercial. Themistocles hoped that the results of his policy would enable the Athenians to gain over their own offspring, the Ionian colonies, and by their means to deliver from the Persian yoke, and permanently attach to the Athenian interest, all the Asiatic Greeks. Extending his views, he beheld the various insular states united to Athens by a vast maritime power, severing themselves from Lacedæmon, and following the lead of the Attican republic. He saw his native city thus supplanting, by a naval force, the long-won pre-eminence and iron supremacy of Sparta upon land, and so extending her own empire, while she sapped secretly and judiciously the authority of the most formidable of her rivals.

IX. But in the execution of these grand designs Themistocles could not but anticipate considerable difficulties: first, in the jealousy of the Spartans; and, second, in the popular and long-rooted prejudices of the Athenians themselves. Hitherto they had discouraged maritime affairs, and their more popular leaders had directed attention to agricultural pursuits. We may suppose, too, that the mountaineers, or agricultural party, not the least powerful, would resist so great advantages to the faction of the coastmen, if acquainted with all the results which the new policy would produce. Nor could so experienced a leader of mankind be insensible of those often not insalutary consequences of a free state in the changing humours of a wide democracy—their impatience at pecuniary demands—their quick and sometimes uncharitable apprehensions of the motives of their advisers. On all, accounts it was necessary, therefore, to act with as much caution as the task would admit—rendering the design invidious neither to foreign nor to domestic jealousies. Themistocles seemed to have steered his course through every difficulty with his usual address. Stripping the account of Diodorus[12] of its improbable details, it appears credible at least that Themistocles secured, in the first instance, the co-operation of Xanthippus and Aristides, the heads of the great parties generally opposed to his measures, and that he won the democracy to consent that the outline of his schemes should not be submitted to the popular assembly, but to the council of Five Hundred. It is perfectly clear, however, that, as soon as the plan was carried into active operation, the Athenians could not, as Diodorus would lead us to suppose, have been kept in ignorance of its nature; and all of the tale of Diodorus to which we can lend our belief is, that the people permitted the Five Hundred to examine the project, and that the popular assembly ratified the approbation of that senate without inquiring the reasons upon which it was founded.

12 Diod. Sic., xi.

X. The next care of Themistocles was to anticipate the jealousy of Sparta, and forestall her interference. According to Diodorus, he despatched, therefore, ambassadors to Lacedæmon, representing the advantages of forming a port which might be the common shelter of Greece should the barbarian renew his incursions; but it is so obvious that Themistocles could hardly disclose to Sparta the very project he at first concealed from the Athenians, that while we may allow the fact that Themistocles treated with the Spartans, we must give him credit, at least, for more crafty diplomacy than that ascribed to him by Diodorus.[13] But whatever the pretexts with which he sought to amuse or beguile the Spartan government, they appear at least to have been successful. And the customary indifference of the Spartans towards maritime affairs was strengthened at this peculiar time by engrossing anxieties as to the conduct of Pausanias. Thus Themistocles, safe alike from foreign and from civil obstacles, pursued with activity the execution of his schemes. The Piræus was fortified by walls of amazing thickness, so as to admit two carts abreast. Within, the entire structure was composed of solid masonry, hewn square, so that each stone fitted exactly, and was further strengthened on the outside by cramps of iron. The walls were never carried above half the height originally proposed. But the whole was so arranged as to form a fortress against assault, too fondly deemed impregnable, and to be adequately manned by the smallest possible number of citizens; so that the main force might, in time of danger, be spared to the fleet.

Thus Themistocles created a sea-fortress more important than the city itself, conformably to the advice he frequently gave to the Athenians, that, if hard pressed by land, they should retire to this arsenal, and rely, against all hostilities, on their naval force.[14]

The new port, which soon bore the ambitious title of the Lower City, was placed under the directions of Hippodamus, a Milesian, who, according to Aristotle,[15] was the first author who, without any knowledge of practical affairs, wrote upon the theory of government. Temples,[16] a market-place,

13 Diod. Sic., xi. The reader will perceive that I do not agree with Mr Thirlwall and some other scholars, for whose general opinion I have the highest respect, in rejecting altogether, and with contempt, the account of Diodorus as to the precautions of Themistocles. It seems to me highly probable that the main features of the story are presented to us faithfully: first, that it was not deemed expedient to detail to the popular assembly all the objects and motives of the proposed construction of the new port; and, second, that Themistocles did not neglect to send ambassadors to Sparta, though certainly not with the intention of dealing more frankly with the Spartans than he had done with the Athenians.
14 Thucyd., i.
15 Aristot. Pol., ii. Aristotle deems the speculations of the philosophical architect worthy of a severe and searching criticism.
16 Of all the temples, those of Minerva and Jupiter were the most remarkable in the time of Pausanias. There were then two market-places. See Paus., i. 1.

even a theatre, distinguished and enriched the new town. And the population that filled it were not long before they contracted and established a character for themselves different in many traits and attributes from the citizens of the ancient Athens—more bold, wayward, innovating, and tumultuous.

But if Sparta deemed it prudent, at present, to avoid a direct assumption of influence over Athens, her scheming councils were no less bent, though

PROPOSITION OF THE SPAR-
TANS IN THE AMPHICTYO-
NIC COUNCIL DEFEATED BY
THEMISTOCLES

by indirect and plausible means, to the extension of her own power. To use the simile applied to one of her own chiefs, where the lion's skin fell short, she sought to eke it by the fox's.

At the assembly of the Amphictyons, the Lacedæmonian delegates moved that all those states who had not joined in the anti-Persic confederacy should be expelled the council. Under this popular and patriotic proposition was sagaciously concealed the increase of the Spartan authority; for had the Thessalians, Argives, and Thebans (voices ever counter to the Lacedæmonians) been expelled the assembly, the Lacedæmonian party would have secured the preponderance of votes, and the absolute dictation of that ancient council.[17]

But Themistocles, who seemed endowed with a Spartan sagacity for the foiling the Spartan interests, resisted the proposition by arguments no less popular. He represented to the delegates that it was unjust to punish states for the errors of their leaders—that only thirty-one cities had contributed to the burden of the war, and many of those inconsiderable—that it was equally dangerous and absurd to exclude from the general Grecian councils the great proportion of the Grecian states.

The arguments of Themistocles prevailed, but his success stimulated yet more sharply against him the rancour of the Lacedæmonians; and, unable to resist him abroad, they thenceforth resolved to undermine his authority at home.

XI. While, his danger invisible, Themistocles was increasing with his own power that of the state, the allies were bent on new enterprises and

ALLIED FLEET AT CYPRUS
AND BYZANTIUM

continued retribution. From Persia, now humbled and exhausted, it was the moment to wrest the Grecian towns, whether in Europe or in Asia, over which she yet arrogated dominion—it was resolved, therefore, to fit out a fleet, to which the Peloponnesus contributed twenty and Athens thirty vessels. Aristides presided over the latter; Pausanias was commander-in-chief; many other of the allies joined the expedition. They sailed to Cyprus, and

---

17 Yet at this time the Amphictyonic Council was so feeble that, had the Spartans succeeded, they would have made but a hollow acquisition of authority; unless, indeed, with the project of gaining a majority of votes, they united another for reforming or reinvigorating the institution.

reduced with ease most of the towns in that island. Thence proceeding to Byzantium, the main strength and citadel of Persia upon those coasts, and the link between her European and Asiatic dominions, they blockaded the town and ultimately carried it.

But these foreign events, however important in themselves, were trifling in comparison with a revolution which accompanied them, and which, in suddenly raising Athens to the supreme command of allied Greece, may be regarded at once as the author of the coming greatness—and the subsequent reverses—of that republic.

XII. The habits of Sparta—austere, stern, unsocial—rendered her ever more effectual in awing foes than conciliating allies; and the manners of the PAUSANIAS—ALTERATION soldiery were at this time not in any way redeemed or counterbalanced by those of the chief. Since the IN HIS CHARACTER battle of Platæa a remarkable change was apparent in Pausanias. Glory had made him arrogant, and sudden luxury ostentatious. He had graven on the golden tripod, dedicated by the confederates to the Delphic god, an inscription, claiming exclusively to himself, as the general of the Grecian army, the conquest of the barbarians—an egotism no less at variance with the sober pride of Sparta, than it was offensive to the just vanity of the allies. The inscription was afterward erased by the Spartan government, and another, citing only the names of the confederate cities, and silent as to that of Pausanias, was substituted in its place.

XIII. To a man of this arrogance, and of a grasping and already successful ambition, circumstances now presented great and irresistible temptation Though leader of the Grecian armies, he was but the uncle and proxy of the young Spartan king—the time must come when his authority would cease, and the conqueror of the superb Mardonius sink into the narrow and severe confines of a Spartan citizen. Possessed of great talents and many eminent qualities, they but served the more to discontent him with the limits of their legitimate sphere and sterility of the Spartan life. And this discontent, operating on a temper naturally haughty, evinced itself in a manner rude, overbearing, and imperious, which the spirit of his confederates was ill calculated to suffer or forgive.

But we can scarcely agree with the ancient historians in attributing the ascendency of the Athenians alone, or even chiefly, to the conduct of Pausanias. The present expedition was naval, and the greater part of the confederates at Byzantium were maritime powers. The superior fleet and the recent naval glories of the Athenians could not fail to give them, at this juncture, a moral pre-eminence over the other allies; and we shall observe that the Ionians, and those who had lately recovered their freedom from the Persian yoke,[18] were especially desirous to exchange the Spartan for the Athenian command.

18 Thucyd., i. 96.

Connected with the Athenians by origin—by maritime habits—by a kindred suavity and grace of temperament—by the constant zeal of the Athenians for their liberties (which made, indeed, the first cause of the Persian war)— it was natural that the Ionian Greeks should prefer the standard of Athens to that of a Doric state; and the proposition of the Spartans (baffled by the Athenian councils) to yield up the Ionic settlements to the barbarians, could not but bequeath a lasting resentment to those proud and polished colonies.

XIV. Aware of the offence he had given, and disgusted himself alike with his allies and his country, the Spartan chief became driven by nature and necessity to a dramatic situation, which a future Schiller may perhaps render yet more interesting than the treason of the gorgeous Wallenstein, to whose character that of Pausanias has been indirectly likened.[19] The capture of Byzantium brought the Spartan regent into contact with many captured and noble Persians,[20] among whom were some related to Xerxes himself. With these conversing, new and dazzling views were opened to his ambition. He could not but recall the example of Demaratus, whose exile from the barren dignities of Sparta had procured him the luxuries and the splendour of oriental pomp, with the delegated authority of three of the fairest cities of Æolia. Greater in renown than Demaratus, he was necessarily more aspiring in his views. Accordingly, he privately released his more exalted prisoners, pretending they had escaped, and finally explained whatever messages he had entrusted by them to Xerxes, in a letter to the king, confided to an Eretrian named Gongylus, who was versed in the language and the manners of Persia, and to whom he had already deputed the government of Byzantium. In this letter Pausanias offered to assist the king in reducing Sparta and the rest of Greece to the Persian yoke, demanding, in recompense, the hand of the king's daughter, with an adequate dowry of possessions and of power.

XV. The time had passed when a Persian monarch could deride the loftiness of a Spartan's pretensions—Xerxes received the communications with delight, and despatched Artabazus to succeed Megabates in Phrygia, and to concert with the Spartan upon the means whereby to execute their joint design.[21] But while Pausanias was in the full flush of his dazzled and grasping hopes, his fall was at hand. Occupied with his new projects, his natural haughtiness increased daily. He never accosted the officers of the allies but with abrupt and overbearing insolence; he insulted the military pride by sentencing many of the soldiers to corporeal chastisement, or to stand all day with an iron anchor on their shoulders.[22] He permitted none to

HIS AMBITIOUS VIEWS AND TREASON

---

19 Heeren, Pol. Hist. of Greece.
20 Corn. Nep., in Vit. Paus.
21 Thucyd., i. 129.
22 Plut., in Vit. Arist.

seek water, forage, or litter, until the Spartans were first supplied—those who attempted it were driven away by rods. Even Aristides, seeking to remonstrate, was repulsed rudely. "I am not at leisure", said the Spartan, with a frown.[23]

Complaints of this treatment were despatched to Sparta, and in the meanwhile the confederates, especially the officers of Chios, Samos, and Lesbos, pressed Aristides to take on himself the general command, and protect them from the Spartan's insolence. The Athenian artfully replied, that he saw the necessity of the proposition, but that it ought first to be authorized by some action which would render it impossible to recede from the new arrangement once formed.

THE REVOLT OF THE ION-
IANS FROM THE SPARTAN
COMMAND

The hint was fiercely taken; and a Samian and a Chian officer, resolving to push matters to the extreme, openly and boldly attacked the galley of Pausanias himself at the head of the fleet. Disregarding his angry menaces, now impotent, this assault was immediately followed up by a public transfer of allegiance; and the aggressors, quitting the Spartan, arrayed themselves under the Athenian, banners. Whatever might have been the consequences of this insurrection were prevented by the sudden recall of Pausanias. The accusations against him had met a ready hearing in Sparta, and that watchful government had already received intimation of his intrigues with the Mede. On his arrival in Sparta, Pausanias was immediately summoned to trial, convicted in a fine for individual and private misdemeanours, but acquitted of the principal charge of treason with the Persians—not so much from the deficiency as from the abundance of proof;[24] and it was probably prudent to avoid, if possible, the scandal which the conviction of the general might bring upon the nation.

PAUSANIAS RECALLED

The Spartans sent Dorcis, with some colleagues, to replace Pausanias in the command; but the allies were already too disgusted with the yoke of that nation to concede it. And the Athenian ascendency was hourly confirmed by the talents, the bearing, and the affable and gracious manners of Aristides. With him was joined an associate of high hereditary name and strong natural abilities, whose character it will shortly become necessary to place in detail before the reader. This co-mate was no less a person than Cimon, the son of the great Miltiades.

DORCIS REPLACES HIM

XVI. Dorcis, finding his pretensions successfully rebutted, returned home; and the Spartans, never prone to foreign enterprise, anxious for excuses to free themselves from prosecuting further the Persian war, and fearful that renewed contentions might only render yet more unpopular the Spartan name, sent forth no fresh claimants to the command; they

THE ATHENIANS RISE TO
THE HEAD OF THE IONIAN
LEAGUE

23 Ibid.
24 Thucyd., i.

affected to yield that honour, with cheerful content, to the Athenians. Thus was effected without a blow, and with the concurrence of her most dreaded rival, that eventful revolution, which suddenly raised Athens, so secondary a state before the Persian war, to the supremacy over Greece. So much, when nations have an equal glory, can the one be brought to surpass the other by the superior wisdom of individuals. The victory of Platæa was won principally by Sparta, then at the head of Greece. And the general who subdued the Persians surrendered the results of his victory to the very ally from whom the sagacious jealousy of his countrymen had sought most carefully to exclude even the precautions of defence!

XVII. Aristides, now invested with the command of all the allies, save those of the Peloponnesus who had returned home, strengthened the Athenian power by every semblance of moderation.

DELOS MADE THE SENATE AND TREASURY OF THE ALLIES

Hitherto the Grecian confederates had sent their deputies to the Peloponnesus. Aristides, instead of naming Athens, which might have excited new jealousies, proposed the sacred isle of Delos, a spot peculiarly appropriate, since it once had been the navel of the Ionian commerce, as the place of convocation and the common treasury: the temple was to be the senate house. A new distribution of the taxes levied on each state, for the maintenance of the league, was ordained. The objects of the league were both defensive and offensive: first, to guard the Ægæan coasts and the Grecian isles; and, second, to undertake measures for the further weakening of the Persian power. Aristides was elected arbitrator in the relative proportions of the general taxation. In this office, which placed the treasures of Greece at his disposal, he acted with so disinterested a virtue, that he did not even incur the suspicion of having enriched himself, and with so rare a fortune that he contented all the allies. The total, raised annually, and with the strictest impartiality, was four hundred and sixty talents (computed at about one hundred and fifteen thousand pounds).

Greece resounded with the praises of Aristides; it was afterward equally loud in reprobation of the avarice of the Athenians. For with the appointment of Aristides commenced the institution of officers styled Hellenotamiæ, or treasurers of Greece; they became a permanent magistracy—they were under the control of the Athenians; and thus that people were made at once the generals and the treasurers of Greece. But the Athenians, unconscious as yet of the power they had attained—their allies yet more blind— it seemed now, that the more the latter should confide, the more the former should forbear. So do the most important results arise from causes uncontemplated by the providence of statesmen, and hence do we learn a truth which should never be forgotten—that that power is ever the most certain of endurance and extent, the commencement of which is made popular by moderation.

ABLE AND PRUDENT MANAGEMENT OF ARISTIDES

XVIII. Thus, upon the decay of the Isthmian congress, rose into existence the great Ionian league; and thus was opened to the ambition of Athens the splendid destiny of the empire of the Grecian seas.

CIMON SUCCEEDS TO THE COMMAND OF THE FLEET

The pre-eminence of Sparta passed away from her, though invisibly and without a struggle, and, retiring within herself, she was probably unaware of the decline of her authority; still seeing her Peloponnesian allies gathering round her, subordinate and submissive, and, by refusing assistance, refusing also allegiance to the new queen of the Ionian league. His task fulfilled, Aristides probably returned to Athens, and it was at this time and henceforth that it became his policy to support the power of Cimon against the authority of Themistocles.[25] To that eupatrid, joined before with himself, was now entrusted the command of the Grecian fleet.

To great natural abilities, Cimon added every advantage of birth and circumstance. His mother was a daughter of Olorus, a Thracian prince; his father the great Miltiades. On the death of the latter,

CHARACTER OF CIMON

it is recorded, and popularly believed, that Cimon, unable to pay the fine to which Miltiades was adjudged, was detained in custody until a wealthy marriage made by his sister Elpinice, to whom he was tenderly, and ancient scandal whispered improperly, attached, released him from confinement, and the brother-in-law paid the debt. "Thus severe and harsh", says Nepos, "was his entrance upon manhood."[26] But it is very doubtful whether Cimon was ever imprisoned for the state-debt incurred by his father—and his wealth appears to have been considerable even before he regained his patrimony in the Chersonesus, or enriched himself with the Persian spoils.[27]

In early youth, like Themistocles, his conduct had been wild and dissolute;[28] and with his father from a child, he had acquired, with the experience, something of the licence, of camps. Like Themistocles also, he was little skilled in the graceful accomplishments of his countrymen; he cultivated neither the art of music, nor the brilliancies of Attic conversation; but power and fortune, which ever soften nature, afterward rendered his habits intellectual and his tastes refined. He had not the smooth and artful affability of Themistocles, but to a certain roughness of manner was conjoined that hearty and ingenuous frankness which ever conciliates mankind, especially in free states, and which is yet more popular when united to rank. He had

---

25 Plut., in Vit. Cimon. Before this period, Cimon, though rising into celebrity, could scarcely have been an adequate rival to Themistocles.

26 Corn. Nep., in Vit. Cim.

27 According to Diodorus, Cimon early in life made a very wealthy marriage; Themistocles recommended him to a rich father-in-law, in a witticism, which, with a slight variation, Plutarch has also recorded, though he does not give its application to Cimon.

28 Corn. Nep., in Vit. Cim.

distinguished himself highly by his zeal in the invasion of the Medes, and the desertion of Athens for Salamis; and his valour in the sea-fight had confirmed the promise of his previous ardour. Nature had gifted him with a handsome countenance and a majestic stature, recommendations in all, but especially in popular, states—and the son of Miltiades was welcomed, not less by the people than by the nobles, when he applied for a share in the administration of the state. Associated with Aristides, first in the embassy to Sparta, and subsequently in the expeditions to Cyprus and Byzantium, he had profited by the friendship and the lessons of that great man, to whose party he belonged, and who saw in Cimon a less invidious opponent than himself to the policy or the ambition of Themistocles.

By the advice of Aristides, Cimon early sought every means to conciliate the allies, and to pave the way to the undivided command he afterward obtained. And it is not improbable that Themistocles might willingly have ceded to him the lead in a foreign expedition, which removed from the city so rising and active an opponent. The appointment of Cimon promised to propitiate the Spartans, who ever possessed a certain party in the aristocracy of Athens—who peculiarly affected Cimon, and whose hardy character and oligarchical policy the blunt genius and hereditary prejudices of that young noble were well fitted to admire and to imitate. Cimon was, in a word, precisely the man desired by three parties as the antagonist of Themistocles, viz., the Spartans, the nobles, and Aristides, himself a host. All things conspired to raise the son of Miltiades to an eminence beyond his years, but not his capacities.

XIX. Under Cimon the Athenians commenced their command,[29] by marching against a Thracian town called Eion, situated on the banks of the river

EION BESIEGED

Strymon, and now garrisoned by a Persian noble. The town was besieged, and the inhabitants pressed by famine, when the Persian commandant, collecting his treasure upon a pile of wood, on which were placed his slaves, women, and children—set fire to the pile.[30] After this suicide, seemingly not an uncommon mode of self-slaughter in the East, the garrison surrendered, and its defenders, as usual in such warfare, were sold for slaves.

From Eion the victorious confederates proceeded to Scyros, a small island in the Ægæan, inhabited by the Dolopians, a tribe addicted to piratical

SCYROS COLONIZED
BY ATTICANS

practices, deservedly obnoxious to the traders of the Ægæan, and who had already attracted the indignation and vengeance of the Amphictyonic assembly. The isle occupied, and the pirates expelled, the territory was colonized by an Attic population.

29 Thucyd., i.
30 Ibid.; Plut., in Vit. Cim.; Diod. Sic., xi.

An ancient tradition had, as we have seen before, honoured the soil of Scyros with the possession of the bones of the Athenian Theseus—some

SUPPOSED DISCOVERY OF THE BONES OF THESEUS

years after the conquest of the isle, in the archonship of Aphepsion,[31] or Apsephion, an oracle ordained the Athenians to search for the remains of their national hero, and the skeleton of a man of great stature, with a lance of brass and a sword by its side was discovered, and immediately appropriated to Theseus. The bones were placed with great ceremony in the galley of Cimon, who was then probably on a visit of inspection to the new colony, and transported to Athens. Games were instituted in honour of this event, at which were exhibited the contests of the tragic poets; and, in the first of these, Sophocles is said to have made his earliest appearance, and gained the prize from Æschylus.

XXI. It is about the period of Cimon's conquest of Eion and Scyros that we must date the declining power of Themistocles. That remarkable man had

DECLINING POWER OF THEMISTOCLES

already added, both to domestic and to Spartan enmities, the general displeasure of the allies. After baffling the proposition of the Spartans to banish from the Amphictyonic assembly the states that had not joined in the anti-Persic confederacy, he had sailed round the isles and extorted money from such as had been guilty of Medizing: the pretext might be just, but the exactions were unpopularly levied. Nor is it improbable that the accusations against him of enriching his own coffers as well as the public treasury had some foundation. Profoundly disdaining money save as a means to an end, he was little scrupulous as to the sources whence he sustained a power which he yet applied conscientiously to patriotic purposes. Serving his country first, he also served himself; and honest upon one grand and systematic principle, he was often dishonest in details.

His natural temper was also ostentatious; like many who have risen from an origin comparatively humble, he had the vanity to seek to outshine his superiors in birth—not more by the splendour of genius than by the magnificence of parade. At the Olympic Games, the baseborn son of Neocles surpassed the pomp of the wealthy and illustrious Cimon; his table was hospitable, and his own life soft and luxuriant;[32] his retinue numerous beyond those of his contemporaries; and he adopted the manners of the noble exactly in proportion as he courted the favour of the populace. This habitual ostentation could not fail to mingle with the political hostilities of the aristocracy the disdainful jealousies of offended pride; for it is ever the weakness of the highborn to forgive less easily the being excelled in genius than the being outshone in state by those of inferior origin. The same haughtiness which offended the nobles began also to displease the people;

31 See Clinton, Fasti Hellenici, vol. ii, p. 34, in comment upon Bentley.
32 Athenæus, xii.

the superb consciousness of his own merits wounded the vanity of a nation which scarcely permitted its greatest men to share the reputation it arrogated to itself. The frequent calumnies uttered against him obliged Themistocles to refer to the actions he had performed; and what it had been illustrious to execute, it became disgustful to repeat. "Are you weary", said the great man, bitterly, "to receive benefits often from the same hand?"[33] He offended the national conceit yet more by building, in the neighbourhood of his own residence, a temple to Diana, under the name of Aristobule, or "Diana of the best counsel"; thereby appearing to claim to himself the merit of giving the best counsels.

It is probable, however, that Themistocles would have conquered all party opposition, and that his high qualities would have more than counterbalanced his defects in the eyes of the people, if he had still continued to lead the popular tide. But the time had come when the demagogue was outbid by an aristocrat—when the movement he no longer headed left him behind, and the genius of an individual could no longer keep pace with the giant strides of an advancing people.

XXII. The victory at Salamis was followed by a democratic result. That victory had been obtained by the seamen, who were mostly of the lowest of the populace—the lowest of the populace began, therefore, to claim, in political equality, the reward of military service. And Aristotle, whose penetrating intellect could not fail to notice the changes which an event so glorious to Greece produced in Athens, has adduced a similar instance of change at Syracuse, when the mariners of that state, having, at a later period, conquered the Athenians, converted a mixed republic to a pure democracy. The destruction of houses and property by Mardonius—the temporary desertion by the Athenians of their native land—the common danger and the common glory, had broken down many of the old distinctions, and the *spirit* of the nation was already far more democratic than the *constitution*. Hitherto, qualifications of property were demanded for the holding of civil offices. But after the battle of Platæa, Aristides, the leader of the aristocratic party, proposed and carried the abolition of such qualifications, allowing to all citizens, with or without property, a share in the government, and ordaining that the archons should be chosen out of the whole body; the form of investigation as to moral character was still indispensable. This change, great as it was, appears, like all aristocratic reforms, to have been a compromise[34] between concession and demand. And the prudent Aristides yielded what was inevitable, to prevent the greater danger of resistance. It may be ever remarked, that the people value more a concession from the aristocratic party than a boon from their

DEMOCRATIC CHANGE IN THE CONSTITUTION

33 Plut., in Vit. Them.
34 Plut., in Vit. Arist.

own popular leaders. The last can never equal, and the first can so easily exceed, the public expectation.

XXIII. This decree, uniting the aristocratic with the more democratic party, gave Aristides and his friends an unequivocal ascendancy over Themistocles, which, however, during the absence of Aristides and Cimon, and the engrossing excitement of events abroad, was not plainly visible for some years; and although, on his return to Athens, Aristides himself prudently forbore taking an active part against his ancient rival, he yet lent all the influence of his name and friendship to the now powerful and popular Cirnon. The victories, the manners, the wealth, the birth of the son of Miltiades were supported by his talents and his ambition. It was obvious to himself and to his party that, were Themistocles removed, Cimon would become the first citizen of Athens.

XXIV. Such were the causes that long secretly undermined, that at length openly stormed, the authority of the hero of Salamis; and at this juncture we may conclude, that the vices of his character avenged themselves on the virtues. His duplicity and spirit of intrigue, exercised on behalf of his country, it might be supposed, would hereafter be excited against it. And the pride, the ambition, the craft that had saved the people might serve to create a despot.

THEMISTOCLES OSTRACIZED

Themistocles was summoned to the ordeal of the ostracism and condemned by the majority of suffrages. Thus, like Aristides, not punished for offences, but paying the honourable penalty of rising by genius to that state of eminence which threatens danger to the equality of republics.

He departed from Athens, and chose his refuge at Argos, whose hatred to Sparta, his deadliest foe, promised him the securest protection.

XXV. Death soon afterward removed Aristides from all competitorship with Cimon; according to the most probable accounts, he died at Athens; and at the time of Plutarch his monument was still to be seen at Phalerum. His countrymen, who, despite all plausible charges, were never ungrateful except where their liberties appeared imperilled (whether rightly or erroneously our documents are too scanty to prove), erected his monument at the public charge, portioned his three daughters, and awarded to his son Lysimachus a grant of one hundred minæ of silver, a plantation of one hundred plethra[35] of land, and a pension of four drachmæ a day (double the allowance of an Athenian ambassador).

DEATH OF ARISTIDES

---

35 About twenty-three English acres. This was by no means a despicable estate in the confined soil of Attica.

CHAPTER II

Popularity and policy of Cimon—Naxos revolts from the
Ionian league—is besieged by Cimon—conspiracy and fate of
Pausanias—flight and adventures of Themistocles—his death

I. The military abilities and early habits of Cimon naturally conspired
with past success to direct his ambition rather to warlike than to civil
distinctions. But he was not inattentive to the arts which
were necessary in a democratic state to secure and confirm
his power. Succeeding to one, once so beloved and ever so
affable as Themistocles, he sought carefully to prevent all disadvantageous
contrast. From the spoils of Byzantium and Sestos he received a vast addition to his hereditary fortunes. And by the distribution of his treasures, he
forestalled all envy at their amount. He threw open his gardens to the
public, whether foreigners or citizens—he maintained a table to which men
of every rank freely resorted, though probably those only of his own tribe[1]—
he was attended by a numerous train, who were ordered to give mantles to
what citizen soever—aged and ill clad—they encountered; and to relieve
the necessitous by alms delicately and secretly administered. By these artful
devices he rendered himself beloved, and concealed the odium of his politics
beneath the mask of his charities. For while he courted the favour, he
advanced not the wishes, of the people. He sided with the aristocratic party,
and did not conceal his attachment to the oligarchy of Sparta. He sought to
content the people with himself, in order that he might the better prevent
discontent with their position. But it may be doubted whether Cimon did
not, far more than any of his predecessors, increase the dangers of a democracy
by vulgarizing its spirit. The system of general alms and open tables had
the effect that the abuses of the Poor Laws[2] have had with us. It accustomed
the native poor to the habits of indolent paupers, and what at first was
charity soon took the aspect of a right. Hence much of the lazy turbulence,
and much of that licentious spirit of exaction from the wealthy, that in
a succeeding age characterized the mobs of Athens. So does that servile

POPULARITY AND
POLICY OF CIMON

---

1 Aristot., apud Plut., Vit. Cim.
2 Produced equally by the anti-popular party on popular pretexts. It was under the sanction
of Mr Pitt that the prostitution of charity to the able-bodied was effected in England.

generosity, common to an anti-popular party, when it affects kindness in order to prevent concession, ultimately operate against its own secret schemes. And so much less really dangerous is it to exalt, by constitutional enactments, the authority of a people, than to pamper, by the electioneering cajoleries of a selfish ambition, the prejudices which thus settle into vices, or the momentary exigences thus fixed into permanent demands.

II. While the arts or manners of Cimon conciliated the favour, his integrity won the esteem, of the people. In Aristides he found the example, not more of his aristocratic politics than of his lofty honour. A deserter from Persia having arrived at Athens with great treasure, and being harassed by informers, sought the protection of Cimon by gifts of money.

"Would you have me" said the Athenian, smiling, "your mercenary or your friend?"

"My friend!" replied the barbarian.

"Then take back your gifts."[3]

III. In the meanwhile the new ascendency of Athens was already endangered. The Carystians in the neighbouring isle of Eubœa openly defied her fleet, and many of the confederate states, seeing themselves delivered from all immediate dread of another invasion of the Medes, began to cease contributions both to the Athenian navy and the common treasury. For a danger not imminent, service became burdensome and taxation odious. And already some well-founded jealousy of the ambition of Athens increased the reluctance to augment her power. Naxos was the first island that revolted from the conditions of the league, and thither Cimon, having reduced the Carystians, led a fleet numerous and well equipped.

NAXOS REVOLTS FROM THE IONIAN LEAGUE—IS BESIEGED BY CIMON

Whatever the secret views of Cimon for the aggrandizement of his country, he could not but feel himself impelled by his own genius and the popular expectation not lightly to forego that empire of the sea, rendered to Athens by the profound policy of Themistocles and the fortunate prudence of Aristides; and every motive of Grecian, as well as Athenian, policy justified the subjugation of the revolters—an evident truth in the science of state policy, but one somewhat hastily lost sight of by those historians who, in the subsequent and unlooked-for results, forgot the necessity of the earlier enterprise. Greece had voluntarily entrusted to Athens the maritime command of the confederate states. To her, Greece must consequently look for no diminution of the national resources committed to her charge; to her, that the conditions of the league were fulfilled, and the common safety of Greece ensured. Commander of the forces, she was answerable for the deserters. Nor, although Persia at present remained tranquil and inert, could the confederates be considered safe from her revenge. No compact of peace had

3 Plut., in Vit. Cim.

been procured. The more than suspected intrigues of Xerxes with Pausanias were sufficient proofs that the great king did not yet despair of the conquest of Greece. And the peril previously incurred in the want of union among the several states was a solemn warning not to lose the advantages of that league, so tardily and so laboriously cemented. Without great dishonour and without great imprudence, Athens could not forego the control with which she had been invested; if it were hers to provide the means, it was hers to punish the defaulters; and her duty to Greece thus decorously and justly sustained her ambition for herself.

IV. And now it is necessary to return to the fortunes of Pausanias, involving in their fall the ruin of one of far loftier virtues and more unequivocal

CONSPIRACY AND
FATE OF PAUSANIAS

renown. The recall of Pausanias, the fine inflicted upon him, his narrow escape from a heavier sentence, did not suffice to draw him, intoxicated as he was with his hopes and passions, from his bold and perilous intrigues. It is not improbable that his mind was already tainted with a certain insanity.[4] And it is a curious physiological fact, that the unnatural constraints of Sparta, when acting on strong passions and fervent imaginations, seem, not unoften, to have produced a species of madness. An anecdote is recorded,[5] which, though romantic, is not perhaps wholly fabulous, and which invests with an interest yet more dramatic the fate of the conqueror of Platæa.

At Byzantium, runs the story, he became passionately enamoured of a young virgin named Cleonice. Awed by his power and his sternness, the parents yielded her to his will. The modesty of the maiden made her stipulate that the room might be in total darkness when she stole to his embraces. But unhappily, on entering, she stumbled against the light, and the Spartan, asleep at the time, imagined, in the confusion of his sudden waking, that the noise was occasioned by one of his numerous enemies seeking his chamber with the intent to assassinate him. Seizing the Persian cimeter[6] that lay beside him, he plunged it in the breast of the intruder, and the object of his passion fell dead at his feet. "From that hour", says the biographer, "he could rest no more!" A spectre haunted his nights—the voice of the murdered girl proclaimed doom to his ear. It is added, and, if we extend our belief further we must attribute the apparition to the skill of the priests, that, still tortured by the ghost of Cleonice, he applied to those celebrated necromancers who, at Heraclea[7] summoned by gloomy spells the manes of the dead, and by their aid invoked the spirit he sought to appease. The shade

---

4 His father's brother, Cleomenes, died raving mad, as we have already seen. There was therefore insanity in the family.

5 Plut., in Vit. Cim.; Paus., iii. 17.

6 Paus., iii. 17.

7 Phigalea, according to Pausanias.

of Cleonice appeared and told him "that soon after his return to Sparta he would be delivered from all his troubles."[8]

Such was the legend repeated, as Plutarch tells us, by many historians; the deed itself was probable, and conscience, even without necromancy, might supply the spectre.

V. Whether or not this story have any foundation in fact, the conduct of Pausanias seems at least to have partaken of that inconsiderate recklessness which, in the ancient superstition, preceded the vengeance of the gods. After his trial he had returned to Byzantium without the consent of the Spartan government. Driven thence by the resentment of the Athenians,[9] he repaired, not to Sparta, but to Colonæ, in Asia Minor, and in the vicinity of the ancient Troy; and there he renewed his negotiations with the Persian king. Acquainted with his designs, the vigilant ephors despatched to him a herald with the famous scytale. This was an instrument peculiar to the Spartans. To every general or admiral, a long black staff was entrusted; the magistrates kept another exactly similar. When they had any communication to make, they wrote it on a roll of parchment, applied it to their own staff, fold upon fold—then cutting it off, dismissed it to the chief. The characters were so written that they were confused and unintelligible until fastened to the stick, and thus could only be construed by the person for whose eye they were intended, and to whose care the staff was confided.

The communication Pausanias now received was indeed stern and laconic. "Stay", it said, "behind the herald, and war is proclaimed against you by the Spartans."

On receiving this solemn order, even the imperious spirit of Pausanias did not venture to disobey. Like Venice, whose harsh, tortuous, but energetic policy her oligarchy in so many respects resembled, Sparta possessed a moral and mysterious power over the fiercest of her sons. His fate held him in her grasp, and, confident of acquittal, instead of flying to Persia, the regent hurried to his doom, assured that by the help of gold he could baffle any accusation. His expectations were so far well founded, that, although, despite his rank as regent of the kingdom and guardian of the king, he was thrown into prison by the ephors, he succeeded, by his intrigues and influence, in procuring his enlargement: and boldly challenging his accusers, he offered to submit to trial.

The government, however, was slow to act. The proud caution of the Spartans was ever loth to bring scandal on their home by public proceedings against any freeborn citizen—how much more against the uncle of their monarch and the hero of their armies! His power, his talents, his imperious character awed alike private enmity and public distrust. But his haughty

8 Plut., in Vit. Cim.
9 Thucyd., i.

385

disdain of their rigid laws, and his continued affectation of the barbarian pomp, kept the government vigilant; and though released from prison, the stern ephors were his sentinels. The restless and discontented mind of the expectant son-in-law of Xerxes could not relinquish its daring schemes. And the regent of Sparta entered into a conspiracy, on which it were much to be desired that our information were more diffuse.

VI. Perhaps no class of men in ancient times excite a more painful and profound interest than the Helots of Sparta. Though, as we have before seen, we must reject all rhetorical exaggerations of the savage cruelty to which they were subjected, we know, at least, that their servitude was the hardest imposed by any of the Grecian states upon their slaves,[10] and that the iron soldiery of Sparta were exposed to constant and imminent peril from their revolts—a proof that the curse of their bondage had passed beyond the degree which subdues the spirit to that which arouses, and that neither the habit of years, nor the swords of the fiercest warriors, nor the spies of the keenest government of Greece had been able utterly to extirpate from human hearts that law of nature which, when injury passes an allotted, yet rarely visible, extreme, converts suffering to resistance.

Scattered in large numbers throughout the rugged territories of Laconia —separated from the presence, but not the watch, of their master, these singular serfs never abandoned the hope of liberty. Often pressed into battle to aid their masters, they acquired the courage to oppose them. Fierce, sullen, and vindictive, they were as droves of wild cattle, left to range at will, till wanted for the burden or the knife—not difficult to butcher, but impossible to tame.

We have seen that a considerable number of these Helots had fought as light-armed troops at Platæa; and the common danger and the common glory had united the slaves of the army with the chief. Entering into somewhat of the desperate and revengeful ambition that, under a similar constitution, animated Marino Faliero, Pausanias sought, by means of the enslaved multitude, to deliver himself from the thraldom of the oligarchy which held prince and slave alike in subjection. He tampered with the Helots, and secretly promised them the rights and liberties of citizens of Sparta, if they would co-operate with his projects and revolt at his command.

Slaves are never without traitors; and the ephors learned the premeditated revolution from Helots themselves. Still, slow and wary, those subtle and haughty magistrates suspended the blow—it was not without the fullest proof that a royal Spartan was to be condemned on the word of Helots: they continued their vigilance—they obtained the proof they required.

VII. Argilius, a Spartan, with whom Pausanias had once formed the vicious connexion common to the Doric tribes, and who was deep in his

10 Plato, Leg. vi.

confidence, was entrusted by the regent with letters to Artabazus. Argilius called to mind that none entrusted with a similar mission had ever returned. He broke open the seals and read what his fears foreboded, that, on his arrival at the satrap's court, the silence of the messenger was to be purchased by his death. He carried the packet to the ephors. That dark and plotting council were resolved yet more entirely to entangle their guilty victim, and out of his own mouth to extract his secret; they therefore ordered Argilius to take refuge as a suppliant in the sanctuary of the Temple of Neptune, on Mount Tænarus. Within the sacred confines was contrived a cell, which, by a double partition, admitted some of the ephors, who, there concealed, might witness all that passed.

Intelligence was soon brought to Pausanias that, instead of proceeding to Artabazus, his confidant had taken refuge as a suppliant in the Temple of Neptune. Alarmed and anxious, the regent hastened to the sanctuary. Argilius informed him that he had read the letters, and reproached him bitterly with his treason to himself. Pausanias, confounded and overcome by the perils which surrounded him, confessed his guilt, spoke unreservedly of the contents of the letter, implored the pardon of Argilius, and promised him safety and wealth if he would leave the sanctuary and proceed on the mission.

The ephors, from their hiding-place, heard all.

On the departure of Pausanias from the sanctuary, his doom was fixed. But, among the more public causes of the previous delay of justice, we must include the friendship of some of the ephors, which Pausanias had won or purchased. It was the moment fixed for his arrest. Pausanias, in the streets, was alone and on foot. He beheld the ephors approaching him. A signal from one warned him of his danger. He turned—he fled. The Temple of Minerva Chalciœcus at hand proffered a sanctuary—he gained the sacred confines, and entered a small house hard by the temple. The ephors—the officers—the crowd pursued; they surrounded the refuge, from which it was impious to drag the criminal. Resolved on his death, they removed the roof—blocked up the entrances (and if we may credit the anecdote, that violating human love was characteristic of Spartan nature, his mother, a crone of great age,[11] suggested the means of punishment, by placing, with her own hand, a stone at the threshold)—and, setting a guard around, left the conqueror of Mardonius to die of famine. When he was at his last gasp, unwilling to profane the sanctuary by his actual death, they bore him out into the open air, which he only breathed to expire.[12] His corpse, which some of the fiercer Spartans at first intended to cast in the place of burial for

---

11 Corn. Nep., in Vit. Paus.
12 Pausanias observes that his renowned namesake was the only suppliant taking refuge at the sanctuary of Minerva Chalciœcus who did not obtain the divine protection, and this because he could never purify himself of the murder of Cleonice.

malefactors, was afterward buried in the neighbourhood of the temple. And thus ended the glory and the crimes—the grasping ambition and the luxurious ostentation—of the bold Spartan who first scorned and then imitated the effeminacies of the Persian he subdued.

VIII. Amid the documents of which the ephors possessed themselves after the death of Pausanias was a correspondence with Themistocles, then residing in the rival and inimical state of Argos. Yet vindictive against that hero, the Spartan government despatched ambassadors to Athens, accusing him of a share in the conspiracy of Pausanias with the Medes. It seems that Themistocles did not disavow a correspondence with Pausanias, nor affect an absolute ignorance of his schemes; but he firmly denied by letter, his only mode of defence, all approval and all participation of the latter. Nor is there any proof, nor any just ground of suspicion, that he was a party to the betrayal of Greece. It was consistent, indeed, with his astute character, to plot, to manœuvre, to intrigue, but for great and not paltry ends. By possessing himself of the secret, he possessed himself of the power of Pausanias; and that intelligence might perhaps have enabled him to frustrate the Spartan's treason in the hour of actual danger to Greece. It is possible that, so far as Sparta alone was concerned, the Athenian felt little repugnance to any revolution or any peril confined to a state whose councils it had been the object of his life to baffle, and whose power it was the manifest interest of his native city to impair. He might have looked with complacency on the intrigues which the regent was carrying on against the Spartan government, and which threatened to shake that Doric constitution to its centre. But nothing, either in the witness of history or in the character or conduct of a man profoundly patriotic, even in his vices, favours the notion that he connived at the schemes which implicated, with the Grecian, the Athenian welfare. Pausanias, far less able, was probably his tool. By an insight into his projects, Themistocles might have calculated on the restoration of his own power. To weaken the Spartan influence was to weaken his own enemies at Athens; to break up the Spartan constitution was to leave Athens herself without a rival. And if, from the revolt of the Helots, Pausanias should proceed to an active league with the Persians, Themistocles knew enough of Athens and of Greece to foresee that it was to the victor of Salamis and the founder of the Grecian navy that all eyes would be directed. Such seem the most probable views which would have been opened to the exile by the communications of Pausanias. If so, they were necessarily too subtle for the crowd to penetrate or understand. The Athenians heard only the accusations of the Spartans; they saw only the treason of Pausanias; they learned only that Themistocles had been the correspondent of the traitor. Already suspicious of a genius whose deep and intricate wiles they were seldom able to fathom, and trembling at the seeming danger they had escaped, it was natural enough that the Athenians should accede to the demands of the

FLIGHT AND ADVENTURES OF THEMISTOCLES

ambassadors. An Athenian, joined with a Lacedæmonian troop, was ordered to seize Themistocles wherever he should be found. Apprised of his danger, he hastily quitted the Peloponnesus and took refuge at Corcyra. Fear of the vengeance at once of Athens and of Sparta induced the Corcyreans to deny the shelter he sought, but they honourably transported him to the opposite continent. His route was discovered—his pursuers pressed upon him. He had entered the country of Admetus, king of the Molossians, from whose resentment he had everything to dread. For he had persuaded the Athenians to reject the alliance once sought by that monarch, and Admetus had vowed vengeance.

Thus situated, the fugitive formed a resolution which a great mind only could have conceived, and which presents to us one of the most touching pictures in ancient history. He repaired to the palace of Admetus himself. The prince was absent. He addressed his consort, and, advised by her, took the young child of the royal pair in his hand, and sat down at the hearth— "THEMISTOCLES THE SUPPLIANT!"[13] On the return of the prince he told his name, and bade him not wreak his vengeance on an exile. "To condemn me now", he said, "would be to take advantage of distress. Honour dictates revenge only among equals upon equal terms. True that I opposed you once, but on a matter not of life, but of business or of interest. Now surrender me to my persecutors, and you deprive me of the last refuge of life itself."

IX. Admetus, much affected, bade him rise, and assured him of protection. The pursuers arrived; but, faithful to the guest who had sought his hearth, after a form peculiarly solemn among the Molossians, Admetus refused to give him up, and despatched him, guarded, to the sea-town of Pydna, over an arduous and difficult mountain-road. The sea-town gained, he took ship, disguised and unknown to all the passengers, in a trading vessel bound to Ionia. A storm arose—the vessel was driven from its course, and impelled right towards the Athenian fleet, that then under Cimon, his bitterest foe, lay before the isle of Naxos.

Prompt and bold in his expedients, Themistocles took aside the master of the vessel—discovered himself; threatened, if betrayed, to inform against the master as one bribed to favour his escape; promised, if preserved, everlasting gratitude; and urged that the preservation was possible, if no one during the voyage were permitted, on any pretext, to quit the vessel.

The master of the vessel was won—kept out at sea a day and a night to windward of the fleet, and landed Themistocles in safety at Ephesus.

In the meanwhile the friends of Themistocles had not been inactive in Athens. On the supposed discovery of his treason, such of his property as could fall into the hands of the government was, as usual in such offences, confiscated to the public use; the amount was variously estimated at eighty

13 Thucyd., i. 136.

and a hundred talents.[14] But the greater part of his wealth—some from Athens, some from Argos—was secretly conveyed to him at Ephesus.[15] One faithful friend procured the escape of his wife and children from Athens to the court of Admetus, for which offence of affection, a single historian, Stesimbrotus (whose statement even the credulous Plutarch questions, and proves to be contradictory with another assertion of the same author), has recorded that he was condemned to death by Cimon. It is not upon such dubious chronicles that we can suffer so great a stain on the character of a man singularly humane.[16]

X. As we have now for ever lost sight of Themistocles on the stage of Athenian politics, the present is the most fitting opportunity to conclude the history of his wild and adventurous career.

Persecuted by the Spartans, abandoned by his countrymen, excluded from the whole of Greece, no refuge remained to the man who had crushed the power of Persia, save the Persian court. The generous and high-spirited policy that characterized the oriental despotism towards its foes proffered him not only a safe, but a magnificent asylum. The Persian monarchs were ever ready to welcome the exiles of Greece, and to conciliate those whom they had failed to conquer. It was the fate of Themistocles to be saved by the enemies of his country. He had no alternative. The very accusation of connivance with the Medes drove him into their arms.

Under guidance of a Persian, Themistocles traversed the Asiatic continent; and, ere he reached Susa, contrived to have a letter, that might prepare the way for him, delivered at the Persian court. His letter ran somewhat thus, if we may suppose that Thucydides preserved the import, though he undoubtedly fashioned the style.[17]

"I, Themistocles, who of all the Greeks have inflicted the severest wounds upon your race, so long as I was called by fate to resist the invasion of the Persians, now come to you." (He then urged, on the other hand, the services he had rendered to Xerxes in his messages after Salamis, relative to the breaking of the bridges, assuming a credit to which he was by no means entitled—and insisted that his generosity demanded a return.) "Able", he

---

14 Plut., in Vit. Them.

15 Thucyd., i. 137.

16 Mr Mitford, while doubting the fact, attempts, with his usual disingenuousness, to raise upon the very fact that he doubts, reproaches against the horrors of democratical despotism. A strange practice for an historian to allow the premises to be false, and then to argue upon them as true!

17 The brief letter to Artaxerxes, given by Thucydides (i. 137), is as evidently the composition of Thucydides himself as is the celebrated oration which he puts into the mouth of Pericles. Each has the hard, rigid, and grasping style so peculiar to the historian, and to which no other Greek writer bears the slightest resemblance. But the matter may be more genuine than the diction.

proceeded, "to perform great services—persecuted by the Greeks for my friendship for you—I am near at hand. Grant me only a year's respite, that I may then apprise you in person of the object of my journey hither."

The bold and confident tone of Themistocles struck the imagination of the young king (Artaxerxes), and he returned a favourable reply. Themistocles consumed the year in the perfect acquisition of the language, and the customs and manners of the country. He then sought and obtained an audience.[18]

Able to converse with fluency, and without the medium of an interpreter, his natural abilities found their level. He rose to instant favour. Never before had a stranger been so honoured. He was admitted an easy access to the royal person—instructed in the learning of the Magi—and when he quitted the court it was to take possession of the government of three cities—Myus, celebrated for its provisions; Lampsacus, for its vineyards; and Magnesia, for the richness of the soil; so that, according to the spirit and phraseology of oriental taxation, it was not unaptly said that they were awarded to him for meat, wine, and bread.

XI. Thus affluent and thus honoured, Themistocles passed at Magnesia the remainder of his days—the time and method of his death uncertain; whether cut off by natural disease, or, as is otherwise related,[19] by a fate than which fiction itself could have invented none more suited to the consummation of his romantic and great career. It is said, that when afterward Egypt revolted, and that revolt was aided by the Athenians; when the Grecian navy sailed as far as Cilicia and Cyprus; and Cimon upheld, without a rival, the new sovereignty of the seas; when Artaxerxes resolved to oppose the growing power of a state which, from the defensive, had risen to the offending, power; Themistocles received a mandate to realize

HIS DEATH

18 At the time of his arrival in Asia, Xerxes seems to have been still living. But he appeared at Susa during the short interval between the death of Xerxes and the formal accession of his son, when, by a sanguinary revolution, yet to be narrated, Artabanus was raised to the head of the Persian empire: ere the year expired Artaxerxes was on the throne.

19 I relate this latter account of the death of Themistocles, not only because Thucydides (though preferring the former) does not disdain to cite it, but also because it is evident, from the speech of Nicias, in the "Knights" of Aristophanes, lines 83, 84, that in the time of Pericles it was popularly believed by the Athenians that Themistocles died by poison; and from motives that rendered allusion to his death a popular claptrap. It is also clear that the death of Themistocles appears to have reconciled him at once to the Athenians. The previous suspicions of his fidelity to Greece do not seem to have been kept alive even by the virulence of party; and it is natural to suppose that it must have been some act of his own, real or imagined, which tended to disprove the plausible accusations against him, and revive the general enthusiasm in his favour. What could that act have been but the last of his life, which, in the lines of Aristophanes referred to above, is cited as the ideal of a glorious death! But if he died by poison, the draught *was not bullock's blood*—the deadly nature of which was one of the vulgar fables of the ancients. In some parts of the continent it is, in this day, even used as medicine.

the vague promises he had given, and to commence his operations against Greece. Then (if with Plutarch we accept this version of his fate), neither resentment against the people he had deemed ungrateful, nor his present pomp, nor the fear of life, could induce the lord of Magnesia to dishonour his past achievements,[20] and demolish his immortal trophies. Anxious only to die worthily—since to live as became him was no longer possible—he solemnly sacrificed to the gods—took leave of his friends, and finished his days by poison.

His monument long existed in the forum of Magnesia; but his bones are said by his own desire to have been borne back privately to Attica, and have rested in the beloved land that exiled him from her bosom. And this his last request seems touchingly to prove his loyalty to Athens, and to proclaim his pardon of her persecution. Certain it is, at least, that however honoured in Persia, he never perpetrated one act against Greece; and that, if sullied by the suspicion of others, his fame was untarnished by himself. He died, according to Plutarch, in his sixty-fifth year, leaving many children, and transmitting his name to a long posterity, who received from his memory the honours they could not have acquired for themselves.

XII. The character of Themistocles has already in these pages unfolded itself—profound, yet tortuous in policy—vast in conception—subtle, patient, yet prompt in action; affable in manner, but boastful, ostentatious and disdaining to conceal his consciousness of merit; not brilliant in accomplishment, yet master not more of the Greek wiles than the Attic wit; sufficiently eloquent, but greater in deeds than words, and penetrating, by an almost preternatural insight, at once the characters of men and the sequences of events. Incomparably the greatest of his own times, and certainly not surpassed by those who came after him. Pisistratus, Cimon, Pericles, Aristides himself, were of noble and privileged birth. Themistocles was the first, and, except Demosthenes, the greatest of those who rose from the ranks of the people, and he drew the people upward in his rise. His fame was the creation of his genius only. To paraphrase the unusual eloquence of Diodorus:

> What other man could in the same time have placed Greece at the head of nations, Athens at the head of Greece, himself at the head of Athens?—in the most illustrious age the most illustrious man. Conducting to war the citizens of a state in ruins, he defeated all the arms of Asia. He alone had the power to unite the most discordant materials, and to render danger itself salutary to his designs. Not more remarkable in war than peace—in the one he saved the liberties of Greece, in the other he, created the eminence of Athens.

20 Plut., in Vit. Them.

After him, the light of the heroic age seems to glimmer and to fade, and even Pericles himself appears dwarfed and artificial beside that masculine and colossal intellect which broke into fragments the might of Persia, and baffled with a vigorous ease the gloomy sagacity of Sparta. The statue of Themistocles, existent six hundred years after his decease, exhibited to his countrymen an aspect as heroical as his deeds.[21]

We return to Cimon.

21 Plut., in Vit. Them.

CHAPTER III

Reduction of Naxos—battle of Eurymedon—actions off
Cyprus—manners of Cimon—improvements in Athens—
colony at the Nine Ways—siege of Thasos—earthquake in
Sparta—revolt of Helots, occupation of Ithomë, and third
Messenian war—rise and character of Pericles—prosecution
and acquittal of Cimon—the Athenians assist the Spartans at
Ithomë—Thasos surrenders—breach between the Athenians
and Spartans—constitutional innovations at Athens—ostracism
of Cimon

I. At the time in which Naxos refused the stipulated subsidies, and was,
in consequence, besieged by Cimon, that island was one of the most wealthy
and populous of the confederate states. For some time
the Naxians gallantly resisted the besiegers; but, at
length reduced, they were subjected to heavier conditions than those previously imposed upon them. No conqueror contents himself with acquiring
the objects, sometimes frivolous and often just, with which he commences
hostilities. War inflames the passions, and success the ambition. Cimon, at
first anxious to secure the Grecian, was now led on to desire the increase of
the Athenian power. The Athenian fleet had subdued Naxos, and Naxos was
rendered subject to Athens. This was the first of the free states which the
growing republic submitted to her yoke.[1] The precedent once set, as occasion tempted, the rest shared a similar fate.

II. The reduction of Naxos was but the commencement of the victories of
Cimon. In Asia Minor there were many Grecian cities in which the Persian
ascendency had never yet been shaken. Along the
Carian coast Cimon conducted his armament, and the
terror it inspired sufficed to engage all the cities, originally Greek, to revolt
from Persia; those garrisoned by Persians he besieged and reduced. Victorious
in Caria, he passed with equal success into Lycia,[2] augmenting his fleet and
forces as he swept along. But the Persians, not inactive, had now assembled
a considerable force in Pamphylia, and lay encamped on the banks of the

REDUCTION OF NAXOS

BATTLE OF EURYMEDON

1 Thucyd., i.
2 Diod. Sic., xi.

Eurymedon, whose waters, sufficiently wide, received their fleet. The expected re-enforcement of eighty Phœnician vessels from Cyprus induced the Persians to delay[3] actual hostilities. But Cimon, resolved to forestall the anticipated junction, sailed up the river, and soon forced the barbarian fleet, already much more numerous than his own, into active engagement. The Persians but feebly supported the attack; driven up the river, the crews deserted the ships, and hastened to join the army arrayed along the coast. Of the ships thus deserted, some were destroyed; and two hundred triremes, taken by Cimon, yet more augmented his armament. But the Persians, now advanced to the verge of the shore, presented a long and formidable array, and Cimon, with some anxiety, saw the danger he incurred in landing troops already much harassed by the late action, while a considerable proportion of the hostile forces, far more numerous, were fresh and unfatigued. The spirit of the men, and their elation at the late victory, bore down the fears of the general; yet warm from the late action, he debarked his heavy-armed infantry, and with loud shouts the Athenians rushed upon the foe. The contest was fierce—the slaughter great. Many of the noblest Athenians fell in the action. Victory at length declared in favour of Cimon; the Persians were put to flight, and the Greeks remained masters of the battle and the booty—the last considerable. Thus, on the same day, the Athenians were victorious on both elements—an unprecedented glory, which led the rhetorical Plutarch to declare that Platæa and Salamis were outshone. Posterity, more discerning, estimates glory not by the greatness of the victory alone, but the justice of the cause. And even a skirmish won by men struggling for liberty on their own shores is more honoured than the proudest battle in which the conquerors are actuated by the desire of vengeance or the lust of enterprise.

III. To the trophies of this double victory were soon added those of a third, obtained over the eighty vessels of the Phœnicians off the coast of Cyprus. These signal achievements spread the terror of the Athenian arms on remote as on Grecian shores. Without adopting the exaggerated accounts of injudicious authors as to the number of ships and prisoners,[4] it seems certain at least that the amount of the booty was sufficient in some degree to create in Athens a moral revolution—swelling to a vast extent the fortunes of individuals, and augmenting the general taste for pomp, for luxury, and for splendour, which soon afterward rendered Athens the most magnificent of the Grecian states.

ACTIONS OFF CYPRUS

The navy of Persia thus broken, her armies routed, the scene of action transferred to her own dominions, all designs against Greece were laid aside. Retreating, as it were, more to the centre of her vast domains, she left the

---

3 Plut., in Vit. Cim.

4 Diod. Sic. (xi) reckons the number of prisoners at twenty thousand! These exaggerations sink glory into burlesque.

Asiatic outskirts to the solitude, rather of exhaustion than of peace. "No troops", boasted the later rhetoricians, "came within a day's journey, on horseback, of the Grecian seas." From the Chelidonian isles on the Pamphylian coast, to those[5] twin rocks at the entrance of the Euxine, between which the sea, chafed by their rugged base, roars unappeasably through its mists of foam, no Persian galley was descried. Whether this was the cause of defeat or of acknowledged articles of peace, has been disputed. But, as will be seen hereafter, of the latter all historical evidence is wanting.

In a subsequent expedition, Cimon, sailing from Athens with a small force, wrested the Thracian Chersonesus from the Persians—an exploit which restored to him his own patrimony.

IV. Cimon was now at the height of his fame and popularity. His share of the booty, and the recovery of the Chersonesus, rendered him by far the wealthiest citizen of Athens; and he continued to use his wealth to cement his power. His intercourse with other nations, his familiarity with the oriental polish and magnificence, served to elevate his manners from their early rudeness, and to give splendour to his tastes. If he had spent his youth among the wild soldiers of Miltiades, the leisure of his maturer years was cultivated by an intercourse with sages and poets. His passion for the sex, which even in its excesses tends to refine and to soften, made his only vice. He was the friend of every genius and every art; and, the link between the lavish ostentation of Themistocles and the intellectual grace of Pericles, he conducted, as it were, the insensible transition from the age of warlike glory to that of civil pre-eminence. He may be said to have contributed greatly to diffuse that atmosphere of poetry and of pleasure which even the meanest of the free Athenians afterward delighted to respire. He led the citizens more and more from the recesses of private life; and carried out that social policy commenced by Pisistratus, according to which all individual habits became merged into one animated, complex, and excited public. Thus, himself gay and convivial, addicted to company, wine, and women, he encouraged shows and spectacles, and invested them with new magnificence; he embellished the city with public buildings, and was the first to erect at Athens those long colonnades—beneath the shade of which, sheltered from the western suns, that graceful people were accustomed to assemble and converse. The Agora, that universal home of the citizens, was planted by him with the oriental planes; and the groves of Academe, the immortal haunt of Plato, were his work. That celebrated garden, associated with the grateful and bright remembrances of all which poetry can lend to wisdom, was, before the time of Cimon, a waste and uncultivated spot. It was his hand that intersected it with walks and alleys,

MANNERS OF CIMON

5 The Cyaneæ. Pliny, vi. 12; Herod. iv. 85, &c. &c.

and that poured through its green retreats the ornamental waters so refreshing in those climes, and not common in the dry Attic soil, which now meandered in living streams, and now sparkled into fountains. Besides these works to embellish, he formed others to fortify the city. He completed the citadel, hitherto unguarded on the south side; and it was from the barbarian spoils deposited in the treasury that the expenses of founding the long walls, afterward completed, were defrayed.

V. In his conduct towards the allies, the natural urbanity of Cimon served to conceal a policy deep-laid and grasping. The other Athenian generals were stern and punctilious in their demands on the confederates; they required the allotted number of men, and, in default of the supply, increased the rigour of their exactions. Not so Cimon—from those whom the ordinary avocations of a peaceful life rendered averse to active service, he willingly accepted a pecuniary substitute, equivalent to the value of those ships or soldiers they should have furnished. These sums, devoted indeed to the general service, were yet appropriated to the uses of the Athenian navy; thus the states, hitherto warlike, were artfully suffered to lapse into peaceful and luxurious pursuits; and the confederates became at once, under the most lenient pretexts, enfeebled and impoverished by the very means which strengthened the martial spirit and increased the fiscal resources of the Athenians. The tributaries found too late, when they ventured at revolt, that they had parted with the facilities of resistance.[6]

In the meanwhile it was the object of Cimon to sustain the naval ardour and discipline of the Athenians; while the oar and the sword fell into disuse

IMPROVEMENTS IN ATHENS

with the confederates, he kept the greater part of the citizens in constant rotation at maritime exercise or enterprise—until experience and increasing power with one, indolence and gradual subjection with the other, destroying the ancient equality in arms, made the Athenians masters and their confederates subjects.[7]

VI. According to the wise policy of the ancients, the Athenians never neglected a suitable opportunity to colonize, thus extending their dominion while they drafted off the excess of their population, as well as the more enterprising spirits whom adventure tempted or poverty aroused. The conquest of Eion had opened to the Athenians a new prospect of aggrandizement, of which they were now prepared to seize the advantages. Not far from Eion, and on the banks of the Strymon, was a place called the Nine Ways, afterward Amphipolis, and which, from its locality and maritime conveniences, seemed especially calculated for the site of a new city. Thither ten thousand persons, some confederates, some Athenians, had been sent to establish a colony. The views of the Athenians were not, however, in this

6 Thucyd., i. 99.
7 Plut., in Vit. Cim.

enterprise, bounded to its mere legitimate advantages. About the same time they carried on a dispute with the Thasians relative to certain mines and places of trade on the opposite coasts of Thrace. The dispute was one of considerable nicety. The Athenians, having conquered Eion and the adjacent territory, claimed the possession by right of conquest. The Thasians, on the other hand, had anciently possessed some of the mines and the monopoly of the commerce; they had joined in the confederacy; and, asserting that the conquest had been made, if by Athenian arms, for the federal good, they demanded that the ancient privileges should revert to them. The Athenian government was not disposed to surrender a claim which proffered to avarice the temptation of mines of gold. The Thasians renounced the confederacy, and thus gave to the Athenians the very pretext for hostilities which the weaker state should never permit to the more strong. While the colony proceeded to its destination, part of the Athenian fleet, under Cimon, sailed to Thasos—gained a victory by sea—landed on the island—and besieged the city.

Meanwhile the new colonizers had become masters of the Nine Ways, having dislodged the Edonian Thracians, its previous habitants. But hostil-
COLONY AT THE NINE WAYS ity following hostility, the colonists were eventually utterly routed and cut off in a pitched battle at Drabescus, in Edonia, by the united forces of all the neighbouring Thracians.

VII. The siege of Thasos still continued, and the besieged took the precaution to send to Sparta for assistance. That sullen state had long viewed
SIEGE OF THASOS with indignation the power of Athens; her younger warriors clamoured against the inert indifference with which a city, for ages so inferior to Sparta, had been suffered to gain the ascendency over Greece. In vain had Themistocles been removed; the inexhaustible genius of the people had created a second Themistocles in Cimon. The Lacedæmonians, glad of a pretext for quarrel, courteously received the Thasian ambassadors, and promised to distract the Athenian forces by an irruption into Attica. They were actively prepared in concerting measures for this invasion, when sudden and complicated afflictions, now to be related, forced them to abandon their designs, and confine their attention to themselves.

VIII. An earthquake, unprecedented in its violence, occurred in Sparta. In many places throughout Laconia the rocky soil was rent asunder. From
EARTHQUAKE IN SPARTA Mount Taygetus, which overhung the city, and on which the women of Lacedæmon were wont to hold their bacchanalian orgies, huge fragments rolled into the suburbs. The greater portion of the city was absolutely overthrown; and it is said, probably with exaggeration, that only five houses wholly escaped the shock. This terrible calamity did not cease suddenly as it came; its concussions were repeated; it buried alike men and treasure: could we credit Diodorus, no less than twenty thousand persons perished in the shock. Thus depopulated, impoverished, and

distressed, the enemies whom the cruelty of Sparta nursed within her bosom resolved to seize the moment to execute their vengeance and consummate her destruction. Under Pausanias we have seen before that the Helots were already ripe for revolt. The death of that fierce conspirator checked, but did not crush, their designs of freedom. Now was the moment, when Sparta lay in ruins—now was the moment to realize their dreams. From field to field, from village to village, the news of the earthquake became the watchword of revolt. Up rose the Helots—they armed themselves, they poured on—a wild, and gathering, and relentless multitude, resolved to slay by the wrath of man all whom that of nature had yet spared. The earthquake that levelled Sparta rent her chains; nor did the shock create one chasm so dark and wide as that between the master and the slave.

It is one of the sublimest and most awful spectacles in history—that city in ruins—the earth still trembling—the grim and dauntless soldiery collected amid piles of death and ruin; and in such a time, and such a scene, the multitude sensible, not of danger, but of wrong, and rising, not to succour, but to revenge: all that should have disarmed a feebler enmity, giving fire to theirs; the dreadest calamity their blessing—dismay their hope: it was as if the Great Mother herself had summoned her children to vindicate the long-abused, the all inalienable heritage derived from her; and the stir of the angry elements was but the announcement of an armed and solemn union between Nature and the Oppressed.

REVOLT OF HELOTS, OCCU-
PATION OF ITHOMË, AND
THIRD MESSENIAN WAR

IX. Fortunately for Sparta, the danger was not altogether unforeseen. After the confusion and horror of the earthquake, and while the people, dispersed, were seeking to save their effects, Archidamus, who, four years before, had succeeded to the throne of Lacedæmon, ordered the trumpets to sound as to arms. That wonderful superiority of man over matter which habit and discipline can effect, and which was ever so visible among the Spartans, constituted their safety at that hour. Forsaking the care of their property, the Spartans seized their arms, flocked around their king, and drew up in disciplined array. In her most imminent crisis, Sparta was thus saved. The Helots approached, wild, disorderly, and tumultuous; they came intent only to plunder and to slay; they expected to find scattered and affrighted foes—they found a formidable army; their tyrants were still their lords. They saw, paused, and fled, scattering themselves over the country—exciting all they met to rebellion, and soon, joined with the Messenians, kindred to them by blood and ancient reminiscences of heroic struggles, they seized that same Ithomë which their hereditary Aristomenes had before occupied with unforgotten valour. This they fortified; and, occupying also the neighbouring lands, declared open war upon their lords. As the Messenians were the more worthy enemy, so the general insurrection is known by the name of the third Messenian war.

X. While these events occurred in Sparta, Cimon, entrusting to others the continued siege of Thasos, had returned to Athens.[8] He found his popularity already shaken, and his power endangered. The demo-

RISE AND CHARACTER
OF PERICLES

cratic party had of late regained the influence it had lost on the exile of Themistocles. Pericles, son of Xanthippus (the accuser of Miltiades), had, during the last six years, insensibly risen into reputation: the house of Miltiades was fated to bow before the race of Xanthippus, and hereditary opposition ended in the old hereditary results. Born of one of the loftiest families of Athens, distinguished by the fame as the fortunes of his father, who had been linked with Aristides in command of the Athenian fleet, and in whose name had been achieved the victory of Mycale, the young Pericles found betimes an easy opening to his brilliant genius and his high ambition. He had nothing to contend against but his own advantages. The beauty of his countenance, the sweetness of his voice, and the blandness of his address, reminded the oldest citizens of Pisistratus; and this resemblance is said to have excited against him a popular jealousy which he found it difficult to surmount. His youth was passed alternately in the camp and in the schools. He is the first of the great statesmen of his country who appears to have prepared himself for action by study; Anaxagoras, Pythoclides, and Damon were his tutors, and he was early eminent in all the lettered accomplishments of his time. By degrees, accustoming the people to his appearance in public life, he became remarkable for an elaborate and impassioned eloquence, hitherto unknown. With his intellectual and meditative temperament all was science; his ardour in action regulated by long forethought, his very words by deliberate preparation. Till his time, oratory, in its proper sense, as a study and an art, was uncultivated in Athens. Pisistratus is said to have been naturally eloquent, and the vigorous mind of Themistocles imparted at once persuasion and force to his counsels. But Pericles, aware of all the advantages to be gained by words, embellished words with every artifice that his imagination could suggest. His speeches were often written compositions, and the novel dazzle of their diction, and that consecutive logic which preparation alone can impart to language, became irresistible to a people that had itself become a Pericles. Universal civilization, universal poetry, had rendered the audience susceptible and fastidious; they could appreciate the ornate and philosophical harangues of Pericles; and, the first to mirror to themselves the intellectual improvements they had made, the first to represent the grace and enlightenment, as Themistocles had been the first to represent the daring and enterprise, of his time, the son of Xanthippus began already to eclipse that very Cimon whose qualities prepared the way for him.

8 For the siege of Thasos lasted three years; in the second year we find Cimon marching to the relief of the Spartans; in fact, the siege of Thasos was not of sufficient importance to justify Cimon in a very prolonged absence from Athens.

XI. We must not suppose, that in the contests between the aristocratic and popular parties, the aristocracy were always on one side. Such a division is never to be seen in free constitutions. There is always a sufficient party of the nobles whom conviction, ambition, or hereditary predilections will place at the head of the popular movement; and it is by members of the privileged order that the order itself is weakened. Athens in this respect, therefore, resembled England, and as now in the latter state, so then at Athens, it was often the proudest, the wealthiest, the most highborn of the aristocrats that gave dignity and success to the progress of democratic opinion. There, too, the vehemence of party frequently rendered politics an hereditary heirloom; intermarriages kept together men of similar factions; and the memory of those who had been the martyrs or the heroes of a cause mingled with the creed of their descendants. Thus, it was as natural that one of the race of that Clisthenes who had expelled the Pisistratidæ, and popularized the constitution, should embrace the more liberal side, as that a Russell should follow out in one age the principles for which his ancestor perished in another. So do our forefathers become sponsors for ourselves. The mother of Pericles was the descendant of Clisthenes; and though Xanthippus himself was of the same party as Aristides, we may doubt, by his prosecution of Miltiades as well as by his connexion with the Alcmæonidæ, whether he ever cordially co-operated with the views and the ambition of Cimon. However this be, his brilliant son cast himself at once into the arms of the more popular faction, and opposed with all his energy the aristocratic predilections of Cimon. Not yet, however, able to assume the lead to which he aspired (for it had now become a matter of time as well as intellect to rise), he ranged himself under Ephialtes, a personage of whom history gives us too scanty details, although he enjoyed considerable influence, increased by his avowed jealousy of the Spartans and his own unimpeachable integrity.

XII. It is noticeable, that men who become the leaders of the public, less by the spur of passion than by previous study and conscious talent—men whom thought and letters prepare for enterprise—are rarely eager to advance themselves too soon. Making politics a science, they are even fastidiously alive to the qualities and the experience demanded for great success; their very self-esteem renders them seemingly modest; they rely upon time and upon occasion; and, pushed forward rather by circumstance than their own exertions, it is long before their ambition and their resources are fully developed. Despite all his advantages, the rise of Pericles was gradual.

PROSECUTION AND ACQUITTAL OF CIMON

On the return of Cimon, the popular party deemed itself sufficiently strong to manifest its opposition. The expedition to Thasos had not been attended with results so glorious as to satisfy a people pampered by a series of triumphs. Cimon was deemed culpable for not having taken advantage of the access into Macedonia, and added that country to the Athenian empire. He was even suspected and accused of receiving bribes from Alexander, the king of Macedon. Pericles[9] is said to have taken at first an active part in this prosecution; but when the cause came on, whether moved by the instances of Cimon's sister, or made aware of the injustice of the accusation, he conducted himself favourably towards the accused. Cimon himself treated the charges with a calm disdain; the result was worthy of Athens and himself. He was honourably acquitted.

XIII. Scarce was this impeachment over, when a Spartan ambassador arrived at Athens to implore her assistance against the Helots; the request produced a vehement discussion.

THE ATHENIANS ASSIST
THE SPARTANS AT ITHOMË

Ephialtes strongly opposed the proposition to assist a city, sometimes openly, always heartily, inimical to Athens. "Much better", he contended, "to suffer her pride to be humbled, and her powers of mischief to be impaired." Ever supporting and supported by the Lacedæmonian party, whether at home or abroad, Cimon, on the other hand, maintained the necessity of marching to the relief of Sparta. "Do not", he said, almost sublimely—and his words are reported to have produced a considerable impression on that susceptible assembly—"do not suffer Greece to be mutilated, nor deprive Athens of *her companion!*"

The more generous and magnanimous counsel prevailed with a generous and magnanimous people; and Cimon was sent to the aid of Sparta at the head of a sufficient force. It may be observed, as a sign of the political morality of the time, that the wrongs of the Helots appear to have been forgotten. But such is the curse of slavery, that it unfits its victims to be free, except by preparations and degrees. And civilization, humanity, and social order are often enlisted on the wrong side, in behalf of the oppressors, from the licence and barbarity natural to the victories of the oppressed. A conflict between the negroes and the planters in modern times may not be unanalogous to that of the Helots and Spartans; and it is often a fatal necessity to extirpate the very men we have maddened, by our own cruelties, to the savageness of beasts.

It would appear that, during the revolt of the Helots and Messenians, which lasted ten years, the Athenians, under Cimon, marched twice[10] to the aid of the Spartans. In the first they probably drove

THASOS SURRENDERS

the scattered insurgents into the city of Ithomë; in the second they besieged the city. In the interval Thasos surrendered; the inhabitants were compelled to level their walls, to give up their shipping, to pay the arrear of tribute, to defray the impost punctually in future, and to resign all claims on the continent and the mines.

9 Plut., in Vit. Cim.
10 Plut., in Vit. Cim.

XIV. Thus did the Athenians establish their footing on the Thracian continent, and obtain the possession of the golden mines, which they mistook for wealth. In the second expedition of the Athenians, the long-cherished jealousy between themselves and the Spartans could no longer be smothered. The former were applied to especially from their skill in sieges, and their very science galled perhaps the pride of the martial Spartans. While, as the true art of war was still so little understood, that even the Athenians were unable to carry the town by assault, and compelled to submit to the tedious operations of a blockade, there was ample leisure for those feuds which the uncongenial habits and long rivalry of the nations necessarily produced. Proud of their Dorian name, the Spartans looked on the Ionic race of Athens as aliens. Severe in their oligarchic discipline, they regarded the Athenian demus as innovators; and, in the valour itself of their allies, they detected a daring and restless energy which, if serviceable now, might easily be rendered dangerous hereafter. They even suspected the Athenians of tampering with the Helots—led, it may be, to that distrust by the contrast, which they were likely to misinterpret, between their own severity and the Athenian mildness towards the servile part of their several populations, and also by the existence of a powerful party at Athens, which had opposed the assistance Cimon afforded. With their usual tranquil and wary policy, the Spartan government attempted to conceal their real fears, and simply alleging they had no further need of their assistance, dismissed the Athenians. But that people, constitutionally irritable, perceiving that despite this hollow pretext the other allies, including the obnoxious Æginetans, were retained, received their dismissal as an insult. Thinking justly that they had merited a nobler confidence from the Spartans, they gave way to their first resentment, and disregarding the league existing yet between themselves and Sparta against the Mede—the form of which had survived the spirit—they entered into an alliance with the Argives, hereditary enemies of Sparta, and in that alliance the Aleuads of Thessaly were included.

XV. The obtaining of these decrees by the popular party was the prelude to the fall of Cimon. The talents of that great man were far more eminent in war than peace; and despite his real or affected liberality of demeanour, he wanted either the faculty to suit the time, or the art to conceal his deficiencies. Raised to eminence by Spartan favour, he had ever too boldly and too imprudently espoused the Spartan cause. At first, when the Athenians obtained their naval ascendency—and it was necessary to conciliate Sparta —the partiality with which Cimon was regarded by that state was his recommendation; now, when, no longer to be conciliated, Sparta was to be dreaded and opposed, it became his ruin. It had long been his custom to laud the Spartans at the expense of the Athenians, and to hold out their manners as an example to the admiration of his countrymen. It was a favourite mode of reproof with him—"The Spartans would not have done this."

It was even remembered against him that he had called his son Lacedæmonius. These predilections had of late rankled in the popular mind; and now, when the Athenian force had been contumeliously dismissed, it was impossible to forget that Cimon had obtained the decree of the relief, and that the mortification which resulted from it was the effect of his counsels.

Public spirit ran high against the Spartans, and at the head of the Spartan faction in Athens stood Cimon.

XVI. But at this time, other events, still more intimately connected with the Athenian politics, conspired to weaken the authority of this able general.

CONSTITUTIONAL INNOVA-
TIONS AT ATHENS

Those constitutional reforms, which are in reality revolutions under a milder name, were now sweeping away the last wrecks of whatever of the old aristocratic system was still left to the Athenian commonwealth.

We have seen that the democratic party had increased in power by the decree of Aristides, which opened all offices to all ranks. This, as yet, was productive less of actual than of moral effects. The liberal opinions possessed by a part of the aristocracy, and the legitimate influence which in all countries belongs to property and high descent (greatest, indeed, where the countries are most free)—secured, as a general rule, the principal situations in the state to rank and wealth. But the *moral* effect of the decree was to elevate the lower classes with a sense of their own power and dignity, and every victory achieved over a foreign foe gave new authority to the people whose voices elected the leader—whose right arms won the battle.

The constitution previous to Solon was an oligarchy of birth. Solon rendered it an aristocracy of property. Clisthenes widened its basis from property to population; as we have already seen, it was, in all probability, Clisthenes also who weakened the more illicit and oppressive influences of wealth, by establishing the ballot or secret suffrage instead of the open voting, which was common in the time of Solon. It is the necessary constitution of society, that when one class obtains power, the ancient checks to that power require remodelling. The Areopagus was designed by Solon as the aristocratic balance to the popular assembly. But in all states in which the people and the aristocracy are represented, the great blow to the aristocratic senate is given less by altering its own constitution than by infusing new elements of democracy into the popular assembly. The old boundaries are swept away, not by the levelling of the bank, but by the swelling of the torrent. The checks upon democracy ought to be so far concealed as to be placed in the representation of the democracy itself; for checks upon its progress from *without* are but as fortresses to be stormed; and what, when latent, was the influence of a friend, when apparent, is the resistance of a foe.

The Areopagus, the constitutional bulwark of the aristocratic party of Athens, became more and more invidious to the people. And now, when Cimon resisted every innovation on that assembly, he only ensured his own destruction, while he expedited the policy he denounced. Ephialtes directed all the force of the popular opinion against this venerable senate; and at length, though not openly assisted by Pericles,[11] who took no prominent part in the contention, that influential statesman succeeded in crippling its functions and limiting its authority.

XVII. I do not propose to plunge the reader into the voluminous and unprofitable controversy on the exact nature of the innovations of Ephialtes which has agitated the students of Germany. It appears to me most probable that the Areopagus retained the right of adjudging cases of homicide,[12] and little besides of its ancient constitutional authority, that it lost altogether its most dangerous power in the *indefinite police* it had formerly exercised over the habits and morals of the people, that any control of the finances was wisely transferred to the popular senate,[13] that its irresponsible character was abolished, and it was henceforth rendered accountable to the people. Such alterations were not made without exciting the deep indignation of the aristocratic faction.

In all state reforms a great and comprehensive mind does not so much consider whether each reform is just, as what will be the ultimate ascendency given to particular principles. Cimon preferred to all constitutions a limited aristocracy, and his practical experience regarded every measure in its general tendency towards or against the system which he honestly advocated.

XVIII. The struggle between the contending parties and principles had commenced before Cimon's expedition to Ithomë; the mortification connected with that event, in weakening Cimon, weakened the aristocracy itself. Still his fall was not

OSTRACISM OF CIMON

11 Those historians who presume upon the slovenly sentences of Plutarch, that Pericles made *"an instrument"* of Ephialtes in assaults on the Areopagus, seem strangely to mistake both the character of Pericles, which was dictatorial, not crafty, and the position of Ephialtes, who at that time was the leader of his party, and far more influential than Pericles himself. Plato (apud Plut., in Vit. Per.) rightly considers Ephialtes the true overthrower of the Areopagus; and although Pericles assisted him (Aristot., ii. 9), it was against Ephialtes as the chief, not "the instrument," that the wrath of the aristocracy was directed.

12 See Dem., adv. Aristocr., p. 642, ed. Reisk. Hermann ap. Heidelb. Jahrb., 1830, No. 44. Forchhammer de Areopago, &c. against Boeckh. I cannot agree with those who attach so much importance to Æschylus, in the tragedy of the "Furies", as an authority in favour of the opinion that the innovations of Ephialtes deprived the Areopagus of jurisdiction in cases of homicide. It is true that the play turns upon the origin of the tribunal—it is true that it celebrates its immemorial right of adjudication of murder, and that Minerva declares this court of judges shall remain for ever. But would this prophecy be risked at the very time when this court was about to be abolished? In the same speech of Minerva, far more direct allusion is made to the police of the court in the fear and reverence due to it; and strong exhortations follow, not to venerate anarchy or tyranny, or banish "all fear from the city", which apply much more forcibly to the council than to the court of the Areopagus.

13 That the Areopagus did, prior to the decree of Ephialtes, possess a power over the finances, appears from a passage in Aristotle (apud Plut., in Vit. Them.), in which it is said that, in the expedition to Salamis, the Areopagus awarded to each man eight drachmæ.

immediate,[14] nor did it take place as a single and isolated event, but as one of the necessary consequences of the great political change effected by Ephialtes. All circumstances, however, conspired to place the son of Miltiades in a situation which justified the suspicion and jealousy of the Athenians. Of all the enemies, how powerful soever, that Athens could provoke, none were so dangerous as Lacedæmon.

Dark, wily, and implacable, the rugged queen of the Peloponnesus reared her youth in no other accomplishments than those of stratagem and slaughter. Her enmity against Athens was no longer smothered. Athens had everything to fear, not less from her influence than her armies. It was not, indeed, so much from the unsheathed sword as from the secret councils of Sparta that danger was to be apprehended. It cannot be too often remembered, that among a great portion of the Athenian aristocracy, the Spartan government maintained a considerable and sympathetic intelligence. That government ever sought to adapt and mould all popular constitutions to her own oligarchic model; and where she could not openly invade, she secretly sought to undermine, the liberties of her neighbours. Thus, in addition to all fear from an enemy in the field, the Athenian democracy were constantly excited to suspicion against a spy within the city: always struggling with an aristocratic party, which aimed at regaining the power it had lost, there was just reason to apprehend that that party would seize any occasion to encroach upon the popular institutions; every feud with Sparta consequently seemed to the Athenian people, nor without cause, to subject to intrigue and conspiracy their civil freedom; and (as always happens with foreign interference, whether latent or avowed) exasperated whatever jealousies already existed against those for whose political interests the interference was exerted. Bearing this in mind, we shall see no cause to wonder at the vehement opposition to which Cimon was now subjected. We are driven ourselves to search deeply into the causes which led to his prosecution, as to that of other eminent men in Athens, from want of clear and precise historical details. Plutarch, to whom, in this instance, we are compelled chiefly to resort, is a most equivocal authority. Like most biographers, his care is to exalt his hero, though at the expense of that hero's countrymen; and though an amiable writer, nor without some semi-philosophical views in morals, his mind was singularly deficient in grasp and in comprehension. He never penetrates the subtle causes of effects. He surveys the past, sometimes as a scholar, sometimes as a tale-teller, sometimes even as a poet, but never as a statesman. Thus, we learn from him little of the true reasons for the ostracism, either of Aristides, of Themistocles, or of Cimon—points now intricate, but which might then, alas! have been easily cleared up by a profound inquirer,

---

14 Plutarch attributes his ostracism to the resentment of the Athenians on his return from Ithomë; but this is erroneous. He was not ostracized till two years after his return.

to the acquittal alike of themselves and of their judges. To the natural deficiencies of Plutarch we must add his party predilections. He was opposed to democratic opinions—and that objection, slight in itself, or it might be urged against many of the best historians and the wisest thinkers, is rendered weighty in that he was unable to see, that in all human constitutions perfection is impossible, that we must take the evil with the good, and that what he imputes to one form of government is equally attributable to another. For in what monarchy, what oligarchy, have not great men been misunderstood, and great merits exposed to envy!

Thus, in the life of Cimon, Plutarch says that it was on a slight pretext[15] that that leader of the Spartan party in Athens was subjected to the ostracism. We have seen enough to convince us that, whatever the pretext, the reasons, at least, were grave and solid—that they were nothing short of Cimon's unvarying ardour for, and constant association with, the principles and the government of that state most inimical to Athens, and the suspicious policy of which was, in all times—at that time especially—fraught with danger to her power, her peace, and her institutions. Could we penetrate farther into the politics of the period, we might justify the Athenians yet more. Without calling into question the integrity and the patriotism of Cimon, without supposing that he would have entered into any intrigue against the Athenian independence of foreign powers—a supposition his subsequent conduct effectually refutes—he might, as a sincere and warm partisan of the nobles, and a resolute opposer of the popular party, have sought to restore at home the aristocratic balance of power, by whatever means his great rank, and influence, and connexion with the Lacedæmonian party could afford him. We are told, at least, that he not only opposed all the advances of the more liberal party—that he not only stood resolutely by the interests and dignities of the Areopagus, which had ceased to harmonize with the more modern institutions, but that he expressly sought to restore certain prerogatives which that assembly had formally lost during his foreign expeditions, and that he earnestly endeavoured to bring back the whole constitution to the more aristocratic government established by Clisthenes. It is one thing to preserve, it is another to restore. A people may be deluded under popular pretexts out of the rights they have newly acquired, but they never submit to be openly despoiled of them. Nor can we call that ingratitude which is but the refusal to surrender to the merits of an individual the acquisitions of a nation.

All things considered, then, I believe, that if ever ostracism was justifiable, it was so in the case of Cimon—nay, it was perhaps absolutely essential to the preservation of the constitution. His very honesty made him resolute in

---

15 Μικρᾶς ἐπιλαβόμενοι προφάσεως—Plut., in Vit. Cim., 17.

his attempts against that constitution. His talents, his rank, his fame, his services, only rendered those attempts more dangerous.

XIX. Could the reader be induced to view, with an examination equally dispassionate, the several ostracisms of Aristides and Themistocles, he might see equal causes of justification, both in the motives and in the results. The first was absolutely necessary for the defeat of the aristocratic party, and the removal of restrictions on those energies which instantly found the most glorious vents for action; the second was justified by a similar necessity that produced similar effects. To impartial eyes a people may be vindicated without traducing those whom a people are driven to oppose. In such august and complicated trials the accuser and defendant may be both innocent.

CHAPTER IV

War between Megara and Corinth—Megara and Pegæ
garrisoned by Athenians—review of affairs at the Persian
court—accession of Artaxerxes—revolt of Egypt under Inarus
—Athenian expedition to assist Inarus—Ægina besieged—
the Corinthians defeated—Spartan conspiracy with the Athenian oligarchy—battle of Tanagra—campaign and successes
of Myronides—plot of the oligarchy against the republic—
recall of Cimon—long walls completed—Ægina reduced—
expedition under Tolmides—Ithomë surrenders—the insurgents are settled at Naupactus—disastrous termination of the
Egyptian expedition—the Athenians march into Thessaly to
restore Orestes the Tagus—campaign under Pericles—truce of
five years with the Peloponnesians—Cimon sets sail for Cyprus
—pretended treaty of peace with Persia—death of Cimon

I. Cimon, summoned to the ostracism, was sentenced to its appointed
term of banishment—ten years. By his removal, the situation of Pericles
became suddenly more prominent and marked, and
he mingled with greater confidence and boldness
in public affairs. The vigour of the new administration was soon manifest. Megara had hitherto been
faithful to the Lacedæmonian alliance—a dispute
relative to the settlement of frontiers broke out between that state and
Corinth. Although the Corinthian government, liberal and enlightened, was
often opposed to the Spartan oligarchy, it was still essential to the interest of
both those Peloponnesian states to maintain a firm general alliance, and to
keep the Peloponnesian confederacy as a counterbalance to the restless ambition of the new head of the Ionian league. Sparta could not, therefore, have
been slow in preferring the alliance of Corinth to that of Megara. On the
other hand, Megara, now possessed of a democratic constitution, had long
since abandoned the Dorian character and habits. The situation of its territories, the nature of its institutions, alike pointed to Athens as its legitimate
ally. Thus, when the war broke out between Megara and Corinth, on the
side of the latter appeared Sparta, while Megara naturally sought the assistance
of Athens. The Athenian government eagerly availed itself of the occasion
to increase the power which Athens was now rapidly extending over Greece.

WAR BETWEEN MEGARA
AND CORINTH—MEGARA
AND PEGÆ GARRISONED BY
ATHENIANS

409

If we cast our eyes along the map of Greece, we shall perceive that the occupation of Megara proffered peculiar advantages. It became at once a strong and formidable fortress against any incursions from the Peloponnesus, while its sea-ports of Nisæa and Pegæ opened new fields, both of ambition and of commerce, alike on the Saronic and the Gulf of Corinth. The Athenians seized willingly on the alliance thus offered to them, and the Megarians had the weakness to yield both Megara and Pegæ to Athenian garrisons, while the Athenians fortified their position by long walls that united Megara with its harbour at Nisæa.

II. A new and more vast enterprise contributed towards the stability of the government by draining off its bolder spirits, and diverting the popular attention from domestic to foreign affairs.

REVIEW OF AFFAIRS AT THE PERSIAN COURT

It is necessary to pass before us, in brief review, the vicissitudes of the Persian court. In republican Greece, the history of the people marches side by side with the biography of great men. In despotic Persia, all history dies away in the dark recesses and sanguinary murthers of a palace governed by eunuchs and defended but by slaves.

In the year BC 465 the reign of the unfortunate Xerxes drew to its close. On his return to Susa, after the disastrous results of the Persian invasion,

ACCESSION OF ARTAXERXES

he had surrendered himself to the indolent luxury of a palace. An able and daring traitor, named Artabanus,[1] but who seems to have been a different personage from that Artabanus whose sagacity had vainly sought to save the armies of Xerxes from the expedition to Greece, entered into a conspiracy against the feeble monarch. By the connivance of a eunuch, he penetrated at night the chamber of the king—and the gloomy destinies of Xerxes were consummated by assassination. Artabanus sought to throw the guilt upon Darius, the eldest son of the murdered king; and Artaxerxes, the younger brother, seems to have connived at a charge which might render himself the lawful heir to the throne. Darius accordingly perished by the same fate as his father. The extreme youth of Artaxerxes had induced Artabanus to believe that but a slender and insecure life now stood between himself and the throne; but the young prince was already master of the royal art of dissimulation: he watched his opportunity—and by a counter-revolution Artabanus was sacrificed to the manes of his victims.[2]

Thus Artaxerxes obtained the undisturbed possession of the Persian throne. The new monarch appears to have derived from nature a stronger intellect

1 Neither Aristotle (Pol., v. 10), nor Justin, nor Ctesias, nor Diodorus speak of the assassin as kinsman to Xerxes. In Plutarch (Vit. Them.) he is Artabanus the Chiliarch.
2 Ctesias, xxx; Diod. Sic., xi; Justin, iii. 1. According to Aristotle, Artabanus, as captain of the king's guard, received an order to make away with Darius, neglected the command, and murdered Xerxes from fears for his own safety.

than his father. But the abuses, so rapid and rank of growth in eastern despotisms, which now ate away the strength of the Persian monarchy, were already, perhaps, past the possibility of reform. The enormous extent of the ill-regulated empire tempted the ambition of chiefs who might have plausibly hoped, that as the Persian masters had now degenerated to the effeminacy of the Assyrians they had supplanted, so the enterprise of a second Cyrus might be crowned by a similar success.

Egypt had been rather overrun by Xerxes than subdued—and the spirit of its ancient people waited only the occasion of revolt. A Libyan prince, of the

REVOLT OF EGYPT
UNDER INARUS

name of Inarus, whose territories bordered Egypt, entered that country, and was hailed by the greater part of the population as a deliverer. The recent murder of Xerxes—the weakness of a new reign, commenced in so sanguinary a manner, appeared to favour their desire of independence; and the African adventurer beheld himself at the head of a considerable force. Having already secured foreign subsidiaries, Inarus was anxious yet more to strengthen himself abroad; and more than one ambassador was despatched to Athens, soliciting her assistance, and proffering, in return, a share in the government for whose establishment her arms were solicited: a singular fatality, that the petty colony which, if we believe tradition, had so many centuries ago settled in the then obscure corners of Attica, should now be chosen the main auxiliary of the parent state in her vital struggles for national independence.

III. In acceding to the propositions of Inarus, Pericles yielded to considerations wholly contrary to his after policy, which made it a principal object

ATHENIAN EXPEDITION
TO ASSIST INARUS

to confine the energies of Athens within the limits of Greece. It is probable that that penetrating and scientific statesman (if indeed he had yet attained to a position which enabled him to follow out his own conceptions) saw that every new government must dazzle either by great enterprises abroad or great changes at home—and that he preferred the former. There are few sacrifices that a wary minister, newly established, from whom high hopes are entertained, and who can justify the destruction of a rival party only by the splendour of its successor—will not hazard rather than incur the contempt which follows disappointment. He will do something that is dangerous rather than do nothing that is brilliant.

Neither the hatred nor the fear of Persia was at an end in Athens; and to carry war into the heart of her empire was a proposition eagerly hailed. The more democratic and turbulent portion of the populace, viz., the seamen, had already been disposed of in an expedition of two hundred triremes against Cyprus. But the distant and magnificent enterprise of Egypt—the hope of new empire—the lust of undiscovered treasures—were more alluring than the reduction of Cyprus. That island was abandoned, and the fleet, composed both of Athenian and confederate ships, sailed up the Nile. Masters of that river, the Athenians advanced to Memphis, the capital of Lower

Egypt. They stormed and took two of the divisions of that city; the third, called the White Castle (occupied by the Medes, the Persians, and such of the Egyptians as had not joined the revolt), resisted their assault.

IV. While thus occupied in Egypt, the Athenian arms were equally employed in Greece. The whole forces of the commonwealth were in demand—war on every side. The alliance with Megara not only created an enemy in Corinth, but the Peloponnesian confederacy became involved with the Attic: Lacedæmon herself, yet inert, but menacing; while the neighbouring Ægina, intent and jealous, prepared for hostilities soon manifest.

The Athenians forestalled the attack—made a descent on Haliæ, in Argolis—were met by the Corinthians and Epidaurians, and the result of

ÆGINA BESIEGED—THE CORINTHIANS DEFEATED

battle was the victory of the latter. This defeat the Athenians speedily retrieved at sea. Off Cecryphalea, in the Saronic Gulf, they attacked and utterly routed the Peloponnesian fleet. And now Ægina openly declared war and joined the hostile league. An important battle was fought by these two maritime powers with the confederates of either side. The Athenians were victorious—took seventy ships and, pushing the advantage they had obtained, landed in Ægina and besieged her city. Three hundred heavy-armed Peloponnesians were despatched to the relief of Ægina; while the Corinthians invaded the Megarian territory, seized the passes of Geranea, and advanced to Megara with their allies. Never was occasion more propitious. So large a force in Egypt, so large a force at Ægina—how was it possible for the Athenians to march to the aid of Megara? They appeared limited to the choice either to abandon Megara or to raise the siege of Ægina: so reasoned the Peloponnesians. But the advantage of a constitution widely popular is, that the whole community become soldiers in time of need. Myronides, an Athenian of great military genius, not unassisted by Pericles, whose splendid qualities now daily developed themselves, was well adapted to give direction to the enthusiasm of the people. Not a man was called from Ægina. The whole regular force disposed of, there yet remained at Athens those too aged and those too young for the ordinary service. Under Myronides, boys and old men marched at once to the assistance of their Megarian ally. A battle ensued; both sides retiring, neither considered itself defeated. But the Corinthians retreating to Corinth, the Athenians erected a trophy on the field. The Corinthian government received its troops with reproaches, and, after an interval of twelve days, the latter returned to the scene of contest, and asserting their claim to the victory, erected a trophy of their own. During the work the Athenians sallied from Megara, where they had ensconced themselves, attacked and put to flight the Corinthians; and a considerable portion of the enemy turning into ground belonging to a private individual, became entangled in a large pit or ditch, from which was but one outlet, viz., that by which they had entered. At this passage the Athenians stationed their heavy-armed troops, while the light-armed soldiers surrounded the ditch, and with the missiles

412

of darts and stones put the enemy to death. The rest (being the greater part) of the Corinthian forces effected a safe but dishonourable retreat.

V. This victory effected and Megara secured—although Ægina still held out, and although the fate of the Egyptian expedition was still unknown—the wonderful activity of the government commenced what even in times of tranquillity would have been a great and arduous achievement. To unite their city with its sea-ports, they set to work at the erection of the long walls, which extended from Athens both to Phalerum and Piræus. Under Cimon, preparations had already been made for the undertaking, and the spoils of Persia now provided the means for the defence of Athens.

Meanwhile, the Spartans still continued at the siege of Ithomë. We must not imagine that all the Helots had joined in the revolt. This, indeed, would be almost to suppose the utter disorganization of the Spartan state. The most luxurious subjects of a despotism were never more utterly impotent in procuring for themselves the necessaries of life, than were the hardy and abstemious freemen of the Dorian Sparta. It was dishonour for a Spartan to till the land—to exercise a trade. He had all the prejudices against any calling but that of arms which characterized a noble of the middle ages.

As is ever the case in the rebellion of slaves, the rise was not universal; a sufficient number of these wretched dependents remained passive and inert to satisfy the ordinary wants of their masters, and to assist in the rebuilding of the town. Still the Spartans were greatly enfeebled, crippled, and embarrassed by the loss of the rest: and the siege of Ithomë sufficed to absorb their attention, and to make them regard without open hostilities, if with secret enmity, the operations of the Athenians. The Spartan alliance formally dissolved—Megara, with its command of the Peloponnesus seized—the Doric city of Corinth humbled and defeated—Ægina blockaded; all these—the Athenian proceedings—the Spartans bore without any formal declaration of war.

VI. And now, in the eighth year of the Messenian war, piety succeeded where pride and revenge had failed, and the Spartans permitted other objects to divide their attention with the siege of Ithomë. It was one of the finest characteristics of that singular people, their veneration for antiquity. For the little, rocky, and obscure territory of Doris, whence tradition derived their origin, they felt the affection and reverence of sons. A quarrel arising between the people of this state and the neighbouring Phocians, the latter invaded Doris, and captured one of its three towns.[3] The Lacedæmonians marched at once to the assistance of their reputed fatherland, with an army of no less than fifteen hundred heavy-armed Spartans and ten thousand of their Peloponnesian allies,[4] under the command of Nicomedes, son of

---

3 Thucyd., i. 107. The three towns of Doris were, according to Thucydides, Bæum, Cytenium, and Erineus. The scholiast on Pindar (Pyth., i. 121) speaks of six towns.
4 Thucyd., i.

Cleombrotus, and guardian of their king Pleistoanax, still a minor. They forced the Phocians to abandon the town they had taken; and having effectually protected Doris by a treaty of peace between the two nations, prepared to return home. But in this they were much perplexed; the pass of Geranea was now occupied by the Athenians: Megara, too, and Pegæ were in their hands. Should they pass by sea through the Gulf of Crissa, an Athenian squadron already occupied that passage. Either way they were intercepted.[5] Under all circumstances, they resolved to halt a while in Bœotia, and watch an opportunity to effect their return. But with these ostensible motives for that sojourn assigned by Thucydides, there was another more deep and latent. We have had constant occasion to remark how singularly it was the Spartan policy to plot against the constitution of free states, and how well founded was the Athenian jealousy of the secret interference of the Grecian Venice.

Halting now in Bœotia, Nicomedes entered into a clandestine communication with certain of the oligarchic party in Athens, the object of the latter
SPARTAN CONSPIRACY WITH
THE ATHENIAN OLIGARCHY
being the overthrow of the existent popular constitution. With this object was certainly linked the recall of Cimon, though there is no reason to believe that great general a party in the treason. This conspiracy was one main reason of the halt in Bœotia. Another was, probably, the conception of a great and politic design, glanced at only by historians, but which, if successful, would have ranked among the masterpieces of Spartan statesmanship. This design was—while Athens was to be weakened by internal divisions, and her national spirit effectually curbed by the creation of an oligarchy, the tool of Sparta—to erect a new rival to Athens in the Bœotian Thebes. It is true that this project was not, according to Diodorus, openly apparent until after the battle of Tanagra. But such a scheme required preparation; and the sojourn of Nicomedes in Bœotia afforded him the occasion to foresee its possibility and prepare his plans. Since the Persian invasion, Thebes had lost her importance, not only throughout Greece, but throughout Bœotia, her dependent territory. Many of the states refused to regard her as their capital, and the Theban government desired to regain its power. Promises to make war upon Athens rendered the Theban power auxiliary to Sparta: the more Thebes was strengthened, the more Athens was endangered: and Sparta, ever averse to quitting the Peloponnesus, would thus erect a barrier to the Athenian arms on the very frontiers of Attica.

VII. While such were the designs and schemes of Nicomedes, the conspiracy of the aristocratic party could not be so secret in Athens but what some rumour, some suspicion, broke abroad. The people became alarmed

---

5 Thucydides, in mentioning these operations of the Athenians, and the consequent fears of the Spartans, proves to what a length hostilities had gone, though war was not openly declared.

and incensed. They resolved to anticipate the war; and, judging Nicomedes cut off from retreat, and embarrassed and confined in his position, they marched against him with a thousand Argives, with a band of Thessalian horse, and some other allied troops drawn principally from Ionia, which, united to the whole force of the armed population within their walls, amounted, in all, to fourteen thousand men.

VIII. It is recorded by Plutarch, that during their march Cimon appeared, and sought permission to join the army. This was refused by the senate of Five Hundred, to whom the petition was referred, not from any injurious suspicion of Cimon, but from a natural fear that his presence, instead of inspiring confidence, would create confusion; and that it might be plausibly represented that he sought less to resist the Spartans than to introduce them into Athens—a proof how strong was the impression against him, and how extensive had been the Spartan intrigues. Cimon retired, beseeching his friends to vindicate themselves from the aspersions cast upon them. Placing the armour of Cimon—a species of holy standard—in their ranks, a hundred of the warmest supporters among his tribe advanced to battle conscious of the trust committed to their charge.

IX. In the territory of Tanagra a severe engagement took place. On that day Pericles himself fought in the thickest part of the battle; exposing himself to every danger, as if anxious that the loss of Cimon should not be missed. The battle was long, obstinate, and even: when in the midst of it, the Thessalian cavalry suddenly deserted to the Spartans. Despite this treachery, the Athenians, well supported by the Argives, long maintained their ground with advantage. But when night separated the armies,[6] victory remained with the Spartans and their allies.[7]

BATTLE OF TANAGRA

The Athenians were not, however, much disheartened by defeat, nor did the Spartans profit by their advantage. Anxious only for escape, Nicomedes conducted his forces homeward, passed through Megara, destroying the fruit trees on his march; and, gaining the pass of Geranea, which the Athenians had deserted to join the camp at Tanagra, arrived at Lacedæmon.

Meanwhile the Thebans took advantage of the victory to extend their authority, agreeably to the project conceived with Sparta. Thebes now attempted the reduction of all the cities of Bœotia. Some submitted, others opposed.

X. Aware of the necessity of immediate measures against a neighbour, brave, persevering, and ambitious, the Athenian government lost no time in recruiting its broken forces. Under Myronides, an army, collected from the allies and dependent states,

CAMPAIGN AND SUCCESSES OF MYRONIDES

6 Diod. Sic., xi.
7 Thucyd., i.

was convened to assemble upon a certain day. Many failed the appointment, and the general was urged to delay his march till their arrival. "It is not the part of a general", said Myronides, sternly, "to await the pleasure of his soldiers! By delay I read an omen of the desire of the loiterers to avoid the enemy. Better rely upon a few faithful than on many disaffected."

With a force comparatively small, Myronides commenced his march, entered Bœotia sixty-two days only after the battle of Tanagra, and, engaging the Bœotians at Œnophyta, obtained a complete and splendid victory. This battle, though Diodorus could find no details of the action, was reckoned by Athens among the most glorious she had ever achieved; preferred by the vain Greeks even to those of Marathon and Platæa, inasmuch as Greek was opposed to Greek, and not to the barbarians. Those who fell on the Athenian side were first honoured by public burial in the Ceramicus—"as men", says Plato, "who fought against Grecians for the liberties of Greece". Myronides followed up his victory by levelling the walls of Tanagra. All Bœotia, except Thebes herself, was brought into the Athenian alliance—as democracies in the different towns, replacing the oligarchical governments, gave the moral blow to the Spartan ascendency. Thus, in effect, the consequences of the battle almost deserved the eulogies bestowed upon the victory. Those consequences were to revolutionize nearly all the states in Bœotia; and, by calling up a democracy in each state, Athens at once changed enemies into allies.

From Bœotia, Myronides marched to Phocis, and, pursuing the same policy, rooted out the oligarchies, and established popular governments. The Locrians of Opus gave a hundred of their wealthiest citizens as hostages. Returned to Athens, Myronides was received with public rejoicings,[8] and thus closed a short but brilliant campaign, which had not only conquered enemies, but had established everywhere garrisons of friends.

XI. Although the banishment of Cimon had appeared to complete the triumph of the popular party in Athens, his opinions were not banished also. Athens, like all free states, was ever agitated by the feud of parties, at once its danger and its strength. Parties in Athens were, however, utterly unlike many of those that rent the peace of the Italian republics; nor are they rightly understood in the vague declamations of Barthélemy or Mitford; they were not only parties of names and men—they were also parties of principles—the parties of restriction and of advance. And thus the triumph of either was invariably followed by the triumph of the principle it espoused. Nobler than the bloody contests of mere faction, we do not see in Athens the long and sweeping proscriptions, the atrocious massacres that attended the party strifes of ancient Rome or of modern Italy. The ostracism, or the fine, of some obnoxious and eminent partisans, usually contented the wrath of the victorious politicians. And in the advance of a cause the people

8 Diod. Sic., xi.

found the main vent for their passions. I trust, however, that I shall not be accused of prejudice when I state as a fact, that the popular party in Athens seems to have been much more moderate and less unprincipled even in its excesses than its antagonists. We never see it, like the Pisistratidæ, leagued with the Persian, nor with Isagoras, betraying Athens to the Spartan. What the oligarchic faction did when triumphant, we see hereafter in the establishment of the Thirty Tyrants. And compared with their offences, the ostracism of Aristides, or the fine and banishment of Cimon, lose all their colours of wrong.

XII. The discontented advocates for an oligarchy, who had intrigued with Nicomedes, had been foiled in their object, partly by the conduct of Cimon in disavowing all connexion with them, partly by the rereat of Nicomedes himself. Still their spirit was too fierce to suffer them to forego their schemes without a struggle, and after the battle of Tanagra they broke out into open conspiracy against the republic.

PLOT OF THE OLIGARCHY AGAINST THE REPUBLIC

The details of this treason are lost to us; it is one of the darkest passages of Athenian history. From scattered and solitary references we can learn, however, that for a time it threatened the democracy with ruin.[9]

The victory of the Spartans at Tanagra gave strength to the Spartan party in Athens; it also inspired with fear many of the people; it was evidently desirable rather to effect a peace with Sparta than to hazard a war. Who so likely to effect that peace as the banished Cimon? Now was the time to press for his recall. Either at this period, or shortly afterward, Ephialtes, his most vehement enemy, was barbarously murdered—according to Aristotle, a victim to the hatred of the nobles.

XIII. Pericles had always conducted his opposition to Cimon with great dexterity and art; and indeed the aristocratic leaders of contending parties are rarely so hostile to each other as their subordinate followers suppose. In the present strife for the recall of his

RECALL OF CIMON

9 Certain German historians, Müller among others, have built enormous conclusions upon the smallest data, when they suppose Cimon was implicated in this conspiracy. Meirs (Historia Juris de bonis Damnatis, p. 4, note 11) is singularly unsuccessful in connecting the supposed fine of fifty talents incurred by Cimon with the civil commotions of this period. In fact, that Cimon was ever fined at all is very improbable; the supposition rests upon most equivocal ground: if adopted, it is more likely, perhaps, that the fine was inflicted after his return from Thasos, when he was accused of neglecting the honour of the Athenian arms, and being seduced by Macedonian gold (a charge precisely of a nature for which a fine would have been incurred). But the whole tale of this imaginary fine, founded upon a sentence in Demosthenes, who, like many orators, was by no means minutely accurate in historical facts, is possibly nothing more than a confused repetition of the old story of the fine of fifty talents (the same amount) imposed upon Miltiades, and really paid by Cimon. This is doubly, and, indeed, indisputably clear, if we accept Bekker's reading of Παρίων for πάτριον in the sentence of Demosthenes referred to.

rival, amid all the intrigues and conspiracies, the open violence and the secret machination, which threatened not only the duration of the government, but the very existence of the republic, Pericles met the danger by proposing himself the repeal of Cimon's sentence.

Plutarch, with a childish sentimentality common to him when he means to be singularly effective, bursts into an exclamation upon the generosity of this step, and the candour and moderation of those times, when resentments could be so easily laid aside. But the profound and passionless mind of Pericles was above all the weakness of a melodramatic generosity. And it cannot be doubted that this measure was a compromise between the government and the more moderate and virtuous of the aristocratic party. Perhaps it was the most advantageous compromise Pericles was enabled to effect; for by concession with respect to individuals, we can often prevent concession as to things. The recall[10] of the great leader of the anti-popular faction may have been deemed equivalent to the surrender of many popular rights. And had we a deeper insight into the intrigues of that day and the details of the oligarchic conspiracy, I suspect we should find that, by recalling Cimon, Pericles saved the constitution.[11]

XIV. The first and most popular benefit anticipated from the recall of the son of Miltiades in a reconciliation between Sparta and Athens, was not immediately realized further than by an armistice of four months.[12]

LONG WALLS COMPLETED —ÆGINA REDUCED

About this time the long walls of the Piræus were completed, and shortly afterward Ægina yielded to the arms of the Athenians, upon terms which subjected the citizens of that gallant and adventurous isle (whose achievements and commerce seem no less a miracle than the

---

10 If we can attach any credit to the Oration on Peace ascribed to Andocides, Cimon was residing on his patrimonial estates in the Chersonesus at the time of his recall. As Athens retained its right to the sovereignty of this colony, and as it was a most important position as respected the recent Athenian conquests under Cimon himself, the assertion, if true, will show that Cimon's ostracism was attended with no undue persecution. Had the government seriously suspected him of any guilty connivance with the oligarchic conspirators, it could scarcely have permitted him to remain in a colony, the localities of which were peculiarly favourable to any treasonable designs he might have formed.

11 In the recall of Cimon, Plutarch tells us, some historians asserted that it was arranged between the two parties that the administration of the state should be divided; that Cimon should be invested with the foreign command of Cyprus, and Pericles remain the head of the domestic government. But it was not until the sixth year after his recall (viz., in the archonship of Euthydemus, see Diod. Sic. xii.) that Cimon went to Cyprus; and before that event Pericles himself was absent on foreign expeditions.

12 Plutarch, by a confusion of dates, blends this short armistice with the five years' truce some time afterward concluded. Mitford and others have followed him in his error. That the recall of Cimon was followed by no peace, not only with the Spartans, but the Peloponnesians generally, is evident from the incursions of Tolmides presently to be related.

greatness of Athens when we survey the limits of their narrow and rocky domain) to the rival they had long so fearlessly, nor fruitlessly braved. The Æginetans surrendered their shipping, demolished their walls, and consented to the payment of an annual tribute. And so was fulfilled the proverbial command of Pericles, that Ægina ought not to remain the eyesore of Athens.

XV. Ægina reduced, the Athenian fleet of fifty galleys, manned by four thousand men,[13] under the command of Tolmides, circumnavigated the Peloponnesus—the armistice of four months had expired—and, landing in Laconia, Tolmides burnt Gythium, a dock of the Lacedæmonians; took Chalcis, a town belonging to Corinth, and, debarking at Sicyon, engaged and defeated the Sicyonians. Thence proceeding to Cephallenia, he mastered the cities of that isle; and descending at Naupactus, on the Corinthian gulf, wrested it from the Ozolian Locrians.

EXPEDITION UNDER TOLMIDES

In the same year with this expedition, and in the tenth year of the siege, Ithomë surrendered to Lacedæmon. The long and gallant resistance of that town, the precipitous site of which nature herself had fortified, is one of the most memorable and glorious events in the Grecian history; and we cannot but regret that the imperfect morality of those days, which saw glory in the valour of freemen, rebellion only in that of slaves, should have left us but frigid and scanty accounts of so obstinate a siege. To posterity neither the cause nor the achievements of Marathon or Platæa, seem the one more holy, the other more heroic, than this long defiance of Messenians and Helots against the prowess of Sparta and the aid of her allies. The reader will rejoice to learn that it was on no dishonourable terms that the city at last surrendered. Life and free permission to depart was granted to the besieged, and recorded by a pillar erected on the banks of the Alpheus.[14] But such of the Helots as had been taken in battle or in the neighbouring territory were again reduced to slavery—the ringleaders so apprehended alone executed.[15]

ITHOMË SURRENDERS

The gallant defenders of Ithomë having conditioned to quit for ever the Peloponnesus, Tolmides invested them with the possession of his new conquest of Naupactus. There, under a democratic government, protected by the power of Athens, they regained their ancient freedom, and preserved their hereditary name of Messenians—long distinguished from their neighbours by their peculiar dialect.

THE INSURGENTS ARE SETTLED AT NAUPACTUS

13 Diod. Sic., xi.
14 See Müller's Dorians, and the authorities he quotes, i. 1.
15 For so I interpret Diodorus.

XVI. While thus, near at home, the Athenians had extended their conquests and cemented their power, the adventurers they had despatched to the Nile were maintaining their strange settlement with more obstinacy than success. At first, the Athenians and their ally, the Libyan Inarus, had indeed, as we have seen, obtained no inconsiderable advantage.

DISASTROUS TERMINATION OF THE EGYPTIAN EXPEDITION

Anxious to detach the Athenians from the Egyptian revolt, Artaxerxes had despatched an ambassador to Sparta, in order to prevail upon that state to make an excursion into Attica, and so compel the Athenians to withdraw their troops from Egypt. The liability of the Spartan government to corrupt temptation was not unknown to a court which had received the Spartan fugitives; and the ambassador was charged with large treasures to bribe those whom he could not otherwise convince. Nevertheless, the negotiation failed; the government could not be induced to the alliance with the Persian king. There was indeed a certain spirit of honour inherent in that haughty nation which, if not incompatible with cunning and intrigue, held at least in profound disdain an alliance with the barbarian, for whatsoever ends. But, in fact, the Spartans were then entirely absorbed in the reduction of Ithomë, and the war in Arcady; and it would, further, have been the height of impolicy in that state, if meditating any designs against Athens, to assist in the recall of an army which it was its very interest to maintain employed in distant and perilous expeditions.

The ambassador had the satisfaction indeed of wasting some of his money, but to no purpose; and he returned without success to Asia. Artaxerxes then saw the necessity of arousing himself to those active exertions which the feebleness of an exhausted despotism rendered the final, not the first resort. Under Megabyzus an immense army was collected; traversing Syria and Phœnicia, it arrived in Egypt, engaged the Egyptian forces in a pitched battle, and obtained a complete victory. Thence marching to Memphis, it drove the Greeks from their siege of the White Castle till then continued, and shut them up in Prosopitis, an island in the Nile, around which their ships lay anchored. Megabyzus ordered the channel to be drained by dykes, and the vessels, the main force of the Athenians, were left stranded. Terrified by this dexterous manœuvre, as well as by the success of the Persians, the Egyptians renounced all further resistance; and the Athenians were deprived at once of their vessels and their allies.[16]

XVII. Nothing daunted, and inspired by their disdain no less than by their valour, the Athenians were yet to the barbarian what the Norman knights were afterward to the Greeks. They burnt their vessels that they might be as useless to the enemy as to themselves, and, exhorting each other not to dim

16 Diod. Sic., xi.

the glory of their past exploits, shut up still in the small town of Byblus situated in the isle of Prosopitis, resolved to defend themselves to the last.

The blockade endured a year and a half, such was the singular ignorance of the art of sieges in that time. At length, when the channel was drained, as I have related, the Persians marched across the dry bed, and carried the place by a land assault. So ended this wild and romantic expedition. The greater part of the Athenians perished; a few, however, either forced their way by arms, or, as Diodorus more probably relates, were permitted by treaty to retire, out of the Egyptian territory. Taking the route of Libya, they arrived at Cyrene, and finally reached Athens.

Inarus, the author of the revolt, was betrayed, and perished on the cross, and the whole of Egypt once more succumbed to the Persian yoke, save only that portion called the marshy or fenny parts (under the dominion of a prince named Amyrtæus), protected by the nature of the soil and the proverbial valour of the inhabitants. Meanwhile a squadron of fifty vessels, despatched by Athens to the aid of their countrymen, entered the Mendesian mouth of the Nile too late to prevent the taking of Byblus. Here they were surprised and defeated by the Persian troops and a Phœnician fleet, and few survived a slaughter which put the last seal on the disastrous results of the Egyptian expedition.

At home the Athenians continued, however, their military operations. Thessaly, like the rest of Greece, had long shaken off the forms of kingly government, but the spirit of monarchy still survived in a country where the few were opulent and the multitude enslaved. The Thessalian republics, united by an assembly of deputies from the various towns, elected for their head a species of protector—who appears to have possessed many of the characteristics of the podesta of the Italian states. His nominal station was that of military command—a station which, in all save the most perfect constitutions, comprehends also civil authority. The name of Tagus was given to this dangerous chief, and his power and attributes so nearly resembled those of a monarch, that even Thucydides confers on a Tagus the title of king. Orestes, one of these princes, had been driven from his country by a civil revolution. He fled to Athens, and besought her assistance to effect his restoration. That the Athenians should exert themselves in favour of a man whose rank so nearly resembled the odious dignity of a monarch, appears a little extraordinary. But as the Tagus was often the favourite of the commonalty and the foe of the aristocratic party, it is possible that, in restoring Orestes, the Athenians might have seen a new occasion to further the policy so triumphantly adopted in Bœotia and Phocis— to expel a hostile oligarchy and establish a friendly democracy.[17] Whatever

THE ATHENIANS MARCH INTO THESSALY TO RESTORE ORESTES THE TAGUS

17 There was a democratic party in Thessaly always favourable to Athens. See Thucyd., iv. 88.

their views, they decided to yield to the exile the assistance he demanded, and under Myronides an army in the following year accompanied Orestes into Thessaly. They were aided by the Bœotians and Phocians. Myronides marched to Pharsalus, a Thessalian city, and mastered the surrounding country; but the obstinate resistance of the city promising a more protracted blockade than it was deemed advisable to await, the Athenians raised the seige without effecting the object of the expedition.

XVIII. The possession of Pegæ and the new colony of Naupactus[18] induced the desire of extending the Athenian conquests on the neighbouring coasts, and the government were naturally anxious to repair the military honours of Athens—lessened in Egypt, and certainly not increased in Thessaly. With a thousand Athenian soldiers, Pericles himself set out for Pegæ. Thence the fleet, there anchored, made a descent on Sicyon; Pericles defeated the Sicyonians in a pitched battle, and besieged the city; but, after some fruitless assaults, learning that the Spartans were coming to the relief of the besieged, he quitted the city, and, re-enforced by some Achæans, sailed to the opposite side of the continent, crossed over the Corinthian Bay, besieged the town of Œniadæ in Acarnania (the inhabitants of which Pausanias[19] styles the hereditary enemies of the Athenians), ravaged the neighbouring country, and bore away no inconsiderable spoils. Although he reduced no city, the successes of Pericles were signal enough to render the campaign triumphant;[20] and it gratified the national pride and resentment to have insulted the cities and wasted the lands of the Peloponnesus.

CAMPAIGN UNDER PERICLES

These successes were sufficient to render a peace with Sparta and her allies advisable for the latter, while they were not sufficiently decided to tempt the Athenians to prolong irregular and fruitless hostilities. Three years were consumed without further aggressions on either side, and probably in negotiations for peace. At the end of that time, the influence and intervention of Cimon obtained a truce of five years between the Athenians and the Peloponnesians.

TRUCE OF FIVE YEARS WITH THE PELOPONNESIANS

XIX. The truce with the Peloponnesians removed the main obstacle to those more bright and extensive prospects of enterprise and ambition which the defeat of the Persians had opened to the Athenians. In that restless and unpausing energy, which is the characteristic of an intellectual republic, there seems, as it were, a kind of destiny: a power impossible to resist urges the state from action to action, from progress to progress, with a rapidity dangerous while it dazzles; resembling in this the career of individuals

18 Now Lepanto.
19 Paus., ii. 28.
20 Plut., in Vit. Per.

impelled onward, first to obtain, and thence to preserve, power, and who cannot struggle against the fate which necessitates them to soar, until, by the moral gravitation of human things, the point which has no beyond is attained; and the next effort to rise is but the prelude of their fall. In such states Time indeed moves with gigantic strides; years concentrate what would be the epochs of centuries in the march of less popular institutions. The planet of their fortunes rolls with an equal speed through the cycle of internal civilization as of foreign glory. The condition of their brilliant life is the absence of repose. The accelerated circulation of the blood beautifies but consumes, and action itself, exhausting the stores of youth by its very vigour, becomes a mortal but divine disease.

XX. When Athens rose to the ascendancy of Greece, it was necessary to the preservation of that sudden and splendid dignity that she should sustain the naval renown by which it had been mainly acquired. There is but one way to *sustain* reputation, viz., to *increase* it: and the memory of past glories becomes dim unless it be constantly refreshed by new. It must also be borne in mind that the maritime habits of the people had called a new class into existence in the councils of the state. The seamen, the most democratic part of the population, were now to be conciliated and consulted; it was requisite to keep them in action, for they were turbulent—in employment, for they were poor: and thus the domestic policy and the foreign interests of Athens alike conspired to necessitate the prosecution of maritime enterprise.

XXI. No longer harassed and impeded by fears of an enemy in the Peloponnesus, the lively imagination of the people readily turned to more dazzling and profitable warfare. The island of Cyprus had (we have seen) before attracted the ambition of the mistress of the Ægæan. Its possession was highly advantageous, whether for military or commercial designs, and once subjected, the fleet of the Athenians might readily retain the dominion. Divided into nine petty states, governed, not by republican, but by monarchical institutions, the forces of the island were distracted, and the whole proffered an easy as well as glorious conquest; while the attempt took the plausible shape of deliverance, inasmuch as Persia, despite the former successes of Cimon, still arrogated the supremacy over the island, and the war was, in fact, less against Cyprus than against Persia. Cimon, who ever affected great and brilliant enterprises, and whose main policy it was to keep the Athenians from the dangerous borders of the Peloponnesus, hastened to cement the truce he had formed with the states of that district, by directing the spirit of enterprise to the conquest of Cyprus.

CIMON SETS SAIL FOR CYPRUS

Invested with the command of two hundred galleys, he set sail for that island.[21] But designs more vast were associated with this enterprise. The

21 Thucyd., i. 112.

objects of the late Egyptian expedition still tempted, and sixty vessels of the fleet were despatched to Egypt to the assistance of Amyrtæus, who, yet unconquered in the marshy regions, sustained the revolt against the Persian king.

Artabazus commanded the Persian forces, and with a fleet of three hundred vessels he ranged himself in sight of Cyprus. Cimon, however, landing

PRETENDED TREATY OF PEACE WITH PERSIA— DEATH OF CIMON

on the island, succeeded in capturing many of its principal towns. Humbled and defeated, it was not the policy of Persia to continue hostilities with an enemy from whom it had so much to fear and so little to gain. It is not, therefore, altogether an improbable account of the later authorities, that ambassadors with proposals of peace were formally despatched to Athens. But we must reject as a pure fable the assertions that a treaty was finally agreed upon, by which it was decreed, on the one hand, that the independence of the Asiatic Greek towns should be acknowledged, and that the Persian generals should not advance within three days' march of the Grecian seas; nor should a Persian vessel sail within the limit of Phaselis and the Cyanean rocks; while, on the other hand, the Athenians were bound not to enter the territories of Artaxerxes.[22] No such arrangement was known to Thucydides; no reference is ever made to such a treaty in subsequent transactions with Persia. A document, professing to be a copy of this treaty, was long extant; but it was undoubtedly the offspring of a weak credulity or an ingenious invention. But while negotiations, if ever actually commenced, were yet pending, Cimon was occupied in the siege of Citium, where famine conspired with the obstinacy of the besieged to protract the success of his arms. It is recorded among the popular legends of the day that Cimon[23] sent a secret mission to the oracle of Jupiter Ammon. "Return", was the response to the messengers; "Cimon is with me!" The messengers did return to find the son of Miltiades was no more. He expired during the blockade of Citium. By his orders his death was concealed, the siege raised, and, still under the magic of Cimon's name, the Athenians engaging the Phœnicians and Cilicians off the Cyprian Salamis, obtained signal victories both by land and sea. Thence, joined by the squadron despatched to Egypt, which, if it did not share, did not retrieve, the misfortunes of the previous expedition, they returned home.

The remains of Cimon were interred in Athens, and the splendid monument consecrated to his name was visible in the time of Plutarch.

22 Diod. Sic., xi; Plut., in Vit. Cim.; Heeren, Manual of Ancient History; but Mr Mitford and Mr Thirlwall properly reject this spurious treaty.
23 Plut., in Vit. Cim.

CHAPTER V

Change of manners in Athens—begun under the Pisistratidæ
—effects of the Persian war, and the intimate connexion
with Ionia—the Hetæræ—the political eminence lately acquired by Athens—the transfer of the treasury from Delos
to Athens—latent dangers and evils—first, the artificial
greatness of Athens not supported by natural strength—
second, her pernicious reliance on tribute—third, deterioration
of national spirit commenced by Cimon in the use of bribes
and public tables—fourth, defects in popular courts of law
—progress of general education—history—its Ionian origin—
early historians—Acusilaus—Cadmus—Eugeon—Hellanicus
—Pherecydes—Xanthus—view of the life and writings of
Herodotus—progress of philosophy since Thales—philosophers
of the Ionian and Eleatic schools—Pythagoras—his philosophical tenets and political influence—effect of these philosophers on Athens—school of political philosophy continued
in Athens from the time of Solon—Anaxagoras—Archelaus
—philosophy not a thing apart from the ordinary life of the
Athenians

I. Before we pass to the administration of Pericles—a period so brilliant
in the history not more of Athens than of art—it may not be unseasonable
to take a brief survey of the progress which the Athenians
had already made in civilization and power.

CHANGE OF MANNERS
IN ATHENS

The comedians and the rhetoricians, when at a later
period they boldly represented to the democracy, in a mixture of satire and
of truth, the more displeasing features of the popular character, delighted to
draw a contrast between the new times and the old. The generation of men
whom Marathon and Salamis had immortalized were, according to these
praisers of the past, of nobler manners and more majestic virtues than their
degenerate descendants. "Then", exclaimed Isocrates, "our young men did
not waste their days in the gambling-house, nor with music-girls, nor in the
assemblies, in which whole days are now consumed . . . then did they shun
the Agora, or, if they passed through its haunts, it was with modest and
timorous forbearance—then, to contradict an elder was a greater offence
than nowadays to offend a parent—then, not even a servant of honest repute
would have been seen to eat or drink within a tavern!" "In the good old

times", says the citizen of Aristophanes,[1] "our youths breasted the snow without a mantle—their music was masculine and martial—their gymnastic exercises decorous and chaste. Thus were trained the heroes of Marathon!"

In such happy days we are informed that mendicancy and even want were unknown.[2]

It is scarcely necessary to observe, that we must accept these comparisons between one age and another with considerable caution and qualification. We are too much accustomed to such declamations in our own time not to recognize an ordinary trick of satirists and declaimers. As long as a people can bear patiently to hear their own errors and follies scornfully proclaimed, they have not become altogether degenerate or corrupt. Yet still, making every allowance for rhetorical or poetic exaggeration, it is not more evident than natural that the luxury of civilization—the fervour of unbridled competition, in pleasure as in toil—were attended with many changes of manners and life favourable to art and intellect, but hostile to the stern hardihood of a former age.

II. But the change was commenced, not under a democracy, but under a tyranny—it was consummated, not by the vices, but the virtues of the nation. It began with the Pisistratidæ,[3] who first introduced into Athens the desire of pleasure and the habits of ostentation, that refine before they enervate; and that luxury which, as in Athenæus it is well and profoundly said, is often the concomitant of freedom, "as soft couches took their name from Hercules",—made its rapid progress with the result of the Persian war. The plunder of Platæa, the luxuries of Byzantium, were not limited in their effect to the wild Pausanias. The decay of old and the rise of new families tended to give a stimulus to the emulation of wealth—since it is by wealth that new families seek to eclipse the old. And even the destruction of private houses, in the ravages of Mardonius, served to quicken the career of art. In rebuilding their mansions, the nobles naturally availed themselves of the treasures and the appliances of the gorgeous enemy they had vanquished and despoiled. Few ever rebuild their houses on as plain a scale as the old ones. In the city itself the residences of the great remained plain and simple; they were mostly built of plaster and unburnt brick, and we are told that the houses of Cimon and Pericles were scarcely distinguishable from those of the other citizens. But in their villas in Attica, in which the Athenians took a passionate delight, they exhibited their taste and displayed their wealth.[4]

BEGUN UNDER THE PIS-ISTRATIDÆ—EFFECTS OF THE PERSIAN WAR, AND THE INTIMATE CONNEXION WITH IONIA

1 The "Clouds".
2 Isoc., Areop., 44.
3 Idomen., apud Athen., xii.
4 Thucyd., ii. 16; Isoc., Areop., 52.

426

And the lucrative victories of Cimon, backed by his own example of ostentation, gave to a vast number of families, hitherto obscure, at once the power to gratify luxury and the desire to parade refinement. Nor was the eastern example more productive of emulation than the Ionian. The Persian war, and the league which followed it, brought Athens into the closest intercourse with her graceful but voluptuous colonies. Miletus fell, but the manners of Miletus survived her liberties. That city was renowned for the peculiar grace and intellectual influence of its women; and it is evident that there must have been a gradual change of domestic habits and the formation of a new class of female society in Athens before Aspasia could have summoned around her the power, and the wisdom, and the wit of Athens—before an accomplished mistress could have been even suspected of urging the politic Pericles into war—and, above all, before an Athenian audience could have assented in delight to that mighty innovation on their masculine drama— which is visible in the passionate heroines and the sentimental pathos of Euripides.

But this change was probably not apparent in the Athenian matrons themselves, who remained for the most part in primitive seclusion; and though, I think, it will be shown hereafter that modern writers

THE HETÆRÆ

have greatly exaggerated both the want of mental culture and the degree of domestic confinement to which the Athenian women[5] were subjected, yet it is certain, at least, that they did not share the social freedom or partake the intellectual accomplishments of their lords. It was the new class of "female friends" or "Hetæræ", a phrase ill translated by the name of "courtesans" (from whom they were indubitably, but not to our notions very intelligibly, distinguished), that exhibited the rarest union of female blandishment and masculine culture. "The wife for our house and honour", implies Demosthenes, "the Hetæra for our solace and delight." These extraordinary women, all foreigners, and mostly Ionian, made the main phenomenon of Athenian society. They were the only women with whom an enlightened Greek could converse as equal to himself in education. While the law denied them civil rights, usage lavished upon them at once admiration and respect. By stealth, as it were, and in defiance of legislation, they introduced into the ambitious and restless circles of Athens many of the

---

5 If we believe with Plutarch that wives accompanied their husbands to the house of Aspasia (and it was certainly a popular charge against Pericles that Aspasia served to corrupt the Athenian matrons), they could not have been so jealously confined as writers, judging from passages in the Greek writers that describe not what women *were*, but what women *ought to be*, desire us to imagine. And it may be also observed, that the popular anecdotes represent Elpinice as a female intriguante, busying herself in politics, and mediating between Cimon and Pericles: anecdotes, whether or not they be strictly faithful, that at least tend to illustrate the state of society.

effects, pernicious or beneficial, which result from the influence of educated women upon the manners and pursuits of men.[6]

III. The alteration of social habits was not then sudden and startling (such is never the case in the progress of national manners), but, commencing with the graces of a polished tyranny, ripened with the results of glorious but too profitable victories. Perhaps the time in which the state of transition was most favourably visible was just prior to the death of Cimon. It was not then so much the over-refinement of a new and feebler generation, as the polish and elegance which wealth, art, and emulation necessarily imparted to the same brave warriors who exchanged posts with the Spartans at Platæa, and sent out their children and old men to fight and conquer with Myronides.

IV. A rapid glance over the events of the few years commemorated in the last book of this history will suffice to show the eminence which Athens had attained over the other states of Greece. She was the head of the Ionian league—the mistress of the Grecian seas; with Sparta, the sole rival that could cope with her armies and arrest her ambition, she had obtained a peace; Corinth was humbled, Ægina ruined, Megara had shrunk into her dependency and garrison. The states of Bœotia had received their very constitution from the hands of an Athenian general—the democracies planted by Athens served to make liberty itself subservient to her will, and involved in her safety. She had remedied the sterility of her own soil by securing the rich pastures of the neighbouring Eubœa. She had added the gold of Thasos to the silver of Laurion, and established a footing in Thessaly which was at once a fortress against the Asiatic arms and a mart for Asiatic commerce. The fairest lands of the opposite coast—the most powerful islands of the Grecian seas—contributed to her treasury, or were almost legally subjected to her revenge. Her navy was rapidly increasing in skill, in number, and renown; at home, the recall of Cimon had conciliated domestic contentions, and the death of Cimon dispirited for a while the foes to the established constitution. In all Greece, Myronides was perhaps the ablest general—Pericles (now rapidly rising to the sole administration of affairs[7]) was undoubtedly the most highly educated, cautious, and commanding statesman.

THE POLITICAL EMINENCE LATELY ACQUIRED BY ATHENS

But a single act of successful daring had, more than all else, contributed to the Athenian power. Even in the lifetime of Aristides it had been proposed

6 As I propose, in a subsequent part of this work, to enter at considerable length into the social life and habits of the Athenians, I shall have full opportunity for a more detailed account of these singular heroines of Alciphron and the later comedians.
7 It was about five years after the death of Cimon that Pericles obtained that supreme power which resembled a tyranny, but was only the expression and concentration of the democratic will.

THE TRANSFER OF THE
TREASURY FROM DELOS TO
ATHENS

to transfer the common treasury from Delos to Athens.[8] The motion failed—perhaps through the virtuous opposition of Aristides himself. But when at the siege of Ithomë the feud between the Athenians and Spartans broke out, the fairest pretext and the most favourable occasion conspired in favour of a measure so seductive to the national ambition. Under pretence of saving the treasury from the hazard of falling a prey to the Spartan rapacity or need, it was at once removed to Athens;[9] and while the enfeebled power of Sparta, fully engrossed by the Messenian war, forbade all resistance to the transfer from that the most formidable quarter, the conquests of Naxos and the recent reduction of Thasos seem to have intimidated the spirit, and for a time even to have silenced the reproaches, of the tributary states themselves. Thus, in actual possession of the tribute of her allies, Athens acquired a new right to its collection and its management; and while she devoted some of the treasures to the maintenance of her strength, she began early to uphold the prerogative of appropriating a part to the enhancement of her splendour.[10]

As this most important measure occurred at the very period when the power of Cimon was weakened by the humiliating circumstances that attended his expedition to Ithomë, and by the vigorous and popular measures of the opposition, so there seems every reason to believe that it was principally advised and effected by Pericles, who appears shortly afterward presiding over the administration of the finances.[11]

---

8 Theophrast., apud Plut., in Vit. Per.

9 Justin, iii. 6.

10 For the transfer itself there were excuses yet more plausible than that assigned by Justin. First, in the year following the breach between the Spartans and Athenians (BC 460), probably the same year in which the transfer was effected, the Athenians were again at war with the great king in Egypt; and there was therefore a show of justice in the argument noticed by Boeckh (though in the source whence he derives it the argument applies to the earlier time of Aristides), that the transfer provided a place of greater security against the barbarians. Second, Delos itself was already and had long been under Athenian influence. Pisistratus had made a purification of the island (Herod., i. 64), Delian soothsayers had predicted to Athens the sovereignty of the seas (Semius Delias, apud Athen., viii.), and the Athenians seem to have arrogated a right of interference with the temple. The transfer was probably, therefore, in appearance, little more than a transfer from a place under the power of Athens to Athens itself. Third, it seems that when the question was first agitated, during the life of Aristides, it was at the desire of one of the allies themselves (the Samians). Plut., in Vit. Arist. Boeckh (vol. i., p. 135, translation) has no warrant for supposing that Pericles influenced the Samians in the expression of this wish, because Plutarch refers the story to the time of Aristides, during whose life Pericles possessed no influence in public affairs.

11 The assertion of Diodorus (xii. 35), that to Pericles was confided the superintendence and management of the treasure, is corroborated by the anecdotes in Plutarch and elsewhere, which represent Pericles as the principal administrator of the funds.

Though the Athenian commerce had greatly increased, it was still principally confined to the Thracian coasts and the Black Sea. The desire of enterprises, too vast for a state whose power reverses might suddenly destroy, was not yet indulged to excess; nor had the turbulent spirits of the Piræus yet poured in upon the various barriers of the social state and the political constitution, the rashness of sailors and the avarice of merchants. Agriculture, to which all classes in Athens were addicted, raised a healthful counteraction to the impetus given to trade. Nor was it till some years afterward, when Pericles gathered all the citizens into the town, and left no safety-valve to the ferment and vices of the Agora, that the Athenian aristocracy gradually lost all patriotism and manhood, and an energetic democracy was corrupted into a vehement though educated mob. The spirit of faction, it is true, ran high, but a third party, headed by Myronides and Tolmides, checked the excesses of either extreme.

V. Thus, at home and abroad, time and fortune, the concurrence of events, and the happy accident of great men, not only maintained the present eminence of Athens, but promised, to ordinary foresight, a long duration of her glory and her power. To deeper observers, the picture might have presented dim but prophetic shadows. It was clear that the command Athens had obtained was utterly disproportioned to her natural resources—that her greatness was altogether artificial, and rested partly upon moral rather than physical causes, and partly upon the fears and the weakness of her neighbours. A sterile soil, a limited territory, a scanty population—all these—the drawbacks and disadvantages of nature—the wonderful energy and confident daring of a free state might conceal in prosperity; but the first calamity could not fail to expose them to jealous and hostile eyes. The empire delegated to the Athenians they must naturally desire to retain and to increase; and there was every reason to forbode that their ambition would soon exceed their capacities to sustain it. As the state became accustomed to its power, it would learn to abuse it. Increasing civilization, luxury, and art, brought with them new expenses, and Athens had already been permitted to indulge with impunity the dangerous passion of exacting tribute from her neighbours. Dependance upon other resources than those of the native population has ever been a main cause of the destruction of despotisms, and it cannot fail, sooner or later, to be equally pernicious to the republics that trust to it. The resources of taxation, confined to freemen and natives, are almost incalculable; the resources of tribute, wrung from foreigners and dependents, are sternly limited and terribly precarious—they rot away the true spirit of industry in the people that demand the impost—they implant ineradicable hatred in the states that concede it:

LATENT DANGERS AND EVILS —FIRST, THE ARTIFICIAL GREATNESS OF ATHENS NOT SUPPORTED BY NATURAL STRENGTH—SECOND, HER PERNICIOUS RELIANCE ON TRIBUTE

430

VI. Two other causes of great deterioration to the national spirit were also at work in Athens. One, as I have before hinted, was the policy commenced by Cimon, of winning the populace by the bribes and exhibitions of individual wealth. The wise Pisistratus had invented penalties—Cimon offered encouragement—to idleness. When the poor are once accustomed to believe they have a right to the generosity of the rich, the first deadly inroad is made upon the energies of independence and the sanctity of property. A yet more pernicious evil in the social state of the Athenians was radical in their constitution—it was their courts of justice. Proceeding upon a theory that must have seemed specious and plausible to an inexperienced and infant republic, Solon had laid it down as a principle of his code, that as all men were interested in the preservation of law, so all men might exert the privilege of the plaintiff and accuser. As society grew more complicated, the door was thus opened to every species of vexatious charge and frivolous litigation. The common informer became a most harassing and powerful personage, and made one of a fruitful and crowded profession; and in the very capital of liberty there existed the worst species of espionage. But justice was not thereby facilitated. The informer was regarded with universal hatred and contempt; and it is easy to perceive, from the writings of the great comic poet, that the sympathies of the Athenian audience were as those of the English public at this day, enlisted against the man who brought the inquisition of the law to the hearth of his neighbour.

VII. Solon committed a yet more fatal and incurable error when he carried the democratic principle into judicial tribunals. He evidently considered that the very strength and life of his constitution rested in the Heliæa—a court the numbers and nature of which have been already described. Perhaps, at a time when the old oligarchy was yet so formidable, it might have been difficult to secure justice to the poorer classes while the judges were selected from the wealthier. But justice to all classes became a yet more capricious uncertainty when a court of law resembled a popular hustings.[12]

If we entrust a wide political suffrage to the people, the people at least hold no trust for others than themselves and their posterity—they are not responsible to the public, for they *are* the public. But in law, where there are two parties concerned, the plaintiff and defendant, the judge should not

The side note reads: THIRD, DETERIORATION OF NATIONAL SPIRIT COMMENCED BY CIMON IN THE USE OF BRIBES AND PUBLIC TABLES—FOURTH, DEFECTS IN POPULAR COURTS OF LAW

---

12 The political nature and bias of the Heliæa is apparent in the very oath, preserved in Dem., contra Tim., p. 746, ed. Reiske. In this the heliast is sworn never to vote for the establishment of tyranny or oligarchy in Athens, and never to listen to any proposition tending to destroy the democratic constitution. That is, a man entered upon a judicial tribunal by taking a political oath!

only be incorruptible, but strictly responsible. In Athens the people became the judge; and, in offences punishable by fine, were the very party interested in procuring condemnation; the numbers of the jury prevented all responsibility, excused all abuses, and made them susceptible of the same shameless excesses that characterize self-elected corporations—from which appeal is idle, and over which public opinion exercises no control. These numerous, ignorant, and passionate assemblies were liable at all times to the heats of party, to the eloquence of individuals—to the whims and caprices, the prejudices, the impatience, and the turbulence which must ever be the characteristics of a multitude orally addressed. It was evident, also, that from service in such a court, the wealthy, the eminent, and the learned, with other occupation or amusement, would soon seek to absent themselves. And the final blow to the integrity and respectability of the popular judicature was given at a later period by Pericles, when he instituted a salary, just sufficient to tempt the poor and to be disdained by the affluent, to every dicast or juryman in the ten ordinary courts.[13] Legal science became not the profession of the erudite and the laborious few, but the livelihood of the ignorant and idle multitude. The canvassing—the cajoling—the bribery—that resulted from this, the most vicious institution of the Athenian democracy—are but too evident and melancholy tokens of the imperfection of human wisdom. Life, property, and character were at the hazard of a popular election. These evils must have been long in progressive operation; but perhaps they were scarcely visible till the fatal innovation of Pericles, and the flagrant excesses that ensued allowed the people themselves to listen to the branding and terrible satire upon the popular judicature, which is still preserved to us in the comedy of Aristophanes.

At the same time, certain critics and historians have widely and grossly erred in supposing that these courts of "the sovereign multitude" were partial to the poor and hostile to the rich. All testimony proves that the fact was lamentably the reverse. The defendant was accustomed to engage the persons of rank or influence whom he might number as his friends, to appear in court on his behalf. And property was employed to procure at the bar of justice the suffrages it could command at a political election. The greatest vice of the democratic Heliæa was, that by a fine the wealthy could purchase pardon—by interest the great could soften law. But the chances were against the poor man. To him litigation was indeed cheap, but justice dear. He had

---

13 These courts have been likened to modern juries; but they were very little bound by the forms and precedents which shackled the latter. What a jury, even nowadays, a jury of only twelve persons, would be if left entirely to impulse and party feeling, any lawyer will readily conceive. How much more capricious, uncertain, and prejudiced a jury of five hundred, and, in some instances, of one thousand or fifteen hundred! By the junction of two or more divisions, as in cases of Eisangelia. Poll., viii. 53 and 123; also Tittman.

much the same inequality to struggle against in a suit with a powerful antagonist, that he would have had in contesting with him for an office in the administration. In all trials resting on the voice of popular assemblies, it ever has been and ever will be found, that, *cæteris paribus*, the aristocrat will defeat the plebeian.

VIII. Meanwhile the progress of general education had been great and remarkable. Music,[14] from the earliest time, was an essential part of instruction; and it had now become so common an acquirement, that Aristotle[15] observes, that at the close of the Persian war there was scarcely a single freeborn Athenian unacquainted with the flute. The use of this instrument was afterward discontinued, and indeed proscribed in the education of freemen, from the notion that it was not an instrument capable of music sufficiently elevated and intellectual;[16] yet it was only succeeded by melodies more effeminate and luxurious. And Aristophanes enumerates the change from the old national airs and measures among the worst symptoms of Athenian degeneracy. Besides the musician, the tutor of the gymnasium and the grammarian still made the nominal limit of scholastic instruction.[17] But life itself had now become a school. The passion for public intercourse and disputation, which the gardens and the Agora, and exciting events, and free institutions, and the rise of philosophy, and a serene and lovely climate, made the prevalent characteristic of the matured Athenian, began to stir within the young. And in the meanwhile the tardy invention of prose literature worked its natural revolution in intellectual pursuits.

PROGRESS OF GENERAL EDUCATION

IX. It has been before observed, that in Greece, as elsewhere, the first successor of the poet was the philosopher, and that the oral lecturer preceded the prose writer. With written prose HISTORY commenced. Having found a mode of transmitting that species of knowledge which could not, like rhythmical tales or sententious problems, be accurately preserved by the memory alone, it was natural that a present age should desire to record and transmit the past—κτῆμα ἐς ἀεί—an everlasting heirloom to the future.

HISTORY

To a semi-barbarous nation history is little more than poetry. The subjects to which it would be naturally devoted are the legends of religion—the

---

14 "Designed by our ancestors", says Aristotle (Pol., viii. 3), "not, as many now consider it, merely for delight, but for discipline; that so the mind might be taught not only how honourably to pursue business, but how creditably to enjoy leisure; for such enjoyment is, after all, the end of business and the boundary of active life."

15 See Aristot., Pol., viii. 6.

16 An anecdote in Gellius, xv. 17, refers the date of the disuse of this instrument to the age of Pericles and during the boyhood of Alcibiades.

17 Drawing was subsequently studied as a branch of education essential to many of the common occupations of life.

deeds of ancestral demigods—the triumphs of successful war. In recording these themes of national interest, the poet is the first historian. As philosophy —or rather the spirit of conjecture, which is the primitive and creative breath of philosophy— becomes prevalent, the old credulity directs the new research to the investigation of subjects which the poets have not sufficiently explained, but which, from their remote and religious antiquity, are mysteriously attractive to a reverent and inquisitive population, with whom long descent is yet the most flattering proof of superiority. Thus genealogies, and accounts of the origin of states and deities, made the first subjects of history, and inspired the Argive Acusilaus,[18] and, as far as we can plausibly conjecture, the Milesian Cadmus.

X. The Dorians—a people who never desired to disturb tradition, unwilling carefully to investigate, precisely because they superstitiously venerated, the past, little inquisitive as to the manners or the chronicles of alien tribes, satisfied, in a word, with themselves, and incurious as to others—were not a race to whom history became a want. Ionia—the subtle, the innovating, the anxious, and the restless—nurse of the arts, which the mother country ultimately reared, boasts in Cadmus the Milesian the first writer of history and of prose;[19] Samos, the birthplace of Pythagoras, produced Eugeon, placed by Dionysius at the head of the early historians; and Mitylene claimed Hellanicus, who seems to have formed a more ambitious design than his predecessors. He wrote a history of the ancient kings of the earth, and an account of the founders of the most celebrated cities in each kingdom.[20] During the early and crude attempts of these and other writers, stern events contributed to rear from tedious research and fruitless conjecture the true genius of history; for it is as a people begin to struggle for rights, to comprehend political relations, to contend with neighbours abroad, and to wrestle with obnoxious institutions at home, that they desire to secure the sanction of antiquity, to trace back to some illustrious origin the rights they demand, and to stimulate hourly exertions by a reference to departed fame. Then do mythologies, and genealogies, and geographical definitions, and the traditions that concern kings and heroes, ripen into chronicles that commemorate the convulsions or the progress of a nation.

During the stormy period which saw the invasion of Xerxes, when everything that could shed lustre upon the past incited to present struggles,
flourished Pherecydes. He is sometimes called of Leria, which seems his birthplace—sometimes of Athens, where he resided thirty years, and to which state his history refers. Although

---

18 Suidas.
19 Hecatæus was also of Miletus.
20 Paus., ii. 3; Cic., de Orat., ii. 53; Aulus Gellius, xv. 23.

his work was principally mythological, it opened the way to sound historical composition, inasmuch as it included references to later times—to existent struggles—the descent of Miltiades—the Scythian expedition of Darius. Subsequently, Xanthus, a Lydian, composed a work on his own country, of which some extracts remain, and from which Herodotus did not disdain to borrow.

XI. It was nearly a century after the invention of prose and of historical composition, and with the guides and examples of many writers not

VIEW OF THE LIFE AND WRITINGS OF HERODOTUS

uncelebrated in their day before his emulation, that Herodotus first made known to the Grecian public, and, according to all probable evidence, at the Olympic Games, a portion of that work which drew forth the tears of Thucydides, and furnishes the imperishable model of picturesque and faithful narrative. This happened in a brilliant period of Athenian history; it was in the same year as the battle of Œnophyta, when Athens gave laws and constitutions to Bœotia, and the recall of Cimon established for herself both liberty and order. The youth of Herodotus was passed while the glory of the Persian war yet lingered over Greece, and while with the ascendency of Athens commenced a new era of civilization. His genius drew the vital breath from an atmosphere of poetry. The desire of wild adventure still existed, and the romantic expedition of the Athenians into Egypt had served to strengthen the connexion between the Greeks and that imposing and interesting land. The rise of the Greek drama with Æschylus probably contributed to give effect, colour, and vigour to the style of Herodotus. And something almost of the art of the contemporaneous Sophocles may be traced in the easy skill of his narratives, and the magic yet tranquil energy of his descriptions.

XII. Though Dorian by ancient descent, it was at Halicarnassus, in Caria, a city of Asia Minor, that Herodotus was born; nor does his style, nor do his views, indicate that he derived from the origin of his family any of the Dorian peculiarities. His parents were distinguished alike by birth and fortune. Early in life those internal commotions, to which all the Grecian towns were subjected, and which crushed for a time the liberties of his native city, drove him from Halicarnassus and, suffering from tyranny, he became inspired by that enthusiasm for freedom which burns throughout his immortal work. During his exile he travelled through Greece, Thrace, and Macedonia—through Scythia, Asia, and Egypt. Thus he collected the materials of his work, which is, in fact, a book of travels narrated historically. If we do not reject the story that he read a portion of his work at the Olympian Games, when Thucydides, one of his listeners, was yet a boy, and if we suppose the latter to have been about fifteen, this anecdote is calculated[21] to

21 Fasti Hellenici, vol. ii.

bear the date of the eighty-first Olympiad, BC 456, when Herodotus was twenty-eight.

The chief residence of Herodotus was at Samos, until a revolution broke out in Halicarnassus. The people conspired against their tyrant Lygdamis. Herodotus repaired to his native city, took a prominent part in the conspiracy, and finally succeeded in restoring the popular government. He was not, however, long left to enjoy the liberties he had assisted to acquire for his fellow-citizens: some intrigue of the counterparty drove him a second time into exile. Repairing to Athens, he read the continuation of his history at the festival of the Panathenæa. It was received with the most rapturous applause; and we are told that the people solemnly conferred upon the man who had immortalized their achievements against the Mede the gift of ten talents. The disposition of this remarkable man, like that of all travellers, inclined to enterprise and adventure. His early wanderings, his later vicissitudes, seem to have confirmed a temperament originally restless and inquisitive. Accordingly, in his forty-first year, he joined the Athenian emigrators that in the south of Italy established a colony at Thurium.

XIII. At Thurium Herodotus apparently passed the remainder of his life, though whether his tomb was built there or in Athens is a matter of dispute. These particulars of his life, not uninteresting in themselves, tend greatly to illustrate the character of his writings. Their charm consists in the earnestness of a man who describes countries as an eyewitness, and events as one accustomed to participate in them. The life, the raciness, the vigour of an adventurer and a wanderer glow in every page. He has none of the refining disquisitions that are born of the closet. He paints history rather than descants on it; he throws the colourings of a mind, unconsciously poetic, over all he describes. Now a soldier—now a priest—now a patriot—he is always a poet, if rarely a philosopher. He narrates like a witness, unlike Thucydides, who sums up like a judge. No writer ever made so beautiful an application of superstitions to truths. His very credulities have a philosophy of their own; and modern historians have acted unwisely in disdaining the occasional repetition even of his fables. For if his truths record the events, his fables paint the manners and the opinions of the time; and the last fill up the history, of which events are only the skeleton.

To account for his frequent use of dialogue and his dramatic effects of narrative, we must remember the tribunal to which the work of Herodotus was subjected. Every author, unconsciously to himself, consults the tastes of those he addresses. No small coterie of scholars, no scrupulous and critical inquirers, made the ordeal Herodotus underwent. His chronicles were not dissertations to be coldly pondered over and sceptically conned: they were read aloud at solemn festivals to listening thousands; they were to arrest the curiosity—to amuse the impatience—to stir the wonder of a lively and motley crowd. Thus the historian imbibed naturally the spirit of the tale-teller. And he was driven to embellish his history with the romantic legend—the awful superstition—the gossip anecdote—which yet characterize the stories of the popular and oral fictionist, in the bazaars of the Mussulman, or on the sea-sands of Sicily. Still it has been rightly said that a judicious reader is not easily led astray by Herodotus in important particulars. His descriptions of localities, of manners and customs, are singularly correct; and modern travellers can yet trace the vestiges of his fidelity. As the historian, therefore, was in some measure an orator, so his skill was to be manifest in the arts which keep alive the attention of an audience. Hence Herodotus continually aims at the picturesque; he gives us the very words of his actors, and narrates the secrets of impenetrable palaces with as much simplicity and earnestness as if he had been placed behind the arras.[22]

That it was impossible for the wandering Halicarnassean to know what Gyges said to Candaules, or Artabanus to Xerxes, has, perhaps, been too confidently asserted. Heeren reminds us, that both by Jewish and Grecian writers there is frequent mention of the scribes or secretaries who constantly attended the person of the Persian monarch—on occasion of festivals,[23] of public reviews,[24] and even in the tumult of battle; and, with the idolatrous respect in which despotism was held, noted down the words that fell from the royal lip. The ingenious German then proceeds to show that this custom was common to all the Asiatic nations. Thus were formed the chronicles or archives of the Persians; and by reference to these minute and detailed documents, Herodotus was enabled to record conversations and anecdotes, and preserve to us the memoirs of a court. And though this conjecture must be received with caution, and, to many passages unconnected with Persia or the East, cannot be applied, it is sufficiently plausible, in some very important parts of the history, not to be altogether dismissed with contempt.

But it is for another reason that I have occasionally admitted the dialogues of Herodotus, as well as the superstitious anecdotes current at the

22 A brilliant writer in the Edinburgh Review (Mr Macaulay) would account for the use of dialogue in Herodotus by the childish simplicity common to an early and artless age—as the boor always unconsciously resorts to the dramatic form of narration, and relates his story by a *series* of "says he's" and "says I's." But does not Mr Macaulay, in common with many others, insist far too much on the artlessness of the age and the unstudied simplicity of the writer? Though history itself was young, art was already at its zenith. It was the age of Sophocles, Phidias, and Pericles. It was from the Athenians, in their most polished period, that Herodotus received the most rapturous applause. Do not all accounts of Herodotus, as a writer, assure us that he spent the greater part of a long life in composing, polishing, and perfecting his history; and is it not more in conformity with the characteristic spirit of the times, and the masterly effects which Herodotus produces, to conclude, that what we suppose to be artlessness was, in reality, the premeditated elaboration of art?
23 Esther, iii. 12; viii. 9; Ezra, vi. 1.
24 Herod., vii. 100.

day. The truth of history consists not only in the relation of events, but in preserving the character of the people, and depicting the manners of the time. *Facts*, if too nakedly told, may be very different from *truths*, in the impression they convey; and the spirit of Grecian history is lost if we do not feel the Greeks themselves constantly before us. Thus when, as in Herodotus, the agents of events converse, every word reported may not have been spoken; but what we lose in accuracy of details we more than gain by the fidelity of the whole. We acquire a lively and accurate impression of the general character—of the thoughts, and the manners, and the men of the age and the land. It is so also with legends, sparingly used, and of which the nature is discernible from fact by the most superficial gaze; we more sensibly feel that it was the Greeks who were engaged at Marathon when we read of the dream of Hippias or the apparition of Theseus. Finally, an historian of Greece will, almost without an effort, convey to the reader a sense of the mighty change, from an age of poetical heroes to an age of practical statesmen, if we suffer Herodotus to be his model in the narrative of the Persian war, and allow the more profound and less imaginative Thucydides to colour the pictures of the Peloponnesian.

XIV. The period now entered upon is also remarkable for the fertile and rapid development of one branch of intellectual cultivation in which the

PROGRESS OF PHILOSOPHY SINCE THALES—PHILOSOPHERS OF THE IONIAN AND ELEATIC SCHOOLS

Greeks were pre-eminently illustrious. In history, Rome was the rival of Greece; in philosophy, Rome was never more than her credulous and reverend scholar.

We have seen the dawn of philosophy with Thales; Miletus, his birthplace, bore his immediate successors. Anaximander, his younger contemporary,[25] is said, with Pherecydes, to have been the first philosopher who availed himself of the invention of writing. His services have not been sufficiently appreciated—like those of most men who form the first steps in the progress between the originator and the perfector. He seems boldly to have differed from his master, Thales, in the very root of his system. He rejected the original element of water or humidity, and supposed the great primary essence and origin of creation to be in that EVERYTHING or NOTHING which he called the INFINITE, and which we might perhaps render as the "Chaos";[26] that of this vast element, the parts are changed—the whole immutable, and all things arise from and return unto that universal source.[27] He pursued his researches into physics, and attempted to account for the thunder, the lightning, and the winds. His conjectures are usually shrewd and keen; and sometimes, as in his assertion, "that the moon shone in

25 About twenty-nine years younger.—Fasti Hellenici, vol. ii, p. 7.
26 Cic., Acad. Quæst., 4; Abbé de Canaye, Mem. de l'Acad. d'Inscrip., tom. x., &c.
27 Diog. Laert., cap. 6; Cic., Acad. Quæst., 4, &c.

light borrowed from the sun", may deserve a higher praise. Both Anaximander and Pherecydes concurred in the principles of their doctrines, but the latter seems to have more distinctly asserted the immortality of the soul.[28]

Anaximenes, also of Miletus, was the friend and follower of Anaximander. He seems, however, to have deserted the abstract philosophical dogmas of his tutor, and to have resumed the analogical system commenced by Thales —like that philosopher, he founded axioms, upon observations, bold and acute, but partial and contracted. He maintained that air was the primitive element. In this theory he united the Zeus, or *ether*, of Pherecydes, and the *Infinite* of Anaximander, for he held the air to be God in itself, and infinite in its nature.

XV. While these wild but ingenious speculators conducted the career of that philosophy called the Ionian, to the later time of the serene and lofty spiritualism of Anaxagoras, two new schools arose, both founded by Ionians, but distinguished by separate names—the Eleatic and the Italic. The first was founded by Xenophanes of Colophon, in Elea, a town in western Italy. Migrating to an alien shore, colonization seems to have produced in philosophy the same results which it produced in politics: it emancipated the reason from all previous prejudice and prescriptive shackles. Xenophanes was the first thinker who openly assailed the popular faith. He divested the Great Deity of the human attributes which human vanity, assimilating God to man, had bestowed upon him. The divinity of Xenophanes is that of modern philosophy—eternal, unalterable, and alone: graven images cannot represent his form. His attributes are—ALL HEARING, ALL SIGHT, and ALL THOUGHT.

To the Eleatic school, founded by Xenophanes, belong Parmenides, Melissus the Samian, Zeno, and Heraclitus of Ephesus. All these were thinkers remarkable for courage and subtlety. The main metaphysical doctrines of this school approach, in many respects, to those that have been familiar to modern speculators.

Their predecessors argued, as the basis of their system, from experience of the outward world, and the evidence of the senses; the Eleatic school, on the contrary, commenced their system from the reality of ideas, and *thence* argued on the reality of external objects; experience with them was but a show and an appearance; knowledge was not in things without, but in the mind; they were the founders of idealism. With respect to the deity, they imagined the whole universe filled with it—God was ALL IN ALL. Such, though each philosopher varied the system in detail, were the main metaphysical dogmas of the Eleatic school. Its masters were high-wrought, subtle, and religious thinkers; but their doctrines were based upon a theory that necessarily led to

28 Aristot., Metaph.; Diog. Laert.; Cic., Acad. Quæst., 4, &c.

paradox and mysticism; and finally conduced to the most dangerous of all the ancient sects—that of the sophists.

We may here observe, that the spirit of poetry long continued to breathe in the forms of philosophy. Even Anaximander, and his immediate followers in the Ionic school, while writing in prose, appear, from a few fragments left to us, to have had much recourse to poetical expression, and often convey a dogma by an image; while, in the Eleatic school, Xenophanes and Parmenides adopted the form itself of verse, as the medium for communicating their theories; and Zeno, perhaps from the new example of the drama, first introduced into philosophical dispute that fashion of dialogue which afterward gave to the sternest and loftiest thought the animation and life of dramatic pictures.

XVI. But even before the Eleatic school arose, the most remarkable and ambitious of all the earlier reasoners, the arch uniter of actual politics with enthusiastic reveries—the hero of a thousand legends—a demigod in his ends and an impostor in his means—Pythagoras of Samos—conceived and partially executed the vast design of establishing a speculative wisdom and an occult religion as the keystone of political institutions.

PYTHAGORAS—HIS PHILO-SOPHICAL TENETS AND POLITICAL INFLUENCE

So mysterious is everything relating to Pythagoras, so mingled with the grossest fables and the wildest superstitions, that he seems scarcely to belong to the age of history, or to the advanced and practical Ionia. The date of his birth—his very parentage, are matters of dispute and doubt. Accounts concur in considering his father not a native of Samos; and it seems a probable supposition that he was of Lemnian or Pelasgic origin. Pythagoras travelled early into Egypt and the East, and the system most plausibly ascribed to him betrays something of oriental mystery and priestcraft in its peculiar doctrines, and much more of those alien elements in its pervading and general spirit. The notion of uniting a state with religion is especially eastern, and essentially anti-Hellenic. Returning to Samos, he is said to have found the able Polycrates in the tyranny of the government, and to have quitted his birthplace in disgust. If, then, he had already conceived his political designs, it is clear that they could never have been executed under a jealous and acute tyrant; for, in the first place, radical innovations are never so effectually opposed as in governments concentrated in the hands of a single man; and, secondly, the very pith and core of the system of Pythagoras consisted in the establishment of an oligarchic aristocracy—a constitution most hated and most persecuted by the Grecian tyrants. The philosopher migrated into Italy. He had already, in all probability, made himself renowned in Greece. For it was then a distinction to have travelled into Egypt, the seat of mysterious and venerated learning; and philosophy, like other novelties, appears to have passed into fashion even with the multitude. Not only all the traditions respecting this extraordinary man, but the certain fact of the mighty effect that, in his single person, he afterward wrought in Italy, prove him also to have possessed that nameless art of making a personal impression upon mankind, and creating individual enthusiasm, which is necessary to those who obtain a moral command, and are the founders of sects and institutions. It is so much in conformity with the manners of the time and the objects of Pythagoras to believe that he diligently explored the ancient religions and political systems of Greece, from which he had long been a stranger, that we cannot reject the traditions (however disfigured with fable) that he visited Delos, and affected to receive instructions from the pious ministrants of Delphi.[29]

At Olympia, where he could not fail to be received with curiosity and distinction, the future lawgiver is said to have assumed the title of philosopher, the first who claimed the name. For the rest, we must yield our faith to all probable accounts, both of his own earnest preparations for his design, and of the high repute he acquired in Greece, that may tend to lessen the miracle of the success that awaited him in the cities of the West.

XVII. Pythagoras arrived in Italy during the reign of Tarquinius Superbus, according to the testimony of Cicero and Aulus Gellius,[30] and fixed his residence in Croton, a city in the Bay of Tarentum, colonized by Greeks of the Achæan tribe.[31] If we may lend a partial credit to the extravagant fables

---

29 It must ever remain a disputable matter how far the Ionian Pythagoras was influenced by affection for Dorian policy and customs, and how far he designed to create a state upon the old Dorian model. On the one hand, it is certain that he paid especial attention to the rites and institutions most connected with the Dorian deity, Apollo—that, according to his followers, it was from that god that he derived his birth, a fiction that might be interpreted into a Dorian origin; he selected Croton as his residence, because it was under the protection of "his household god"; his doctrines are said to have been delivered in the Dorian dialect; and much of his educational discipline, much of his political system, bear an evident affinity to the old Cretan and Spartan institutions. But, on the other hand, it is probable that Pythagoras favoured the god of Delphi, partly from the close connexion which many of his symbols bore to the metaphysical speculations the philosopher had learned to cultivate in the schools of oriental mysticism, and partly from the fact that Apollo was the patron of the medical art, in which Pythagoras was an eminent professor. And in studying the institutions of Crete and Sparta, he might rather have designed to strengthen by examples the system he had already adopted, than have taken from those Dorian cities the primitive and guiding notions of the constitution he afterward established. And in this Pythagoras might have resembled most reformers, not only of his own, but of all ages, who desire to go back to the earliest principles of the past as the sources of experience to the future. In the Dorian institutions was preserved the original character of the Hellenic nation; and Pythagoras, perhaps, valued or consulted them less because they were Dorian than because they were ancient. It seems, however, pretty clear, that in the character of his laws he sought to conform to the spirit and mode of legislation already familiar in Italy, since Charondas and Zaleucus, who flourished before him, are ranked by Diodorus and others among his disciples.
30 Livy dates it in the reign of Servius Tullus.
31 Strabo.

of later disciples, endeavouring to extract from florid superaddition some original germ of simple truth, it would seem that he first appeared in the character of a teacher of youth;[32] and, as was not unusual in those times, soon rose from the preceptor to the legislator.

Dissensions in the city favoured his objects. The senate (consisting of a thousand members, doubtless of a different race from the body of the people; the first the posterity of the settlers, the last the native population) availed itself of the arrival and influence of an eloquent and renowned philosopher. He lent himself to the consolidation of aristocracies, and was equally inimical to democracy and tyranny. But his policy was that of no vulgar ambition; he refused, at least for a time, ostensible power and office, and was contented with instituting an organized and formidable society—not wholly dissimilar to that mighty order founded by Loyola in times comparatively recent. The disciples admitted into this society underwent examination and probation; it was through degrees that they passed into its higher honours, and were admitted into its deeper secrets. Religion made the basis of the fraternity— but religion connected with human ends of advancement and power. He selected the three hundred who, at Croton, formed his order, from the noblest families, and they were professedly reared to know themselves, that so they might be fitted to command the world. It was not long before this society, of which Pythagoras was the head, appears to have supplanted the ancient senate and obtained the legislative administration. In this institution, Pythagoras stands alone—no other founder of Greek philosophy resembles him. By all accounts, he also differed from the other sages of his time in his estimate of the importance of women. He is said to have lectured to and taught them. His wife was herself a philosopher, and fifteen disciples of the softer sex rank among the prominent ornaments of his school. An order based upon so profound a knowledge of all that can fascinate or cheat mankind, could not fail to secure a temporary power. His influence was unbounded in Croton—it extended to other Italian cities—it amended or overturned political constitutions; and had Pythagoras possessed a more coarse and personal ambition, he might, perhaps, have founded a mighty dynasty, and enriched our social annals with the results of a new experiment. But his was the ambition, not of a hero, but a sage. He wished rather to establish a system than to exalt himself; his immediate followers saw not all the consequences that might be derived from the fraternity he founded: and the political designs of his gorgeous and august philosophy, only for a while successful, left behind them but the mummeries of an impotent freemasonry and the enthusiastic ceremonies of half-witted ascetics.

XVIII. It was when this power, so mystic and so revolutionary, had, by the means of branch societies, established itself throughout a considerable

32 Iamblichus, viii, ix. See also Plato, de Repub., x.

portion of Italy, that a general feeling of alarm and suspicion broke out against the sage and his sectarians. The anti-Pythagorean risings, according to Porphyry, were sufficiently numerous and active to be remembered for long generations afterward. Many of the sage's friends are said to have perished, and it is doubtful whether Pythagoras himself fell a victim to the rage of his enemies, or died a fugitive among his disciples at Metapontum. Nor was it until nearly the whole of Lower Italy was torn by convulsions, and Greece herself drawn into the contest, as pacificator and arbiter, that the ferment was allayed—the Pythagorean institutions were abolished, and the timocratic democracies[33] of the Achæans rose upon the ruins of those intellectual but ungenial oligarchies.

XIX. Pythagoras committed a fatal error when, in his attempt to revolutionize society, he had recourse to aristocracies for his agents. Revolutions, especially those influenced by religion, can never be worked out but by popular emotions. It was from this error of judgment that he enlisted the people against him—for, by the account of Neanthes, related by Porphyry,[34] and, indeed, from all other testimony, it is clearly evident that to popular, not party commotion, his fall must be ascribed. It is no less clear that, after his death, while his philosophical sect remained, his political code crumbled away. The only seeds sown by philosophers which spring up into great states are those that, whether for good or evil, are planted in the hearts of the many.

XX. The purely intellectual additions made by Pythagoras to human wisdom seem to have been vast and permanent. By probable testimony, he added largely to mathematical science; and his discoveries in arithmetic, astronomy, music, and geometry, constitute an era in the history of the mind. His metaphysical and moral speculations are not to be separated from the additions or corruptions of his disciples. But we must at least suppose that Pythagoras established the main proposition of the occult properties of NUMBERS, which were held to be the principles of all things. According to this theory, unity is the abstract principle of all perfection, and the ten elementary numbers contain the elements of the perfect system of nature. By numbers the origin and the substance of all things could be explained.[35] Numbers make the mystery of earth and heaven—of the gods themselves. And this part of his system, which long continued to fool mankind, was a sort of monstrous junction between arithmetic and magic—the most certain

---

33 That the Achæan governments were democracies appears sufficiently evident; nor is this at variance with the remark of Xenophon, that timocracies were "according to the laws of the Achæans"; since timocracies were but modified democracies.

34 The Pythagoreans assembled at the house of Milo, the wrestler, who was an eminent general, and the most illustrious of the disciples were stoned to death, the house being fired. Lapidation was essentially the capital punishment of mobs—the mode of inflicting death that invariably stamps the offender as an enemy to the populace.

35 Aristot., Metaph., i. 3.

of sciences with the most fantastic of chimeras. The Pythagoreans supposed the sun, or central fire, to be the seat of Jupiter and the principle of life. The stars were divine. Men, and even animals, were held to have within them a portion of the celestial nature. The soul, emanating from the celestial fire,[36] can combine with any form of matter, and is compelled to pass through various bodies. Adopting the Egyptian doctrine of transmigration, the Pythagoreans coupled it with the notion of future punishment or reward.

Much of the doctrinal morality of Pythagoras is admirable; but it is vitiated by the ceremonial quackery connected with it. Humanity to all things— gentleness—friendship—love—and, above all the rest, SELF-COMMAND— form the principal recommendations of his mild and patriarchal ethics. But, perhaps from his desire to establish a political fraternity—perhaps from his doubt of the capacity of mankind to embrace Truth unadorned, enamoured only of her own beauty—these doctrines were united with an austere and frivolous asceticism. And virtue was but to be attained by graduating through the secret and rigid ceremonies of academical imposture. His disciples soon pushed the dogmas of their master into an extravagance at once dangerous and grotesque; and what the sage designed but for symbols of a truth were cultivated to the prejudice of the truth itself. The influence of Pythagoras became corrupt and pernicious in proportion as the original tenets became more and more adulterated or obscure, and served, in succeeding ages, to invest with the sanctity of a great name the most visionary chimeras and the most mischievous wanderings of perverted speculation. But, looking to the man himself—his discoveries—his designs—his genius—his marvellous accomplishments—we cannot but consider him as one of the most astonishing persons the world ever produced; and, if in part a mountebank and an impostor, no one, perhaps, ever deluded others with motives more pure— from an ambition more disinterested and benevolent.

XXI. Upon the Athenians the effect of these various philosophers was already marked and influential. From the time of Solon there had existed in

EFFECT OF THESE PHILO-
SOPHERS ON ATHENS—
SCHOOL OF POLITICAL
PHILOSOPHY CONTINUED IN
ATHENS FROM THE TIME OF
SOLON — ANAXAGORAS —
ARCHELAUS

Athens a kind of school of political philosophy.[37] But it was not a school of refining dogmas or systematic ethics; it was too much connected with daily and practical life to foster to any great extent the abstract contemplations and recondite theories of metaphysical discoveries. Mnesiphilus, the most eminent of these immediate successors of Solon, was the instructor of Themistocles, the very antipodes of rhetoricians and refiners. But now a new age of philosophy was at

36 Diog. Laert., viii. 28.
37 Plut., in Vit. Them. The sophists were not, therefore, as is commonly asserted, the first who brought philosophy to bear upon politics.

hand. Already the Eleatic sages, Zeno and Parmenides, had travelled to Athens, and there proclaimed their doctrines, and Zeno numbered among his listeners and disciples the youthful Pericles. But a far more sensible influence was exercised by Anaxagoras of the Ionian school. For thirty years, viz., from BC 480 to BC 450, during that eventful and stirring period intervening between the battle of Thermopylæ and the commencement of the five years' truce with Sparta, followed by the death of Cimon (BC 449), this eminent and most accomplished reasoner resided in Athens.[38] His doctrines were those most cherished by Pericles, who ranked the philosopher among his intimate friends. After an absence of some years, he again returned to Athens; and we shall then find him subjected to a prosecution in which religious prejudice was stimulated by party feud. More addicted to physics than to metaphysical research, he alarmed the national superstition by explaining on physical principles the formation even of the celestial bodies. According to him, the sun itself—that centre of divine perfection with the Pythagoreans—was ejected from the earth and heated into fire by rapid motion. He maintained that the proper study of man was the contemplation of nature and the heavens:[39] and he refined the Author of the universe into an intellectual principle ($No\hat{u}s$), which went to the root of the material causes mostly favoured by his predecessors and contemporaries. He admitted the existence of matter, but INTELLIGENCE was the animating and prevailing principle, creating symmetry from chaos, imposing limit and law on all things, and inspiring life, and sensation, and perception. His predecessors in the Ionian school, who left the universe full of gods, had not openly attacked the popular mythology. But the assertion of One Intelligence, and the reduction of all else to material and physical causes, could not but have breathed a spirit wholly inimical to the numerous and active deities of Hellenic worship. Party feeling against his friend and patron Pericles ultimately drew the general suspicion into a focus; and Anaxagoras was compelled to quit Athens, and passed the remainder of his days at Lampsacus. But his influence survived his exile. His pupil Archelaus was the first *native Athenian* who taught philosophy at Athens, and from him we date the foundation of those brilliant and imperishable schools which secured to Athens an intellectual empire long after her political independence had died away.[40] Archelaus himself (as was the usual custom of the earlier sages) departed widely from the tenets of his master. He supposed that two discordant principles, fire and water, had, by their operation, drawn all things

38 See, for evidence of the great gifts and real philosophy of Anaxagoras, Drucker de Sect. Ion., xix.
39 Aristot., Eth. Eud., i. 5.
40 Archelaus began to teach during the interval between the first and second visit of Anaxagoras. See Fasti Hellenici, vol. ii, BC 450.

445

from chaos into order, and his metaphysics were those of unalloyed materialism. At this period, too, or a little later, began slowly to arise in Athens the sect of the sophists, concerning whom so much has been written and so little is known. But as the effects of their lessons were not for some time widely apparent, it will be more in the order of this history to defer to a later era an examination of the doctrines of that perverted but not wholly pernicious school.

XXII. Enough has been now said to convey to the reader a general notion of the prodigious rise which, in the most serene of intellectual departments,

PHILOSOPHY NOT A THING APART FROM THE ORDINARY LIFE OF THE ATHENIANS

had been made in Greece, from the appearance of Solon to the lectures of Archelaus, who was the master of Socrates. With the Athenians philosophy was not a thing apart from the occupations of life and the events of history—it was not the monopoly of a few studious minds, but was cultivated as a fashion by the young and the well-born, the statesman, the poet, the man of pleasure, the votary of ambition.[41] It was inseparably interwoven with their manners, their pursuits, their glory, their decay. The history of Athens includes in itself the history of the human mind. Science and art—erudition and genius—all conspired—no less than the trophies of Miltiades, the ambition of Alcibiades—the jealousy of Sparta—to the causes of the rise and fall of Athens. And even that satire on themselves, to which, in the immortal lampoons of Aristophanes, the Athenian populace listened, exhibits a people whom, whatever their errors, the world can never see again—with whom philosophy was a pastime—with whom the Agora itself was an Academe—whose coarsest exhibitions of buffoonery and caricature sparkle with a wit, or expand into a poetry, which attest the cultivation of the audience no less than the genius of the author; a people, in a word, whom the Stagirite unconsciously individualized when he laid down a general proposition, which nowhere else can be received as a truism—that the common people are the most exquisite judges of whatever in art is graceful, harmonious, or sublime.

41 See the evidence of this in the "Clouds" of Aristophanes.

446

Book V

FROM THE DEATH OF CIMON,
BC 449, TO THE DEATH
OF PERICLES, IN THE
THIRD YEAR OF THE
PELOPONNESIAN
WAR, BC 429

CHAPTER I

Thucydides chosen by the aristocratic party to oppose Pericles—
his policy—munificence of Pericles—Sacred war—battle of
Coronea—revolt of Eubœa and Megara—invasion and retreat
of the Peloponnesians—reduction of Eubœa—punishment
of Histiæa—a thirty years' truce concluded with the
Peloponnesians—ostracism of Thucydides

I. On the death of Cimon the aristocratic party in Athens felt that the position of their antagonists and the temper of the times required a leader

THUCYDIDES CHOSEN BY
THE ARISTOCRATIC PARTY
TO OPPOSE PERICLES—HIS
POLICY—MUNIFICENCE OF
PERICLES

of abilities widely distinct from those which had characterized the son of Miltiades. Instead of a skilful and enterprising general, often absent from the city on dazzling but distant expeditions, it was necessary to raise up a chief who could contend for their enfeebled and disputed privileges at home, and meet the formidable Pericles, with no unequal advantages of civil experience and oratorical talent, in the lists of the popular assembly, or in the stratagems of political intrigue. Accordingly their choice fell neither on Myronides nor Tolmides, but on one who, though not highly celebrated for military exploits, was deemed superior to Cimon, whether as a practical statesman or a popular orator. Thucydides, their new champion, united with natural gifts whatever advantage might result from the memory of Cimon; and his connexion with that distinguished warrior, to whom he was brother-in-law, served to keep together the various partisans of the faction, and retain to the eupatrids something of the respect and enthusiasm which the services of Cimon could not fail to command, even among the democracy. The policy embraced by Thucydides was perhaps the best which the state of affairs would permit; but it was one which was fraught with much danger. Hitherto the eupatrids and the people, though ever in dispute, had not been absolutely and totally divided; the struggles of either faction being headed by nobles, scarcely permitted to the democracy the perilous advantage of the cry, that the people were on one side, and the nobles on the other. But Thucydides, seeking to render his party as strong, as compact, and as united as possible, brought the main bulk of the eupatrids to act together in one body. The means by which he pursued and attained this object are not very clearly narrated; but it was probably by the formation of a political club—

449

a species of social combination, which afterward became very common to all classes in Athens. The first effect of this policy favoured the aristocracy, and the energy and union they displayed restored for a while the equilibrium of parties; but the aristocratic influence, being thus made clear and open, and brought into avowed hostility with the popular cause, the city was rent in two, and the community were plainly invited to regard the nobles as their foes.[1] Pericles, thus more and more thrown upon the democracy, became identified with their interests, and he sought, no less by taste than policy, to prove to the populace that they had grown up into a wealthy and splendid nation, that could dispense with the bounty, the shows, and the exhibitions of individual nobles. He lavished the superfluous treasures of the state upon public festivals, stately processions, and theatrical pageants. As if desirous of elevating the commons to be themselves a nobility, all by which he appealed to their favour served to refine their taste and to inspire the meanest Athenian with a sense of the Athenian grandeur. It was said by his enemies, and the old tale has been credulously repeated, that, his own private fortune not allowing him to vie with the wealthy nobles whom he opposed, it was to supply his deficiencies from the public stock that he directed some part of the national wealth to the encouragement of the national arts and the display of the national magnificence. But it is more than probable that it was rather from principle than personal ambition that Pericles desired to discountenance and eclipse the interested bribes to public favour with which Cimon and others had sought to corrupt the populace. Nor was Pericles without the means or the spirit to devote his private fortune to proper objects of generosity. "It was his wealth and his prudence", says Plutarch, when, blaming the improvidence of Anaxagoras, "that enabled him to relieve the distressed." What he spent in charity he might perhaps have spent more profitably in display, had he not conceived that charity was the province of the citizen, magnificence the privilege of the state. It was in perfect consonance with the philosophy that now began to spread throughout Greece, and with which the mind of this great political artist was so deeply imbued, to consider that the graces ennobled the city they adorned, and that the glory of a state was intimately connected with the polish of the people.

II. While, at home, the divisions of the state were progressing to that point in which the struggle between the opposing leaders must finally terminate in the ordeal of the ostracism—abroad, new causes of hostility broke out between the Athenians and the Spartans. The sacred city of Delphi formed a part of the Phocian nation; but, from a remote period, its citizens appear to have exercised the independent right of

SACRED WAR

---

1 Plut., in Vit. Per.

managing the affairs of the temple,[2] and to have elected their own super-intendents of the oracle and the treasures. In Delphi yet lingered the trace of the Dorian institutions and the Dorian blood, but the primitive valour and hardy virtues of the ancestral tribe had long since mouldered away. The promiscuous intercourse of strangers, the contaminating influence of unrelaxing imposture and priestcraft—above all, the wealth of the city, from which the natives drew subsistence, and even luxury, without labour,[3] contributed to enfeeble and corrupt the national character. Unable to defend themselves by their own exertions against any enemy, the Delphians relied on the passive protection afforded by the superstitious reverence of their neighbours, or on the firm alliance that existed between themselves and the great Spartan representatives of their common Dorian race. The Athenian government could not but deem it desirable to wrest from the Delphians the charge over the oracle and the temple, since that charge might at any time be rendered subservient to the Spartan cause; and accordingly they appear to have connived at a bold attempt of the Phocians, who were now their allies. These hardier neighbours of the sacred city claimed and forcibly seized the right of superintendence of the temple. The Spartans, alarmed and aroused, despatched an armed force to Delphi, and restored their former privileges to the citizens. They piously gave to their excursion the name of the Sacred war. Delphi formally renounced the Phocian league, declared itself an independent state, and even defined the boundaries between its own and the Phocian domains. Sparta was rewarded for its aid by the privilege of precedence in consulting the oracle, and this decree the Spartans inscribed on a brazen wolf in the sacred city. The Athenians no longer now acted through others—they recognized all the advantage of securing to their friends and wresting from their foes the management of an oracle, on whose voice depended fortune in war and prosperity in peace. Scarce had the Spartans withdrawn, than an Athenian force, headed by Pericles, who is said to have been freed by Anaxagoras from superstitious prejudices, entered the city, and restored the temple to the Phocians. The same image which had recorded the privilege of the Spartans now bore an inscription which awarded the right of precedence to the Athenians. The good fortune of this expedition was soon reversed.

III. When the Athenians, after the battle of Œnophyta, had established in the Bœotian cities democratic forms of government, the principal members

---

2 See Thucyd., v. 16, in which the articles of peace state that the temple and fane of Delphi should be independent, and that the citizens should settle their own taxes, receive their own revenues, and manage their own affairs as a sovereign nation (αὐτοτελεῖς καὶ αὐτοδίκους),[4] according *to the ancient laws* of their country. Consult on these words Arnold's Thucydides, vol. ii, p. 256, n. 4.

3 Müller's Dorians, vol. ii, p. 422; Athenæus, iv.

of the defeated oligarchy, either from choice or by compulsion, betook themselves to exile. These malcontents, aided, no doubt, by partisans who did not share their banishment, now seized upon Chæronea, Orchomenus, and some other Bœotian towns. The Athenians, who had valued themselves on restoring liberty to Bœotia, and, for the first time since the Persian war, had honoured with burial at the public expense those who fell under Myronides, could not regard this attempt at counter-revolution with indifference. Policy aided their love of liberty; for it must never be forgotten that the change from democratic to oligarchic government in the Grecian states was the formal exchange of the Athenian for the Spartan alliance. Yet Pericles, who ever unwillingly resorted to war, and the most remarkable attribute of whose character was a profound and calculating caution, opposed the proposition of sending an armed force into Bœotia. His objections were twofold—he considered the time unseasonable, and he was averse to hazard upon an issue not immediately important to Athens the flower of her hoplites, or heavy-armed soldiery, of whom a thousand had offered their services in the enterprise. Nevertheless, the counsel of Tolmides, who was eager for the war, and flushed with past successes, prevailed. "If", said Pericles, "you regard not my experience, wait, at least, for the advice of time, that best of counsellors." The saying was forgotten in the popular enthusiasm it opposed—it afterward attained the veneration of a prophecy.[4]

IV. Aided by some allied troops, and especially by his thousand volunteers, Tolmides swept into Bœotia—reduced Chæronea—garrisoned the captured town, and was returning homeward, when, in the territory of Coronea, he suddenly fell in with a hostile ambush,[5] composed of the exiled bands of Orchomenus, of Opuntian Locrians, and the partisans of the oligarchies of Eubœa. Battle ensued—the Athenians received a signal and memorable defeat; many were made prisoners, many slaughtered: the pride and youth of the Athenian hoplites were left on the field; the brave and wealthy Clinias (father to the yet more renowned Alcibiades), and Tolmides himself, were slain. But the disaster of defeat was nothing in comparison with its consequences. To recover their prisoners, the Athenian government were compelled to enter into a treaty with the hostile oligarchies and withdraw their forces from Bœotia. On their departure, the old oligarchies everywhere replaced the friendly democracies, and the nearest neighbours of Athens were again her foes. Nor was this change confined to Bœotia. In Locris and Phocis the popular party fell with the fortunes of

BATTLE OF CORONEA

---

4 A short change of administration, perhaps, accompanied the defeat of Pericles in the debate on the Bœotian expedition. He was evidently in power, since he had managed the public funds during the opposition of Thucydides; but when beaten, as we should say, "on the Bœotian question", the victorious party probably came into office.

5 An ambush, according to Diodorus, xii.

Coronea—the exiled oligarchies were re-established—and, when we next read of these states, they are the allies of Sparta. At home, the results of the day of Coronea were yet more important. By the slaughter of so many of the hoplites, the aristocratic party in Athens were greatly weakened, while the neglected remonstrances and fears of Pericles, now remembered, secured to him a respect and confidence which soon served to turn the balance against his competitor Thucydides.

V. The first defeat of the proud mistress of the Grecian sea was a signal for the revolt of disaffected dependents. The isle of Euboea, the pasturages of which were now necessary to the Athenians, encouraged by the success that at Coronea had attended the arms of the Euboean exiles, shook off the Athenian yoke. In the same year expired the five years' truce with Sparta, and that state forthwith prepared to avenge its humiliation at Delphi. Pericles seems once more to have been called into official power—he was not now supine in action. At the head of a sufficient force he crossed the channel, and landed in Euboea. Scarce had he gained the island, when he heard that Megara had revolted—that the Megarians, joined by partisans from Sicyon, Epidaurus, and Corinth, had put to the sword the Athenian garrison, save a few who had ensconced themselves in Nisæa, and that an army of the Peloponnesian confederates was preparing to march to Attica. On receiving these tidings, Pericles re-embarked his forces and returned home. Soon appeared the Peloponnesian forces, commanded by the young Pleistoanax, king of Sparta, who, being yet a minor, was placed under the guardianship of Cleandridas; the lands by the western frontier of Attica, some of the most fertile of that territory, were devastated, and the enemy penetrated to Eleusis and Thria. But not a blow was struck—they committed the aggression and departed. On their return to Sparta, Pleistoanax and Cleandridas were accused of having been bribed to betray the honour or abandon the revenge of Sparta; Cleandridas fled the prosecution, and was condemned to death in his exile. Pleistoanax also quitted the country, and took refuge in Arcadia, in the sanctuary of Mount Lycæum. The suspicions of the Spartans appear to have been too well founded, and Pericles, on passing his accounts that year, is stated to have put down ten talents[6] as devoted to a certain use—an item which the assembly assented to in conscious and sagacious silence. This formidable enemy retired, Pericles once more entered Euboea, and reduced the isle. In Chalcis he is said by Plutarch to have expelled the opulent landowners, who, no doubt, formed the oligarchic chiefs of the revolt, and colonized Histiæa with Athenians, driving out at

REVOLT OF EUBŒA AND MEGARA—INVASION AND RETREAT OF THE PELOPON-NESIANS—REDUCTION OF EUBŒA—PUNISHMENT OF HISTIÆA

---

6 Twenty talents, according to the scholiast of Aristophanes. Suidas states the amount variously at fifteen and fifty.

least the greater part of the native population.[7] For the latter severity was given one of the strongest apologies that the stern justice of war can plead for its harshest sentences—the Histiæans had captured an Athenian vessel and murdered the crew. The rest of the island was admitted to conditions, by which the amount of tribute was somewhat oppressively increased.[8]

VI. The inglorious result of the Peloponnesian expedition into Attica naturally tended to make the Spartans desirous of peace upon honourable terms, while the remembrance of dangers, eluded rather than crushed, could not fail to dispose the Athenian government to conciliate a foe from whom much was to be apprehended and little gained. Negotiations were commenced and completed. The Athenians surrendered some of the most valuable fruits of their victories in their hold on the Peloponnesus. They gave up their claim on Nisæa and Pegæ—they renounced the footing they had established in Trœzene—they abandoned alliance or interference with Achæa, over which their influence had extended to a degree that might reasonably alarm the Spartans, since they had obtained the power to raise troops in that province, and Achæan auxiliaries had served under Pericles at the siege of Œniadæ.[9] Such were the conditions upon which a truce of thirty years was based.[10] The articles were ostensibly unfavourable to Athens. Bœotia was gone—Locris, Phocis, an internal revolution (the result of Coronea) had torn from their alliance. The citizens of Delphi must have regained the command of their oracle, since henceforth its sacred voice was in favour of the Spartans. Megara was lost—and now all the holds on the Peloponnesus were surrendered. These reverses, rapid and signal, might have taught the Athenians how precarious is ever the military eminence of small states. But the treaty with Sparta, if disadvantageous, was not dishonourable. It was founded upon one broad principle, without which, indeed, all peace would have been a mockery—viz., that the Athenians should not interfere with the affairs of the Peloponnesus. This principle acknowledged, the surrender of advantages or conquests that were incompatible with it was but a necessary detail. As Pericles was at this time in office,[11] and as he had struggled against an armed interference with the Bœotian towns, so it is probable that he followed out his own policy in surrendering all right to interfere with the Peloponnesian states. Only by peace with Sparta could he accomplish his vast designs for the greatness of Athens—designs which rested not upon

A thirty years' truce concluded with the Peloponnesians

---

7 Who fled into Macedonia.—Theopomp. apud Strabo. The number of Athenian colonists was one thousand, according to Diodorus—two thousand, according to Theopompus.
8 Aristoph., Nub., 213.
9 Thucyd., i, iii.
10 Idem, i. 115.
11 As is evident, among other proofs, from the story before narrated, of his passing his accounts to the Athenians with the item of ten talents employed as secret service money.

her land-forces, but upon her confirming and consolidating her empire of the sea; and we shall shortly find, in our consideration of her revenues, additional reasons for approving a peace essential to her stability.

VII. Scarce was the truce effected ere the struggle between Thucydides and Pericles approached its crisis. The friends of the former never omitted an occasion to charge Pericles with having too lavishly squandered the public funds upon the new buildings which adorned the city. This charge of extravagance, ever an accusation sure to be attentively received by a popular assembly, made a sensible impression. "If you think", said Pericles to the great tribunal before which he urged his defence, "that I have expended too much, charge the sums to my account, not yours—but on this condition, let the edifices be inscribed with my name, not that of the Athenian people." This mode of defence, though perhaps but an oratorical hyperbole,[12] conveyed a rebuke which the Athenians were an audience calculated to answer but in one way—they dismissed the accusation, and applauded the extravagance.

VIII. Accusations against public men, when unsuccessful, are the fairest stepping-stones in their career. Thucydides failed against Pericles. The death of Tolmides—the defeat of Coronea—the slaughter of the hoplites—weakened the aristocratic party; the democracy and the democratic administration seized the occasion for a decisive effort. Thucydides was summoned to the ostracism, and his banishment freed Pericles from his only rival for the supreme administration of the Athenian empire.

OSTRACISM OF
THUCYDIDES

---

12 The Propylæa alone (not then built) cost two thousand and twelve talents (Harpocrat., in προπύλαια ταῦτα), and some temples cost a thousand talents each. [Plut., in Vit. Per.] If the speech of Pericles referred to such works as these, the offer to transfer the account to his own charge was indeed but a figure of eloquence. But, possibly, the accusation to which this offer was intended as a reply was applicable only to some individual edifice or some of the minor works, the cost of which his fortune might have defrayed. We can scarcely indeed suppose, that if the affected generosity were but a bombastic flourish, it could have excited any feeling but laughter among an audience so acute.

CHAPTER II

Causes of the power of Pericles—judicial courts of the dependent allies transferred to Athens—sketch of the Athenian
revenues—public buildings the work of the people rather than
of Pericles—vices and greatness of Athens had the same sources
—principle of payment characterizes the policy of the period—
it is the policy of civilization—colonization, cleruchiæ

I. In the age of Pericles there is that which seems to excite, in order to
disappoint, curiosity. We are fully impressed with the brilliant variety of his
gifts—with the influence he exercised over his times.
He stands in the midst of great and immortal names,
at the close of a heroic, and yet in the sudden meridian
of a civilized age. And scarcely does he recede from our gaze, ere all the evils
which only his genius could keep aloof, gather and close around the city which
it was the object of his life not less to adorn as for festival than to crown
as for command. It is almost as if, with Pericles, her very youth departed
from Athens. Yet so scanty are our details and historical materials, that the
life of this surprising man is rather illustrated by the general light of the
times than by the blaze of his own genius. His military achievements are not
dazzling. No relics, save a few bold expressions, remain of the eloquence
which awed or soothed, excited or restrained, the most difficult audience in
the world. It is partly by analysing the works of his contemporaries—partly
by noting the rise of the whole people—and partly by bringing together and
moulding into a whole the scattered masses of his ambitious and thoughtful
policy, that we alone can gauge and measure the proportions of the master-
spirit of the time. The age of Pericles is the sole historian of Pericles.

This statesman was now at that period of life when public men are usually
most esteemed—when, still in the vigour of manhood, they have acquired
the dignity and experience of years, outlived the earlier prejudices and
jealousies they excited, and see themselves surrounded by a new generation,
among whom rivals must be less common than disciples and admirers. Step
by step, through a long and consistent career, he had ascended to his present
eminence, so that his rise did not startle from its suddenness; while his
birth, his services, and his genius presented a combination of claims to
power that his enemies could not despise, and that justified the enthusiasm
of his friends. His public character was unsullied; of the general belief in his

CAUSES OF THE POWER
OF PERICLES

456

integrity there is the highest evidence;[1] and even the few slanders afterward raised against him—such as that of entering into one war to gratify the resentment of Aspasia, and into another to divert attention from his financial accounts, are libels so unsupported by any credible authority, and so absurd in themselves, that they are but a proof how few were the points on which calumny could assail him.

II. The obvious mode to account for the moral power of a man in any particular time, is to consider his own character, and to ascertain how far it is suited to command the age in which he lived and the people whom he ruled. No Athenian, perhaps, ever possessed so many qualities as Pericles for obtaining wide and lasting influence over the various classes of his countrymen. By his attention to maritime affairs, he won the sailors, now the most difficult part of the population to humour or control; his encouragement to commerce secured the merchants and conciliated the alien settlers; while the stupendous works of art, everywhere carried on, necessarily obtained the favour of the mighty crowd of artificers and mechanics whom they served to employ. Nor was it only to the practical interests, but to all the more refined, yet scarce less powerful sympathies of his countrymen, that his character appealed for support. Philosophy, with all parties, all factions, was becoming an appetite and passion. Pericles was rather the friend than the patron of philosophers. The increasing refinement of the Athenians—the vast influx of wealth that poured into the treasury from the spoils of Persia and the tributes of dependent cities, awoke the desire of art; and the graceful intellect of Pericles at once indulged and directed the desire, by advancing every species of art to its perfection. The freedom of democracy—the cultivation of the drama (which is the oratory of poetry)—the rise of prose literature—created the necessity of popular eloquence—and with Pericles the Athenian eloquence was born. Thus his power was derived from a hundred sources; whether from the grosser interests—the mental sympathies—the vanity—ambition—reason—or imagination of the people. And in examining the character of Pericles, and noting its harmony with his age, the admiration we bestow on himself must be shared by his countrymen. He obtained a greater influence than Pisistratus, but it rested solely on the free will of the Athenians—it was unsupported by armed force—it was subject to the laws—it might any day be dissolved; and influence of this description is only obtained in free states by men who are in themselves the likeness and representative of the vast majority of the democracy they wield. Even the

---

1 The testimony of Thucydides (ii. 5) alone suffices to destroy all the ridiculous imputations against the honesty of Pericles which arose from the malice of contemporaries, and are yet perpetuated only by such writers as cannot weigh authorities. Thucydides does not only call him incorrupt, but "clearly or notoriously honest" (Χρημάτων τε διαφανῶς ἀδωρότατος). Plutarch and Isocrates serve to corroborate this testimony.

aristocratic party that had so long opposed him appear, with the fall of Thucydides, to have relaxed their hostilities. In fact, they had less to resent in Pericles than in any previous leader of the democracy. He was not, like Themistocles, a daring upstart, vying with, and eclipsing their pretensions. He was of their own order. His name was not rendered odious to them by party proscriptions or the memory of actual sufferings. He himself had recalled their idol Cimon—and in the measures that had humbled the Areopagus, so discreetly had he played his part, or so fortunately subordinate had been his co-operation, that the wrath of the aristocrats had fallen only on Ephialtes. After the ostracism of Thucydides, "he became", says Plutarch,[2] "a new man—no longer so subservient to the multitude—and the government assumed an aristocratical, or rather monarchical, form." But these expressions in Plutarch are not to be literally received. The laws remained equally democratic—the Agora equally strong—Pericles was equally subjected to the popular control; but having now acquired the confidence of the people, he was enabled more easily to direct them, or, as Thucydides luminously observes, "Not having obtained his authority unworthily, *he* was not compelled to flatter or to sooth the popular humours, but, when occasion required, he could even venture vehemently to contradict them."[3] The cause which the historian assigns to the effect is one that deserves to be carefully noted by ambitious statesmen—because the authority of Pericles was *worthily* acquired, the people often suffered it to be even unpopularly exercised. On the other hand, this far-seeing and prudent statesman was, no doubt, sufficiently aware of the dangers to which the commonwealth was exposed, if the discontents of the great aristocratic faction were not in some degree conciliated, to induce his wise and sober patriotism, if not actually to seek the favour of his opponents, at least cautiously to shun all idle attempts to revenge past hostilities or feed the sources of future irritation. He owed much to the singular moderation and evenness of his temper; and his debt to Anaxagoras must have been indeed great, if the lessons of that preacher of those cardinal virtues of the intellect, serenity and order, had assisted to form the rarest of all unions—a genius the most fervid, with passions the best regulated.

III. It was about this time, too, in all probability, that Pericles was enabled to consummate the policy he had always adopted with respect to the tributary allies. We have seen that the treasury had been removed from Delos to Athens; it was now resolved to make Athens also the seat and centre of the judicial authority. The subject allies were compelled, if not on minor, at least on all important cases, to resort to Athenian

JUDICIAL COURTS OF THE DEPENDENT ALLIES TRANSFERRED TO ATHENS

2 Plut., in Vit. Per.
3 Thucyd., ii. 25.

courts of law for justice.[4] And thus Athens became, as it were, the metropolis of the allies. A more profound and sagacious mode of quickly establishing her empire it was impossible for ingenuity to conceive; but as it was based upon an oppression that must have been daily and intolerably felt—that every affair of life must have called into irritating action, so, with the establishment of the empire was simultaneously planted an inevitable cause of its decay. For though power is rarely attained without injustice, the injustice, if continued, is the never-failing principle of its corruption. And, in order to endure, authority must hasten to divest itself of all the more odious attributes of conquest.

IV. As a practical statesman, one principal point of view in which we must regard Pericles is in his capacity of a financier. By English historians his policy and pretensions in this department have not been sufficiently considered; yet, undoubtedly, they made one of the most prominent features of his public character in the eyes of his countrymen. He is the first minister in Athens who undertook the scientific management of the national revenues, and partly from his scrupulous integrity, partly from his careful wisdom, and partly from a fortunate concurrence of circumstances, the Athenian revenues, even when the tribute was doubled, were never more prosperously administered. The first great source of the revenue was from the tributes of the confederate cities.[5] These, rated at four hundred and sixty talents in the time of Aristides, had increased to six hundred in the time of Pericles; but there is no evidence to prove that the increased sum was unfairly raised, or that fresh exactions

SKETCH OF THE ATHENIAN REVENUES

---

4 "The model of this regulation, by which Athens obtained the most extensive influence, and an almost absolute dominion over the allies, was possibly found in other Grecian states which had subject confederates, such as Thebes, Elis, and Argos. But on account of the remoteness of many countries, it is impossible that every trifle could have been brought before the court at Athens; we must therefore suppose that each subject state had an inferior jurisdiction of its own, and that the supreme jurisdiction alone belonged to Athens. Can it, indeed, be supposed that persons would have travelled from Rhodes or Byzantium, for the sake of a lawsuit of fifty or a hundred drachmas? In private suits a sum of money was probably fixed, above which the inferior court of the allies had no jurisdiction, while cases relating to higher sums were referred to Athens . . . There can be no doubt that public and penal causes were to a great extent decided in Athens, and the few definite statements which are extant refer to lawsuits of this nature" (Boeckh, Pol. Econ. of Athens, vol. ii, pp. 142, 143, translation).

5 In calculating the amount of the treasure when transferred to Athens, Boeckh (Pol. Econ. of Athens, vol. i, p. 193, translation) is greatly misled by an error of dates. He assumes that the fund had only existed ten years when brought to Athens: whereas it had existed about seventeen, viz., from BC 477 to BC 461, or rather BC 460. And this would give about the amount affirmed by Diodorus, xii. 38 (viz., nearly 8000 talents), though he afterward raises it to 10,000. But a large portion of it must have been consumed in war before the transfer. Still Boeckh rates the total of the sum transferred far too low, when he says it cannot have exceeded 1800 talents. It more probably doubled that sum.

were levied, save in rare cases,[6] on the original subscribers to the league. The increase of a hundred and forty talents is to be accounted for partly by the quota of different confederacies acquired since the time of Aristides, partly by the exemption from military or maritime service, voluntarily if unwisely purchased, during the administration of Cimon, by the states themselves. So far as tribute was a sign of dependance and inferiority, the impost was a hardship; but for this they who paid it are to be blamed rather than those who received. Its practical burden on each state at this period appears, in most cases, to have been incredibly light; and a very trifling degree of research will prove how absurdly exaggerated have been the invectives of ignorant or inconsiderate men, whether in ancient or modern times, on the extortions of the Athenians, and the impoverishment of their allies. Aristophanes[7] attributes to the empire of Athens a thousand tributary cities: the number is doubtless a poetical licence; yet, when we remember the extent of territory which the league comprehended, and how crowded with cities were all the coasts and islands of Greece, we should probably fall short of the number of tributary cities if we estimated it at six hundred; so that the tribute would not in the time of Pericles average above a talent, or 241*l*. 13*s*. 4*d*.[8] English money, for each city! Even when in a time of urgent demand on the resources of the state,[9] Cythera fell into the hands of the Athenians,[10] the tribute of that island was assessed but at four talents. And we find, by inscriptions still extant, that some places were rated only at two thousand, and even one thousand drachmas.[11]

Finally, if the assessment by Aristides, of four hundred and sixty talents, was such as to give universal satisfaction from its equity and moderation, the additional hundred and forty talents in the time of Pericles could not have been an excessive increase, when we consider how much the league had extended, how many states had exchanged the service for the tribute, and how considerable was the large diffusion of wealth throughout the greater part of Greece, the continued influx of gold,[12] and the consequent fall in value of the precious metals.

6 Such as Eubœa, see ch. I sec. V.
7 Aristoph., Vesp., 795.
8 Knight's Prolegomena to Homer; see also Boeckh (translation), vol. i, p. 25.
9 Viz., BC 424; 89th Olympiad.
10 Thucyd., iv. 57.
11 See Chandler's Inscript.
12 In the time of Alcibiades the tribute was raised to one thousand three hundred talents, and even this must have been most unequally assessed, if it were really the pecuniary hardship the allies insisted upon and complained of. But the resistance made to imposts upon matters of *feeling* or *principle* in our own country, as, at this day, in the case of church-rates, may show the real nature of the grievance. It was not the amount paid, but partly the degradation of paying it, and partly, perhaps, resentment in many places at some unfair assessment. Discontent exaggerates every burden, and a feather is as heavy as

V. It was not, then, the amount of the tribute which made its hardship, nor can the Athenian government be blamed for having continued a claim voluntarily conceded to them. The original object of the tribute was the maintenance of a league against the barbarians—the Athenians were constituted the heads of the league and the guardians of the tribute; some states refused service and offered money—their own offers were accepted; other states refused both—it was not more the interest than the duty of Athens to maintain, even by arms, the condition of the league—so far is her policy justifiable. But she erred when she reduced allies to dependents—she erred when she transferred the treasury from the central Delos to her own state— she erred yet more when she appropriated a portion of these treasures to her own purposes. But these vices of Athens are the vices of all eminent states, monarchic or republican—for they are the vices of the powerful. "It was", say the Athenian ambassadors in Thucydides, with honest candour and profound truth—"it was from the nature of the thing itself that we were at first *compelled* to advance our empire to what it is—chiefly through fear— next for honour—and, lastly, for interest; and then it seemed no longer safe for us to venture to let go the reins of government, for the revolters would have gone over to you" (viz., to the Spartans).[13] Thus does the universal lesson of history teach us that it is the tendency of power, in what hands soever it be placed, to widen its limits, to increase its vigour, in proportion as the counteracting force resigns the security for its administration, or the remedy for its abuse.

VI. Pericles had not scrupled, from the date of the transfer of the treasury to Athens, to devote a considerable proportion of the general tribute to public buildings and sacred exhibitions—purposes purely Athenian. But he did so openly—he sought no evasion or disguise—he maintained in the face of Greece that the Athenians were not responsible to the allies for these contributions; that it was the Athenians who had resisted and defended the barbarians, while many of the confederate states had supplied neither ships nor soldiers; that Athens was now the head of a mighty league; and

---

a mountain when laid on unwilling shoulders. When the new arrangement was made by Alcibiades or the later demagogues, Andocides asserts that some of the allies left their native countries and emigrated to Thurii. But how many Englishmen have emigrated to America from objections to a peculiar law or a peculiar impost, which state policy still vindicates, or state necessity still maintains! The Irish Catholic peasant, in reality, would not, perhaps, be much better off, in a pecuniary point of view, if the tithes were transferred to the rental of the landlord, yet Irish Catholics have emigrated in hundreds from the oppression, real or imaginary, of Protestant tithe-owners. Whether in ancient times or modern, it is not the amount of taxation that makes the grievance. People will pay a pound for what they like, and grudge a farthing for what they hate. I have myself known men quit England because of the stamp-duty on newspapers!

13 Thucyd., i. 75; Bloomfield's translation.

that, to increase her glory, to cement her power, was a duty she owed no less to the allies than to herself. Arguments to which armies, and not orators, could alone reply.[14]

The principal other sources whence the Athenian revenue was derived, it may be desirable here to state as briefly and as clearly as the nature of the subject will allow. By those who would search more deeply, the long and elaborate statistics of Boeckh must be carefully explored. Those sources of revenue were:

1   rents from corporate estates—such as pastures, forests, rivers, saltworks, houses, theatres, &c., and mines, let for terms of years, or on heritable leases;

2   tolls, export and import duties, probably paid only by strangers, and amounting to two per cent, a market excise, and the twentieth part of all exports and imports levied in the dependent allied cities—the last a considerable item;

3   tithes, levied only on lands held in usufruct, as estates belonging to temples;

4   a protection tax,[15] paid by the settlers, or Metœci, common to most of the Greek states, but peculiarly productive in Athens from the number of strangers that her trade, her festivals, and her renown attracted. The policy of Pericles could not fail to increase this source of revenue;

5   a slave tax of three obols per head;[16]
    (Most of these taxes appear to have been farmed out.)

6   judicial fees and fines;
    (As we have seen that the allies in most important trials were compelled to seek justice in Athens, this, in the time of Pericles, was a profitable source of income. But it was one, the extent of which necessarily depended upon peace. Fines were of many classes, but not, at least in this period, of very great value to the state. Sometimes (as in all private accusations) the fine fell to the plaintiff, sometimes a considerable proportion enriched

14 A sentiment thus implied by the Athenian ambassadors: "We are not the first who began the custom which has ever been an established one, that the weaker should be kept under by the stronger." The Athenians had, however, an excuse more powerful than that of the ancient Rob Roys. It was the general opinion of the time that the revolt of dependent allies might be fairly punished by one that could punish them—(so the Corinthians take care to observe). And it does not appear that the Athenian empire at this period was more harsh than that of other states to their dependents. The Athenian ambassadors (Thucyd., i. 78) not only quote the far more galling oppressions the Ionians and the isles had undergone from the Mede, but hint that the Spartans had been found much harder masters than the Athenians.

15 Only twelve drachmæ each yearly; the total, therefore, is calculated by the inestimable learning of Boeckh not to have exceeded twenty-one talents.

16 Total estimated at thirty-three talents.

the treasury of the tutelary goddess. The task of assessing the files was odious, and negligently performed by the authorities, while it was easy for those interested to render a false account of their property.)

7   the state received the aid of annual contributions, or what were termed "liturgies", from individuals for particular services.

The ordinary liturgies were:

1   the choregia, or duty of furnishing the chorus for the plays—tragic, comic, and satirical—of remunerating the leader of the singers and musicians—of maintaining the latter while trained—of supplying the dresses, the golden crowns and masks, and, indeed, the general decorations and equipments of the theatre. He on whom this burdensome honour fell was called choregus; his name, and that of his tribe, was recorded on the tripod which commemorated the victory of the successful poet, whose performances were exhibited;[17]

2   the Gymnasiarchy, or charge of providing for the expense of the torch-race, celebrated in honour of the gods of fire, and some other sacred games. In later times the gymnasiarchy comprised the superintendence of the training schools, and the cost of ornamenting the arena;

3   the architheoria, or task of maintaining the embassy to sacred games and festivals;

4   the hestiasis, or feasting of the tribes, a costly obligation incurred by some wealthy member of each tribe for entertaining the whole of the tribe at public, but not very luxurious, banquets. This last expense did not often occur. The hestiasis was intended for sacred objects, connected with the rites of hospitality, and served to confirm the friendly intercourse between the members of the tribe.

These three ordinary liturgies had all a religious character; they were compulsory on those possessed of property not less than three talents—they were discharged in turn by the tribes, except when volunteered by individuals.

VII. The expenses incurred for the defence or wants of the state were not regular, but *extraordinary* liturgies—such as the trierarchy, or equipment of ships, which entailed also the obligation of personal service on those by whom the triremes were fitted out. Personal service was indeed the characteristic of all liturgies, a property tax, which was not yet invented, alone excepted; and this, though bearing the name, has not the features, of a liturgy. Of the extraordinary liturgies, the trierarchy was the most important. It was of very

17 The state itself contributed largely to the plays, and the lessee of the theatre was also bound to provide for several expenses, in consideration of which he received the entrance money.

early origin. Boeckh observes[18] that it was mentioned in the time of Hippias. At the period of which we treat each vessel had one trierarch. The vessel was given to the trierarch, sometimes ready equipped; he also received the public money for certain expenses; others fell on himself.[19] Occasionally, but rarely, an ambitious or patriotic trierarch defrayed the whole cost; but in any case he rendered strict account of the expenses incurred. The cost of a whole trierarchy was not less than forty minas, nor more than a talent.

VIII. Two liturgies could not be demanded simultaneously from any individual, nor was he liable to any one more often than every other year. He who served the trierarchies was exempted from all other contributions. Orphans were exempted till the year after they had obtained their majority, and a similar exemption was, in a very few instances, the reward of eminent public services. The nine archons were also exempted from the trierarchies.

IX. The moral defects of liturgies were the defects of a noble theory, which almost always terminates in practical abuses. Their principle was that of making it an honour to contribute to the public splendour or the national wants. Hence, in the earlier times, an emulation among the rich to purchase favour by a liberal, but often calculating and interested ostentation; hence, among the poor, actuated by an equal ambition, was created so great a necessity for riches as the means to power,[20] that the mode by which they were to be acquired was often overlooked. What the theory designed as the munificence of patriotism, became in practice but a showy engine of corruption; and men vied with each other in the choregia or the trierarchy, not so much for the sake of service done to the state, as in the hope of influence acquired over the people. I may also observe, that in a merely fiscal point of view, the principle of liturgies was radically wrong; that principle went to tax the few instead of the many; its operation was therefore not more unequal in its assessments than it was unproductive to the state in proportion to its burden on individuals.

X. The various duties were farmed—a pernicious plan of finance common to most of the Greek states. The farmers gave sureties, and punctuality was rigorously exacted from them, on penalty of imprisonment, the doubling of the debt, the confiscation of their properties, the compulsory hold upon their sureties.

18 On the authority of Pseud. Aristot., Œcon., 2–4.

19 In the expedition against Sicily the state supplied the vessel and paid the crew. The trierarchs equipped the ship and gave voluntary contributions besides (Thucyd., vi. 31).

20 Liturgies, with most of the Athenian laws that seemed to harass the rich personally, enhanced their station and authority politically. It is clear that wherever wealth is made most obviously available to the state, there it will be most universally respected. Thus is it ever in commercial countries—in Carthage of old, where, according to Aristotle, wealth was considered virtue, and in England at this day, where wealth, if not virtue, is certainly *respectability*.

XI. Such were the main sources of the Athenian revenue. Opportunities will occur to fill up the brief outline and amplify each detail. This sketch is now presented to the reader as comprising a knowledge necessary to a clear insight into the policy of Pericles. A rapid glance over the preceding pages will suffice to show that it was on a rigid avoidance of all unnecessary war— above all, of distant and perilous enterprises, that the revenue of Athens rested. Her commercial duties—her tax on settlers—the harvest of judicial fees, obtained from the dependent allies—the chief profits from the mines— all rested upon the maintenance of peace: even the foreign tribute, the most productive of the Athenian resources, might fail at once, if the Athenian arms should sustain a single reverse, as indeed it did after the fatal battle of Ægospotamos.[21] This it was which might have shown to the great finance minister that peace with the Peloponnesus could scarce be too dearly purchased.[22] The surrender of a few towns and fortresses was nothing in comparison with the arrest and paralysis of all the springs of her wealth, which would be the necessary result of a long war upon her own soil. For this reason Pericles strenuously checked all the wild schemes of the Athenians for extended empire. Yet dazzled with the glories of Cimon, some entertained the hopes of recovering Egypt, some agitated the invasion of the Persian coasts; the fair and fatal Sicily already aroused the cupidity and ambition of others; and the vain enthusiasts of the Agora even dreamed of making that island the base and centre of a new and vast dominion, including Carthage on one hand and Etruria on the other.[23] Such schemes it was the great object of Pericles to oppose. He was not less ambitious for the greatness of Athens than the most daring of these visionaries; but he better understood on what foundations it should be built. His objects were to strengthen the possessions already acquired, to confine the Athenian energies within the frontiers of Greece, and to curb, as might better be done by peace than war, the Peloponnesian forces to their own rocky barriers. The means by which he sought to attain these objects were, first, by a maritime force; and, second, by that inert and silent power which springs as it were from the moral

21 And so well aware of the uncertain and artificial tenure of the Athenian power were the Greek statesmen, that we find it among the arguments with which the Corinthians some time after supported the Peloponnesian war, "that the Athenians, if they lost one sea-fight, would be utterly subdued"; (Thucyd., i. 121) nor, even without such a mischance, could the flames of a war be kindled, but what the obvious expedient (as the Corinthians indeed suggested, Thucyd., i. 122) of the enemy would be to excite the Athenian allies to revolt, and the stoppage or diminution of the tribute would be the necessary consequence.
22 If the courts of law among the allies were not removed to Athens till after the truce with Peloponnesus, and indeed till after the ostracism of Thucydides, the rival of Pericles, the value of the judicial fees did not, of course, make one of the considerations for peace; but there would then have been the mightier consideration of the design of that transfer which peace only could effect.
23 Plut., in Vit. Per.

dignity and renown of a nation; whatever, in this latter respect, could make Athens illustrious, made Athens formidable.

XII. Then rapidly progressed those glorious fabrics which seemed, as Plutarch gracefully expresses it, endowed with the bloom of a perennial youth. Still the houses of private citizens remained simple and unadorned; still were the streets narrow and irregular; and even centuries afterward, a stranger entering Athens would not at first have recognized the claims of the mistress of Grecian art. Put to the homeliness of her common thoroughfares and private mansions, the magnificence of her public edifices now made a dazzling contrast. The Acropolis, that towered above the homes and thoroughfares of men—a spot too sacred for human habitation—became, to use a proverbial phrase, "a city of the gods". The citizen was everywhere to be reminded of the majesty of the state—his patriotism was to be increased by the pride in her beauty—his taste to be elevated by the spectacle of her splendour. Thus flocked to Athens all who throughout Greece were eminent in art. Sculptors and architects vied with each other in adorning the young empress of the seas;[24] then rose the masterpieces of Phidias, of Callicrates, of Mnesicles,[25] which even, either in their broken remains, or in the feeble copies of imitators less inspired, still command so intense a wonder, and furnish models so immortal. And if, so to speak, their bones and relics excite our awe and envy, as testifying of a lovelier and grander race, which the deluge of time has swept away, what, in that day, must have been their brilliant effect—unmutilated in their fair proportions—fresh in all their lineaments and hues? For their beauty was not limited to the symmetry of arch and column, nor their materials confined to the marbles of Pentelicus and Paros. Even the exterior of the temples glowed with the richest harmony of colours, and was decorated with the purest gold; an atmosphere peculiarly favourable both to the display and the preservation of art, permitted to external pediments and friezes all the minuteness of ornament—all the brilliancy of colours, such as in the interior of Italian churches may yet be seen—vitiated, in the last, by a gaudy and barbarous taste. Nor did the Athenians spare any cost upon the works that were, like the tombs and tripods of their heroes, to be the monuments of a nation to distant ages, and to transmit the most irrefragable proof "that the power of ancient Greece was not an idle legend".[26] The whole democracy were animated with the passion of Pericles; and when Phidias recommended

PUBLIC BUILDINGS THE WORK OF THE PEOPLE RATHER THAN OF PERICLES

24 "As a vain woman decked out with jewels", was the sarcastic reproach of the allies (Plut., in Vit. Per.).

25 The Propylæa was built under the direction of Mnesicles. It was begun BC 437, in the archonship of Euthymenes, three years after the Samian war, and completed in five years. Harpocrat. in προπύλαια ταύτα.

26 Plut., in Vit. Per.

marble as a cheaper material than ivory for the great statue of Minerva, it was for that reason that ivory was preferred by the unanimous voice of the assembly. Thus, whether it were extravagance or magnificence, the blame in one case, the admiration in another, rests not more with the minister than the populace. It was, indeed, the great characteristic of those works, that they were entirely the creations of the people: without the people, Pericles could not have built a temple or engaged a sculptor. The miracles of that day resulted from the enthusiasm of a population yet young—full of the first ardour for the beautiful—dedicating to the state, as to a mistress, the trophies honourably won or the treasures injuriously extorted—and uniting the resources of a nation with the energy of an individual, because the toil, the cost, were borne by those who succeeded to the enjoyment and arrogated the glory.

XIII. It was from two sources that Athens derived her chief political vices: first, her empire of the seas and her exactions from her allies; second, an unchecked, unmitigated democratic action, void of the two vents known in all modern commonwealths —the press, and a representative, instead of a popular, assembly. But from these sources she now drew all her greatness also, moral and intellectual. Before the Persian war, and even scarcely before the time of Cimon, Athens cannot be said to have eclipsed her neighbours in the arts and sciences. She became the centre and capital of the most polished communities of Greece, and she drew into a focus all the Grecian intellect; she obtained from her dependents the wealth to administer the arts, which universal traffic and intercourse taught her to appreciate; and thus the Odeon, and the Parthenon, and the Propylæa arose! During the same administration, the fortifications were completed, and a third wall, parallel[27] and near to that uniting Piræus with Athens, consummated the works of Themistocles and Cimon, and preserved the communication between the twofold city, even should the outer walls fall into the hands of an enemy.

VICES AND GREATNESS OF ATHENS HAD THE SAME SOURCES

But honour and wealth alone would not have sufficed for the universal emulation, the universal devotion to all that could adorn or exalt the nation. It was the innovations of Aristides and Ephialtes that breathed into that abstract and cold formality, the state, the breath and vigour of a pervading people, and made the meanest citizen struggle for Athens with that zeal with which an ambitious statesman struggles for himself.[28] These two causes united reveal to us the true secret why Athens obtained a pre-eminence in intellectual grandeur over the rest of Greece. Had Corinth obtained the

---

27 See Arnold's Thucydides, ii. 13, n. 12.
28 "Their bodies, too, they employ for the state as if they were any one's else but their own; but with minds completely their own, they are ever ready to render it service" (Thucyd., i. 70; Bloomfield's translation).

command of the seas and the treasury of Delos—had Corinth established abroad a power equally arbitrary and extensive, and at home a democracy equally broad and pure—Corinth might have had her Pericles and Demosthenes, her Phidias, her Sophocles, her Aristophanes, her Plato—and posterity might not have allowed the claim of Athens to be the ἔλλας ἑλλάδος, "the Greece of Greece."

XIV. But the increase of wealth bounded not its effects to these magnificent works of art—they poured into and pervaded the whole domestic policy of Athens. We must recollect, that as the greatness of the state was that of the democracy, so its treasures were the property of the free population. It was *the people* who were rich; and according to all the notions of political economy in that day, the people desired practically to enjoy their own opulence. Thus was introduced the principle of payment for service, and thus was sanctioned and legalized the right of a common admission to spectacles, the principal cost of which was defrayed from common property. That such innovations would be the necessary and unavoidable result of an overflowing treasury in a state thus democratic is so obvious, that nothing can be more absurd than to lay the blame of the change upon Pericles. He only yielded to, and regulated the irresistible current of the general wish. And we may also observe, that most of those innovations, which were ultimately injurious to Athens, rested upon the acknowledged maxims of modern civilization; some were rather erroneous from details than principles; others, from the want of harmony between the new principles and the old constitution to which they were applied. Each of the elements might be healthful—amalgamated, they produced a poison.

XV. It is, for instance, an axiom in modern politics that judges should receive a salary.[29] During the administration of Pericles, this principle was applied to the dicasts in the popular courts of judicature. It seems probable that the vast accession of law business which ensued from the transfer of the courts in the allied states to the Athenian tribunal was the cause of this enactment. Lawsuits became so common, that it was impossible, without salaries, that the citizens could abandon their own business for that of others. Payment was, therefore, both equitable and unavoidable, and, doubtless, it would have seemed to the Athenians, as now to us, the best means, not only of securing the attention, but of

PRINCIPLE OF PAYMENT CHARACTERIZES THE POLICY OF THE PERIOD

---

29 With us, juries as well as judges are paid, and, in ordinary cases, at as low a rate as the Athenian dicasts (the different value of money being considered), viz., common jurymen one shilling for each trial, and, in the sheriffs' court, fourpence. What was so pernicious in Athens is perfectly harmless in England; it was the large number of the dicasts which made the mischief, and not the system of payment itself, as unreflecting writers have so often asserted.

strengthening the integrity, of the judges or the jurors. The principle of salaries was, therefore, right, but its results were evil, when applied to the peculiar constitution of the courts. The salary was small—the judges numerous, and mostly of the humblest class—the consequences I have before shown.[30] Had the salaries been high and the number of the judges small, the means of a good judicature would have been attained. But, then, according to the notions, not only of the Athenians, but of all the Hellenic democracies, the democracy itself, of which the popular courts were deemed the constitutional bulwark and the vital essence, would have been at an end. In this error, therefore, however fatal it might be, neither Pericles nor the Athenians, but the theories of the age, are to be blamed.[31] It is also a maxim formerly acted upon in England, to which many political philosophers now incline, and which is yet adopted in the practice of a great and enlightened portion of the world, that the members of the legislative assembly should receive salaries. This principle was now applied in Athens.[32] But there the people themselves were the legislative assembly, and thus a principle, perhaps sound in itself, became vitiated to the absurdity of the people as sovereign paying the people as legislative. Yet even this might have been necessary to the preservation of the constitution, as meetings became numerous and business complicated; for if the people had not been tempted and even driven to assemble in large masses, the business of the state would have been jobbed away by active minorities, and the life of a democracy been lost.[33] The payment was first one obolus—afterward increased to three. Nor must we suppose, as the ignorance or effrontery of certain modern historians has strangely asserted, that in the new system of payments the people were munificent only to themselves. The senate was paid—the public advocates and orators were paid—so were the ambassadors, the inspectors of the youths in the trading schools, the nomothetæ or law commissioners, the physicians, the singers, even the poets; all the servants of the different officers received salaries. And now, as is the inevitable consequence of that civilization in a commercial society which multiplies and strongly demarcates the divisions

30 See Book IV ch. V sec. VII.
31 At first the payment of the dicasts was one obolus (Aristoph. Nub., 861). Afterward, under Cleon, it seems to have been increased to three; it is doubtful whether it was in the interval ever *two* obols. Constant mistakes are made between the pay, and even the constitution, of the ecclesiasts and the dicasts. But the reader must carefully remember that the former were the popular *legislators*, the latter, the popular *judges* or jurors—their functions were a mixture of both.
32 $Mισθòς \ ἐκκλησιαστικός$—the pay of the ecclesiasts, or popular assembly.
33 We know not how far the paying of the ecclesiasts was the work of Pericles: if it were, it must have been at, or after, the time we now enter upon, as, according to Aristophanes (Eccles., 302), the people were not paid during the power of Myronides, who flourished, and must have fallen with Thucydides, the defeated rival of Pericles.

of labour, the safety of the state no longer rested solely upon the unpurchased arms and hearts of its citizens—but not only were the Athenians themselves who served as soldiers paid, but foreign mercenaries were engaged—a measure in consonance with the characteristic policy of Pericles, which was especially frugal of the lives of the citizens. But peculiar to the Athenians of all the Grecian states was the humane and beautiful provision for the poor, commenced under Solon or Pisistratus. At this happy and brilliant period few were in need of it—war and disaster, while they increased the number of the destitute, widened the charity of the state.

XVI. Thus, then, that general system of payment which grew up under Pericles, and produced many abuses under his successors, was, after all, but the necessary result of the increased civilization and opulence of the period. Nor can we wonder that the humbler or the middle orders, who, from their common stock, lavished generosity upon genius,[34] and alone, of all contemporaneous states, gave relief to want—who maintained the children of all who died in war— who awarded remunerations for every service, should have deemed it no grasping exaction to require for their own attendance on offices forced on them by the constitution a compensation for the desertion of their private affairs, little exceeding that which was conferred upon the very paupers of the state.[35]

IT IS THE POLICY OF CIVILIZATION

XVII. But there was another abuse which sprang out of the wealth of the people, and that love for spectacles and exhibitions which was natural to the lively Ionic imagination, and could not but increase as leisure and refinement became boons extended to the bulk of the population—an abuse trifling in itself—fatal in the precedent it set. While the theatre was of wood, free admissions were found to produce too vast a concourse for the stability of the building; and once, indeed, the seats gave way. It was, therefore, long before the present period, deemed advisable to limit the number of the audience by a small payment of two obols for each seat; and this continued after a stately edifice of stone replaced the wooden temple of the earlier drama.

But as riches flowed into the treasury, and as the drama became more and more the most splendid and popular of the national exhibitions, it seemed but just to return to the ancient mode of gratuitous admissions. It was found, however, convenient, partly, perhaps, for greater order and for the better allotment of the seats—partly, also, for the payment of several expenses

---

34 The Athenians could extend their munificence even to foreigners, as their splendid gift, said to have been conferred on Herodotus, and the sum of ten thousand drachmas, which Isocrates declares them to have bestowed on Pindar (Isoc., de Antidosi).

35 The pay of the dicast and the ecclesiast was, as we have just seen, first one, then three obols; and the money paid to the infirm was never less than one, nor more than two obols a day. The common sailors, in time of peace, received four obols a day. Neither an ecclesiast nor a dicast was, therefore, paid so much as a common sailor.

which fell not on the state, but individuals and partly, no doubt, to preserve the distinctions between the citizens and the strangers, to maintain the prices, but to allow to those whose names were enrolled in the book of the citizens the admittance money from the public treasury. This fund was called the theoricon. But the example once set, theorica were extended to other festivals besides those of the drama,[36] and finally, under the plausible and popular pretext of admitting the poorer classes to those national or religious festivals, from which, as forming the bulk of the nation, it was against the theory of the constitution to exclude them, paved the way to lavish distributions of the public money, which at once tended to exhaust the wealth of the state, and to render effeminate and frivolous the spirit of the people. But these abuses were not yet visible: on the contrary, under Pericles, the results of the theoricon were highly favourable to the manners and genius of the people. Art was thus rendered the universal right, and while refinement of taste became diffused, the patriotism of the citizens was increased by the consciousness that they were the common and legitimate arbiters of all which augmented the splendour and renown of Athens.

Thus, in fact, the after evils that resulted from the more popular part of the internal policy of Pericles, it was impossible to foresee; they originated not in a single statement, but in the very nature of civilization. And as in despotisms, a coarse and sensual luxury, once established, rots away the vigour and manhood of a conquering people, so in this intellectual republic it was the luxury of the intellect which gradually enervated the great spirit of the victor race of Marathon and Salamis, and called up generations of eloquent talkers and philosophical dreamers from the earlier age of active freemen, restless adventurers, and hardy warriors. The spirit of poetry, or the pampered indulgence of certain faculties to the prejudice of others, produced in a whole people what it never fails to produce in the individual: it unfitted them—just as they grew up into a manhood exposed to severer struggles than their youth had undergone—for the stern and practical demands of life; and suffered the love of the beautiful to subjugate or soften away the common knowledge of the useful. Genius itself became a disease, and poetry assisted towards the euthanasia of the Athenians.

XVIII. As all the measures of Pericles were directed towards consolidating the Athenian empire, so under his administration was not omitted the

COLONIZATION, CLERUCHIÆ

politic expedient of colonization. Of late years, states having become confirmed and tribes settled, the Grecian migrations were far less frequent than of old; and one principal cause of colonization, in the violent feud of parties, and the expulsion of a considerable number of citizens, arose from the disasters of infant communities, and was no longer in force under the free but strong government of Athens.

---

36 Such as the Panathenæa and Hieromeniæ.

As with the liberties fell the commerce of Miletus and Ionia, so also another principal source of the old colonization became comparatively languid and inert. But now, under the name of cleruchi,[37] a new description of colonists arose—colonists by whom the mother country not only drafted off a redundant population, or rid herself of restless adventurers, but struck the roots of her empire in the various places that came under her control. In the classic as in the feudal age, conquest gave the right to the lands of the conquered country. Thus had arisen, and thus still existed, upon the plundered lands of Laconia, the commonwealth of Sparta—thus were maintained the wealthy and luxurious nobles of Thessaly—and thus, in fine, were created all the ancient Dorian oligarchies. After the Return of the Heraclidæ, this mode of consummating conquest fell into disuse, not from any moral conviction of its injustice, but because the wars between the various states rarely terminated in victories so complete as to permit the seizure of the land and the subjugation of the inhabitants. And it must be ever remembered, that the old Grecian tribes made war to procure a settlement, and not to increase dominion. The smallness of their population rendered human life too valuable to risk its waste in the expeditions that characterized the ambition of the leaders of oriental hordes. But previous to the Persian wars, the fertile meadows of Eubœa presented to the Athenians a temptation it could scarcely be expected that victorious neighbours would have the abstinence to forego; and we have seen that they bestowed the lands of the Hippobotæ on Athenian settlers. These colonists evacuated their possessions during the Persian war: the Hippobotæ returned, and seem to have held quiet, but probably tributary, possession of their ancient estates, until after the recent retreat of the Peloponnesians. Pericles defeated and displaced them; their lands fell once more to Athenian colonists; and the north of Eubœa was protected and garrisoned by the erection of Oreus, a new town that supplanted the old Histiæa. Territories in Scyros, Lemnos, and Imbros had been also bestowed on Athenian settlers during the earlier successes of the Athenian arms—and the precedent thus set, examples became more numerous, under the profound and systematic policy of Pericles. This mode of colonization, besides the ordinary advantages of all colonization, proffered two peculiar to itself. In the first place, it supplied the deficiency of land, which was one of the main inconveniences of Attica, and rewarded the meritorious or appeased the avaricious citizens, with estates which it did not impoverish the mother country to grant. Second, it secured the conquests of the state by planting garrisons which it cost little to maintain.[38] Thus were despatched by Pericles

---

37 From κλῆροι, lots. The estates and settlements of a cleruchia were divided among a certain number of citizens by lot.

38 The state only provided the settlers with arms, and defrayed the expenses of their journey. See Boeckh, Pol. Econ. of Athens, vol. ii, p. 170 (translation).

a thousand men to the valuable possessions in the Chersonesus, two hundred and fifty to Andros, five hundred to Naxos, a thousand to Thrace. At another period, the date of which is uncertain, but probably shortly subsequent to the truce with the Peloponnesians, a large fleet, commanded by Pericles, swept the Euxine, in order to awe and impress the various states and nations along the adjacent coasts, whether Greek or barbarian, with the display of the Athenian power; and the city of Sinope, being at that time divided with contentions for and against its tyrant Timesilaus, the republican party applied to the head of the Greek democracies for aid. Lamachus, a warrior to whose gallant name, afterward distinguished in the Peloponnesian war, Aristophanes has accorded the equal honour of his ridicule and his praise, was entrusted with thirteen galleys and a competent force for the expulsion of the tyrant and his adherents. The object effected, the new government of Sinope rewarded six hundred Athenians with the freedom of the city and the estates of the defeated faction.

While thus Athens fixed her footing on remoter lands, gradually her grasp extended over the more near and necessary demesnes of Euboea, until the lands of more than two-thirds of that island were in the possession of Athenians.[39] At a later period, new opportunities gave rise to new cleruchiæ.[40]

XIX. Besides these cleruchiæ, in the second year of the supreme administration of Pericles a colony, properly so called, was established in western Italy—interesting alike from the great names of its early adventurers, the beauty of its site, and from the circumstance of its being, besides that at Amphipolis, the only pure and legitimate colony,[41] in contradistinction to the cleruchiæ, founded by Athens, since her ancient migrations to Ionia and

---

39 Andoc., Orat. de Pace.

40 These institutions differed, therefore, from colonies principally in this: the mother country retained a firm hold over the cleruchi—could recall them or reclaim their possessions, as a penalty of revolt: the cleruchi retained all the rights, and were subject to most of the conditions, of citizens (except, for instance, the liturgies). Lands were given without the necessity of quitting Athens—departure thence was voluntary, although it was the ordinary choice. But whether the cleruchi remained at home or repaired to their settlement, they were equally attached to Athenian interests. From their small number, and the enforced and unpopular nature of their tenure, their property, unlike that of ordinary colonists, depended on the power and safety of the parent state: they were not so much transplanted shoots as extended branches of one tree, taking their very life from the same stem. In modern times, Ireland suggests a parallel to the old cleruchiæ—in the gift of lands to English adventurers—in the long and intimate connexion which subsisted between the manners, habits, and political feeling of the English settlers and the parent state—in the separation between the settlers and the natives; and in the temporary power and subsequent feebleness which resulted to the home government from the adoption of a system which garrisoned the land, but exasperated the inhabitants.

41 Nor were even these composed solely of Athenians, but of mixed and various races. The colony to Amphipolis (BC 465) is the first recorded colony of the Athenians after the great Ionic migrations.

the Cyclades. Two centuries before, some Achæans, mingled with Trœzenians, had established, in the fertile garden of Magna Græcia, the state of Sybaris. Placed between two rivers, the Crathis and the Sybaris—possessing extraordinary advantages of site and climate, this celebrated colony rose with unparalleled rapidity to eminence in war and luxury in peace. So great were its population and resources, that it is said by Diodorus to have brought at one time three hundred thousand men into the field—an army which doubled that which all Greece could assemble at Platæa! The exaggeration is evident; but it still attests the belief of a populousness and power which must have rested upon no fabulous foundation. The state of Sybaris had prospered for a time by the adoption of a principle which is ever apt to force civilization to premature development, and not unfrequently to end in the destruction of national character and internal stability—viz., it opened its arms to strangers of every tribe and class. Thronged by mercantile adventurers, its trade, like that of Agrigentum, doubtless derived its sources from the oil and wine which it poured into the harbours of Africa and Gaul. As with individuals, so with states, wealth easily obtained is prodigally spent, and the effeminate and voluptuous ostentation of Sybaris passed into a proverb more enduring than her prosperity. Her greatness, acquired by a tempered and active democracy, received a mortal blow by the usurpation of a tyrant named Telys, who, in BC 510, expelled five hundred of the principal citizens. Croton received the exiles, a war broke out, and in the same year, or shortly afterward, the Crotoniates, under Milo, defeated the Sybarites with prodigious slaughter, and the city was abandoned to pillage, and left desolate and ruined. Those who survived fled to Laos and Scidrus. Fifty-eight years afterward, aided by some Thessalians, the exiled Sybarites again sought possession of their former settlement, but were speedily expelled by the Crotoniates. It was now that they applied to Sparta and Athens for assistance. The former state had neither population to spare, nor commerce to strengthen, nor ambition to gratify, and rejected the overtures of the Sybarite envoys. But a different success awaited the exiles at Athens. Their proposition, timed in a period when it was acceptable to the Athenian policy, was enforced by Pericles. Adventurers from all parts of Greece, but invited especially from the Peloponnesus, swelled the miscellaneous band: eminent among the rest were Lysias, afterward so celebrated as a rhetorician,[42] and Herodotus, the historian.

As in the political code of Greece the religious character of the people made a prevailing principle, so in colonization the deity of the parent state transplanted his worship with his votaries, and the relation between the new and the old country was expressed and perpetuated by the touching symbol of taking fire from the Prytaneum of the native city. A renowned diviner,

---

42 In the year in which the colony of Thurium or Thurii was founded, the age of Lysias was fifteen, that of Herodotus forty-one.

named Lampon,[43] whose sacred pretensions did not preserve him from the ridicule of the comic poets,[44] accompanied the emigrants, and an oracle dictated the site of the new colony near the ancient city, and by the fountain of Thurium. The Sybarites, with the common vanity of men whose ancestors have been greater than themselves, increased their pretensions in proportion as they lost their power; they affected superiority over their companions, by whose swords alone they again existed as a people; claimed the exclusive monopoly of the principal offices of government, and the first choice of lands; and were finally cut off by the very allies whose aid they had sought, and whose resentment they provoked. New adventurers from Greece replaced the Sybarites, and the colonists of Thurium, divided into ten tribes (four, the representatives of the united Ionians, Euboeans, islanders, and Athenians; three of the Peloponnesians; and three of the settlers from northern Greece)— retained peaceable possession of their delightful territory, and harmonized their motley numbers by the adoption of the enlightened laws and tranquil institutions of Charondas. Such was the home of Herodotus, the historian.

---

43 Plut., in Vit. Per.; Schol. Aristoph., Av., 521.

44 Viz., Callias, Lysippus, and Cratinus. See Athenæus, viii. 344. The worthy man seems to have had the amiable infirmities of a *bon vivant*.

CHAPTER III

Revision of the census—Samian war—sketch of the rise and
progress of the Athenian comedy to the time of Aristophanes

I. In proportion as it had become matter of honourable pride and lucrative
advantage to be a citizen of Athens, it was natural that the laws defining and
limiting the freedom of the city should increase
in strictness. Even before the time of Themistocles,
those only were considered legitimate[1] who, on either side, derived parentage
from Athenian citizens. But though illegitimate, they were not therefore
deprived of the rights of citizenship; nor had the stain upon his birth been a
serious obstacle to the career of Themistocles himself. Under Pericles, the
law became more severe, and a decree was passed (apparently in the earlier
period of his rising power), which excluded from the freedom of the city those
whose parents were not both Athenian. In the very year in which he attained
the supreme administration of affairs, occasion for enforcing the law occurred:
Psammetichus, the pretender to the Egyptian throne, sent a present of corn
to the Athenian people; the claimants for a share in the gift underwent
the ordeal of scrutiny as to their titles to citizenship, and no less than five
thousand persons were convicted of having fraudulently foisted themselves
into rights which were now tantamount to property; they were disfranchised;[2]

REVISION OF THE CENSUS

---

1 Plut., in Vit. Them.
2 Historians, following the received text in Plutarch, have retailed the incredible story
   that the rejected claimants were sold for slaves; but when we consider the extraordinary
   agitation it must have caused to carry such a sentence against so many persons, amounting
   to a fourth part of the free population—when we remember the numerous connexions,
   extending throughout at least four times their own number, which five thousand persons
   living long undisturbed and unsuspected as free citizens must have formed, it is impossible
   to conceive that such rigour could even have been attempted without creating revolution,
   sedition, or formidable resistance. Yet this measure, most important if attended with such
   results—most miraculous if not—is passed over in total silence by Thucydides and by
   every other competent authority. A luminous emendation by Mr Clinton (Fasti Hellenici,
   vol. ii, second edition, p. 52 and 390, note p) restores the proper meaning. Instead of
   $\dot{\epsilon}\pi\rho\acute{a}\theta\eta\sigma a\nu$, he proposes $\dot{a}\pi\eta\lambda\acute{a}\theta\eta\sigma a\nu$—the authorities from Lysias quoted by Mr Clinton
   (p. 390) seem to decide the matter. "These five thousand disfranchised citizens, in BC 444,
   partly supplied the colony to Thurium in the following year, and partly contributed to
   augment the number of the Metœci."

and the whole list of the free citizens was reduced to little more than fourteen thousand.[3]

II. While under this brilliant and energetic administration Athens was daily more and more concentrating on herself the reluctant admiration and the growing fears of Greece, her policy towards her dependent allies involved her in a war which ultimately gave, if not a legal, at least an acknowledged, title to the pretensions she assumed. Hostilities between the new population of Miletus and the oligarchic government of Samos had been for some time carried on; the object of contention was the city of Priene—united, apparently, with rival claims upon Anæa, a town on the coast opposite Samos. The Milesians, unsuccessful in the war, applied to Athens for assistance. As the Samians were among the dependent allies, Pericles, in the name of the Athenian people, ordered them to refer to Athens the decision of the dispute; on their refusal an expedition of forty galleys was conducted against them by Pericles in person. A still more plausible colour than that of the right of dictation was given to this interference; for the prayer of the Milesians was backed and sanctioned by many of the Samians themselves, oppressed by the oligarchic government which presided over them. A ridiculous assertion was made by the libellers of the comic drama and the enemies of Pericles, that the war was undertaken at the instigation of Aspasia, with whom that minister had formed the closest connexion; but the expedition was the necessary and unavoidable result of the twofold policy by which the Athenian government invariably directed its actions: first, to enforce the right of ascendency over its allies; second, to replace oligarchic by democratic institutions. Nor, on this occasion, could Athens have remained neutral or supine without materially weakening her hold upon all the states she aspired at once to democratize and to govern.

III. The fleet arrived at Samos—the oligarchic government was deposed— one hundred hostages (fifty men—fifty boys) from its partisans were taken and placed at Lemnos, and a garrison was left to secure the new constitution of the island. Some of the defeated faction took refuge on the Asiatic continent—entered into an intrigue with the Persian Pissuthnes, satrap of Sardis; and having, by continued correspondence with their friends at Samos, secured connivance at their attempt, they landed by night at Samos with a hired force of seven hundred soldiers, and succeeded in mastering the Athenian garrison, and securing the greater part of the chiefs of the new

(margin note) SAMIAN WAR

---

3 Fourteen thousand two hundred and forty, according to Philochorus. By the term "free citizens" is to be understood those male Athenians above twenty—that is, those entitled to vote in the public assembly. According to Mr Clinton's computation, the women and children being added, the fourteen thousand two hundred and forty will amount to about fifty-eight thousand six hundred and forty, as the total of the free population.

administration; while, by a secret and well-contrived plot, they regained their hostages left at Lemnos. They then openly proclaimed their independence —restored the oligarchy—and, as a formal proof of defiance, surrendered to Pissuthnes the Athenians they had captured. Byzantium hastened to join the revolt. Their alliance with Pissuthnes procured the Samians the promised aid of a Phœnician fleet, and they now deemed themselves sufficiently strong to renew their hostilities with Miletus. Their plans were well laid, and their boldness made a considerable impression on the states hostile to Athens. Among the Peloponnesian allies it was debated whether or not, despite the treaty, the Samians should be assisted: opinions were divided, but Corinth,[4] perhaps, turned the scale, by insisting on the right of every state to deal with its dependents. Corinth had herself colonies over which she desired to preserve a dictatorial sway; and she was disposed to regard the Samian revolution less as the gallantry of freemen than the enterprise of rebels. It was fortunate, too, perhaps, for Athens, that the Samian insurgents had sought their ally in the Persian satrap; nor could the Peloponnesian states at that time have decorously assisted the Persian against the Athenian arms. But short time for deliberation was left by a government which procured for the Athenians the character to be not more quick to contrive than to execute—to be the only people who could simultaneously project and acquire—and who even considered a festival but as a day on which some necessary business could be accomplished.[5] With a fleet of sixty sail, Pericles made for Samos; some of the vessels were stationed on the Carian coast to watch the movements of the anticipated Phœnician re-enforcement; others were despatched to collect aid from Chios and Lesbos. Meanwhile, though thus reduced to forty-four sail, Pericles, near a small island called Tragia, engaged the Samian fleet returning from Miletus, consisting of seventy vessels, and gained a victory. Then, re-enforced by forty galleys from Athens, and twenty-five from Lesbos and Chios, he landed on the island, defeated the Samians in a pitched battle, drove them into their city, invested it with a triple line of ramparts, and simultaneously blockaded the city by sea. The besieged were not, however, too discouraged to sally out; and, under Melissus, who was at once a philosopher and a hero, they even obtained advantage in a sea-fight. But these efforts were sufficiently unimportant to permit Pericles to draw off sixty of his vessels, and steer along the Carian coast to meet the expected fleet of the Phœnicians. The besieged did not suffer the opportunity thus afforded them to escape—they surprised the naval blockading force, destroyed the guard-ships, and joining battle with the rest of the fleet, obtained a decisive victory, which for fourteen days left them the mastery of the open sea, and enabled them to introduce supplies.

4 Thucyd., i. 40.
5 See the speech of the Corinthians (Thucyd., i. 70).

IV. While lying in wait for the Phœnician squadron, which did not, however, make its appearance, tidings of the Samian success were brought to Pericles. He hastened back and renewed the blockade—fresh forces were sent to his aid—from Athens, forty-eight ships, under three generals, Thucydides,[6] Agnon, and Phormio; followed by twenty more under Tlepolemus and Anticles, while Chios and Lesbos supplied an additional squadron of thirty. Still the besieged were not disheartened; they ventured another engagement, which was but an ineffectual struggle, and then, shut up within their city, stood a siege of nine months.

With all the small Greek states it had ever been the policy of necessity to shun even victories attended with great loss. This policy was refined by Pericles into a scientific system. In the present instance, he avoided all assaults which might weaken his forces, and preferred the loss of time to the loss of life. The tedious length of the blockade occasioned some murmurs among the lively and impatient forces he commanded; but he is said to have diverted the time by the holiday devices, which in the middle ages often so graced and softened the rugged aspect of war. The army was divided into eight parts, and by lot it was decided which one of the eight divisions should, for the time, encounter the fatigues of actual service; the remaining seven passed the day in sports and feasting.[7] A concourse of women appear to

6 Who was this Thucydides? The rival of Pericles had been exiled less than ten years before in fact, about four years ago; viz., BC 444; and it is difficult to suppose that he could have been recalled before the expiration of the sentence, and appointed to command, at the very period when the power and influence of Pericles were at their height. Thucydides, the historian, was about thirty-one, an age at which so high a command would scarcely, at that period, have been bestowed upon any citizen, even in Athens, where men mixed in public affairs earlier than in other Hellenic states; Thucydides himself (v. 43) speaks of Alcibiades as a mere youth (at least one who would have been so considered in any other state), at a time when he could not have been much less, and was probably rather more than thirty. Besides, had Thucydides been present, would he have given us no more ample details of an event so important? There were several who bore this name. The scholiast on Aristophanes (Acharn., 703) says there were four, whom he distinguishes thus—first, the historian; second, the Gargettian; third, the Thessalian; fourth, the son of Melesias. The scholiast on the "Vespæ" (991) enumerates the same, and calls them all *Athenians*. The son of Melesias is usually supposed the opponent of Pericles—he is so called by Androtion. Theopompus, however, says that it was the son of Pantanus. Marcellinus (in Vit. Thucyd., p. xi) speaks of many of the name, and also selects four for special notice: first, the historian; second, the son of Melesias; third, a Pharsalian; fourth, a poet of the ward of Acherdus, mentioned by Androtion, and called the son of Ariston. Two of this name, the historian and the son of Melesias, are well known to us; but, for the reasons I have mentioned, it is more probable that one of the others was a general in the Samian war. A third Thucydides (the Thessalian or Pharsalian) is mentioned by the historian himself (viii. 92). I take the Gargettian (perhaps the son of Pantanus named by Theopompus) to have been the commander in the expedition.

7 Plut., in Vit. Per.

have found their way to the encampment,[8] and a Samian writer ascribes to their piety or their gratitude the subsequent erection of a temple to Venus. The siege, too, gave occasion to Pericles to make experiment of military engines, which, if invented before, probably now received mechanical improvement. Although, in the earlier contest, mutual animosities had been so keen that the prisoners on either side had been contumeliously branded,[9] it was, perhaps, the festive and easy manner in which the siege was afterward carried on, that, mitigating the bitterness of prolonged hostilities, served to procure, at last, for the Samians articles of capitulation more than usually mild. They embraced the conditions of demolishing their fortifications, delivering up their ships, and paying by instalments a portion towards the cost of the siege.[10] Byzantium, which, commanding the entrance of the Euxine, was a most important possession to the Athenians,[11] whether for ambition or for commerce, at the same time accepted, without resistance, the terms held out to it, and became once more subject to the Athenian empire.

V. On his return, Pericles was received with an enthusiasm which attested the sense entertained of the value of his conquest. He pronounced upon those who had fallen in the war a funeral oration.[12] When he descended from the rostrum, the women crowded round and showered fillets and chaplets on the eloquent victor. Elpinice, the sister of Cimon, alone shared not the general enthusiasm. "Are these actions," she said to Pericles, "worthy of chaplets and

---

8 Alexis, apud Athenæus, xiii.

9 At this period the Athenians made war with a forbearance not common in later ages. When Timotheus besieged Samos, he maintained his armament solely on the hostile country, while a siege of nine months cost Athens so considerable a sum.

10 Plut., in Vit. Per. The contribution levied on the Samians was two hundred talents, proportioned, according to Diodorus, to the full cost of the expedition. But as Boeckh (Pol. Econ. of Athens, vol. i, p. 386, translation) well observes, "This was a very lenient reckoning; a nine months' siege by land and sea, in which one hundred and ninety-nine triremes were employed, or, at any rate, a large part of this number, for a considerable time, must evidently have caused a greater expense, and the statement, therefore, of Isocrates and Nepos, that twelve hundred talents were expended on it, appears to be by no means exaggerated." (Boeckh states the number of triremes at one hundred and ninety-nine, but, in fact, there were two hundred and fifteen vessels employed, since we ought not to omit the sixteen stationed on the Carian coast or despatched to Lesbos and Chios for supplies).

11 It was on Byzantium that they depended for the corn they imported from the shores of the Euxine.

12 The *practice* of funeral orations was probably of very ancient origin among the Greeks: but the *law* which ordained them at Athens is referred by the scholiast on Thucydides (ii. 35) to Solon; while Diodorus, on the other hand, informs us it was not passed till after the battle of Platæa. It appears most probable that it was a usage of the heroic times, which became obsolete while the little feuds among the Greek states remained trivial and unimportant; but, after the Persian invasion, it was solemnly revived, from the magnitude of the wars which Greece had undergone, and the dignity and holiness of the cause in which the defenders of their country had fallen.

garlands? actions purchased by the loss of many gallant citizens—not won against the Phœnician and the Mede, like those of Cimon, but by the ruin of a city united with ourselves in amity and origin." The ready minister replied to the invective of Elpinice by a line from Archilochus, which, in alluding to the age and coquetry of the lady, probably answered the oratorical purpose of securing the laugh on his own side.[13]

While these events confirmed the authority of Athens and the Athenian government, a power had grown up within the city that assumed a right, the grave assertion of which without the walls would have been deeply felt and bitterly resented—a power that sat in severe and derisive judgment upon Athens herself, her laws, her liberties, her mighty generals, her learned statesmen, her poets, her sages, and her arrogant democracy—a power that has come down to foreign nations and distant ages as armed with irresistible weapons—which now is permitted to give testimony, not only against individuals, but nations themselves, but which, in that time, was not more effective in practical results than at this day a caricature in St James's street, or a squib in a weekly newspaper—a power which exposed to relentless ridicule, before the most susceptible and numerous tribunal, the loftiest names in rank, in wisdom, and in genius—and which could not have deprived a beggar of his obol or a scavenger of his office: the power of the Comic Muse.

VI. We have seen that in the early village festivals, out of which grew the tragedy of Phrynichus and Æschylus, there were, besides the dithyramb and

SKETCH OF THE RISE AND PROGRESS OF THE ATHENIAN COMEDY TO THE TIME OF ARISTOPHANES

the satyrs, the phallic processions, which diversified the ceremony by the lowest jests mingled with the wildest satire. As her tragedy had its origin in the dithyramb—as her satyric after piece had its origin in the satyric buffooneries—so out of the phallic processions rose the comedy of Greece.[14] Susarion is asserted by some to have been a Megarian by origin; and while the democracy of Megara was yet in force he appears to have roughly shaped the disorderly merriment of the procession into a rude farce, interspersed with the old choral songs. The close connexion between Megara and Athens soon served to communicate to the latter the improvements of Susarion; and these improvements obtained for the Megarian the title of inventor of comedy, with about the same justice as a similar degree of art conferred upon the later Thespis the distinction of

13 Οὐκ ἂν μύροισι γραῦσ᾿ ἐοῦς ἠλείφεο. This seems the only natural interpretation of the line, in which, from not having the context, we lose whatever wit the sentence may have possessed—and witty we must suppose it was, since Plutarch evidently thinks it a capital joke. In corroboration of this interpretation of an allusion which has a little perplexed the commentators, we may observe, that ten years before, Pericles had judged a sarcasm upon the age of Elpinice the best way to silence her importunities. The anecdote is twice told by Plutarch, in Vit. Cim., 14, and in Vit. Per., 10.

14 Aristot., Poet., iv.

the origin of tragedy. The study of Homer's epics had suggested its true province to tragedy; the study of the Margites, attributed also to Homer, seems to have defined and enlarged the domain of comedy. Eleven years after Phrynichus appeared, and just before the first effort of Æschylus, Epicharmus, who appears to have been a native of Cos,[15] produced at Syracuse the earliest symmetrical and systematic form of comic dialogue and fable. All accounts prove him to have been a man of extraordinary genius, and of very thoughtful and accomplished mind. Perhaps the loss of his works is not the least to be lamented of those priceless treasures which time has destroyed. So uncertain, after all, is the great tribunal of posterity, which is often as little to be relied upon as the caprice of the passing day!

We have the worthless "Electra" of Euripides—we have lost all, save the titles and a few sententious fragments, of thirty-five comedies of Epicharmus! Yet if Horace inform us rightly, that the poet of Syracuse was the model of Plautus, perhaps in the "Amphitryon" we can trace the vein and genius of the father of true comedy; and the thoughts and the plot of the lost Epicharmus may still exist, mutilated and disguised, in the humours of the greatest comic poet[16] of modern Europe.

VII. It was chiefly from the rich stores of mythology that Epicharmus drew his fables; but what was sublimity with the tragic poet, was burlesque with the comic. He parodied the august personages and venerable adventures of the gods of the Greek pantheon. By a singular coincidence, like his contemporary Æschylus,[17] he was a Pythagorean, and it is wonderful to observe how rapidly and how powerfully the influence of the mysterious Samian operated on the most original intellects of the age. The familiar nature of the Hellenic religion sanctioned, even in the unphilosophical age of Homer, a treatment of celestial persons that to our modern notions would, at first glance, evince a disrespect for the religion itself. But wherever homage to "dead men" be admitted, we may, even in our own times, find that the most jocular legends are attached to names held in the most reverential awe. And he who has listened to an Irish or an Italian Catholic's familiar stories of some favourite saint, may form an adequate notion of the manner in which a pious Greek could jest upon Bacchus today and sacrifice to Bacchus tomorrow. With his mythological travesties the Pythagorean mingled, apparently,

---

15 "As he was removed from Cos in infancy, the name of his adopted country prevailed over that of the country of his birth, and Epicharmus is called of Syracuse, though born at Cos, as Apollonius is called the Rhodian, though born at Alexandria" (Fasti Hellenici vol. ii, introduction).

16 Molière.

17 Laertius, viii. For it is evident that Epicharmus the philosopher was no other than Epicharmus the philosophical poet—the delight of Plato, who was himself half a Pythagorean—see Bentley, Diss. Phal., p. 201; Laertius, viii. 78; Fynes Clinton, Fasti Hellenici vol. ii, introduction, p. 36 (note *g*).

many earnest maxims of morality,[18] and though not free, in the judgment of Aristotle, from a vice of style usually common only to ages the most refined,[19] he was yet proverbial, even in the most polished period of Grecian letters, for the graces of his diction and the happy choice of his expressions.

Phormis, a contemporary of Epicharmus, flourished also at Syracuse, and though sometimes classed with Epicharmus, and selecting his materials from the same source, his claims to reputation are immeasurably more equivocal. Dinolochus continued the Sicilian school, and was a contemporary of the first Athenian comic writer.

VIII. Hence it will be seen that the origin of comedy does not rest with the Athenians; that Megara, if the birthplace of Susarion, may fairly claim whatever merit belongs to the first rude improvement, and that Syracuse is entitled to the higher distinction of raising humour into art. So far is comedy the offspring of the Dorians—not the Dorians of a sullen oligarchy, with whom to vary an air of music was a crime—not the Dorians of Lacedæmon— but of Megara and Syracuse—of an energetic, though irregular democracy —of a splendid, though illegitimate monarchy.[20]

But the comedy of Epicharmus was not altogether the old comedy of Athens. The last, as bequeathed to us by Aristophanes, has features which bear little family resemblance to the philosophical parodies of the Pythagorean poet. It does not confine itself to mythological subjects—it avoids the sententious style—it does not preach, but ridicule philosophy—it plunges amid the great practical business of men—it breathes of the Agora and the Piræus—it is not a laughing sage, but a bold, boisterous, gigantic demagogue, ever in the thickest mob of human interests, and wielding all the various humours of a democracy with a brilliant audacity, and that reckless ease which is the proof of its astonishing power.

IX. Chionides was the first Athenian comic writer. We find him before the public three years after the battle of Marathon, when the final defeat of Hippias confirmed the stability of the republic; and when the improvements of Æschylus in tragedy served to communicate new attractions to the comic stage. Magnes, a writer of great wit, and long popular, closely followed, and the titles of some of the plays of these writers confirm the belief that Attic comedy, from its commencement, took other ground than that occupied by the mythological burlesques of Epicharmus. So great was the impetus given to the new art, that a crowd of writers followed simultaneously, whose very names it is wearisome to mention. Of these the most eminent were Cratinus and

---

18 A few of his plays were apparently not mythological, but they were only exceptions from the general rule, and might have been written after the less refining comedies of Magnes at Athens.

19 A love of false antithesis.

20 In Syracuse, however, the republic existed when Epicharmus first exhibited his comedies. His genius was therefore formed by a republic, though afterward fostered by a tyranny.

Crates. The earliest *recorded* play of Cratinus, though he must have exhibited many before,[21] appeared the year prior to the death of Cimon. Plutarch quotes some lines from this author, which allude to the liberality of Cimon with something of that patron-loving spirit which was rather the characteristic of a Roman than an Athenian poet. Though he himself, despite his age, was proverbially of no very abstemious or decorous habits, Cratinus was unsparing in his attacks upon others, and wherever he found or suspected vice, he saw a subject worthy of his genius. He was admired to late posterity, and by Roman critics, for the grace and even for the grandeur of his hardy verses; and Quintilian couples him with Eupolis and Aristophanes as models for the formation of orators. Crates appeared two years before the first *recorded* play of Cratinus. He had previously been an actor, and performed the principal characters in the plays of Cratinus. Aristophanes bestows on him the rare honour of his praise, while he sarcastically reminds the Athenian audience of the ill reception that so ingenious a poet often received at their hands. Yet, despite the excellence of the earlier comic writers, they had hitherto at Athens very sparingly adopted the artistical graces of Epicharmus. Crates, who did not write before the five years' truce with Sparta, is said by Aristotle not only to have been the first who abandoned the iambic form of comedy, but the first *Athenian* who invented systematic fable or plot—a strong argument to show how little the Athenian borrowed from the Sicilian comedy, since, if the last had been its source of inspiration, the invented stories of Epicharmus (by half a century the predecessor of Crates) would naturally have been the most striking improvement to be imitated. The Athenian comedy did not receive the same distinctions conferred upon tragedy. So obscure was its rise to its later eminence, that even Aristotle could not determine when or by whom the various progressive improvements were made and, regarded with jealous or indifferent eyes by the magistrature as an exhibition given by private competitors, nor calling for the protection of the state, which it often defied, it was long before its chorus was defrayed at the public cost.

Under Cratinus and Crates,[22] however, in the year of the Samian war, the comic drama assumed a character either so personally scurrilous, or so

21 For Crates acted in the plays of Cratinus before he turned author (see above). Now the first play of Crates dates two years *before* the first recorded play (the "Archilochi") of Cratinus; consequently Cratinus must have been celebrated long previous to the exhibition of the "Archilochi"—indeed, his earlier plays appear, according to Aristophanes, to have been the most successful, until the old gentleman, by a last vigorous effort, beat the favourite play of Aristophanes himself.

22 That the magistrature did not at first authorize comedy seems a proof that it was not at the commencement considered, like tragedy, of a religious character. And, indeed, though modern critics constantly urge upon us its connexion with religion, I doubt whether at any time the populace thought more of its holier attributes and associations than the Neapolitans of today are impressed with the sanctity of the carnival when they are throwing sugarplums at each other.

politically dangerous, that a decree was passed interdicting its exhibitions. The law was repealed three years afterward.[23] Viewing its temporary enforcement, and the date in which it was passed, it appears highly probable that the critical events of the Samian expedition may have been the cause of the decree. At such a time the opposition of the comic writers might have been considered dangerous. With the increased stability of the state, the law was, perhaps, deemed no longer necessary. And from the recommencement of the comic drama, we may probably date both the improvements of Crates and the special protection of the state; for when, for the first time, Comedy was formally authorized by the law, it was natural that the law should recognize the privileges it claimed in common with its sister Tragedy. There is no authority for supposing that Pericles, whose calm temper and long novitiate in the stormy career of public life seem to have rendered him callous to public abuse, was the author of this decree. It is highly probable, indeed, that he was absent at the siege of Samos[24] when it was passed; but he was the object of such virulent attacks by the comic poets that we might consider them actuated by some personal feeling of revenge and spleen, were it not evident that Cratinus at least (and probably Crates, his disciple) was attached to the memory of Cimon, and could not fail to be hostile to the principles and government of Cimon's successor. So far at this period had comedy advanced; but, in the background, obscure and undreamed of, was one, yet in childhood, destined to raise the comic to the rank of the tragic muse; one who, perhaps, from his earliest youth, was incited by the noisy fame of his predecessors, and the desire of that glorious, but often perverted power, so palpable and so exultant, which rides the stormy waves of popular applause.[25]

---

23 In the interval, however, the poets seem to have sought to elude the law, since the names of two plays (the Σάτυροι and the Κολεόφοροι) are recorded during this period—plays which probably approached comedy without answering to its legal definition. It might be that the difficulty rigidly to enforce the law against the spirit of the times and the inclination of the people was one of the causes that led to the repeal of the prohibition.
24 Since that siege lasted nine months of the year in which the decree was made.
25 Aristophanes thus vigorously describes the applauses that attended the earlier productions of Cratinus. I quote from the masterly translation of Mr Mitchell:

> Who Cratinus may forget, or the storm of whim and wit,
> Which shook theatres under his guiding;
> When Panegyric's song poured her flood of praise along,
> Who but he on the top wave was riding?
> ....
> His step was as the tread of a flood that leaves its bed,
> And his march it was rude desolation, &c.
> Mitchell's Aristoph., The Knights, p. 204.

The man who wrote thus must have felt betimes—when, as a boy, he first heard the roar of the audience—what it is to rule the humours of eighteen thousand spectators!

About thirteen years after the brief prohibition of comedy appeared that wonderful genius, the elements and attributes of whose works it will be a pleasing, if arduous task, in due season, to analyse and define; matchless alike in delicacy and strength, in powers the most gigantic, in purpose the most daring—with the invention of Shakespeare—the playfulness of Rabelais—the malignity of Swift—need I add the name of Aristophanes?

X. But while comedy had thus progressed to its first invidious dignity, that of proscription, far different was the reward that awaited the present representative and master of the tragic school. In the year that the muse of Cratinus was silenced, Sophocles was appointed one of the colleagues with Pericles in the Samian war.

CHAPTER IV

I. It was in the very nature of the Athenian drama, that, when once established, it should concentrate and absorb almost every variety of the poetical genius. The old lyrical poetry, never much cultivated in Athens, ceased in a great measure when tragedy arose, or rather tragedy was the complete development, the new and perfected consummation of the dithyrambic ode. Lyrical poetry transmigrated into the choral song, as the epic merged into the dialogue and plot, of the drama. Thus, when we speak of Athenian poetry, we speak of dramatic poetry—they were one and the same. As Helvetius has so luminously shown,[1] genius ever turns towards that quarter in which fame shines brightest, and hence, in every age, there will be a sympathetic connexion between the taste of the public and the direction of the talent.

THE TRAGEDIES OF SOPHOCLES

Now in Athens, where audiences were numerous and readers few, every man who felt within himself the inspiration of the poet would necessarily desire to see his poetry put into action—assisted with all the pomp of spectacle and music, hallowed by the solemnity of a religious festival, and breathed by artists elaborately trained to heighten the eloquence of words into the reverent ear of assembled Greece.

Hence the multitude of dramatic poets, hence the mighty fertility of each; hence the life and activity of this—the comparative torpor and barrenness of every other—species of poetry. To add to the pre-eminence of the art, the applauses of the many were sanctioned by the critical canons of the few. The drama was not only the most alluring form which the divine spirit could assume—but it was also deemed the loftiest and the purest; and when Aristotle ranked[2] the tragic higher than even the epic muse, he probably did

1 De l'esprit, passim.
2 Poet., xxvi.

but explain the reasons for a preference which the generality of critics were disposed to accord to her.[3]

II. The career of the most majestic of the Greek poets was eminently felicitous. His birth was noble, his fortune affluent; his natural gifts were the rarest which nature bestows on man, genius and beauty. All the care which the age permitted was lavished on his education. For his feet even the ordinary obstacles in the path of distinction were smoothed away. He entered life under auspices the most propitious and poetical. At the age of sixteen he headed the youths who performed the triumphant pæan round the trophy of Salamis. At twenty-five, when the bones of Theseus were borne back to Athens in the galley of the victorious Cimon, he exhibited his first play, and won the prize from Æschylus. That haughty genius, whether indignant at the success of a younger rival, or at a trial for impiety before the Areopagus, to which (though acquitted) he was subjected, or at the rapid ascendency of a popular party, that he seems to have scorned with the disdain at once of an eupatrid and a Pythagorean, soon after retired from Athens to the Syracusan court; and though he thence sent some of his dramas to the Athenian stage,[4] the absent veteran could not but excite less enthusiasm than the young aspirant, whose artful and polished genius was more in harmony with the reigning taste than the vast but rugged grandeur of Æschylus, who, perhaps from the impossibility tangibly and visibly to body forth his shadowy Titans and obscure sublimity of design, does not appear to have obtained a popularity on the stage equal to his celebrity as a poet.[5] For three-and-sixty years did Sophocles continue to exhibit; twenty times he obtained the first prize, and he is said never to have been degraded to the third. The ordinary persecutions of envy itself seem to have spared this fortunate poet. Although his moral character was far from pure,[6] and even in extreme old age he sought after the pleasures of

---

3 The oracle that awarded to Socrates the superlative degree of wisdom, gave to Sophocles the positive, and to Euripides the comparative degree,

Σοφὸς Σοφοκλῆς· σοφώτερος δ' Εὐριπίδης·
Ἀνδρῶν δὲ πάντων Σωκράτης σοφώτατος.

Sophocles is wise—Euripides wiser—but wisest of all men is Socrates.

4 The Oresteia.

5 For out of seventy plays by Æschylus only thirteen were successful; he had exhibited fifteen years before he obtained his first prize; and the very law passed in honour of his memory, that a chorus should he permitted to any poet who chose to re-exhibit his dramas, seems to indicate that a little encouragement of such exhibition was requisite. This is still more evident if we believe, with Quintilian, that the poets who exhibited were permitted to correct and polish up the dramas, to meet the modern taste, and play the Cibber to the Athenian Shakespeare.

6 Athenæus, xiii. 603, 604.

his youth,[7] yet his excesses apparently met with a remarkable indulgence from his contemporaries. To him were known neither the mortifications of Æschylus nor the relentless mockery heaped upon Euripides. On his fair name the terrible Aristophanes himself affixes no brand.[8] The sweetness of his genius extended indeed to his temper, and personal popularity assisted his public triumphs. Nor does he appear to have keenly shared the party animosities of his day; his serenity, like that of Goethe, has in it something of enviable rather than honourable indifference. He owed his first distinction to Cimon, and he served afterward under Pericles; on his entrance into life, he led the youths that circled the trophy of Grecian freedom—and on the verge of death, we shall hereafter see him calmly assent to the surrender of Athenian liberties. In short, Aristophanes perhaps mingled more truth than usual with his wit, when even in the shades below he says of Sophocles, "He was contented here—he's contented there." A disposition thus facile, united with an admirable genius, will, not unoften, effect a miracle, and reconcile prosperity with fame.[9]

At the age of fifty-seven, Sophocles was appointed, as I before said,[10] to a command as one of the ten generals in the Samian war; but history is silent as to his military genius.[11] In later life we shall again have occasion to refer to him, condemned as he was to illustrate (after a career of unprecedented brilliancy—nor ever subjected to the caprice of the common public) the melancholy moral inculcated by himself,[12] and so often obtruded upon us by the dramatists of his country, "never to deem a man happy till death itself denies the hazard of reverses". Out of the vast, though not accurately known, number of the dramas of Sophocles, seven remain.

III. A great error has been committed by those who class Æschylus and Sophocles together as belonging to the same era, and refer both to the age

---

7 He is reported, indeed, to have said that he rejoiced in the old age which delivered him from a severe and importunate taskmaster (Athenæus, xii. 510). But the poet, nevertheless, appears to have retained his amorous *propensities*, at least, to the last (see Athenæus, xiii. 523).

8 He does indeed charge Sophocles with avarice, but he atones for it very handsomely in the "Frogs".

9 M. Schlegel is pleased to indulge in one of his most declamatory rhapsodies upon the life, "so dear to the gods", of this "pious and holy poet". But Sophocles, in private life, was a profligate, and in public life a shuffler and a trimmer, if not absolutely a renegade. It was, perhaps, the very laxity of his principles which made him thought so agreeable a fellow. At least, such is no uncommon cause of personal popularity nowadays. People lose much of their anger and envy of genius when it throws them down a bundle or two of human foibles by which they can climb up to its level.

10 It is said, indeed, that the appointment was the reward of a successful tragedy; it was more likely due to his birth, fortune, and personal popularity.

11 It seems, however, that Pericles thought very mainly of his warlike capacities (see Athenæus, xiii. 604).

12 Œdip. Tyr., 1429, &c.

of Pericles, because each was living while Pericles was in power. We may as well class Dr Johnson and Lord Byron in the same age, because both lived in the reign of George III. The Athenian rivals were formed under the influences of very different generations; and if Æschylus lived through a considerable portion of the career of the younger Sophocles, the accident of longevity by no means warrants us to consider them the children of the same age—the creatures of the same influences. Æschylus belonged to the race and the period from which emerged Themistocles and Aristides— Sophocles to those which produced Phidias and Pericles. Sophocles indeed, in the calmness of his disposition, and the symmetry and stateliness of his genius, might almost be entitled the Pericles of poetry. And as the statesman was called the Olympian, not from the headlong vehemence, but the serene majesty of his strength, so of Sophocles also it may be said, that his power is visible in his repose, and his thunders roll from the depth of a clear sky.

IV. The age of Pericles is the age of art.[13] It was not Sophocles alone that was an artist in that time; he was but one of the many who, in every department, sought, in study and in science, the secrets of the wise or the beautiful. Pericles and Phidias were in their several paths of fame what Sophocles was in his. But it was not the art of an emasculate or effeminate period—it grew out of the example of a previous generation of men astonishingly great. It was art still fresh from the wells of nature. Art with a vast field yet unexplored, and in all its youthful vigour and maiden enthusiasm. There was, it is true, at a period a little later than that in which the genius of Sophocles was formed, one class of students among whom a false taste and a spurious refinement were already visible—the class of rhetoricians and philosophical speculators. For, in fact, the art which belongs to the imagination is often purest in an early age; but that which appertains to the reason and intellect is slow before it attains mature strength and manly judgment. Among these students was early trained and tutored the thoughtful mind of Euripides; and hence that art which in Sophocles was learned in more miscellaneous and active circles, and moulded by a more powerful imagination, in Euripides often sickens us with the tricks of a pleader, the quibbles of a schoolman, or the dullness of a moralizing declaimer. But as, in the peculiar attributes and character of his writings, Euripides somewhat forestalled his age—as his example had a very important influence upon his successors—as he did not exhibit till the fame of Sophocles was already confirmed—and as his name is intimately associated with the later age of Aristophanes and Socrates—it may be more convenient to confine our critical examination at present to the tragedies of Sophocles.

13 When Sophocles (Athenæus, i. 22) said that Æschylus composed befittingly, but without knowing it, his saying evinced the study his compositions had cost himself.

Although the three plays of the "Œdipus Tyrannus", the "Œdipus at Colonus", and the "Antigone", were composed and exhibited at very wide intervals of time, yet, from their connexion with each other, they may almost be said to form one poem. The "Antigone", which concludes the story, was the one earliest written; and there are passages in either "Œdipus" which seem composed to lead up, as it were, to the catastrophe of the "Antigone", and form a harmonious link between the several dramas. These three plays constitute, on the whole, the greatest performance of Sophocles, though in detached parts they are equalled by passages in the "Ajax" and the "Philoctetes".

V. The "Œdipus Tyrannus" opens thus. An awful pestilence devastates Thebes. Œdipus, the king, is introduced to us, powerful and beloved: to him whose wisdom had placed him on the throne, look up the priest and the suppliants for a remedy even amid the terrors of the plague. Œdipus informs them that he has despatched Creon (the brother of his wife Jocasta) to the Pythian god to know by what expiatory deed the city might be delivered from its curse. Scarce has he concluded, when Creon himself enters, and announces "glad tidings" in the explicit answer of the oracle. The god has declared that a pollution had been bred in the land, and must be expelled the city—that Laius, the former king, had been murdered—and that his blood must be avenged. Laius had left the city never to return; of his train but one man escaped to announce his death by assassins. Œdipus instantly resolves to prosecute the inquiry into the murder, and orders the people to be summoned. The suppliants arise from the altar, and a solemn chorus of the senators of Thebes (in one of the most splendid lyrics of Sophocles) chant the terrors of the plague—*"that unarmed Mars"*—and implore the protection of the divine averters of destruction. Œdipus then, addressing the chorus, demands their aid to discover the murderer, whom he solemnly excommunicates, and dooms, deprived of aid and intercourse, to waste slowly out a miserable existence; nay, if the assassin should have sought refuge in the royal halls, there too shall the vengeance be wreaked and the curse fall.

"For I", continued Œdipus,

I, who the sceptre which he wielded, wield;—
I, who have mounted to his marriage bed;—
I, in whose children (had he issue known)
His would have claimed a common brotherhood;—
Now that the evil fate hath fallen o'er him,
I am the heir of that dead king's revenge,
Not less than if these lips had hailed him "father!"

A few more sentences introduce to us the old soothsayer Tiresias—for whom, at the instigation of Creon, Œdipus had sent. The seer answers the adjuration of the king with a thrilling and ominous burst:

Woe—woe!—how fearful is the gift of wisdom,
When to the wise it bears no blessing!—Woe!

The haughty spirit of Œdipus breaks forth at the gloomy and obscure warnings of the prophet. His remonstrances grow into threats. In his blindness he even accuses Tiresias himself of the murder of Laius—and out speaks the terrible diviner:

Ay—is it so? Abide then by thy curse
And solemn edict,—never from this day
Hold human commune with these men or me;
Lo, where thou standest—lo, the land's polluter!

A dialogue of great dramatic power ensues. Œdipus accuses Tiresias of abetting his kinsman, Creon, by whom he had been persuaded to send for the soothsayer, in a plot against his throne—and the seer, who explains nothing and threatens all things, departs with a dim and fearful prophecy.

After a song from the chorus, in which are embodied the doubt, the trouble, the terror which the audience may begin to feel—and here it may be observed, that with Sophocles the chorus always carries on, not the physical, but the moral, progress of the drama[14]—Creon enters, informed of the suspicion against himself which Œdipus had expressed. Œdipus, whose whole spirit is disturbed by the weird and dark threats of Tiresias, repeats the accusation, but wildly and feebly. His vain worldly wisdom suggests to him that Creon would scarcely have asked him to consult Tiresias, nor Tiresias have ventured on denunciations so tremendous, had not the two conspired against him: yet a mysterious awe invades him—he presses questions on Creon relative to the murder of Laius, and seems more anxious to acquit himself than accuse another.

While the princes contend, the queen, Jocasta, enters. She chides their quarrel, learns from Œdipus that Tiresias had accused him of the murder of the deceased king, and, to convince him of the falseness of prophetic lore, reveals to him, that long since it was predicted that Laius should be murdered by his son—joint offspring of Jocasta and himself. Yet, in order to frustrate the prophecy, the only son of Laius had been exposed to perish upon solitary and untrodden mountains, while, in after years, Laius himself had fallen, in a spot where three roads met, by the hand of a stranger; so that the prophecy had not come to pass.

---

14 "The chorus should be considered as one of the persons in the drama, should be a part of the whole, and a sharer in the action, not as in Euripides, but as in Sophocles" (Aristot., Poet., Twining's translation). But even in Sophocles, at least in such of his plays as are left to us, the chorus rarely, if ever, is a sharer in the outward and positive action of the piece; it rather carries on and expresses the progress of the emotions that spring out of the action.

At this declaration terror seizes upon Œdipus. He questions Jocasta eagerly and rapidly—the place where the murder happened, the time in which it occurred, the age and personal appearance of Laius—and when he learns all, his previous arrogant conviction of innocence deserts him; and as he utters a horrid exclamation, Jocasta fixes her eyes upon him, and "shudders as she gazes".[15] He inquires what train accompanied Laius—learns that there were five persons; that but one escaped; that on his return to Thebes, seeing Œdipus on the throne, the survivor had besought the favour to retire from the city. Œdipus orders this witness of the murder to be sent for, and then proceeds to relate his own history. He has been taught to believe that Polybus of Corinth and Merope of Doris were his parents. But once at a banquet he was charged with being a supposititious child; the insult galled him, and he went to Delphi to consult the oracle. It was predicted to him that he should commit incest with his mother, and that his father should fall by his hand. Appalled and horror-stricken, he resolves to fly the possible fulfilment of the prophecy, and return no more to Corinth. In his flight by the triple road described by Jocasta he meets an old man in a chariot, with a guide or herald, and other servitors. They attempt to thrust him from the road—a contest ensues—he slays the old man and his train. Could this be Laius? Can it be to the marriage couch of the man he slew that he has ascended? No, his fears are too credulous! He clings to a straw; the herdsman who had escaped the slaughter of Laius and his attendants may prove that it was not the king whom *he* encountered. Jocasta sustains this hope—she cannot believe a prophecy—for it had been foretold that Laius should fall by the hand of his son, and that son had long since perished on the mountains. The queen and Œdipus retire within their palace; the chorus resume their strains; after which, Jocasta reappears on her way to the Temple of Apollo, to offer sacrifice and prayer. At this time a messenger arrives to announce to Œdipus the death of Polybus, and the wish of the Corinthians to elect Œdipus to the throne! At these tidings Jocasta is overjoyed:

> Predictions of the gods, where are ye now?
> Lest by the son's doomed hand the sire should fall,
> The son became a wanderer on the earth,
> Lo, not the son, but Nature, gives the blow!

Œdipus, summoned to the messenger, learns the news of his supposed father's death! It is a dread and tragic thought, but the pious Œdipus is *glad* that his father is no more, since he himself is thus saved from parricide; yet the other part of the prediction haunts him. His mother!—she yet lives.

15 ὀκνῶ τοι πρός σ᾽ ἀποσκοποῦσ᾽ ἄναξ—Œdip. Tyr., 711. This line shows how much of emotion the actor could express in spite of the mask.

He reveals to the messenger the prophecy and his terror. To cheer him, the messenger now informs him that he is *not* the son of Merope and Polybus. A babe had been found in the entangled forest-dells of Cithæron by a herdsman and slave of Laius—he had given the infant to another—that other, the messenger who now tells the tale. Transferred to the care of Polybus and Merope, the babe became to them as a son, for they were childless. Jocasta hears—stunned and speechless—till Œdipus, yet unconscious of the horrors still to come, turns to demand of her if she knew the herdsman who had found the child. Then she gasps wildly out:

> Whom speaks he of? Be silent—heed it not—
> Blot it out it out from thy memory!—it is evil!
> *Œdipus*: It cannot be—the clue is here; and I
> Will trace it through that labyrinth—my birth.
> *Jocasta*: By all the gods I warn thee; for the sake
> Of thine own life, beware; it is enough
> For me to hear and madden!

Œdipus (suspecting only that the pride of his queen revolts from the thought of her husband's birth being proved base and servile) replies:

>   Nay, nay, cheer thee!
> Were I through three descents threefold a slave,
> My shame would not touch thee.
> *Jocasta*:   I do implore thee,
> This once obey me—this once.
> *Œdipus*:   I will not!
> To truth I grope my way.
> *Jocasta*:   And yet what love
> Speaks in my voice! Thine ignorance is thy bliss.
> *Œdipus*:   A bliss that tortures!
> *Jocasta*:   Miserable man!
> Oh couldst thou never learn the thing thou art!
> *Œdipus*:   Will no one quicken this slow herdsman's steps!
> The unquestioned birthright of a royal name
> Let this proud queen possess!
> *Jocasta*:   Woe! woe! thou wretch!
> Woe! my last word!—words are no more for me!

With this Jocasta rushes from the scene. Still Œdipus misconstrues her warning; he ascribes her fears to the royalty of her spirit. For himself, *Fortune* was his mother, and had blessed him; nor could the accident of birth destroy his inheritance from nature. The chorus give way to their hopes! their wise, their glorious Œdipus might have been born a *Theban!*

The herdsman enters: like Tiresias, he is loth to speak. The fiery king extorts his secret. Œdipus is the son of Laius and Jocasta—at his birth the terrible prophecies of the Pythian induced his own mother to expose him on the mountains—the compassion of the herdsman saved him—saved him to become the bridegroom of his mother, the assassin of his sire. The astonishing art with which, from step to step, the audience and the victim are led to the climax of the discovery, is productive of an interest of pathos and of terror which is not equalled by the greatest masterpieces of the modern stage,[16] and possesses that species of anxious excitement which is wholly unparalleled in the ancient. The discovery is a true catastrophe—the physical denouement is but an adjunct to the moral one. Jocasta, on quitting the scene, had passed straight to the bridal-chamber, and there, by the couch from which had sprung a double and accursed progeny, perished by her own hands. Meanwhile, the predestined parricide, bursting into the chamber, beheld, as the last object on earth, the corpse of his wife and mother! Once more Œdipus reappears, barred for ever from the light of day. In the fury of his remorse, he "had smote the balls of his own eyes", and the wise baffler of the sphinx, Œdipus, the haughty, the insolent, the illustrious, is a forlorn and despairing outcast. But amid all the horror of the concluding scene, a beautiful and softening light breaks forth. Blind, powerless, excommunicated, Creon, whom Œdipus accused of murder, has now become his judge and his master. The great spirit, crushed beneath its intolerable woes, is humbled to the dust; and the "wisest of mankind" implores but two favours—to be thrust from the land an exile, and once more to embrace his children. Even in translation the exquisite tenderness of this passage cannot altogether fail of its effect.

> For *my* fate, let it pass! My children, Creon!
> My sons—nay, they the bitter wants of life
> May master—*they* are MEN?—my *girls*—my darlings—
> Why never sat I at my household board
> Without their blessed looks—our very bread
> We brake together; thou'lt be kind to them
> For my sake, Creon—and (O latest prayer!)
> Let me but touch them—feel them with these hands,
> And pour such sorrow as may speak farewell
> O'er ills that must be theirs! By thy pure line—
> For thine is pure—do this, sweet prince. Methinks
> I should not miss these eyes, could I but touch them.

16 "Of all discovering, the best is that which arises from the action itself, and in which a striking effect is produced by probable incidents. Such is that in the Œdipus of Sophocles" (Aristot., Poet., Twining's translation).

What shall I say to move thee?
                    Sobs!—And do I,
Oh do I hear my sweet ones? Hast thou sent,
In mercy sent, my children to my arms?
Speak—speak—I do not dream!
Creon: They are thy children;
I would not shut thee from the dear delight
In the old time they gave thee.
Œdipus: Blessings on thee!
For this one mercy mayst thou find above
A kinder god than I have. Ye—where are ye?
My children—come!—nearer and nearer yet, &c.

The pathos of this scene is continued to the end; and the very last words Œdipus utters as his children cling to him, implore that they at least may not be torn away.

It is in this concluding scene that the art of the play is consummated; the horrors of the catastrophe, which, if a last impression, would have left behind a too painful and gloomy feeling, are softened down by this beautiful resort to the tenderest and holiest sources of emotion. And the pathos is rendered doubly effective, not only from the immediate contrast of the terror that preceded it, but from the masterly skill with which all display of the softer features in the character of Œdipus is reserved to the close. In the breaking up of the strong mind and the daring spirit, when empire, honour, name, are all annihilated, the heart is seen, as it were, surviving the wrecks around it, and clinging for support to the affections.

VI. In the "Œdipus at Colonus", the blind king is presented to us, after the lapse of years, a wanderer over the earth, unconsciously taking his refuge in the grove of the Furies[17]—"the awful goddesses, daughters of Earth and

---

17 But the spot consecrated to those deities which men "tremble to name", presents all the features of outward loveliness that contract and refine, as it were, the metaphysical terror of the associations. And the beautiful description of Colonus itself, which is the passage that Sophocles is said to have read to his judges, before whom he was accused of dotage, seems to paint a home more fit for the Graces than the Furies. The chorus inform the stranger that he has come to "the white Colonos":

> Where ever and aye, through the greenest vale
> Gush the wailing notes of the nightingale
> From her home where the dark-hued ivy weaves
> With the grove of the god a night of leaves;
> And the vines blossom out from the lonely glade,
> And the suns of the summer are dim in the shade,
> And the storms of the winter have never a breeze,
> That can shiver a leaf from the charmed trees;

Darkness". His young daughter, Antigone, one of the most lovely creations of poetry, is his companion and guide; he is afterward joined by his other daughter, Ismene, whose weak and selfish character is drawn in strong contrast to the heroism and devotion of Antigone. The ancient prophecies that foretold his woes had foretold also his release. His last shelter and resting-place were to be obtained from the dread deities, and a sign of thunder, or earthquake, or lightning was to announce his parting hour. Learning the spot to which his steps had be guided, Œdipus solemnly feels that his doom approaches: thus, at the very opening of the poem, he stands before us on the verge of a mysterious grave.

The sufferings which have bowed the parricide to a premature old age[18] have not crushed his spirit; the softness and self-humiliation which were the first results of his awful affliction are passed away. He is grown once more vehement and passionate, from the sense of wrong; remorse still visits him, but is alternated with the yet more human feeling of resentment at the unjust severity of his doom.[19] His sons, who, "by a word", might have saved him from the expulsion, penury, and wanderings he has undergone, had deserted his cause—had looked with indifferent eyes on his awful woes— had joined with Creon to expel him from the Theban land. They are the Goneril and Regan of the classic Lear, as Antigone is the Cordelia on whom he leans—a Cordelia he has never thrust from him. "When", says Œdipus, in stern bitterness of soul:

> For there, O ever there,
> With that fair mountain throng,
> Who his sweet nurses were, [the Nymphs of Nisa]
> Wild Bacchus holds his court, the conscious woods among!
> Daintily, ever there,
> Crown of the mighty goddesses of old,
> Clustering Narcissus with his glorious hues
> Springs from his bath of heaven's delicious dews,
> And the gay crocus sheds his rays of gold.
> And wandering there for ever,
> The fountains are at play,
> And Cephisus feeds his river
> From their sweet urns, day by day.
> The river knows no dearth;
> Adown the vale the lapsing waters glide,
> And the pure rain of that pellucid tide
> Calls the rife beauty from the heart of earth;
> While by the banks the Muses' choral train
> Are duly heard—and there, Love checks her golden rein.

18 Γέροντα δ' ὀρθοῦν, φλαῦρον, ὃς νέος πέσῃ—Œdip. Col., 396. Thus, though his daughter had only grown up from childhood to early womanhood, Œdipus has passed from youth to age since the date of the Œdipus Tyrannus.
19 See his self-justification, 960–1000.

When my soul boiled within me—when "to die"
Was all my prayer—and death was sweetness, yea,
Had they but stoned me like a dog, I'd blessed them;
Then no man rose against me—but when time
Brought its slow comfort—when my wounds were scarred—
All my griefs mellow'd, and remorse itself
Judged my self-penance mightier than my sins,
Thebes thrust me from her breast, and they, my sons,
My blood, mine offspring, from their father shrunk:
A word of theirs had saved me—one small word—
They said it not—and lo! the wandering beggar!

In the meanwhile, during the exile of Œdipus, strife had broken out
between the brothers: Eteocles, here represented as the younger, drove out
Polynices, and seized the throne; Polynices takes refuge at Argos, where he
prepares war against the usurper: an oracle declares that success shall be with
that party which Œdipus joins, and a mysterious blessing is pronounced on
the land which contains his bones. Thus, the possession of this wild tool
of fate—raised up in age to a dread and ghastly consequence—becomes the
argument of the play, as his death must become the catastrophe. It is the deep
and fierce revenge of Œdipus that makes the passion of the whole. According
to a sublime conception, we see before us the physical Œdipus in the lowest
state of destitution and misery—in rags, blindness, beggary, utter and abject
impotence. But in the moral, Œdipus is all the majesty of a power still
royal. The oracle has invested one, so fallen and so wretched in himself, with
the power of a god—the power to confer victory on the cause he adopts,
prosperity on the land that becomes his tomb. With all the revenge of age,
all the grand malignity of hatred, he clings to this shadow and relic of
a sceptre. Creon, aware of the oracle, comes to recall him to Thebes. The
treacherous kinsman humbles himself before his victim—he is the suppliant
of the beggar, who defies and spurns him. Creon avenges himself by seizing
on Antigone and Ismene. Nothing can be more dramatically effective than
the scene in which these last props of his age are torn from the desolate old
man. They are ultimately restored to him by Theseus, whose amiable and
lofty character is painted with all the partial glow of colouring which an
Athenian poet would naturally lavish on the Athenian Alfred. We are next
introduced to Polynices. He, like Creon, has sought Œdipus with the selfish
motive of recovering his throne by means of an ally to whom the oracle
promises victory. But there is in Polynices the appearance of a true penitence,
and a mingled gentleness and majesty in his bearing which interests us in
his fate despite his faults, and which were possibly intended by Sophocles to
give a new interest to the plot of the "Antigone", composed and exhibited
long before. Œdipus is persuaded by the benevolence of Theseus, and the
sweet intercession of Antigone, to admit his son. After a chant from the

chorus on the ills of old age,[20] Polynices enters. He is struck with the wasted and miserable appearance of the old man, and bitterly reproaches his own desertion.

"But since", he says, with almost a Christian sentiment:

Since o'er each deed, upon the Olympian throne,
Mercy sits joint presider with great Jove,—
Let her, oh father, also take her stand
Within thy soul—and judge me! The past sins
Yet have their cure—ah, would they had recall!
Why are you voiceless? Speak to me, my father?
Turn not away—will you not answer me! &c.

Œdipus retains his silence in spite of the prayers of his beloved Antigone, and Polynices proceeds to narrate the wrongs he has undergone from Eteocles, and, warming with a young warrior's ardour, paints the array that he has mustered on his behalf—promises to restore Œdipus to his palace—and, alluding to the oracle, throws himself on his father's pardon.

Then, at last, outspeaks Œdipus, and from reproach bursts into curses.

And now you weep; you wept not at these woes
Until you wept your own. But I—*I* weep not.
These things are not for tears, but for endurance.
My son is like his sire—a parricide!
Toil, exile, beggary—daily bread doled out
From stranger hands—these are your gifts, my son!
My uncles, guardians—they who share the want,
Or earn the bread, are daughters; call them not
Women, for they to me are men. Go to!—
Thou art not mine—I do disclaim such issue.
Behold, the eyes of the avenging god
Are o'er thee! but their ominous light delays
To blast thee yet. March on—march on—to Thebes!
Not—not for thee, the city and the throne;
The earth shall first be reddened with thy blood—
Thy blood and *his*, thy foe—thy brother! Curses!
Not for the first time summoned to my wrongs—
Curses! I call ye back, and make ye now
Allies with this old man!

....

20 As each poet had but three actors allowed him, the song of the chorus probably gave time for the representative of Theseus to change his dress, and reappear as Polynices.

Yea, curses shall possess thy seat and throne,
If antique Justice o'er the laws of earth
Reign with the Thunder God. March on to ruin!
Spurned and disowned—the basest of the base—
And with thee bear this burthen: o'er thine head
I pour a prophet's doom; nor throne nor home
Waits on the sharpness of the levelled spear:
Thy very land of refuge hath no welcome;
Thine eyes have looked their last on hollow Argos.
Death by a brother's hand—dark fratricide,
Murdering thyself a brother—shall be thine.
Yea, while I curse thee, on the murky deep
Of the primeval hell, I call! Prepare
These men their home, dread Tartarus! Goddesses,
Whose shrines are round me—ye avenging Furies!
And thou, oh Lord of Battle, who hast stirred
Hate in the souls of brethren, hear me—hear me!—
And now, 'tis past!—enough!—depart and tell
The Theban people, and thy fond allies,
What blessings, from his refuge with the Furies,
The blind old Œdipus awards his sons![21]

As is usual with Sophocles, the terrific strength of these execrations is immediately followed by a soft and pathetic scene between Antigone and her brother. Though crushed at first by the paternal curse, the spirit of Polynices so far recovers its native courage that he will not listen to the prayer of his sister to desist from the expedition to Thebes, and to turn his armies back to Argos. "What", he says:

Lead back an army that could deem I trembled!

Yet he feels the mournful persuasion that his death is doomed; and a glimpse of the plot of the "Antigone" is opened upon us by his prayer to his sister, that if he perish, they should lay him with due honours in the tomb. The exquisite loveliness of Antigone's character touches even Polynices, and he departs, saying:

With the Gods rests the balance of our fate;
But thee, at least—O never upon thee
May evil fall! Thou art too good for sorrow!

---

21 The imagery in the last two lines has been amplified from the original in order to bring before the reader what the representation would have brought before the spectator.

The chorus resume their strains, when suddenly thunder is heard, and
Œdipus hails the sign that heralds him to the shades. Nothing can be
conceived more appalling than this omen. It seems as if Œdipus had been
spared but to curse his children and to die. He summons Theseus, tells him
that his fate is at hand, and that without a guide he himself will point out
the spot where he shall rest. Never may that spot be told—that secret and
solemn grave shall be the charm of the land and a defence against its foes.
Œdipus then turns round, and the instinct within guides him as he gropes
along. His daughters and Theseus follow the blind man, amazed and awed.
"Hither", he says:

> Hither—by this way come—for this way leads
> The unseen conductor of the dead[22]—and she
> Whom shadows call their queen![23] O Light, sweet Light,
> Rayless to me—mine once, and even now
> I feel thee palpable, round this worn form,
> Clinging in last embrace—I go to shroud
> The waning life in the eternal Hades!

Thus the stage is left to the chorus, and the mysterious fate of Œdipus is
recited by the Nuntius, in verses which Longinus has not extolled too highly.
Œdipus had led the way to a cavern, well known in legendary lore as the
spot where Perithous and Theseus had pledged their faith, by the brazen
steps which make one of the entrances to the infernal realms:

> Between which place and the Thorician stone—
> The hollow thorn, and the sepulchral pile
> He sat him down.

And when he had performed libations from the stream, and laved, and decked
himself in the funereal robes, Jove thundered beneath the earth, and the old
man's daughters, aghast with horror, fell at his knees with sobs and groans.

> Then o'er them as they wept, his hands he clasped,
> And "O my children", said he, "from this day
> Ye have no more a father—all of me
> Withers away—the burthen and the toil
> Of mine old age fall on ye nevermore.
> Sad travail have ye borne for me, and yet
> Let one thought breathe a balm when I am gone—

22 Mercury.
23 Proserpine.

> The thought that none upon the desolate world
> Loved you as I did; and in death I leave
> A happier life to you!"
>   Thus movingly,
> With clinging arms and passionate sobs, the three
> Wept out aloud, until the sorrow grew
> Into a deadly hush—nor cry nor wail
> Starts the drear silence of the solitude.
> Then suddenly a bodiless voice is heard,—
> It call'd on him, it call'd; and over all
> Horror fell cold, and stirr'd the bristling hair!
> Again, the voice—again—"Ho! Œdipus,
> Why linger we so long? Come—hither—come."

Œdipus then solemnly consigns his children to Theseus, dismisses them, and Theseus alone is left with the old man.

> So groaning we depart—and when once more
> We turned our eyes to gaze, behold, the place
> Knew not the man! The king *alone* was there,
> Holding his spread hands o'er averted brows
> As if to shut from out the quailing gaze
> The horrid aspect of some ghastly thing
> That nature durst not look on. So we paused
> Until the king awakened from the terror,
> And to the mother Earth, and high Olympus,
> Seat of the gods, he breathed awe-stricken prayer
> But, how the old man perished, save the king,
> Mortal can ne'er divine; for bolt, nor levin,
> Nor blasting tempest from the ocean borne,
> Was heard or seen; but either was he rapt
> Aloft by wings divine, or else the shades,
> Whose darkness never looked upon the sun,
> Yawned in grim mercy, and the rent abyss
> Engulf'd the wanderer from the living world.

Such, sublime in its wondrous power, its appalling mystery, its dim, religious terror, is the catastrophe of the "Œdipus at Colonus." The lines that follow are devoted to the lamentations of the daughters, and appear wholly superfluous, unless we can consider that Sophocles desired to indicate the connexion of the "Œdipus" with the "Antigone", by informing us that the daughters of Œdipus are to be sent to Thebes at the request of Antigone herself, who hopes, in the tender courage of her nature, that she may perhaps prevent the predicted slaughter of her brothers.

VII. Coming now to the tragedy of "Antigone", we find the prophecy of Œdipus has been fulfilled—the brothers have fallen by the hand of each other—the Argive army has been defeated—Creon has obtained the tyranny, and interdicts, on the penalty of death, the burial of Polynices, whose corpse remains guarded and unhonoured. Antigone, mindful of her brother's request to her in their last interview, resolves to brave the edict, and perform those rites so indispensably sacred in the eyes of a Greek. She communicates her resolution to her sister Ismene, whose character, still feeble and commonplace, is a perpetual foil to the heroism of Antigone. She acts upon her resolutions, baffles the vigilant guards, buries the corpse. Creon, on learning that his edict has been secretly disobeyed, orders the remains to be disinterred, and in a second attempt Antigone is discovered, brought before him, and condemned to death. Hæmon, the son of Creon, had been affianced to Antigone. On the news of her sentence he seeks Creon, and after a violent scene between the two, which has neither the power nor the dignity common to Sophocles, departs with vague menaces. A short but most exquisite invocation to love from the chorus succeeds, and in this, it may be observed, the chorus express much left not represented in the action—they serve to impress on the spectator all the irresistible effects of the passion which the modern artist would seek to represent in some moving scene between Antigone and Hæmon. The heroine herself now passes across the stage on her way to her dreadful doom, which is that of living burial in "the cavern of a rock". She thus addresses the chorus:

Ye, of the land wherein my fathers dwelt,
Behold me journeying to my latest bourne!
Time hath no morrow for these eyes. Black Orcus,
Whose court hath room for all, leads my lone steps,
E'en whilst I live, to Shadows. Not for me
The nuptial blessing or the marriage hymn:—
Acheron, receive thy bride!
Chorus: Honoured and mourned
Nor struck by slow disease or violent hand,
Thy steps glide to the grave! Self-judged, like Freedom,[24]
Thou, above mortals gifted, shalt descend,
All living to the shades.
Antigone: Methinks I have heard—
So legends go—how Phrygian Niobe
(Poor stranger) on the heights of Sipylus,
Mournfully died. The hard rock, like the tendrils

24 Αὐτόνομος—Antig., 821.

O' the ivy, clung and crept unto her heart:—
Her, nevermore, dissolving into showers,
Pale snows desert;—and from her sorrowful eyes,
As from unfailing founts, adown the cliffs,
Fall the eternal dews. Like her, the god
Lulls me to sleep, and into stone!

Afterward she adds in her beautiful lament, "that she has one comfort—that she shall go to the grave dear to her parents and her brother".

The grief of Antigone is in perfect harmony with her character—it betrays no repentance, no weakness—it is but the natural sorrow of youth and womanhood, going down to that grave which had so little of hope in the old Greek religion. In an Antigone on our stage we might have demanded more reference to her lover; but the Grecian heroine names him not, and alludes rather to the loss of the woman's lot of wedlock than the loss of the individual bridegroom. But it is not for that reason that we are to conclude, with M. Schlegel and others, that the Greek women knew not the sentiment of love. Such a notion, that has obtained an unaccountable belief, I shall hereafter show to be at variance with all the poetry of the Greeks—with their drama itself—with their modes of life—and with the very elements of that human nature, which is everywhere the same. But Sophocles, in the character of Antigone, personifies duty, not passion. It is to this, her leading individuality, that whatever might weaken the pure and statue-like effect of the creation is sacrificed. As she was to her father, so is she to her brother. The sorrows and calamities of her family have so endeared them to her heart that she has room for little else. "Formed", as she exquisitely says of herself, "to love, not to hate",[25] she lives but to devote affections the most sacred to sad and pious tasks, and the last fulfilled, she has done with earth.

When Antigone is borne away, an august personage is presented to us, whose very name to us who usually read the "Œdipus Tyrannus" before the "Antigone", is the foreteller of omen and doom. As in the "Œdipus Tyrannus", Tiresias the soothsayer appears to announce all the terrors that ensue—so now, at the crowning desolation of that fated house, he, the solemn and mysterious surviver of such dark tragedies, is again brought upon the stage. The auguries have been evil—birds battle with each other in the air—the flame will not mount from the sacrificial victim—and the altars and hearths are full of birds and dogs, gathering to their feast on the corpse of Polynices. The soothsayer enjoins Creon not to war against the dead, and to accord the rites of burial to the prince's body. On the obstinate refusal of Creon, Tiresias utters prophetic maledictions and departs. Creon, whose vehemence of temper

---

25 Οὔ τοι συνέχθειν, ἀλλὰ συμφιλεῖν ἔφυν—Antig., 523.

is combined with a feeble character, and strongly contrasts the mighty spirit of Œdipus, repents, and is persuaded by the chorus to release Antigone from her living prison, as well as to revoke the edict which denies sepulture to Polynices. He quits the stage for that purpose, and the chorus burst into one of their most picturesque odes, an invocation to Bacchus, thus inadequately presented to the English reader:

> Oh thou, whom earth by many a title hails,
> Son of the thunder-god, and wild delight
>   Of the wild Theban maid!
> Whether on far Italia's shores obey'd,
>   Or where Eleusis joins thy solemn rites
> With the Great Mother's,[26] in mysterious vales,—
> Bacchus in Bacchic Thebes best known,
> Thy Thebes, who claims the Thyads as her daughters;
> Fast by the fields with warriors dragon-sown,
> And where Ismenus rolls his rapid waters.
>   It saw thee, the smoke,
>   On the horned height—[27]
>   It saw thee, and broke
>   With a leap into light;—
> Where roam Corycian nymphs the glorious mountain,
> And all melodious flows the old Castalian fountain:
>   Vocal with echoes wildly glad,
>   The Nysian steeps with ivy clad,
> And shores with vineyards greenly blooming,
>   Proclaiming, steep to shore,
>   That Bacchus evermore
>   Is guardian of the race,
>   Where he holds his dwelling-place
>   With her,[28] beneath the breath
>   Of the thunder's glowing death,
>   In the glare of her glory consuming.
>
> O now with healing steps along the slope
>   Of lov'd Parnassus, or in gliding motion,
>   O'er the far-sounding deep Eubœan ocean—

26 Ceres.
27 Ὑπὲρ διλόφον πέτρας—viz., Parnassus. The Bacchanalian light on the double crest of Parnassus, which announced the god, is a favourite allusion with the Greek poets.
28 His mother, Semele.

Come! for we perish—come!—our Lord and hope!
  Leader of the stately choir
Of the great stars, whose very breath is light,
  Who dost with hymns inspire
Voices, oh youngest god, that sound by night;
  Come, with thy Maenad throng,
Come with the maidens of thy Naxian isle,
Who chant their Lord Iacchus—all the while,
Maddening, with mystic dance, the solemn midnight long!

At the close of the chorus the Nuntius enters to announce the catastrophe, and Eurydice, the wife of Creon, disturbed by rumours within her palace, is made an auditor of the narration. Creon and his train, after burying Polynices, repair to the cavern in which Antigone had been immured. They hear loud wailings within "that unconsecrated chamber"—it is the voice of Hæmon. Creon recoils—the attendants enter—within the cavern they behold Antigone, who, in the horror of that deathlike solitude, had strangled herself with the zone of her robe; and there was her lover lying beside, his arms clasped around her waist. Creon at length advances, perceives his son, and conjures him to come forth:

Then, glaring on his father with wild eyes,
The son stood dumb, and spat upon his face,
And clutched the unnatural sword—the father fled,
And, wroth, as with the arm that missed a parent,
The wretched man drove home unto his breast
The abhorrent steel; yet ever, while dim sense
Struggled within the fast-expiring soul—
Feebler, and feebler still, his stiffening arms
Clung to that virgin form—and every gasp
Of his last breath with bloody dews distained
The cold white cheek that was his pillow. So
Lies death embracing death![29]

29 Aristotle finds fault with the incident of the son attempting to strike his father, as being shocking, yet not tragic—that is, the violent action is episodical, since it is not carried into effect; yet, if we might connect the plot of the "Antigone" with the former plays of either "Œdipus", there is something of retribution in the attempted parricide when we remember the hypocritical and cruel severity of Creon to the involuntary parricide of Œdipus. The whole description of the son in that living tomb, glaring on his father with his drawn sword, the dead form of his betrothed, with the subsequent picture of the lovers joined in death, constitutes one of the most masterly combinations of pathos and terror in ancient or modern poetry.

In the midst of this description, by a fine stroke of art, Eurydice, the mother of Hæmon, abruptly and silently quits the stage.[30] When next we hear of her, she has destroyed herself, with her last breath cursing her husband as the murderer of her child. The end of the play leaves Creon the surviver. He himself does not perish, for he himself has never excited our sympathies.[31] He is punished through his son and wife—they dead, our interest ceases in him, and to add his death to theirs and to that of Antigone would be bathos.

VIII. In the tragedy of "Electra", the character of the heroine stands out in the boldest contrast to the creation of the Antigone; both are endowed with surpassing majesty and strength of nature—they are loftier than the daughters of men, their very loveliness is of an age when gods were no distant ancestors of kings—when, as in the early sculptors of Pallas, or even of Aphrodite, something of the severe and stern was deemed necessary to the realization of the divine; and the beautiful had not lost the colossal proportions of the sublime. But the strength and heroism of Antigone is derived from love—love, sober, serene, august—but still love. Electra, on the contrary, is supported and exalted above her sex by the might of her hatred. Her father, "the king of men", foully murdered in his palace—herself compelled to consort with his assassins—to receive from their hands both charity and insult—the adulterous murderer on her father's throne, and lord of her father's marriage bed[32]—her brother a wanderer and an outcast. Such are the thoughts unceasingly before her!—her heart and soul have for years fed upon the bitterness of a resentment, at once impotent and intense, and nature itself has turned to gall. She sees not in Clytemnestra a mother, but the murderess of a father. The doubt and the compunction of the modern Hamlet are unknown to her more masculine spirit. She lives on but in the hope of her brother's return and of revenge. The play opens with the appearance of Orestes, Pylades, and an old attendant—arrived at break of day at the habitation of the Pelopidæ—"reeking with blood"—the seats of Agamemnon. Orestes, who had been saved in childhood by his sister from the designs of Clytemnestra and Ægisthus, has now returned in manhood. It is agreed that, in order to lull all suspicion in the royal adulterers, a false account of the death of Orestes by an accident in the Pythian Games shall be given to Clytemnestra; and Orestes and Pylades themselves are afterward to be introduced in the character of Phocians, bearing the ashes of the supposed dead.

30 This is not the only passage in which Sophocles expresses feminine woe by silence. In the "Trachiniæ", Deianira vanishes in the same dumb abruptness when she hears from her son the effect of the centaur's gift upon her husband.
31 According to that most profound maxim of Aristotle, that in tragedy a very bad man should never be selected as the object of chastisement, since his fate is not calculated to excite our sympathies.
32 Electra, 250–300.

Meanwhile the two friends repair to the sepulchre of Agamemnon to offer libations, &c. Electra then appears, indulges her indignant lamentations at her lot, and consoles herself with the hope of her brother's speedy return.

She is joined by her sister Chrysothemis, who is bearing sepulchral offerings to the tomb of Agamemnon; and in this interview, Sophocles, with extraordinary skill and deep knowledge of human nature, contrives to excite our admiration and sympathy for the vehement Electra by contrasting her with the weak and selfish Chrysothemis. Her very bitterness against her mother is made to assume the guise of a solemn duty to her father. Her unfeminine qualities rise into courage and magnanimity—she glories in the unkindness and persecution she meets with from Clytemnestra and Ægisthus—they are proofs of her reverence to the dead. Woman as she is, she is yet the daughter of a king—she cannot submit to a usurper—"she will not add cowardice to misery". Chrysothemis informs Electra that on the return of Ægisthus it is resolved to consign her to a vault "where she may chant her woes unheard". Electra learns the meditated sentence undismayed—she will not moderate her unwelcome woe—"she will not be a traitress to those she loves". But a dream has appalled Clytemnestra—Agamemnon has appeared to her as in life. In the vision he seemed to her to fix his sceptre on the soil, whence it sprouted up into a tree that overshadowed the whole land. Disquieted and conscience-stricken, she now sends Chrysothemis with libations to appease the manes of the dead. Electra adjures Chrysothemis not to render such expiations—to scatter them to the winds or on the dust—to let them not approach the resting-place of the murdered king. Chrysothemis promises to obey the injunction, and departs. A violent and powerful scene between Clytemnestra and Electra ensues, when the attendant enters (as was agreed on) to announce the death of Orestes. In this recital he portrays the ceremony of the Pythian races in lines justly celebrated, and which, as an animated and faithful picture of an exhibition so renowned, the reader may be pleased to see, even in a feeble and cold translation. Orestes had obtained five victories in the first day—in the second he starts with nine competitors in the chariot-race—an Achæan, a Spartan, two Libyans—he himself with Thessalian steeds—a sixth from Ætolia, a Magnesian, an Ænian, an Athenian, and a Bœotian complete the number:

> They took their stand where the appointed judges
> Had cast their lots, and ranged the rival cars;
> Rang out the brazen trump! Away they bound,
> Cheer the hot steeds and shake the slackened reins;
> As with a body the large space is filled
> With the huge clangour of the rattling cars:
> High whirl aloft the dust-clouds; blent together
> Each presses each—and the lash rings—and loud
> Snort the wild steeds, and from their fiery breath,

Along their manes and down the circling wheels,
Scatter the flaking foam. Orestes still,
Aye, as he swept around the perilous pillar
Last in the course, wheel'd in the rushing axle;
The left rein curbed—that on the dexter hand
Flung loose. So on erect the chariots rolled!
Sudden the Ænian's fierce and headlong steeds
Broke from the bit—and, as the seventh time now
The course was circled, on the Libyan car
Dash'd their wild fronts:—then order changed to ruin:
Car crashed on car—the wide Crissæan plain
Was, sealike, strewn with wrecks: the Athenian saw,
Slackened his speed, and, wheeling round the marge,
Unscathed and skilful, in the midmost space,
Left the wild tumult of that tossing storm.
Behind, Orestes, hitherto the last,
Had yet kept back his coursers for the close;
Now one sole rival left—on, on he flew,
And the sharp sound of the impelling scourge
Rang in the keen ears of the flying steeds.
He nears—he reaches—they are side by side:
Now one—the other—by a length the victor.
The courses all are past—the wheels erect—
All safe—when as the hurrying coursers round
The fatal pillar dash'd, the wretched boy
Slackened the *left* rein; on the column's edge
Crash'd the frail axle—headlong from the car,
Caught and all meshed within the reins he fell;
And masterless, the mad steeds raged along!

Loud from that mighty multitude arose
A shriek—a shout! But yesterday such deeds—
To-day such doom! Now whirled upon the earth,
Now his limbs dash'd aloft, they dragged him—those
Wild horses—till all gory from the wheels
Released,—and no man, not his nearest friends,
Could in that mangled corpse have traced Orestes.

They laid the body on the funeral pyre,
And while we speak, the Phocian strangers bear,
In a small, brazen, melancholy urn,
That handful of cold ashes to which all
The grandeur of the beautiful hath shrunk.
Hither they bear him—in his father's land
To find that heritage—a tomb!

509

It is much to be regretted that this passage, so fine in the original, is liable to one great objection—it has no interest as connected with the play, because the audience know that Orestes is not dead; and though the description of the race retains its animation, the report of the catastrophe loses the terror of reality, and appears but a highly coloured and elaborate falsehood.

The reader will conceive the lamentations of Electra and the fearful joy of Clytemnestra at a narrative by which the one appears to lose a brother and a friend—the other a son and an avenging foe.

Chrysothemis joyfully returns to announce, that by the tomb of Agamemnon she discovers a lock of hair; libations yet moisten the summit of the mound, and flowers of every hue are scattered over the grave. "These", she thinks, "are signs that Orestes is returned." Electra, informing her of the fatal news, proposes that they, women as they are, shall attempt the terrible revenge which their brother can no longer execute. When Chrysothemis recoils and refuses, Electra still nurses the fell design. The poet has more than once, and now again with judgment, made us sensible of the mature years of Electra;[33] she is no passionate, wavering, and inexperienced girl, but the eldest born of the house; the guardian of the childhood of its male heir; unwedded and unloving, no soft matron cares, no tender maiden affections, have unbent the nerves of her stern, fiery, and concentrated soul. Year after year has rolled on to sharpen her hatred—to disgust her with the present—to root her to one bloody memory of the past—to sour and freeze up the gentle thoughts of womanhood—to unsex

And fill her from the crown to the toe, top-full
Of direst cruelty—make thick her blood—
Stop up the access and passage to remorse,[34]

and fit her for one crowning deed, for which alone the daughter of the king of men lives on.

33 When (line 614) Clytemnestra reproaches Electra for using insulting epithets to a mother—and "Electra, too, at such a time of life"—I am surprised that some of the critics should deem it doubtful whether Clytemnestra meant to allude to her being too young or too mature for such unfilial vehemence. Not only does the age of Orestes, so much the junior to Electra, prove the latter signification to be the indisputable one, but the very words of Electra herself to her younger sister, Chrysothemis, when she tells her that she is "growing old, unwedded":

Ἐς τοσόνδε τοῦ χρόνου
ἄλεκτρα γηράσκουσαν ἀνυμέναιά τε.

Brunck has a judicious note on Electra's age, line 614.
34 Macbeth, act i, scene 5.

At length the pretended Phocians enter, bearing the supposed ashes of Orestes; the chief of the train addresses himself to Electra, and this is the most dramatic and touching scene in the whole tragedy. When the urn containing, as she believes, the dust of her brother, is placed in the hands of Electra, we can well overleap time and space, and see before us the great actor who brought the relics of his own son upon the stage, and shed no mimic sorrows[35]—we can well picture the emotions that circle round the vast audience—pity itself being mingled with the consciousness to which the audience alone are admitted, that lamentation will soon be replaced by joy, and that the living Orestes is before his sister. It is by a most subtle and delicate art that Sophocles permits this struggle between present pain and anticipated pleasure, and carries on the passion of the spectators to wait breathlessly the moment when Orestes shall be discovered. We now perceive why the poet at once, in the opening of the play, announced to us the existence and return of Orestes—why he disdained the vulgar source of interest, the gross suspense we should have felt, if we had shared the ignorance of Electra, and not been admitted to the secret we impatiently long to be communicated to her. In this scene, our superiority to Electra, in the knowledge we possess, refines and softens our compassion, blending it with hope. And most beautifully here does Sophocles remove far from us the thought of the hard hatred that hitherto animates the mourner—the strong, proud spirit is melted away—the woman and the sister alone appear. He whom she had loved more dearly than a mother—whom she had nursed, and saved, and prayed for, is "a nothing" in her hands; and the last rites it had not been hers to pay. He had been

By strangers honoured and by strangers mourned.

All things had vanished with him—"vanished in a day"—"vanished as by a hurricane"—she is left with her foes alone. "Admit me", she cries, "to thy refuge—make room for me in thy home."

In these lamentations, the cold, classic drama seems to warm into actual life. Art, exquisite because invisible, unites us at once with imperishable nature—we are no longer delighted with Poetry—we are weeping with Truth.

At length Orestes reveals himself, and now the plot draws to its catastrophe. Clytemnestra is alone in her house, preparing a caldron for the burial; Electra and the chorus are on the stage; the son—the avenger, is within; suddenly the cries of Clytemnestra are heard. Again—again! Orestes re-enters a parricide![36] He retires as Ægisthus is seen approaching; and the

---

35 See below n. 46.

36 Sophocles skilfully avoids treading the ground consecrated to Æschylus. He does not bring the murder before us with the struggles and resolve of Orestes.

adulterous usurper is now presented to us for the first and last time—the crowning victim of the sacrifice. He comes flushed with joy and triumph. He has heard that the dreaded Orestes is no more. Electra entertains him a few moments with words darkly and exultingly ambiguous. He orders the doors to be thrown open, that all Argos and Mycenæ may see the remains of his sole rival for the throne. The scene opens. On the threshold (where, with the Greeks, the corpse of the dead was usually set out to view) lies a body covered with a veil or pall. Orestes (the supposed Phocian) stands beside.

> *Ægisthus*: Great Jove! a grateful spectacle!—if thus
> May it be said unsinning; yet if she,
> The awful Nemesis, be nigh and hear,
> I do recall the sentence!—Raise the pall.
> The dead was kindred to me, and shall know
> A kinsman's sorrow.
> *Orestes*: Lift thyself the pall;
> Not mine, but thine, the office to survey
> That which lies mute beneath, and to salute,
> Lovingly sad, the dead one.
> *Ægisthus*: Be it so—
> It is well said. Go thou and call the queen:
> Is she within?
> *Orestes*: Look not around for her—
> She is beside thee!

Ægisthus lifts the pall, and beholds the body of Clytemnestra! He knows his fate at once. He knows that Orestes is before him. He attempts to speak. The fierce Electra cuts him short, and Orestes, with stern solemnity, conducts him from the stage to the spot on which Ægisthus had slain Agamemnon, so that the murderer might die by the son's hand in the place where the father fell. Thus artistically is the catastrophe not lessened in effect, but heightened, by removing the deed of death from the scene—the poetical justice, in the calm and premeditated selection of the place of slaughter, elevates what on the modern stage would be but a spectacle of physical horror into the deeper terror and sublimer gloom of a moral awe; and vindictive murder, losing its aspect, is idealized and hallowed into religious sacrifice.

IX. Of the seven plays left to us, the "Trachiniæ" is usually considered the least imbued with the genius of Sophocles; and Schlegel has even ventured on the conjecture, singularly destitute of even plausible testimony, that Sophocles himself may not be the author. The plot is soon told. The play is opened by Deianira, the wife of Hercules, who indulges in melancholy reflections on the misfortunes of her youth, and the continual absence of her husband, of whom no tidings have been heard for months. She soon learns from her son, Hyllus, that Hercules is said to be leading an expedition into Eubœa; and our interest is immediately excited by Deianira's reply, which informs us that oracles had foretold that this was to be the crisis[37] in the life of Hercules—that he was now to enjoy rest from his labours, either in a peaceful home or in the grave; and she sends Hyllus to join his father, share his enterprise and fate. The chorus touchingly paint the anxious love of Deianira in the following lines:

> Thou, whom the starry-spangled night did lull
>   Into the sleep from which—her journey done—
> Her parting steps awake thee—Beautiful
>   Fountain of flame, O Sun!
> Say, on what sea-girt strand, or inland shore
>   (for earth is bared before thy solemn gaze),
>   In orient Asia, or where milder rays
> Tremble on western waters, wandereth he
>   Whom bright Alcmena bore?
> Ah! as some bird within a lonely nest
>   The desolate wife puts sleep away with tears;
>   And ever ills to be
>   Haunting the absence with dim hosts of fears,
> Fond fancy shapes from air dark prophets of the breast.

In her answer to the virgin chorus, Deianira weaves a beautiful picture of maiden youth as a contrast to the cares and anxieties of wedded life:

> Youth pastures in a valley of its own;
> The scorching sun, the rains and winds of heaven,
> Mar not the calm—yet virgin of all care;
> But ever with sweet joys it buildeth up
> The airy halls of life.

Deianira afterward receives fresh news of Hercules. She gives way to her joy. Lichas, the herald, enters, and confides to her charge some maidens whom the hero had captured. Deianira is struck with compassion for their

---

37 This is very characteristic of Sophocles: he is especially fond of employing what maybe called "a crisis in life" as a source of immediate interest to the audience. So in the "Œdipus at Colonus", Œdipus no sooner finds he is in the grove of the Furies than he knows his hour is approaching; so, also, in the "Ajax", the Nuntius announces from the soothsayer, that if Ajax can survive the one day which makes the crisis of his life, the anger of the goddess will cease. This characteristic of the peculiar style of Sophocles might be considered as one of the proofs (were any wanting) of the authenticity of the "Trachiniæ".

lot, and with admiration of the noble bearing of one of them, Iole. She is about to busy herself in preparation for their comfort, when she learns that Iole is her rival—the beloved mistress of Hercules. The jealousy evinced by Deianira is beautifully soft and womanly.[38] Even in uttering a reproach on Hercules, she says she cannot feel anger with him, yet how can she dwell in the same house with a younger and fairer rival:

> She in whose years the flower that fades in mine
> Opens the leaves of beauty.

Her affection, her desire to retain the love of the hero, suggests to her remembrance a gift she had once received from a centaur who had fallen by the shaft of Hercules. The centaur had assured her that the blood from his wound, if preserved, would exercise the charm of a filter over the heart of Hercules, and would ever recall and fix upon her his affection. She had preserved the supposed charm—she steeps with it a robe that she purposes to send to Hercules as a gift; but Deianira, in this fatal resolve, shows all the timidity and sweetness of her nature; she even questions if it be a crime to regain the heart of her husband; she consults the chorus, who advise the experiment (and here, it may be observed, that this is skilfully done, for it conveys the excuse of Deianira, the chorus being, as it were, the representative of the audience). Accordingly, she sends the garment by Lichas. Scarce has the herald gone, ere Deianira is terrified by a strange phenomenon: a part of the wool with which the supposed filter had been applied to the garment was thrown into the sunlight, upon which it withered away—"crumbling like sawdust"—while on the spot where it fell a sort of venomous foam froths up. While relating this phenomenon to the chorus, her son, Hyllus, returns,[39] and relates the agonies of his father under the poisoned garment: he had indued the robe on the occasion of solemn sacrifice, and all was rejoicing, when,

> As from the sacred offering and the pile
> The flame broke forth,

---

38 M. Schlegel rather wantonly accuses Deianira of "levity"—all her motives, on the contrary, are pure and high, though tender and affectionate.
39 Observe the violation of the unity which Sophocles, the most artistical of all the Greek tragedians, does not hesitate to commit whenever he thinks it necessary. Hyllus, at the beginning of the play, went to Cenæum; he has been already there and back—viz., a distance from Mount Œta to a promontory in Eubœa, during the time about seven hundred and thirty lines have taken up in recital! Nor is this all: just before the last chorus—only about one hundred lines back—Lichas set out to Cenæum; and yet sufficient time is supposed to have elapsed for him to have arrived there—been present at a sacrifice—been killed by Hercules—and after all this, for Hyllus, who tells the tale, to have performed the journey back to Trachis.

the poison began to work, the tunic clung to the limbs of the hero, glued as if by the artificer, and, in his agony and madness, Hercules dashes Lichas, who brought him the fatal gift, down the rock, and is now on his way home. On hearing these news and the reproaches of her son, Deianira steals silently away, and destroys herself upon the bridal-bed. The remainder of the play is very feeble. Hercules is represented in his anguish, which is but the mere raving of physical pain; and after enjoining his son to marry Iole (the innocent cause of his own sufferings), and to place him yet living upon his funeral pyre, the play ends.

The beauty of the "Trachiniæ" is in detached passages, in some exquisite bursts by the chorus, and in the character of Deianira, whose artifice to regain the love of her consort, unhappily as it terminates, is redeemed by a meekness of nature, a delicacy of sentiment, and an anxious, earnest, unreproachful devotion of conjugal love, which might alone suffice to show the absurdity of modern declamations on the debasement of women, and the absence of pure and true love in that land from which Sophocles drew his experience.

X. The "Ajax" is far superior to the "Trachiniæ". The subject is one that none but a Greek poet could have thought of or a Greek audience have admired. The master-passion of a Greek was emulation—the subject of the "Ajax" is emulation defeated. He has lost to Ulysses the prize of the arms of Achilles, and the shame of being vanquished has deprived him of his senses.

In the fury of madness he sallies from his tent at night—slaughters the flocks, in which his insanity sees the Greeks, whose award has galled and humbled him—and supposes he has slain the Atridæ and captured Ulysses. It is in this play that Sophocles has, to a certain extent, attempted that most effective of all combinations in the hands of a master—the combination of the ludicrous and the terrible:[40] as the chorus implies, "it is to laugh and to weep". But when the scene, opening, discovers Ajax sitting amid the slaughtered victims—when that haughty hero awakens from his delirium— when he is aware that he has exposed himself to the mockery and derision of his foes—the effect is almost too painful even for tragedy. In contrast to Ajax is the soothing and tender Tecmessa. The women of Sophocles are, indeed, gifted with an astonishing mixture of majesty and sweetness. After a very pathetic farewell with his young son, Ajax affects to be reconciled to his lot, disguises the resolution he has formed, and by one of those artful transitions of emotion which at once vary and heighten interest on the stage, the chorus, before lamenting, bursts into a strain of congratulation and joy. The heavy affliction has passed away—Ajax is restored. The Nuntius arrives from the camp. Calchas, the soothsayer, has besought Teucer, the hero's

40 Even Ulysses, the successful rival of Ajax, exhibits a reluctance to face the madman which is not without humour.

brother, not to permit Ajax to quit his tent that day, for on that day only Minerva persecutes him; and if he survive it, he may yet be preserved and prosper. But Ajax has already wandered away, none know whither. Tecmessa hastens in search of him, and, by a very rare departure from the customs of the Greek stage, the chorus follow.

Ajax appears again. His passions are now calm and concentrated, but they lead him on to death. He has been shamed, dishonoured—he has made himself a mockery to his foes. Nobly to live or nobly to die is the sole choice of a brave man. It is characteristic of the Greek temperament, that the personages of the Greek poetry ever bid a last lingering and half-reluctant farewell to the sun. There is a magnificent fulness of life in those children of the beautiful West; the sun is to them as a familiar friend—the affliction or the terror of Hades is in the thought that its fields are sunless. The orb which animated their temperate heaven, which ripened their fertile earth, in which they saw the type of eternal youth, of surpassing beauty, of incarnate poetry—human in its associations, and yet divine in its nature—is equally beloved and equally to be mourned by the maiden tenderness of Antigone or the sullen majesty of Ajax. In a Chaldæan poem the hero would have bid farewell to the stars!

It is thus that Ajax concludes his celebrated soliloquy:

> And thou that mak'st high heaven thy chariot-course,
> Oh Sun—when gazing on my father-land,
> Draw back thy golden rein, and tell my woes
> To the old man, my father—and to her
> Who nursed me at her bosom—my poor mother!
> There will be wailing thro' the echoing walls
> When—but away with thoughts like these!—the hour
> Brings on the ripening deed.—Death, death, look on me!
> Did I say death?—it was a waste of words;
> *We* shall be friends hereafter.
>   —'Tis the DAY,
> Present and breathing round me, and the car
> Of the sweet sun, that never shall again
> Receive my greeting!—henceforth time is sunless,
> And day a thing that is not! Beautiful light,
> My Salamis—my country—and the floor
> Of my dear household-hearth—and thou, bright Athens,
> Thou—for thy sons and I were boys together—
> Fountains and rivers, and ye Trojan plains,
> I loved ye as my fosterers—fare ye well!
> Take in these words, the last earth hears from Ajax—
> All else unspoken, in a spectre land
> I'll whisper to the dead!

Ajax perishes on his sword—but the interest of the play survives him. For with the Greeks, burial rather than death made the great close of life. Teucer is introduced to us, the protector of the hero's remains: and his character, at once fierce and tender, is a sketch of extraordinary power. Agamemnon, on the contrary—also not presented to us till after the death of Ajax—is but a boisterous tyrant.[41] Finally, by the generous intercession of Ulysses, who redeems his character from the unfavourable conception we formed of him at the commencement of the play, the funeral rites are accorded, and a didactic and solemn moral from the chorus concludes the whole.

XI. The "Philoctetes" has always been ranked by critics among the most elaborate and polished of the tragedies of Sophocles. In some respects it deserves the eulogies bestowed on it. But one great fault in the conception will, I think, be apparent on the simple statement of the plot.

Philoctetes, the friend and armour-bearer of Hercules, and the heir of that hero's unerring shafts and bow, had, while the Grecian fleet anchored at Chryse (a small isle in the Ægæan), been bitten in the foot by a serpent; the pain of the wound was insufferable—the shrieks and groans of Philoctetes disturbed the libations and sacrifices of the Greeks. And Ulysses and Diomed, when the fleet proceeded, left him, while asleep, on the wild and rocky solitudes of Lemnos. There, till the tenth year of the Trojan siege, he dragged out an agonizing life. The soothsayer, Helenus, then declared that Troy could not fall till Philoctetes appeared in the Grecian camp with the arrows and bow of Hercules. Ulysses undertakes to effect this object, and, with Neoptolemus (son of Achilles), departs for Lemnos. Here the play opens. A wild and desolate shore—a cavern with two mouths (so that in winter there might be a double place to catch the sunshine, and in summer a twofold entrance for the breeze), and a little fountain of pure water, designate the abode of Philoctetes.

Agreeably to his character, it is by deceit and stratagem that Ulysses is to gain his object. Neoptolemus is to dupe him whom he has never seen with professions of friendship and offers of services, and to snare away the consecrated weapons. Neoptolemus—whose character is a sketch which Shakespeare alone could have bodied out—has all the generous ardour and

---

41 Potter says, in common with some other authorities, that "we may be assured that the political enmity of the Athenians to the Spartans and Argives was the cause of this odious representation of Menelaus and Agamemnon". But the Athenians had, at that time, no political enmity with the Argives, who were notoriously jealous of the Spartans; and as for the Spartans, Agamemnon and Menelaus were not their heroes and countrymen. On the contrary, it was the thrones of Menelaus and Agamemnon which the Spartans overthrew. The royal brothers were probably sacrificed by the poet, not the patriot. The dramatic effects required that they should be made the foils to the manly fervour of Teucer and the calm magnanimity of Ulysses.

honesty of youth, but he has also its timid irresolution—its docile submission to the great—its fear of the censure of the world. He recoils from the base task proposed to him; he would prefer violence to fraud; yet he dreads lest, having undertaken the enterprise, his refusal to act should be considered treachery to his coadjutor. It is with a deep and melancholy wisdom that Ulysses, who seems to contemplate his struggles with compassionate and not displeased superiority, thus attempts to reconcile the young man:

> Son of a noble sire!—*I* too, in youth,
> Had a slow tongue and an impatient arm:
> But now, life tried, I hail in words, not deeds,
> The universal rulers of mankind.

Neoptolemus is overruled. Ulysses withdraws, Philoctetes appears. The delight of the lonely wretch on hearing his native language; on seeing the son of Achilles—his description of his feelings when he first found himself abandoned in the desert—his relation of the hardships he has since undergone, are highly pathetic. He implores Neoptolemus to bear him away, and when the youth consents, he bursts into an exclamation of joy, which, to the audience, in the secret of the perfidy to be practised on him, must have excited the most lively emotions. The characteristic excellence of Sophocles is, that in his most majestic creations he always contrives to introduce the sweetest touches of humanity. Philoctetes will not even quit his miserable desert until he has returned to his cave to bid it farewell—to kiss the only shelter that did not deny a refuge to his woes. In the joy of his heart he thinks, poor dupe, that he has found faith in man—in youth. He trusts the arrows and the bow to the hand of Neoptolemus. Then, as he attempts to crawl along, the sharp agony of his wound completely overmasters him. He endeavours in vain to stifle his groans; the body conquers the mind. This seems to me, as I shall presently again observe, the blot of the play; it is a mere exhibition of physical pain. The torture exhausts, till insensibility or sleep comes over him. He lies down to rest, and the young man watches over him. The picture is striking. Neoptolemus, at war with himself, does not seize the occasion. Philoctetes wakes. He is ready to go on board; he implores and urges instant departure. Neoptolemus recoils—the suspicions of Philoctetes are awakened; he thinks that this stranger, too, will abandon him. At length the young man, by a violent effort, speaks abruptly out, "Thou must sail to Troy—to the Greeks—the Atridae".

"The Greeks—the Atridae!", the betrayers of Philoctetes—those beyond pardon—those whom for ten years he has pursued with the curses of a wronged, and deserted, and solitary spirit. "Give me back", he cries, "my bow and arrows." And when Neoptolemus refuses, he pours forth a torrent of reproach. The son of the truth-telling Achilles can withstand no longer.

He is about to restore the weapons, when Ulysses rushes on the stage and prevents him.

At length, the sufferer is to be left—left once more alone in the desert. He cannot go with his betrayers—he cannot give glory and conquest to his inhuman foes; in the wrath of his indignant heart even the desert is sweeter than the Grecian camp. And how is he to sustain himself without his shafts! Famine adds a new horror to his dreary solitude, and the wild beasts may now pierce into his cavern: but *their* cruelty would be mercy! His contradictory and tempestuous emotions, as the sailors that compose the chorus are about to depart, are thus told.

The chorus entreat him to accompany them:

Philoctetes: Begone.
Chorus: It is a friendly bidding—we obey—
Come, let us go. To ship, my comrades.
Philoctetes: No—
No, do not go—by the great Jove, who hears
Men's curses—do not go.
Chorus: Be calm.
Philoctetes: Sweet strangers!
By the Gods, leave me not.

Chorus: But now you bade us!
Philoctetes: Ay—meet cause for chiding,
That a poor desperate wretch, maddened with pain,
Should talk as madmen do!
Chorus: Come, then, with us.
Philoctetes: Never! oh—never! Were the veriest bolts
Of the fire-darting Thunderer hurl'd against me,
Still would I answer "Never!" Perish Troy,
And all beleaguered round its walls—yea, all
Who had the heart to spurn a wounded wretch;
But, but—nay—yes—one prayer, one boon accord me.
Chorus: What wouldst thou have?
Philoctetes: A sword, an axe, a something;
So it can strike, no matter!
Chorus: Nay—for what?
Philoctetes: What!—for this hand to hew me off this head—
These limbs!—To death, to solemn death, at last
My spirit calls me.
Chorus: Why?
Philoctetes: To seek my father.
Chorus: Whither?
Philoctetes: In Hades.

519

Having thus worked us up to the utmost point of sympathy with the abandoned Philoctetes, the poet now gradually sheds a gentler and holier light over the intense gloom to which we had been led. Neoptolemus, touched with generous remorse, steals back to give the betrayed warrior his weapons—he is watched by the vigilant Ulysses—an angry altercation takes place between them. Ulysses finding he cannot intimidate, prudently avoids personal encounter with the son of Achilles, and departs to apprise the host of the backsliding of his comrade. A most beautiful scene, in which Neoptolemus restores the weapons to Philoctetes—a scene which must have commanded the most exquisite tears and the most rapturous applauses of the audience, ensues; and, finally, the god so useful to the ancient poets brings all things, contrary to the general rule of Aristotle,[42] to a happy close. Hercules appears and induces his former friend to accompany Neoptolemus to the Grecian camp, where his wound shall be healed. The farewell of Philoctetes to his cavern—to the nymphs of the meadows—to the roar of the ocean, whose spray the south wind dashed through his rude abode—to the Lycian stream and the plain of Lemnos—is left to linger on the ear like a solemn hymn, in which the little that is mournful only heightens the majestic sweetness of all that is musical. The dramatic art in the several scenes of this play Sophocles has never excelled, and scarcely equalled. The contrast of character in Ulysses and Neoptolemus has in it a reality, a human strength and truth, that is more common to the modern than the ancient drama. But still the fault of the story is partly that the plot rests upon a base and ignoble fraud, and principally that our pity is appealed to by the coarse sympathy with physical pain: the rags that covered the sores, the tainted corruption of the ulcers, are brought to bear, not so much on the mind as on the nerves; and when the hero is represented as shrinking with corporeal agony—the blood oozing from his foot, the livid sweat rolling down the brow—we sicken and turn away from the spectacle; we have no longer that *pleasure* in our own pain which ought to be the characteristic of true tragedy. It is idle to vindicate this error by any dissimilarity between ancient and modern dramatic art. As Nature, so Art, always has some universal and permanent laws. Longinus rightly considers pathos a part of the sublime, for pity ought to elevate us; but there is nothing to elevate us in the noisome wounds, even of a mythical hero; our human nature is too much forced back into itself—and a proof that in this the ancient art did not differ from the modern, is in the exceeding rarity with which bodily pain is made the instrument of compassion with the

---

42 That the catastrophe should be unhappy! Aristot., Poet., xiii. In the same chapter Aristotle properly places in the second rank of fable those tragedies which attempt the trite and puerile moral of punishing the bad and rewarding the good.

Greek tragedians. The examples of Philoctetes and Hercules are among the exceptions that prove the rule.[43]

XII. Another drawback to our admiration of the "Philoctetes" is in the comparison it involuntarily courts with the "Prometheus" of Æschylus. Both are examples of fortitude under suffering—of the mind's conflict with its fate. In either play a dreary waste, a savage solitude, constitute the scene. But the towering sublimity of Prometheus dwarfs into littleness every image of hero or demigod with which we contrast it. What are the chorus of mariners, and the astute Ulysses, and the boyish generosity of Neoptolemus —what is the lonely cave on the shores of Lemnos—what the high-hearted old warrior, with his torturing wound and his sacred bow—what are all these to the vast Titan, whom the fiends chain to the rock beneath which roll the rivers of hell, for whom the daughters of Ocean are ministers, to whose primeval birth the gods of Olympus are the upstarts of a day, whose soul is the treasure-house of a secret which threatens the realm of heaven, and for whose unimaginable doom earth reels to its base, all the might of divinity is put forth, and Hades itself trembles as it receives its indomitable and awful guest! Yet, as I have before intimated, it is the very grandeur of Æschylus that must have made his poems less attractive on the stage than those of the humane and flexible Sophocles. No visible representation can body forth his thoughts—they overpower the imagination, but they do not come home to our household and familiar feelings. In the contrast between the "Philoctetes" and the "Prometheus" is condensed the contrast between Æschylus and Sophocles. They are both poets of the highest conceivable order; but the one seems almost above appeal to our affections—his tempestuous gloom appals the imagination, the vivid glare of his thoughts pierces the innermost recesses of the intellect, but it is only by accident that he strikes upon the heart. The other, in his grandest flights, remembers that men make his audience, and seems to feel as if art lost the breath of its life when aspiring beyond the atmosphere of human intellect and human passions. The difference between the creations of Æschylus and Sophocles is like the difference between the Satan of Milton and the Macbeth of Shakspeare. Æschylus is equally artful with Sophocles—it is the criticism of ignorance that has said otherwise. But there is this wide distinction—Æschylus is artful as a dramatist to be read, Sophocles as a dramatist to be acted. If we get rid of actors, and stage, and audience, Æschylus will thrill and move us no less than Sophocles, through a more intellectual if less passionate medium.

43 When Aristophanes (in the character of Æschylus) ridicules Euripides for the vulgarity of deriving pathos from the rags, &c., of his heroes, he ought not to have omitted all censure of the rags and sores of the favourite hero of Sophocles. And if the Telephus of the first is represented as a beggar, so also is the Œdipus at Colonus of the latter. Euripides has great faults, but he has been unfairly treated both by ancient and modern hypercriticism.

A poem may be dramatic, yet not theatrical—may have all the effects of the drama in perusal, but by not sufficiently enlisting the skill of the actor—nay, by soaring beyond the highest reach of histrionic capacities, may lose those effects in representation. The storm in "Lear" is a highly dramatic agency when our imagination is left free to conjure tip the angry elements,

> Bid the winds blow the earth into the sea,
> Or swell the curled waters.

But a storm on the stage, instead of exceeding, so poorly mimics the reality, that it can never realize the effect which the poet designs, and with which the reader is impressed. So is it with supernatural and fanciful creations, especially of the more delicate and subtle kind. The Ariel of the "Tempest", the fairies of the "Midsummer Night's Dream", and the Oceanides of the "Prometheus", are not to be represented by human shapes. We cannot say that they are not dramatic, but they are not theatrical. We can sympathize with the poet, but not with the actor. For the same reason, in a lesser degree, all creations, even of human character, that very highly task the imagination, that lift the reader wholly out of actual experience, and above the common earth, are comparatively feeble when reduced to visible forms. The most metaphysical plays of Shakespeare are the least popular in representation. Thus the very genius of Æschylus, that kindles us in the closet, must often have militated against him on the stage. But in Sophocles all—even the divinities themselves—are touched with humanity; they are not too subtle or too lofty to be submitted to mortal gaze. We feel at once that on the stage Sophocles ought to have won the prize from Æschylus; and, as a proof of this, if we look at the plays of each, we see that scarcely any of the great characters of Æschylus could have called into sufficient exercise the powers of an actor. Prometheus on his rock, never changing even his position, never absent from the scene, is denied all the relief, the play and mobility, that an actor needs. His earthly representative could be but a grand reciter. In the "Persians", not only the theatrical, but the dramatic effect is wanting—it is splendid poetry put into various mouths, but there is no collision of passions, no surprise, no incident, no plot, no rapid dialogue in which words are but the types of emotions. In the "Suppliants" Garrick could have made nothing of Pelasgus. In the "Seven before Thebes" there are not above twenty or thirty lines in the part of Eteocles in which the art of the actor could greatly assist the genius of the poet. In the trilogy of the "Agamemnon", the "Chœphori", and the "Orestes", written in advanced years, we may trace the contagious innovation of Sophocles; but still, even in these tragedies, there is no part so effective in representation as those afforded by the great characters of Sophocles. In the first play the hypocrisy and power of Clytemnestra would, it is true, have partially required and elicited the talents of the player; but Agamemnon himself is but a thing of pageant, and the splendid bursts of Cassandra might have been effectively uttered by a very inferior histrionic artist. In the second play, in the scene between Orestes and his mother, and in the gathering madness of Orestes, the art of the poet would unquestionably task to the uttermost the skill of the performer. But in the last play (the Furies), perhaps the sublimest poem of the three, which opens so grandly with the parricide at the sanctuary, and the Furies sleeping around him, there is not one scene from the beginning to the end in which an eminent actor could exhibit his genius.

But when we come to the plays of Sophocles, we feel that a new era in the drama is created; we feel that the artist poet has called into full existence the artist actor. His theatrical effects[44] are tangible, actual—could be represented tomorrow in Paris—in London—everywhere. We find, therefore, that with Sophocles has passed down to posterity the name of the great actor[45] in his principal plays. And I think the English reader, even in the general analysis and occasional translations with which I have ventured to fill so many pages, will perceive that all the exertions of subtle, delicate, and passionate power, even in a modern actor, would be absolutely requisite to do justice to the characters of Œdipus at Colonus, Antigone, Electra, and Philoctetes.

This, then, was the distinction between Æschylus and Sophocles—both were artists, as genius always must be, but the art of the latter adapts itself better to representation. And this distinction in art was not caused merely by precedence in time. Had Æschylus followed Sophocles, it would equally have

---

44 The single effects, not the plots.
45 "Polus, celebrated", says Gellius, "throughout all Greece, a scientific actor of the noblest tragedies". Gellius relates of him an anecdote, that when acting the Electra of Sophocles, in that scene where she is represented with the urn supposed to contain her brother's remains, he brought on the stage the urn and the relics of his own son, so that his lamentations were those of real emotion. Polus acted the hero in the plays of "Œdipus Tyrannus" and "Œdipus at Colonus" (Arrian. apud Stob., xcvii. 28). The actors were no less important personages on the ancient than they are on the modern stage. Aristotle laments that good poets were betrayed into episodes, or unnecessarily prolonging and adorning parts not wanted in the plot, so as to suit the rival performers (Aristot., Poet., ix). Precisely what is complained of in the present day. The Attic performers were the best in Greece—all the other states were anxious to engage them, but they were liable to severe penalties if they were absent at the time of the Athenian festivals (Plut., in Vit. Alex.). They were very highly remunerated. Polus could earn no less than a talent in two days (Plut., in Rhet. Vit.), a much larger sum (considering the relative values of money) than any English actor could now obtain for a proportionate period of service. Though in the time of Aristotle actors as a body were not highly respectable, there was nothing highly derogatory in the profession itself. The high birth of Sophocles and Æschylus did not prevent their performing in their own plays. Actors often took a prominent part in public affairs; and Aristodemus, the player, was sent as ambassador to King Philip. So great, indeed, was the importance attached to this actor, that the state took on itself to send ambassadors in his behalf to all the cities in which he had engagements (Æschin., de Fals. Legat., pp. 30–203, ed. Reiske).

existed—it was the natural consequence of the distinctions in their genius —the one more sublime, the other more impassioned—the one exalting the imagination, the other appealing to the heart. Æschylus is the Michael Angelo of the drama, Sophocles the Raffaele.

XIII. Thus have I presented to the general reader the outline of all the tragedies of Sophocles. In the great length at which I have entered in this, not the least difficult, part of my general task, I have widely innovated on the plan pursued by the writers of Grecian history. For this innovation I offer no excuse. It is her poetry at the period we now examine, as her philosophy in a later time, that makes the *individuality* of Athens. In Sophocles we behold the age of Pericles. The wars of that brilliant day were as pastimes to the mighty carnage of oriental or northern battle. The reduction of a single town, which, in our time, that has no Sophocles and no Pericles, a captain of artillery would demolish in a week, was the proudest exploit of the Olympian of the Agora; a little while, and one defeat wrests the diadem of the seas from the brows of the "Violet Queen"; scanty indeed the ruins that attest the glories of the "Propylæa, the Parthenon, the Porticoes, and the Docks", to which the eloquent orator appealed as the "indestructible possessions" of Athens; along the desolate site of the once tumultuous Agora the peasant drives his oxen—the champion deity[46] of Phidias, whose spectral apparition daunted the barbarian Alaric,[47] and the gleam of whose spear gladdened the mariner beneath the heights of Sunium, has vanished from the Acropolis; but, happily, the age of Pericles has its stamp and effigy in an art more imperishable than that of war—in materials more durable than those of bronze and marble, of ivory and gold. In the majestic harmony, the symmetrical grace of Sophocles, we survey the true portraiture of the genius of the times, and the old man of Colonus still celebrates the name of Athens in a sweeter song than that of the nightingale,[48]—and in melodies that have survived the muses of Cephisus.[49] Sophocles was allegorically the prophet when he declared that in the grave of Œdipus was to be found the sacred guardian and the everlasting defence of the city of Theseus.

46 The Minerva *Promachus*—ἡ μεγάλη Ἀθήνα.
47 Zosimus, v. 294.
48 Œdip. Col., 671, &c.
49 Œdip. Col., 691.

Book VI (a fragment)

FROM THE START OF THE PELOPONNESIAN WAR TO THE BATTLE OF DELIUM, BC 432/1–BC 424/3

Transcribed and edited by Oswyn Murray

INTRODUCTION

Oswyn Murray

At an early stage in my researches, I came across a remark in one of the biographies of Bulwer Lytton that, although only the first two volumes of his *Athens* had ever been published, he had in fact completed the entire work in manuscript. This not unnaturally excited my curiosity, since he had proclaimed that his work would continue in two additional volumes, "and close the records of Athens at that period when the annals of the world are merged into the chronicle of the Roman Empire"; and I was especially anxious to discover how, having so successfully idealized Athens in the period of its rise and zenith, he would manage to treat of its "Fall".

Further research led to the discovery of the manuscript of *Athens* in the Hertfordshire Archives, where it had been deposited (along with many other papers) for safe keeping by the Lytton family. It was a tense moment when, one day in autumn 2002, I travelled to Hertford to inspect the brown paper parcel which contained the manuscript. There indeed was the complete manuscript of the published section of *Athens*, a bundle of many hundred pages of closely written text, covered with multiple corrections and additions, such that it was effectively indecipherable—although presumably the copyist or printer had managed to create the published text from it.

But there too was another parcel, with a note on the cover sheet in a hand not that of Bulwer Lytton, stating, "'History of Athens' Vol. III. Never Published. Probably Finished in *1837*." In fact a number of indications show that the manuscript derives from the early 1840s: a statement in Lytton's handwriting on the cover of ms. 2/3, which is a fair copy of the beginning of the book, reads "Athens—1843"; this presumably was the date at which he began (and laid aside) the preliminary revision of the work that he was currently working on. A letter to Bulwer Lytton preserved with the ms. (2/14a) is dated "20th March, 1844" (see below); this is a reply to a query on the topography of Pylus, which must have been solicited by him at the time when he was writing that section of his narrative, one of the latest episodes in the text. Again a section of manuscript which is on lighter and smaller paper has been inserted in 2/14; its content is drawn from a work hitherto unknown to me, but clearly of importance to Bulwer Lytton, which he referred to as "St John's Manners of antient Greece"; this work, J.A. St John, *The History of the Manners and Customs of Ancient Greece* (3 vols) was published in London in 1842. It seems therefore that he was still at work on the manuscript between 1842 and 1844; the account given in the preface of the posthumous Knebworth edition (quoted above, pp. 15–16), of Bulwer's gradual abandonment of his *Athens* in the face of the competition from first Thirlwall and finally Grote, is correct: the unpublished section refers to the later volumes of Thirlwall (whose work was completed in 1844), and may well have been finally abandoned around 1846, on the publication of the first two volumes of Grote's *History of Greece*, to which it does not refer, in the expectation that Grote's work would one day reach the Peloponnesian war. These first volumes of Grote containing his theory of Greek myth were indeed so far in advance of Bulwer's views of 1837 that he might well fear (unnecessarily, as it turned out) that the later volumes would supersede rather than complement his own efforts. What is now revealed is in fact how completely Bulwer anticipated all the main points of Grote's narrative of Greek political history, and how his own sense of political life makes his narrative of this period infinitely more convincing than that of Grote.

The unpublished manuscript D/EK/W12/2 consists of a large number of quarto sheets loosely made up into booklets, and written on one side of the paper only—approximately 500 manuscript pages, with occasional insertions and notes on the opposite page. This manuscript is clearly the first draft of the third volume; it contains few alterations, and is relatively easy to read. It offers a fascinating insight into Bulwer Lytton's method of composition.

The hand is fluent and confident; the words are usually legible, but the letters are not well formed: it is the general shape of the word, rather than a careful calligraphy that enables one to read the text, and sometimes one can be grossly misled at first reading. The author composed as he wrote, in a phrase or a sentence at a time: he used a quill pen, well filled with ink, and the pen would continue in action with a series of dashes or dots, as he waited for the next phrase to come into his mind. From time to time the pen would degenerate into a broad brush, until it was resharpened with a penknife, or another pen taken up. Apart from these running marks on the page there is little punctuation; words are capitalized almost at random;[1] the ampersand is used instead of "and" almost universally. It is clear that the author is thinking as he writes, with an extraordinary fluency and a remarkable turn of phrase; he leaves it to his amanuensis or typesetter to normalize the punctuation. There is indeed a half-suppressed excitement and an immediacy of response to the subject matter, which explain the vividness and dramatic

---

1 His teacher at preparatory school, "Dr Hooker had an inordinate fondness for capital letters; his pupil was often rallied in later life for continuing to make that peculiarity his own" (T.H.S. Escott, *Edward Bulwer, First Baron Lytton of Knebworth* (London 1910) p. 24).

impact of his style: he writes as he thinks, in short bursts as the phrases come fully formed into his mind. The author is completely caught up in his subject; and, even when he is following a source such as Thucydides closely, he imparts a new vivacity to the original.

The unpublished section of Bulwer Lytton's *Athens* is a narrative history of the period from the events leading up to the start of the Peloponnesian war in 431 BC to the ninth year of the war (423 BC). It covers the events recorded in the first four books of Thucydides' *History*; there are full accounts of the causes of the war, the evacuation of the Attic countryside in the face of invasion, the siege of Platæa, the funeral oration of Pericles, the Great Plague of Athens, the death of Pericles, the struggle of rival Athenian leaders and the rise of the demagogues, the growth of the "revolutionary spirit" throughout Greece, and the great Athenian victory over the Spartans at Pylus. The later stages of the narrative are concerned with the rise of Cleon, his character and his military and political successes. This is the first positive picture of Cleon known to me. The story breaks off with the preparations for the northern campaign in which both Brasidas and Cleon were killed, and the way was opened for the conclusion of the first part of the war with the Peace of Nicias concluded in 421 BC. The narrative of the first war, known as the Archidamian war (after King Archidamus, the Spartan royal general), is therefore virtually complete.

But Athens remains at the height of her power: we are not really in a position to understand how Bulwer would have envisaged its fall, still less how he would have dealt with the succeeding three centuries before the Roman conquest. In the course of his account he gives us some clues as to how he would have treated the revolutionary oligarchical movements in Athens of the period 411–404 BC—from a radical perspective, and in terms of the *trahison des clercs* (betrayal by the intellectuals) which modern writers agree destroyed Athens.[2] Perhaps the most fascinating aspect of this story would have been how he dealt with "the splendid Alcibiades" (Book VI ch. IV sec. I), whose youthful excesses as an Athenian dandy he begins to describe, and whose character so closely resembled that of Bulwer Lytton himself: his contemporaries often noted the parallel with "the young Alcibiades" for praise or criticism, and Bulwer was clearly flattered by it. He would surely have offered a critical self-portrait worthy of the author of *Pelham*; we might compare the dramatic presentation as a Regency masque of the great scandal of the profanation of the Eleusinian Mysteries, in the youthful fragment *Scenes from "Athenian Revels"* (1824) by his contemporary Lord Macaulay.[3]

2 This view is expressed most dramatically in the clandestine work written in hiding during the régime of Marshal Pétain by the famous protagonist of Jewish-Catholic relations, Jules Isaac, *Les Oligarques. Essai d'histoire partiale* (Paris 1946).
3 *Macaulay's Complete Works vol. XI. Speeches, Poems and Miscellaneous Writings* I (1898), pp. 228–53.

The main source of Bulwer Lytton's narrative is of course Thucydides, studied in the newly published (1830–35) three-volume edition of Thomas Arnold, Lytton Strachey's "eminent Victorian", reforming headmaster of Rugby, and Regius Professor of Modern History at Oxford (now chiefly remembered as the father of Matthew Arnold). He also made extensive and intelligent use of other authors such as Aristophanes and Euripides, as well as the biographies of Plutarch and the parallel historical narrative of Diodorus. References to modern works are relatively common, and include especially the work of St John mentioned above and the English translation of August Boeckh's *Public Economy of Athens* (1828).

Since Thucydides is the main source for this section of his history, I have not thought it worth reproducing the more simple narrative sections: there is much on military events, especially in north Greece, which is merely a retelling in exuberant early Victorian prose of the narrative in Thucydides; and there are a number of speeches which Bulwer Lytton has translated or adapted at length from his author. My selection of passages from the manuscripts concentrates on those aspects of the history of the period where Bulwer Lytton reveals his own opinions and comments on events. I have included a small number of characteristic comments; the longer passages are concerned with the siege of Athens, the plague, and the development of Athenian political life within the beleagured city—a series of imaginative recreations of the mental state of Athenian society which are of outstanding vividness and insight. Finally I have included a full account of the events at Pylus in 425, in order to demonstrate the power of Bulwer Lytton's narrative technique and his emotional involvement in these dramatic events.

This section of his narrative in particular was immediately relevant to the greatest contemporary event in the history of modern Greece, the destruction by the combined fleets of Britain, France, and Russia, of the Turkish fleet at the battle of Navarino in 1826—an event which was surrounded by controversy at the time, when it was both alleged and denied that the British admiral in charge had exceeded his orders (in fact the British Foreign Secretary had died during the campaign, and British policy had changed), and also insinuated that the French fleet had surreptitiously shelled the Russians in an act of "friendly fire" in revenge for Napoleon's retreat from Moscow. Whatever the undoubtedly devious and conflicting intentions of the ill-matched allies, the destruction of the new Ottoman fleet ensured the liberation of Greece from Turkish rule and the creation of the modern kingdom of Greece. No contemporary European could fail to be moved by Bulwer's dramatic representation of an earlier battle in what he firmly and correctly believed, against the opinion of contemporary scholarship, was a virtually unchanged Bay of Navarino.

It was therefore with considerable excitement that I found a loose letter inserted in Bulwer Lytton's manuscript from someone whom (after a brief period of puzzlement) I recalled was actually the British admiral in charge at the battle of Navarino. Edward Codrington had been removed from active service as a result of his heroic exploit or monumental blunder, and spent the rest of his life in a vain attempt to vindicate his reputation. At this date he was in fact a fellow Member of the reformed Parliament; and it is clear that Bulwer Lytton, worried by the scholarly controversy about the ancient topography of the Bay of Pylus that he found in Arnold's commentary on Thucydides, had written to his colleague requesting the opinion of one who had actually fought in the bay. Codrington's response is hardly conclusive, but nevertheless historically interesting:

2/14a Letter on black-edged mourning paper from Sir Edward Codrington commander of the allied forces at the battle of Navarino, and from 1832–9 liberal MP for Davenport.

92 Eaton Square
20th March, 1844

Dear Sir Edward,

You have led me into a view of Navarin which I did not contemplate. I have read the references in both the books & also the description of Col. Leake; I must say his description seems to me very good. The map in Doctor Arnold's book appears to me quite correct, as indeed it must be, being copied from Captain Smith's survey. As to the width of the entrances round Sphacteria, historians are very subject to mistakes of that sort, even in these times: but certainly it would require many more such craft as those people had to fill up the space than is calculated on by Thucydides. The result however of my perusal of these books, is, a conviction that I am much less capable of deciding the knotty points in dispute than yourself or either of the authors before me.—I certainly understood when in the harbor of Navarin, that it was the ancient Pylus, & that what the map marks Paliocastro was old Navarin.

Your very sincere & faithful
Edwd Codrington

As you are good enough to mention my proceedings in those parts favorably, I would propose your perusing my defensive papers: but that someone has borrowed them without my recollecting whom, & has not yet returned them.

The manuscript

I give the selections from the manuscript in the correct order of the various sections, with brief notes on the manuscript. The punctuation and capitalization have been normalized in the spirit of the published sections of the work, although I have allowed the author to retain his capitals when they appear to be used for dramatic effect. The author began numbering his chapters and paragraphs, with the assumption that book V would continue (as originally stated in the published version) to the death of Pericles. Chapter divisions continue to chapter III; paragraphs are numbered as far as chapter III paragraph IX (see my note there). In the transcription I have renumbered the chapters to begin as Book VI, while respecting Bulwer Lytton's paragraph divisions and their numeration as far as possible until they run out. All changes to his numeration are printed in italics, with the original numbering in square brackets.

The manuscript is numbered D/EK/W12/2, and consists of a series of separate manuscript sections beginning as follows:

2/1 A loose page of notes headed "Preliminary Chapter" giving a set of topics to be covered.

2/2 A miscellaneous set of notes not all about Athens. They concern Euripides: two pages bound in with various quotations and excerpts relating to Pericles, etc., Athenian manners and dress. Miscellaneous notes on gardening, agriculture, linguistic expressions, etc.; notes on Neopythagoreans; Horace Satires and Odes: approx 80 pages. Some of these notes appear to be in part notes of preliminary reading for Athens, but the booklet has also been used for a number of other purposes.

2/3 16 sheets with cover inscription: Athens 1843
This is clearly a second draft of the start of 2/4. Transcript as follows:

CHAPTER I
[VOL III BOOK V
CONTINUED: CH. IV]

*Introduction—events leading to war—the Athenian character
—speeches in Thucydides—the night attack on Platæa—the nature
of Greek city government—preparations for the siege—reflections on
the true causes of the war*

I. We have traced the rise of the Athenian commonwealth—we have now
before us its meridian and decline. In the Peloponnesian war we approach
events not more memorable in the annals of the ancient world,
than instructive to the societies of the modern. For as it has
been justly said, "there is an ancient and a modern period in the History of
every People, the ancient differing, and the modern in many essential points
agreeing with that in which we live".[4] In Greece then, as through Europe
now, a great popular spirit was at work. To the earlier times, when aristocracy
protects freedom from the single tyrant, to the later æra of civilization when
wealth becomes the innovating principle and enfeebles by extending the
privileges of nobility and birth, now succeeded the graver struggle between
property and numbers—that struggle which has produced the greatest
calamities in the past, and with which unreasoning fanaticism and speculative
philosophy have alike threatened the futures of existing nations. Whatever
our several opinions and predilections, we can only profit by the lessons
which the history of this struggle in the most brilliant period of Grecian
civilization should bestow, by preserving the disproportionate judgment
which distinguishes the guide who bequeathed to mankind the narrative of
the Peloponnesian war—κτῆμα ἐς αἰεί—"an everlasting possession", not
to subserve the aims of malignant partisans, but to enrich the experience of
every statesman and warn the factions of every land.

INTRODUCTION

---

4 "Thus the largest portion of that history which we commonly call ancient is practically
modern, as it describes society in a stage analogous to that in which it now is; while on the
other hand, much of what is called modern history is practically ancient, as it relates to a
state of things which has passed away." Appendix I. Arnold's Thucyd. vol. I. p. 630.

II. We left Athens in the enjoyment of that peace which is advantageous to nations in proportion to the civilization they possess, in proportion as empire can be extended by commerce, and prosperity ennobled by the arts. But to the eyes of the discerning the peace was hollow and insecure. In the thirty years' truce established between Athens and the Peloponnesian confederacy, it had been agreed that any state not already allied to one of the two great powers might join either as it pleased,[5]—a provision which evinces the demarcation still existing between both, and the desire of each to strengthen its power for war in the very articles which composed the peace. But by this provision it is clear that neither Athens nor Sparta could assist or receive those states already in alliance with its rival—an advantage of immense importance to the Athenians, whose allies were in fact dependents, and who were thus enabled to defy the desertion and complete the subjugation of the numerous commonwealths that supplied their treasury and swelled their fleets. Thus they had been permitted to enforce the submission of Samos, and thus the Spartans were obliged to refuse aid to the aristocracy of Mitylene who desired to free their city from the ascendency of Athens.[6] A peace that thus served to consolidate the ascendency of the Athenians could hardly fail to dispose to war, by augmenting the jealous apprehensions of the rival powers. The reduction of Samos, which established amidst the silence of Greece the maritime sovereignty of Athens[7]—the rapid growth of the settlements by which the Athenians multiplied their facilities of commerce and of conquest—and obtained by Thurii in the West, by Naxos in the East, by the Chersonesus in the North, the openings to wider empire—the calm but obvious policy of Pericles at once to concentrate and to restrain the energies of his countrymen—restrain from distant and hazardous enterprise —concentrate upon the attainment of the general supremacy of Greece; and more than all, perhaps the democratic institutions which the Athenians established wherever their influence could prevail—concurred to alarm the Peloponnesian states with fears of a power that menaced them without by its undisguised ambition, and within by the all penetrating contagion of popular innovation. Already in Greece the expectation of coming war was general;[8] and as in times of revolutions the conduct of individuals becomes what men predict that it will be[9]—so events are ripened by the common presentiment of their necessity. Perhaps in every war, certainly in every revolution (the struggle now to be narrated was war and revolution both) the causes are of slow growth—and the pretext is but the excuse for determinations

5 Thucyd., i. 35.
6 Thucyd., iii. 2.
7 Wachsmuth para. 61.
8 Cf. Thucyd., i. 1–ii. 8.
9 Mignet.

already ripened, and passions long silently inflamed. Here as is usual the pretext was found amidst events least to be foreseen and not materially connected with the real causes which rendered the peace of Athens incompatible with the jealousies of confederate rivals opposed to her polity and distrusting her ambition.

II–III. BC 432. Discussion of the events leading to the Peloponnesian war, as described in Thucydides: Ægina—Megara—Corcyra.

EVENTS LEADING TO WAR   *2/4: This starts with a crossed out section "Vol III Book V continued. The causes of the Peloponnesian War" on Corcyra (as rewritten in 2/3). The first three pages are crossed out, then the ms. continues with the Corcyra episode (27 pages); 7 inserted pages are a second draft of Potidæa, then 11 pages on Potidæa. On p. 7 of this a note, concerning the breach of the alliance between Perdiccas and Athens (Thucyd., i. 62):*

Mr Mitford says with a dishonesty not rarely shewn by him—that "probably some gross insolence of the Athenian government which the contemporary historian would prudently avoid to notice offended him!!"—there is not only no ground, however shadowy, for this accusation—but the very suddenness of the Macedonian king's desertion left no time for the display of insolence on the part of the Athenian government; and Mr Mitford must have read Thucydides to very little purpose, if he could seriously suppose that that candid historian would have refrained from imputing blame to the government, if there were any cause for it. In fact there would have been no prudence in the case: the affair was sufficiently remote at the time Thucydides wrote, to allow the truth to be safely spoken. Dishonest assumptions are almost worse because less easily perceived than distorted facts. The attack on Beroa by the Athenian army may furnish excuse to Perdiccas. But we should be very wary in the absence of all authority, in supposing with Arnold that this was perfidiously made. It is quite as possible that Perdiccas had already broken the treaty, as that he broke it after the attack on Beroa; in fact it is much more probable, for it was not the habit of the Athenians shamelessly to violate any treaty, while the whole character of Perdiccas is that of a thoroughly unprincipled person.

2/14 is misplaced: it belongs at this point. The last numbered page in 2/4 is 28, and there is an insert on smaller paper; but if this is ignored the remainder of the ms. reaches to an unnumbered p. 43. 2/14 follows on directly. It starts with a paragraph numbered XV and a page numbered "p. 44", and continues the Corinthian speech in favour of war at Sparta.

IV. On the description of Athens in the Corinthian speech (Thucyd., i. 70) there is a note:

THE ATHENIAN
CHARACTER

It must be confessed that this masterly sketch of the Ionian character drawn by the unfriendly hand of the Corinthian furnishes the best explanation of the growth of Athenian greatness. If we compare it with the more flattering likenesses subsequently submitted to our attention in the orations of Pericles, and strike the medium between the two, it would be impossible to withhold admiration from a national character so vigorous and so brilliant. The student of the attributes of Race cannot but be struck with the similarity which in many points the Ionian character bears to the Anglo-Saxon: and few modern works will perhaps throw more light upon the causes that engendered feud and agitation amongst the mingled colonies of Greece —nay even less directly upon those which divided with lines of iron the two great confederacies verging to war—than the Report upon Lower Canada published by the late Earl of Durham: contrast the distinctions of the Anglo-Saxon and French race, so ably therein depicted.[10] Examine those qualities of the former, which tend as it were to devour all power in whatever land or amidst whatever population they fix their settlements; and turning then to the history of ancient Greece, a better notion of the contests that rent and exhausted its two main families will be obtained, than by half the voluminous learning of Closet Scholars and Academic Critics.

Ms. p. 62: The speeches in Thucydides (Thucyd., i. 22).

V. [XXI.] The speeches ascribed by Thucydides to Pericles have other claims to authenticity than those harangues which he ascribes to strangers in the assemblies of foreign states. What Thucydides him-
SPEECHES IN THUCYDIDES
self says with regard to the harangues or speeches that adorn his history is as follows:

> As for the several speeches of individuals, either when about to enter on the war or when engaged in it, it were indeed hard both for me, when present, and to others who retailed them to me, to remember with exactness and precision the words that were spoken. But according as it appeared to me that the several persons could most befittingly have expressed themselves on the matters successively before them, adhering at the same time as closely as possible to the general sense of what was actually spoken—so have I recorded their speeches.

10 "They (the French Canadians) remain an old and stationary society in the midst of a new and progressive world." Lord Durham's report.

It is clear then that Thucydides, both as frequently himself one of the audience, and as having much more ample means of information from his fellow-citizens, had a very superior advantage in reporting the speeches made at Athens compared with those delivered by foreigners in other states; considering especially that in the Spartan debates, the foreign envoys and deputies were excluded, it is difficult to know how he arrived at even the general sense of what was said by such speakers as Archidamus and Sthenelaidas; yet the speech of the latter—it must be owned—bears strong marks of individuality.

It is even by no means impossible that of such speeches, though not published by Pericles himself—crude and sketched reports were taken at the time.[11] At all events the substance of his harangues, with the very words of the more striking passages, would long dwell in the minds of many of his hearers—at a day when the faculty of memory was infinitely more cultivated and tenacious than it is at present. Yet it is clear that Thucydides, writing for men many of whom had heard the very speeches professed to be delivered, could not venture much to add or to invent. In the case of Corinthians or Spartans, he might reasonably embody the best arguments his own wisdom could suggest; but he could only, with propriety and grace, ascribe to Pericles the very statements he uttered. And he who has so well depicted the laconic energy of Sthenelaidas, must have assayed also much of the manner of his more congenial countryman. We are justified therefore in drawing a most interesting distinction between the orations of Pericles and those elsewhere given—although no doubt the style of the orator is often merged with that of the historian, we may yet reasonably believe that in the main we are listening to the mind of him[12] who persuaded the most gifted, versatile, and fiery audience which eloquence ever delighted or patriotism aroused. And if from these remains the grace of Thucydides has not refined away the rhetorical dross common to the greatest orators—humour, the passionate declamation, the personal allusions and dexterous retorts by which statesmen addressing large and miscellaneous assemblies are usually compelled to give effect to the simplicity of argument—the audience itself seems yet more worthy of admiration than the orator, so inestimably does the whole substance as well as manner of the speech upon this occasion address itself to the intellect and reason—eloquent from the absence of all vulgar eloquence, and striking home to the common understanding simply from the clearness of its views, the earnestness of its purpose, and the peculiar

11 "There is some reason to suppose that stenography which was commonly practised at no long period afterwards was then to some degree known." Bloomfield, vol. I p. 52.

12 I desire therefore, on mature consideration, to correct an opinion too hastily advanced in the first edition of this work, Vol II . . . viz., to the effect that we cannot accept as genuine specimens of the eloquence of Pericles the orations given to him in Thucydides.

closeness with which it grapples with the strongest arguments of the opposing parties.

The speech of Pericles on the necessity of war (Thucyd., i. 140–4) is given in extenso in direct speech, with notes relating to Arnold's edition of Thucydides.

VI. [XXIII.] *The narrative continues with preparations for war.* BC 431: *description of Platæa (Thucyd., ii. 2ff.) and the night attack on*

THE NIGHT ATTACK
ON PLATÆA

Platæa by the Thebans, which was repulsed by the Platæans.

The Thebans retired from the country; the Platæans in all haste removed their effects without into the protection of their walls, and then put to death their prisoners to the number of one hundred and eighty, among whom was Eurymachus.[13] By the laws of all nations ancient or modern the Platæans were amply justified in the execution of the perpetrators of so insidious and criminal an attempt. But the justification ceases if they had entered into any compact to the contrary with the Thebans.[14]

[*The following passage is deleted in the ms.:*]

VII. Greek history is often rendered obscure by the habit of the historian to speak generally of the acts of the *people* instead of the acts of the *government.*

THE NATURE OF GREEK
CITY GOVERNMENT

"The Athenians did this, and the Platæans did that"— when in fact it was the administration that acted for either. What scope would there be for the blackest accusations against the English or any modern people, if in the gloomier passages of their history the same mode of statement were resorted to; if the people were to be judged for the excesses of faction, the crimes of tyrants, the absurdities of governments, if the fires of Smithfield or the barbarities committed in Ireland, if the massacre of St Bartholemew—if the atrocities of Pizarro in the new world—if the heartless butcheries of Ezelino Romano or the Borgia, were ascribed indifferently to the people and not to the individuals or the parties by whom the guilt was incurred.

Even in that latter case some excuse must be made for the excitement of the population: the compact agreed to by their leaders—those leaders might be unable to enforce upon the inflamed multitude, yet quivering under its

---

13 Diodorus says that the Platæans restored their prisoners. I wish that we could believe Diodorus instead of Thucydides—confirmed as the latter is by Demosthenes and Polyænus. Diodorus might have been misled by the fact that the Platæans gave up the *bodies* of the Thebans.

14 And even by their own account they are not free from blame. It was a subterfuge to promise release to the prisoners provided a treaty were executed—and then to make treaty impossible by their execution.

own deliverance from servitude or massacre. In the history of every people and under every form of government are to be found the follies of human infirmity and the criminal excesses of human passion. To judge of states as of individuals, the evil must be compared with the good, the glory with the shame; and a brave and generous spirit will not be reluctant to admit such palliation as Reason will allow for a single act of violence or frenzy in that scanty but illustrious population[15] who shared the laurels of the Athenians at Marathon, Salamis, and Platæa.

VIII. [XXV.] The Platæans had contrived on the admission of the Thebans —to despatch a messenger to Athens, and a second upon the defeat and capture of the enemy. The prompt and vigilant administration under Pericles, upon the arrival of the first messenger, had given orders to seize all the Bœotians who were in Attica; on the arrival of the second, foreseeing the excitement of the victors they despatched a herald to the Platæans, enjoining them not to proceed to any extremities with the Theban prisoners, till they themselves had consulted on the matter. This humane mandate arrived too late; and the Athenian government, perceiving that the first blow of the war was struck, hastened to provision and garrison Platæa for the anticipated siege. The women (except one hundred and ten—left to cook the victuals, &c.), the children, and the aged or infirm among the men of the little commonwealth found an asylum at Athens.

PREPARATIONS FOR THE SIEGE

IX. [XXVI.] Such were the causes, such the commencement of that long and eventful war, fatal to the best blood and the fairest lands of Greece, exhausting her strength and ultimately ruinous to her liberties. Yet is it difficult to perceive what wisdom could at that crisis have averted the calamity. The dragon-seed had been sown long before the armed men sprang up. If we look to the ostensible causes—the alliance with Corcyra, the orders sent to Potidæa, and lastly the Theban assault on Platæa—it is impossible to fix blame on the Athenians. They could not have permitted Corinth to subdue and annex to her own maritime power the fleet of Corcyra without the most serious and certain danger to their dominion of the seas—a danger perhaps extending to the internal security of Athens itself. They could not have permitted their tributary town of Potidæa to retain the magistrature

REFLECTIONS ON THE TRUE CAUSES OF THE WAR

15 After all it is amusing to see historians lavishing virtuous indignation on an act of equivocal justice, or if they please dishonourable frenzy, committed by a population on the very day after a midnight invasion of their liberties and homes—yet pass briefly and indifferently by the far more horrible and long premeditated design of the oligarchic faction to massacre their fellow-citizens in their sleep.

and be submitted to the influence of the hostile Corinth, without resigning the stronghold to their most valuable possessions in Thrace. Whatever the guilt of the Thebans or the unjust revenge of the Platæans, they were innocent of the one and had sought to avert the other; even in regard to the stern decree against the Megarians, the speech of Pericles will probably have convinced the reader that, as a free state, Athens could not listen to the imperious dictates of a hostile equal—and for the rest, that as a great empire she could not have foregone without a struggle the dominion she had acquired. From first to last the Athenian administration adhered indeed to the precise stipulation of the existing treaty, viz., that all causes of dispute should be referred to judicial arbitrament.

But we have already seen that the ostensible were not the real and irremediable causes of the war. "The Spartans", says Thucydides, "were influenced in their vote that the war was to be commenced, not so much from the representation of their allies as from their fear of the growing power of the Athenians." In this apprehension the Spartans are not to blame. Doubtless the time had come when it might be reasonably feared that the most active, wealthy, and adventurous of the Hellenic states would rapidly absorb the rest—that in a word all Greece would be one Athens; yet, as the Athenian envoys are said to have remarked at Sparta, the increase of the Power was in the nature of the Power itself. Its commencement was in the pre-eminent services of Athens in the Persian war; the consequent fortification of their city and the Piræan harbour, the advantages of Nature in their threefold port, their early maritime habits, the victory of Salamis, the genius of Themistocles, opened to their energies the wide realm of the ocean. The incapable excesses of the Spartan Pausanias, the popular virtues of Aristides, drew to them the voluntary allegiance of the allies and formally raised them to the acknowledged empire of the seas. The safety of Greece, and the probable danger of renewed aggression from the Persians, rendered the maintenance of a fleet indispensable. Athens by common consent was empowered to raise the necessary tribute from the various states. On their refusal she had an excuse to enforce the demand. In human affairs power never rests at the limit to which excuse is confined: the allies, too often unwilling to serve in person, granted as we have already seen subsidies, which went as intended to the increase of the Athenian navy; and general supineness checked the power of the individual state. In all this there ran the universal law, which leads some races to rise at the expense of others, and proportions political power to national energies. In her judicial treatment of her dependencies, Athens was rigorous rather than unjustly aggressive: as her ambassadors observed at Sparta, in lawsuits against them in their own courts there was sufficient impartiality to make her often the losing party; while as to fiscal tyranny, the amount levied from each state appears to have been inconsiderable. And in fine, if we look to the example and to the maxims of other contemporaneous states, Athens was at least as moderate as they in the exercise of her power, while more justified in its original foundation.[16]

But there, as I have elsewhere enforced, our excuses for this illustrious commonwealth must rest. Power usurped, under whatever pretext or however exercised, brings its own punishments and retribution. It was no sin peculiar in her form of government; monarchies as in Macedon, aristocracies as in Thebes, were yet more unscrupulous in their ambition; it was no sin peculiar even to the vices and errors of the age. For that one state should subject its neighbours is no uncommon spectacle in the history of the modern world. But a sin it was no less—though general in the constitution of mortal affairs—that Athens had found states free, and retained them subject, that she had imposed her own institutions, however popular, on commonwealths not always prepared to receive them, and that she pampered her own arts by tributes originally intended against a common foe. Hence deservedly did she attract the odium as well as the admiration of her rivals —hence naturally did she excite the hatred, amidst the reluctant allegiance, of her allies—hence, though innocent in the ostensible causes of the Peloponnesian war, was she primarily guilty in the one less patent and avowed. Hence, as she had founded her right on force, force as employed against her had its rights in turn; and the curse of the Peloponnesian war was but the slow and predestined avenger of the subjugation of Naxos and the seizure of the common treasury of Delos.

It is true that, in addition to the causes of the war already enumerated, there was one yet more vast and permanent than all, in which to a lover of the more popular systems of government, Athens might at the first glance be considered the Defender of Liberty. It was a war partly of policy, partly of race, partly also of *opinion*—a great struggle between the elements of Oligarchy —enlisted with Sparta—of Democracy with Athens. But the latter vitiated the solemn interests she professed to advocate; for the democracies she planted

16 Isocrates (Panathen.) very fairly sums up the principal authorities for the Athenian sovereignty. He observes that no state had a right to blame the Athenians, unless it had been milder in the exercise of its own rule—that it was impossible to preserve the obedience of so many cities without punishing the disobedient, that after all, they had long retained their sovereignty and yet how few were the examples of their severity, that (and this is highly important in their defence) such of their subject allies as remained faithful, had been most prosperous, and that they had never sought jealously to weaken them by sowing internal dissensions like the Spartans, further than to assist the population in establishing popular government—that the Peloponnesians in three months had put to death without legal condemnation more than Athens had arraigned during its whole sovereignty. All this is true, and all, nevertheless, subordinate to the main apology—viz., a state never can voluntarily part with what it has once obtained. Who could ask England to surrender Ireland, or India, or Canada? True, the relation between Athens and her allies was not precisely the same as that between England and her possessions; but in both the main distinction is identical, viz., sovereignty and subjection.

and maintained were often forced and exotic, not the natural growth of the public spirit of the states thus revolutionized; more than this, they were democracies subjected to the principality—a kind of municipal liberty controlled by remote and imperial despotism. Thus she did not secure to herself even the love of the populations she had enfranchised with the one hand, to hold dependent by the other; the popular enthusiasm without which the democratic principle is the weakest of all was not enlisted on her side; and instead of regarding the Arch Republic of their land as the generous champion of enlightened Freedom, the Greeks for the most part looked to the formal Sparta, with her combination of oligarchies, as the destined liberator of Hellas from the assumptions [*sic*] of an aspiring Power—which planted democracies only as the outguards to her towering and solitary citadel.

CHAPTER II
[CHAPTER VI: TO THE PLAGUE]

Preparations for war—omens—the Peloponnesian strength—the Athenian—Peloponnesian army assemble at the Isthmus—Archidamus sends a messenger to Athens who is refused an audience—Pericles commander-in-chief persuades the Athenians to desert their farms and villages—sketch of Athenian rural life—effects of crowding the population within the walls—Archidamus invades Attica—resentment and agitation of the Athenians—first public appearance of Cleon the demagogue—wisdom of Pericles and retreat of Archidamus—retaliations of the Athenians—siege of Methone—the rise of Brasidas—operations at Phia and Sollium—Astacus and Cephallenia—incursions on the Locrians—fortification of Atalante, and expulsion of the Æginetans to whom Sparta gives refuge in Thyrea—alliance with Sitalces and reconciliation with Perdiccas—invasion of Megara—funeral at the Ceramicus—the celebrated oration of Pericles—eclipse of the sun—the "Medea" of Euripides

I–III. Description of the allies and resources of each. Numbers of Athenian soldiers according to Boeckh; forts; Pericles was the first to institute soldiers' pay (a reference to Boeckh, vol I. p. 363). Financial resources of Athens. Archidamus invades.

IV. Before this, and while the enemy were yet assembling, Pericles, who was appointed commander in chief with, as was customary, nine colleagues,

PERICLES COMMANDER-IN-CHIEF PERSUADES THE ATHENIANS TO DESERT THEIR FARMS AND VILLAGES — SKETCH OF ATHENIAN RURAL LIFE

having at a public assembly supported the courage and hopes of the citizens by a faithful and detailed account of their resources, had induced the Athenians to forestall the march of the foe by removing from the farms and villas which they held in Attica into the walls of the city. This was the most painful and ungracious of all the preparations for the war. From the earliest period, the Athenians had been attached to rural occupation and a country life. Though for many ages the Attic burghs had been incorporated with the city, yet all the beautiful associations of religion connected the various families with the rustic hearths of their ancestors and the altars of their peculiar gods. To drive such men within the walls was not only to compel them to abandon their homes but their usages and manners, their patriarchal fanes, their very city itself—for the burgh and not the metropolis was their city.[1] This fondness for rural life was felt by most of the Athenians—and doubtless not only the wealthier, but many of the middle class engaged in trade at shops or warehouses within the walls,[2] had their proper homes with their families in the neighbouring country. After the Persian war the Athenians settled back to their old haunts with increased affection. Their villas, destroyed by the invader, were restored with the elegance of the new refinement and the costliness of increased wealth; with such predilections, it need scarcely be said that no less a care was lavished upon the land itself than on the villa. The very difficulties in the nature of the soil[3]—in great parts poor and stony—tended but to sharpen the ingenuities of industry and increase a knowledge of agricultural science. For the variety of the produce in Attica sufficiently attests the artificial means that were used to enrich the original thinness of the land. From the easy and copious supply of corn from abroad, it is clear that corn would not have been grown at a profit in the unfavourable soil of Attica without considerable art in the management of the ground and the creation of a new stratum; yet it produced barley and even wheat,[4] though the main staple consisted of olives, wine, and figs. The devastation of these fruits of an artificial soil must in many places have undone the work of long years; and thus, besides the pang of abandoning his home, the rural Athenian must have contemplated the most ruinous injury to his property.

The following section is on smaller paper, and is clearly a later insert, derived from reading of St John:

V. Perhaps indeed the imagination can scarcely exaggerate the charm of the country life which the Athenians were compelled to abandon. The landscapes around the city were scarcely more blest by Nature than adorned by the elegance of Art. Amidst groves of pine stood the graceful villas surrounded with the peristyles that shaded from the sun. On the gardens that stretched behind, the Athenian taste lavished its fondest care; between copses, alleys

---

1 And the Athenian usually subjoined to his own name the burgh to which he belonged.
2 The Dicæopolis of Aristophanes—that is the Personation of the Athenian People, is an instance of the half and half life of a citizen of that commonwealth. At the commencement of the play ("Acharnians") he is one of the turbulent Assembly at the Pnyx, even there cursing the town and sighing for the fields and peace; and the very next shift of the scene places him in his native burgh, sacrificing not very decorously to Bacchus.
3 Thucyd., i. 2.
4 It was even judged necessary to institute a law strictly prohibiting the exportation of corn: Ulpian, ad Demosth., in Timocr.

and arcades of the many trees which luxuriated under the delicious climate, bloomed parterres of flowers, the hues of which were assimilated or contrasted with the nicest art; there abounded the golden crocuses[5] dear to Athenian poets, the lilies, whether in their natural silver or crimsoned by cinnabar or purpled by the lees of wine,[6] the natural violet and abundant roses that blossomed in several varieties with every month, the iris, the hyacinth, the narcissus—in a word the "omnis copia narium"—the whole wealth of sweets; the mild winter had its separate garden, as well as the glowing summer. From the hills the breeze scattered the odours of the pomegranate.[7] Under the arcades, the fountains diffused the coldness—or the stream wound its silver way—by violet banks and wild thyme, and fragrant reeds and overhanging willows; statues and fanes crowned the eminences or closed the vistas. Beneath the porticoes, and gazing on these scenes, the owner held banquets with guests crowned with chaplets—now, as the lyre and myrtle circled round, listening to lively impromptu song; now conversing on the brilliant themes which in the age of Aspasia and Pericles, of Socrates and Gorgias, of Euripides and Aristophanes, united pleasure and wit with philosophy and the muse. Beyond the garden extended the orchard with its briary fence, enriched by all the fruits which commerce could collect from distant shores—the peach and the nectarine, the citron, the fig, the pear, the mulberry, the pistachio—and hallowed by the monuments of the dead.

From the orchard might extend the vineyard—usually trained into arches —terrace upon terrace on sunny slopes; or the silvery olives, which marked the boundary, ripened in venerable groves and were hung with votive offerings. If from these more luxurious abodes the eye turned to the busier landscape, it saw everywhere the happy industry of a population secure and free. The narrow limits of the soil occupied those small subdivisions, and that eager desire for land, which produce minute and careful cultivation. Nothing known to the art of husbandry was neglected. The most barren hillock still could be cultured into a vineyard, or at the least serve for the hives of the renowned Athenian bees. It was a favourite speculation to purchase bad land, and improve it into good.[8] The Athenian exhibited in his farm the same energy he displayed in the Agora; his resources of gain were wonderful. From the skilful breeding of cattle or the elaborate study of manures,[9] to the fattening of partridges, quails, and thrushes, the produce

5 Soph., Oedip.Col.
6 St John's *Manners of Antient Greece* Book V ch. II p. 309, to which eloquent and erudite work generally throughout this passage I beg to acknowledge my obligations.
7 St John's *Greece* Vol. II, bk. v, ch. 2.
8 Xen., Œcon., xx. 22.
9 St John's *Greece* Vol. II, pp. 383f.

from the milk of cows, goats, and sheep, the filling of each interstice of ground, with something to turn to profit, even if only parsley and rue, or lentils, vetches and lupins—everything attested their love of labour, their enjoyment of rural life, their ingenuity, thrift, and patience.

VI. From homes so dear to the luxurious and employments so pleasing to the industrious, great was the reluctance and severe the hardship to be torn. But to the poorer freemen in many cases the change must have been that from welcome labour to dejected pauperism. Such men could only, for the most part, have found their existence in a city crowded with every subdivision of work, from the bounty of their tribe, or the charity of the state.

[*End of smaller insert, back to the main ms. with a deleted sentence identical to above.*]

But the inevitable necessity of a war carried to their gates left the Athenians no option but to subscribe to the exhortations of Pericles; and their leader sought to reconcile them to the evil by his own sacrifices. A relation peculiar to the Greeks was that between Host and Guest; arising in remote periods, before inns and accommodation for strangers were created by the intercourse and wants of civilized commerce, from the absolute necessity of inculcating hospitality as a part of religion, it still existed as an enduring and inviolable connexion. Sometimes a wealthy and eminent individual acted as host to a whole state, receiving its envoys, &c.; sometimes on the other hand a whole state considered itself the host of an individual. This was the public connexion: a more private and yet more sacred one existed between man and man, and now bound together Archidamus and Pericles. And the minister foreseeing that either through private regard, or from some political device to bring him into suspicion with his countrymen, Archidamus might spare his lands amidst the general ravage, publicly declared that if this were done they should pass from that time to the property of the state.

With much reluctance and dejection the Athenians now removed their flocks and cattle to Eubœa and the neighbouring islands, their families with their furniture and portable effects—nay, the very timber of their houses—into Athens. But the ancient cities, closely confined within walls, the public edifices occupying considerable space, and the private houses small and incommodious, could not so readily as the modern accommodate themselves to a great influx of newcomers. Some of the dislodged Atticans found a refuge with their friends and relations; but far the greater part were compelled to content themselves with the rudest shelter on whatever ground they could find unoccupied—some in those temples and fanes that usage left open, some in the towers of the walls. The patches of vacant ground throughout the city were thus covered with temporary sheds

EFFECTS OF CROWDING
THE POPULATION WITHIN
THE WALLS

and huts—even that which superstition had from the remotest period set apart and forbidden to mortal habitation. A space at the foot of the rocks on the northern side of the city, had received from the ancient builders of the wall it adjoined the name of the Pelasgian: a curse was pronounced on whomsoever should tenant it, and there was yet extant the fragment of a Pythian oracle which said darkly "Pelasgian—best untrodden!"[10] Even this was now seized upon and filled thickly with sheds and hovels. By degrees the new settlers found more enlarged accommodation in the space between the long walls, and the skirts of those that fortified the Piræus.[11] Fortunately it was yet summer, and in that delightful climate the evil was not yet felt in its full extent. It was not long before a more dismal calamity than even war itself was found, its aggravation if not its cause in this huddled and unwholesome superflux to an already crowded population.

VII. *Archidamus besieges Œnoe, lays waste Eleusis and the Thriasian plain and camps at Acharnæ.*
VIII. *Indignation of Acharnians but Pericles prevents battle; cavalry skirmishes, Archidamus withdraws.*

The popular feeling seems to have found a principal organ in a man destined shortly afterwards to hold a very prominent position in the democracy of
FIRST PUBLIC APPEARANCE
OF CLEON THE DEMAGOGUE Athens, and who, with all his deficiencies or vices, possessed many of the qualities which in free countries give weight and force to the excesses of a demagogue. That man was Cleon.[12]

IX. *Athenian defensive measures and counter-attacks.*
X. *Naval expeditions (using Diodorus as well as Thucydides).*
XI. *Pericles' expedition to the Megarid.*

XII. An usage peculiar among the Greek states to Athens had long, perhaps immemorially, prevailed—to honour with a public funeral those who had

10 It is has been supposed with much ingenious plausibility that policy invented the superstition—that buildings on the site might have been rendered useful to an enemy in besieging the citadel, and that therefore the rude statesmanship and craft of a remote day laid it under an interdict. But had that been the case I think the acute Athenians would soon have perceived it and the "searching" Thucydides would have hinted at the true cause. More probably the interdict originated in some early and forgotten crime which had polluted the spot.
11 The modern traveller who has seen the sheds or huts built within the huge space of the Coliseum may have some notion of those for which the Atticans now surrendered their farms and villas.
12 Hermippus, apud Plut., in Vit. Per.

FUNERAL AT THE
CERAMICUS

fallen in the service of their country:[13] so noble a method of stimulating the national enthusiasms was the less likely to be omitted at a time when the Athenians required more than ordinary encouragement in the prosecution of a war that, while it threatened long duration, interfered with all their most established habits and their most cherished pursuits. For three days the remains of the slain were exposed to view under an awning; thither the friends and relations of each bore to the departed the funeral offerings.[14] The relics were then deposited in coffins of cypress—one to each of the ten tribes, while an empty bier covered with a pall was consecrated to those whose bodies had not been discovered in the field. All who chose, strangers as well as citizens might join in the procession, which [was] rendered yet more pathetic by the wailings of the women and the presence of the sons of the dead. The deceased were then borne to the Ceramicus—without the walls, esteemed the most beautiful of the suburbs—to rest among the illustrious ashes of all who had fallen for Athens since the Persian war—except only those to whom the tumulus of Marathon had been consecrated as a yet more holy burial place. When the earth was thrown over them, it was the duty of one of the most eminent citizens to pronounce such an oration as might at once console and animate the survivors. It was upon this occasion that Pericles uttered an oration, the severe and thoughtful beauty of which may indeed defy translation, but which as containing the most vivid character yet extant of the Athenian People— as uttered by an Athenian who, while he could correct the errors, could appreciate the virtues of the Athenians—cannot be wholly omitted by any historian of ancient Greece, without injustice to the most eminent of her states.

From a bema, or stand so elevated that his voice might penetrate as far as possible, through that large and mingled assembly Pericles thus spoke:

XIII. *Report of the funeral oration of Pericles, Thucyd., ii. 35, from which I have selected the following footnotes provided by Bulwer Lytton:*

THE CELEBRATED
ORATION OF PERICLES

(a) In these remarks the quiet but severe allusion to the different habits of the Spartans is sufficiently obvious. Freedom, with the Athenians is said to extend to liberty of tastes and pursuits, of private life—whereas in Sparta, the state controlled and moulded all private life, into one form.

---

13 Thucyd., ii. 34; Dem., Lept., p. 499; Philostratus, Heroicus.

14 The following trait of resemblance between the ancient and modern Greeks is interesting and touching: "Before the body is covered with earth, the relations approach in turn, and lifting the corpse in their arms, indulge like Andromache in the full pleasure of their grief, while they call in vain on the friend they have lost, or the fate by which that loss has been occasioned." Douglas.

The austere bearing and mien of the Spartan was proverbial; but that censorship of countenance to which the orator refers, cannot punish the shameless though it can wound the modest.

(b) The scholiast says there was only one day in the year agreed at Athens without sacrifices, so many were the public shows and amusements that Athenian life was said to be one holy day—Idomeneus apud Athenaeus, 532 refers the invention of these public exhibitions to the sons of Pisistratus. The generous and easy Cimon kept a public table, confined however according to Aristotle to his own tribe (Plut., in Vit. Cim.); and his liberality was said almost to revive the Saturnian community of goods. Plutarch says (in Vit. Per.) that, in order to vie with the greater wealth of Cimon, Pericles employed the public treasures in national feasts and diversions. But it is quite clear from the whole character of Pericles that he deemed it a part of a wise and enlightened policy to humanize and refine the population, by the graces of amusement, leisure, and the arts.

(c) That is—with us, we do not have a privileged class as in Sparta, who monopolize the public administration and leave private affairs to Periœci and Helots; nor do we consider even the labourer and mechanic incompetent to have a due share and exercise a sound judgment in political concerns.

XIV. Such, imperfectly rendered, was the purport of that renowned oration—a masterpiece in ancient art characterized by the completeness and progress of the most polished poem, but more admirable far in thought than language. It is observable that, from the first to the last, not one mean idea, one vulgar consolation, finds a place. And noble sentiments must indeed have been habitually cherished in the time and land which produced a statesman who could utter, an historian who could report, and an audience who could appreciate, an eloquence that appealed but to generous minds and could kindle only the loftiest emotions. Still more valuable is this relic of the genius of that day as a thoughtful and elaborate picture of the Athenian character, drawn unquestionably by a partial hand, but not so much magnifying virtues, as omitting the darker shadows of defects.

Thus closed that memorable year. Amongst its external phenomena Thucydides records an eclipse of the sun during the summer; a more signal

ECLIPSE OF THE SUN—THE "MEDEA" OF EURIPIDES

event, apart from the stormy calamities it introduced, was the appearance of perhaps the greatest tragedy of Euripides—the "Medea"—a work not only replete with the singular beauties that attest a great poet, but worthy of peculiar study as showing how far the philosophy of the time had penetrated into those subtler and more tender secrets of human nature which the earlier masters of the dramatic art had left unconjectured. The Gods spoke in Æschylus—Art in Sophocles—Society in Euripides.

CHAPTER III

The plague—physical symptoms—moral degeneration—Athenian expeditions—Pericles is blamed—his speech in reply—he is fined—further activities—death of Pericles

I. As soon as the spring commenced, the Peloponnesians again appeared in Attica under the command of Archidamus. After ravaging the plain of Attica, destroying the fruit trees[1] and setting fire to the granaries, they marched on to the silver-mines of Laurion, and continued the work of devastation even to the plain of Marathon with its four burghs. These, however, they spared in memory of the tradition which consecrated the place and its vicinity to the refuge of the Heraclidæ in their march against Eurystheus. For forty days they remained in Attica, and might still longer have desolated the country and harassed the citizens, if a more deadly enemy had not now appeared, which struck terror even to the invaders, and before which the tide of war itself rolled backward from the land. A pestilence had seized on Athens. This Horrible Disease was said to have begun in Æthiopia beyond Egypt,[2] to have spread thence over Egypt, Libya, and a considerable portion of the dominions of the Persian king, to have ravaged Lemnos and the neighbouring isles, and finally to have burst forth suddenly in the crowded port of the Athenian Piræus—whence it rapidly spread to the upper city.

THE PLAGUE

The season had been more than usually healthy in regard to other disorders, and all previous maladies turned from their ordinary channels merged in this. So inexorable a mortality amongst the human race had never been known in Greece; its effects were sudden: it commenced with violent and feverish heats in the head, redness and inflammation in the eyes, then the throat and tongue assumed a raw and sanguineous appearance, the breath became intolerably fœtid, sneezing and hoarseness followed; the disease descended to the breast with a violent cough, and settled finally in the stomach with bilious vomiting and the most agonizing pain. A hollow exhausted hiccup succeeded with choleric spasms and convulsions varying in duration. The body did not feel hot to the touch but

PHYSICAL SYMPTOMS

---

1 Diod. Sic., xii.1. They spared the olives as sacred.
2 i.e. Nubia, Cinnaar, and perhaps Abyssinia. Bloomfield.

the skin was lead-coloured and bespeckled with small pustules and running sores. So inflamed were the internal parts that the lightest clothing was intolerable. Many devoured by a burning thirst threw themselves into wells, but the thirst was unappeasable. A perturbed restlessness forbade sleep and harassed the sufferers with a perpetual vigil. What seemed most strange while the disease was at its height—the body did not grow more emaciated but surprisingly fought up against the terrible disorder, so that many, dying of the internal fever on the seventh or ninth day, still retained something of strength; or if indeed they passed that period, the disease, falling into the bowels, manifested itself by violent ulceration and diarrhœa, and carried off numbers by the debility that ensued.

Thus the disorder, first establishing itself in the head, descended downwards till it seized and spread through the whole body. Some escaping with life yet lost the extremities, as the fingers, the toes etc.—some the eyes, some memory itself—so that on their first recovery they had no knowledge of others nor even of their own identity. The birds and beasts of prey either shunned the carcasses, or if they tasted, perished. The virulence of the disorder, which, in the strong language of the historian, human nature itself was unequal to bear, baffled all aid and derided all precaution. The weak and the strong were alike devoured by it; the medicine that relieved one but aggravated the miseries of another. But in all this multiplied affliction no symptom was worse than the consternation and despair that seized those who were attacked— rendering themselves, without a struggle, to their preternatural enemy, the infection rotted them away, helpless and hopeless as diseased sheep.

The Athenian humanity which made one of the noblest attributes of the national character still, however, exhibited its virtues the more admirably as it was unsupported by that sublime and self-scorning faith which in Florence, the Athens of Italy, brought the ministers of Christ to the relief of the rich and the spiritual comfort of the dying. True that some left the wretched to languish and expire alone. But they who arrogated to themselves the virtue of a more generous disposition spared not their own lives in tending their friends, and, ashamed of selfish caution, fell the martyrs of their courage. Those especially who had recovered from the pestilence were remarkable for their compassion for the sufferings they had experienced. The disease indeed did not attack twice the same person, so at least as to be mortal; and they who escaped so direful an infection almost flattered themselves with the hope that their frames would be free henceforth from the ordinary complaints of humanity.

Whatever the origin and commencement of this pestilence, it seems clear that the peculiar virulence it displayed in Athens was caused by the thronged and stifling population of the city: the numbers driven from their rural homes into the walls, some without shelter, others swarming on each other in close huts, must have rendered the very atmosphere unwholesome, and while feeding the pestilence diminished all power of guarding against its infection. Corpses lay huddled together in the street, the half dead were seen staggering against each other; the fountains to which they had rushed for water, the temples in which they had fixed their habitation, were filled with carcasses. The peculiar and touching piety of the Greeks in all that related to the rites of sepulture—a piety which foe with foe respected, and which after every battle produced a truce that the slain might be removed and interred by their own friends—*this* even was forgotten in that horrible medley of death. The corpses were thrust anywhere, hasty convenience the only law: on the funeral pile, which some more religious love consecrated to the clay over which it had watched in vain, irreverent hands would throw hurriedly the corpses they neglected themselves to honour.

II. More fatal and more lasting than the plague to the body was the moral plague that it left behind: the same relaxation of religious bonds and social virtues, which Boccaccio has made so fearfully visible in Christian Florence, produced also its licentious revolution in heathen Athens. Men, regarding life and property but the tenure of a day, began to live but for the day itself—why devote labour to honourable pursuits, when death might come so suddenly between the labour and the end? The rich dying in shoals, some distant and hitherto needy relative grew wealthy in an hour—to spend licentiously what he had thus fearfully acquired. All punishment was relaxed, all public opinion dead: the decent hypocrisy with which vice had hitherto concealed its disputes was thrown aside for audacious and reckless indulgence. The culprit laughed at the slow Law; he might be dead before it could chastise; a heavier doom hung over him—he would snatch some darling vices before it come. The gods themselves ceased to awe the miserable multitude; for blind alike to the devout or the blaspheming, no worship seemed to arrest and no impiety to expedite the sentence.

MORAL DEGENERATION

This change in the manners and morals of the city was not, nor could be merely for a season. In modern nations of large extent, and with a scattered population, the example of vices contrary to the ancient character can neither strike deep nor endure long. Even the dissolute court of Louis XV failed to corrupt the manners of the remoter provinces; and when after the first madness the Bourbons regained their throne, they found the general morals even of the capital itself far purer and manlier than at any previous period since the reign of Henri IV. Far less effective—since neither the court nor the capital in England have ever possessed that influence over the provinces and the great bulk of the population which they have exercised in France—was the profligate example of Charles II and his unprincipled nobility. The plague in London produced for a short time the same demoralization which Thucydides records at Athens and Boccaccio at Florence; but the people soon settled back to its pristine manners under the re-established vigour of opinion and of law.

It was otherwise in small and ancient states, where the people itself was cooped within the walls of a fortified city—where the moral infection, having no outlet, spread no less rapidly than the physical—where the current of population was not kept in constant change and freshness by an habitual and regular influx from the healthier manners of the provinces—where licentiousness once introduced had not to contend against the great varieties of sect, of class, of rank, almost of race, that prevail in a numerous and mingled population. At Florence therefore, as in Athens, the moral effects of the plague were profound and lasting. In Athens they were yet more so, from the circumstance that as absolute poverty was unknown amongst the citizens, as much of the ruder drudgeries of life were left to the slaves and metics, and to a certain degree even the poorer classes indulged in a leisure unknown to their equals in the republics of Italy—so idleness itself tempted to sensual indulgence and momentary pleasures.

It may indeed be remarked that not one of the Greek states, the hardy Doric less than any, ever thoroughly redeemed its purer and manlier character, when the bonds of its national morals were once loosened. In addition to political causes for this inevitable tendency to deteriorate (the poison once imbibed), must unquestionably be ranked the religious. In a people whose faith places its hopes mainly in the present life, and estimates the justice of heaven in proportion as it seems to them manifest below, national misfortune, undeserved and sweeping, loosens permanently the solemn chains of religion itself. The creed, not only sublimer, but more true to the actual experience of human dispensations, that transfers to a future life the justice and mercy of the deity, saves mankind from despair under existing evils, and preserves the morality that guides the earth by undiminished confidence in the ultimate heritage of heaven—so that by a larger application of His August title the Divine Founder of the Creed of Modern Europe may be justly called not only of Men—but of Governments and Nations—the Redeemer!

III. *Pericles' expedition to Epidaurus and Trœzen, Agnon & Cleopompus to Chalcidice.*

IV. It was not only natural—it was almost inevitable that amidst such calamities the public mind should become irritated against the government of Pericles. The two natural afflictions, the war and the pestilence, might well by the opposite party be ascribed to his counsels. By his advice they had rejected the preliminary overtures and demands of the Spartans, by his advice they had crowded the city with the rural population; and the throng, the discomfort, and the squalor consequent on that immigration, if they had not caused, had unquestionably aggravated the disease. True that the war could not have been avoided without concessions disgraceful to the authority and perhaps fatal to the empire of Athens; true that, when the war was declared, the safety of the state could alone be consulted by confining defence to the city, and offensive warfare to the unrivalled naval power of the Piræus. But what free population was ever reasonable and just to the policy of its statesmen in the midst of disasters which that policy had occasioned? Their spirit broken by suffering

PERICLES IS BLAMED

and disease, the ruin of many apparent in the ravages of the farms and the vineyards which constituted their property—they even sent ambassadors to Sparta, to attempt conciliatory negotiations. As might be expected, this confession of weakness but increased the pride and encouraged the hopes of their enemy, and the overtures were rejected.

In the midst of universal discontent Pericles, being still general, summoned a general assembly; he boldly reproved the people for their resentment against HIS SPEECH IN REPLY himself and their dejection under their misfortunes; he observed to the resentful sufferers in the devastation of the territory that the only permanent distress of individuals was in the downfall or ruin of a state, and that, while the state prospered, a thousand occasions for the retrieval of their affairs were afforded to its citizens; that in this crisis it became them therefore to bear their private and unavoidable sacrifices, and think only of the best means to preserve the state. He reminded them with the arrogance which the character of the man and the nature of the occasion justified, and which was probably provoked by the counters of his inferior adversaries, of his own claims to their confidence and respect. He contended that the war itself was necessary if they desired to preserve their independence: a voluntary war was folly; but when the choice was between a war and subjection, the wisest counsel was boldly to face the lesser evil of the two. He touched with a noble sarcasm on their changed opinions—brave till the sufferings of war began—weak and unstable when actually experienced.

> I grant that that affliction which is sudden, unforeseen, uncalculated upon, such as the Pestilence, may well bow down the mind. Yet it becomes you, who are citizens of so great a state, and educated in a spirit worthy of your institutions, to sustain with fortitude the gravest calamities, and not efface the dignity of your fame: opinion condemns those who desert the glory that they have obtained by their cowardice, no less than it hates those who arrogate a reputation not their due.

Pericles proceeded with particular earnestness to show them not only that their alarm was unreasonable but that their true power remained unimpeached, that they were still supreme Lords of that half the World—the Sea; that their dominion was thus not limited to their subject allies alone; that in their fleet existed the means to extend, if they so pleased, almost without bounds, their sway; that their villas and estates formed no portion of their real power, and ought to be regarded rather as the trappings, the idle flower-gardens of authority and wealth. Freedom, if they clung fast to that, would easily recover losses so unworthy of their care. They were proud of their dominion—it behoved them to sustain its dignity; if they arrogated its honours, they must sustain its toils; they were not only threatened with the loss of empire, but with the revenge of those whom empire itself had irritated and provoked. Even if they would now divest themselves of dominion for the sake of peace, it was not in their power to do so safely. "Like a tyranny, the empire you possess it may have been unjust to acquire—but it is perilous to relinquish." The principle of tranquil acquiescence was not that suited for a dominant but a subject state: those citizens who had argued to the contrary would soon ruin the commonwealth; and he cautioned them against such counsel. It was the height of injustice to impute blame to their minister, if the plague he had no power to avert had befallen them. They must submit to the ills of Heaven as a necessity—the enmity of men they might resist by courage. Fortitude under affliction had been hitherto the very life and principle of their commonwealth: by that virtue they had alone gained their power and a name that (though all human greatness must decay) would, even when the state was no more, be remembered to the latest age. Theirs was the glory of having as Greeks possessed dominion not over barbarians, but Greeks themselves, of having maintained against them singly and collectively the severest contests, of being citizens of the largest and the wealthiest community of Greece. This very greatness inert and feeble politicians might affect to lament and blame; but the statesman of higher ambition for his country would see in it only matter for emulation: partizans defeated in their object might envy and calumniate—envy and calumny were the everlasting destiny of men who aspired to be superior to the herd. But hatred so acquired was not lasting and its legacies were present renown and an eternal name—"You therefore", confirmed Pericles,

> casting your doubts beforehand, prepare for the present and avoid disgrace; provide for the future and attain to glory. Courage and alacrity are your means to these ends. Send no more embassies to Sparta, betray not that you are oppressed by your existing troubles. With states, as with individuals, they who least succumb to calamity, they who resist with the bravest spirit, are the most illustrious.

V. These arguments and remonstrances produced an effect—as great at least as could reasonably have been anticipated amidst so universal a discontent—the rich despoiled of their superfluities—the poor of their most ordinary comforts. No further embassies were sent to Sparta: the war was prosecuted with greater heart. In public they yielded to their minister—in private they murmured over their ills.

In the jurisprudence of Athens, as of most Greek states, there had existed from the time of Solon an inherent defect which could not fail to lead to the

HE IS FINED grossest abuses: it was the system of punishment by fine. It is probable that at the commencement the national humanity had no less a share than apparent policy in this assessment of offences. Many crimes that in modern states are inexorably punished with death were in

Athens atoned for by a pecuniary mulct,[3] especially those to which the laws of Europe in this day are the least lenient—political offences including various cases of state treason itself. A state with a small population is ever chary of life; a state with small fixed resources is ever prone to make crime itself subservient to the public treasury. But this system of fines became, both privately and nationally, an unavoidable source of corruption: it tended to produce and accumulate a swarm of spies and informers, feeding upon the sores that they first made—even men of less sordid callings were tempted to the accusation of the wealthy by an avarice that disguised itself under the name of zeal. All of you know, says Isocrates, that they who are skilled in public speaking, but are without fortune, are ever apt to accuse others who have no eloquence, but who can pay money.[4] So that the system tended inevitably to an undue oppression of the rich man, for his offences were profitable in proportion to his wealth; but worse than all, it was calculated to incline the public mind to receive with avidity charges which, without dishonouring their principal citizens—for these fines when paid ordinarily entailed little or no loss of reputation[5]—enriched the revenues at their expense. And as in Athens the poorer classes benefited by frequent distributions from the common stock, so the accusations against a rich man added the stimulus of prospective gain to the natural and eternal disposition of poverty to welcome the course of law when directed against wealth. The distress of all classes at Athens, at this time, aided the bitterness of the party against Pericles, of which the rude but eloquent Cleon was one of the most vehement leaders; nor did his enemies rest until they had subjected him to a fine—the amount is variously stated, the highest sum according to Plutarch was fifty talents, the lowest fifteen—the former probably the assessment of his accuser, the latter that to which it was commuted by the court.[6]

3 The embezzlement of the public money was punished by a fine of double the amount: the conviction of Miltiades would have led to capital punishment in most modern states; Timotheus was fined one hundred talents for conviction of treason in taking bribes, nine-tenths were remitted to his son (Boeckh, vol. II, p. 116); Cimon was convicted of an attempt to overthrow the constitution—a capital offence in other countries, but punished by a fine of fifty talents in his case. I do not say whether these offences were *committed*. But the supposed offenders were *convicted*—a matter that seems overlooked by declaimers on the ingratitude of the Athenians.
4 Isocr., contra Euthyn.
5 If the defendant could not pay the public he incurred *atimia*. Thus it is observable that Isocrates in the oration composed for the son of Alcibiades draws a strong distinction between those who can pay the fine and those who cannot. He treats of the former carelessly as if no disgrace attended the mere affliction of the fine if paid, but makes his highborn client declare that exile was a less calamity than the *atimia* incurred by incapacity to pay (Isoc., de Bigis).
6 Boeckh, *Pub. Econ.* vol. II, 117—Diodorus, always exaggerating, computes it at eighty talents.

The public discontent was not only appeased by this sacrifice, but the momentary triumph of the hostile party was followed by immediate reaction. And Pericles was re-elected general with supremacy over his nine colleagues and with apparently new and higher powers, not only military but civil; the noble mind of this great statesman was above the petty resentments for a wrong to which every public man in every free state must be subjected. For wherever there are liberal institutions there will be difference of opinion: differing opinions produce animosities of party, and it is the unhappy but uncontrollable nature of party often to interrupt justice and blind the reason of the people.

VI. BC *430. Activities of Peloponnesians around Zacynthos. Peloponnesian envoys to Persia at court of Sitalces captured and handed over to Athens.*

VII. "The Spartans if slow to commence the war had been peculiarly barbarous in its conduct." *Spartan envoys executed at Athens, execution of Corinthian commander at Potidæa. Story of Talthybius and earlier embassy of Persians.*

VIII. *Phormio at Naupactus. Surrender of Potidæa.*

IX. [XI apparently in error for IX, added later. There are no further section numbers in the ms.] BC *429 Peloponnesian army at Platæa; siege of Platæa. Stratagems of besiegers and besieged. Athenian disaster in Chalcidice; Phormio in Ambracia defeats Peloponnesians. Athenian reinforcements sail via Crete. Second battle and defeat of Phormio, finally turned into victory. Brasidas attacks Piræus.*

X. The descent upon Salamis had surprised the Athenians in their affliction for a loss no victory could compensate, no time repair, the death of the illustrious Pericles. He had been long afflicted by an DEATH OF PERICLES illness, which, though it did not manifest the ordinary symptoms of the plague, was confounded with that terrible disorder. Slow and lingering, with frequent intermissions, it concurred with, if it was not caused by, domestic calamities and wasting sorrow. The pestilence had robbed him of his nearest relations, of his trusted counsellors and friends. The peculiar dignity which belonged to a character that seems to have been at once gentle and firm without parallel in Grecian history had supported him through all but the last and intolerable affliction—the death of Paralus, his younger son. The elder, Xanthippus, had grieved and harassed him all his life prodigal and malignant, he had retaliated on the frugality which refused to supply his expenses, by irreverent ribaldry and calumnious abuse. According to Stesimbrotus, he hated his father to his latest breath; it might require less resignation in Pericles to bear the death than to witness the life of such a son. And when the plague removed Xanthippus, he beheld an heir worthy his affection and his name in the sole survivor of his legitimate children; but when Paralus also fell a victim to the pestilence, his heart gave way. In vain he struggled for the pride and the fortitude which made the serene Philosophy of the School in which his virtues had been trained. He placed the funeral garland upon the temples of his dead son and sobbed aloud—a passion never known in him before.

Thus deprived of his legitimate offspring, and seeing his fame and his race ending in himself, the unhappy statesman centred his last hopes in the child borne to him by Aspasia—but excluded as a bastard by the very law which Pericles himself had carried, or rather perhaps revised, from the privileges of an Athenian citizen. Moved by the sorrows of their great man, the popular assembly exempted him from the general law: his natural son was formally legitimated, registered in his own phratria, and permitted to bear the name of Pericles. This boon we may trust consoled the fatal illness by which it was succeeded. At the point of death and when he seemeed no longer conscious, as his friends grouping around his bed discoursed of his virtues, his power, and the nine trophies he had erected to the honour of the Athenian name, he roused himself from his lethargy to say, "In these acts Fortune had her share, and others have been as favoured—but you omit the most honourable quality in my career: I have never caused an Athenian to put on mourning."

Although in this manly boast, the dying statesman possibly meant, as a recent and learned historian has supposed, a reference simply to the main character of a policy averse to all unnecessary wars, yet it might not unjustly bear the nobler sense in which it is interpreted by Plutarch: clemency to enemies and humane moderation in the midst of angry factions. To the integrity of this great Athenian we have the strong and unquestionable authority of Thucydides. Though frugal in his habits, he impaired his fortune, but enriched the public; a lover of Art, his mansion was not known by its splendour from that of an ordinary citizen, but his magnificence and his taste were visible in the buildings he caused to be erected for the people and the gods. Among the noblest by his birth, his sympathies, as those of all men at once clear to reason and warm to feel ever are and must be, with the broad and general interests of his country. A popular champion, he never pandered to the popular passions, and stands singularly free alike from the fierceness and the servility of the demagogues. That he incurred great errors has been allowed already; but we are scarcely aware how far they were necessitated by the time, still less how far their consequences the most sagacious could have foreseen. In genius, he was more remarkable for the union of qualities rarely found combined, than for the brilliancy of each separately considered. His intellect embraced both letters and action; exquisite in art, enlightened in philosophy, sagacious and temperate in war, artful without guile and commanding without insolence in peace. Power is grander and craft is subtler in Themistocles, Aristides is more rigid in his justice, Demosthenes more eloquent, Alcibiades more dazzling in accomplishments, versatility, and wit. But in the name of Pericles is implied something of them all—great where they are greatest, and where we deem them deficient often chiefly to be admired. And as a character thus rounded, as it were, polished and harmonious, does not present to the superficial the angles that strike the eye—so ordinary minds have considered his actions scarcely worthy his renown. But with his age he was identified, and in the character of that age, we contemplate his own. In the most splendid period of Athenian Civilization he appears the most splendid Citizen. As such, by the admiration of the ancient world Greek and Roman he was regarded; and if some portion of his glory is dimmed by his distance from the modern gaze, enough remains to kindle no ordinary enthusiasm at the mention of Pericles and his age. Of all the Grecian heroes he is the one that most commands our love—the one that best represents the Athenian *Kaloskagathos*—and approaches nearest to the somewhat correspondent expression of the English gentleman in all its ideal grace and courage of genial humanity and intellectual beauty. Many circumstances concurred, to make the generation of which the ornament and the flower close with himself. From the Pestilence and the War arose a new and ignobler race, at once looser in their manners and more ferocious in their temper. With Pericles passed away much of the beauty of the Athenian character.

CHAPTER IV

I. The most eminent of the Athenians for command in war after the death of Pericles was unquestionably Phormio; but this great admiral was now far advanced in years,[1] and, in common with many other of the strategi or commanders, he seems to have taken no active part in the civil government or the popular assemblies. As yet the splendid Alcibiades was alternating between the disputes of philosophy and the pleasures of debauch, notorious for his beauty and his steeds, his loose flowing robes and his sauntering gait,[2] for his magnificence and his profligacy, and distinguished in spite of all by the discerning few for the promise of qualities that save or ruin states, when riper years should admit him into the practical affairs of men.

THE RISE OF THE TRADING CLASSES

But at present the most prominent persons in the popular assemblies belonged to that class which had naturally increased in power, with the commercial prosperity and enterprise of their native city. From the moment that Athens became the Mistress of the Seas, the rise and influence of the trading class were assured; and it was in the very nature of things that from this class popular leaders should emerge, to struggle with the wellborn for political consideration. Whoever in our country has taken share, whether as voter or candidate in contests for the Parliamentary representation of a burgh or city, will understand Athenian life more readily than many a mere scholar of intellect, assisted only by abstract meditation and learned commentators. Public life in Athens was like one eternal election. And as in an English town, we see the most powerful electors less among the haughty and idle gentlemen than among the more opulent traders who give employment to many hands, who form daily connexions with various interests, who are brought familiarly into contact with the mass of the voters, and become

---

1 For his son Asopus must have been at least thirty, probably much older, since in this year we find him appointed instead of Phormio to the command of a fleet.
2 Archippus, apud Plut., in Vit. Alcibiad.; Aristoph., Δαιταλεῖς exhibited this year BC 427.

intimately acquainted with the means by which now to secure gratitude, now to intimidate hostility,—so at Athens precisely the same order of men, precisely from the same causes, had begun to win ascendancy in the popular meetings, and to confront the ancient aristocracy with more active, if less elegant and accomplished leaders. As the privileges peculiar to nobility (save in certain houses to which a high priesthood was annexed)[3] were either abrogated or had died away, so it was perhaps natural, that the young patricians should seek, by additional insolence and presumption, to distinguish themselves and their order from the commons. For the aristocracy is ever more exclusive in spirit, in proportion as it is less fenced around by demarcations of Law; and Aristophanes with all his aristocratic predilections has left us a striking picture of the arrogant pretensions, little supported by practical merits, of the noble Athenian youths in his comedy of the "Knights". While the young generation of the wellborn, deserting the ancient and manly forms of education, forsaking the moral discipline and hardy habits of the gymnasia for the babble of gaudy sophists or the enervating allurements of the Hetæræ, thus gradually frittered away the political honour of their class, the rising generation of the middle order were trained with a jealous sense of their importance into a vehement passion for public business, with the exercise of all those active, busy, restless energies which found their vent in the tumultuous roar of the popular assembly.[4] In conformity then with the necessary and moral laws that ever regulate this peculiar crisis of society in free states, every sound thinker may be prepared to find the leaders of the trading class most prominent in contest for the political power left to competition by the death of Pericles.

II. Two candidates from this class soon appeared upon the stage of Party. The one Eucrates,[5] a flax-dealer—the other Lysicles, a grazier or dealer in sheep.[6] The last had married Aspasia after the death of
THE DEMAGOGUES   Pericles,[7] and either the experience of that remarkable woman in the party contests of the day, or the ascendancy she still preserved

---

3 Wachsmuth vol. II, sec. 64.
4 The character of the Commons is forcibly painted by a single word that seems to have come into use about this time—to *agorize*—i.e. to frequent, to haunt the Agora.
5 Aristoph., Equit., 129. 154.
6 Ibid., 132.
7 It seems evident that the Lysicles who, according to Plutarch, married Aspasia, and rose by her means to eminence, is the same Lysicles who according to Aristophanes preceded Cleon in popular favour, and the same whose death Thucydides records iii. 19. If so, we must in some degree qualify Plutarch's assertion that he owed his rise to Aspasia, for he had no time to rise from insignificance to power between his marriage and his death. He was most probably one of the partizans of Pericles, and, at the death of the latter, holding such a position common in the lives of all public men whom a sudden addition to influence, either by a powerful marriage or the death of the party chieftain, raised them at once from a well-known subordinate to the station of Leader.

amongst the friends of Pericles, joined possibly to the advantage of her lessons, probably to that of her fortune, raised Lysicles for a short time to the highest importance in the state.[8] Lysicles, who seems very rapidly to have supplanted Eucrates, probably retained the popular favour till his death, which happened within the year we now enter; for he was appointed to the command of a naval squadron with five colleagues and perished on the Carian coast.[9] And again it was one of the trading class who struggled for, and in part obtained the sovereignty of the people.

A tanner or leather-dealer had risen to considerable notoriety, nay to much public influence, in the latter days of Pericles; he had been the boldest opponent of that great statesman; it was in his nature to take the more vulgar, which is ever the more violent side, of every question; and he had secured popularity in joining the popular rage kindled against Pericles when he declined to meet the Spartans in the field on their first invasion. That he had acquired a certain station during the life of Pericles, and in contrast to the majesty of so great an intellect, is in itself proof that he possessed powers of a nature more easily conjectured by active and practical men, than conceded by the fastidious elegance of scholars. This tanner's name, Cleon the son of Cleænetus, is transmitted to us by the terrific ribaldry of Aristophanes and the calm disdain of Thucydides, echoed by later and feebler writers, as a byeword the most odious and contemptible. But we must not forget that upon matters of character Aristophanes is no authority whatsoever, that according to him Socrates is a foul and bestial corrupter of youth, Euripides a miserable scribbler, and the Olympian Pericles a profligate rogue. And although Thucydides is a historian unrivalled for temperance and for candour—still he was by birth, by fortune, and by party opposed to those of whom Cleon was the most vehement and obnoxious champion— those from whose hostility the illustrious writer had suffered calumny, and though Thucydides may not have exaggerated the gross faults of the demagogue, it is not presuming too far to suppose that, had a portrait of Cleon's character been drawn by a writer as honest as Thucydides, but belonging to the same faction as "the god-detested Tanner"—we should see at least more plainly drawn those redeeming qualities which in the most civilized age of Athens could alone have made him the most influential leader of the demus. The nature of the man was evidently coarse, and his policy narrow from the deficiency of his intellectual culture, and at times brutal from the violence of his passions. But he seems to have possessed the most essential qualities of a successful chief in stormy times, and amidst turbulent factions. His boldness as a speaker was carried into the hardiest effrontery, but boldness it still was; and all factions love a champion who shrinks from no antagonist and is awed

^{CLEON}

8 Aeschines Socraticus, apud Plut., in Vit. Per., 24.
9 Thucyd., iii. 19.

by no authority from speaking plainly the mind of his adherents. His eloquence, which Cicero allows—whatever its sins against the *Senatorius Decor* that had hitherto characterized the Athenian orators—must even from the hostile description of his enemies have had the appearance of earnestness and passion,[10] after one of those stately speeches, delivered with little action, and addressed to the nobler sentiments in serene language, by which Pericles charmed the higher order of intellect, or still more, after the timid sentences of Nicias (whom we shall presently consider as the immediate rival of Cleon), stammered forth by a man brave in action and a trembler on the hustings: anyone accustomed to public assemblies can comprehend the effect produced when the burly tanner rose, with a voice that came out from brazen lungs thundering over the whole audience, and accompanied by gesticulations and starts, and passionate apostrophes which seemed to show to them how much the vehement speaker had at heart the course which he enforced.

The condition of Cleon had its advantages; for while it belonged to the people, and identified his success with their vanity as to class, his birth and parentage were respectable.[11] He is said upon no very sufficient authority to

10 Cleon would spring from one end of the bema to the other, strike his thigh, throw back his gown, &c; and these traits of a vehement speaker, and a passionate temper, are noticed by Plutarch with a tone of censure which succeeding historians have enlarged into actual accusation. Yet precisely the same anecdotes are recorded of Caius Gracchus, the first of the Romans who threw his gown off his shoulders and moved from one end of the stand to the other (Plut., in Vit. Tib. Grac.). In the noble Roman this delivery is called energy & passion, in the Athenian Tanner, coarseness and vulgarity. Such is the unexamining spirit of depreciation with which the son of Cleænetus has been judged.

Cicero classes Cleon among the early Athenian Orators & describes him, no doubt with discrimination and accuracy as "Turbulentum quidem civem, sed tamen eloquentem" (Cic., in Brut.) Bloomfield says truly that Mitford (in common, that learned Commentator might have added, with all our modern historians) scarcely does justice to Cleon's abilities. It requires perhaps some experience of public life, and the qualities which obtain success in a political career, to distinguish the talents Cleon must necessarily have had amidst the cloud which rests upon a character that, with every allowance for party exaggeration, must remain sufficiently displeasing. But it would be scarcely fair to deny to the Athenian demagogue that dispassionate discrimination which historians of all shades in politics have in our day sought to exercise in their judgment even of the Revolutionary leaders of the French Reign of Terror:—Cleon is surely as much entitled as Danton to the judgment that can analyse even in condemning.

11 Mr Mitford says incorrectly "Bred among the lowest of the People". Thirlwall, with a just choice of words and a proper understanding of the importance the middle class had obtained, observes "that he was of reputable though not of high condition". It may be remarked that Thucydides, though treating the character of Cleon with great contempt, in no way extends that contempt to his powers of speaking, nor intimates that there was the slightest trace of mean origin or of vulgar breeding in his language. On the contrary, in the speech he assigns to Cleon for the debate with regard to the Prisoners of Mitylene, some of the most elegant atticisms in the whole of the history are introduced: the diction is scholastic and compact, even to obscurity, and the arguments (considering the badness

have entered party life crippled with mortgages and debts[12]—an assertion which proves at all events that he had inherited the fortune without which no man can become very largely in debt. However this may be, he soon became rich in his career as a demagogue; and this wealth, however acquired, enabled him to gratify the wants of his poorer supporters: with his fierceness against her enemies and his insolence in the assemblies were united the arts which conciliated his own party. He paid peculiar attention to the older citizens, and his courtesy to the populace was carried to an extent to be called by his enemies servility and fawning. In fine he seems to have been one of those men who seldom fail to rise in free states, possessing not indeed the qualities which are noble, but those which are popular and vigorous: intolerant to all enemies of himself and his party, abusive and foul-mouthed to his opponents, but braving with a bull's hide and a brazen front their worst obloquy in return; having sufficient instruction to express strong opinions in strong language, and varnish a bad cause with specious rhetoric, active, restless, and if greedy and self-seeking, no less ready to give than avid to grasp, enjoying all physical advantage of strength and voice, and above all, possessing to a degree probably not equalled by any other in the interval between the death of Pericles and the rise of Alcibiades, the uncommon and valuable, though not lofty, faculty of addressing with readiness, power, and courage a large, miscellaneous, and stormy audience in the open air.[13]

III. As Lysicles only attained to the leadership of the party through the influence brought to him by Aspasia, and as we find Eucrates afterwards the

---

of his cause) are ingenious and subtle. And although Thucydides does not of course give us the precise speech which Cleon delivered, he has shown us in his specimen of Laconic oratory that he can individualize where the peculiar character of the orator is to be distinguished. Nor is it at all probable that Thucydides would have imparted to the sentiments of Cleon a polish of language or a refinement of reasoning which would have been ludicrous to those who remembered the demagogue, if in strong contrast to his ordinary style.

12 Aelian., Var., x. 17 mentions two Athenians as having enriched themselves at the expense of the state, the first Themistocles, the second Cleon. Of the latter he says that he left the considerable balance of fifty talents. Aristophanes in the "Knights" says wittily enough that he entered the Prytaneum thin and went out of it fat.

13 The descriptions given of Cleon's delivery imply extempore speaking. It was violent to indecorum—he would throw open his upper garment, strike his thigh, spring across the stand, or (as we should phrase it) hustings—the redundance of action at variance with previous speakers. But anyone who has closely observed the different classes of public oratory, will have noted that extempore speaking, especially in the open air, is always accompanied by a much greater licence and energy of gesticulation than are characteristic of a speaker who has prepared his language, or even composed his thoughts on the subject: the suddenness with which a pertinent thought or a lofty expression flashes across a man of some warmth and passion leads involuntarily to abrupt and vehement action.

THE OPPOSITION OF THE WELLBORN — THE TIMIDITY OF NICIAS

principal opponent of Cleon, so it is evident that the immediate successors to Pericles in the public assemblies attempted to follow the same policy as their great predecessor. And when Cleon, heading the popular party, supplanted his feebler rivals, the aristocracy looked around for one of their own rank, to oppose the demagogue and defend their interests. It was evidently politic to select a man whose fortune would enable him to oppose the popular virtues of splendour and charity to the popular energies and wiles of Cleon. It was desirable also to choose one, who should rally round him the scattered partizans of Pericles: they united both these objects in Nicias the son of Niceratus. He was one of the wealthiest citizens of Athens. He held in fee farm[14] some silver-mines in Laurion upon which were employed no less than a thousand slaves;[15] he had been several times associated with Pericles as a colleague in the war. He was willing to devote his fortune to the purposes of his party, and professed a natural taste for splendour and magnificence; he indulged the populace with exhibitions, exceeding in pomp and art all that had hitherto been known.[16] None applied to him for alms, and went away empty-handed. He dreaded calumny and purchased its silence; and the comic poet implies that when the poor man was seen with Nicias, the public informer was on the scent to detect the sale of a vote.[17] Nicias was an irresolute man and a craven speaker; he hung down his head when he walked the streets;[18] the great vice of his character was moral fear. This pervaded his whole nature. His piety was carried to superstition: he maintained a diviner in his house whom he consulted equally about the offerings to the gods and the success or the safety of his silver-mines. He was so in dread of informers (the Pest of Athens) that he did not venture to mix in general society, and resorted to various quackeries to obtain the reputation of exclusive attention to public affairs.[19] He was so afraid of incurring the popular displeasure, even in his military operations, that he even sought less to obtain renown than to avoid failure. In short, during his whole career he

---

14 See Boeckh, *Dissertation on the Silver Mines of Laurion*, for the tenure upon which these mines were held by the proprietor.
15 Athenaeus, vi, and Xen., Memorab., ii. 5.2; de Vectig., iv. 14. The wealth and munificence of Nicias are described also by Thucydides and Plutarch.
16 Plut., in Vit. Nic.
17 Eupolis, Maricas, apud Plut., in Vit. Nic., 4 Nicias had good reason to dread the informers. For Cleon was a rough enemy, and it was a part of his policy to provide donations for the poor from the fines of the rich. Moreover the chief source of wealth to Nicias was his mines, which he held in fee, and these reverted to the state "upon violation of the Laws and non-performance of the duties under which they were held". See Boeckh, *Pol. Econ. of Athens*, Book III., 14.
18 Phrynichus, apud Plut., in Vit. Nic.
19 Plut., in Vit Nic.

seems to have been haunted by a foreboding of misfortune—a terror of the future—which his melancholy end strangely justified. Such a man, with all his wealth and all his virtues, was not fitted, either to wrestle with the robust demagoguery of Cleon, or to guide the destinies of Athens in a crisis, above all then requiring a decision. Yet in a happier and calmer time there was much in the character of Nicias that might have served his country and achieved his fame. His very defeats arose in part from a singular amiability of temper, an incapability to opinion never found but in natures delicate and refined; humane, munificent, prudent, of unimpeachable integrity, of abilities above the ordinary level, and thoroughly Attic in the elegance of his tastes, he might with credit and felicity have succeeded Cimon; but far other qualities were needed in the man who was called upon to defend the liberties and preserve the morale of the Athenian people—when the Spartan was in the field and the demagogue within the city.

(The above section on Cleon gives evidence of many additions and much rewriting.)

IV. 4th year of the war: invasion of Attica. Revolt of Lesbos, siege of Mitylene; their appeal to Sparta. 2nd Spartan invasion planned, counter-attack by Athens. Mitylene blockaded. Financial problems in Athens; death of Lysicles collecting tribute. Siege of Platæa continued: escape of most of the besieged.
BC 427 Expedition of Alcidas. Mutiny of commons at Mitylene, fall of city. End of ms. 14.

2/5 follows on from 14, concerns the forced surrender of Mitylene as a result of the mutiny of the commons; Alcidas at Colophon; Notium and Paches' exploits. Mitylenean debate. Speech of Cleon given in extended form (10 pages), comment on p. 7:

The speech reminds us of the policy of Danton when he vindicated the system of terror as the sole salvation of the state. Note NB Find some suitable quotations from Macchiavel.

THE TRUE NATURE *Speech of Diodotus (4 pp.), end of revolt (1 p.); p.16:*
OF CLERUCHIÆ

V. The whole island except the Methymnæans was subjected to a penalty that seems rigorous to the superficial, but was in reality rather humiliating in its principle than severe in its practical effect. The land was, no doubt, chiefly in the hands of the aristocratic party so hostile to the Athenians: this was divided into three thousand cleruchiæ or shares—a tithe consecrated to the gods, the rest allotted to Athenian citizens. But with regard to the latter the possession was rather nominal than real—the Lesbians cultivated the land and retained its profits, paying to the Athenian landlord a moderate, permanent, and uniform quit rent—thus, in fact, rather converting the freehold into leasehold than dispossessing the occupiers. By this system three objects were effected: first, the power of the landed aristocracy over the population ceased to be formidable to the sovereign state; second, though it cannot be supposed that in this instance the Athenian shareholders foresook their own country to settle in Lesbos,[20] the general agency they must have established spread a sort of police throughout the island; third, the Athenian people themselves were indemnified for severe burthens they had borne during the ravages in Attica, and under the novel exaction of a direct tax.[21] For the rest, Lesbos remained exempt from tribute, treated rather as a colony than an ally.

VI. One blank page, then an account of the fate of the Platæan garrison at the hands of the Spartans; 6 pages to end of ms. 5.
2/6 Carries on from 5 with Platæans' speech, 4pp. to end of episode.

20 Mr Mitford seems singularly ignorant of the nature of the Cleruchiae—in his emphasis that this mode of allotment was calculated rather for private emolument than public advantage, being rather required by the common people as an indulgence or proposed by some leading men as a bribe. Macchiavelli's keen eye saw the immense advantage to states in so cheap a form of colonization; and unhappily it was that advantage to the state far more than the emoluments to individuals which blinded Athens to its equivocal morality and justice. It may be as well here to observe that it was not under this democratic period in Athenian history that the system of Cleruchiae was introduced : so far from its being the novelty Mr Mitford so innocently deems it, he might have seen in Herodotus v. 77. vi. 100, the same system existing before the Persian War, when to 4000 Athenian citizens were allotted the lands of the Knights of Chalcis; and it was under the almost dictatorship of Pericles that it flourished in its fullest vigour.

21 The Athenian shareholders went, as Dr Arnold observes, "to ascertain the size and situation of their respective shares—and arrange with their future tenants— . . . but it is clear that they did not continue to live in the island from all the subsequent story of the revolts in Lesbos: Thucyd. viii. 22, 23; Xenophon i.6–ii. 2". Besides at the time the population of Athens had been so thinned by the plague that it could never have spared two thousand one hundred citizens. Nay very shortly afterwards the Athenians were compelled to extend their franchise to aliens &c in order to repair their losses. In the previous cleruchiæ established by Pericles such as Histiæa in Eubœa, Potidæa in the Chersonesus, Naxos, Andros, Thrace &c the Cleruchi did reside upon their shares; for Pericles had then in view precisely the object which would have been contemplated by any statesman at the time as now—viz., the opening a vent to a redundant population. Aristophanes himself was a Cleruchus in Ægina, while living in Athens (See Boeckh, Bk. iii. ch. 18 for other & more unquestionable examples). We may reasonably suppose, however, with Boeckh (ibid.) that a part of the settlers, probably a very few, might have stayed in Lesbos, but only as a garrison, and serving with the former inhabitants to compose the commonwealth.

CHAPTER V

2/6 P.5: new heading "Chapter" (no number) for the section on the corruption of political morals.

I. On the national character of Greece was already visible the baleful influence of this disastrous conflict. The war of one foreign nation upon

THE EFFECTS OF FACTION

another rarely exhibits the same features of violence and malignity as that in which men speaking the same tongue, and belonging essentially to the same land, bring into the field the envy of rivals, the feuds of neighbours, the familiar and the hereditary associations which make friendship dear but hatred deadly. No event had more ennobled the Greek character than the Persian war, none more depraved it than the Peloponnesian. Already, as we have unhappily seen, the old humanity and the simple faith had ceased to distinguish the Greek from the Barbarian; Athens could no longer boast of superior mildness, nor Sparta assume the attributes of manly honesty. Nor was it only in the calamities inflicted by the sword, in the struggle between state and state, that the virtue and the happiness of Greece wasted rapidly away: it was, as we have before stated, not a war simply between Athens and Sparta, Dorian and Ionian; it was a war of opinion: with one was Democracy, with the other the Aristocrat, or the Oligarch. A war like this is inflamed by all the passions of party, and into every state it inevitably introduced treason: not a city, but the aristocracy inclined to Sparta—the democracy to Athens. Such divisions had existed before the war, and ever must exist in all states not held in thraldom by the alternate vigour and paralysis of absolute power. But in peace the passions of party had found a natural and not perhaps unhealthful vent, and constitutions settled down amidst contests of more noise than danger into those forms best adapted to the genius and the habits of the several states. The war between Athens and Sparta—the actual appearance in the field—the armed impersonation, as it were, of the two great principles most nicely balanced in the human intellect—promised to either party a more rapid succour than debate. Either party—if impatient of the constitutional domination of the other—became eager to invoke the aid of the Spartan or the Athenian according to its political predilections.

568

Thus it was not only a state of War, it was a crisis of Revolution. A fever kindred to that which burned through Italy in the fiercest days of the strife between Guelf and Ghibelline—nay, little less passionate and delirious than that disordered frenzy which existed in the various towns of France, while the Jacobins and the Girondists contended for empire in the capital—began to rage throughout the communities of Greece. Sedition in the city and war through the land inflamed the passions, till the character itself grew congenial to the fiery atmosphere it breathed. In this new and revolutionary strife of party, man—to use a homely and strong expression—felt that he lived fast; the slow-growing objects of a rational ambition ceased to tempt: he must hasten to subdue his enemy, or his enemy would subdue him. Thus even words lost their old character and a morality was shaped correspondent to the evils of the time. Brutal ferocity was considered true courage—a slow discretion was specious cowardice—the violent man was thought the honest —emulation consisted in the competition of knavery and craft, and he was deemed the wisest man, who succeeded best in deceiving his fellow rogue. In such a state of evil frequent in civil war, common in revolutions, and foulest as in Greece and in France, where both war and revolution have been united, true relationship itself is weakened. Clubs became numerous, and then true brotherhood was political association.

Breathing this element of constant danger, religion lost its great hold on the sanctity of oaths: they were regarded by the weak as long only as they served to protect—they were broken by the strong as soon as they had the power to destroy. A modern politician can scarcely conceive the passion for public life, for political power, that made up the very character of the ancient Greek: the course of his energies and the self-excuse for his crimes. His life was so thoroughly urban, so entirely in public, the applause of a popular assembly was so exciting and so immediate a reward; his attention was so impelled by the constant activity at work around him to public business; if a patriot, every month so teemed with events sinister or favour- able to his little commonwealth, and if a sordid self-seeker, such pecuniary advantages were open to the dishonest in the administration of affairs, that all the motives, which with us separately move men of active minds to separate careers, combined to confine the lively passion and exuberant energy of the Greek to the one turbulent field of Political Ambition. And in proportion to the intensity of the ambition was necessarily the fierceness of the rivalry: as the struggle was desperate, so the revenge grew terrific. In all such times pure intellect cannot thrive; vehemence and cunning secure success, and in revolutions no man can command a party unless he go to its extremes. The moderate were suspected by all, to be neutral was to be odious and proscribed; sincerity and truth were impracticable, for human nature clings to self-preservation. And who could frankly own an opinion that would destroy him? All union between the two great ranks was neces- sarily sundered. If we could see before us one of the many states agitated and accursed by the influence, direct and indirect, of the Peloponnesian war, we should behold the demagogue presiding at his club—thundering against the rich and the wellborn, and the wellborn mutiny in secret to plot how to destroy all elements of civil freedom, and to admit the Peloponnesian into the city. The great and almost universal crime of the higher classes at this period, was unquestionably a hearty hatred of their own country, caring nothing for its independence, willing to render it to Spartan or to Mede—so that they could root and branch destroy the popular faction. On the other hand their almost unanswerable excuse is that the popular faction made their property insecure and their life intolerable. It was as great a mockery to ask them to love the state, as to accuse a French nobleman of disaffection to the Reign of Terror.

II. But the main calamity of this war of opinion in the internal commotions it created elsewhere was as yet unfelt by its two principal leaders, Athens and Sparta. In Sparta, the severe and primitive form of government was still unquestioned—no Athenian, that is no democratic faction, could be found; nor was it possible that the spirit of innovation could endanger its venerable institutions—until the whole framework of its society had become corrupted by the final ulterior consequences of the war, and until its own chiefs and authorities became the innovators. In Athens, it is true, that there existed then as it had always, a Spartan faction; but at this time it was latent and insignificant. The higher classes had a pre-eminent interest in bringing the war to a conclusion, either by honourable peace, or decisive conquest; for as they were the landowners, it was chiefly their possessions which the yearly invasion spoiled and wasted. Nor were they dishonoured or oppressed by the democracy: on the contrary, they still held, from the free popular voice, their full share of the great offices of state. And the indulgent admiration that gathered round the brilliant type of their rising generation, the young Alcibiades, is a proof of the lenity towards those follies peculiar to rank, of which, when an aristocracy is once unpopular, the subordinate classes are the least tolerant.

SPARTA AND ATHENS

At Athens now, in the meridian of her democracy, there was a greater unison of feeling, a stronger bond of patriotism than had existed in the earlier period of the popular struggles with the eupatrids, when Solon was called upon to conciliate the have-nots and the haves—or when, even in the Persian invasion, the loftiest of her nobles was supposed to hold treacherous correspondence with the Mede. Aristocracy and populace were equally in earnest against the common danger; and while the demagogue roused the wrath of the assembly against the Spartan, against the Spartans the noble led the armies to the field. With all the many defects of her institutions, and despite the growing corruption and the looser manners, which we shall hereafter describe, Athens was still then the best and healthiest of all the Greek commonwealths—her energies the greatest, her patriotism the strongest, her councils the wisest, her ordinary life the most polished and enjoyable. Still, in this very year of extended war, and amidst the langour of recent disease about to be renewed—still while in other states, sedition shook the walls, and slaughter dyed the streets—Athens exhibited within all the liberal arts and genial splendour of her marvellous civilization. Nicias, leader of the aristocracy, was attracting to his party all whom charity could bribe and magnificence could dazzle; Aristophanes, himself nobly born, was defending the interests of his order with the most exuberant wit ever bestowed on man; Sophocles was at the height of his fame, and Euripides was struggling his noble but melancholy way to the third throne of the Grecian drama; Gorgias was intoxicating the lively and subtle students with the brilliant novelties of his rhetoric; Socrates was laying the foundations of the philosophy which gave to Athens a second, a vaster and a less perishable empire; and the very idlers in the market-place were repeating the anecdotes of the pleasures, the whims, and the genius of Alcibiades. So little were the population altogether engrossed by the turbulent spirit of party politics— so little were they brutalized by the rude vigour and fierce temperament of their Cleon—so large a leisure could they find still amidst the broils of faction and the lust of empire, for all the graces, the refinements, the intellectual joys which the dispassionate inquirer and the genuine scholar will always comprehend in the life of an Athenian citizen while Athens preserved her freedom.

III. But from this picture we are summoned to contemplate in their worst and most revolting form those effects of civil discord, of atrocious treachery, fierce revenge and thirst of blood, which the Greek historian has CORCYRA traced, in other states, to the demoralization of the Peloponnesian war, and which were first distinctly visible in the island, in whose quarrels the war itself had arisen. The fleet under Alcidas, after baffling the pursuit of Paches[1] and weathering a storm off Crete, reached Cyllene, where the Spartan admiral was joined by Brasidas despatched to him as a colleague, with orders to sail at once to Corcyra. And it is the condition of parties in this island that we are now to survey.

Revolutionary activities at Corcyra: the Corcyrean aristocratic exiles from Corinth persuade the assembly to ally with Corinth. Pithias Athenian proxenus accused, acquitted; counter-accusations. The conspiracy of the aristocrats and murder of the democratic leaders. Counter-embassies at Athens. The aristocrats fire the city; arrival of Athenian vessels. Nicostratus' attempts at reconciliation fail. The battle with the Peloponnesian ships. The Corcyreans retreat.

2/7 Corcyra stasis continued.

1 Paches, see Plut., in Vit. Arist.; Vit. Nic.—Cam. Philological Mus. Vol II, p. 236.

Such was the calamitous condition to which the greatest maritime state of Greece, next to Athens, was reduced, ostensibly and directly, as is obvious to the shallow, by the rage of democratic faction, but primarily though less evidently, by that system of foreign interference in civil institutions, which was the most prevalent curse of the Peloponnesian war. Had Corinth not instigated the aristocratic party to overset the popular constitution, and had she not subsequently supported them by the arrival of her galleys, party difference how violent soever could never have led to outrages so atrocious. And it is remarkable that while the interference of Corinth sufficed to throw the state into anarchy, that of Nicostratus proved wholly unavailing to restore tranquillity and peace. So dangerous and so terrible a responsibility rests ever upon the state that, whether by intrigue or by force, attempts what it calls the settlement, but what produces in reality, the revolution of another.

IV. The Athenian designs on Sicily are deferred. The return of the plague. Expeditions of BC 426: Nicias attacks Melos unsuccessfully, ravaging of plain of Tanagra. Demosthenes at Naupactus; his exploits in northwest, designs on Bœotia; his defeat by Ætolians. The Spartan foundation of Heraclea. Attacks on Naupactus repelled. 2/8: Demosthenes in Acarnania cont.

CHAPTER VI

> *The invasion of Agis is cut short by news of Pylus—the Athenian expedition to Sicily stops at Pylus—Pylus is fortified—the reaction of the Spartans—the battle for Pylus and the return of the Athenian fleet—the Spartans on Sphacteria are cut off—dismay at Sparta —the embassy to Athens—reflections on the situation—Cleon's response—the siege—Cleon accepts command—the assault on Sphacteria and the surrender of the Spartans—the end of the affair—Cleon vindicated*

I. With Sophocles and Eurymedon sailed the boldest and ablest captain Athens then possessed—Demosthenes. On his return from Acarnania he had escaped all prosecution for his calamitous enter-

THE ATHENIAN EXPEDI-
TION TO SICILY STOPS AT
PYLUS

prise in Ætolia; but had not been re-promoted to any official command. He had requested leave, how-ever, to accompany Eurymedon and Sophocles, and given the government to understand that he had devised an advantageous plan upon Laconia—to be executed as the fleet sailed by the Peloponnesus. The Athenians were doubtless willing to employ the services of a man of such unquestionable talents, and to suffer still further successes than those which had effaced his offence to justify his formal restoration to military command. As long, therefore, as the fleets should be on the Peloponnesian coast,[1] it was arranged that Demosthenes, without superseding the commanders, in their ultimate destination to Corcyra and to Sicily, should advise them with regard to its employment. As the Athenian squadron were on the coast of Laconia, Demosthenes desired the admirals to bring to at a stony promontory called Pylus, constituting the northern horn of the modern

---

1 Περὶ τὴν Πελοπόννησον—Thucyd., iv. 3. It is evident that the commission of Demosthenes was limited to the Peloponnesian coast, and did not *irregularly* supersede the command of Eurymedon and Sophocles. He had the use of their fleet only for a special purpose, the nature of which he had no doubt explained to the government—but the success of which depended upon secrecy till the moment of execution.

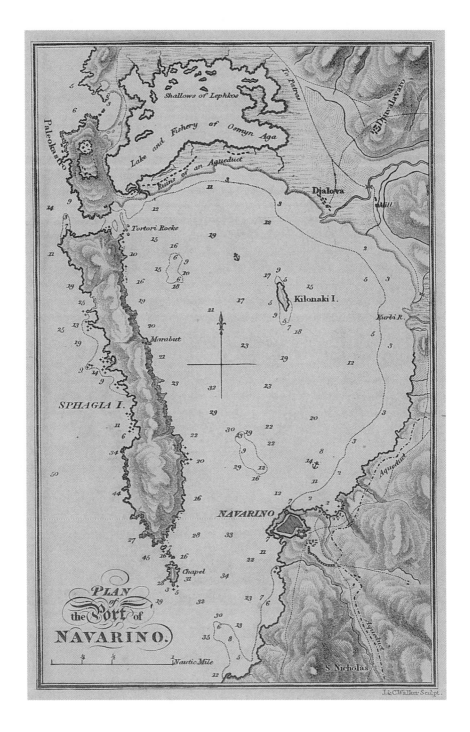

PLAN
of
the Port of
NAVARINO.

Shallows of Lephkos

Lake and Fishery of Osmyn Aga

Ruins of an Aqueduct

Paleokastro

To Patras

Djavlaram

Djalova

Mill

Tortori Rocks

Kilonaki I.

Kurbi R.

Marabut

SPHAGIA I.

NAVARINO

Chapel

S. Nicholas

Aqueduct

Nautic Mile

J. & C. Walker Sculpt.

Navarino.[2] At this very time the intelligence was received that the Peloponnesian fleet had already arrived at Corcyra; and Sophocles and Eurymedon would have hastened thither but for the rough weather which actually drove them to Pylus. Demosthenes then urged them instantly to fortify the place. "For this", he said, "For this expressly he had taken part in the voyage". He pointed out the extraordinary advantages of the place, not more than fifty miles from Sparta itself—the strength of its position, the materials in timber and large stones for the construction of a fort which the soil supplied, its excellence as an harbour—the most spacious indeed in Greece—and suggested the expediency of manning the garrison, if built, with the Naupactan Messenians—the old inhabitants of the very district, speaking the same Doric dialect as the Spartans, thoroughly acquainted with the country, whose hostility to Sparta would lead them to constant incursions, whose fidelity to Athens would render them hardy guardians of so important a post in the enemy's domains.

No doubt this idea had been long cherished by Demosthenes, suggested first by the Messenians themselves during his residence at Naupactus, confirmed by his opportunities of inspecting the coast as he PYLUS IS FORTIFIED had sailed home from Acarnania, and having now every practical advantage for execution, in the absence of the Spartan army, employed in Attica. But neither Eurymedon nor Sophocles appears to have had the military statesmanship even to comprehend the arguments addressed to them by the genius of this most able tactician. Finding he could not persuade the leaders he addressed the captains—a breach of discipline, which the words of Thucydides imply was unusual in that day as in this[3]—but excused perhaps by the nature of his authority while on the Peloponnesian coast, and quite in conformity with the earnest and somewhat presumptuous character of the man. With these he succeeded no better, and the scheme might have altogether failed, but from the continued hostility of wind and weather, which detained the fleet in the desert and unpopulated post. From that lively impatience of idleness which characterized the ancient Athenian, the common men began to amuse themselves with putting into practice the masterly idea of Demosthenes. The labour once begun, an enthusiasm swayed the workmen to complete it before the Spartans could interrupt them. They had no tools for masonry, but they piled the stones as they found them, filling them in as they best could; the smaller stones and shingles alone

---

2 For the discussion on the site of the Fort at Pylus and the neighbourhood of Sphacteria, see the Memoir annexed to vol. II of Arnold's *Thucydides*. The suggestion which the candour of this lamented scholar and admirable writer offers, thrown out against his own arguments in the last page of the memoir, appears the most satisfactory answer to every objection to the belief, certainly most consistent with the account in Thucydides, viz., that Sphacteria is the modern Sphagia, and the harbour the Bay of Navarino.

3 ὕστερον καὶ τοῖς ταξιάρχοις κοινώσας.

would have required mortar or cement—and this for want of baskets they brought on their backs, bending forward their bodies and clasping their hands behind them, that the load might not fall off.

In short such was their energy and goodwill in the work that a rude wall was completed in six days; the greater part of the place nature itself had fortified. The weather then grew favourable, the fleet sailed leaving five ships, their crews and Demosthenes himself to guard this sudden settlement on the hitherto uninvaded Sparta.

II. All this while the Spartans themselves were keeping one of their religious festivals; their army was in Attica, and the government treated with contempt the news of a settlement on their coast,
THE REACTION OF
THE SPARTANS
which they deemed the first assault would dislodge. But a messenger was sent to Agis with the intelligence, and the Spartan king deemed it of greater importance than the government at home. He hastened, then, as we have before said, back to Sparta; and on his return a body of the pure Spartan citizens, and such of the neighbouring Periœci as could be readily collected, marched to Pylus. At the same time appeared the formidable fleet of sixty ships destined for Corinth, but recalled in haste—and who had eluded the armament of Eurymedon and Sophocles then at Zacynthus. No want of action now indeed!—all Lacedæmon was astir. Here and there, up and down, throughout went the messengers that were to collect all the strength not only of Laconia but of the Peloponnesus round the six-days' plaything of the Athenian soldiers.

III. The alert Demosthenes was fully equal to the danger he had courted: he despatched two of his vessels to Zacynthus to summon back to his aid the Athenian fleet. The position of the fort, and the strategy of the Spartans were as follows: across the harbour lay an islet called Sphacteria, which thus closing up the centre left two entrances, one on either side; the smaller of these two openings admitted only two ships abreast, the larger only eight or nine. The plan of the Spartans was therefore: first, to block up these entrances with their vessels moored close, so as to preclude the Athenian fleet, the arrival of which they foresaw, from sailing into the harbour to the relief of the fortress; second, to man the islet of Sphacteria itself with their own soldiers—and here they placed a strong detachment of heavy-armed troops, drafted from the divisions (*lochoi*) of the Lacedæmonian army, and comprising a large number of pure Spartans, many of them considerable from rank or repute, with their Helot attendants; third, so to dispose their men on the continent as to assault the fort from the land, while, as the rest of the surrounding coast was without creek or inlet, no other place for debarking was left to the Athenians. All these precautions they effected except the first—viz., securing the two entrances to the harbour—a neglect seemingly owing to the impetuosity with which they poured their whole squadron into the wide space of the bay within.

Demosthenes, nothing daunted by this formidable array, which boasted the terrible arm and heroic valour of Brasidas—the Achilles of the time[4]— prepared for defences: he hauled up his three galleys on the beach close by the fort, protecting them by a strong stockade. His force consisted of the crews of these vessels, and forty Messenians who had chanced, in cruising about and carrying on the petty warfare by which they fully subsisted, to put into the port in two vessels, a privateer and a pinnace. These Messenians were regularly armed, and had brought with them a supply of shields, chiefly of wickerwork, which Demosthenes distributed amongst his Athenian sailors. The greater part of this little force, he planted round the walls, where the assault inland was to be expected, but where the defence was strongest. But foreseeing that the main attack would be from the sea, where the fort was least guarded, he stationed himself in person, with sixty heavy-armed troops and a few archers, right on the rocky verge of the sea. In a few spirited words he encouraged his little band, bidding them not compute the danger, but rather to proportion their hope to their peril. Though they were but few, the place was beset with difficulties for the landing of the enemy if they would but stand firm; and the enemy could only advance a few at a time for want of room for anchorage, so that the difficulties of their opponent matched the paucity of their own numbers. They must know well enough how difficult indeed it was for men to debark in the teeth of a resolute few who kept their ground.

The men responded to the courage of their leader; and now the attack began, both by land and from sea—but especially, as Demosthenes had foreseen, on the very part he himself had taken.

THE BATTLE FOR PYLUS AND THE RETURN OF THE ATHENIAN FLEET

Only a few ships could approach at a time; but each division passed on to relieve the other. Chiefly distinguished above all the assailants was Brasidas himself—indignant to perceive the wariness of the captains and shipmasters in approaching their ships to the difficult and rocky shore, he shouted forth "that that was no time, when a hostile fort was planted in Laconia, to be sparing of hulls of timber, that in return for the services of Sparta the allies should not grudge the sacrifice of their ships, rather let them shatter and split, and land anyhow, so as to master the place and the men". Aiding exhortations by example, he compelled his own master to run ashore, and advanced forth on the steps or plank by which the Greeks descended from their galleys. Instantly the missiles of the Athenians showered round him, and their pressure stopped his way. Wounded in several places he at length fell fainting with loss of blood back into the ship—his shield dropped from

---

4 Οἷος γὰρ Ἀχιλλεὺς ἐγένετο, ἀπεικάσειεν ἄν τις καὶ Βρασίδαν, Plato, Symp., 221c.

his arm and was carried ashore by the breakers to furnish afterwards the trophy of the Athenians.[5] The conflict still continued, fought on both sides with equal obstinacy till nightfall, and renewed part of the next day, when the Spartans suspended the attack and sent ships to Asine for timber wherewith to construct machines for attempting the Fort, where the wall was highest but the landing much more favourable.

Meanwhile the Athenian fleet, reinforced by vessels from Chios and Naupactus, arrived at the scene of action. Seeing the coast and the isle of

THE SPARTANS ON SPHACTERIA ARE CUT OFF

Sphacteria beset with the enemy and their ships within the harbour, the commanders anchored for the night in the neighbouring island of Prote; and the next day, finding the Peloponnesians would not come into the open sea and had neglected to guard the mouths of the harbour, the Athenians sailed in by both entrances. The Peloponnesians had taken so little precautions against the proverbial alertness of an Athenian navy that some of their ships drawn ashore were not even manned. The first charge of the Athenians put to flight the foremost range of the Peloponnesian vessels, damaged many and took five; then, pressing upon those drawn ashore, they seized on some that were empty, the crews saving themselves by flight. But the Spartans on land, now roused to all that national spirit that made them so terrible to encounter in close conflict, waded into the sea, seized the ships as they were being hauled away, and finally rescued all except the five first taken. The parties then returned to their several encampments; the Athenians as victors erected their trophy and gave back the dead. But the material object was effected: the Athenian squadron had cut off the islet of Sphacteria, with the Spartan detachment there placed, from all hope of rescue; and they now sailing round the island kept watch upon it, converting, in fact, the post into a prison.

IV. Sparta was seized with consternation at the intelligence of the transactions at Pylus. The condition of their countrymen in Sphacteria was their

DISMAY AT SPARTA

main care: to that republic of gentlemen and warriors, the probable destruction of men of their order, comprehending some of its very prime and flower, was an evil exceeding an hundredfold larger loss of less valuable lives. For a state so jealous of the pure blood of its citizens, and in which the franchise was so narrowed that the Spartan people were in fact a nobility, the loss of a few hundreds was attended with a shock to the whole constitution. Formidable war without, and a discontented Helot population at home, required more than the usual chariness with which the Spartan policy watched over the privileged garrison that it called its citizens. Compared with the largest slaughter of Helots or even Periœci, the danger

---

5 Thucyd., iv. 12; Diod. Sic., xii. According to the latter in this fainting his buckler-arm naturally drooped on the side of the ship—and the buckler slipped off.

of the prisoners of Sphacteria created more dismay than would have been occasioned to William the Conqueror by the jeopardy of a proportionate number of Norman knights and barons—as compared with the unimportant havoc amidst the mere Saxon population. The Spartan ephors came themselves to the spot, and when they beheld the condition of their warriors at Sphacteria, the impossiblity of guarding against the double danger— famine in delay and the certainty of death or captivity if the Athenians poured their superior numbers on the island—they decided at once on demanding a truce, until an embassy could be sent and return from Athens, and humbled their pride to its conditions. They agreed, first, to bring to Pylus and deliver up to the Athenians not only all the warships employed in the late engagement, but all then on the Laconian territory; second, to suspend all hoplite operations on the Fort by land or sea.

2/9.

On their part the Athenians agreed to permit the Spartans to supply the besieged in Sphacteria (the blockade still existing) with ample and allotted rations of bread, meat, and wine, submitted to the inspection of Athenians, to restore the ships as delivered, on the return of the embassy from Athens, which was to be conducted in an Athenian galley. If any article in the treaty were infringed, the whole should be from that moment null and void.

V. It could scarcely fail to flatter the vanity and excite the pride of the Athenians, when, in the seventh year of the war, the ambassadors of Sparta arrived in their city, to confess disaster and invite to peace. For three years in those seven the Athenians THE EMBASSY TO ATHENS had been subjected by two separate visitations to the deadliest pestilence recorded in the Grecian annals; five times had their territory been invaded, and their lands wasted. They had stood almost alone, with the dependencies subdued by their valour or governed by their arts, against the confederacy of nearly all the principal free states in Greece, commanded by the power most approved for valour and military experience, backed by the oracle of Delphi, and secretly favoured amongst her own allies by every party opposed to democracy, and aided by the open revolt of the important Mitylene. In spite of all, her triumphs had been signal; her vigour had coped with every danger, had subdued rebellion in the islands, defeated the Peloponnesian navies on the sea and the Peloponnesian armies on the land, had planted her fortress on the virgin coast of Sparta, held some of the most eminent of the Spartan chiefs imprisoned in sight of their own shores, retained as a hostage the fleet of her foe, and now heard before her assembled people the envoys of Lacedæmon appealing to her generosity for peace: "The vicissitudes of Fortune", said the Spartan ambassadors, "you may well acknowledge by regarding our disasters. We who though of highest station amongst the Greeks address ourselves to you, we who before thought it more in our power to give, what we now come to ask." They proceeded then to comment on the wisdom of moderation in prosperity, and finally, on behalf of their country, invited the Athenians to an amicable settlement of all difference, and a cordial peace between Athens and Sparta. But to effect this peace, the ambassadors asked—the release of the besieged at Sphacteria, and proffered nothing in return but the amity of Sparta, deceiving themselves with the remembrance that Athens had once desired the peace that Sparta had refused, and the strange belief that the success of the one party would not alter the position of both. The Spartans, I say, offered nothing; but they hinted much—which would have been significant to a council, but seemed meaningless to a popular assembly. In words which Thucydides has left studiously delicate and covert, and the importance of which, though escaping the general commentator and historian, was seized at once by the profound sagacity of Hobbes, they concluded their harangue by observing that if Athens and Sparta were united, the rest of Greece, being inferior to them in power, must pay them deference and respect.[6]

VI. In any state, even in the most mild and far-sighted policy by which modern governments are guided in their relations with foreign powers, the administration of a people who, after unparalleled exertions and multiple calamities, had obtained the superiority in a war forced upon them, and accompanied by five invasions of their country, would naturally answer a request for peace by a demand for advantages more or less correspondent with the position they had won. But it is precisely in such treaties with foreign powers that the defects of a democracy are the most apparent. Even in the modified democracy of an English House of Commons, every practical statesman of every party is aware that the silent address of an able administration can effect more than all the popular eloquence, which rather serves to increase the difficulties by irritating the passions. Whatever belongs to finance cannot be too largely confided to the people; whatever belongs to diplomacy and to war cannot be too generously consigned to a responsible executive. It was not to be expected that the vigorous demagogy of Cleon would omit so favourable an occasion for enforcing the power of the Athenians, and extorting further concessions

REFLECTIONS ON
THE SITUATION

6 ἡμῶν γὰρ καὶ ὑμῶν ταὐτὰ λεγόντων τό γε ἄλλο Ἑλληνικὸν ἴστε ὅτι ὑποδεέστερον ὂν τὰ μέγιστα τιμήσει Thucyd., iv. 2. τὰ μέγιστα τιμήσει: "either will honour us in the highest degree, or being inferior will pay respect to the greatest powers"—Arnold. Of this passage Hobbes says "it conveyed to the understanding of the wiser sort of hearer the consideration of tyrannizing over the rest of Greece; for by the highest honour he means tyranny, but avoiding the envy of the word because if he had said it plainly the confederates would see that they who termed themselves the deliverers of Greece would now out of private interest be content to join with the Athenians." The meaning is still more clear in iv. 22, where Thucydides says that, by making offers not accepted, the Spartans might provoke the censure of their allies.

from the humbled foe. Still less was it to be expected from any popular assembly, flushed and intoxicated with sudden triumph after calamities so prolonged, to err rather on the side of moderation than that of presumption. The answer of the Athenian assembly accordingly was that the men at Sphacteria might be removed, and a peace for as long a term as both parties might judge expedient be effected—provided that the Spartans would surrender Nisæa, Pegæ, Trœzen—places which they had taken in the former war, and which the weakness of the Athenians at that time had conceded in the treaty or truce for thirty years; that in the meanwhile (and seemingly as hostages) the men at Sphacteria should be brought to Athens.

The true conditions by which peace could be obtained lay between the speech of the Spartans, in which nothing was openly proffered, and the reply of the Athenians, in which too much was imperiously exacted. And this the Spartan ambassadors probably felt, for they made no objections to the terms proposed, but requested that commissioners might be appointed to treat with them, and finally agree on such articles as might be mutually approved. Whoever has studied the humours and infirmities of the multitude (no matter in which country, provided it be free), must have perceived the proneness to jealous suspicion, whenever it is proposed to consign its interests to the arbitration of a few—especially upon any course in which its passions are engaged and its judgment has been pronounced. This is one of the unhappiest but one of the most invariable attributes of democracy; and in Athens perhaps it had the more excuse from the faithlessness which Sparta had so notoriously manifested[7]—she did not even answer the charge when at a later period reproached with it by her own allies—and from the

---

7 The opinion entertained at Athens of Spartan perfidy is shown in the "Andromache" of Euripides, who never missed a favourable opportunity of introducing allusions to the affairs of the time:

> O bitterest Foes (exclaims the persecuted Andromache)
> O bitterest Foes to all mankind—ye Spartans!
> Frauds are your counsels . . . o'er the realm of Lies
> Ye reign as Kings . . . cunning Artificers
> Of evils . . . winding thro' your torturous wiles
> To worthless ends . . . unmerited the rank
> Ye hold in Hellas—What of crime is known,
> Nor known in ye?—What slaughter and what greed?
> With tongues belying what your thoughts conceal
> Are ye not ever caught. Destruction seize ye!

Eurip., Andr., 446–50. Our language has no words to express the energy of the single word ὄλοισθ'! so feebly diluted into "destruction seize ye!"—with which the indignant description winds up. With such notions of the Spartan character the distrust felt by the assembly and expressed by Cleon is natural enough. The date of this play is plausibly assigned by Petit to BC 419—but the Spartans were quite as unpopular at Athens in BC 425.

fact that in Athens itself there existed still a party, entertaining the strongest predilections to Sparta, and boasting amongst its numbers no less a person than the already rising Alcibiades.[8]

VII. This weakness of distrust Cleon, in himself the personation of a populace, was sure even honestly to feel—to such a weakness he was sure

CLEON'S RESPONSE

proportionately and effectively to appeal. He exclaimed with bitter vehemence, that he had been persuaded before that the intentions of the Spartans had not been fair and upright, that their duplicity was clear now, since they could not speak openly to the people, but desired only a hole and corner conference with the few. "Let them say what they had to say if in truth it was sincere and honest manfully to the people." The Spartan honour could not concede to the popular demands, the Spartan gravity could not manage the popular humour. Of themselves their desire for peace might have conceded much, but they hesitated to offend their allies, by a clear exposition of the intentions they had so ambiguously hinted, viz., to purchase peace for themselves, not only to the exclusion but the prospective subjection of their confederates.[9] The envoys therefore, seeing no probability of moderate compromise, reluctantly quitted Athens.

VIII. On their return to Pylus, the treaty of truce of course expired, and the Spartans re-demanded their ships. But the Athenians charged them with

THE SIEGE

a violent attack upon the Fort, and some other not very important matters of complaint; and contending that according to the express treaty[10] the violation of one article nullified the others, refused to yield up the ships. Hostilities were at once renewed: Sphacteria was kept closely guarded by the Athenian galleys. But high rewards induced some of the Laconians, and the promise of liberty especially the Helots, to brave every danger in carrying over provisions to the besieged: seizing advantage of night, the position of the wind, baffling the watch-ships, diving under water, drawing after them skins filled with nutrial aliments, such as bruised linseed &c., these bold peasants sustained their haughty masters. On the other hand the Athenians in the six-days' fort of Pylus began themselves to suffer the privations of thirst and hunger. There was but one small spring within the fort, and the main supply of water, necessarily brackish and unwholesome, was procured by digging pits in the gravelly beach.

8 For at this time Alcibiades, as we shall hereafter notice, had all the bias of his family towards Sparta.

9 Hobbes; Bloomfield.

10 Οἱ δ' Ἀθηναῖοι ἐγκλήματα ἔχοντες ἐπιδρομήν τε τῶι τεχίσματι παράσπονδον καὶ ἄλλα οὐκ ἀξιόλογα δοκοῦντα εἶναι οὐκ ἀπεδίδοσαν &c: ἐπιδρομήν cannot bear any other interpretation than a violent assault or attack (NB strengthen this remark from instances &c). The other matters of complaint Thucydides considers of small consequence; but the construction of the passage does not imply that he also so considered the attack on the fort.

Though by the accession of twenty fresh ships from Athens, the force about the garrison was strengthened, yet the increase of numbers in so confined a space only swelled the inconveniences to which all were subject. The crews lived in the vessels which rode at anchor and went ashore in reliefs for their meals, while the Peloponnesians encamped round the Fort harassed it by frequent assaults. Thus several weeks passed since Sphacteria had been blockaded, and still Demosthenes was as far as ever from the actual capture of the men virtually imprisoned.

It seems strange at first that, with so large an armament and so ample a force, the Athenians did not at once land on the island and proceed to actual engagement with the little band it contained. But Demosthenes, taught prudence by his disaster in Ætolia, overestimated perhaps the difficulties of the attempt. The island was overgrown with wood, which would serve to conceal the enemy and enable their inferior numbers, if well placed, to plant the most formidable ambushes. Should the Athenians on landing keep to the open ground, all their movements could be detected, all their errors perceived; should they penetrate the pathless covert, they would be exposed to all the surprises of which an able soldiery thoroughly acquainted with the ground would avail themselves; and as they must necessarily from the nature of the place march in detachments, their numbers would be of little avail. Demosthenes had apparently another motive in diffidence of his operations: he desired, if possible, to take alive those Spartans whose rank rendered them so precious to their country. The possession of their persons might command terms of peace the most advantageous, their slaughter might make peace impossible by the revenge it would bequeathe. It never was supposed that Spartans would surrender with arms in their hands— but if attacked, die fighting to the last. Thus, as he somewhat underrated their numbers, he had long cherished the hope, that if supplies could be cut off, their countrymen, knowing their inability to resist an assault, would consent to any treaty by which they might be preserved from famine or the sword.

But in the meanwhile the Athenians at home were alarmed and disturbed by the unsatisfactory slowness of the operations at Pylus. It was difficult even in summer to bring the supplies to the fort along the capes of the Peloponnesus; when winter approached it would be impossible. The besieged at Sphacteria might contrive, in some stormy weather which would hinder the movements of the fleet, to escape in the light rafts and boats in which the Helots had brought them provisions. Encouraged by the supineness of the Athenians, Sparta, especially if the besieged should escape from Sphacteria, would no longer be disposed to the peace she had before proffered. In short the Athenians repented their hasty rejection of the Spartan embassy, and with the usual caprice and injustice of all public bodies evinced to Cleon their displeasure for having enforced the opinion they themselves had entertained. The able demagogue took a short and a bold course of defence: he affected utter disbelief of the report of the messengers from Pylus; and when, at the request of the messengers themselves, he was appointed with a colleague to inquire into their veracity, he replied with sense and truth that it was absurd to lose time by commissions of inquiry: if the report were true, why, the more necessity for prompt action—put to sea, and seize at once the troop at Sphacteria; then glancing at Nicias, one of the ten official generals and the object of his perpetual opposition, he added that, if the generals were but there, it would be easy to take the persons on the island, and that, if he were general, it should be soon done. The assembly murmured, and voices were heard asking why, if it appeared so easy, he did not himself go. Nicias drily observed that he and his fellow generals would, with the sanction of the people, permit him to take what force he pleased for the attempt. Cleon might very naturally think his military experience scarcely adapted to the enterprise he urged upon the professional commanders, and replied that, not he, but Nicias held the office of general. Nicias waived his right to the command of Pylus. The people pressed on the seemingly reluctant demagogue, and shouted to him to be gone.[11]

IX. Whether (as Thucydides informs us) Cleon had really shrunk from performing his boast, or whether, as seems equally probable, his reluctance had been an artful game to secure his object, Cleon then at once accepted the command. He declared that so little did he fear the Spartans, that he would not even withdraw one Athenian from the city, but, with some Lemnian and Imbrian auxiliaries, and a body of foreign targeteers and archers, in addition only to the force at Pylus, he would either put the Spartans at Sphacteria to the sword, or bring

CLEON ACCEPTS COMMAND

11 Thucydides says that he was afraid lest he should be obliged to confirm the accounts of those whom his disbelief had slandered, or if he contradicted, be convicted of falsehood. But whatever the impartiality of the great historian he could not read the heart of Cleon, and his answer was that which any man of sense and spirit would have made. A commission of inquiry obviously was a weak and frivolous waste of time, at the very moment when time was most essential. In the disbelief of the account of the messengers which Cleon professes it is obviously meant from what follows that he disbelieved in the difficulties of the attempt on Sphacteria. And in that disbelief he was quite right. Through his whole course on this occasion, one cannot but suspect that he was in secret correspondence with Demosthenes, and acted by his intelligence and advice. We have seen before the little unison that existed between Demosthenes and the commanders of the fleet, Eurymedon and Sophocles. It is highly probable that, among the reasons which deterred Demosthenes from assault on Sphacteria, was the non co-operation of these two commanders. From what follows Cleon evidently had been acquainted with the plan formed by Demosthenes: he names him as his colleague in the expedition. What more likely than that Demosthenes really stood in need of Cleon's influence with the popular assembly, to force the rival commanders to the clever measures he meditated? If Thucydides is not clear in this somewhat intricate business we must remember that he was in opposition to Cleon, and that the most penetrating investigator cannot discover all the true springs of conduct in the party he opposes.

them alive to Athens within twenty days. The boast moved even to partial laughter an assembly which, with all its vehemence, seldom gave way to that indecorum. But the men of graver minds who, with hostility to Cleon, could unite love to their country, were pleased to think that if the expedition failed, Cleon was destroyed; if he succeeded, that the Spartans would be in the power of Athens.

As soon as Cleon was formally empowered, he named Demosthenes as his colleague and departed. He was already apprised that the able captain he had associated with himself was disposed to attempt the island, from which the main obstacle had been removed by accident. Some Athenian sailors had landed to dine on the outskirts of Sphacteria, guarding themselves with a piquet. By chance one amongst them set fire to a part of the wood; a brisk wind fanned the flame till it overspread the greater part of the wild forest land that had hitherto concealed the enemy, and the position and numbers of the Spartans were thus revealed.

As soon as Cleon reached Pylus, a herald was despatched to the Peloponnesian camp on the land to require them to avoid extremities by

THE ASSAULT ON SPHAC-
TERIA AND THE SURRENDER
OF THE SPARTANS

ordering the besieged to surrender, on condition of mild custody until a treaty between the two states could be concluded. The proposal, which at least was honourable and humane, being rejected, on the night of the following day, Cleon and Demosthenes transported their heavy-armed troops to Sphacteria: they landed to the number of eight hundred in two divisions on opposite parts of the island. The besieged were thus stationed: in the middle and most level part of the island, Epitadas, the Spartan leader, had collected his principal force round the water spring which supplied his little army, a vanguard of thirty men, with part at one of the extremities, and another body entrenched themselves upon steep and rocky ground opposite to Pylus—strong against assault, landward and seaward—a site defended by the ruins of some ancient fortress, apparently Cyclopean. The Athenians surprised the vanguard while yet on their couches, and put them to the sword. By daybreak the rest of the Athenian force had landed from the whole armament, leaving only the necessary garrison at the fort.

X. The plan of Demosthenes was equally simple and skilful. He formed his light-armed men, amongst whom were eight hundred archers, into detachments of two hundred each, ordered to harass the enemies, while with his heavy-armed troops he marched on towards the main station of Epitadas. The Spartans on their part drew up in battle array, and advanced upon the Athenian hoplites. But now the light-armed men, having gained the heights, assailed them with missiles on the flanks and rear. Thus disabled from preserving that order and displaying that skill which rendered the Spartan encounter so formidably renowned, the band of Epitadas was compelled to repel the desultory warfare of these harassing and agile skirmishers, who fled when charged, but turned again to assail them in their turn from rough

places where the Spartans could not follow, and with the darts and arrows
against which the Spartan sword was terrible in vain.

2/10.

Thus leaving the enemy to exhaust itself in vain against his light-armed
soldiers, Demosthenes kept his hoplites immovable. The heavy panoply of
the Spartans concurred with the constant harassments of their nimble foes to
weary their endurance, and slacken the vigour of their retort. The assailants,
whom the martial renown of the Spartans had at first awed and daunted,
gathered boldness at the continuance of the strife, their own superiority
of numbers, and the embarrassment of their opponents; at length, with a
loud shout and a simultaneous rush, and a shower of stones and darts,
they closed upon Epitadas. The dust from the embers of the woodland so
recently burned rose in clouds under the feet of the trampling throng—to
confuse and blind the disheartened Lacedæmonians; the orders of the
leaders were drowned in the clamour of the enemy's halloo—their armour
was pierced by the broken shafts which, where they failed to wound, served
at least to impede. The Spartans at last closed their ranks, and retreated
towards the ruined fort at the north extremity of the island. Hotly pursued,
some perished in the march, most gained the fort and joined their comrades.
The place was strong and open to assault only in front, so that it could not
be encompassed. And though the Athenians pressed on with untiring
energy, there seemed no prospect of carrying it by storm. At length Como,
the captain of the Messenian auxiliaries, obtained the consent of Demosthenes
and Cleon to an attempt which decided the fortunes of the day.[12] With
a detachment of light-armed archers, Como wound unobserved along the
curving line of the rocky coast, and at length appeared upon a height behind
the ruin, on which the Spartans, confiding in the strength of the spot, had
placed no guard.

Thus exposed without shelter in the rear, and menaced by the fresh
vigour with which this sight inspired the Athenians in the front, nothing
seemed left to the Spartans but certain and honourable death. The humanity,
or the policy, of Cleon and Demosthenes preserved them. These commanders
checked their assault, and summoned the enemy by herald to surrender their
arms, and yield at discretion. The state of the besieged was indeed desperate
—their chief Epitadas was slain, his second-in-command lay dying amidst
the dead. Most of them grounded their shields and waved their hands in

---

12 This Como was afterwards the leader of his countrymen in a migration into Libya—and
   the Dreamer of a Dream prefiguring the restoration of the noble and gallant people to
   which he belonged to their ancient land—Paus. (Messenics), iv. 26.

token of acquiescence. A conference between the Athenian generals and Stypho, who had succeeded, by the fate of his superiors, to the command of this little band, ensued: he, in the spirit of the discipline which distinguished his race, demanded first to send over to the Peloponnesian camp on the mainland for the directions of his countrymen. The Athenian generals consented to send for heralds from the hostile camp, to bear Stypho's message, and report the answer. After two or three interrogations thus exchanged, the final message from the mainland camp was this—truly Laconic and truly ambiguous in its import: "The Spartans direct you to consult for yourselves provided you preserve your honour." The besieged interpreted the reply as self-preservation prompted, and yielded to the Athenians. Of the four hundred and twenty garrisoned on the island, one hundred and twenty-eight had fallen and two hundred and ninety-two surrendered, of whom one hundred and twenty were pure Spartans.

XI. The Peloponnesian camp on the mainland broke up, the Athenian fleet under Eurymedon and Sophocles departed for Corcyra; and as he had promised, so within twenty days Cleon brought the Sphacteria garrison triumphantly to Athens. Without depriving Demosthenes of his due share, probably by far the larger, in the plan and execution of this enterprise, it would be injustice to Cleon to deny that through the whole he appears to considerable advantage: the suspicion of personal timidity, caused by his real or feigned reluctance to accept the command, was removed by his leading an enterprise which the Athenian soldiers considered dangerous and even desperate; and he contrasted his usual fierceness in seeking first to negotiate with the Peloponnesian allies, and interfering afterwards with his gallant colleague to save the lives of the enemy. The party opposed to the demagogue would naturally seek, however, to depreciate and ridicule his success; and their language may well be conjectured by the amusing caricature of their champion Aristophanes. The comedy of the "Knights" is opened by Demosthenes and Nicias in humorous complaint of "the Paphlagonian". Alluding to the affair at Sphacteria, Demosthenes exclaims:

THE END OF THE AFFAIR—
CLEON VINDICATED

> It was but t'other day these hands had mixt
> A Spartan pudding for him. There at Pylus
> Slily and craftily the knave stole on me
> Ravished the Feast and to my Master bore it.[13]

---

13 The "Knights", Mitchell's translation. A few lines afterwards Aristophanes tells off in his own lively satire the extreme energy of Cleon, in which lay the secret of much of his success: "Nothing", says Demosthenes "can be hid from the Paphlagonian: he has one leg in Pylus, another in the Assembly."

And doubtless there were some who thought that to Demosthenes belonged the honour which Cleon assumed. But with the mass of the people, who could not but compare the vigour which had followed, with the languor which had preceded his arrival at Pylus the reputation of the popular favourite was not unreasonably increased. A service indeed at once more brilliant and more important had not been rendered to Athens since the war began.[14] An effect was produced upon the whole of Greece, highly injurious to the moral power of the Spartans: it had never been supposed that any armed body of that soldier-nation would yield in battle to a force, however superior. And had the Athenians and their government wisely hastened to found a treaty of peace upon the advantage they had gained, their posterity might have lived to bless the fortunate demagogue, whose name is now surrendered to the ridicule of malignant wit, and the graver contumely of that aristocracy of letters, so rarely indulgent to the coarse merits which win the populace and command the hour.

XII. On the arrival of the prisoners from Sphacteria, the Athenians decreed that they should be kept in custody until accommodation with Sparta could be made, and, agreeably to the warfare of the time, that they should be put to death if before a treaty could be established, the Peloponnesians should invade Attica. The latter decree was stern, but the sternness which places a new barrier between a land and the invasion requires no excuse. In the meanwhile the prisoners were mildly treated,[15] and found in the young and wealthy Alcibiades, whose family had anciently been connected with their country in the hospitable relations of the age, a friend able and willing to soften their captivity. The Athenian government hastened also to confirm their invaluable settlement at Pylus. A party of the Naupactan Messenians were sent to form its garrison, and, inveterate foes to Sparta, were enabled by the purity of their Doric dialect, which afforded them the facilities of stratagem and the advantage of being mistaken for the Lacedæmonians themselves—as in the surprise of the Ambracians before related—to aid by the ingenuity of ambush and surprise the harassments continually prompted by revenge. The little fort of Pylus was strengthened by the disaffection which the severity of Sparta engendered amongst her servile population. Thither for shelter and for vengeance the Helots began to flock. Alarmed and embarrassed, but still, as ever, dignified and proud, the Spartan government,

---

14 The shields of the Spartans were shown to Pausanias amongst the relics of the better days and braver generations of the then fallen Athens (Paus., i. 15). And so highly did the Messenians value their share in the achievement that Pausanias tells us their descendants still pointed to a statue of Victory in Olympia, which they asserted had been dedicated by the Messenians in commemoration of their joint success with the Athenians at Sphacteria (Paus., v. 26).

15 Plut., in Vit. Alc.

without stooping to confess apprehension or acknowledge weakness, became more and more in earnest in its negotiations with Athens. But unhappily the haughtiness of the one state and the overwrought expectations of the other prevented the peace so desirable to both.

XIII. It is impossible to ascertain the exact degree in which the influence of Cleon activated the practical measures of the Athenian state. But it is undeniable that, during his ascendency over the assembly and the popular party, the policy of Athens exhibited a vigour and a promptitude never excelled, never perhaps equalled, in any period of her history. Scarcely had this victory at Sphacteria been effected, before an Athenian armament was within eight miles of Corinth.

Operations at Corinth; events at Corcyra. Sicily, Chios, end of a year of great success for Athens.

CHAPTER VII

Capture of Cythera—expedition to Thyrea by Nicias—the fate of the prisoners—Hippocrates' attack on Megara—the capture of Nisæa —the arrival of Brasidas—the Delium campaign—the character of Brasidas

I. 2/11 New chapter (no number) begins with capture of Cythera. 2/12 Megara continued.

And Megara became an oligarchy which endured long. For whether in Oligarchies, Tyrannies or Democracies, cruelty is often a great consolidator of established wrong, and where Violence or Fraud usurps a government, its odious security can be only purchased by the extermination of its foes.

Demosthenes in Bœotia, Delium campaign and battle. 2/13 Negotiations after the battle continued.

II. Hitherto we have seen that Sparta with all her military discipline, all the comparative compactness of her institutions, all the fleets and armies of her allies, and all the moral influence she secretly exercised, whether over the Athenian dependencies by the character she assumed of the general emancipator of Greece, or over the nobler classes in every state as the enemy of popular innovation, had been mortified and humbled more and more, year after year, by the brilliancy and vigour of Athenian operations. But now she obtained that advantage hitherto monopolized by her foe, the advantage which redeems the defects and heightens the merits of institutions, without which neither discipline nor fleets nor armies nor the dignity of a cause avail against those by whom it is possessed, the advantage of genius and intellect in leaders, the glorious felicity of great men. The first of those who appeared to prove in Sparta the universal truth—how much the History of Nations depends on the life of an individual Man—was Brasidas. Till now the powers of this young Spartan had found no sufficient field for their development; in this year they emerged with a splendour which threw into shade all the living statesmen and generals whom the rest of Greece could boast.

In the peculiar institutions of Sparta it had, as yet, been difficult for anyone not of the Royal Race to rise to the first military distinctions. For by her usages no army of pure Spartans left the Peloponnesus, except under command of one of her kings; and her policy ever seeking self-defence, rather than aggrandizement, was reluctantly drawn into the hazard of distant expeditions. But, just prior to the revolution at Megara, circumstances had concurred to induce the Spartan government, without infringing its law, to place an army, not composed of the pure Spartans, but of Peloponnesian allies and Helots, under the command of Brasidas.

Here the manuscript of 2/13 breaks off; there are seven blank pages to the end, which suggests that this is as far as Bulwer Lytton progressed with his work. (As stated above, 2/14 is misplaced: it starts with the numbering "XV p. 44" and concerns the Corinthian speech at Sparta. It follows on directly from 2/4).

CHAPTER VIII

2/15–21. A series of loose pages, which are a draft or perhaps part of a separate lecture, containing a partial repetition of a passage on the origins of historical writing in Greece, which occurs in the published text in Book IV chapter V; together with a comparison of Herodotus and Thucydides. The passage, though fragmentary, with its striking introduction and its comparison of Herodotus and Thucydides, may serve as an ideal summing up of Bulwer Lytton's romantic image of history.

Philosophy everywhere has preceded History, and men were desirous of deciphering the enigmas of the world before they paid much attention to the transactions of its past inhabitants. But if we examine the ways of an infant we shall cease to wonder at those of an infant civilization. The first questions that arouse and arrest the intellect of the child are scrupulously speculative, before you can make him take pleasure in the History of England; long before he can be taught to care about Magna Charta or the Bill of Rights, he questions you of the world—how he came into it—what is the nature of God—why it thunders and rains—and why the rainbow accompanies the shower. The Why perpetually torments him, and every child is born a philosopher. The child is the analogy of a people yet in childhood.

As for History, it presents to semi-barbarous tribes no other attraction than that of celebrating the deeds of their ancestors and the triumphs of some successful war. These subjects fall naturally to the province of the poet, and thus the first commemoration of facts ever blends itself with the embellishments of fable. Gradually however, as Philosophy abandons conjecture for experience, and as written prose becomes the medium of factual observation or inductive reasoning, the past is no longer the undisputed property of the poet. A people begins to struggle for rights, to contend with neighbours, to be avid of glory; it desires to trace back the rights it demands to a distant origin, or to learn more accurately than by tradition the result of its former contentions, or to sanction present ambition by former fame. Then is created the demand and the necessity for History. And then, yet half blended with the fiction from which it emerges, and all unconscious of its own importance, History is born. In the wonderful rapidity of the intellectual progress in Greece, History, however seen, forestalled its usual date, and very shortly followed the dawn of Philosophy.

The Dorians—a people who never desired to disturb tradition, willing not to investigate precisely because they implicitly venerated the past—little inquisitive as to the manners or the chronicles of other tribes—satisfied in a word with themselves, and incurious as to others—were not a race to whom History became a want. Ionia, the subtle, the innovating, the polished and the restless nurse of the arts which the mother country perfected, claims its origin. Miletus, which early profited by its connection with the civilized and luxurious Lydia, boasts the first writer of prose history in Cadmus:[1] he appears to have flourished about the time of Crœsus—he wrote concerning some cities of Ionia in four books. Contemporary with him was an Argive, Acusilaus, who wrote genealogies rather perhaps than history.[2] The whole of that century was sufficiently fertile in these chroniclers whose works are lost to us, and who probably treated rather of mythology or of genealogies than of history properly so called; and though indeed the affairs of Persia and the history of the great Darius naturally caught the attention and furnished the themes of the historians of Ionia, then subject to the Persian yoke, the Grecian colonies continued to produce the greater number of these historians; and Eugeon of Samos, the illustrious isle from which Pythagoras drew his birth, is placed by Dionysius at the head of the early writers of history. Hellanicus of Mitylene (BC 496 to 411—he lived to eighty-five according to Lucian) appears to have formed a more ambitious design than his predecessors. He wrote the History of the Ancient Kings of the Known Earth and of the founders of the most celebrated cities:[3] the subject, so nearly allied to fable, leads us to suspect that he, like his predecessors, dealt rather with the traditions of poetry than in the proper province of History. At length in Athens (BC 480), and during the stormy period of the invasion of Xerxes, when everything that could shed lustre upon the past incited to present struggles, Pherecydes the historian rose. He is sometimes called of Ionia—sometimes of Athens. His History related to the latter state. It was a mythological work, in which however he introduced references to later times—the pedigree of Miltiades, and the Scythian expedition of Darius.[4] In BC 463 we next find a Greek historian of Lydia—Xanthus: he wrote a history of his country of which some fragments remain and from which Herodotus did not disdain to borrow.

Such were the principal predecessors of that great historian [who] conceived and executed that work which has become the first model of historical

1 Pliny, H.N., vii. 56.
2 Suidas—Cic., de Orat.
3 Paus., ii. 3; Cic., de Orat., Aul. Gell., 15.
4 See Clinton's Grecian Chronology p. 325 and the authorities he quotes.

composition. We see from the brief outline which ushers him to our notice how little he deserves the vulgar title of Father of History. He was not the father—he was the educator. For nearly eighty years preceding him, [*there*] had been many historians so called, sufficiently eminent in their time. What he owed to them we know not—we know at least from the consent of fame that he surpassed them. Neither in Letters nor in Science does the first inventor obtain the prize—it is reserved for him who first makes the fitting application of inventions. That regarded merely as histories, the works preceding the immortal labours of the Halicarnassean must have been rather curious than valuable, I gather partly from the general notion of their subjects, principally from the qualities of Herodotus himself. That mixture of truth with fable—of shrewdness with superstition—of observation with credulity, which characterize his delightful chronicles—are to me a proof how completely the mists of poetry yet clung around the dawning of research. The strange and rambling manner of his narrative is no less a proof how little the philosophy of method had yet breathed order into the arrangement of facts. The strong and homely sense of Herodotus—his quickness of apprehension—and that practical aptitude which a life cast from youth amongst then in action scenes must have brought him, would never have allowed him to neglect any improvement that his predecessors had wrought. And the fame he suddenly acquired is the evidence how. . . . [*ms breaks off*].

2/16.

Herodotus is the earliest of the historians preserved to us—he thus appears (however erroneously) to modern times as the originator of History—and yet he is no historian's model. He rather originated works of travels than works of history. Modern writers have formed their study in Thucydides, or in the Roman authors, and have accessed to Herodotus only in reference or for delight. He stands in this respect like Froissart, whom in many things he resembles: he is read as a describer of the past and not as an example of how things past should be described. Where one man would be charmed with Macchiavelli a hundred would be charmed with Froissart—but to this day mediately and immediately Macchiavelli forms all Historical Disquisition, and Froissart is but the model of the Novelist. Macchiavelli is to Froissart what Thucydides is to Herodotus—the influence of Herodotus upon our thought and on style is nugatory—that of Thucydides pervading and imperishable.

2/17.

Still though Thucydides and Herodotus have written immortal and admirable works, those works are but imperfect attempts at History. And regarded solely as *Histories*, I consider that they are surpassed by the writings of Tacitus and Livy, and not less so by the great historians of Italy and England. This is the only branch of letters in which the Romans can be said to exceed the Greeks, and the only form of composition which the Greeks in originating did not perfect. The epic—the drama—the lyric—oratory—philosophy—sprung up at once under the influence of their creative genius to full and complete excellence, each in its several kind. History alone appears not to have developed its true and entire properties, and rather to have suggested in Herodotus how much it requires of the poet, and with Thucydides how much it demands of the statesman, than to have made that happy amalgamation of those contrasted but not antagonist qualities, the reason and the imagination, without which a chronicle may be flowing or a disquisition profound—but a History is not complete.

2/18.

And it seems at first somewhat singular that the origin of Prose should commence with the origin of Philosophy. That subtle and laborious Science, calculated only for the few, appears less likely to have called forth the arts of composition in a rude and unpolished age than subjects more adapted to the senses and the passions of the multitude. Yet so it is: in all countries wild and speculative inquiry seems to have commenced, with the dawn of Letters. In India—in China—in the East some philosophy is the characteristic of the earliest masters preserved to us—sometimes moral in its precepts—sometimes allegorically shadowing forth, sometimes plainly expressing the opinions of the author on the Mysteries of Life, of Nature and the Universe. Even with us the dawn of Letters broke on the dark ages of northern torpor by speculative disquisitions and the ingenious mimicries of Philosophy. The Arabian and the Aristotelian subtleties engaged the attention of the earliest cultivators of modern literature as distinct from the fictions of Poetry, and the first instinct of the awakened reason was to grope through the misty twilight after *Truth*.

BIBLIOGRAPHY OF WORKS CITED
BY THE AUTHOR

This bibliography contains the details of those works cited by the author in his notes, in the editions which he is most likely to have used: the reader should remember that these are not always the last edition, and that many references are to translated works. Apart from facilitating checking statements in the notes, the bibliography is intended to demonstrate the range of books that were available to Bulwer Lytton for the writing of his history. The list has been compiled largely from the pre-1920 catalogue of the Bodleian Library, Oxford, in which library most of the originals may be found.

Barthélemy, Jean-Jacques, *Travels of Anacharsis the younger in Greece*, tr. [by W. Beaumont]. 5th edn: revised, with Memoirs of the life of J.J. Barthélemy written by himself. 6 vols. London, 1817.

Bentley, Richard, *A Dissertation upon the Epistles of Phalaris: with an answer to the objections of C. Boyle. To which are added, Dr Bentley's dissertation on the Epistles of Themistocles, and others; and the Fables of Æsop.* New edn. London, 1817.

Boeckh, August, *The Public Economy of Athens; to which is added, a dissertation on the silver mines of Laurion*, trans. [by G.C. Lewis]. 2 vols. London, 1828.

Brucker, Johann Jacob, *The History of Philosophy, drawn up from Brucker's Historia critica philosophiæ* by W. Enfield. 2 vols. London, 1791.

Chandler, Richard, *Marmora Oxoniensia*. Oxford, 1763.

Clinton, Henry Fynes, *Fasti Hellenici, the civil and literary chronology of Greece from the earliest accounts to the death of Augustus*. 2nd edn. Oxford, 1834.

Coleridge, Henry Nelson, *Introductions to the Study of the Greek Classic Poets*. Pt. 1. [No more published]. London 1830.

Dodwell, Edward, *A Classical and Topographical Tour through Greece, during . . . 1801, 1805 and 1806*. 2 vols. London, 1819.

Forchhammer, Peter Wilhelm, *De Areopago non privato per Ephialten homicidii judiciis contra Boeckhium disputatio*. Diss. Kiel, 1828.

Gell, Sir William, *The Itinerary of Greece, with a commentary on Pausanias and Strabo and an account of the monuments of antiquity at present existing*. London, 1810.

—— *Itinerary of the Morea*. London, 1817.

—— *The Itinerary of Greece, containing 100 routes in Attica, Bœotia, Phocis, Locris, and Thessaly*. London, 1819.

—— *The Topography of Rome and its Vicinity*. London, 1834.

Heeren, Arnold Hermann L., *A Sketch of the Political History of Ancient Greece*, trans. [by G. Bancroft from Vol. 3, Pt. 1 of *Ideen über die Politik, den Verkehr und den Handel der vornehmsten Völker der alten Welt*]. Oxford, 1829.

—— *Historical Researches into the Politics, Intercourse, and Trade of the Carthaginians, Ethiopians, and Egyptians*, trans. [by D.A. Talboys from Vol. 2 of *Ideen über die Politik, den Verkehr und den Handel der vornehmsten Völker der alten Welt*]. 2 vols. Oxford, 1832.

—— *Historical Researches into the Politics, Intercourse, and Trade of the Principal Nations of Antiquity. Asiatic nations* [trans. from vol. 1 of *Ideen über die Politik, den Verkehr und den Handel der vornehmsten Völker der alten Welt*]. 3 vols. Oxford, 1833.

Helvétius, Claude Adrien, *De l'esprit: or, Essays on the mind, and its several faculties*, trans., London, 1759.

Herodotus, *Herodoti . . . historiarum libri ix. Gr. et Lat. ex L. Vallae interpretatione cum adnotationibus T. Galei et I. Gronovii. Ed. curavit et suas itemque L.C. Valckenarii notas adiecit P. Wesselingius.* Amsterdam, 1763.

Hermann, Karl Friedrich, "Ueber die neueren Streitschriften rücksichtlich der Blutgerichtsbarkeit des Areopags", *Heidelberger Jahrbücher der Literatur* 23 (1830) no. 44, pp. 689–701.

Heyne, Christian Gottlob, *Excursus in Homerum. Accedunt Godofredi Hermanni dissertationes de legibus quibusdam subtilioribus sermonis Homerici.* Oxford, 1822.

Hobhouse, John Cam, Baron Broughton, *A Journey through Albania and other Provinces of Turkey to Constantinople during 1809 and 1810.* 2 vols. London, 1813.

Homer, *Carmina Homerica, Ilias et Odyssea, in pristinam formam redacta; cum notis ac prolegomenis, opera et studio R.P. Knight.* [3 pt.]. London, 1820.

Hume, David, *Essays Moral, Political and Literary*, Edinburgh 1777.

Larcher, Pierre Henri, *Histoire d'Hérodote, tr. avec des remarques historiques et critiques*, 7 vols. Paris, 1786. New edn, 9 vols. Paris, 1802.

Lennep, Johan Daniel van, *Etymologicum linguae Graecae sive Observationes ad singulas verborum nominumque stirpes secundum ordinem lexici compilati olim a I. Scapula. Ed. curavit E. Scheid.* 2 vols. Utrecht, 1790.

Lobeck, Christian August, *Aglaophamus; sive, de theologiæ mysticæ Græcorum causis libri tres, idemque poetarum Orphicorum dispersas reliquias collegit.* 2 vols. Kaliningrad (Regiomonti Pruss.), 1829.

Machiavelli, Niccolò, *Machiavels Discourses, upon the first decade of T. Livius translated out of the Italian; with animadversions by E.D. To which is added his* Prince. London, 1663.

Mignet, François Auguste, *History of the French Revolution.* 2 vols., trans., London, 1826.

Milton, John, *The History of Britain, that part especially now call'd England, continu'd to the Norman conquest.* London, 1670.

Mitford, William, *The History of Greece. To which is prefixed a brief memoir of the author, by Lord Redesdale.* New edn, with additions [by W.K.]. 8 vols. London, 1829.

Montfaucon, Bernard de, *Antiquity Explained, and Represented in Sculptures*, trans. D. Humphreys. 5 vols. London, 1721–2.

—— *The supplement to Antiquity explained*, trans. by D. Humphreys. London, 1725.

Müller, Carl Otfried, *The History and Antiquities of the Doric Race*, trans. H. Tufnell and G.C. Lewis. 2 vols. Oxford, 1830. (See also Vol. I, Appendix IV, "History of the Greek Congress").

Philological Museum, ed. by J.C. H[are]. Vols. 1, 2. Cambridge, 1832, 1833.

Potter, John, *Archaeologia Graeca, or The antiquities of Greece. {&c.}* by G. Dunbar. *New edn; with a life of the author, by R. Anderson, and an appendix, containing a concise history of the Grecian states,* 2 vols. Edinburgh, 1824.

Prideaux, Humphrey (ed.), *Marmora Oxoniensia, ex Arundellianis Seldenianis, aliisque conflata, recensuit & commentario explicavit H. Prideaux. Appositis ad eorum nonnulla Seldeni & Lydiati annotationibus. Accessit Sertorii Ursati De notis Romanorum commentarius.* Oxford, 1676.

Rennel, James, *The geographical system of Herodotus examined and explained by a comparison with those of other ancient authors and with modern geography.* London, 1800.

Richardson, Robert, *Travels along the Mediterranean and parts adjacent; in company with the Earl of Belmore . . . 1816–17–18.* 2 vols. London, 1822.

Robertson, William, *The History of America.* 2 vols. London, 1777; *The history of America. In which is included the posthumous volume, containing the history of Virginia, to the year 1688; and of New England, to the year 1652.* 10th edn. 4 vols. London, 1803.

Schlegel, Friedrich Carl W. von, *Lectures on the History of Literature, Ancient and Modern,* trans., 2 vols. Edinburgh, 1818.

St. John, James Augustus, *The History of the Manners and Customs of Ancient Greece.* 3 vols. London, 1842.

Thirlwall, Connop, *A History of Greece.* 8 vols. (Cabinet cyclopedia). London, 1835–44; new edn. 8 vols. London, 1845–52.

Thucydides, *The history of Thucydides, newly translated and illustrated with annotations {&c.}* by S.T. Bloomfield. 3 vols. London, 1829.

—— *The History of the Peloponnesian War, with notes by T. Arnold. {With} Additional notes.* 3 vols. Oxford 1830–42.

Turner, Sharon, *The Sacred History of the World, attempted to be philosophically considered, in a series of letters.* 3 vols. London, 1832–37.

Wachsmuth, Ernst Wilhelm G., *The Historical Antiquities of the Greeks with reference to their political institutions,* trans. E. Woolrych. 2 vols. Oxford, 1837.

Welcker, Friedrich Gottlieb, *Sappho von einem herrschenden Vorurtheil befreyt.* Göttingen, 1816.

Wilkins, William, *Atheniensia, or Remarks on the topography and buildings of Athens.* London, 1816.

Wordsworth, Christopher, *Athens and Attica: journal of a residence there.* London, 1836.

INDEX

Atossa (Persian queen) 294, 299
Attica 43f., 543–6; evacuation of 546
Aulus Gellius 173, 234, 433, 441, 523

Babylonians 112, 224
Bacchiadæ 118
Bacchus 74, 101, 263f.
Barthélemy, J.-J. 416
Bekker, I. 417
Bellerophon and writing 167
Bentley, Richard 264
Bernal, Martin 15f., 19f.
Bias of Priene 174
Bloomfield, S.T. 461, 563
Boccaccio 552
Boeckh, August 13, 32, 190, 191, 261, 290f., 369, 405, 429, 459, 460, 462–4, 472, 480, 530, 556, 565–7
Bœotia 69, 106, 115f., 149, 227f.; and Hesiod 164; medizes 311; rebels against Athens 452f.
Brahmins 85
Brasidas 577f., 590f.
brigands 95f.
British Empire compared to Athenian 541
Byblus 421
Bulwer Lytton, Edward: political opinions 2f., 17f., 38f., 152, 533; *Athens* intended terminal date 31, 527; reviews 31; translations and editions 18f.; *Pelham* 2, 3, 15, 529; views on culture and government 110f.
Byron, Lord 3, 9, 18, 19, 29, 32, 33
Byzantium 373, 478, 480

Cadmus 51, 115
Cadmus of Miletus 171, 593
'Callias, Peace of' 395f., 424
Callicrates 466
Callimachus (polemarch) 250
Callinus 166
Cambyses 226, 294f.
Canada 536
Caria, Carians 86, 237f., 394
Carlyle, Thomas 27–9, 30
Carneian festival 318
Carthage 464
Carystus 247, 338, 383
Catholicism 289

Cecrops 19, 47, 48–52, 58, 68, 83f., 102f.
Cecryphalia (battle) 412
Ceres 55
Chalcis 227f., 567; Chalcidians at Artemisium 317; settled after revolt 453
Chandler, Richard 460
Charles II 532
Charon 65
Charondas 441
Chersonesus 211f., 240f., 534
Chileus of Tegea 313, 345
Chil-Menar (Persepolis) 298
Chilo the ephor 173
Chionides (comic poet) 483
Chios 226, 239f., 341
choragus 268
choregia 463
chorus: Schlegel on chorus in theatre 269; role in Sophocles 492, 503
Christianity 76, 551–3
Cicero 76, 204, 439, 441, 563
Cimmerians 222
Cimon (brother of Miltiades) 217
Cimon (son of Miltiades) 260, 345, 375, 377–83, 389, 391–8, 400; ostracism 405–9; recall 414f., 416, 417f., 422; in Cyprus 423f.; his death 424, 428, 431; compared with Pericles 458, 465, 549; compared with Nicias 566
Cirrha 183, 201; *see also* Crissa
citizenship under Clisthenes 220; Pericles' citizenship law 476f.
city-state 148f.
Cleandridas 453
Cleombrotus 333, 345
Cleomenes 126, 132, 220f., 227–31, 243–5
Cleon 16, 528, 547, 562–89; as orator 562–4, 571
Cleonice 384f.
Cleruchiæ 471–3, 566f.
Clidemus 101
Clinias 326
Clinton, Henry Fynes 21, 36f., 91, 106, 112, 144, 145, 156, 159, 171, 179, 181, 201f., 340, 345, 369, 379, 435, 438, 476f.
Clisthenes of Athens 217, 284; his reforms 219–21
Clisthenes of Sicyon 118, 183

women: in Sparta 90, 136, 138; in the theatre 269; their portrayal on stage 515
Wordsworth, Christopher 250
Wordsworth, William 34
working classes 151

Xanthippus, father of Pericles 260, 341, 345, 357, 370
Xanthippus, son of Pericles 557
Xanthus of Lydia 435, 593

Xenophanes 439f.
Xenophon 318
Xerxes 294, 302; expedition to Greece 303–37; death 391, 410

Zaleucus of Locri 75, 441
Zeno 439, 445
zeugitæ 191
Zopyrus 300, 309
Zoroaster 63; Zoroastrianism in Persia 300
Zosimus 524